Florida's First Law School

Florida's First Law School

History of Stetson University College of Law

Michael I. Swygert

and

W. Gary Vause

Carolina Academic Press

Durham, North Carolina

Library of Congress Cataloging-in-Publication Data

Swygert, Michael I.
Florida's first law school : history of Stetson University College of Law / by Michael I. Swygert, W. Gary Vause.
p. cm.
Includes bibliographical references and index.
Ten Digit ISBN 1-59460-316-2 (alk. paper)
Thirteen Digit ISBN 978-1-59460-316-7
1. Stetson University. College of Law. 2. Law schools--Florida--History. I. Vause, W. Gary. II. Title.

KF292.S744S99 2006
340.071'175921--dc22

2006024058

Carolina Academic Press
700 Kent Street
Durham, North Carolina 27701
Telephone (919) 489-7486
Fax (919) 493-5668
www.cap-press.com

Printed in the United States of America

This book is dedicated to Jeffrey, Gregory, Megan, and Paige Swygert, and to Celia Vause, widow of W. Gary Vause.

Contents

FOREWORD

Florida's Oldest Law School

Dean Darby Dickerson

The story of a law school is a story about people—students, faculty, alumni, staff, donors, and friends whose dreams, hopes, hard work, and ongoing support make the school a reality. In the pages that follow, you will read about the remarkable people who have graced the halls, courtyards, and piazzas of Stetson University College of Law.

The College of Law opened in DeLand, Florida on October 2, 1900, with five male students from Florida. In many ways, our first graduates would not recognize their alma mater today. The school's main campus is now located in Gulfport, a small community adjacent to St. Petersburg; we also have a satellite campus near downtown Tampa. The student body exceeds 950, and many students are women and minorities. In other ways, the original graduates would be very comfortable at today's Stetson law school: from the very beginning, we emphasized the importance of skills training, professionalism, and service—tenets to which we still adhere.

Stetson's story is fascinating, and I thank the co-authors for their vision and perseverance. My predecessor, Dean Gary Vause, wrote about Stetson's early history in a 1987 law-review article. In the late 1990s, he started preparing to write a book for the College of Law's centennial in 2000. In 1999, he became dean, which slowed his progress; although he continued to research and work on the book, he succumbed to cancer in 2003. We were fortunate that Michael Swygert, a long-time Stetson law professor who had just completed a book about his law school alma mater, enthusiastically agreed to continue the project. Mike has spent the better part of three years researching, writing, and editing. His ability to organize vast amounts of raw information, his love of history, his determination to be as complete and true as possible, and his fascination with the subjects of this work were truly an inspiration. Due to Mike's and Gary's talent and hard work, the story of Stetson's history is ready to share.

From establishing formal legal training in Florida, to producing outstanding judges and attorneys, to helping to build fields such as advocacy, elder law, and higher-education law and policy, Stetson's impact has been long-lasting and significant—and continues to grow. The path has not always been smooth, but the challenges have made us a stronger institution. As you read this history, always remember the people, because they have been the key to every success we have been fortunate enough to experience.

Acknowledgments

May 11, 2006

The genesis of this history of Stetson University College of Law began with the late Dean W. Gary Vause. In 1998, as the 100th anniversary of the founding of the College approached, Dean Vause began to research the Stetson law school in preparation for writing a comprehensive history. Unfortunately, his illness and death intervened. Subsequently, Dean Darby Dickerson asked me to take over the project, a happy task that has taken all my time for over two years. The work has benefitted from the guidance of Dean Emeritus Bruce R. Jacob (who took oral histories of a dozen prominent law school alumni) and from the research and assistance of Dean Emeritus Richard T. Dillon.

Others who assisted Dean Vause included Dorothy Bishop, former administrative assistant to five Stetson deans; Roxane Latoza, assistant to Dean Darby Dickerson; and Velaine Paryzek of the Office of Graduate and International Programs. Dean Vause also utilized the services of student research assistants Barbara Cowherd and Kristina Gles.

After taking over in January 2004, I worked with Sharon Gisclair, a paralegal in the Office of Faculty Support Services, until she left for a job with a judge in Washington, D.C. Ms. Gisclair's many excellent contributions are greatly appreciated. Silvia Manzanero, also a paralegal, then took over. She is a recipient of the Carnegie Endowment for International Peace Fellowship. Ms. Manzanero consistently provided outstanding research and editorial support. A third person whose assistance was invaluable was my research assistant, Lisa Smith, a former Stetson law student and now a member of The Florida Bar. Besides research, Ms. Smith (at one time a magazine editor) provided needed editorial corrections and suggestions. Ms. Connie Evans, Director of Faculty Support Services, coordinated the services of all these people and, in doing so, did a yeoman's job. I also acknowledge and thank Ms. Evans' entire Faculty Support Staff, in particular, Shannon Mullins, for their combined efforts in producing this volume.

Two others who provided critical assistance were Dean Emeritus Lizabeth Moody and Distinguished Professor Emeritus of Law William Eleazer. Each spent considerable effort in reviewing the manuscripts. Several members of the law faculty also read segments of the work-in-process and offered suggestions. Meanwhile, Pamela Burdett and Sally Waters, professional librarians, found obscure sources, and worked with librarians in DeLand in obtaining records from the University. Additional support came from Frank Klim, Director of Communications, and his assistants Davina Gould and Lizz Angello; Dotti Bressi, Director of College Relations; Michael Sepe, paralegal; and Brooke Bowman, Instructor of Legal Research and Writing, and Special Assistant to the Dean. Professor Bowman canvassed and scrutinized all 4,500 plus footnotes, which *Stetson Law Review* associates James Kushner and Frances Shefter had written.

Finally, I wish to recognize those who read the manuscript prior to its going to the publisher: James Beasley, Executive Vice President and Chief Operating Officer, Stetson University; Deborah Brown, Associate Vice President for Human Resources and Legal Affairs, Stetson College of Law; Dean Darby Dickerson; Frank Klim, Executive Director of Communications; and my always helpful wife, Dianne. I thank each of the people listed above as well as all the others who offered assistance. Finally, I thank Dean Darby Dickerson for granting me a year's leave to work exclusively on this project and for her continuing encouragement and support over the past two-and-one-half years (the last year of which I have been allegedly in retirement).

Michael I. Swygert,
Professor Emeritus of Law
St. Petersburg, May 11, 2006

Florida's First Law School

PROLOGUE

Teddy Roosevelt, Rocking on the Verandah

The evening of June 3, 1898, was warm and muggy. Wiping sweat off his brow, Theodore Roosevelt rocked in an "elegant bentwood" on the verandah of the grand Tampa Bay Hotel.[1] Built by Florida railroad tycoon Morton Plant, the "lavish palace" (according to some) or "ostentatious folly" (in the view of others) had opened seven years earlier amidst "fanfare and celebration."[2] Whether palace or folly, Plant's luxurious hotel accommodated well-to-do guests, many of whom traveled to it on the Plant's recently completed Tampa-to-Jacksonville "Florida Southwest Railroad."[3]

The dazzling Tampa Bay Hotel was something to behold. The exterior of the gingerbread-adorned, 500-room edifice was sheathed with reddish-brown bricks, topped with Moorish minarets, silver domes, and lighted cupolas.[4] The inviting interior—which included elegant staircases, a casino, a circular ball-

---

1. President Roosevelt and his wife spent three nights at the Tampa Bay Hotel. *See generally* Edmund Morris, *The Rise of Theodore Roosevelt* 624–628 (Coward, McCann & Geoghegan 1979).

2. *Id.* at 626; *see* U. Tampa, *History*, www.utampa.edu/aboutut/history-museum.html (accessed May 6, 2004).

3. Samuel Proctor, *Prelude to the New Florida, 1877–1919*, in *The New History of Florida* 1, 268 (Michael Gannon ed., U. Press Fla. 1996); James W. Covington, *The Tampa Bay Hotel*, 26 Tequesta 1 (1966); Dudley S. Johnson, *Henry Bradley Plant and Florida*, 45 Fla. Historical Q. 118 (Oct. 1966).

> Henry B. Plant, a Connecticut Yankee, developed the Plant System—railroads, hotels, and steamship lines—along the Gulf Coast and into central Florida ... Plant's Tampa Bay Hotel ... with its Moorish architecture and its ornate furnishings, became world famous for its accommodations and excellent service.

Proctor, *supra* n. 3, at 268.

4. *See* Henry B. Plant Museum, *The History*, www.plantmuseum.com/history/index.shtml; *select* "The History"; "The Henry B. Plant Bio"; "1891 Hotel" (accessed Feb. 6, 2004) (de-

room with crystal chandeliers, and even a swimming pool—was framed in varnished red mahogany accentuated by massive ten-foot-tall, intricately carved doors with sculptured glass insets and shiny brass hardware.

Looking beyond the hotel's splendor, Theodore Roosevelt could see "Army and Navy officers, newspaper correspondents, foreign attachés, and pretty Cuban women sipping iced tea and champagne."[5] These were not the hotel's customary guests. Nor, for that matter, was the future President of the United States on a holiday. Instead, Roosevelt and the hotel's residents were on a mission.

In June 1898, federal troops had taken over Plant's hotel to use it as a military command post. The plush inn was served as the operations center for the Army's 25,000 soldiers billeted on the outskirts of Tampa, and for the Navy's flotilla of ships anchored in nearby Tampa Bay. America was at war, and President William McKinley had designated Tampa, Florida, to be the principal embarkation point for an American invasion of the island of Spanish-controlled Cuba.

McKinley chose Brigadier General William Rufus Shafer to lead the Army's Fifth Corps. Lieutenant-Colonel Roosevelt (who earlier had served as Secretary of the Navy) was not pleased. Historian Edmund Morris describes the General, and adds Roosevelt's opinion of the man:

> Conspicuous among the elite, who daily crossed the Tampa Bay Hotel lobby, was dropsical, gouty old Brigadier General Shafer. At three-hundred pounds, or one-seventh of a ton, Schafer was barely able to heave himself up the grand stairway ... "Not since the campaign of Crassus against the Parthians," in Roosevelt's later opinion, "has there been so criminally incompetent a General as Shafer."[6]

Roosevelt's disparaging opinion not withstanding, Shafer mapped out the planned invasion of Cuba from the hotel's third-floor "cockpit." His forces included a volunteer unit of African-Americans,[7] regular Army brigades, and a contingent of cavalry, "the Rough Riders." Colonel Roosevelt had personally assembled nearly 1,000 members of the unit. Roosevelt biographer Edmund Morris writes that the Rough Riders, besides consisting of former soldiers, cowboys, and Native Americans, included 50 Eastern "Nickerbockers," or

---

scriptions of Plant's development of railroads in Florida and of the construction and history of the Tampa Bay Hotel).

5. Morris, *supra* n. 1, at 626.

6. *Id.* For that matter, at that time, Roosevelt did not like President McKinley either, declaring that the President had the "backbone of a chocolate éclair." Charles A. Beard & Mary R. Beard, *A Basic History of the United States* 343 (Garden City Publg. 1944).

7. Morris, *supra* n. 1, at 628.

"Gentlemen Rankers," along with the world's greatest polo player (Joseph Stevens), the world's tennis champion (Bob Wrenn), a former Harvard quarterback (Dudley Dean), and other athletes from Princeton and Yale, all young men seeking adventure.[8]

For a time, some people at Stetson thought that a Rough Rider named Charles Dana was the same person who five decades later gave over $2 million to the College of Law.[9] But the Rough Rider and the donor were not the same. Dana's first gift to the school enabled it to build a law library.[10]

In June 1898, Roosevelt and the Rough Riders had traveled to Tampa from San Antonio, Texas. Within a few days, they became part of America's assault on Spanish Cuba. The plan was simple: the soldiers would embark on the naval ships in the Gulf of Mexico, then sail to Cuba, and the soldiers would liberate the island from Spanish rule.

How had America come to war? Roosevelt might have been pondering that very question as he sat on Tampa Bay Hotel's verandah on the evening of June 3. He may have been thinking about "the shocking news" eleven weeks earlier, news that had precipitated the present crisis. The catalyst occurred at 9:40 p.m., on the evening of February 15, 1898. At that moment, the United States battleship *U.S.S. Maine*, loaded with gunpowder in Havana's harbor, blew up in a fiery explosion and sank. Those aboard included 262 Americans who lost their lives.[11]

Was the sinking of the *Maine* the result of sabotage or was it accidental? If sabotage, who was responsible? Many assumed (including Roosevelt) that Spanish agents had mined the ship. In short order, investigators found that the *Maine* indeed was the victim of an "external [explosive] device," though there was no proof of who or what had precipitated the explosion. Eventually, it was concluded that a boiler malfunction caused the *Maine*'s demise. At the time of the disaster, however, the public was convinced that Spanish agents had sabotaged the vessel. Americans cried in outrage: "*Remember the Maine; the hell with Spain.*"[12]

The consequences of the *Maine*'s explosion and loss of American lives were far reaching. Of immediate impact was that the incident became the defining

---

8. *Id.* at 620–621.

9. Bruce R. Jacob, *Remembering a Great Dean: Harold L. "Tom" Sebring*, 30 Stetson L. Rev. 71, 143 (2000) [hereinafter Jacob, *Remembering Sebring*] (citing *The Charles A. Dana Foundation, Incorporated: A Review 1963–1967*, at 5–6 (Found. 1967)).

10. *Infra* nn. 2117–2143 and accompanying text.

11. Morris, *supra* n. 1, at 598.

12. Beard & Beard, *supra* n. 6, at 342.

impetus for America's invasion of Cuba.[13] The United States' preparations for war included the strengthening of shoreline defenses. On Egmont Key at the mouth of Tampa Bay, the Army constructed a concrete fort to ward off possible naval attack by Spanish forces.[14] Though that did not happen, as America's troops took the offensive and invaded Cuba. The Spanish-American War followed, but not for long.

Fortunately, the war on Cuban soil ended after a few weeks of fighting, but not without the sacrifice of hundreds of American and Spanish lives. According to one report, half of Roosevelt's Rough Riders died.[15] Though the price of victory had been high, America's goal of a "free Cuba" was achieved. Following the conflict, the United States emerged as a global power, having gained control over Puerto Rico, Guam, the Philippines, and Cuba, all pursuant to the Treaty of Paris.[16]

As a result of "the splendid little war" (as many called it), Theodore Roosevelt and the Rough Riders became national heros, largely due to their success in the decisive battle of the conflict—their triumphant "charge up San Juan Hill."[17] One historian writes that because of the successful "charge," Roosevelt became "the most famous man in America."[18] Given this popularity, President William McKinley offered the war hero the position of Vice President of the United States on the Republican ticket in the 1900 presidential election. They won, and on January 1, 1901, Theodore Roosevelt took office as Vice President. Then, less than nine months later, Roosevelt unexpectedly was thrust into the presidency as a result of President McKinley's assassination in Buffalo, New York, on September 14, 1901.[19] By historical coincidence, the same year that Roosevelt was elected Vice President of the United States, Florida's first school of law opened in a small town named DeLand. The school started with five white males, the first students to study law at a Florida-based law school.

---

13. Morris, *supra* n. 1, at 604–608.

14. Proctor, *supra* n. 3, at 268. Regarding Florida's contributions, see William J. Schellings, *The Role of Florida in the Spanish-American War 1898,* (unpublished Ph.D. dissertation, U. Fla. 1958) (located in Smathers Library, Special Collections); *see also* Tampa Bay History Ctr., *Tampa's Contributions to the Spanish-American War*, www.tampabayhistorycenter.org/spanam.htm (accessed Oct. 27, 2004).

15. Proctor, *supra* n. 3, at 268.

16. Beard & Beard, *supra* n. 6, at 344.

17. Morris, *supra* n. 1, at 650–651.

18. *Id.* at 662; *see* Beard & Beard, *supra* n. 6, at 348.

19. Edmund Morris, *Theodore Rex* 3 (Random House 2001).

More than 100 years later, that same school—the Stetson University College of Law—opened a second campus called the Tampa Law Center, one mile down the Hillsborough River from the former Tampa Bay Hotel. In contrast to the law school's 1900 initial enrollment, in the fall of 2005 the school enrolled in excess of 1,000 students in Gulfport and Tampa. Over half were women. The 2004 Stetson student body included 165 minority students (consisting of 52 African-Americans, 83 Hispanics, 27 Asians, and three Native Americans), in addition to international students from nine countries.[20]

When the law school was in its third decade in the 1920s, another grand hotel was being built, thirty miles southwest of Tampa in the Pasadena Estates section of Gulfport, Florida. Called the Rolyat Hotel,[21] the warm and welcoming resort, like the Tampa Bay Hotel, was conceived in a distinctive architectural style. While the Moorish Tampa Bay Hotel sprouted gingerbread, silver turrets, minarets, and domes, the newer Spanish, Mediterranean Revival Rolyat Hotel reveled in towers, arcades, arches, fountains, passageways, and piazzas. Although the Rolyat never was commandeered as a military center during a war, it did serve for 23 years as the home for the Florida Military Academy for boys.[22]

Over time, the two architecturally distinctive hotels—one on each side of Tampa Bay—surrendered to Florida's periodic land busts. Eventually, new owners transformed each of the former inns into academic institutions. The Tampa Bay Hotel became, and remains, the University of Tampa.[23] In time, the former Rolyat Hotel became the principal location of Stetson University College of Law, the first and, thereby, oldest law school in the State of Florida.[24]

From its founding and for sixty years thereafter, the College's student body consisted of all white and overwhelmingly male students. Of course, attitudes change over time. Today, 105 years after Stetson's College of Law opened, a law student rocking in a chair on the second-floor porch of Stetson's Tampa Law Center might be thinking about America's military presence in Iraq. Viewing the former Tampa Bay Hotel in the distance, the Stetson law student might imagine Theodore Roosevelt, a century earlier, rocking in a chair on the hotel's

---

20. These figures came from data provided by Stetson University College of Law Admissions Office, August 13, 2004.

21. The name "Rolyat" was Taylor spelled backwards. *See infra* nn. 1765–1766 and accompanying text.

22. *See infra* nn. 1839–1873 and accompanying text.

23. Ed Hirshberg, *Tampa Bay Transformations: Hotels to Universities,* Fla. Gulf Coast Living 20, 21 (Apr./May 1981).

24. *See infra* nn. 292–302 and accompanying text.

verandah, pondering the impending Spanish-American War. Today, the Stetson student, in thinking about the lessons of history, might conclude that education ultimately trumps wars, hotels, and cultural biases. And she, an African-American honors law student, would be correct.

CHAPTER ONE

Stetson University in Historical Perspective

1.1 12,000-Year History in a Nutshell

Twelve thousand years ago, ancient hunters and gatherers lived in what today is the State of Florida. "Great armadillos, camels, and saber-tooth tigers" roamed the land.[25] They traveled great distances, since Florida's peninsula was twice its present size due to lower sea levels.

Eleven thousand years later, in 1513, Spanish explorer Ponce de Leon waded onto the beach near present-day St. Augustine, the oldest city in the United States. He named the land "Florida," after the Spanish "Pascua Florida," which means "feast of flowers."[26]Subsequently, French and English venturers came to the Florida peninsula, but not always with good will. In 1586, English explorer Sir Francis Drake burned the tiny community of St. Augustine.[27]

English and French forays notwithstanding, Spanish domination lasted throughout the sixteenth and seventeenth centuries, and for half of the eighteenth century. Then, Spain's dominion quickly came to an end—but only

---

25. Off. of Cultural & Historical Programs, *A Brief History of Florida*, "Early Human Inhabitants," http://dhr.dos.state.fl.us/facts/history/summary/ (2004). As a matter of comparison, in 2004, thousands of lawyers roamed the Florida peninsula. In no way does this suggest that members of the legal profession are like saber-tooth tigers, giant armadillos, or camels. It merely demonstrates evolutionary change.

As to evidence of the first human communities in Florida, see generally Robert S. Carr & John G. Beriault, *Prehistoric Man in South Florida*, in *Environments of South Florida: Present and Past* 1, 1–14 (P.J. Gleason ed., 2d ed., Miami Geological Socy. 1984).

For a detailed bibliography of Florida historical resources, see *A Guide to the History of Florida* (Paul S. George ed., Greenwood Press 1989).

26. Off. of Cultural & Historical Programs, *supra* n. 25, at "European Exploration & Colonization."

27. *Id.* at "First Spanish Period."

temporarily. In 1702, England began threatening Spain's sovereignty. English colonialists from Carolina, with the assistance of Creole (later called "Seminole") Indians, ransacked St. Augustine, historically not a safe place to live before Florida's statehood. The invaders, however, failed to capture Fort Castillo de San Marcos, because the fort was constructed of concrete-like coquina stone, making it impervious to cannonball fire.[28]Then, in 1719, French troops invaded from the west and took control of Pensacola. These forays represented the beginning of the end of the "first Spanish period" in Florida's history.

The British continued to make military incursions into the territory. From 1756 through 1763, England intensified its attacks during the "Seven-Years' War."[29]The hostilities ended with the English victorious. Consequently, Spain ceded Florida to England in exchange for it giving Cuba back to Spain. Thereby, the English period of Florida's history commenced.

After Spain abandoned its claim to Florida, Spanish inhabitants, including those residing in the small towns of Pensacola and St. Augustine, fled, followed by English settlers quickly taking control. Because St. Augustine and Pensacola were hundreds of miles apart, England divided Florida into two sections—East and West. East Florida was administered from St. Augustine, and West Florida from Pensacola. But England's occupation of its two Floridas lasted only twenty-one years.

In 1776, the American colonies and Great Britain became combatants embroiled in America's War for Independence. France, an American ally, seized the opportunity to expand its Louisiana territory eastward and allied with Spain against British control of Florida.[30]In the meantime, Great Britain concentrated its armies to the north in its war against the American revolutionaries. Given minimal British resistance, and with France's encouragement, Spain retook Florida in 1781. That same year, British General Cornwallis surrendered to American colonialists, thereby ending the War for Independence.[31]

Nearly two years passed before a peace treaty among America, Great Britain, and France was signed in Paris in 1783.[32] The treaty's provisions included one requiring Britain to cede both East and West Florida to Spain, beginning Spain's "second period" of governing Florida. But it would last for only a few decades.

For the next thirty-five years, Spain's influence in Florida waned while America's prominence rose, primarily because of America's response to Indian

---

28. *Id.*
29. *Id.* at "British Florida."
30. *Id.* at "British Florida."
31. *Id.*
32. Beard & Beard, *supra* n. 6, at 112.

marauders who were attacking America.[33]The first significant military invasion of Spanish East Florida by American militia, who were chasing "renegade Indians," occurred in 1814. It was led by General Andrew Jackson, "Old Hickory," whose forces took control of the region and then remained. Four years later, America's militia defeated the Indians for a second time in what is called the "First Seminole War."[34] As a result of America's military success, Spain had little choice but to cede all of Florida to the United States in return for Spain being released from more than $5 million in outstanding debts owed America. On February 22, 1819, the two countries signed the Adams-Onis Treaty,[35] but it would take three more years until American sovereignty over the new Florida "territory" became official.

President James Madison appointed "Old Hickory"—hero of the Battle of New Orleans—to be first governor of the Territory.[36] After first turning down the appointment, Jackson changed his mind and the newly appointed governor of the Florida Territory left for Pensacola.[37] On the morning of July 17, 1821, American and Spanish troops faced each other on the grounds of Pensacola's Government House. Andrew Jackson stood at attention as the American Fourth Infantry Band played *The Star Spangled Banner.*[38] As Federal soldiers raised the red, white, and blue American banner to half mast, the red and yellow Spanish flag was lowered to half mast. Meanwhile, in the harbor, the American battleship *Hornet* fired a twenty-one gun salute. Then, the Spanish flag was lowered the remainder of the way, while America's banner was raised to the top of its mast. As Jackson biographer Marquis James put it, at that moment "Florida was ours."[39] Many thought statehood would quickly follow, but not so. Opposition from northern interests forced a delay for several years.

---

33. *Id.* at 113; *see also* Daniel L. Schafer, *U.S. Territory and State*, in *The New History of Florida*, *supra* n. 3, at 207.

34. Off. of Cultural & Historical Programs, *supra* n. 25, at "Second Spanish Period."

35. Marquis James, *The Life of Andrew Jackson: Part One—The Border Captain* 301 (Bobbs-Merrill Co. 1938).

36. General Jackson defeated British forces in the Battle of New Orleans in 1814 at the end of the War of 1812 between America and Britain. *Id.* Actually, the war had ended with the signing of the Treaty of Ghent in late 1814, but the news did not reach the invading British forces in time to stem the battle in which the British invaders were decimated by the American defenders. *Id.*

37. *Id.* at 310–11.

38. *Id.* at 317–18.

39. *Id.* at 318. Negotiations dragged on for months before Spain finally agreed to hand over West and East Florida. The East Florida Spanish governor, Jose Coppinger, transferred power to American authorities on July 10, 1821. Jackson had to wait until July 17 for West

Andrew Jackson served only one year as Florida's first territorial governor. His successor was William P. Duval, who took office in 1822.[40] Duval was present at the first session of the Florida Legislative Council that met in Pensacola on July 22, 1822. To travel to Pensacola, council members from St. Augustine spent fifty-nine days sailing around the Florida peninsula. Needless to say, they were disheartened by the hardships and length of time it took. The following year, Pensacola's delegates sailed around the peninsula by way of the straits of Florida to reach St. Augustine. The Pensacolans found the voyage equally unpleasant.[41] Consequently, Duval and his advisors selected Tallahassee as a compromise site for the territory's capital. Located in far northern Florida, a few miles south of Georgia's border, the region, known by some as "the Red Hills," was sparsely populated except for a few homes and council houses of the Apalachee Indians. Hernando De Soto in 1539 encamped in the area.[42] Tallahassee was chosen primarily because it was exactly half-way between Pensacola and St. Augustine (the territory's two population centers at that time), and also because it was free of yellow fever, then rampant in Florida's coastal communities.[43] One year later, in 1824, Florida's Legislative Council met in Tallahassee[44] and enacted territorial laws and established a court system.[45] Statehood would not come for two decades.

Soon after the Florida territory was established, troubles between Native Americans and white immigrant settlers intensified. Creeks and Miccosukees lived and roamed on lands that white settlers desired.[46] Pressures to relocate Native Americans to outside the Florida Territory mounted. While many left on their own, one tenacious group—the Seminoles—strongly resisted the forced move to Oklahoma.[47] Led by their legendary leader, Osceola, the Seminoles ferociously fought against relocation in the "Second Seminole War," lasting from 1835 through 1842.[48]

Florida governor Jose Callava to abandon his territorial office. *See* Schafer, *supra* n. 33, at 207. The population of the Florida Territory in 1821 was fewer than 8,000, including slaves.

40. Michael V. Gannon, *Florida: A Short History* 28 (U. Press Fla. 1993).

41. *Id.*

42. Schafer, *supra* n. 33, at 210.

43. Gannon, *supra* n. 40, at 30–31.

44. *Id.*

45. *See* Charles D. Farvis, *The Courts of Territorial Florida*, 19 Fla. Historical Q. 346, 346–367 (Apr. 1941).

46. Off. of Cultural & Historical Programs, *supra* n. 25, at "Territorial Period."

47. Mary Young, *Indian Removal and Land Allotment: The Civilized Tribes and Jacksonian Justice*, 64 Am. Historical Rev. 31, 31–45 (Oct. 1958).

48. Off. of Cultural & Historical Programs, *supra* n. 25, at "Territorial Period."

The "Indian difficulties," especially involving the Seminoles, continued even after statehood status was attained in 1845. William D. Mosley, Florida's first governor under statehood, warned the State Assembly that "Indians had not confined themselves within their prescribed limits."[49] In response, the Assembly passed a law calling "for the removal" of the State's Indians. The act made it unlawful for any Native Americans to remain in Florida except for the few "Indians and half-breeds residing among the whites."[50] Subsequently, the federal government spent $20 million during Andrew Jackson's presidency to remove by persuasion or force, if necessary, the State's Native Americans. It turned out force was needed. In the removal, hundreds of Indians were killed. Though many of those who survived were forced to relocate west of the Mississippi, others escaped into the Everglades, waiting for government-sanctioned reservations to be established.[51] It would be a long wait.

In 1891, the Florida legislature mandated the State to donate 5,000 acres of land for "the sole and permanent use and benefit of the Seminole Indians in South Florida."[52] Nonetheless, the legislature did not appropriate the necessary funds to purchase the lands.[53] Eventually, the State and federal governments set aside large tracts for reservations for Florida's relatively few remaining Native Americans. By then, Florida had attained statehood.

Florida became the twenty-seventh state of the Union on March 3, 1845, as a consequence of persistent efforts of articulate and determined statehood proponents. One was David Levy Yulee. After statehood had been won, Yulee's popularity was such that he was elected Florida's first United States Senator.

The population of the twenty-seventh state was diverse.[54] In 1845, African-Americans comprised nearly half of its residents.[55] By 1860, the State's population had grown to 87,500, including 1,000 free African-Americans and 39,000 African-American slaves.[56] Northern and Southern states were sharply divided over slavery. In 1859, John Brown raided Harper's Ferry, followed by

49. Caroline Mays Brevard, *A History of Florida: From the Treaty of 1763 to Our Times* 10 (James Alexander Robertson ed., Fla. St. Historical Socy. 1924).

50. *Id.* at 9.

51. Off. of Cultural & Historical Programs, *supra* n. 25, at "Territorial Period."

52. Brevard, *supra* n. 49, at 200; *see also* Charles H. Coe, *The Seminoles Right to Lands* (1897) (indexed pamphlet located in the National Archives, Washington, D.C.).

53. Brevard, *supra* n. 49, at 200–201.

54. Off. of Cultural & Historical Programs, *supra* n. 25, at "Territorial Period."

55. Proctor, *supra* n. 3, at 282.

56. Off. of Cultural & Historical Programs, *supra* n. 25, at "Statehood." In addition to African-Americans, over the next fifty years thousands of immigrants came to Florida. In particular, Spanish-speaking Cubans, along with southern Italians, immigrated to the com-

Abraham Lincoln being elected president in 1860. Then the Southern states, including Florida, seceded from the Union, and formed the Confederate States of America. These events led to the "War between the States" (a historically more accurate phrase than the "Civil War"). This tragic conflict ended in 1865, with the Union forces victorious.

Although most Floridians were sympathetic to the Confederate cause, many were not. The State sent 15,000 men to the Confederate Forces, but some 2,000 Floridians—both African-Americans and whites—joined the Union Army.[57] Although secessionism was strong in the State's middle plantation belt (Jackson, Leon, Jefferson, and Madison counties), opponents of secession lived throughout Florida, primarily on the east coast.[58]

Even though only two major battles took place on Florida soil—Olustee and Natural Bridge—the number killed during the war on both sides was enormous. Florida reportedly lost more than 5,000 men.[59] Distraught by the pending Confederate defeat on April 1, 1865, the State's Confederate Governor, John Milton, killed himself, having said "death was preferable to reunion."[60] Six weeks later, Union troops occupied Tallahassee shortly following the Confederate Army of Tennessee's surrender to William Tecumseh Sherman.[61] The Union was saved, but a desired way of life for many had ended; more importantly, so too had the despicable "peculiar institution" of slavery.[62]

The post-war era brought rapid and sweeping changes to the South, especially in Florida. Tourism, citrus, cattle, and the railroad industry all grew in importance, while the growing of cotton diminished. Within three years of the war's end, a Republican-controlled federal government commenced "Reconstruction." Although strongly resented by most Floridians, reconstruction opened the possibilities of developing the State's vast frontier to northern investors.[63] When federal troops left Florida in January 1877, reconstruction efforts in the State had ceased. By then, Florida's Democrats had gained control

---

munity named Ybor City (part of Tampa) where, by 1905, cigar manufacturing was thriving. Charlton W. Tebeau, *A History of Florida* 286 (U. Miami Press 1980).

57. Off. of Cultural & Historical Programs, *supra* n. 25, at "Civil War and Reconstruction."

58. Proctor, *supra* n. 3, at 245.

59. *Id.*

60. *Id.*

61. For an excellent account of the Civil War, see Bruce Catton, *The Civil War* (Am. Heritage Press 1971); *see also* Paul Johnson, *A History of the American People* (Weidenfeld & Nicolson 1997).

62. *Id.*

63. Proctor, *supra* n. 3, 530–531.

of the state government.[64] Consequently, political power returned to the Democrats who, some said, had "redeemed the state from carpetbag-Scalawag-Negro government."[65]

The overwhelmingly white dominance of Florida government during this period is known as the "Bourbon Era," although others call it the "Gilded Age." Regardless, Florida's political leaders of the era longed for the "Old South." The recently passed Emancipation Proclamation amounted to nothing in practice and this period was especially oppressive for African-Americans. First, the State's leaders resisted giving newly enfranchised African-Americans voting rights. Second, and more tragic, hateful vigilante groups, including members of the Ku Klux Klan, attacked African-Americans and white sympathizers.

Although racial hatred had been a fact for a long time in Florida, lynchings became common from the 1870s onward.[66] The slaughter only worsened in the new century. Between 1900 and 1917, as many as ninety African-Americans were lynched by Klansmen and vigilantes.[67] The worse occurred in 1923, when lynchings and riots swept the small community of Rosewood, Florida, in Leon County. Six African-Americans died along with two whites. Homes and churches owned by African-Americans also were burned.[68]

Given these travesties and the wide-spread denial of voting rights of African-Americans, the Bourbon Era in Florida's history must be considered a low point. Nonetheless, the State's politicians did spur economic development in the State. Northern speculators—and their cash—descended upon Florida. One was Union Army General Henry S. Sanford, a developer of or-

64. Fla. Heritage Collection, *Economics and Society: Post-Civil War Florida 1865–1913: Reconstruction Era, 1865–1877*, http://palmm.fcla.edu/fh/outline/1865recon.html (last updated Jan. 7, 2002); Tebeau, *supra* n. 56, at 273.

65. Tebeau, *supra* n. 56, at 273–274.

66. *See e.g.* Robert P. Ingalls, *General Joseph H. Wall and Lynch Law in Tampa*, 63 Fla. Historical Q. 51, 52 (July 1984); *see also* Robert P. Ingalls, *Urban Vigilantes in the New South: Tampa, 1882–1936* (U. Tenn. Press 1988).

67. Maxine D. Jones, *The African-American Experience in Twentieth Century America*, in *The History of Florida*, *supra* n. 3, at 373, 379. Another major racial incident occurred at Ocoee, west of Orlando. Conversation between Michael I. Swygert, Prof. Emeritus of L., Stetson U. College of L., & Bruce R. Jacob, Dean Emeritus and Prof. of L. (July 10, 2005).

68. Jones, *supra* n. 67, at 379. In 1994—seventy-one years after the Rosewood killings—the Florida Legislature finally enacted the Rosewood Compensation Act for the victims and families of the killings and riots. *Id.; see also* William W. Rodgers, *A Documented History of the Incident Which Occurred at Rosewood, Florida, in January 1923* (Dec. 1993) (report submitted to the Florida Board of Regents) (available at http://dlis.dos.state.fl.us/fgils/rosewood.html).

ange groves who, in 1870, founded a town named after him—Sanford, Florida.[69]

In 1881, Governor William Bloxham, pursuant to the Florida Internal Improvement Act, authorized the State to sell a million acres of wetlands to northern industrialist Hamilton Disston at the bargain price of twenty-five cents per acre. Disston drained his newly purchased properties and resold portions to other northern developers looking for investment opportunities.[70]

Having an even greater impact on Florida's future were railroad developers, in particular, Henry Morrison Flagler. During one decade, more than 2,000 miles of new railroad lines were laid.[71] With the help of federal and state subsidies, Flagler, along with Henry B. Plant and William D. Chipley, purchased land and right-of-ways from one end of the State to the other. In time, the combined inter-connected railroads made most of the State's regions, especially those along the East Coast, accessible and, consequently, ripe for development. The symbolic triumph of Florida's new railroads occurred on January 22, 1912, when the first train on Flagler's "overseas railroad" arrived in Key West, thereby linking the pristine island community with Florida's mainland.[72]

---

69. William W. Rodgers, *Fortune and Misfortune: The Paradoxical Twenties*, in *The New History of Florida*, *supra* n. 3, at 287, 288-289; *see also* Gannon, *supra* n. 40, at 53.

70. The Disston purchase of one million acres in Florida for twenty-five cents per acre has to be added to the great land deals in American history, including the Native-American sale of Manhattan to Dutch Colonialists, the French sale of the Louisiana Territory, and America's procurement of the Alaskan Territory from Russia. For more information about wealthy northerners flocking to Florida during and after Reconstruction, see Maurice M. Vance, *Northerners in the Late Nineteenth Century Florida: Carpetbaggers or Settlers?* 38 Fla. Historical Q. 1 (July 1959).

71. Much has been written about the late nineteenth-century development of Florida's railroads. *See e.g.* Edward N. Akin, *Flagler: Rockefeller Partner and Florida Baron* (Kent St. U. Press 1988); David Leon Chandler, *Henry Flagler: The Astonishing Life and Times of the Visionary Robber Baron Who Founded Florida* (MacMillan Publg. Co. 1986) (a bit of hyperbole in the title); Sidney Walter Martin, *Florida's Flagler* (U. Ga. Press 1949); George W. Pettengill, Jr., *The Story of Florida Railroads 1834–1903* (Ry. & Locomotive Historical Socy. 1952); Proctor, *supra* n. 3, at 266, 268–71; Henry J. Doherty, *Jacksonville as a Nineteenth Century Railroad Center*, 58 Fla. Historical Q. (Apr. 1980); Off. of Cultural & Historical Programs, *supra* n. 25 at "Florida Development."

72. Gannon, *supra* n. 40, at 53. According to the Florida Office of Cultural and Historical Programs, Florida's economic transformation began in 1855 when the Legislature enacted the Internal Improvement Act, by which the State made public land available to investors (notably those who were interested in railroads and steamboats) at extremely low prices. Off. of Cultural & Historical Programs, *supra* n. 25, at "Florida Development."

With steel rails traversing Florida by the early 1900s, the State's economic and population growth accelerated. Its population at the beginning of the railroad boom in 1880 was 269,500. When Henry Flagler's train arrived in Key West in 1912, the state had nearly one million residents.[73] Prior to Florida's railroad-driven boom, the State's sparse populous, for the most part, harvested cotton, grew citrus, and raised cattle. The citrus industry had been introduced by the Spanish near St. Augustine. As a consequence, until the mid-1890s, Volusia County was the State's primary orange-growing area.[74]

Meanwhile, "cowmen" (as some described them versus Texan "cowboys") raised cattle in west-central and southwest Florida.[75] The cowmen were financially successful, as open-range grazing fostered expansion of the cattle industry. As a result, Florida became one of the largest cattle-producing states east of the Mississippi.[76] During the 1880s and early 1890s, however, cattle wars were common occurrences, especially in DeSoto County. A few Floridians took law into their own hands; in one instance, eight men died consequent to a Sarasota vigilante rampage.[77] Cattle wars notwithstanding, some, including at least one well-known resident—Thomas Edison—claimed that the end product of Florida cattle raising—the meat—was not of high quality.[78] In any event, as the cattle industry flourished, a very different industry—education—was growing.

---

73. Brevard, *supra* n. 49, at 198. "The once lonely city was now united to the continent." *Id.* The next major impetus for increased growth and development came decades later with the arrival of indoor air-conditioning.

74. Gannon, *supra* n. 40, at 30, 54; *see* Jerry Woods Weeks, *Florida Gold: Emergence of the Florida Citrus Industry, 1865–1895* (unpublished Ph.D dissertation, U.N.C. 1977) (available at Davis Microforms Coll Microfilm U.N.C.).

75. Gannon, *supra* n. 40, at 61. According to historian Michael Gannon, one theory about the genesis of the phrase "Florida Cracker" related to cowmen who "worked their herds with ... buckskin whips, [which] when cracked, sounded like rifle shots." *Id.* It may be that Florida's cowmen were the original "Crackers." Today, the phrase "Florida Cracker" typically refers to native Floridians (who are relatively few in comparison with the State's millions of non-Crackers, i.e., those who moved to Florida from other states or countries). *Id.*

76. *Id.*

77. *See* Janet Snyder Matthews, *He Carried His Life in His Hands: The Sarasota Assassination Society of 1884,* 58 Fla. Historical Q. 1 (July 1979).

78. Thomas Edison—the State's most famous inventor (for example, the incandescent lamp in 1879)—was quoted as saying, "They [the cattle] were poor specimens.... It took a sharp knife to even cut the gravy, much less the meat." Peter B. Gallagher, *Jim Bob Tinsley Chronicles Life and Music of Cowboys,* St. Pete. Times n.p. (n.d.) (on file at the Stetson U. College of L., Gulfport, Fla.).

1.2 Florida's Early Colleges and Universities

According to historian Charlton Tebeau, Florida established two all-white seminaries pursuant to an 1851 act of the legislature.[79] It was not unusual to call colleges "seminaries" in the mid-nineteenth century.[80] Though most seminaries were created to educate women for teaching, a few proclaimed they had a broader mission. For example, the stated objectives of Florida's two seminaries were to instruct students in the "art of teaching ... in the mechanical arts, in husbandry and [in] agricultural chemistry ... and [in the] arts which ennoble man and make him truly independent."[81] East Florida Seminary opened its doors in Gainesville in 1853, while West Florida Seminary opened in Tallahassee in 1856.[82]

Gainesville's East Seminary later moved to Lake City, then back to Gainesville, and ultimately became the University of Florida, the oldest *public* institution of higher learning in the State.[83] In addition to these two seminaries, a third public institution for higher learning—Florida Agricultural College—opened in 1870, followed by a fourth—Florida Normal School at DeFuniak Springs—in 1887.[84] That same year, South Florida Educational and Military Institute began in Bartow. Initially privately owned, the State took it over in 1895.[85] At the beginning of the twentieth century, Florida was supporting five white-only institutions of higher education. African-Americans had been ignored,[86] though not entirely.

In 1883, the Florida Legislature appropriated money to establish normal schools to train elementary school teachers. [87] Besides the white-only normal school at DeFuniak Springs, two state-funded schools for African-Americans opened in 1884. Unlike the "white" schools, the "Negro" normal schools were open for only two months of the year. One was located in Gainesville and the other in Tallahassee. In 1887, the Tallahassee school was renamed "State Normal School for Negroes."[88]

---

79. Tebeau, *supra* n. 56, at 305.

80. *See* Michael Irven Swygert, *And, We Must Make Them Noble: A Contextual History of the Valparaiso University School of Law 1879–2004*, at 18 (Carolina Academic Press 2004).

81. Tebeau, *supra* n. 56, at 305.

82. U. Fla. Archives, *University of Florida Timeline*, www.uflib.edu/spec/archome/Timeline.htm (last updated Apr. 27, 2000).

83. *Id.* at 1.

84. *Id.*

85. Tebeau, *supra* n. 56, at 305.

86. *See generally* J. Irving Scott, *The Education of Black People in Florida* (Dorrance Publg. Co. 1974).

87. *Id.*

88. *Id.*

In 1901, Florida took over what had been a privately owned "graded" school in St. Petersburg, renaming it St. Petersburg Normal and Industrial School.[89] Also in 1901, one year after Stetson University College of Law was founded,[90] the Legislature renamed East Florida Seminary, "Florida State College." The changing of the schools' names and moving them from one location to another became the norm. Historian Tebeau notes that Florida Southern College (in Lakeland) went by four different names and over time was located in five different communities.[91]

In 1905, the Florida Legislature enacted the Buckman Act,[92] a law that consolidated all seven existing state-financed schools into four, each having a new name and serving a defined segment of the State's populous. One of the four institutions was called "Florida Female College" (for white women only), located in Tallahassee and occupying the campus of the former Florida State College for Women. In time, this institution became co-educational and was renamed Florida State University.[93]

The Buckman Act renamed another existing school to the "University of the State of Florida," later shortened to the "University of Florida." The third renamed institution was "State Normal School for Negroes," located in Tallahassee. In 1909, this "colored school" became a four-year college and was renamed Florida Agricultural and Mechanical College. Then, in 1953, the name was changed to the Florida A & M University, as it is known today. Finally, a state-funded institution called "School for the Deaf, Dumb, and Blind," was opened in St. Augustine.[94] Today, the highly respected school continues, and offers classes at nearby Flagler College.[95]

Private colleges and universities in Florida developed more slowly than did public institutions. The first private school in the State to become a university—Stetson—began as a Baptist-affiliated school that opened in Volusia County in 1883. Named "DeLand Academy," it subsequently became "DeLand College," then "John B. Stetson University," and finally, "Stetson University." The interesting and somewhat improbable story of the founding of Stetson

89. U. Fla. Archives, *supra* n. 82.

90. *See infra* nn. 342–343 and accompanying text.

91. Tebeau, *supra* n. 56, at 306.

92. *See* 1969 Fla. Laws ch. 69–106, §§ 15, 35 (repealed 1979).

93. Gannon, *supra* n. 40, at 71.

94. *Id.*

95. Telephone Interview with Lisa Smith, Stetson U. College of L. student & Flagler College alumna (Aug. 27, 2004).

University, the oldest private university in Florida, is discussed in the next chapter.[96]

After Stetson was founded, other private colleges established during the nineteenth century included: Rollins College, which opened in 1885 at Winter Park under the auspices of Florida Congregationalists;[97] South Florida Seminary in Orlando, commencing in 1893 (followed by several subsequent name changes and relocation—today it is Florida Southern College at Lakeland);[98] and St. Leo Abbey, later, St. Leo College, in San Antonio, opened by Benedictine monks.[99] In addition, the University of Miami held its first classes in 1925. All five of these institutions admitted whites only.[100]

African-Americans (with no state assistance) opened their own schools. Historian Samuel Proctor notes that the first African-American school in Florida was started in Jacksonville during the 1860s. It was founded and run by Edward Waters, for whom the institution was named.[101] The school still remains open.

Then, in 1904, African-American educator Mary McLeod Bethune opened the "Daytona Literary and Industrial Training School for Negro Girls," renamed in 1923 Bethune-Cookman College. This highly regarded college continues today.[102] Historians recognize Mary McLeod Bethune as a leading pioneer in Florida education. Among scores of accolades, several articles have been written about her monumental contributions to Florida education and to the State's African-American children.[103]

1.3 Founding of John B. Stetson University

a. The Vanishing of Persimmon Hollow

The year 1876 was America's Centennial, and folks across much of the Nation were celebrating. However, in post-Civil War Florida, one of the former Confederate States of America, the anniversary was subdued, not only because of the South's defeat by the Union Army in the Civil War, but also because wealthy northerners were coming into Florida and buying massive amounts

96. *See infra* nn. 134–156 and accompanying text.

97. Tebeau, *supra* n. 56, at 306. Population was only 140,000 residents.

98. *Id.* at 307.

99. *Id.*

100. Gannon, *supra* n. 40, at 71.

101. Proctor, *supra* n. 3, at 266.

102. *Id.*

103. *See* Gannon, *supra* n. 40, at 71; *see also* Rackham Holt, *Mary McLeod Bethune* (Doubleday 1964).

of land for investment, a development many Floridians found irksome. This trend made the State's white residents less than enthusiastic about the Nation's Centennial. In referring to the northerners coming into the State, Floridians used various epithets, among which "carpetbaggers" was the kindest.[104] Nonetheless, though many viewed their former enemies from the north as renegades, others saw them as "investors" who would help revive Florida from the Civil War's economic aftershocks. Many of these "investors" came from New York, New Jersey, and New England.

During March 1876, a wealthy New York manufacturer named Henry Addison DeLand traveled to Florida for the first time. Accompanied by his brother-in-law, O.P. Terry from South Carolina, DeLand scrutinized scrub lands on his journey as he inspected prospective property he might purchase in Volusia County.[105] A short distance east of the St. John's River, DeLand and Terry came upon uplands of rolling pine-covered hills, wild persimmon trees, and natural springs, all bathed in the soft fog of a typical March morning in northern Florida.[106] To some travelers, the idyllic landscape might have reminded them of a Monet canvas, spewed with a palate of varied and indistinct hues. To others—as was true of the approaching two men—this pristine land, with its rich soil, awakened thoughts of profitably harvesting oranges. Unlike areas DeLand had previously inspected, these lands were well drained and had little underbrush, making passage among the pine trees "very agreeable."[107] Located sixteen miles from the Atlantic coast and 115 miles south of Jacksonville, this largely (though not entirely) uninhabited segment of Florida's frontier was known as "Persimmon Hollow."[108]

---

104. Vance, *supra* n. 70, at 1.

105. W.S. Gordis, *John B. Stetson University: History and Reminiscences* ch. 7, 12–13 (unpublished ms. 1946) (on file at Stetson U. Archives, DeLand, Fla.).

106. Three springs existed in Volusia County: two at DeLeon Springs and another near Lake Monroe. *Id.* at 3. The warm springs had perfect transparency, unpleasant [sulfuric] odor, and blueish water. *Id.* Volusia County is "situated between the beautiful and historic St. John's River and the stretch of ocean [from] St. Augustine to the north [to] Cape Canaveral, a little to the south." *Id.* at 42.

107. *Id.* at 4.

108. Bill Keeler, *DeLand Florida 1876–1896: A Tale of Two Families*, www.angelfire.com/ny5/fairporthistmuseum/deland.htm (accessed Oct. 22, 2004). For the founding of Volusia County, see Florida Heritage Collection, *Florida Counties*, http://fdl.fcla.edu/fh/counties.html (updated Jan. 7, 2002).

Being a part of America's developing frontier distinguished Florida from other southern states, and contributed to its rapid economic development from 1870 onward. Florida reflected characteristics of frontier America. A state of 54,000 square miles with 1,200 miles of coastline, Florida was the least populous state in the South.

Approaching the Hollow in a horse-drawn buggy,[109] DeLand saw the rolling highlands under the blanket of a pine-green forest.[110] There being no roads, he and his brother-in-law traveled on a seldom-used trail. Since the nearest railroad was twenty miles away, to reach these highlands the men took a paddle-driven steamboat down the St. John's River to a settlement called Enterprise. After disembarking from the vessel, they stayed one night in the Brock House Hotel (not far down the St. John's River from a place that later would become Alexander's Landing).[111]

Seeing the rolling highlands, Henry DeLand was enthralled by a scene more friendly and inviting than the typical wet and brush-covered scrub lands he had recently traversed.[112] The native New Yorker was unaware of the name of this lovely countryside—"Persimmon Hollow"—and, of course, could not imagine that in a few years the landscape at which he was gazing would bear his name, "DeLand," Florida.[113]

On this, his first trip to the Sunshine State, Henry Addison DeLand, forty-two years old, was considering buying Florida acreage to grow oranges and to speculate on the future development of a new community. DeLand came to

---

109. Gilbert L. Lycan, *Stetson University: The First 100 Years* (Stetson U. Press 1983) [hereinafter Lycan, *History of Stetson*]. One historical account of this journey—an account written by the curator of the Fairport, New York, Historical Museum—says that the men were both riding horses. Another, contained in Professor Lycan's 1983 *Stetson University: The First 100 Years*, describes the men hiring a horse and buggy to travel from the St. John's River. Lycan, however, offers no specific reference material for his assertion, but neither does the curator of the Fairmont Historical Museum.

110. Several other sources for the story of DeLand's coming to, purchasing land around, settling in, and promoting the community named after him have been used by the authors in addition to Professor Lycan's history of the University. *Id.* These include Internet biographical data on various web pages, as well as previous historical records in the Stetson University Archives (both at the main campus in DeLand, Fla., and at the Law School in Gulfport, Fla.) and historical summaries of the founding of the University, including those of former Stetson University President Ollie Edmunds; the co-author of this volume, former Stetson University College of Law Dean W. Gary Vause; and Dean Emeritus and Professor of Law Bruce Jacob. *Id.*

111. For a history of Volusia County, see Michael G. Schene, *Hopes, Dreams and Promises: A History of Volusia County, Florida* (News-J. Corp. 1976).

112. *Id.* at 2.

113. "Persimmon Hollow" was simply a name given by a few homesteaders in this part of Florida and was due to the number of persimmon trees intermingled among the pines, the persimmons typically being near water in the lower areas of the rolling hills. *See* Volusia County Heritage, *Henry DeLand*, http://volusiahistory.com/deland1.htm (accessed Oct. 22, 2004); *see also* Keeler, *supra* n. 108; Planet Fla., *The History of DeLand*, www.planet-florida.net/deland-hist/ (accessed Oct. 22, 2004).

the State at the urging of Terry, who had convinced the retired manufacturer to explore Florida's investment possibilities.[114] The brother-in-law had earlier purchased land for orange groves not far from Persimmon Hollow. At this period in Florida's history, the land south and west of St. Augustine was the principal citrus-growing region of the State.[115]

Based on what he saw and at the urging of Terry, DeLand purchased 160 acres, only to return six months later and acquire substantially larger tracts.[116] He soon resold these newly acquired properties to other investors desiring to grow citrus for profit. DeLand's land purchases, however, were not his only investments in Florida's future. It turned out that his most significant investment was his subsequent founding of a university.

b. Henry Addison DeLand

Henry Addison DeLand was born October 25, 1834, in Newark County, New York.[117] His ancestors primarily were French Huguenots who, in the 1600s in response to persecution by the Catholic majority, escaped France and immigrated to Holland, Eastern Europe, England, and the United States.[118] One

---

114. *See infra* n. 116 and accompanying text.

115. Jack Fortes, *In Heyday, DeLand Was King for Citrus Cultivation*, www.informed-volusian.com/2003/Issue_3/Volusia%20History%20Fortes3A.htm (accessed Oct. 22, 2004). Fortes notes,

> In the 1880s through the mid-1890s, "the orange was king" in the area around DeLand. DeLand's first newspaper, called the *Orange Ridge Echo,* in an 1883 article noted that Volusia County was "the home of the orange," adding that DeLand was the "center of a business for a large and rapidly increasing community of orange [growers] who have found here the most favorable conditions for the culture of the orange and kindred fruits." *Id.*

In 1879, Judge Isaac Stone planted a new variety of orange tree from a parent seedling in a grove near DeLand. A few years later, the grove was purchased by A.G. Hamlin, who subsequently became a member of the first Board of Trustees of Stetson University in the early 1900s. The oranges from his grove became known as "Hamlins," and today are one of top two varieties of oranges grown in Florida. Jené's Tropicals, *Hamlin Orange*, www.tropical-fruit.com/tfc/product.asp?ID=174 (accessed Oct. 22, 2004).

116. Gordis, *supra* n. 105, at 14.

117. Olga Bowen, *Memorandum on "Henry A. DeLand"* (1969) (cited in Lycan, *History of Stetson, supra* n. 109, at 15). For a detailed biography of Henry A. DeLand, see Helen Parce DeLand, *Story of DeLand and Lake Helen, Florida* (Academic Press 1928).

118. *See* Frederick DeLand Leete, *The DeLand Family in America, A Biographical Genealogy* (DeLand, Fla. 1943); *see also* Rob DeLand, *The DeLand Family in America*, http://home2.owc.net/-rdeland/DeLandHome.html (last updated Oct. 24, 2003); *Biography of Henry A. DeLand*, http://ourworld.compuserve.com/homepages/ndeland/Biography.htm (accessed May 26, 2004).

Huguenot who relocated was Claude Charles DeLand, a resident of Lamballe in Brittany, who came to North America in 1665. He was an ancestor of Henry DeLand. Indeed, those DeLands who live in the United States today trace their heritage back to Claude Charles DeLand.[119]

Raised on a farm in upstate New York close to Buffalo, Henry DeLand moved at a young age to the nearby small town of Fairport.[120] He soon became interested in commerce and, after turning twenty, began working as a salesman for a company that his older brother, Daniel DeLand, had founded. The company manufactured baking soda and its product was sold throughout the country.[121] Henry DeLand was associated with this manufacturing enterprise for twenty-two years, first as an employee, then—following Daniel's death in 1872—as its remaining owner.[122]

But within only four years, after taking charge, Henry DeLand grew weary of his New York baking soda business. By then he had become independently wealthy. It was said that his Fairport "saleratus and soda" business earned him in excess of twenty-five thousand dollars a year in profit, a huge amount in today's terms.[123]

Following his first trip to Florida in March 1876, DeLand decided to relocate to Volusia County. He then made it his goal to plan, finance, and develop a new community of growers, many of whom, like himself, were coming to Florida from the Northeast.[124] To concentrate his efforts on Florida land purchases and sales, DeLand sold his baking soda business in Fairport and came to Florida with money and intentions, including a desire to remain for the rest of his life. This, however, did not happen.[125]

Before being forced to leave and after settling in Volusia County, DeLand began to broker land deals with buyers, most of whom used their newly purchased properties to grow citrus. DeLand promised the buyers that the lands would produce a specified minimum annual yield of citrus, with the understanding that if the guaranteed levels were not reached, he would buy back the properties at their original price. Making this promise turned out to be the worst business decision of Henry DeLand's life.

119. DeLand, *supra* n. 118, at 1.
120. Gordis, *supra* n. 105, at 12.
121. DeLand, *supra* n. 118, at 1.
122. *Id.*
123. Gordis, *supra* n. 105, at 12.
124. Bowen, *supra* n. 117, at 14.
125. *See infra* n. 127 and accompanying text.

In the winter of 1885–1886, two devastating freezes—only weeks apart—killed Volusia County's entire citrus groves to the ground. DeLand, a man of integrity and honor, made good on his guarantees and bought back the lands he had previously sold.[126] As a result, he lost the remainder of his fortune, said then to be $250,000. Having no financial assets and without any source of income—his own groves having been destroyed—DeLand returned to Fairport, New York, and looked for a job in industry. Brian Meddaugh of the Fairport, New York, History Museum notes that DeLand's dreams of fostering a Florida citrus empire had turned into a "frozen nightmare."[127]

c. Emergence of Town and College

For the quarter of a century that DeLand lived in Florida—1876 through 1899—he made a name for himself, literally, before returning to his native New York. His philanthropy and public service in developing the town of DeLand (and later the University) were extensive and magnanimous. He gave land for the community's first elementary school;[128] built the town's first hotel ("Parceland," later "College Arms"); and donated funds to help construct the town's first Baptist Church.[129] Moreover, he laid out a grid for the town's streets, naming most after states, and donated land for a thoroughfare through the middle (Woodland Avenue).[130] In gratitude for DeLand's vision, generosity, and efforts, town officials named the community after him. In 1881, DeLand, Florida, was officially incorporated.

In 1883, a watershed event occurred in Henry DeLand's life when he met with Colonel C.O. Codrington, editor of a regional agricultural paper.[131] The two discussed ways to make the town "distinctive," and decided that DeLand, Florida, held both the opportunity and the potential of becoming an "outstanding educational center."[132] Stetson University historian Gilbert Lycan explains why:

> [T]here was not a single four-year college anywhere in the State of Florida ... [The] State Superintendent of Public Instruction in his bien-

126. Brian Meddaugh, *Central New Yorkers Who Helped Develop Central Florida,* in Keeler, *supra* n. 108, at 2–3; *see also* DeLand, *supra* n. 118.

127. Meddaugh, *supra* n. 126, at 3.

128. Lycan, *History of Stetson, supra* n. 109, at 3.

129. *Id.* at 4.

130. Meddaugh, *supra* n. 126, at 3.

131. The paper was called the *Florida Agriculturist* and was published by Colonel Codrington in DeLand. The paper lasted from 1873 until 1911. Schene, *supra* n. 111, at 90–91.

132. Lycan, *History of Stetson, supra* n. 109, at 4.

> nial report for 1881–82 had lamented that "thousands of Florida parents desired to educate their children, but institutions of higher learning were not available."[133]

Enticed by the prospect of promoting education, DeLand started to make arrangements for a town learning center. On November 5, 1883, he opened a new school—DeLand Academy—in a room of the town's First Baptist Church, and welcomed five enrollees consisting of both primary and secondary students.

In late nineteenth century America, it was common for institutions calling themselves "colleges" or "seminaries" to enroll students who had little if any formal school education when admitted. As the students became older, some stayed for "upper-level" instruction, the forerunner of today's college or university-level training.[134] Thus, the claim that DeLand Academy was the first *private* college (later, university) in Florida, is historically correct, though no actual college-level students, as classified by today's criteria, initially attended.

DeLand brought in Reverend John H. Griffith, an experienced educator and an ordained Baptist pastor from Troy, New York, as the Academy's principal. In addition to heading the Academy, he assumed the responsibilities of pastor at the town's First Baptist Church.[135] Though a few people consider Griffith to be Stetson's first president, the assertion is disputed by Stetson University historian Gilbert Lycan.[136] The weight of opinion, as well as University records, support Lycan's view. On the other hand, the University's origin occurred in 1883, the year of the institution's founding. Griffith was the head of DeLand Academy from 1883 through 1885 and, thus, in a *de facto* sense, was the first leader of the institution that evolved into Stetson University. In any event, Reverend Griffith resigned his principalship at the DeLand Academy in 1885, but he continued on as pastor of the town's Baptist Church.[137]

d. Florida Baptist Convention

Historian Lycan observes that if Henry A. DeLand was "the father" of Stetson University, then Florida's Baptist Convention was "the mother."[138] The Convention's 1854 constitution stated that the promotion of Baptist educa-

---

133. *Id.*

134. Swygert, *supra* n. 80, at 15–16.

135. Lycan, *History of Stetson, supra* n. 109, at 4–5; *see also* Meddaugh, *supra* n. 126, at 3.

136. Lycan, *History of Stetson, supra* n. 109, at 3–4.

137. *Id.* at 5.

138. *Id.*

tion within Florida was a Convention priority. The aspiration was delayed, however, due to the Civil War.

Two decades after the war, in 1884, the Florida Baptist Convention, under the leadership of Reverend F.B. Moodie, authorized the creation of a Baptist women's college in the State. Henry DeLand was both a member of the Convention and a friend of Reverend Moodie. DeLand suggested to Moody that the proposed Baptist school be combined with his DeLand Academy. Specifically, DeLand offered the use of DeLand Hall along with cash and an endowment to match $10,000 pledged by the Convention.[139] He insisted, however, that the college be co-educational. Moody and the Convention accepted the proposal and, at its 1885 meeting, named Henry DeLand, along with eight other Baptist men, to serve as "DeLand College's" initial Board of Trustees.[140] Thus, in quick fashion, the Baptist-affiliated DeLand College was established.

That it would have a strong religious affiliation is not surprising. Christian colleges and universities were springing up throughout the country during the latter part of the nineteenth century. The proliferation of church-related colleges occurred in response to the "Protestant impulse," explained as follows:[141]

> [E]vangelical Protestant Christianity had become the largest single subculture in the United States ... The popular churches such as the Methodists and the Baptists exhibited a passion to convert the ... frontier population and create the moral commitments to build civilized communities.[142]

The sectarian Christian, church-related DeLand College, therefore, was not atypical of private colleges and universities of the period; it was the norm. Many of today's best-known universities (i.e., Duke, Vanderbilt, Northwestern, Chicago, Southern Methodist, Georgetown, Notre Dame, Boston College, Rice, Yale, Princeton, and Harvard) all began as sectarian institutions. At its

139. *Id.* at 7.

140. For a comprehensive treatment of the beginning and subsequent turbulent relationship between Stetson University and Florida Baptists, see Dr. Harry C. Garwood, *Stetson University and Florida Baptists: A Documentary History of Relations between Stetson University and the Florida Baptist Convention* (Fla. Baptist Historical Socy. 1962); *see also* John L. Rosser, *A History of Florida Baptists* (Broadman Press 1949); W. Gary Vause, *Foundations for Excellence—The History of Stetson University College of Law,* 16 Stetson L. Rev. 295, 301 (1987).

141. Richard Baepler, *Flame of Faith, Lamp of Learning: A History of Valparaiso University,* 18 (Concordia Publg. House 2002).

142. *Id.*

founding, Harvard University's mission was to educate future members of the clergy to serve New England, an objective the university fulfilled for over fifty years. Similarly, ministers began Yale University to train students for the clergy. Meanwhile, Princeton University academics developed a theological thesis doctrine known as the Hodge-Warfield Doctrine, one that argued for a literal interpretation of the Bible.[143]

When DeLand Academy opened in 1883, the town's Baptist Church was said to be the community's only institution that emphasized not only religious, but also social and civic goals. Before moving to Florida, Henry DeLand had served as Sunday School director and a Baptist deacon in Fairport, New York. As a devout Baptist, DeLand shared the Florida Baptist's goal of establishing a school that would offer students not only the advanced knowledge of the time, but also one that would instill Florida's future citizens with strong religious convictions. Thus, an affiliation between the Florida Baptist Convention and DeLand College appeared advantageous to Henry DeLand, to the State's Baptists, and to the Baptist Convention's hierarchy.

The initial optimism notwithstanding, from the outset the relationship between the Baptist Convention and DeLand College was difficult. The issue of shared control between the College and the Baptist Convention persisted as the single most divisive issue for decades. A more immediate concern in the mid-1880s, however, was the College obtaining sufficient financial support to operate. There also was the matter of finding a worthy person to head it.

e. One of the "Most Learned Men Who Ever Served Stetson"

In 1885, Henry DeLand hired Dr. John F. Forbes to be the College's first president. Years later, John Forbes was described as one of the "five or six most learned men who ever served Stetson University."[144] Previously a professor of Latin and Greek at the State Normal School in Brockport, New York (near Rochester), he has been described as "the ideal man to head up the new College."[145]

John Forbes was born in Middlesex, New York, in 1853.[146] Residing in the Empire State until coming to DeLand, he received an undergraduate degree with honors from the University of Rochester. He later was awarded an hon-

143. David Briggs, *The Sacred & the Secular: A Scholarly Struggle,* St. Pete. Times E4 (Sept. 12, 1992).

144. Lycan, *History of Stetson, supra* n. 109, at 9.

145. *Id.* at 5.

146. Olga Bowen, *John Franklin Forbes* 1 (unpublished ms. 1968) (on file in Stetson U. College of L., Gulfport, Fla.).

President John F. Forbes

orary Ph.D. degree from the same institution. Consequently, Forbes was referred to as "Doctor," though he never earned a degree beyond the Bachelors.[147]

Only thirty-two years old when he assumed the College's presidency, Forbes had a thoroughly modern and sophisticated view of education, one that incorporated principles that at that time were called "the new education."[148] Charles W. Eliot (later to become president of Harvard) espoused the tenants of this new pedagogy in an 1869 article titled "The New Education."[149] Based on the writings of philosophers John Dewey and Herbert Spencer, Elliot articulated a theory of learning that required each student's direct involvement in his or her education, an involvement that would cause the student to observe, think, compare, and reason, rather than to passively sit back and record facts that would be soon forgotten and, in the long run, be of little use.[150]

After becoming president of DeLand College, Forbes described this "new education" philosophy in an article in the Baptist publication *The Florida Baptist Witness.* He wrote that the aim of education was not primarily to impart facts to students, but rather "to use information, general statements, and prin-

---

147. *Id.*

148. John Dewey, *My Pedagogic Creed* (Kellogg 1897) (quoted in Robert M. Hutchins, *The Learning Society* 117 (Frederick A. Praeger 1968)). Dewey wrote,

> Both practically and philosophically, the key [to education] lies in a general reconstruction of school materials and method so as ... to bring out the intellectual and moral content of various forms ... seeing to it that the technical subjects which are now socially necessary acquire humane direction.

Id.

149. Anthony Chase, *The Birth of the Modern Law School,* 23 Am. J. Leg. History329 (1979).

150. *Id.* at 333.

ciples of truth, whether in or out of textbooks ... by which the student is to be trained to observe, to compare, to judge, and to reason." Forbes continued: "Our definition of education is *the development of power,* intellectual and moral power ... We attempt to develop in the student the habit of independent judgment—the habit of investigating statements and principles for himself, and thus for himself discover their truth or falsity."[151]

Despite his having strong Baptist ties, Forbes insisted that the College, although fraternally related to the Florida Baptist Convention, always remain governmentally nonsectarian.[152] He made this point in a letter to the University's Board of Trustees.[153] Forbes' view was in part based on what he saw as the benefits of the College having an intellectual independence, and in part because in his view the College had to remain outwardly nonsectarian for fundraising, a belief shared by Henry DeLand. Forbes and DeLand knew that a large portion of needed funds would have to come from non-Baptist sources.

In the midst of these troubles with the Florida Baptist Convention, a devastating personal problem befell Henry DeLand as a consequence of the State's 1885–1886 freezes. Following mammoth financial losses, DeLand was besieged by creditors. Worried that the College's assets might be jeopardized, he deeded the property to three individuals to hold as trustees until a charter of incorporation setting up a perpetual board of trustees could be obtained.[154] Led by a Philadelphia hatmaker named John B. Stetson, the three appointees were able to persuade the Florida Legislature to grant a charter to DeLand University, a charter that established a twenty-three member perpetual Board of Trustees.[155]

f. The Boss of the Plains

During the winter of 1885–1886, a wealthy Philadelphian named John Batterson Stetson came to DeLand.[156] One of twelve children, and son of a hat maker, the Philadelphian had no formal education.[157] His life experiences, however, overcame this handicap. For example, John Stetson spent some time in Colorado and saw an object that impressed him, a local "ten-gallon hat." After returning to Philadelphia, he began to make a similar hat, one he called

151. *Florida Baptist Witness* 1 (Sept. 10, 1985) (emphasis added).

152. Lycan, *History of Stetson, supra* n. 109, at 11.

153. *Id.* at 12.

154. Bowen, *supra* n. 146, at 5.

155. *Id.* at 6.

156. Memo. from Olga Bowen, Registrar, Stetson U. College of L. to unnamed recipient, *Memorandum on John B. Stetson* (n.d.) (on file in the Stetson U. Archives, DeLand, Fla.); *see also* Gordis, *supra* n. 105 at 35.

157. Bowen, *supra* n. 146, at 3.

Chairman John B. Stetson

"The Boss of the Plains"; it became the company's signature western cowboy hat.[158]

While producing western (and other) hats in Pennsylvania, John Stetson purchased a second home in DeLand, Florida, so he and his wife could escape the harsh Northern winters.[159] Henry DeLand and John Stetson soon became friends. John Stetson also befriended DeLand University President John Forbes, a relationship historian Lycan describes as a "deep, mutual admiration and respect between the two men."[160] DeLand, realizing that Stetson had great wealth, asked the Philadelphia hat maker if he would consider contributing financial support to DeLand University. The maker of "The Boss of the Plains" who, like DeLand, was a devout Baptist, said yes.

As John Stetson's contributions over time increased, so did his involvement with the University. Following Stetson's donation of money in 1886 for a new dormitory, the University's Board of Trustees in gratitude named it Stetson Hall.[161] The following year, Stetson was elected a member of the Board of

158. Lois H. Hirsch, *"The Hat of the West" Is Born: John B. Stetson's Hats*, http://cheltenhamtownship.org/wallhouse/stetson.htm (accessed June 4, 2004).

159. Lycan, *History of Stetson, supra* n. 109, at 13. Stetson's winter home was in Ashbourn, Pennsylvania. *Id.*

160. *Id.* at 48; Elbert Hubbard, *Little Journeys to the Homes of Great Business Men: John B. Stetson* (Roycrofters 1911) (cited in Lycan, *History of Stetson, supra* n. 109, at 19).

161. Lycan, *History of Stetson, supra* n. 109, at 13.

Trustees and soon became its president.[162] The same year, 1889, the Board renamed DeLand University the John B. Stetson University with the full approval and support of Henry DeLand.[163]

From the mid-1880s onward, benefactor John Stetson made numerous modest—as well as several generous—donations to the University bearing his name. The most significant may have been a $50,000 gift made in 1893 to endow a "President's Chair." Later, he gave money to construct Elizabeth Hall, named in honor of his wife Elizabeth, which opened in 1898 and included a 900-seat chapel with a "fine" pipe organ. In appreciation for John B. Stetson's philanthropy, beginning in 1893 and continuing through 1935, the University celebrated each year "Presentation Day" in honor of Stetson and other benefactors.[164] The total dollar amount of John B. Stetson's contributions to the University remains unclear. One account places it at one million dollars.[165] Yet another puts the support at over $200,000.[166] In any event, following his death in 1906, his widow and son continued to give financial gifts to the University for over two decades.

g. University-Baptist Relations: Part Two

As noted earlier, the "marriage" between the Florida Baptist Convention and Stetson University officials was difficult from the start. Relations became further strained after the Florida Legislature in 1887 granted DeLand University a charter that stated that members of the Baptist denomination were guaranteed a significant role in the University's governance. The charter required that three-quarters of the Board of Trustees be members of the Baptist denomination in good standing, and that the University's president be an ordained Baptist minister.[167]

But the charter gave no direct authority to the Baptist Convention or to its Board of Ministers. The University's Board of Trustees, moreover, was to be

---

162. *Id.* at 19.

163. *Id.* at 20.

164. Bowen, *supra* n. 146, at 6.

165. "The wealthy industrialist, John B. Stetson, encouraged by Henry DeLand, donated $1,000,000 to the school over the next few years." Schene, *supra* n. 111, at 89–90 (citing William Bristol Shaw, *John Batterson Stetson*, in *Dictionary of American Biography* vol. 17, 599 (Charles Scribner's Sons 1943).

166. *Presentation Day—A Yearly Occurrence of Great Advantage to a Florida College,* Jacksonville Times Union (Feb. 23, 1902) (copy on file in the Stetson U. Archives, DeLand, Fla.).

167. An Act to Incorporate an Institution of Learning at DeLand, Florida, under the Name of DeLand University, 1887 Fla. Laws ch. 3808, § 128.

self-perpetuating, meaning that its members, rather than the Convention or the State Board of Ministers, elected their successors. Not surprisingly, the Baptist Convention's hierarchy was displeased.[168]

By 1900, confusion over the Baptists' role in directing the University erupted into to open hostilities. Though Chairman John Stetson and President John Forbes sought secular control of the University—an arrangement that would allow it to attract non-Baptist financial support—the Florida Baptist Convention disagreed, believing that the University must operate under the authority and rules of the Baptist State Board of Ministers, and must function totally in accordance with Baptist moral prescibes. One example of the Convention's displeasure with secular control of the University concerned "non-Baptist" activities occurring at the school.[169] Though not permitted under the University rules, drinking and smoking had become frequent "unofficial student pastimes" which, it was said, were usually overlooked.[170]

At the height of the tension over who, or what group, had the right to govern the University, in 1906 John B. Stetson died. Within a month of his death, his widow, Elizabeth Stetson, wrote Henry DeLand in Fairport, New York, seeking to clarify what DeLand believed the Convention's role was, if any, in governing the University. In response, DeLand wrote that he had never intended the Convention to have control, explaining that such an arrangement would not be in the best interests of either the school or the Florida Baptists, adding that the Baptists "cannot, or will not, sustain it in a proper way."[171]

---

168. *Florida Baptist Witness, supra* n. 151, at 3.

169. *Id.*

170. Lycan, *History of Stetson, supra* n. 109, at 42–43.

171. Ltr. from H.A. DeLand, Pres. & Manager, Monroe Co. Chem. Corp. to Mrs. S.E. Stetson, *Regarding Baptist Control of Stetson University* (Mar. 28, 1906) (on file in the Stetson U. Archives, DeLand, Fla.). The letter reads in significant part:

> I never had a thought, or desire or purpose to turn the property of the University over to Florida Baptist Convention. I never knew anyone else who did. I did not have the desire or the purpose when the charter got out under the name of DeLand University to ever turn it over to the Florida Baptist Convention. I never have since. I don't think it's best for the university. I do not think it for the best interest of the Florida Baptists themselves. They cannot or will not sustain it in a proper way. Hence, I am intensely opposed to turning the University or any of its belongings or property of any name or nature over to the Florida Baptist Convention ... I am greatly surprised to learn from your interesting letter that Florida Baptists have only paid $4,000 on the $10,000 they pledged on condition I pay $10,000. My ten thousand dollars ($10,000) was paid in full over twelve years ago.
> Sincerely and heartily,
>
> *H.A. DeLand* [signed]

Id.

Despite the unresolved governance issue, by 1900 the John B. Stetson University was faring rather well. Its enrollment was up, the faculty strong, and the physical plant at least adequate. Moreover, President Forbes was an educationally savvy, highly intelligent, hard working, dedicated, and visionary leader. Concurrently, Board of Trustees Chairman John Stetson was actively involved in the University's operations, as well as being its major benefactor. Florida's first private university was on solid ground. It had come a long way since a handful of students entered DeLand Academy in the fall of 1883. Now, the University was in a position to expand its programs. For President Forbes, it seemed the right moment to establish a law department.

CHAPTER TWO

Founding of College of Law

2.1 Silk Hats Versus Wool Hats

What a decade! Beginning with the enactment of the Sherman Antitrust Act and the election of President Grover Cleveland, the 1890s included: the "gold panic"; the nationwide Pullman strike; the election of President William McKinley; the sinking of the *U.S.S. Maine* (followed by the Spanish-American War); and the re-election of President McKinley (this time with Theodore Roosevelt as Vice President). Meanwhile, in a small town the decade ended and a new century brought with it Florida's first (and today's oldest) law school—the Stetson University College of Law.

The final decade of the nineteenth century is known variously as the Gilded Age,[173] the Gay Nineties, the height of the Robber-Baron Era, the decline of the Bourbon Era, the rise of Populism, and the beginning of the Progressive Age. Though each is applicable to Florida's experience, two in particular describe social and political changes taking place: the rise of populism and the beginning of progressive politics.

According to historian Samuel Proctor, the 1890s was the decade of "Silk Hats" versus "Wool Hats" in Florida.[174] Silk Hats included wealthy investors, speculators, bankers, and corporate executives; men such as Henry Flagler, Henry Plant, William Chipley, and Hamilton Disston. With a green light from Bourbon Democrats, these men, who for the most part were nonresident northern Republicans, benefitted enormously from Florida's *laissez-faire* pol-

---

173. Edward C. Williamson, *Florida Politics in the Gilded Age, 1877–1893,* at 72–78 (U. Press Fla. 1976).

174. Proctor, *supra* n. 3, at 266, 278.

itics of the period.[175] During this Bourbon Era, Florida encouraged and enabled unrestricted development of millions of acres of the State's resources.[176]

But a backlash to these policies developed, and by the mid-1880s, attitudes concerning Florida's enabling of Northern developers were changing. Historian Proctor describes the evolution:

> [By 1884] the Democratic legislature had granted railroads 22,360,000 acres, although only 14,831,739 acres were in the public domain. Patronage-oriented Republicans from the North were horse-trading with Bourbon Democrats to get what they wanted ... but the demand for reform and change was growing.... An anti-Bourbon coalition, consisting of reform-minded white Republicans, Negro-Republicans, and Independent Democrats, became the State's [reform] party.[177]

The anti-Bourbon coalition of "Wool Hats," on the other hand, opposed Florida's land resources being "given away" to wealthy "Silk Hats" at a price as low as twenty-five cents an acre.[178] The "Wool Hats" consisted of farmers, laborers, and small business owners.[179] During the 1880s and 1890s, Florida remained primarily an agricultural state despite railroad expansion, new residents immigrating, and an influx of tourists. As late as 1900, eighty percent of Florida's residents still resided in rural communities.[180]

These rural and small-town residents often felt they were ignored by Florida's political leaders. Wanting to be heard, they became the "Florida Independent" movement, a group that grew in numbers, though not, at first, in political strength. Moreover, in 1885, Florida's Constitution effectively disenfranchised African-American voters by establishing a poll tax. Without the black vote, no anti-Bourbon Republican government could be elected in Florida.[181] Bourbon Democrats were taking all the steps they thought necessary to remain in political power. Nevertheless, many Floridians were becoming dissatisfied with the status quo.

In addition to a growing restlessness over corporate and banking dominance of politics, populist uneasiness was rising in other parts of the country,

---

175. *Id.*; Tebeau, *A History of Florida, supra* n. 56, at 273.
176. Proctor, *supra* n. 3, at 273.
177. *Id.*
178. *Id.* at 274.
179. *Id.* at 278.
180. *Id.* at 272.
181. *Id.*

especially in the Midwest.[182] American farmers, laborers, and small-town residents, believing that the interests of "the common man" were not being considered, ushered in a new era of American Populism.[183]

The tenets of populism at that time were articulated at the 1896 Democratic National Convention in Chicago. There, William Jennings Bryan delivered his "Cross of Gold Speech," where he emphasized that every person in America, not just eastern bankers and industrialists, was contributing to the Nation's wealth. He focused on the farmer, "who goes forth in the morning and toils all day—who begins in the spring and toils all summer—and who by application of brain and muscle to the natural resources of this country creates wealth."[184] Bryan also included small-town lawyers in his expansive definition of the American businessman.[185] In Florida, small-town lawyers made up the majority of the 400 to 500 attorneys in the State during this period.

Arguably, Florida was where the American Populist movement began.[186] In 1890, representatives of laborers and farmers from across America met in Ocala at what was called the "National Alliance Convention."[187] Attendees drafted a set of proposed reforms referred to as the "Ocala Demands."[188] The platform's goals included protection of farmers' land from eminent domain, prohibition of child labor practices, control of railroads' abuses and privileges, greater emphasis on better road construction, and a maximum ten-hour work day for farm laborers.[189]

These demands, historian Proctor writes, became the political focus of the American Populist Party, founded at the 1891 convention in Cincinnati.[190] Populism quickly became a significant political force in several states—Ohio, Wisconsin, Minnesota, South Dakota, Indiana, and Nebraska, among others. Though populist ideas were slower to influence Florida politics, in time, it occurred. Governor William Bloxham signed legislation in 1897 that did away with the practice of slating candidates for local election. From that point forward, primary elections—rather than party selections—were the means of

182. *Id.*; Arthur M. Schlesinger, Jr., *The Age of Jackson* 322 (Little, Brown & Co. 1945).

183. Proctor, *supra* n. 3, at 272.

184. *Id.*; George McKenna, *American Populism* 95, 99–100 (G.P. Putman's Sons 1974).

185. Proctor, *supra* n. 3, at 272.

186. Samuel Proctor, *The National Farmers' Alliance Convention of 1890 and Its "Ocala Demands,"* 28 Fla. Historical Q. 161, 161–81 (Jan. 1950).

187. *Id.*; Proctor, *supra* n. 3, at 272, 274.

188. Proctor, *supra* n. 3, at 274.

189. *Id.*

190. *Id.*

choosing local candidates.[191] In 1904, primaries for selecting candidates were extended to aspirants for state offices.

Moreover, in response to populist demands, the Florida Legislature established a commission to regulate railroads and, in 1897, the Legislature granted this regulatory body authority to promulgate rules "in the public's interest." The regulations included the prohibition of railroad rebates to favored shippers, and the discontinuance of railroads offering gratuitous passes and other favors to those in power.[192] Yet in time the Populist coalition's influence on Florida politics diminished. There was a transition to a more "Progressive Era," one that responded not only to the concerns of laborers, farmers, and merchants, but also took into consideration business and developmental interests. This progressive turn resulted in the 1904 election of Governor Napoleon Bonaparte Broward.[193]

Broward, a three-time elected sheriff of Duval County, espoused political views that coincided in part with those of the populists. Florida historian Charlton Tebeau notes that Broward shared the "strong Jeffersonian emphasis on farm-labor values."[194] Still, Broward recognized the benefits of growth and economic development. Thus, as leader of a new progressive coalition, he ran for office on a liberal, anti-railroad, and anti-corporation platform, yet one promoting the State's on-going growth and development. Consequently, he won both Wool Hats' and a sufficient number of Silk Hats' votes to win the 1904 election.[195]

The political domination of the Silk Hats—Bourbon Democrats and Northern (some would say "Robber Barons") Republicans—had come to an end. Now, men and women residing in rural communities, small towns, villages, and throughout Florida's frontier interior—citrus growers, cattlemen, homesteaders, cotton farmers, laborers, merchants, and professional people—had a voice in the State's political dialogue.

These folks also had legal problems. Many owned land; others rented; property disputes resulted; accidents occurred; people were injured; entrepreneurs started up businesses, and others sold theirs. Naturally, the people needed advice as their lives became more complex. Some began to question whether attorneys would be available in sufficient numbers to meet the rising demand

---

191. *Id.*; Tebeau, *supra* n. 56, at 304.

192. Tebeau, *supra* n. 56, at 304.

193. *See* Samuel Proctor, *Napoleon Bonaparte Broward: Florida's Fighting Democrat* 240–50 (U. Fla. Press 1950).

194. *Id.*; Gannon, *supra*, n. 40, at 67–69.

195. Proctor, *supra* n. 193, at 280–81.

for legal services. The call for a full-time law school in the State arose, a school that would provide rigorous training thought necessary to turn aspiring lawyers into competent attorneys.

2.2 Foundations of American Legal Education

American academic-based legal education was still in its formative years when Stetson University founded Florida's first law school in 1900.[196] Following America's War for Independence, those who desired to become lawyers in the "new world" did not go to law school.[197] University-related schools of law, as we know them today, did not come into existence until the last decades of the nineteenth century. Then, by 1890, there were sixty-one, increasing to 124 by 1910. The expansion has continued since. In the spring 2006, some 200 American Bar Association-approved, or provisionally approved, law schools, including ten in Florida.[198]

Back when Thomas Jefferson—one of the principal founders of American law schools—began to practice law in 1767, no law schools of any kind existed in the Colonies.[199] The Colonialist lawyers with sufficient financial resources studied the English common law at one of the Inns of Court in London.[200] But for the majority of the aspirants, they read law on their own, served as apprentices to practicing attorneys, or both.[201] Thomas Jefferson studied law as an apprentice, and, though he admired his own tutor, he did not favor the apprenticeship route. In a letter to a nephew, Jefferson advised, "All that is necessary [to become a lawyer] ... is access to a library and directions in what

---

196. For a comprehensive history of American legal education up until the 1980s, see Robert Stevens, *Law School: Legal Education in America from the 1850s to the 1980s* (U.N.C. Press 1983) [hereinafter Stevens, *Law School*].

197. *See* Lawrence M. Friedman: *A History of American Law* (2d ed., Simon & Schuster 1986).

198. These numbers come from the Carnegie Foundation 1921 study of American law schools. *See* Alfred Z. Reed, *Training for the Public Profession of Law* (Charles Scribner's Sons 1921).

199. John Ritchie, *The First Hundred Years: A Short History of the School of Law of the University of Virginia for the Period 1826–1926*, at 4 (U. Press Va. 1978).

200. Among the few fortunate ones who obtained their legal training at the Inns of Court were leading members of the bar in several of the colonies, many of whom were very influential in the Revolutionary War and the subsequent formation of the Union. Friedman, *supra* n. 197, at 97.

201. James Willard Hurst, *The Growth of American Law: The Law Makers* 256 (Little, Brown & Co. 1950).

order the [law] books should be read."[202] Similarly, Abraham Lincoln believed that, for those aspiring to be lawyers, the "cheapest, quickest, and best way" to the legal profession was to read great treatises on the law, such as Sir William Blackstone's *Commentaries on the Law of England*, "then to get a license and go practice and still keep reading."[203]

In spite of Jefferson's general objections to apprenticeship, he had little choice but to follow that path. As it turned out, he had a great tutor—George Wythe, a lawyer and teacher whom Jefferson came to admire greatly, so much so, that Jefferson made Wythe America's first academic law teacher, by naming him to an academic "chair" at the College of William and Mary.[204] In 1779, Jefferson reorganized the curriculum of the College of William and Mary to include a then rarely taught Constitutional law course, to be instructed by Wythe in the College's liberal arts program.[205] In addition to Constitutional law, Wythe taught other courses on government and politics. Professor Paul Carrington of Duke University School of Law, who has written on aspects of early American legal education, notes that the vision of Jefferson and Wythe that the practice of law was a public profession and should be taught as part of a *university* education was subsequently adopted at several other institutions, including Transylvania University in Kentucky.[206]

Jumping ahead to 1815, Harvard University appointed Issac Parker, the Chief Justice of the Massachusetts Supreme Court, to the endowed Royall Professorship of Law. Parker, unlike Wythe, taught law with little concern about Constitutional law and its Bill of Rights, emphasizing instead narrow legal

---

202. Swygert, *supra* n. 80, at 26–27.

203. Friedman, *supra* n. 197, at 606.

204. *Id.* at 320.

205. For an excellent discussion of Thomas Jefferson's and George Wythe's significance to legal education in America , *see* Paul D. Carrington, *The Revolutionary Idea of University Legal Education,* 31 Wm. & Mary L. Rev. 527 (1990). Carrington points out that Wythe was a mentor not only to Thomas Jefferson, but also to John Marshall (later Chief Justice of the United States), and to Henry Clay, *Id.*

In teaching law, Wythe had his students read Blackstone, one of whom was Sr. George Tucker, who later was the American editor of *Blackstone's Commentaries.* Tucker, according to Professor Carrington, added an additional volume to the *Commentaries*,and "made the book useful to Americans." Paul D. Carrington, e-mail from Paul D. Carrington, Henry R. Chadwick, Sr., Professor Emeritus, Duke U. School of L. to Michael I. Swygert, Professor Emeritus, Stetson U. College of L. (March 14, 2006).

206. *See* Paul D. Carrington, *Teaching Law and Virtue at Transylvania University: The George Wythe Tradition in the Antebellum Years,* 41 Mercer L. Rev. 673 (1990). According to Carrington, seven of Transylvania's students were among the fifty U.S. Senators who voted on the Compromise of 1850, which at that time saved the Union.

rules relating to contract and property rights. Parker's narrower vision of law did not survive for long at Harvard. In 1829, the Harvard law program was reestablished as a "law school" under the direction of professor Joseph Story. Story's view of legal education was more in line with that of Jefferson and Wythe, a view, Professor Carrington argues, that grew out of the American Revolution and its declaration and endorsement that individuals have rights.[207] Story's broader intellectual focus at Harvard, however, came to an end when Christopher Langdell became its dean in 1870.

The emphasis of teaching law within the broader context of contract, property, and individual rights continued in 1837, when the Regents of the University of Maryland appointed David Murray Hoffman to a newly established chair in law. Hoffman viewed preparing students for law in much the same manner as Story and Wythe. Hoffman had authored a book setting out a proposed curriculum, titled *A Course of Legal Study*, that drew great attention and remains historically a classic today. The Maryland law program was integrated into the general curriculum, unlike Harvard, where law study had been relegated to a separate and distinct curriculum within its law school. This intergration of law into a general curriculum had began at William and Mary, then was carried on at the University of Virginia (UVA)—founded by Thomas Jefferson—beginning in 1826 as part of its undergraduate liberal studies program.[208] Initially taught by John Taylor Lomax, the course was integrated into UVA's general curriculum, one that included history, music, philosophy, and science.[209]

William and Mary, UVA, and Maryland emphasized what scholars came to call the Jeffersonian tradition of legal education, which encompassed the idea that law should be studied as a component of a diverse curriculum, not as an isolated or narrow subject in itself, and certainly not one designed to teach law *solely* to enable students to become legal technicians.[210] Jefferson perceived law study not just as education in law, but also as preparation for men to become "gentlemen" so as to qualify for leadership in a wide range of fields, law being one.[211]

---

207. Hurst, *supra* n. 201, at 257. Some of the information in the above paragraph was furnished by Professor Paul D. Carrington. *See* Paul D. Carrington, and Henry R. Chadwick, Sr., Professor Emeritus, Duke U. School of L. to Michael I. Swygert, Professor Emeritus, Stetson U. College of L. (March 14, 2006).

208. *See* Ritchie, *supra* n. 199, at 7.

209. Herbert L. Packer & Thomas Ehrlich, *New Directions in Legal Education* 285 (McCraw-Hill 1973) [hereinafter *New Directions*].

210. For Jefferson's philosophy of education, see James B. Conant, *Thomas Jefferson and the Development of American Public Education* (U. Cal. Press 1962).

211. Thomas L. Shaffer & Robert S. Redmount, *Lawyers, Law Students and People* 17 (Shepard's 1977).

In a certain respect, the Jeffersonian concept reflected the first segment of the English approach to academic law study.[212] At Oxford or Cambridge, for examples, the study of law begins as an intellectual component within a broader liberal arts intellectual framework. The training of legal technicians in the technical rules of law and in the skills and nuances of law practice comes later in legal training taken in either the Inns of Court (barristers) or in the Law Society's (solicitors) College of Law. In contrast to this bifurcated system, in America, UVA in the nineteenth century focused almost entirely on the broader intellectual study of law.[213] Other universities that adopted the UVA integrated approach included the University of Michigan, Transylvania University, and the University of Cincinnati.[214]

Meanwhile, a distinctively different kind of legal training—one that minimized academic disciplines outside the law and was vocationally focused—had begun shortly after Jefferson's concept had been implemented at William and Mary. In 1784, Connecticut's Litchfield School of Law opened.[215] Litchfield was America's first entirely practitioner-oriented law school, one not integrated into a university. Using a structured teaching method, Tapping Reeve (the school's founder and a practicing attorney) took a group of students and lectured on various areas of law, but primarily on real estate conveyancing. The lectures were given in a small schoolhouse.[216] Reeve owned the school outright, not an uncommon phenomenon in early American legal education.[217] At Litchfield, students took a fourteen-month course of study, covering superficially a number of doctrinal topics.[218]

Students enrolling in the early proprietary-type law schools like Litchfield usually had no academic education beyond primary or, at most, secondary

---

212. Packer & Ehrlich, *supra* n. 209, at 285.

213. The University of Virginia was established by an act of the Virginia General Assembly on January 25, 1819. *See* Vause, *Centennial History, infra* n. 595.

214. Peter Del Swords & Frank K. Walwer, *The Costs and Resources of Legal Education: A Study of the Management of Educational Resources* 28 (Columbia U. Press 1974).

215. Friedman, *supra* n. 197, at 319. The significance of the Litchfield Law School is also discussed in Robert Stevens, *Two Cheers for 1870: The American Law School,* 5 Persp. Am. History 403, 403–548 (1971).

216. For a thorough discussion of the history and significance of the Litchfield Law School, see Marian C. McKenna, *Tapping Reeve and the Litchfield Law School* (Oceana Publications 1986).

217. Interview by Prof. Michael I. Swygert, Prof. Emeritus, Stetson U. College of L., with Walter F. Pratt., Jr., Assoc. Dean and Prof. of L., Notre Dame L. Sch. (Feb. 2002); *see also* Stevens, *Law School, supra* n. 196, at 5; *infra* n. 224 (regarding Valparaiso).

218. Friedman, *supra* n. 197, at 319.

levels. Consequently, law school education was strictly vocational training with little economic, psychological, philosophical, sociological, or historical undergirdings. This technician's approach to law study was used at Litchfield for nearly fifty years before the school closed in 1833. The few remaining "lecture-type schools" ceased to operate by 1850.[219]

Yet another distinctive style of academic law training first developed during the latter half of the nineteenth century—the *university-related*, rather than the *university-integrated* law program. It was called a university law school, the predominant form today. The first three university-related law schools opened at Harvard, Pennsylvania, and Yale.[220] Both Yale and Harvard law schools followed the Litchfield vocational model during their early years. Yale purchased a proprietary law school, one which had been operated for profit by the New Haven law firm of Stapels & Hitchcock.[221] By the late nineteenth century, however, Yale began to transform its vocational model into a prototype of today's university-related school of law. By 1840, the number of university-related law schools constituted fourteen of seventeen schools in existence, the other three operating as proprietary "evening" law schools.[222]

Turning to the Southern states, in addition to William and Mary, UVA, Maryland, and Transylvania, other early university-related law schools included Georgia (1843), North Carolina (1845), Alabama (1845), Louisville (1846), Tulane (1847), Cumberland (1847), and South Carolina.[223] Among the university-related law schools in the South, perhaps the most significant was the law school associated with the University of South Carolina. Professor Carrington observes that South Carolina was the beneficiary of two formidable intellectual professors within the Jeffersonian tradition: Thomas Cooper and Francis Lieber. Lieber, Carrington notes, became "the intellectual founder of Columbia University Law School."[224] In addition to law, Cooper taught medicine.

Prior to the outbreak of the War between the States, there had been twenty-five university-related law schools. Though the Civil War caused several of these to close, the number of university-related law schools increased sharply after the war. The results were clear by 1900, the year Stetson University Col-

---

219. Hurst, *supra* n. 201, at 258.

220. Reed, *supra* n. 198, at 132–133.

221. *Id.* at 142.

222. Del Swords & Walwer, *supra* n. 214, at 30.

223. *Id.* at 29.

224. *See* Paul D. Carrington, *The Aims of Early American Law Teaching: The Patriotism of Francis Lieber,* 42 J. Leg. Ed. 339 (1992). For a list of law schools that came into existence in the 1840s and 1850s in the South, *see* Del Swords & Walwer, *supra* n. 214, at 30.

lege of Law opened. Twenty percent of America's lawyers held law-school degrees, compared with less than five percent in 1850.[225]

One reason may have been that the university-related model of legal education was evolving into what, in the 1870s, some called the "scientific" analysis of law, a pedagogy of analytic study thought by certain law professors to be distinct from many other academic programs. The Jeffersonian tradition of legal education as a component of an undergraduate "major" curriculum was quickly disappearing, being replaced by a model implemented at Harvard, one emphasizing the "scientific" study of law, a technical course of law study that provided students little exposure to the Jeffersonian broad liberal arts program beyond the doctrinal rules of law. Nonetheless, in time the Harvard "elite model law school" became the prototype from 1870 onward for several decades. But not all law schools emulated the model. A few schools (particularly Columbia) did not follow Harvard and introduced social sciences into their law school curricula, especially from around 1915 onward. Today, most of America's law schools incorporate social science perspectives in teaching law, including those coming from economics, statistics, sociology, and history.

In 1870, Harvard University President Charles Elliot appointed Christopher Columbus Langdell to be dean of Harvard's Law School.[226] Langdell has received credit for changing legal education in America. His philosophy of learning coincided with that of Harvard's President Elliot. Both espoused a pedagogy for teaching and learning that demanded students learn general principles of law from real life situations.[227] In other words, the student begins with facts that lead to theory. "From facts to theory" became and remains one of the pedagogies of the casebook method of learning law. The "theory," however, was seldom nourished by the social sciences.

Langdell introduced the casebook pedagogy to Harvard after he had become dean.[228] As noted earlier, he called his approach "the scientific study of the law." Not all his contemporaries, however, supported the casebook versus

---

225. *Report of the Committee on Legal Education of the American Bar Association,* vol. 14, 318 (ABA 1891); *see also Reports of the American Bar Association*, vol. 17, 462–463 (ABA 1894).

226. Chase, *supra* n. 148, at 342.

227. *Id.* at 333–334 (quoting in part Hugh Hawkins, *Between Harvard and America: The Educational Leadership of Charles W. Eliot* (Oxford U. Press 1972)); *see also* Alain Touraine, *The Academic System in American Society* 46 (McGraw-Hill 1974).

228. Hurst, *supra* n. 201, at 265. One scholar has suggested that Langdell was not the first to introduce the casebook pedagogy into American legal education, but that it was Professor John Norton Pomeroy who did so prior to 1870 at the University of New York City (now New York University). *See* Chase, *supra* n. 149, at 329 n.16.

textbook teaching method, including several of his Harvard colleagues. It should be noted that Harvard was not the first American law school to adopt casebooks. They had been used earlier at Iowa, among other schools.

Nonetheless, according to a 1914 report issued by the Carnegie Foundation for the Advancement of Teaching, the casebook method of instruction was "an entirely original creation of the American mind."[229] The Carnegie report noted that the best learning in law school occurred when the student was made to focus on a series of related cases through an "analytical decomposition" and analysis of each case, and through the "distillation of legal principles."[230] Under the case method, learning is always in a flux, as each case presents a new opportunity to define and refine what the student has learned previously. Most, if not all, university-related law schools such as Harvard in 1870 did not require *any* undergraduate, broad curriculum training. The Langdellian method in essence remained vocationally centered in a narrow sense, even though it was a refined version of the Litchfield tradition and in contrast to the legal education philosophy of Jefferson, Wythe, Cooper, and Hoffman.

Meanwhile, at many university-related law schools, a new teaching pedagogy developed hand-in-hand with case books. The teacher typically would ask the student a series of questions, changing a fact here and there to probe the student's understanding of the principle of law being applied. This method came to be known (in a strict sense, inaccurately) as the "Socratic" teaching style.[231]

Previously, the predominant teaching pedagogies in law schools consisted of the teacher lecturing, and students standing up in class and reciting relevant rules of law learned from textbooks. In contrast, under the so-called Socratic method of learning, ideally the student and teacher continuously interacted in a mutually participatory learning situation. Langdell emphasized that in the classroom, "it is critical that the efforts of the students go hand-in-hand with mine."[232] Students read the cases (rather then passages of a textbook) before class; then in class, they responded directly (or vicariously) to a series of questions from their instructor designed to stimulate analytical thinking. In a

229. Josef Redlich, *The Common Law and the Case Method in American University Law Schools, A Report to the Carnegie Foundation for the Advancement of Teaching* 1 (Found. 1914).

230. *Id.*

231. Hurst, *supra* n. 201, at 265. The teaching method of Socrates required more intuitive learning on the part of a student than is customary in law school classrooms.

232. Christopher Columbus Langdell, *A Selection of Cases on the Law of Contracts* ii–vii (Little, Brown & Co. 1871).

1894 report to the American Bar Association,[233] Harvard Law Professor William A. Keener described the casebook learning process:

> [It is through] the study of cases that one is to acquire the power of legal reasoning, discrimination and judgment, qualities indispensable to the practicing lawyer ... the study of cases best develops the power to analyze and to state clearly and concisely a complicated state of facts.[234]

It took several decades for most American law schools to adopt the combination Langdellian casebook/Socratic pedagogy. Interestingly, the better-known schools—including, Harvard, Yale, Chicago, Michigan, and Columbia—were among the first to deemphasize this narrow focus on analytical study primarily on cases only, when they began to integrate social science principles into a more intellectual study of law.

In recent decades, probably a large majority of law school teachers have relied less on Socratic-style methodology. For one thing, the majority of entering law students in today's era have already developed analytic reasoning in undergraduate courses, though clearly not all. For the better students, the Socratic style of instructors quizzing students day after class day has become tedious and moves too slowly to cover the growing body of legal principles and their cultural, political, and economic foundations.

At Stetson University College of Law, the Socratic quizzing of students about cases read from casebooks first began around 1914, after Richmond A. Rasco became the dean. Though still used at the College today, the Socratic teaching style is much less in evidence in comparison with two decades ago. Today, Stetson law professors supplement the Socratic method with interactive lectures, hypothetical problems, group projects, and simulations of lawyering activities such as pre-trial practice, negotiations, trial practice, and appellate arguments.

2.3 Founding of Stetson University College of Law

a. Florida and DeLand at the Turn of the Century

During the first few years of the twentieth century, changes were occurring both in Florida and in the country. Some were monumental, while others were

233. William A. Keener, *The Inductive Method in Legal Education,* in *Reports of the American Bar Association,* vol. 17, 473, 473 (ABA 1893).

234. *Id.*

anything but. A few examples: women were beginning to wear skirts above their ankles;[235] art nouveau's popularity was coming to an end;[236] Cubans and Italians increasingly were moving into the Ybor City section of Tampa (where the hand-rolled cigar industry was flourishing);[237] William Sherman Jennings was elected Florida's Governor (the progressive era was in full swing);[238] the country elected McKinley and Roosevelt U.S. President and Vice President, folks saw automobiles more frequently;[239] and the John B. Stetson University in DeLand, Florida, expanded, opening the first law school in the State of Florida.[240]

A person born in the United States in 1900 had an average life expectancy of forty-seven years.[241] America's total population was 76,212,168,[242] while Florida's population in 1900, according to the U.S. Census, was 528,542.[243] Tallahassee had 2,091 residents.[244] Duval was the most populous county in Florida—39,733—followed by Hillsborough with 36,013; then Alachua with 32,245.[245] Volusia County's (where DeLand was the county seat) population was 10,003.[246] Meanwhile, southeast Florida lagged behind the comparatively heavily populated northeast section of the State. Consider that in 1900 Dade County's population (where Miami is located) was less than 5,000.[247]

Meanwhile, Jacksonville was the largest city in the State, with 28,249 residents, followed by Pensacola, Key West, then Tampa.[248] Incidentally, one year after the 1900 census, Jacksonville experienced one of the most devastating

235. Proctor, *supra* n. 3, at 70.

236. Johnson, supra n. 61, at 598.

237. *See* Raymond A. Mohl & George E. Pozzetta, *From Migration to Multiculturalism: A History of Florida Immigration*, in *The New History of Florida*, *supra* n. 3, at 391, 398.

238. Proctor, *supra* n. 3, at 178.

239. Morris, *supra* n. 19, at 3–4.

240. *See infra* nn. 342–343 and accompanying text.

241. Johnson, *supra* n. 61, at 590.

242. U.S. Census Bureau, *United States Summary: Population and Housing Units 1790 to 1990*, at tbl 2.2 (Gov. Prtg. Off. 2004) [hereinafter *United States Summary*]; *see also* U.S. Census Bureau, *Twelfth United States Census* vol. 1, pt. 1, 2, 94 (Gov. Prtg. Off. 1900).

243. *United States Summary*, *supra* n. 242, at tbl. 16; *see also* Proctor, *supra* n. 193, at 65. Historian Samuel Proctor lists a lower 1900 Florida population of 421,511 in his book chapter titled *Prelude to a New Florida, 1877–1919*. Proctor, *supra* n. 3, at 282.

244. Clifton Paisley, *The Red Hills of Florida* 212 (U. Ala. 1989).

245. U.S. Census Bureau, *Florida: Population of Counties by Decennial Census: 1900 to 1990*, at 4 (Richard L. Forstal ed., Gov. Prtg. Off.1995).

246. *Id.* at 5.

247. *Id.* at 4.

248. Proctor, *supra* n. 3, at 282.

fires in the State's history. On May 3, 1901, the city's entire downtown, as well as a good portion of the residential sections, was destroyed, leaving 10,000 homeless.[249]

As to rate of growth, Tampa grew from less than 1,000 in 1882 to close to 15,000 by 1900. Hillsborough County's overall population rose 141% between 1890 and 1900 alone.[250] Yet despite this rapid growth, Florida's population was the smallest of all the Southern states at the beginning of the twentieth century.[251]

That new "confangled" invention—the automobile—began to appear in Florida from about 1900 onward; even a few showed up in DeLand. Beginning in 1903, several of these noisy "horse substitutes" appeared on Daytona's beaches to race on the hard sand.[252] Historian Michael Gannon notes that by 1906, 2,906 automobiles were registered in Florida, including seventy-four in Daytona and seventeen in Jacksonville, more evidence of the State's adapting to the new industrial age, especially along Florida's northeast coast.[253] Roads, however, were few and poor in quality. The exception was the road between Pensacola and St. Augustine.[254]

For the most part, however, people still traveled on horseback, in horse-drawn wagons, carriages using oxen to pull high-wheel wagons, and in riverboats.[255] Though electricity was available only in limited areas, the town of DeLand was electrified. Summers (as now) were hot and humid, but unlike today, no air conditioning existed. Relief came by the way of an ocean breeze, a hand-held fan, or sitting under a live-oak tree.

At the turn of the century, winter tourists were increasingly discovering the benefits of Florida's beaches, and Florida was increasingly discovering the benefits of winter tourists. In the midst of these changing times and circumstances in Florida's history, a risky venture sprouted up—a law school.

b. Forbes, Harper, Flagler, and the University of Chicago

In 1887, Stetson University President John Forbes pondered the future expansion of what was then called DeLand University. He considered that some

---

249. *Id.* at 282–283.

250. *Id.* at 282.

251. David R. Colburn, *Florida Politics in the Twentieth Century*, in *The New History of Florida*, *supra* n. 3, at 344, 345.

252. Proctor, *supra* n. 3, at 283.

253. Proctor, *supra* n. 174, at 71.

254. Mark F. Boyd, *The First American Road in Florida: Pensacola-St. Augustine Highway, 1824,* 14 Fla. Historical Q. 73, 106 (Oct. 1935).

255. Proctor, *supra* n. 3, at 274.

day specialized and professional schools might be added. That same year, the Florida Legislature granted a charter giving legal authority to DeLand University and to its Board of Trustees. The Charter also included regulations for the Board's perpetuation and for limiting its locations for dispensing educational services.[256] Interestingly, section eight of the Charter—officially titled "An Act to Incorporate an Institution of Learning at DeLand, Florida, under the name of DeLand University"—provided:

> Sec. 8 ... *however,* the law and medical departments, in case any such shall be established, may by a two-thirds vote of said [Board of] Trustees be located at or near the city of Jacksonville, Florida, in said State of Florida.[257]

Section seven of the 1887 Charter clearly stated that the University's Trustees had legal authority to establish "schools of every description ... and departments devoted to instruction in theology, law, medicine, general or particular sciences and literature of the arts."[258] Stetson's "law department," or "College of Law" (as it also was called), opened thirteen years after enactment of the 1887 Charter. Jacksonville, however, was not the location. Rather, the College opened on the University's DeLand Campus. Perhaps it was a harbinger of things to come. Fifty-three years later, Jacksonville a second time would not be chosen for the College's location following a debate over whether to relocate the College of Law to Jacksonville, Orlando, Tampa, St. Petersburg, or a small community adjacent to St. Petersburg named Gulfport.[259]

In 1897, President Forbes knew that Florida had neither a law nor an engineering school, and thought that the University in DeLand could fill the void.[260] His immediate concern was how money might be raised to finance the expansionary ventures. As Forbes had done on previous occasions, he went to John B. Stetson and argued why the University should establish two new university divisions. Stetson, however, was not persuaded that a law school, in particular, should be attempted. Nor did he wish to finance such a venture. He said to Forbes, "[T]he day had passed [for my giving] these large sums without feeling it and feeling it deeply."[261]

---

256. An Act to Incorporate an Institution of Learning at DeLand, Florida, under the Name of DeLand University, 1887 Fla. Laws ch. 3808, § 128.

257. *Id.* (emphasis added).

258. *Id.* (emphasis added).

259. *See infra* nn. 1655–1700 and accompanying text.

260. Lycan, *History of Stetson, supra* n. 109, at 84.

261. *Id.* at 85 (writing that though Stetson may have been worth five million dollars, he may not have much money "lying in the bank waiting to be spent").

Benefactor Henry Flagler

Fortunately for Forbes, John B. Stetson was not the only multi-millionaire in Florida. Aware of the huge investments railroad magnate Henry Morrison Flagler was making in the State, Forbes went out of his way to befriend the former oil tycoon. On one occasion, Forbes traveled to New York to talk with Flagler about investing in the University.[262] Forbes' efforts in the end were successful. In 1897, Flagler donated $10,000 to DeLand University on the condition that his name not be disclosed until after his death.[263] Stetson's Trustees, in the hope of becoming more closely allied with a business giant who had a deep pocketbook, elected Flagler to the University's board, but he declined.[264] Nonetheless, Flagler became a major benefactor of Stetson University, if only for a short time.

Meantime, on February 10, 1898—a day described in a Jacksonville newspaper as the "most memorable day in connection with higher education in the annals of [Florida]"—President Forbes announced that a fund drive he had directed had raised $100,000 for the University's endowment.[265] He revealed the good news at the University's annual Presentation Day ceremonies.

262. *Id.* at 61–62.

263. *Id.* at 63 (citing a front-page article in the *Jacksonville Florida Times-Union*). Around campus, everyone was aware that the donor was Henry Flagler. *Id.*

264. *Id.*

265. *Id.* at 64.

Flagler Hall

As it turned out, the keynote speaker for that year's Presentation Day was University of Chicago President William Rainey Harper, who offered something other than money to Stetson University—prestige.[266] Historian Lycan summarizes what happened: "Harper liked what he saw at Stetson, and he had so much confidence in the institution's future that he suggested to Forbes that [Chicago and Stetson Universities] become affiliated. Forbes was delighted [with the idea]."[267]

Harper had another reason to be attracted to Stetson. He was a Baptist and had been a Professor of Hebrew at the Baptist Union Theological Seminary in Morgan Park, Illinois. And like Stetson University, the University of Chicago's affiliation with the Baptists was solid; in fact, Chicago's 1892 Charter required that at least one-third (ten) of its thirty trustees be Baptists.[268]

After examining the academic standards in place at Stetson University and the competence of its faculty, Harper was satisfied that Stetson University was qualified to affiliate with the University of Chicago.[269] Chicago had earlier established affiliations with three other Baptist institutions: Kalamazoo College in Michigan, Butler University in Indiana, and Des Moines College in Iowa.[270]

---

266. *Biography of William Rainey Harper*, www.lib.uchicago.edu/projects/centcat/centcats.pres.prescho01_01.html (accessed on June 13, 2004).

267. Lycan, *History of Stetson, supra* n. 109, at 64.

268. *Id.* at 63.

269. Gordis, *supra* n. 105, at 25. After affiliation, "honor graduates of Stetson became at once graduates of the University of Chicago." *Id.* at 26.

270. Lycan, *History of Stetson, supra* n. 109, at 70.

Harper's plan was to expand the University of Chicago's "affiliation program" across the country to bring "uniformity and high standards to college work in America."[271]

Affiliation between the University of Chicago and Stetson University officially began in fall 1899.[272] Students from each school could take courses at the other.[273] Incidentally, one University of Chicago student who spent a winter at Stetson University taking courses, pursuant to the affiliation program, was the father of John Paul Stevens, Associate Justice of the United States Supreme Court.[274]

Despite strong disapproval of Harper's affiliation program by many University of Chicago faculty members, the program continued for eight years before the University of Chicago terminated it. Stetson University, however, was slow in acknowledging that its ties with Chicago had ended, and for several years made erroneous and misleading references, proclaiming Stetson's continuing academic linkage with the institution located on the midway of the Windy City.[275]

However, while it lasted, the University of Chicago and Stetson University affiliation was especially beneficial to Stetson and to its College of Law, impacting favorably on the status of both.[276] Recognized as one of the nation's elite institutions of higher learning, the University of Chicago opened after oil tycoon John D. Rockefeller, a one-time partner of Henry Flagler,[277] magnanimously endowed the institution "to assure [its] best possible management."[278]

271. *Id.* at 73.

272. *Id.*

273. In a full-page advertisement in a 1902 edition of *The Stetson Collegiate*, under the name in bold 36-point type of "Jon. B. Stetson University" appears "in affiliation with" (14-point type), followed again in bold, this time 28-point type, "The University of Chicago." Immediately below in 16-point type is written: "PRO RATA CREDIT GIVEN IN EITHER INSTITUTION FOR WORK IN THE OTHER." At the bottom, the advertisement reads, "For further information address the President, JOHN F. FORBES, Ph. D., DeLand, Fla." *See John. B. Stetson University,* Stetson Collegiate 16 (Apr. 1902) (advertisement).

274. John Paul Stevens, *Remarks* (St. Pete., Fla. 1989) (on file at Stetson U. College of L., Gulfport, Fla.).

275. Lycan, *History of Stetson, supra* n. 109, at 75, 165–172.

276. "It is obvious that such recognition by one of the foremost Universities of the country had tremendous significance for a small young southern university." Gordis, *supra* n. 105, at 26.

277. John P. Howe, Chicago, University of, *Encyclopedia Britannica* vol. 5, 457 (William Yust ed., 1946 U. Chicago, 1946). Rockefeller over the years donated more than $35 million to the university, and the boards of his trust donated countless millions more. *Id.*

278. *Id.*

This meant that Chicago could (and did) attract renowned professors who, in turn, would (and did) help establish a high-quality student body to come to its Gothic-inspired campus.

John D. Rockefeller's relationship with the University of Chicago was helpful to Stetson University. Henry Flagler, prior to building his Florida railroad, steamship, and hotel empire, was Rockefeller's partner in developing the Standard Oil Company, the giant enterprise that for several decades was the world's largest oil conglomerate.[279] In time, the Rockefeller-Flagler company evolved into the most powerful and predatory monopoly in America, one that had world-wide tenacles. By 1890, Standard Oil Company controlled ninety percent of the world's oil refining capacity.[280] But its dominance did not last. In 1911, the United States Supreme Court ordered the break up of the oil giant.[281] The Court held that the company had illegally fixed prices, paid illegal rebates, and engaged in other illegal and predatory practices, all designed to drive competitors out of business.[282] Prior to this judicial dismantling, however, the partnership of Rockefeller and Flagler earned millions of dollars for each. Flagler explained their method: "It was our idea to work night and day making good oil as cheaply as possible and selling it for [as much as] we could."[283] He did not further explain, however, that this was accomplished by driving competitive companies out of the market through predatory pricing and group boycotts.

After dissolving his partnership with Rockefeller, Flagler re-directed his business efforts to Florida. In time, Henry Flagler met, and came to admire, Stetson's president, John Forbes. Flagler was gratified that Stetson University was a Christian-related institution. A devoutly religious Presbyterian, he was raised in a Puritan home where religious observance was a priority.[284] Throughout his life, Flagler said that he lived in accordance with the high moral standards of his faith. He expected that those around him live morally (as he defined the term). He opposed in particular the use of alcohol. Thus, he was pleased that Stetson University prohibited the consumption of alcohol on campus. For that matter, "no licensed saloon" was said to exist in Volusia County.[285]

---

279. Chandler, *supra* n. 71, at 3–5; Akin, *supra* n. 71; Martin, *supra* n. 71.

280. Chandler, *supra* n. 71, at 4.

281. *Stand. Oil Co. v. U.S.*, 221 U.S. 1 (1911).

282. *Id.*

283. *Id.*

284. Martin, *supra* n. 71, at 258.

285. John B. Stetson U. Dept. of L., *Annual Announcement* 10 (1901–1902) (on file at Stetson U. College of L., Gulfport, Fla.).

Given Flagler's strong religiosity, his friendship with Forbes, his connection with Rockefeller, and his proclaimed belief in aspiring to the high standards of personal morality, it is not surprising that Forbes wrote Flagler outlining the University's opportunity to expand and its need for financial assistance in doing so.[286] In a three-page letter, President Forbes asked the Florida developer to fund "first and foremost a School of Technology patterned after the Sheffield Scientific School at Yale."[287] Forbes added, somewhat parenthetically, that "there also [is] an increasing demand for a law department in the University."[288]

After describing the opportunities and needs for these schools, Forbes sought Flagler's financial support for the construction of a building to house the proposed new enterprises.[289] Flagler responded that he would donate $60,000 for the new quarters, but that, just as he had done in his earlier $10,000 gift to the University's endowment,[290] his name not be disclosed until after his death, "fearing that other colleges would also ask him for money."[291] How did Forbes come to believe that a law program in Florida was needed? That story follows.

c. *Encouragement of the State's Attorneys and Florida Supreme Court to Start a Law School*

Beginning around 1897, several Florida lawyers suggested to President Forbes that the University should open a law school, pointing out that none existed in the State. According to Olga Bowen (Stetson University's archivist during the 1970s), the Florida Supreme Court and "The Florida Bar Association" both were urging Forbes and members of the Board of Trustees for the University to commence a program of professional law study.[292]

Bowen's description of the "Florida Bar Association," however, is not entirely accurate. Not until 1907 did the "Florida State Bar Association" come into existence.[293] And not until 1950 was its name changed to "The Florida

---

286. President John Forbes' letter to Henry Flagler was written on March 17, 1899. Lycan, *History of Stetson, supra* n. 109, at 85.

287. *Id.* (citing Ltr. from John Forbes, Pres., Stetson U. to Henry Flagler, *Request for University Funding* (Mar. 17, 1899) (on file at Stetson U. Archives, DeLand, Fla., in *General Correspondence Stetson University* vol. 2, 463)).

288. *Id.*

289. *Id.*

290. *Id.* at 86.

291. Sidney Johnston, *The Historic Stetson University in DeLand, 1884–1934*, 70 Fla. Historical Q. 281, 292–294 (Jan. 1992).

292. Olga Bowen, *The Stetson College of Law* 1 (unpublished ms. 1969) (on file in Stetson U. College of L., Gulfport, Fla).

293. *The Story of the Florida Bar, A History* 2 (Fla. B. n.d.) (circa 1975).

Bar."[294] At that time, the organization became an integrated, compulsory-membership association for all attorneys licensed to practice in Florida.[295]

Yet the earliest assembly of a group of Florida lawyers may have taken place in 1899 when "a small, voluntary group" occasionally met in informal gatherings.[296] Though no evidence has been found suggesting that this loosely organized group had contacted Forbes about establishing a law school, many individual attorneys and judges did so. A few Floridians, moreover, promised Forbes they would assist the new venture financially, a promise that Forbes later had to remind them to fulfill.[297] The importance of Florida's lawyers in encouraging the University's founding of the new law venture is acknowledged in an 1899 announcement of the Law School's opening: "At the request of *prominent members of the Bar* and many others, the College of Law of the John B. Stetson University will be opened in DeLand, October 2, 1900."[298]

The decision was about to be made. In President Forbes' annual report to the University Trustees for 1899, he wrote: "[The] time seems ripe for the establishment of a Law School as a separate department in the University."[299] He continued,

> [T]here had been a steadily growing demand for [a law school] as evidenced by our correspondence for the past five years. I have been inves-

---

294. *Id.* at 3–4. A description of the formation of the compulsory Florida Bar reads:

> In the summer of 1949, the Florida Supreme Court told the State Bar officials to proceed [instituting compulsory membership on admission to practice]. At that time Justice W. Glenn Terrell said: "A new Bar with compulsory membership would benefit the public and the profession", He wrote that the new Bar plan "provides a fair and equitable method for which every lawyer may participate in and help bear the burden of carrying on the activities of the Bar, instead of resting the duty on the voluntary association composed of a minority membership." ... [Subsequently, the 3,758 attorneys in Florida in 1950 automatically became members of the Florida Bar.] *Id.*

295. *Id.*

296. *Id.* at 2–3.

297. Lycan, *History of Stetson, supra* n. 109, at 87 (citing, as an example of Forbes writing, an attorney for support, a letter from Forbes to J.C. Davant, of Brooksville, Florida, dated September 27, 1899).

298. *About Your Law School* 3 (circa 1900) (unsigned document on file in Stetson U. Archives, DeLand, Fla.) (emphasis added).

299. Memo. from John F. Forbes, President, Stetson U. to the Stetson U. Bd. of Trustees, *President's Report to the Board of Trustees of John B. Stetson University* 6 (1899) (copy on file in Stetson U. Archives, DeLand, Fla.).

> tigating this matter ... and have consulted with judges and lawyers throughout the State, and find but one opinion: viz, that such a school would be of great importance and value in raising the standard in the practice of law in Florida, and that the standard sorely needs to be raised.[300]

Forbes emphasized that a law school would "be of immense value to the University" as it would graduate a "large body of alumni among the most influential men in the political life of the State and in public service."[301] (His prediction proved to be prophetic.) Forbes added that a law school would "do a great and beneficent work for the State" and thereby, also bring credit to the University.[302]

Forbes' arguments won over the Trustees, John B. Stetson's previous reservations notwithstanding. In 1899, the Board officially authorized establishment of the Stetson University College of Law (though many referred to the new division as a "law department").

d. Albert J. Farrah, the College of Law's First Dean

Having convinced the Board of Trustees to establish the law school, President Forbes next sought advice on how to go about it. He knew little about law schools, let alone how to organize and start one. Apparently, no one else in Florida did either. Then, serendipity intervened.

In summer 1899, John Forbes and his family were vacationing at the Lake Placid Club in upstate New York.[303] Lake Placid was (and is) a small village in the Adirondack Mountains. The Club was sometimes referred to as a "university in the wilderness," as it was a place that attracted guests "predominantly from educational circles, college professors, teachers, preachers, writers, librarians, etc."[304] By sheer coincidence, Professor E.W. Huffcutt of the Cornell Law School was a guest at the Club. There, Forbes and Huffcutt met, at first no doubt engaging in country-clubbish small talk.[305] But upon learning that

---

300. *Id.*

301. *Id.*

302. *Id.*

303. Bowen, *supra* n. 292, at 1.

304. Lee Manchester, *The Lake Placid Club, 1890–2002*, at 2 (Adirondack Publg. Co. 2003).

305. The owner of the Lake Placid Club at that time, Melvin Dewey (founder of the Dewey Decimal System), hoped that this Club would "provide a place for open-minded people to relax, get healthy and share ideas"—and it certainly did that day. Manchester, *supra* n. 304, at 2; *see generally The Last Dance, Adirondack Life,* Mag. 42 (Apr. 1987).

Huffcutt was an experienced law school professor, Forbes seized the opportunity and asked the legal educator how Stetson University should put together and start up a law program.[306]

Huffcutt was pleased to be asked and was quick to respond. Over the next several days, the two academics discussed many relevant topics, including how the new law school should be organized, what should be included in its curriculum,[307] and "what characteristics a man should have" to be an effective law teacher.[308] In giving advice on these and other matters, Professor Huffcutt became the College of Law's first (and arguably most important) consultant in its history. The Cornell law professor drafted a proposed two-year course that he advised should be the minimum time for a student to obtain a law degree. He then recommended specific textbooks for each course. Moreover, Huffcutt advised Forbes what legal materials would be necessary for assembling the nucleus of a workable law library.[309]

When it came to selecting faculty for the new law school, Forbes also turned to Huffcutt for recommendations, but not until Forbes' own efforts proved fruitless. Forbes' first faculty offer went to W.E. Waltz of Bangor, Maine, at the salary of $1,500 per year (which would have been the highest salary at Stetson University).[310] Waltz was not interested. Then, J.C. Davant of Brooksville, Florida, wrote Forbes to inquire about a law teaching position. Forbes was not interested.[311] With mounting anxiety, the Stetson President wrote Huffcutt asking the Cornell law professor for help "to secure a man to teach in the Law Department."[312]

Though no written response to Forbes' letter has been found, the Cornell professor did offer specific suggestions since Forbes, in a subsequent letter to Huffcutt, acknowledged the latter's suggestions of "several names."[313] Among

306. *Id.*

307. Lycan, *History of Stetson, supra* n. 109, at 87–88.

308. W. Gary Vause, *Foundations for Excellence—The History of Stetson University College of Law*, 16 Stetson L. Rev. 295, 302–303 (1987) [hereinafter Vause, *Foundations for Excellence*].

309. Bowen, *supra* n. 292, at 1–2.

310. Lycan, *History of Stetson, supra* n. 109, at 87.

311. Ltr. from John F. Forbes to J.C. Davant, *Teaching Position at Stetson* (Sept. 27, 1899) (on file at Stetson U. Archives, DeLand, Fla., in *General Correspondence Stetson University* vol. 4, at 290).

312. Ltr. from John F. Forbes to E.W. Huffcutt, *Regarding Qualified Law Professors* (Sept. 27, 1899) (on file at Stetson U. Archives, DeLand, Fla., in *General Correspondence Stetson University* vol. 4, 279–280).

313. Ltr. from John F. Forbes to E.W. Huffcutt, *Regarding Qualified Law Professors* (Oct. 23, 1899) (on file at Stetson U. Archives, DeLand, Fla., in *General Correspondence Stetson University* vol. 4, 421).

Dean Albert J. Farrah

Huffcutt's recommendations were Professor Charles Pickett of the University of Illinois and Professor P.C. Woodward of Dickinson College in Pennsylvania.[314] Neither worked out, as Pickett never responded, and Woodward wanted too much money.

Staffing the College of Law was taking longer than Forbes had expected. Originally, the University planned to open the law school on January 1, 1900, but given Forbes' difficulty in finding "the right man" to be dean (as well as faculty members), the president postponed the opening nine months, until early October.[315]

Huffcutt then suggested a name for a possible dean of the Stetson College of Law, Albert J. Farrah, a University of Michigan Law School graduate and currently a professor of law at that institution. It turned out to be an excellent suggestion.

Albert Farrah was born in the small town of Adrian, Michigan, on July 15, 1863.[316] He became interested in education early in life. Years later, from 1889 through 1894, Farrah served as superintendent of a Michigan school district.[317] He next entered the University of Michigan Law School, graduating with a law degree in 1896. Admitted to the Michigan Bar the same year, Farrah practiced

314. Bowen, *supra* n. 292, at 2.

315. *Id.*

316. Ala. Libr. Assn., *Alabama Authors and Their Works*, www.lib.auburn.edu/madd/docs/ala_authors/f.html (accessed Oct. 29, 2004) (citing *Who Was Who in America*, vol. 2).

317. *Id.*

law in Battle Creek for one year before leaving to join the University of Michigan law faculty.[318] Farrah was teaching law at Michigan when Forbes contacted him and asked whether he might be interested in the deanship at Stetson's new law college.[319] Farrah had just concluded co-authoring one of the first casebooks on domestic relations in America, a 488-page volume with the interesting title *Cases on the Law of Husband and Wife*.[320] Forbes was impressed by Farrah's productivity, but even more so by his being a university law professor, especially at Michigan. By 1899, the University of Michigan's law school had become one of the most visible, high quality, and largest law schools in America.[321] In spite of Farrah's relatively youthful age (thirty-seven), Forbes hired him. Historian Gilbert Lycan wrote:

> [Farrah] won Forbes' respect by asking about the adequacy of the library, the amount of support Stetson University would give the new school, and how a law school would be received in the community and in Florida. [Forbes] judged correctly that the young man was interested in the right points.[322]

Lycan added that Farrah's appointment as the College's first dean "proved to be a good one."[323]

Indeed, Farrah was the right person for the task. After being hired, without delay he began promoting the school. He drafted advertisements and announcements designed to attract prospective students. Farrah also suggested that President Forbes have a circular printed and sent to "all male students in the colleges of Florida, Georgia, Mississippi, and Alabama." Forbes agreed. As a result, the Stetson University distributed 2,000 circulars announcing the opening of the College of Law throughout the four-state area.[324]

---

318. *Id.*

319. Bowen, *supra* n. 292, at 2.

320. Primary Source Microfilm, *Family Law*, http://microformguides.gale.com/browsesubset.asp?colldocid=1017013&Page=1 (accessed Oct. 29, 2004).

321. Henry Wade Rodgers, *Law School of the University of Michigan*, 1 Green Bag 189, 189–208 (1889). For an earlier history by the same author, see Henry Wade Rodgers, *The Law Department of Michigan University*, 3 W. Jurist 129, 129 (1869); *see also* Stevens, *Law School*, *supra* n. 196, at 73, 81–83.

322. Lycan, *History of Stetson*, *supra* n. 109, at 88.

323. *Id.*

324. Ltr. from Albert Farrah to John F. Forbes, *Law School Promotion* (June 22, 1900) (on file at Stetson U. Archives, DeLand, Fla., in *General Correspondence Stetson University* vol. 17, 98).

e. Marketing a New Law School

President Forbes also understood that Stetson's initial success in attracting law students depended on advertising. The President wrote to every newspaper editor in Florida, telling them about the opening of the law school, and asking that each include a story about it in their respective publications.[325] Forbes urged the editors to underscore that Stetson's law school was the first professional school in Florida.[326] Inside each envelope, Forbes inserted a copy of the 1899–1900 Stetson University Annual Catalog, which included a full-page advertisement. The language of the promotive announcement follows:

> **STETSON UNIVERSITY**
> **A SCHOOL OF FIRST RANK**
> **DeLand, Florida**
> **Affiliated With Chicago University**
>
> Work done in one institution gives pro rata credit in the other. The degree of A.B. in Stetson, with a credit of 90 percent in college studies, entitles the student to A.B. in Chicago.
>
> Instruction is Now Offered in ...
>
> THE SCHOOL OF LAW—A complete School of Law, under competent instructors, will be opened Oct. 1, 1900. Excellent law library ...
>
> Stetson University is located in one of the most beautiful towns of beautiful Florida. The location is noted for its great healthfulness.
>
> John F. Forbes, President[327]

Despite Forbes' and Farrah's extensive efforts to advertise and promote the law school, only five students enrolled in Stetson University College of Law's first class on opening day, October 2, 1900.[328] Rationalizations for the few entrants ranged from "Florida did not need law-school-trained attorneys, that 'men' could still read law to enter practices," to "money [for tuition, living expenses and travel] was scarce." Energetic and visionary, Forbes and Farrah, though disappointed, were not deterred. For the next several years, enrollments increased.

---

325. Ltr. from John F. Forbes to Fla. newspaper editors *Opening of Stetson's Law School* (May 16, 1900) (copy on file at Stetson U. Archives, DeLand, Fla.). In the letter, Forbes wrote: "As this is the first professional school of any kind that was ever opened in Florida, we feel that it is a significant event, and would appreciate any notice that you might seem fit to make of it, of any other feature of the [enclosed] catalogue, in your editorial columns." *Id.*

326. *Id.*

327. *Stetson University*, 10 Stetson Collegiate (n.p.) (Dec. 1899) (advertisement).

328. Bowen, *supra* n. 292, at 4; Vause, *supra* n. 308, *Foundations for Excellence*, at 305.

f. Law Books and Law Teachers

Two problems remained prior to the College of Law's opening: needed law books had to be obtained for a law library, and additional instructors had to be hired. Regarding the law library, Forbes and Farrah enlisted the aid of Florida's attorneys. Even though several lawyers had previously donated law books to the College, more volumes were required to establish the core collection that Professor Huffcutt had recommended.[329] Forbes enlisted a member of Stetson University's Board of Trustees—A.G. Hamlin, attorney for the Florida East Coast (Flagler's) Railroad—to lead an effort to raise $1,000 from Florida attorneys to acquire the books.[330] The Trustees, in turn, appointed a committee consisting of James D. Beggs, W.S. Jennings, George P. Raney, and Duncan U. Fletcher to work with Hamlin.[331]

The Hamlin committee's efforts succeeded, raising close to $900 in donations from Florida's roughly 500 attorneys.[332] In a 1901 annual report to the Board of Trustees, President Forbes noted that in addition to the attorneys' contributions, others had donated money to the law book drive.[333] Moreover, two law book publishers—Bancroft-Whitney Company and Banks Law Publishing Company—contributed specific volumes. In all, the value of the gifts exceeded $1,000; thus, Forbes achieved his financial goal for funding Stetson's core law library.[334]

Regarding the additional instructors, Forbes appointed three part-time law faculty members. The first was Robert J. Bonner. After joining the faculty, however, Bonner was asked to teach Latin part-time in the University, since his full-time services in the law program were not needed, given that only five students had enrolled.[335] Forbes next appointed Egford Bly, a local DeLand attorney, to serve on the faculty, who like Farrah was a graduate of the University of Michigan Law School.[336]

---

329. Lycan, *History of Stetson, supra* n. 109, at 88.

330. Memo. from John F. Forbes to the Stetson U. Bd. of Trustees, *President's Report to the Board of Trustees of John B. Stetson University* 2 (Feb. 9, 1900) (copy on file in Stetson U. Archives, DeLand, Fla.).

331. *Id.*

332. *Id.*

333. *Id.* at 3.

334. In reference to raising money, especially for the College of Law, Forbes, in his report to the Board of Trustees, described the progress of the law library fund drive as "the most notable movement of the year [1900]." *Id.* at 2.

335. Bowen, *supra* n. 292, at 4.

336. *Id.*

But Forbes' appointment to have the greatest historical significance was his third: Annie R. MacLean.[337] In 1900, women teaching in law schools were rare. Law historian Robert Stevens[338] points out that "women [either as teachers or students] were not welcome in the law school classroom."[339] There were a few exceptions, and one was the woman law teacher at the first law school in Florida.

Stetson's Annie MacLean taught constitutional law at the College of Law from the moment it opened. At the same time, MacLean served as the University's Dean of Women.[340] Though not a lawyer, MacLean had earned a Ph.D. degree from the University of Chicago. Her being hired by Stetson University likely resulted from a recommendation by University of Chicago President Robert Harper. MacLean's name as "Instructor in Constitutional Law" first appears in the 1901–1902 catalog of the "John B. Stetson University Department of Law."[341] She continued teaching at the College of Law for three years.

When the time came to open what would become the Stetson University College of Law in October 1900, the law school had an adequate library and a strong faculty. President Forbes' and Dean Farrah's efforts had paid off. Forbes' involvement was especially significant. First, he persuaded the Board of Trustees to authorize a law college; next, he raised the needed money for a building; advertised the school's pending opening throughout Florida and, at Farrah's suggestion, in other Southeastern states as well; and, finally, raised sufficient money for a core law library.

But of all his contributions, Forbes' most singular was his recruiting a young, energetic, visionary, and experienced legal educator from the faculty of one of America's most prestigious law schools, Dean Albert J. Farrah. With Dean Farrah at the helm, the Stetson University College of Law was ready to begin its continuing long life.

---

337. *Id.*

338. *See* Stevens, *Law School, supra* n. 196.

339. *Id.* at 82; *see also* Friedman, *supra* n. 197, at 639; Cynthia Grant Bowman, *Women and the Legal Profession*, 7 Am. U. J. Gender Soc. Policy & L. 149, 150–175 (1998).

340. John B. Stetson U. Dept. L., *supra* n. 285, at 8.

341. *Id.*

CHAPTER THREE

A Strong Beginning — Dean Farrah

3.1 The College of Law's Opening Year

a. Prospective Announcement

The 1899–1900 Bulletin of the John B. Stetson University announced the October 1900 opening of "The College of Law,"[342] stating that the school would offer "instruction leading to the degree of Bachelor of Law (LL.B.)." The announcement continued,

> [T]he object of the instruction will be not merely to secure familiarity with the rules of law as actually enforced, but also to develop a legal mind, to train the student in the art of legal reasoning and *to cultivate the faculty of sound legal common sense.*[343]

When President Forbes drafted the text, he had not yet appointed Albert J. Farrah to be the College of Law's first dean. Thus, under the heading "faculty," only two names appear: "John F. Forbes, *President,*" followed by "G. Prentice Carson, A.M., Professor of Political Science and History."[344] Carson, an undergraduate Stetson professor, had neither law training nor background in law teaching. In fact, when the College of Law opened, Carson was not a member of its faculty. Was Carson used as a temporary "filler" until Forbes acquired a law faculty? Though unclear, it is possible. In any event, the 1899–1900 announcement lists no full-time faculty members.[345]

Three "Special Lecturers," however, were identified in the announcement: Judge W.A. Hocker, Fifth District, Florida Circuit Court; Judge James W. Locke,

342. Stetson U., *Annual Catalogue, John B. Stetson University, 1899–1900*, at 36 (1899).
343. *Id.* at 37 (emphasis added).
344. *Id.* at 36.
345. *Id.*

United States District Court; and Judge M.H. Mabry, Supreme Court of Florida.[346] How Forbes persuaded these members of the judiciary to agree to lecture (or at least to have their names appear in the catalog) remains unclear. Whether the listed jurists actually gave lectures during the first year of the College's existence also is not known, for their names do not appear in other College records of that time. Then in the 1900–1901 catalog, three new names were listed as "special lecturers" during that opening year. They were W.A. Blount, D.U. Fletcher, and R.L. Anderson.[347]

b. Minimal Admission Standards

According to the Stetson 1899–1900 catalog, to be admitted to the College of Law, an applicant had to be eighteen years of age or older and have "a previous education at least equivalent to a High School course."[348] But if the applicant could not produce a certificate evidencing high-school-equivalent work, the aspirant might still be admitted by examination. What the examination consisted of, how it was administered, and what it covered were not described.[349] Once admitted, a student was designated a "junior" in the College. Then, if he finished the first year of law study, the student was moved up to "senior" status during the second and final year of law school.[350] After becoming the College of Law's first dean in fall 1900, Farrah raised the minimum age for admission to nineteen (twenty for entering seniors) for the 1901–1902 academic year.[351]

As to what constituted sufficient prior education, the College of Law's admission requirements were vague. The school's announcements stated that candidates for admission "must either have completed an academic course satisfactory to the Faculty ... [or] give satisfactory evidence of educational qualifications sufficient to enable [the applicant] to pursue successfully the study of law."[352] In any event, Dean Farrah, it seems, made all admission decisions following an interview with each prospective student.

---

346. *Id.*

347. Stetson U., *Annual Catalogue, John B. Stetson University, 1900–1901*, at 46 (1900).

348. *Id.* at 37.

349. The early catalogs of the College of Law mention the examination process for admission as an alternative if the applicant did not qualify for admission under the regular admission criteria. Yet, no "entrance examinations" as such have been located in the University archives.

350. *Id.* at 47.

351. *Id.*

352. *Id.*

To be admitted directly into the senior (second-year) class without examination, an applicant who desired to learn Florida procedure and practice had to be either an attorney in good standing who had been admitted in any state, or have completed, in an out-of-state law school, since none existed in Florida, the equivalent of Stetson's required first-year program in law.[353] If neither option were available, the applicant had a third avenue: he could take an examination on the subjects covered in Stetson's first-year law study. The advanced-standing examination took place over a two-day period, but it is uncertain how much time the examination took.[354]

c. Course of Study and Instructional Methods

To earn the LL.B. degree, a Stetson student had to successfully complete a course of study consisting of sixty-six weeks of classes over a two-year period.[355] The school year (not including time for exams) required thirty-three weeks of attendance. But whereas today's law-school year is divided into two semesters and a summer session, for several years after the College of Law opened, Stetson's academic year was divided into three segments: a fall and a winter term of twelve weeks each, and a spring term of nine weeks.[356]

The University's 1900–1901 catalog mentions "three distinct methods of instruction," adding that the faculty of the College of Law would "endeavor to combine" the three, taking the "good features" from each.[357] The pedagogies were listed as (1) lecture, (2) textbook, and (3) case system.[358] No evidence exists that casebooks were used during the College's first several years of operation.

---

353. John B. Stetson U. Dept. of L., *supra* n. 285, at 12–13.

354. *Id.* at 13.

355. *Catalogue, supra* n. 347, at 48–49.

356. *Id.*

357. *Id.* at 48. That the catalog noted three "distinct methods of instruction" were used in law schools shows how significant it was that Forbes' had hired an existing law school academician, Albert Farrah, as dean. Farrah, having taught at a leading law school then (and now), the University of Michigan, was well aware of the various pedagogies that had developed in American legal education.

358. For an early discussion of the lecture-textbook recitation, and casebook methods of instruction, see James B. Scott, *The American Law School* 2–10 (publisher unavailable 1906). Scott was a law professor who correctly forecast that the casebook method would in time become the standard; *see also* Stevens, *Legal Education, supra* n. 196, at 54. President Charles Elliot of Harvard was an early critic of the lecture method, saying at his inauguration as Harvard's president: "[T]he lecturer pumps laboriously into sieves. The water may be wholesome but it runs through." *Id.* (citing *American Higher Education: A Documentary History* vol. 1, 617 (Richard Hofstadter & Wilson Smith eds., U. Chi. Press 1961)).

From the outset, students read assignments from textbooks, listened to and took notes of their professors' lectures, and gave oral recitations of legal principles in class. And, in certain courses, including contracts, criminal law, and torts, an instructor might add selected cases as supplemental sources to the course's basic textbook and to the instructor's class lectures.[359] As noted earlier, these were the predominant teaching pedagogies used in American law schools around the beginning of the twentieth century. Interestingly, at Stetson's College of Law, student class recitations were sometimes called "quizzes."[360] Though a few schools had begun to emulate Harvard Law School's casebook method of instruction, the majority of schools, including Stetson, went several years (in some cases decades) before adopting the casebook system of instruction as the predominant teaching pedagogy.[361]

d. Required Curriculum

When the College of Law opened in 1900, the two-year course of study for the LL.B. degree consisted of required courses; no electives being offered. The College's curriculum for the first (junior) year of law study follows:[362]

First Year

Junior (First) Year		
Semester	Courses	credit/hr.
fall	Bailments and Carriers	3
	Contracts & Quasi Contracts	4
	Criminal Law	3
	Domestic Relations	3
	Elementary Law	2
Winter	Contracts & Quasi Contracts	3
	Criminal Procedure	3
	Elementary Real Property	4
	Torts	4
Spring	Agency	4
	Common Law Pleading	4
	Equity Jurisdiction	4
	Personal Property & Sales	4

359. *Catalogue*, *supra* n. 347, at 49–50.

360. *See generally Stevens*, *supra* n. 215.

361. *See* Hurst, *supra* n. 201, at 262–266. For Stetson's adoption of the casebook method as the predominant teaching pedagogy, see *infra* n. 695–696 and accompanying text.

362. *Catalogue*, *supra* n. 347, at 49.

A student was required to take—during his or her first year of study—forty-five credit hours, fifteen to be completed in the initial fall term, fourteen in the winter, and sixteen in the spring.[363] Rather than giving a single examination at the end of a course, as is the modern custom, testing for the most part consisted of periodic oral examinations and in-class "quizzes."[364] It would be a few years before written examinations were instituted at Stetson.

In addition to successfully completing the first-year courses, a Stetson law student had to take an intensive senior-year prescribed curriculum to earn the LL.B. degree.[365] The required seventeen courses in the student's second year follows:

Second Year

Senior (Second) Year		
Semester	**Courses**	**credit/hr.**
Fall	Evidence	4
	Equity Pleading	3
	Private Corporations	4
	Mortgages	2
	Equity Jurisdiction	3
	Florida Pleading and Practice	2
Winter	Partnership	3
	Negotiable Instruments	3
	Private International Law	3
	Wills & Administration	3
	Real Property	3
	Practice Court	1
	Florida Statute Laws	2
Spring	Practice Court	1
	Florida Statute Laws	2
	Public Corporations	2
	Constitutional Law	5
	Damages	4
	Jurisdiction of U.S. Courts	3

Total credit hours for a student's senior year in law school amounted to fifty-three: eighteen in the fall, eighteen in the winter, and seventeen in the student's spring term.[366]

363. *Id.*

364. *Id.*

365. *Id.* at 49–50.

366. *Id.* The earlier law school announcements listed required course offerings, credit

Two features of Stetson University College of Law's curriculum in its early years are noteworthy of discussion: first, the inclusion of a required trial skills course, and second, a strong emphasis on equity jurisprudence.

e. Stetson's Unique Requirement in Trial Court Practice

At inception, Stetson's College of Law required each student to enroll in a course called "Practice Court," which spanned two terms. This hands-on trial advocacy course was a prerequisite for a student to receive an LL.B. degree. In the evolution of American legal education, Stetson's College of Law appears to be the first university-related law school to require such a course. Although "moots," or mock appellate arguments, had been initiated at Harvard Law School in the 1870s, and though certain schools offered a required, for-credit course in appellate advocacy (called moot court), little evidence has been found that instruction in trial pleading and practice skills was required and given academic credit at other American law schools in 1900.

According to law school historian Robert Stevens, law schools generally did not begin teaching trial practice skills until the late 1970s and early 1980s.[367] Not so, however, at Stetson's College of Law; there, trial court training began at the dawn of the twentieth century. Indeed, the College of Law's announcements for the 1901–1902 academic year proclaims that a "well-organized Practice Court [is] a regular feature of the [law] course in the senior year."[368] It reads:

> Beginning with the winter term, weekly sessions of the [Practice] Court will be held, over which some member of the Faculty will preside. The object of the course in the Practice Court is to give the student practical instructions in pleading and practicing at law and in equity, and actual experience in the preparation and trial of the cause, thus removing the main objection raised to law school training, that it is theoretical and not practical.[369]

The announcement added that work in the Practice Court "[would] be emphasized."[370] Stetson's requirement that students take a course in trial practice did not continue indefinitely. Nonetheless, the College's emphasis on skills training has been consistent throughout its history.[371] Yet, not until the mid-

---

hours of each, and which term specific courses would be taught, but gave no descriptions, other than titles, of what each course covered.

367. Stevens, *supra* n. 215, at 214–215, 240–241.

368. *Catalogue, supra* n. 347, at 47–48.

369. *Id.* at 48.

370. *Id.* at 47.

371. Noting that law schools failed to offer practical or skills training, historian Robert Stevens cites a 1979 report of the American Bar Association revealing one response of the

1980s—a few years following issuance of a report by the American Bar Association's special task force on lawyer competency (known as the Crampton Report)—did skills training become a significant component of most law schools' curricula.[372]

In contrast, Stetson's Practice Court course began decades earlier. It spanned two terms in a student's senior year and consisted of three segments. First, the instructor assigned a story, or a set of "facts," to each student who then had to issue, serve, and return process, prepare pleadings, and bring the cause to court "under an issue of law."[373] Then, "actual controversies [were] arranged and assigned for trial as issues of facts" to be adjudicated. Students then [had to] subpoena the witnesses, impanel the jury, examine and cross-examine the witnesses, and argue the case to the court and jury."[374] Finally, students prepared a mock case for appeal and then argued the legal issues before appellate tribunals comprised of faculty members and practicing attorneys.[375]

f. Emphasis on Equity Jurisprudence

In addition to students taking the required course in trial practice, the College's 1900–1901 first-year curriculum prescribed that students take contracts, torts, property, criminal law, and civil procedure.[376] Today, more than a century later, those same subjects are still included in Stetson's first-year required courses. Though the course in practice court was unique, the College's substantive first-year "core" requirements reflected the curricula of American law schools at the beginning of the twentieth century, a curriculum modeled upon the one used at Harvard Law School.[377]

A slight deviation from Harvard's standardized curriculum, however, was Stetson's emphasis on courses related to equity jurisprudence, including of-

---

bar to the shortfall. "As late as 1951, thirty-five states allowed law office practice in lieu of law school." Stevens, *supra* n. 215, at 255 n. 71 (citing *Annual Review of Legal Education* 71 (ABA 1979)). In 1974, Chief Justice Warren Burger decried the lack of trial skills of lawyers practicing in the federal courts. *See Burger Urges Curbs on Trial Lawyers Not Fully Trained*, N.Y. Times 1 (Nov. 27, 1973).

372. *See American Bar Association on Lawyer Competency* (ABA 1973); *see also Bar Unit Urges Law Schools to Shift Emphasis,* 18 Chron. Higher Educ. 6 (June 1979).

373. John B. Stetson U. Dept. of L., *supra* n. 285, at 17–18.

374. *Id.* at 18.

375. *Id.*

376. *Catalogue, supra* n. 347, at 49–50.

377. By 1900, there had emerged "a remarkable uniformity in curricula" among America's law schools. Stevens, *supra* n. 196, at 39. With respect to the core curriculum, virtually all university-related legal education "had accepted the Harvard model." *Id.* at 41.

ferings pertaining to equity principles, jurisprudence, remedies, and pleadings. Consequently, a Stetson law student was required to take four courses on equitable principles of law.[378] "Equity" historically was considered separate from "law," a separation that arose in England and developed into two different court systems, each having separate jurisdictions, pleading requirements, judicial powers, and remedies. The division of law and equity was part of Colonial America's legal system as well.[379] In time, the two distinct English-based legal systems of law and equity in America merged.[380] Whereas courts of equity in America were once distinct from law courts, today a single court dispenses both law and equitable remedies, and plaintiff attorneys plead both law and equity theories in a complaint.[381]

In summary, since its inception, Stetson University's College of Law offered not only substantive, theoretical instruction in the law, it also *required* students to take an intensive skills course in trial practice. Its program was both comprehensive and innovative, a combination which, at the time, appears to have been unique in American legal education.

g. So, What's the Cost?

For the thirty-three weeks of instruction, access and use of the law library, attendance at special lectures, participation in practice court and moot court arguments, as well as the "status" of being a law student (claimed by some to be a "dating" advantage), a student's tuition was $66 for the year. This was not a small sum at that time.[382] The price went up considerably if a law student lived in a dormitory on Stetson's DeLand campus. Then, a student paid $222 for the school year (thirty-three weeks). In 2003 dollars, this amounts to $4,681.56.[383] This figure included not only tuition, but also the costs of room, board, heat, light, and laundry.[384] Thus, for less than $450, a student could ob-

378. *See Catalogue, supra* n. 347, at 49–50.

379. *See generally* Friedman, *supra* n. 197.

380. *Id.*

381. Over time, the importance of stressing equity courses in law school diminished. Though a few equity courses remain in law schools, including Stetson, they are rarely required. Most law schools have relegated equity jurisprudence to a single course on remedies, or have included equitable remedies and principles as components of courses such as contracts, torts, property, real-estate finance, and family law.

382. Vause, *Foundations for Excellence, supra* n. 308, at 303–304.

383. *The Inflation Calculator*, accessed at http://westegg.com/inflation (accessed on Dec. 31, 2004. This calculation is based on data from *Historical Statistics of the United States* (Govt. Prtg. Off. 1975), and *Statistical Abstracts of the United States* (Govt. Prtg. Off. 2003)).

384. Vause, *Foundations for Excellence, supra* n. 308, at 304.

tain an LL.B. degree, though at graduation, the school assessed an added fee of ten dollars.

h. The First Class

Only five students, all white males from Florida, enrolled in the first entering class at the College of Law, though Forbes and Farrah had hoped for more. William Emery Baker of Thonotosassa, Florida (near Plant City) enrolled first and, at 6' 5" tall, was easily recognizable on campus.[385] Having graduated from Georgia's Harris College,[386] Baker presented Dean Farrah with a certificate of classes he had taken there.[387] After graduating from Stetson's first law class in 1902, Baker moved to Gainesville, where he practiced real estate law for nearly fifty years in the firm of Baker & Chitty. For a brief period, he also served as a part-time instructor at University of Florida College of Law.[388] Baker retired in 1951.[389]

Thomas Fielding of Lake Butler became the second student to enroll in Stetson's initial law class. To be admitted, Fielding also "presented credits" for all the required entrance subjects, after he studied at (but did not graduate from) the University of Georgia.[390] The third student to enroll was Bert Fish, a DeLand resident who had earlier graduated from DeLand Academy (later, Stetson University).[391] The fourth was Frank Pope, Jr., of Jacksonville. Finally, the fifth was Robert L. Turner of Citronelle, Florida. Turner left law school after his first year, having accepted the post of Superintendent of Citrus County (which today would be the chairman of the county's board of commissioners).[392]

Of the five members of Stetson's first graduating class, Bert Fish became the best known. He served ten years as a United States Minister ("ambassador") in three countries: Egypt, Saudi Arabia, and Portugal (where he died).[393] Upon

---

385. *Id.* at 304.

386. *See William Emery Baker,* ftp://ftp.rootsweb.com/pub/usgenweb/fl/hernando/genealogy/baker.txt (accessed May 14, 2004).

387. *Id.*

388. *See generally* Bowen, *supra* n. 292.

389. *Id.*

390. *William Emery Baker, supra* n. 386.

391. *Id.*

392. *Id.*

393. Before entering law school, Bert Fish was superintendent of the public schools of Volusia County. Fish would bicycle back and forth between DeLand and Daytona Beach, the two largest towns within the school district, on a road made of compressed sea shells. Ltr. from Bruce Jacob to Michael Swygert (July 10, 2005) [hereinafter *Jacob July 10 Ltr.*] (on file at Stetson U. College of L., Gulfport, Fla. and original remains in possession of co-author Michael I. Swygert).

Bert Fish (*Courtesy of Bert Fish Medical Center, New Smyrna Beach, Florida*)

receiving his law degree in 1902, Fish and his first-year Stetson law professor Cary D. Landis formed the DeLand law firm of Landis & Fish.[394] Bert Fish also served as superintendent of the Orlando County school system and, for two terms, as county criminal court judge. Fish's law partner, Cary Landis, subsequently became Florida's Attorney General, taking office in 1931. Landis served in that position until his death in 1938.[395]

At the beginning of the 1900–1901 winter term, three additional law students joined the initial class: Verling W. Davis of Marion, Indiana; Benjamin L. Keith of St. Augustine, Florida; and Elbert D. Turner of Gainesville, Florida.[396] The College of Law's 1902 first graduating class consisted of six men: Baker, Fielding, Fish, Pope, Davis, and Turner.[397]

i. Early Members of the Law Faculty

President Forbes' hirings of Dean Albert J. Farrah,[398] Robert J. Bonner, Annie M. MacLean, and Egford Bly have been noted earlier.[399] Nonetheless, some further details of the College's initial faculty are warranted. Albert Farrah held the

394. Bowen, *supra* n. 292, at 4.

395. *Cary D. Landis, State's Attorney General Passes Away Tuesday; One Time on Stetson Law Faculty*, Stetson Rptr. 1 (May 11, 1938) [hereinafter *Landis*].

396. *Id.*

397. Bowen, *supra* n. 292, at 4.

398. *Id.*

399. *See supra* nn. 335–341 and accompanying text.

positions of dean and professor. Robert Bonner was Instructor in Law (and Chair of the Latin Department in the University). Annie MacLean served as an Instructor in Constitutional Law. Finally, Egford Bly was Instructor in Florida Pleading and Practice and Statute Law.[400] For a new law school in what some historians considered a frontier state, it is noteworthy that each member of Stetson's initial law faculty possessed strong qualifications.

Instructor Robert Bonner earned his A.B. degree in Latin from the University of Toronto in 1891. He then took two years of law training at the Osgoode Hall Law School of Toronto.[401] Subsequently, Bonner taught Latin and Greek at the Collingwood Collegiate Institute for five years, and then worked as a "senior fellow," teaching Greek at the University of Chicago for the 1899–1900 academic year.[402]

In 1899, Annie MacLean, the College's Instructor in Constitutional Law, was appointed Stetson University's Dean of Women and Instructor of Sociology and Economics. MacLean was a graduate of the University of Chicago, as was Bonner, and likely had been recommended by President Harper or by other University of Chicago faculty.[403] Forbes and Farrah soon learned that MacLean was a multi-talented woman. A native of Nova Scotia, she earned a bachelor's degree from Arcadia College in 1893, followed by a master's degree the following year.[404] MacLean next earned a Ph.M. in 1897, followed by a Ph.D. in sociology and political science in 1900, both from the University of Chicago.[405] Being dean of women and instructor in law concurrently, MacLean may be a rarity in the annals of higher education.

Egford Bly was a DeLand attorney with a solid legal education. Bly, like Dean Farrah, had graduated from the University of Michigan School of Law.[406] Bly was well-known throughout Florida when he accepted his appointment to the law faculty, as he had practiced law in excess of twenty-five years.[407] His trial experience was relevant, since for several years he taught Stetson's Practice Court course.

Thus, the first teaching faculty of the College of Law (excluding occasional lecturers) consisted of two graduates of the University of Michigan law school,

---

400. *Id.*
401. *Catalogue, supra* n. 347, at 46.
402. *University Opening and New Teachers,* 3 Stetson Collegiate 2 (Oct. 1900).
403. *Id.*
404. *Id.*
405. *Id.*
406. *Id.*
407. *Law Department,* 3 Stetson Collegiate 4, 6 (Oct. 1901).

another who had attended a two-year law program at the Osgoode Hall Law School in Toronto, and a woman Ph.D. graduate of the University of Chicago. Forbes, Farrah, and the students had to be pleased to have a highly credentialed and apparently highly qualified and diverse faculty.

One year later, another strong instructor joined the Stetson law faculty—Cary Landis.[408] Landis was appointed assistant professor to replace Bonner, and became the third member of Stetson's law faculty to graduate from the University of Michigan School of Law.[409] He was raised in the small Indiana town of Huntington. After attending college in the Hoosier State, Landis became superintendent of the Bloomington, Indiana, public schools, "a post he [soon] deserted for the study of law."[410] After receiving his LL.B. degree from Michigan in spring 1899, Landis practiced law in Indiana for two years before coming to Florida to accept appointment in 1901 to the law faculty at Stetson.[411] Years later, Farrah wrote of Landis: "In my thirty-five years of choosing law faculties, I have never found his superior."[412]

3.2 The First Few Years

a. Dean Farrah Faces Challenges

When Stetson University College of Law opened on October 2, 1900, three able leaders were in charge: University President John F. Forbes; Board of Trustees Chairman John B. Stetson; and College of Law Dean Albert J. Farrah. These men at that point respected each other and worked well together to build Stetson University and its law school. Still, John B. Stetson had misgivings over Forbes' decision to start a law school and was likely displeased by Forbes' courting of Henry Flagler, who John B. saw as a rival for influence, especially after Flagler had donated $60,000.[413] Nonetheless, Forbes and Stetson saw eye-to-eye on most issues.

Around the outset of the twentieth century, the United States had international ambitions, following its recent victory in the Spanish-American War.

---

408. *See supra* n. 395 and accompanying text.

409. The other two were Dean Farrah and Professor Egford Bly.

410. *Landis, supra* n. 395, at 1.

411. *Id.*

412. Address at Reunion, Stetson Fla. L. Students, *Albert John Farrah: 1863–1944; Address, Papers, and Letters,* 22 (Ala. L. Sch. Found. 1985) [hereinafter *Address at Reunion*]. Cary Landis died at the age of 65, while Attorney General of Florida, on his birthday, May 10, 1938.

413. Vause, *Foundations for Excellence, supra* n. 308, at 306.

One manifestation was its negotiations with Colombia to permit the U.S. to build and operate a canal across the Isthmus of Panama (the French earlier having failed to do so).[414] Though Panama attempted to proclaim independence from Colombia, the latter ignored Panama's declaration and continued to control the isthmus. Pursuant to the 1903 Hay-Herran Treaty, Colombia granted the United States rights to a six mile-wide, north/south corridor through the isthmus, so that the U.S. could build a canal linking the Atlantic and Pacific oceans. Construction began the following year. Historian David McCullough describes the significance of the undertaking as "a profoundly important historic event ... It represented the largest, most costly single effort ever before mounted on earth."[415] Though contractors assumed that the work would be over within five years, the canal took eleven years to complete due to "*unforseen difficulties*."[416]

Farrah similarly assumed that his deanship at the College of Law would run smoothly, but like the building of the Panama Canal, unforseen difficulties soon arose. Less than two years after the College's opening, growing hostilities among John Forbes, John B. Stetson, and members of the Board of Trustees made Farrah's running and promoting the College of Law problematic.[417] Yet, at the beginning of Farrah's deanship, everything seemed to go right. During the initial month of the law school's operation, he wrote in the University's newspaper—*The Stetson Collegiate*—that the College of Law:

> [p]laces before the young men of Florida an opportunity of acquiring, through a systematic and scientific course of study of two years, not only a theoretical knowledge of the law, but a practical and working knowledge of the law as actually administered in the courts of their own state.[418]

Farrah chided critics who claimed "that the world [would] be better off if there were no lawyers in it [and] that the legal profession, as a whole, is a kind of human parasite feeding on the rest of mankind," by responding that "the legal profession is essential to the business world," and that its members are persons of influence in government.[419] Farrah posed three rhetorical

---

414. George Washington Goethals, Carence Ridley, *Panama Canal, History*, in *Encyclopedia Britannica supra* n. 277, at vol. 171, pgs. 174–175.

415. David McCullough, *The Path Between the Seas: The Creation of the Panama Canal, 1879–1914*, at 11 (Simon & Schuster 1977).

416. *Id.* (emphasis added).

417. *See infra* nn. 440–462 and accompanying text.

418. *Law Department*, Stetson Collegiate (Oct. 1900).

419. *Address at Reunion*, *supra* n. 412, at 22.

questions: First, are schools of law necessary? Second, is a law school in Florida necessary? And third, should a Florida law school be part of a university? Naturally, he answered each of his questions in the affirmative, and in every instance offered a brief explanation.[420] Farrah referred to a resolution adopted at an 1891 meeting of the American Bar Association, from which he quoted:

> It [is] a part of the highest duty and interest of every civilized state [in the Union] to make provisions, when necessary, for the maintenance of law schools and the thorough professional education of all who are admitted to practice law.[421]

Earlier, the ABA reported that "there is little, if any, dispute now as to the relative merit of education by means of law schools." The ABA report concluded that "the verdict of the best informed is in favor of schools."[422] Chief Justice Waite of the Florida Supreme Court added his endorsement of the benefits of law schools: "The time has gone by when an eminent lawyer, in full practice, can take a class of students into his office and become their teacher. Once that was practical, but now it is not. The consequences is [sic] that law schools are now a necessity."[423]

President Forbes was pleased with Stetson law school's first year. At the annual Presentation Day Celebration, Forbes publicly congratulated Farrah:

> The law school, under the able direction of Dean Farrah, has sprung up at once into favor, and has won the confidence and support of the Bench and Bar of the State. There is no doubt about its future, and in its new quarters, it will be amply and elegantly equipped.[424]

A commentary in *The Stetson Collegiate* noted that Stetson's law school "already demonstrated its right to exist."[425] The unnamed student author added that the law school had "splendid instructors" and was under the "efficient direction of Dean Farrah and President Forbes."[426] Such grandiose statements were to be expected from college insiders, but the reality was that the law school had gotten off to a good start.

---

420. *Id.*

421. *Id.*

422. *See Reports of the American Bar Association* vol. 2, 216 (ABA 1879).

423. Stetson U. Dept. of L., *supra* n. 353, at 5.

424. John F. Forbes, *President's Statement—Presentation Day 1902,* at 1-E (Stetson U. 1902).

425. *University Opening and New Teachers, supra* n. 402, at 2.

426. *Id.*

b. The First Graduation at Stetson University College of Law

Stetson University College of Law's first graduates were William Baker, Verling W. Davis, Thomas Wesley Fielding, Bert Fish, Frank Pope, and Elbert D. Turner.[427] Bert Fish, president of the class of 1902, delivered an address at the graduation ceremonies.[428] At the "Senior Class Law Day" during the week of graduation, two students presented "orations": Tom Fielding, on "Imperial America," and Elbert Turner, on "Responsibilities of Citizenship."[429] Bill Baker wrote the class history, while Frank Pope presented an oil portrait of Dean Farrah "enclosed in a gold frame" to the University on behalf of the graduating students. The graduates gave the Farrah portrait in "recognition of the faithful and painstaking work of the dean and as an expression of our love and esteem."[430]

Both current students and the graduates admired Dean Farrah. They knew him as a professional, friendly, and personable teacher and administrator. Farrah often chatted with students about the practical, as well as the theoretical, aspects of being a lawyer.[431] In an address to the Kent Club,[432] Farrah told students to plan on a "modest start" in the legal profession. He described their first few years in practice as the "starvation period through which every lawyer must pass."[433] According to Arthur L. Auvil, class of 1906, Farrah implored students that when they entered law practice to always value and follow the moral imperative of honesty in all matters. Auvil noted that Farrah "warned [students] against laziness, a vice so easily acquired and so strenuously to be avoided by all, especially lawyers."[434]

Incidentally, twenty years after graduating from Stetson Law School, Auvil was elected in 1926 to the Florida House of Representative from Pasco County.

427. Bowen, *supra* n. 292, at 4.

428. *Senior Class Day*, 4 Stetson Collegiate 4 (May 1902). The name of the student publication, *The Stetson Collegiate*, on occasion was published as *Stetson Collegiate*, and for a period, as *The Weekly Stetson Collegiate*. The name was eventually change to the *Stetson Reporter.* (All issues are available at the Stetson U. Archives in DeLand, Fla.). Once the Law School moved to Gulfport, the *Stetson Lawyer* became the predominant student publication for law students. These issues are available at the Stetson University College of Law archives in Gulfport, Florida. Note that for some citations, volume and page numbers are unavailable.

429. *Id.*

430. *Id.*

431. Arthur L. Auvil, *College of Law*, Stetson Collegiate 5 (May 9, 1906).

432. *Id.*

433. *Id.*

434. *Id.*

He was the first of many Stetson law graduates to serve in the Florida Legislature. He died in 1951 at the age of 74, having practiced law for three decades in Dade City.[435]

The College of Law grew during its first decade. Twenty-six students enrolled in 1904, while the decade's high reached twenty-eight in 1908.[436] In 1900, the University's total enrollment was 372 students, consisting of 215 women and 158 men.[437] Of this number, eighty-four were in the University's non-professional colleges and the rest were enrolled in the primary and secondary schools. At that time, Stetson students could go from first grade through college, a fact that one historian describes "an uncommon advantage of the time."[438] Though Stetson's students came from sixteen states and two foreign countries, the large majority were Floridians. Those from outside the state were "mostly children of winter residents."[439]

c. *Honeymoon's End: The Forbes-Mathes-Stetson Scandal*

An episode began in 1901 that Stetson historian Gilbert Lycan describes as being "so sad that people have wept over it more than sixty years later."[440] Excusing Lycan's hyperbole, the episode did culminate in President Forbes being forced to leave the University.

According to various accounts on file in Stetson University's archives,[441] rumors began circulating in the summer of 1901 that Forbes (who was married) had been engaging in sexual relations with a married woman named Lena B. Mathes. Mathes was head of a DeLand normal school that prepared young women to become teachers, a school funded by the Peabody Foundation and located on Stetson's campus.[442] Both Forbes and Mathes taught at the school.

One summer, Forbes' wife and family were residing as per custom in their summer home in Penfield, New York. At the same time, Forbes and Mathes—

---

435. Carol Jeffares Hedman, *Pasco County Politicians Make Mark in Legislature,* Tampa Trib. F6 (Pasco ed.) (July 13, 2004).

436. Bowen, *supra* n. 292, at 3; *see also* Gordis, *supra* n. 105, at 15.

437. Memo. from John F. Forbes to the Stetson U. Bd. of Trustees, *President's Report to the Board of Trustees of John B. Stetson University* app. 1-A (1901) (on file at Stetson U. Archives, DeLand, Fla.).

438. Johnston, *supra* n. 291, at 281–304.

439. *Id.*

440. Lycan, *History of Stetson, supra* n. 109, at 92.

441. *See Forbes-Stetson Controversy Folder* (located in Cabinet D, Stetson U. Archives, DeLand, Fla.). It appears that historian Gilbert Lycan's detailed account of the Forbes-Stetson controversy is based on materials and letters he uncovered in this particular folder.

442. Lycan, *History of Stetson, supra* n. 109, at 92–93.

according to sworn statements of faculty members, students, and a DeLand businessman—were carrying on an illicit affair alternatively in the president's home and in Chaudoin Hall, where Mathes maintained an apartment.[443] Historian Lycan writes that "a large portion of the students became so disgusted with the [alleged] affair that they were at the point of leaving the school."[444]

One person did leave—Mrs. Mathes, who departed after rumors of the tryst surfaced. Despite the campus rancor over the affair, only three months later Forbes announced that he was bringing Mathes back to the University and appointed her professor of education. The affair itself may have been excusable to many faculty members and trustees, but what was perceived to be Forbes' gall in inviting her to return, was not. John B. Stetson, as Chairman of the Board of Trustees, was outraged, and he called for a "hearing" on the adultery charges against Forbes. A committee comprised of Stetson Trustee W.H. Stewart and University of Chicago faculty member Dr. George B. Foster listened to four hours of sworn testimony of several witnesses who included three women instructors at Stetson University. Each testified that the Forbes-Mathes trysts had in fact occurred.[445]

Soon, two camps developed: those supporting Forbes (who proclaimed his innocence, but were convinced that the charges were either untrue or, even if true, had been blown out of proportion); and those who believed the accusers, who felt the affair could not be overlooked—they demanded Forbes' resignation.[446] Despite the near certainty that the Forbes' affair with Mathes had taken place, a majority of the University's Trustees decided not to ask for Forbes' resignation. The campus-wide dispute, however, was far from over, as the battle dragged on for another two long and painful years. Throughout this protracted episode, rancor and divisiveness embroiled the campus, eventually extending to citizens of DeLand and Volusia County, as well as to Baptists throughout Florida.[447] In the midst of the turmoil, Forbes and Mathes filed separate lawsuits for defamation against John B. Stetson personally for $250,000. Shocked, the hat-maker filed counter-suits.[448] The cases, however, were never tried.

In the beginning of the embroilment, a majority of Stetson University's Trustees had sided with Forbes and were angry with John B. Stetson. The

443. *Id.*
444. *Id.*
445. *Id.* at 93.
446. *Id.* at 93–94.
447. *Id.* at 98.
448. *Id.*

Board at that point removed Stetson as Chairman (though he remained a member).[449] This action precipitated a storm, both within and without the University. For example, the treatment of "Mr. Stetson" produced an "angry outcry" from many of the state's newspapers, including the local *Volusia County Record*. An entire front page of the *Record* was devoted to the removal action and included a lengthy editorial criticizing the University Trustees for stripping Mr. Stetson of his Chairmanship.[450] The *Tampa Tribune* also joined the attack, claiming that the Trustees had "abused their power" by removing Stetson from power.[451]

Meanwhile, back on campus the Forbes-Stetson dispute had its effects on Forbes. Despite initial support from a majority of both trustees and faculty (as well as many—but not all—of the town's leading citizens), Forbes reluctantly came to see that his problems with Stetson were not about to end, and that, consequently, the University's reputation and finances would continue to be damaged. Moreover, Forbes was depressed, according to Lycan, because he noticed that when he spoke of Christian principles in Chapel—as he routinely had done throughout his presidency—listeners no longer took him seriously, perceiving him to be a hypocrite.[452]

d. President Forbes—Midwife of the College—Resigns

Concluding that no viable alternative existed, the man who for eighteen years had led the University, submitted his written resignation to the Board of Trustees in August 1903.[453] At first, a majority of the Board did not accept Forbes' tendered resignation. John B. Stetson, however, remained displeased, and the power struggle continued. Neither those supporting Stetson, nor those backing Forbes, would compromise. Within a few months it became clear to the Board that the University faced a disaster if the Forbes-Stetson matter was allowed to fester further. The support that Forbes enjoyed for many years with trustees eroded. Consequently, on February 18, 1904, the trustees belatedly accepted Forbes' tendered resignation from the University.[454]

Three years had passed since rumors began circulating over Forbes' alleged nocturnal activities with Mrs. Mathes. Though the charges of adultery were never adjudicated in a court of law, by 1904 that made little difference, since

449. *Id.* at 99.
450. *Id.*
451. *Id.*
452. *Id.* at 100.
453. *Id.*
454. Bowen, *supra* n. 146, at 10.

the Forbes-Stetson feud by then had become a personal power struggle that eclipsed the earlier charges of adultery. With Forbes' resignation, the scandal and its divisive aftermath came to an end, but not without significant harm to the reputation of the University and, derivatively, to its College of Law. Yet viewing the situation with neutral historical perspective, the greatest harm arguably was the University's loss of John Forbes' vision, dedication, enthusiasm, and skills. Among Forbes' achievements at the University was establishing the College of Law. In essence, he was the "midwife" who oversaw the birth of the Stetson University College of Law.

Looking back sixty-five years later, University Archivist Olga Bowen wrote: "The quarrel between Mr. Stetson and Dr. Forbes was a tragedy for Stetson."[455] She added that "[Forbes' leaving] thus ended the career of a brilliant man who had brought Stetson University from a little one-building school to a real college."[456]

The controversy had wider ramifications than ending Forbes' career. Not only did the episode leave the faculty, students, trustees, and citizens of DeLand angry and divided, it also "added fuel to the controversy between Stetson and the Florida Baptist Convention."[457] Moreover, the scandal damaged the affiliation Stetson had with the University of Chicago, an affiliation that Chicago unilaterally terminated not long after Forbes' departure.[458] Thereafter, Stetson University found it more difficult to attract top-flight faculty prospects like it previously had done. Few, if any, new faculty recommendations came from officials at either Chicago or Cornell universities.

Nonetheless, Forbes had served Stetson University well.[459] During his tenure (1885 through 1903), the University's endowment rose from $15,000 to $225,000; the campus grew from four to twenty-eight acres and from one building (DeLand Hall) to seven, while enrollment increased from fifty-eight to 450 students. During his presidency, the University's music, business, and technology departments opened; the faculty grew from six to thirty-three instructors; a museum of science opened on campus; and, perhaps Forbes' great-

---

455. Olga Bowen, *History of Stetson University* 59 (unpublished Ph.D. dissertation, Stetson U. 1967) (located and cataloged at Stetson U. DuPont-Ball Lib., DeLand, Fla.).

456. Bowen, *supra* n. 146, at 12.

457. *Id.*

458. Lycan, *History of Stetson, supra* n. 109, at 98. Dr. William Rainey Harper, the University of Chicago's president during this period, "expressed alarm" over the Forbes-Stetson controversy, and according to Lycan, considered an immediate end to Chicago's affiliation with Stetson. *Id.*

459. Bowen, *supra* n. 455, at 10.

est achievement, a strong academic affiliation with the prestigious University of Chicago was forged.[460]

Though Dean Farrah had not himself become directly involved in the Forbes-Stetson controversy, he greatly admired and had worked closely with Forbes. In all likelihood, Farrah was a behind-the-scene supporter of the president during Forbes' troubles with Mr. Stetson. Moreover, since Forbes and Stetson continued their dispute for over three years, neither of these University officers could properly attend to helping build the College of Law during its formative period.[461]

In speaking to Stetson College of Law and Florida Law School alumni years later, Dean Farrah praised President John Forbes:

> It required courage on the part of Dr. Forbes to establish the Stetson Law School in view of the limited funds at his disposal ... He felt strongly the need for higher standards for admission to the Bar in [Florida], and his duty to attempt to supply the opportunity.[462]

Following Forbes' departure, Stetson quickly reestablished his power base within the University and regained control of the Board of Trustees. Farrah knew, of course, that the Philadelphia hat maker was not, and never had been, a strong supporter of the College of Law, yet he was hopeful, as a new president would soon be appointed; he would have to wait and see how that sorted out. In the meantime, activities within the College of Law continued.

e. Kent Club Forms: Students Debate World, National, Legal, and Racial Issues

At the beginning of the College's second year, the law school opened with thirteen students (compared with five the previous year).[463] The "Practice Court" class and mock trials continued and remained key components of the law program throughout the decade.[464] Practice Court was described by one student as "the most interesting and instructive feature of the law course."[465] During the winter term, students put on mock civil trials, followed by criminal cases in the spring term.[466]

---

460. *Id.* at 10–11.

461. Vause, *Foundations for Excellence, supra* n. 308, at 306.

462. *Address at Reunion, supra* n. 412, at 22.

463. John B. Stetson U. Dept. of L., *supra* n. 285.

464. *The College of Law: Lawyers Are Busy with Practice Court: Pelot Acquitted of Murder*, Stetson Collegiate 1 (Apr. 18, 1906).

465. *Law School Seniors Plead Cases: Men of '07 Wield Sword of Justice*, Stetson Collegiate 1 (Apr. 24, 1907).

466. *Id.*

Besides participating in practice court, Stetson law students created additional opportunities to develop public speaking skills. In fall 1901, students organized a debating society called the "Kent Club."[467] The Club's objective was to afford members weekly debates to further develop their advocacy skills through public debates. From the beginning, advocacy and oratorical skills were considered by faculty and students to be priorities. In time, this program became known as the "Stetson method."

With support of Dean Farrah, the Kent Club appointed officers and extended honorary memberships to the law faculty and a recently appointed part-time law librarian, Carolyn Palmer.[468] The Club's officers included: W.E. Baker, President; T.W. Fielding, Vice-President; F.W. Pope, Jr., Secretary; O.K. Reeves, Treasurer; and E.D. Turner, Critic.[469]

From 1901 through the remainder of the decade, the Kent Club met during each school term, usually on a weekly basis. Law students debated subjects suggested by the Club's members and the faculty. Topics concerned current political, sociological, historical, and legal issues. The subjects, moreover, reveal various biases and beliefs of the students.[470] Each debate centered on the pros and cons of a controversial proposition. Student proponents of the resolution would present affirmative arguments, followed by opponents making counter-arguments, while judges decided which side had put together the better argument. Topics of debate included:[471]

> <u>Resolved</u>: The everglades should be drained for sugar cane. (April 4, 1906)
> <u>Resolved</u>: Passage of the Buckman Act will be detrimental to education in Florida. (Oct. 25, 1905)

---

467. The club was named for James Kent, author of *American Commentaries on the Law,* an encyclopedic treatise written between 1826 and 1830. Michael I. Swygert & Jon W. Bruce, *The Historical Origins, Founding, and Early Development of Student-Edited Law Reviews,* 36 Hastings L.J. 739, 745 (1985). Kent in 1793 had been appointed Columbia University's first professor of law. *Id.* Based on a series of lectures to law students that had been meticulously drafted, Kent published his *Commentaries* "for the benefit of American students." *See* A.W.B. Simpson, *The Rise and Fall of the Legal Treatise: Legal Principles and the Forms of Legal Literature,* 48 U. Chi. L. Rev. 632, 633–634 (1981). Sixteen editions of *Kent's Commentaries* were published, the twelfth edited by Oliver Wendell Holmes, Jr., who added twenty-five years of American and English case history to the work. Swygert & Bruce, *supra* n. 467, at 745.

468. *Law Department, supra* n. 407.

469. *Id.*

470. *Id.*

471. All of the debate topics listed in the paragraphs below come from items appearing in various issues of *The Stetson Collegiate* during the years 1902 through 1910. After each topic appears in parenthesis the month, date, and year of the issue where that topic was mentioned.

Resolved: Attendance of those under twenty-one should be compulsory in the public schools. (Oct. 16, 1907)
Resolved: Municipal ownership and operation of street railroads is preferable to private ownership and operation. (April 4, 1902)
Resolved: Public ownership of all railroads is preferable to private ownership. (Oct. 25, 1905)
Resolved: The United States government should own all of the country's railroads. (Jan. 13, 1910)
Resolved: The Parcel-Post system is bad. (Feb. 7, 1906)
Resolved: A federal commission should resolve disputes between shippers and interstate carriers. (March 14, 1906)
Resolved: In a case of dispute between a shipper and a carrier, a federal commission shall have power to fix a rate until reviewed by a court of competent jurisdiction. (Nov. 7, 1906)
Resolved: All disputes between labor and capital shall be settled by boards of arbitration. (Oct. 24, 1906)
Resolved: Labor unions as they exist today do more harm than good. (Oct. 17, 1906)
Resolved: Cuba should be annexed to the United States. (Oct. 31, 1906)
Resolved: The Panama Canal is a bad investment for the United States. (Oct. 20, 1910)
Resolved: Perry should be given credit for discovering the North Pole. (Oct. 21, 1909)

Only occasionally was a topic a bit fanciful, for example:

Resolved: City life is preferable to country life. (Nov. 8, 1905)

On the other hand, serious legal issues were debated, several of which remain controversial even today. For example:

Resolved: Capital punishment should be abolished. (Oct. 28, 1909)
Resolved: Corporations should be liable for punitive damages. (Nov. 13, 1907)
Resolved: The issuance of injunctions in federal courts should be forbidden by Congress. (Nov. 24, 1910)
Resolved: Present conditions demand that husband and wife be treated as two distinct parties in all matters relating to civil contracts and estates. (Oct. 15, 1908)
Resolved: The jury system should be abolished. (Oct. 10, 1906).
Resolved: A three-fourth majority rule should be adopted in criminal cases. (Nov. 7, 1906)

f. African-Americans Need Not Apply

When it came to race, many of Stetson's law students of that era held long-embedded attitudes, commonplace in the old South. For example, several of the topics the Kent Club members debated, though requiring each side of the issue to be presented, suggested that white students had severe difficulties in dealing with "the Negro race." The following topics illustrate the point.

> Resolved: The races should be separated. (Nov. 15, 1905)
> Resolved: The Negro should be given industrial rather than liberal training. (April 11, 1906)
> Resolved: Negroes should be colonized. (April 17, 1907)
> Resolved: Theodore Roosevelt has done more for his race than Booker T. Washington has done for his. (Feb. 6, 1908)

As regards national origin bias, consider this topic:

> Resolved: Immigrants are more detrimental to the United States than beneficial. (Oct. 24, 1907)

Yet even more shocking by today's norms is a reference found in *The Stetson Collegiate* under its weekly column on the law school's Kent Club. An item states: "Quite a number of the men [after a Kent Club debate] wished to go over and hear the 'niggers' sing."[472] That this disgusting and derogatory epithet was in common usage at the time makes it no less shocking today.

Of course, discrimination and disparagement of African-Americans by Caucasians were widespread in the South, including Florida.[473] Consequently, African-Americans were afforded little opportunity to hold jobs.[474] Those who did work often did so under horrific conditions. For example, during the 1890s through the 1940s, "turpentine camps" operated across Florida. African-Americans who could not pay their debts were forced to work under a peonage system in pine forests, making turpentine for bosses who "treated them as convicts."[475]

Historian Maxine D. Jones, author of a definitive account of the African-American experience in twentieth-century Florida,[476] writes that in 1900 the State's African-Americans "were politically impotent and voiceless." They were

---

472. *Id.*

473. Gannon, *supra* n. 40, at 74.

474. *See generally* Joe M. Richardson, *The Negro in the Reconstruction of Florida* (Fla. St. U. Studies No. 46, 1965).

475. *Id.* at 73.

476. Maxine D. Jones, *supra* n. 67, at 373.

treated as outcasts. At the start of the new century, out of a total state population of 528,542, Florida's "Negro Population" was 230,730, rising to 308,669 by 1910.[477]

When it came to legal education, African-Americans were unwelcome at all of Florida's "white only" law schools, including Stetson's, until long after the *Brown v. School Board of Topeka, Kansas* case in 1952 was decided by the United States Supreme Court.[478] Earlier, Florida Agricultural and Mechanical University, a university set up by the Florida Legislature primarily for African-Americans, opened a law school in 1951 on its Tallahassee campus.[479] Separate but unequal was the norm. Discrimination against African-Americans being admitted to law schools was not unique to the South; it happened throughout the country.[480]

g. Women Enter the Legal Profession (and Stetson's Law School)

In contrast to African-Americans pervasively being denied access to legal education, the situation in Florida was better for white women. Prior to describing women's entry into Florida's legal profession, however, a brief summary of how women had been relegated to second-class citizenship is presented.

From Colonial times onward, America's women were considered inferior in the eyes of the law. An English legal doctrine, *femme couvert* or *coverture*, became part of America's "received" common law. Under *coverture*, when a woman married, she gave up her separate legal identity. Her legal status merged with that of her husband.[481] This meant that married women could not enter into contracts; own property (including the wages they earned); had no right to inherit from their husband upon their death; nor had a right for custody of their children; and, in the large majority of cases, were not permitted to obtain a divorce.[482] Moreover, women had no voting franchise prior to ratification in 1920 of the Nineteenth Amendment to the United States Constitution.[483]

---

477. *Id.* at 382.

478. *Brown v. Bd. of Educ. of Topeka*, 347 U.S. 483 (1954).

479. *Celebrating Florida's First 150 Women Lawyers* xx (Wendy S. Loquasto ed., Fla. B. & Fla. Assn. of Women Laws., Lexis Publg. 2000) [hereinafter *Florida's Women Lawyers*].

480. *See generally* Ernest Gellhorn, *The Law Schools and the Negro*, 1968 Duke L.J. 1069.

481. *See* Barbara J. Harris, *Beyond Her Sphere: Women and the Professions in American History* 3–28 (Greenwood Press 1978). Harris writes about how legal disabilities of women contributed to an "ideology of inferiority." *Id.*

482. JoEllen Lind, *Trailblazers: The Changing Role of Women in American Legal History*, 7 Amicus 12, 12–14 (Winter 1994).

483. Cynthia L. Cooper, *Suffrage in Year 1900: Women Lawyers at the Start of the Twentieth Century*, in *Florida's Women Lawyers, supra* n. 479, at xii, xiv; *see also* Bowman, *supra*

Despite these imposed, sanctioned, and enforced legal disabilities, women in the early twentieth century began to demand their independence and equality under the law. A few women sought to enter the legal profession, but they found it a difficult road. Among the first women seeking admittance were Myra Bradwell of Illinois and Arabella Mansfield of Iowa, the latter becoming the first woman in America admitted to a state bar.[484] Neither had attended law school, but both "read" the law on their own in the 1860s. Though Bradwell passed the Illinois bar examination in 1869, she was denied admission by the Illinois Supreme Court to practice, simply because she was a woman. Bradwell appealed to the United States Supreme Court, but lost. In language that seems incredulous to today's lawyers and law students, Justice Joseph Bradley wrote:

> The natural and proper timidity and delicacy which belongs to the female sex evidently unfits it for many of the occupations of civil life ... The paramount destiny and mission of women are to fulfill the noble and benign offices of wife and mother.[485]

Other women kept the movement for change alive. The first women to attend law schools in America and earn law degrees were: Ada Kepley, who graduated from the law school at Union College in Chicago (later, Northwestern University) in 1870; then Pheobe Couzins and Lemma Barkaloo, both 1870 graduates of the law school at Washington University at St. Louis (the first law school in the U.S. to actively recruit women); and finally, Belva Lockwood, who studied two years at National University (later called George Washington University) Law School.

Lockwood was denied her earned law degree in 1873 because she was a woman.[486] Not one to give up, Lockwood petitioned U.S. President Ulysses S. Grant, who was a trustee at National University. President Grant intervened on her behalf, and she was belatedly granted a law degree.[487] This did not end her struggles, however. Subsequently denied admission to practice in the Dis-

---

n. 339; Virginia G. Drachman, *Women Lawyers and the Quest for Professional Identity in the Late Nineteenth-Century America,* 88 Mich. L. Rev. 2414 (1990).

484. *Id.* at xii.

485. *Bradwell v. Ill.,* 83 U.S. 130, 141 (1872); *see also* Myra Bradwell, *Admission of Women to the Bar,* 11 Chi. Leg. News 179 (1879).

486. Doris Weatherford, *A History of America's First Women Lawyers,* in *Florida's Women Lawyers, supra* n. 479, at xi, xii.

487. Edith G. Osman, *Awakening: A Celebration of The Florida Bar's 50th Anniversary and of Florida's First 150 Women Lawyers,* in *Florida's Women Lawyers, supra* n. 479, at vii.

trict of Columbia, Lockwood petitioned the United States Supreme Court for admission. Though the Court turned down her petition, in dicta it commented that if Congress enacted a law permitting women to practice in the federal courts, the justices would uphold it. Edith G. Osman, the first woman president of The Florida Bar, relates what happened next:

> Lockwood knew a challenge when she saw one. She successfully lobbied Congress to pass an "Act to Relieve Certain Legal Disabilities of Women." Weeks later, she became the first woman admitted to practice before the United States Supreme Court.[488]

Osman adds that Lockwood was an activist her entire life, until dying at the age of eighty-four. Throughout her lawyering career, she was an advocate for women's rights and prison reform, among other social causes.[489] Shortly before her death, Ms. Lockwood looked back on her extraordinary efforts and commented: "I have not raised the dead, but I have awakened the living."[490] Meanwhile, a few women in Florida also were striving to become lawyers.

In the 1890s, Louise Rebecca Pinnell, a Cuban-born woman, read the law for two years in her father's law office in Bronson, Levy County, Florida.[491] Turning twenty-one in 1898, Pinnell took the oral examination given by the Florida Supreme Court. After waiting five months (an unusually long time, probably due to her gender), she was notified that she was admitted to practice in Florida. Thus, Pinnell became the first woman lawyer in Florida's history.[492] She practiced for fifty years, for the most part in Jacksonville, where she specialized in railroad litigation, working with the "respected railroad attorney, Major St. Clair-Abrams."[493]

The second woman admitted to practice in Florida was Alice Johnson of Live Oak, Florida, though her name appears in neither the Florida Supreme Court Minutes, nor in its Book of Attorneys.[494] Nonetheless, Ms. Johnson's picture appears with her name listed as an attorney in the *Bench and Bar of Florida* of 1899.[495] Neither Pinnell nor Johnson, however, attended law school.

---

488. *Id.; see also* Stevens, *Law School, supra* n. 196 at 82.

489. Osman, *supra* n. 487, at vii.

490. *Id.*

491. *Louise Rebecca Pinnell (1877–1966)*, in *Florida's Women Lawyers, supra* n. 479, at 1, 2.

492. *Id.* at 1.

493. *Id.*

494. *Alice Johnson, Date of Admission: 1898 or 1899*, in *Florida's Women Lawyers, supra* n. 479, at 3.

495. *Id.*

Mary Stewart, First Woman Graduate

h. Mary Stewart—First Woman Law School Graduate Admitted to Practice in Florida

The first woman in Florida to attend law school and to earn a law degree was Mary Stewart Howarth-Hewitt.[496] The daughter of a DeLand attorney (and later judge) Isaac A. Stewart, she received her Bachelor of Arts degree in 1906 at the University of Michigan.[497] That fall, she entered Stetson University College of Law, graduating with an LL.B. degree two years later. The only woman in her law school class, Stewart was admired by her male compatriots. In the fall of 1907, Stewart was elected "Critic" of the Kent Club, the law school's debating society. An article in *The Stetson Weekly Collegiate* describes her as "fair and brilliant."[498] One of Stewart's duties was to summarize the week's news at the Club's weekly meetings. After one such summary, the *Collegiate* noted: "Members who were fortunate to be present had a rare treat ... When [Mary Stewart] had finished, every member felt that he knew more about what was going on in the world at the present time, than he knew before."[499] Her remarks, it was said, were greeted with "hearty applause."[500]

496. *Mary Stewart Howarth-Hewitt (1886–1976),* in *Florida's Women Lawyers, supra* n. 479, at 3.

497. *Id.* at 3.

498. *Kent Club,* Stetson Wkly. Collegiate 6 (Oct. 24, 1907).

499. *Id.* Also present was Stetson University President Lincoln Hulley, who listened attentively to Ms. Stewart's discussion of "Current Events." *Id.*

500. *Id.*

Described as "very determined and strong-willed," after graduating Stewart said that she "encountered no resistance" while studying at Stetson's College of Law.[501] Admitted by the Florida Supreme Court to practice on June 20, 1908 (after having passed an oral examination), Mary Stewart became the first woman lawyer to be entered in the records of the Florida Supreme Court.[502]

During her ninety-year life, she married twice and raised three daughters. One of her daughters, Catherine Stewart Howarth Carter, followed in her mother's footsteps and graduated from Stetson's College of Law in 1934. The daughter was only twenty years old at the time she graduated.[503] Unfortunately, decades later, mother and daughter became embroiled in a property dispute involving several years of litigation.[504] After practicing law in Pennsylvania for a few years, Mary Stewart Howarth returned to DeLand to join her father in the firm of Stewart and Stewart. Later, her daughter, Catherine, joined the family firm after she graduated from Stetson's law school.[505]

Besides practicing law, Mary Stewart Howarth and her first husband owned several businesses, including 700 acres of orange groves, the Surety Bank of DeLand, and a sheet metal foundry. In addition, Mary Stewart taught Constitutional Law on a part-time basis at Stetson. She supported Stetson's College of Law throughout her life. Mary Stewart—Stetson University College of Law's first woman law graduate, and the first woman lawyer in Florida to earn a law degree—died in January 1976 at her home in DeLand. She occupies a special space in the heritage of Florida's first law school.

Another woman enrolled in Stetson's College of Law in the same year in which Stewart graduated—1908. There are only references to her last name—Pitcher. As a member of the Kent Club, she, like Mary Stewart, was assigned the task of "entertaining" the group with the news of the past week. On one occasion, she misplaced a book that she planned to use at her weekly talk. A report said "Miss Pitcher was undaunted by the accident and treated us to an entertaining talk not withstanding."[506] The last reference to her at Stetson appears in spring 1909 in the Report of the Senior Law Class. It reads:

> Miss Pitcher, the only fair co-ed in the class, with the spirit of a martyr, sacrificed her own legal ambition to the best interests of the class. She,

501. *Mary Stewart Howarth-Hewitt, supra* n. 496, at 3, 4.

502. *Id.* at 4.

503. *Catherine Stewart Howarth Carter, Date of Admission: 1934*, in *Florida's Women Lawyers, supra* n. 479, at 66.

504. *See infra* nn. 914–916 and accompanying text.

505. *Catherine Stewart Howarth Carter, supra* n. 503, at 66–67.

506. *Mary Stewart Howarth-Hewitt, supra* n. 496, at 3.

finding herself a rival of Blackstone in the attention of the boys, gracefully withdrew from law school, in order that the work should not suffer.[507]

Despite Pitcher's not completing her legal studies, most women who entered Stetson's law school during the first three decades of the twentieth century did graduate. Consider the following statistics: Out of Florida's first 150 women lawyers, ninety were admitted without formal law school education. They either had read the law or had previously been admitted in other states. Nonetheless, each passed an oral examination required by the Florida Supreme Court. The remaining sixty admitted women lawyers graduated from law schools, located both within and outside Florida. Of this number, thirty-five were graduates of a single law school—the Stetson University College of Law.

Indeed, between 1900 and 1930, Stetson was the only law school in Florida to admit and graduate women attorneys. During these three decades, twenty-six Stetson women lawyers were admitted to practice in the State.[508] Since the graduation of Mary Stewart in 1908, Stetson's women law graduates have made significant contributions to their communities and to the legal profession. For those women who graduated from 1900 through the present, their significance is highlighted in subsequent chapters.

i. The College of Law's Initial Locations: Elizabeth and Flagler Halls

When the College of Law opened in October 1900, students attended classes in Elizabeth Hall, one of two Colonial revival brick buildings erected on the DeLand University campus, the other being Chaudoin Hall.[509] Elizabeth Hall was named in honor of John B. Stetson's wife. Stetson, along with University trustee C.T. Sampson (a shoe manufacturer from Philadelphia), donated funds for both Elizabeth and Chaudoin Halls.[510] The buildings were sited near Stetson University's first building, DeLand Hall, which itself has noted historical significance.

Built in 1884, DeLand Hall is described as "the oldest building in Florida continuously associated with higher education."[511] Designed by John Mace, DeLand Hall since 1983 has been listed in the National Register of Historic Places.

507. *Law Senior Class Report*, Stetson Collegiate 5 (1909).

508. These statistics were gathered by W. Gary Vause, co-author. They were published in *Florida's Women Lawyers, supra* n. 479, at an unnumbered page near the back of the book, a page beginning with the Stetson College of Law letterhead and indicating that it is a salute to "The first 150 Women Lawyers in Florida."

509. Johnston, *supra* n. 291, at 288–290.

510. *Id.*

511. *Id.* at 288.

Meanwhile, Philadelphia architect George T. Pearson designed Elizabeth Hall. According to Florida architectural history expert Sidney Johnston, the building was planned to resemble Independence Hall.[512] Johnston describes Elizabeth Hall as the most "architecturally significant building" on Stetson's DeLand campus.[513]

After being housed in Elizabeth Hall a little over a year, the College of Law moved into the then just-completed Science Hall (later renamed Flagler Hall in recognition that Henry Flagler's donation had financed its construction). President Forbes earlier had hired San Francisco architect William Charles Hays[514] to draw plans for the two-story building, but it ended up being three stories.[515] Flagler told Forbes that he wanted the building to resemble the Spanish-Mediterranean Revival style of hotels he had built in Florida. As a consequence, Flagler Hall resembles the Ponce de Leon Hotel, located in St. Augustine (which subsequently became the home of Flagler College).[516]

Back at Stetson, law students appreciated the new and larger quarters of Flagler Hall. University Archivist Olga Bowen described the new facilities:

> The quarters for the law department in Flagler Hall occupied the south half of the second floor. The large room in the southeast wing was used as the library and as a moot court room. Book stacks lined the walls. There were study tables. The front of the room was *arranged like a courtroom* with a railing enclosing the area occupied by the judges, by the attorneys, and the prisoner. A large portrait of Henry M. Flagler hung over the judge's bench.[517]

While one room served as the school's law library, other rooms housed the new industrial arts (also called technology) division of the University. Flagler Hall served as the College of Law's home for more than four decades. At one point, the law school took over the entire third floor of the building, where it remained until 1947, when it moved to a nearby abandoned Naval Air base.

j. People Say the Strangest Things (Part One)

Studying law has never been tension-free, as one Stetson student in fall 1908 discovered. Depressed by the demands of his studies, he wrote his aunt about

512. *Id.* at 284.

513. *Id.* at 290.

514. *Id.* at 292 (citing *Master Builders: A Guide to Famous American Architects* 185 (Diane Maddex ed., Preservation Press 1985)).

515. *Id.*

516. Lycan, *History of Stetson, supra* n. 109, at 86.

517. Bowen, *supra* n. 292, at 3–4 (emphasis added).

his despondency. Antidepressants or psychiatrists being unavailable in DeLand in 1908, his aunt's reply may have been the best alternative. She wrote:

> Don't get the blues, my dear boy. Do you not think it's a good idea to smile hard when you feel them coming? Stretch the mouth wide and presently you will enjoy the joke and feel like laughing at it and the blues will be lighted up as a blue summer sky with sunshine.[518]

Another incident involved a law student who did not exactly answer a question properly in class. Asked by Dean Farrah what the Latin phrase *filius nullius* meant, the student responded: "That, dean, is a person born with neither mother nor father."[519] In another Farrah-student exchange, the dean called on Thomas Calmes "to summarize that clause of the Declaration of Independence which declared that all men are created equal." A classmate said that Calmes used "about 4,000 words what took our forefathers about 250 to tell."[520]

The same Thomas Calmes became president of the 1904 graduating class. His classmates said that his middle initial "C." stood for "Calamity."[521] Still another story about "Calamity" appeared in *The Stetson Collegiate*:

> Our Class President, Mr. Thomas Calamity Calmes ... says to me, "hold my books until I get back. I don't know when that will be. If I don't get back, tell professor where I have gone; send my trunk back home; you can keep all my books; just write Sallie that my last thoughts were of her; see that Sallie gets all the residue of my property." ... He was gone about two minutes when he returned ... and took his seat by my side. Naturally I asked the cause of his return. ["Calmity"] with a voice as the Rock of Ages, informed me that he ... did not believe in oral wills.[522]

Then there were excuses students made (as there always are) for not being prepared for class. Examples: John C. Gramling replied upon being corrected: "That's what I intended to say"; David Rodgers frequently murmured: "I know [the answer], but I can't speak it"; Wesley Pinnell would assert: "I thought we had only lectures today, without any cases."[523] About the same time students

518. *An Aunt's Letter to Her Nephew*, Stetson Collegiate 2 (Oct. 26, 1908).

519. *College of Law: Little News Notes about Our Lawyers*, Stetson Collegiate 3 (Jan. 16, 1906).

520. *Class History-Law Department*, Stetson Collegiate 8 (Apr. 1902).

521. Lehman McKinney, *Class History-Law Department*, Stetson Collegiate 7, 9 (Apr. 1903).

522. *Id.* at 8.

523. Arthur L. Auvil, *College of Law*, Stetson Collegiate 3 (Feb. 14, 1906).

President Lincoln Hulley

revealed their unpreparedness, the University revealed it had a new president, one who would remain in office for over three decades.

k. Lincoln Hulley Becomes President and Preserves University's Independence

After President John Forbes resigned in 1904 following the debacle with John Stetson, the Board of Trustees appointed Lincoln Hulley to be the University's second president. Hulley assumed his duties only six months following Forbes' departure.[524]

Born in 1865 in Camden, New Jersey, Lincoln Hulley grew up in southeastern Pennsylvania. His father was a foreman in a weaving mill where Lincoln worked, often twelve-hour days, six days a week.[525] The hard work instilled in the young man a habit of discipline and persistence, as well as determination to get a job done. Hulley graduated from Bucknell University in 1888, then from Harvard University the following year. (One of his Harvard class-

---

524. *See generally* Olga Bowen, *Lincoln Hulley* (unpublished ms. 1964) (on file at Stetson U. Archives, DeLand, Fla.). Most of the information about Lincoln Hulley's background comes from an unpublished paper by Stetson University Archivist during the 1960s, Olga Bowen. It was one of several Stetson historical summaries she authored. Others included papers on President Forbes, the College of Law, and a history of the University through 1960.

525. *Id.* at 1–2.

mates was J. Pierpoint Morgan, later to become a famous Wall Street tycoon).[526] Returning to Bucknell, Hulley joined its faculty and taught there two years prior to being admitted into a doctorate program at the University of Chicago. He subsequently earned a Ph.D. in Semitic languages from Chicago. In 1894, Hulley once again returned to teach at Bucknell, this time history.

Hulley's appointment as president of Stetson was due to the recommendation of University of Chicago President Robert Harper. Following Forbes' resignation, the Stetson Board of Trustees contacted Harper, inquiring whom he might suggest as a qualified successor to Forbes. Harper suggested his former student, Lincoln Hulley. Harper noted that he had instructed Hulley in Hebrew during the summers of 1890 and 1891 at Yale, where Harper was a professor and Hulley a student.[527]

Though raised a Methodist, by then Lincoln Hulley had become a devout Baptist. Undoubtedly, this was part of Harper's admiration for the Pennsylvanian. Harper, an active Baptist, persuaded Hulley to spend his summers lecturing at "Chautauguas"—Baptist summer teachers' institutes. Hulley did so for thirty-five years. His teaching topics included great authors, especially poets like Robert Browning, Robert Burns, Alfred Lord Tennyson, Rudyard Kipling, and William Wordsworth.[528]

Upon Harper's recommendation, Stetson's Board of Trustees interviewed Hulley. He made a good impression. Consequently, T.C. Search, Chairman of the Board of Trustees, extended a formal offer and invited the Bucknell professor to become the second president of Stetson University. Though Hulley initially declined the offer, his friend and mentor Harper persuaded him to accept and become head of the small Baptist-affiliated university in Florida.[529] Earlier, Harper had advised Hulley to reject an invitation to be president of Colgate University. Perhaps Harper believed that the Baptist affiliation of Stetson University made the difference.

In any event, in 1904 Lincoln Hulley did become the second president of Stetson University. He could not have imagined that he would remain president for thirty years, nor that he would be the de facto dean of its law school for nine of those years. Moreover, probably Hulley did not foresee that he would be embroiled in controversies from nearly the moment he stepped on campus.[530] Upon arrival, he found the Board of Trustees, the faculty, and the DeLand community

526. *Id.* at 3.
527. *Id.*
528. *Id.*
529. *Id.* at 5.
530. *Id.* at 8.

all divided over the prolonged Forbes-Stetson controversy.[531] In addition, the University's relations with the Florida Baptist Convention were deteriorating as the University Trustees and leaders of the Baptist Convention were engaged in a "bitter fight."[532] Hulley insisted that ownership of the University must remain with the existing Board of Trustees pursuant to its 1897 Charter. The Convention's leadership, on the other hand, took the opposite view and, in 1907, introduced into both the Florida Senate and House a bill seeking enactment of a new Stetson University charter, one that would establish without doubt that the Baptist Convention owned and controlled John B. Stetson University.

Never one to run from a battle, Hulley fought to keep the 1897 Charter unchanged.[533] After the lower house of Florida's Legislature passed the bill that would give Stetson a new Charter, Hulley traveled to Tallahassee and testified before the Senate Judiciary Committee.[534] Former Florida Governor William S. Jennings also testified, but as a strong advocate for a new charter, as he wanted the Baptist Convention to have absolute control of Stetson University.[535]

Hulley's argument before the Senate committee focused on questions of constitutional law. He began by reading Article I, Section 10 of the United States Constitution, the provision which declares that no state shall pass any law impairing the obligations of contracts. Though a nonlawyer (at that time) and having no formal legal training, Hulley made a sound argument. He asked the Committee's members to consider the U.S. Supreme Court decision in the *Dartmouth College* case of 1819.[536] In that landmark opinion, the Court held that the original charter of incorporation of Dartmouth College, granted in 1769 by King George III, was inviolable and that the New Hampshire Legislature had no authority to change the charter, one that had created a private trust against the will of a majority of Dartmouth's trustees.[537] (Legendary American lawyer and statesman Daniel Webster represented the majority of the trustees of Dartmouth College).[538] Hulley pointed out to the Florida leg-

531. Lycan, *History of Stetson*, *supra* n.109, at 109. "When he assumed the presidency of Stetson, he launched into a sea of troubles." *Id.*

532. *Id.*

533. *Id.*

534. *Id.* at 134–35.

535. *Id.* at 137.

536. *Dartmouth College v. Woodward*, 17 U.S. 518 (1819).

537. Charles Evans Hughes, *The Supreme Court of the United States* 201 (Columbia U. Press 1927); *see also* Eugene Francis Clark, *Dartmouth College*, in *Encyclopedia Britannica*, *supra* n. 227, vol. 7, 64.

538. "It [Dartmouth] is, as I said, a small college, and yet there are those who love it." This is a quote from Daniel Webster's U.S. Supreme Court argument in *Dartmouth v. Wood-*

islators that he represented sixteen trustees, a majority of Stetson University's twenty-four, and that these sixteen trustees opposed having Stetson's original Charter altered.

In continuing his argument, Hulley next cited the U.S. Supreme Court case of *Fletcher v. Peck,*[539] describing (in an over-generalization) its holding as imposing restrictions on state legislatures to change state law.[540] Hulley concluded his "legal" argument by declaring that the issue under consideration must be settled on "legal principles, not on sentiment, passion, poetry or oratory."[541]

The Senate's Judiciary Committee members—many of whom were lawyers—were "deeply impressed" with Hulley's legal analysis. Indeed, his skillful and persuasive argument changed the minds of many. As a result, the Judiciary Committee unanimously voted not to send the bill to the floor of the Senate, thereby killing it and guaranteeing the continued independence of Stetson University, at least for the foreseeable future, from direct control and ownership by the Florida Baptist Convention. At Stetson, it was said that "Lincoln" won the day.[542]

One year after Hulley's success in preventing the Convention's takeover of the school, Stetson University founder Henry A. DeLand died on March 13, 1908. At the time of his death, DeLand was in his home community of Fairport, New York, the town where he had made his fortune in the baking soda business.[543] In commenting on DeLand's death, Hattie Austin, a prominent citizen of DeLand, Florida, wrote:

> People from this entire section owe much to Mr. DeLand's noble generosity. He planted orange groves, he opened roads, cut down forests, financed many town enterprises, brought many settlers here every year, landed all sorts of enterprises and was one of the best promoters of good public works that ever came to Florida.[544]

---

ward, 17 U.S. 518 (1819). Upon hearing Webster's utterance, which affected everyone in the courtroom, including Chief Justice John Marshall: "the deep furrows of his cheek expanded with emotion and his eyes suffused with tears." Camaliel Bradford, *Webster, Daniel*, in *Encyclopedia Britannica*, *supra* n. 227, vol. 23, 470–471.

539. 10 U.S. 87 (1810).

540. Lycan, *History of Stetson*, *supra* n. 109, at 137.

541. *Id.*

542. Even before his persuasive discourse, Stetson President Lincoln Hulley was widely acclaimed as an accomplished orator. His parents had aptly named him "Lincoln," said to be in honor of Abraham Lincoln. Bowen, *supra* n. 524, at 1.

543. *See supra* nn. 121–122 and accompanying text.

544. Keeler, *supra* n. 108.

It seems a fitting epitaph for the founder of both the University and the town.

l. Dean Farrah Leaves Stetson and Starts New Law School

After taking the helm as the University, President Lincoln Hulley quickly endeared himself to John B. Stetson. Subsequent to John Stetson's removal two years earlier as Chairman of the Board, the philanthropist had ceased making donations to the University. Within two years of becoming president, however, Hulley convinced Stetson's Trustees to re-elect John B. Stetson as its Chairman.

In gratitude, John Stetson was about to resume his financial support to the University, but only three days after his election, to the shock of President Hulley and the entire University community, he died after suffering a stroke.[545] Fortunately for the University, his widow, Elizabeth, and his son, John B. Stetson, Jr., continued to provide financial support to the University over the next four decades.

Turning to the law school during this period, President Hulley worked well with Albert Farrah, Dean of the College of Law, at least up to the point when Farrah announced that he was leaving Stetson University to establish a new law school at the University of Florida (UF).[546]

University of Florida officials naturally contacted Stetson's Dean Farrah. After all, he was the founding dean of the first law school in the State of Florida. He also had graduated from the prestigious University of Michigan Law School and had been a professor on Michigan's law faculty. More importantly, he had been dean of Stetson's law school for nearly a decade, where he had assembled a first-rate law faculty and had caused the law school to grow from five to twenty-eight students. Moreover, Farrah knew many, if not most, of Florida's prominent jurists, lawyers, and politicians.

It seems only natural that the University of Florida would invite Farrah to become the founding dean of its law school.[547] Why did he accept the UF offer and leave his secure position at Stetson? Farrah explained to Hulley that UF had offered him a "handsome increase in salary," and that the needs of Farrah's family compelled him to accept the new position.[548]

---

545. Lycan, *History of Stetson, supra* n. 109, at 116.

546. *Id.* at 178. Two years earlier, the University of Florida decided to establish a law program, one that would become the second law school in the State at Gainesville.

547. Vause, *Foundations for Excellence, supra* n. 308, at 308.

548. Lycan, *History of Stetson, supra* n. 109, at 178 (citing Ltr. from Albert J. Farrah to Lincoln Hulley (June 21, 1909) (on file at Stetson U. Archives, DeLand, Fla., in *General Correspondence Stetson University* vol. 71, 23)).

But other factors also may have influenced Farrah's decision. Recall that he had been an admirer and strong supporter of President John Forbes. Therefore, Farrah had to be distressed when Forbes was forced to resign following Forbes' feud with John Stetson. Farrah also had to be concerned over Stetson's return to power at the University, knowing that Stetson, though the University's chief benefactor, had never given any money to the law school, and that John B. Stetson had opposed the law school becoming a division of the University at the outset.

There may have been another more personal factor as well. In 1906, President Hulley studied law on his own and, in a sense, became a competitor of Farrah in "knowing the law." Moreover, through political lobbying, Hulley became a member of the Florida Bar Association, even though he never had attended law school nor taken the Supreme Court's examination.[549] Add to this the fact that Hulley and Farrah both were strong-willed, it seems probable that they would come to disagree over the management and the future of the law school, though no documents have been located to substantiate this assumption.

In any event, for whatever combination of reasons, Dean Albert J. Farrah left Stetson's College of Law and accepted the deanship of the University of Florida's new law school in 1909. What made matters worse for the College was that Farrah took a strong member of Stetson's law faculty with him, Harry R. Trusler (who later became Farrah's successor as law dean at UF). In addition, several of Stetson's law students left with Farrah to go to Florida.[550]

Stetson's College of Law, as historian Lycan puts it, "was deeply shaken."[551] And things were not going to get better. Over the next decade, the law school's progress would be hampered not only by the new competition from Gainesville, but also by a lack of attention to University and law school academic standards by a University president who, though multi-talented, was predisposed to micromanage everything within the University, including the College of Law.

549. Bowen, *supra* n. 524.

550. Lycan, *History of Stetson, supra* n. 109, at 179.

551. *Id.* at 178.

CHAPTER FOUR

Confronting New Competition — President Hulley; Dean Rasco

4.1 Growing Pains

a. Dean Farrah Promotes the State's Second Law School

After Stetson College of Law's first dean, Albert J. Farrah, left the University to become founding dean of the University of Florida College of Law, a leadership vacuum developed at Stetson's law school.[552] As noted above, the problem was compounded because Professor Trusler also left Stetson and went with Dean Farrah to Gainesville.[553] Given that several Stetson law students had also transferred to UF,[554] historian Lycan concluded that the exodus created a "damaging situation."[555]

Prior to leaving, Farrah met with Stetson law professors Fred Botts and Egford Bly, and advised them about how to manage with fewer students.[556] Following Farrah's departure, the law school's enrollment fell from twenty-

552. Dean Farrah served as Dean of the University of Florida College of Law from 1909 until 1915, when he moved to the University of Alabama law school to become its dean. At Alabama, he was considered an outstanding dean. After several years, the University of Alabama named the law school building the Albert J. Farrah Hall in his honor. Albert J. Farrah enhanced the academic reputations of each law school he served.

553. Professor Harry Trusler, who accompanied Albert Farrah to Gainesville, succeeded Farrah as Dean of the University of Florida College of Law in 1915. Trusler remained dean until 1947, a term of thirty-two years. *See* Vause, *supra* n. 308, at 308 n. 48. Thus, the first thirty-eight years of the University of Florida's law school was headed by a former Stetson law dean (Farrah) and a former Stetson law professor (Trusler).

554. *Id.*

555. Lycan, *History of Stetson, supra* n. 109, at 178–179.

556. *Id.*

eight to eighteen.[557] The reasons Stetson law students left were, first, out of fondness and respect for Farrah and, second, because of the tuition differential between the two schools. In 1909, UF charged a flat $40 tuition per academic year, compared with Stetson's $66, a significantly higher amount. But it could have been worse. UF officials had hoped that its law school be tuition-free, but Florida Governor Broward disagreed, declaring that "there would be no state law school without a substantial tuition."[558] Had UF instituted free tuition at its law school, Stetson's College of Law likely would not have survived.

There was no doubt that Albert Farrah promoted Stetson's College of Law during his deanship, but he worked just as diligently to advance UF's new law school. A few of his tactics raised some concerns at Stetson, especially his writing first-year Stetson law students, inviting them to transfer to UF. Farrah did so because he believed the State of Florida could support only one law school.[559] He shared this opinion with college undergraduates not only in Florida, but also in other southeastern states.[560]

Making Stetson law school's future even more problematic, President Hulley learned that Florida's Dean Farrah had been contacting Stetson's alumni, suggesting that the future of Stetson's law school was in doubt.[561] Ambrose L. Suhrie, a retired scholar who taught part time at Stetson, served as a consultant to President Hulley. Suhrie communicated the news of Farrah's activities to the Stetson president.[562] Florida's Attorney General James W. Perkins also wrote Hulley that persons across Florida were asking whether Stetson's law school could survive in spite of its "worthwhile [law] program."[563]

According to Lycan, after beginning his duties in Gainesville, Farrah concluded that the Florida tax-based revenues available to finance UF's law school would give that institution a strategic advantage over Stetson's private law

---

557. Bowen, *supra* n. 524, at 2.

558. Ltr. from Ambrose Suhrie to Lincoln Hulley (July 11, 1909) (on file at Stetson U. Archives, DeLand, Fla.).

559. Lycan, *History of Stetson, supra* n. 109, at 179.

560. *Id.* (citing *General Correspondence of Stetson University* vol. 106, 83 (Stetson U. Archives, DeLand, Fla.)).

561. Ltr. from Ambrose Suhrie to Lincoln Hulley (Aug. 1, 1909) (Stetson U. Archives, DeLand, Fla.).

562. Lycan, *History of Stetson, supra* n. 109, at 162, n. 14; *see also* Ambrose L. Suhrie, *Teacher of Teachers* 171 (Richard R. Smith 1955).

563. Lycan, *History of Stetson, supra* n. 109, at 179 (citing Ltr. from James Perkins to Lincoln Hulley (July 1, 1909)).

school, and that, consequently, in time the UF law school would be "the only one left standing." A few at Stetson even believed this to be true.[564] Stetson University Professor W.S. Gordis (who in 1946 wrote the first history of the University) observed that the opening of UF's law school on campus raised the question of whether it would be wise for Stetson to discontinue its College of Law.[565] Ultimately, however, Florida's first law school continued to stand erect in an area once known as Persimmon Cove.[566] The College of Law's survival may fairly be attributed to the tenacity of President Hulley, and to his ability to make legal arguments.

b. A New Challenge

Neither Florida's Attorney General James Perkins nor UF's new law school dean Albert Farrah appreciated Lincoln Hulley's willingness to fight for the survival of Stetson's College of Law.[567] During Hulley's high school days in Pennsylvania, he competed in various sports, notably boxing.[568] It was said that Hulley learned that suffering a knockdown does not prevent one from jumping back up and fighting on. Being next to the youngest of seven siblings, he also learned how to react to ambitious "adversaries."[569]

Following Farrah becoming dean at UF's law school, Hulley assumed the acting deanship of the Stetson College of Law while continuing to serve as the University's president. He remained acting dean of the law school for five years until 1914, when he named Richmond Rasco the dean. Recognizing that financial incentives of the publicly financed UF law school would be attractive to aspiring students, Hulley instituted a scholarship program for Stetson law students, albeit only for a few.[570] More importantly, he lowered Stetson's law school tuition to $40 per year, thereby making it the same as that at UF's law school. To spread the word, Hulley advertised the lower Stetson tuition in papers throughout the State.[571] Next, he sent professors Egford Bly and a recently

564. *Id.*

565. Gordis, *supra*, n. 105, at 34–35.

566. For an explanation of "Persimmon Cove," see *supra* n. 108 and accompanying text.

567. Bowen, *supra* n. 524, at 18. "Dr. Hulley was an aggressive man who loved a fight. He was quick to anger." *Id.*

568. *Id.* at 2.

569. *Id.* at 1.

570. Lycan, *History of Stetson, supra* n. 109, at 179.

571. Lincoln Hulley, President, Stetson U. College of L. (1909) (handwritten ad) (on file in *General Correspondence Stetson University* vol. 84, 36) (on file at Stetson U. College of Law, Gulfport, Fla. and reprinted in *Annual announcement 1910–1911* (John B. Stetson U.)).

hired Richmond Rasco to recruit students, instructing the professors to emphasize to prospective students "the advantages" of attending Stetson's established and tested law program.[572]

Meanwhile, in the summer of 1909, the chairman of the University's Department of Elocution (a.k.a., Department of Public Speaking), Ambrose Suhrie, traveled throughout Florida, canvassing Stetson alumni regarding their opinions and concerns about Stetson's law school and its reputation. Suhrie wrote Hulley that not all was well, suggesting that the president communicate with Stetson alumni to dispel negative impressions that many of them had about the future of the Stetson law program.[573]

Without delay, Hulley sent advertisements to newspapers across Florida, touting the College's established record. He accompanied these advertisements with "news" stories (which he and Suhrie had drafted) to the papers' editors, suggesting that they publish the informative pieces concerning the law school. The Jacksonville *Times-Union* and the *Tampa Tribune* (and perhaps other papers) published portions of what in reality were promotive news releases.[574] Though not all editors chose to print Hulley's advertisements, the messages reached many intended recipients, especially those in Duval County. The news stories emphasized the College's reduced tuition of $40 per year and highlighted its achievements, noting in particular the school's well-known alumni.[575]

In an effort to further enhance the importance of Stetson's College of Law, Hulley wrote to all "Members of the Bench and Bar of Florida," a copy of which letter appears in the College's Annual Announcement for the 1910–1911 academic year.[576] In his letter, he extolled the virtues of Stetson's law program and stressed the importance of incorporating Florida statutes and case decisions "in each subject taught in the Law School."[577] Moreover, Hulley praised the school's "special course in Florida Pleading and Practice," and pointed out that subjects pertaining to Florida law throughout the school's curriculum "are

572. Lycan, *History of Stetson*, *supra* n. 109, at 179.

573. *Id.*

574. Hulley, *supra* n. 571.

575. *Id.*

576. *See generally Foreword: To the Members of the Bench and Bar of Florida,* reprinted in John B. Stetson U. College of L., *Annual Announcement 1910–1911*, at x (1910) [hereinafter *Forward*] (a publication sent out to all applicants and, in many instances, potential applicants to the College of Law, 1910) (copy on file at Stetson U. College of Law, Gulfport, Fla.).

577. *Id.*

of inestimable value to young men intending to practice law in Florida."[578] The Stetson president also directed the readers' attention to "special lectures" given by "prominent members of the Bar of Florida."[579]

Though UF's law school was in operation, Hulley never referred to it in his letter to Florida's judges and lawyers, as he directed his comment only on the law school in DeLand:

> In the work we are doing for the advancement of legal education in Florida, a work carried on with no hope of pecuniary gain, may we not count on the active support of the bench and bar of the State? We will greatly appreciate it if you will send us the names [of] ... any young men of your acquaintance interested in the study of law. May we not hope that pride in our State will cause you to say a good word for her leading educational institution and particularly for her law school?
>
> Very truly yours, LINCOLN HULLEY, President.[580]

Hulley had made his plea: Stetson's College of Law was the State of Florida's law school, albeit private, and it deserved the support of Florida's entire bench and bar. But for his efforts to promote the College of Law in the years following the opening of UF's law school, UF's Dean Farrah might have been proven right—that Florida could support only one law school.[581]

Though his advertising and hyping the College of Law certainly had a positive impact for the school, some of Hulley's hype seemed beyond the fringe. For example, he often accentuated "claimed" health benefits of attending law school in DeLand. In the University's Law School Announcement for the 1910–1911 academic year, an interesting passage, quoted below, appears under the heading, "LOCATION."

> The city [DeLand] is on high pine land, not near any water and is remarkable for its general healthiness. The climate is almost specific for throat and lung troubles, catarrh [sic], rheumatism, etc. Students who are unable, from delicate health, to attend school during the winter in

578. *Id.*

579. *Id.*

580. *Id.*

581. What a difference a century makes. At the end of 2004, ten law schools exist in the State. They are Stetson University College of Law, University of Florida College of Law, University of Miami School of Law, Florida State University College of Law, Nova Southeastern University Law Center, Florida Coastal School of Law, Florida A&M Law School, Florida International University Law School, Barry University School of Law, and St. Thomas University School of Law.

> the North, find it possible to pursue their studies here regularly, and yet constantly improve their health.[582]

Should the above testament not convince a prospective student to choose Stetson's law school for its health spa benefits, the announcement offered yet another reason for students to come study law in DeLand: "Since 1889, there has been no licensed saloon in Volusia County and prosecutions for illegal selling are prompt and vigorous."[583] It is not clear how many, if any, students chose to attend the Stetson law school either because the area's climate was free of respiratory ailments, or because temperance ruled.

Certainly one reason they came was the lowering of Stetson's tuition, making it more in line with that at UF. In the 1910–1911 Law School Announcement under "Expenses," Stetson's tuition was listed at $45 per year. In the following year, however, the school's Announcement listed tuition at $40 per year in accordance with Hulley's earlier declarations in the College's advertisements and news releases.[584] Hulley's promotion of the law school is further evidenced in *An Open Letter to any Person Desiring to Study Law at Stetson,* a publication prominently displayed in each of the school's annual catalogs beginning in 1910 and continuing through 1915.[585] The printed "letter" included sixteen declaratory statements in the form of redundant questions about the school's quality.[586] Each declaration started with the phrase, "Did you know ..." For example, the first inquiry began: "Did you know that the Stetson College of Law offers a few scholarships for part tuition this year to Florida boys who are unable to pay full tuitions?"[587]

In his open letter to prospective students, Hulley underscored seven times that the law school's program concentrated on *Florida* law and practice. One example: "Did you know that Florida Law is taught in the Stetson College of Law by a law school graduate who has been an eminent attorney in Florida for a number of years?"[588] Hulley's letter also pointed out the successes of Stetson's law graduates, such as that of Emmett Wilson from Pensacola, class of

---

582. Stetson U., *Location,* in *Annual Announcement, supra* n. 576, at 3. This passage also appeared in the *Annual Announcement 1911–1912,* but not thereafter.

583. *Id.*

584. *Id.* at 26; see also John B. Stetson College of Law, *Annual Announcement 1911–1912,* 25 (1911) (copy on file at Stetson U. College of Law, Gulfport, Fla.).

585. Hulley, *supra* n. 571 (reprinted in John B. Stetson University College of Law, *Annual Announcement, 1910–1911,* et seq.).

586. *Id.*

587. *Id.*

588. *Id.*

1904. Wilson had been elected a member of Congress in 1917, representing the Congressional District of West Florida.[589] In sum, once Hulley learned that the "folks at Gainesville [were actively] pushing the [UF] Law School, he took action."[590] Both he and Farrah understood that when it came to academic institutions, only those that are promotive and well-managed survive.

Yet during Hulley's years as acting dean of Stetson's College of Law, the school's survival brought with it Hulley's turbulent relations with students, faculty, and especially with a new law dean. Moreover, the University president contributed to the lowering of academic standards at the College of Law.

4.2 Hulley's Years As Acting Dean

a. "Precipitous Decline" in Admissions and Academic Standards

Hulley stayed on as president of Stetson University for thirty years. Not only was he a fierce competitor, he also possessed superb oratorical skills that could change minds and inspire those around him to strive harder. Being a competitor, he cherished winning. Yet, given Hulley's competitiveness, oratorical proficiency, and diplomatic maneuvering, he failed to appreciate that a university, throughout its divisions and schools, must constantly strive to maintain and improve the institution's academic standards. In the crucial area of academic quality, Lincoln Hulley did not serve Stetson University or its College of Law well. Historian Gilbert Lycan writes that, from 1908 until the end of the Hulley era, Stetson University's academic standards failed to rise.[591]

Hulley's approach to law school admissions was clearly ad hoc and, in all likelihood, *ad hominem*.[592] In one case, he admitted a law student, but allowed him to stay at home to study, requiring only that the student come on campus to take examinations. In another instance, Hulley permitted a high-school dropout (ten years after he had left school) to enroll.[593] Still another example:

---

589. *Id.* The class of 1904 also included J. Turner Butler who later served as a Florida Circuit Judge in Jacksonville, and William B. Crawford, who served as Prosecuting Attorney for Kissimmee, Florida. *Alumni of the Law School; All Hold Degrees of LL.B.*, in Stetson U. College of L., *Annual Announcement 1917–1918*, at 20 (1917) (copy on file at Stetson U. College of L., Gulfport, Fla.).

590. *See Foreword*, *supra* n. 576, at x.

591. Lycan, *History of Stetson*, *supra* n. 109, at 182.

592. Vause, *Foundations for Excellence*, *supra* n. 308, at 308. "It was exceedingly easy to secure admission to Stetson Law School." *Id.*

593. Lycan, *History of Stetson*, *supra* n. 109, at 242.

A student who had studied at UF's College of Law and who had been denied a law degree there due to academic deficiency, contacted Hulley, who allowed the excluded former student to enter Stetson's law school, and assured him an LL.B. degree upon completion of required courses.[594]

Though in theory a part-time acting dean, Hulley took over complete control of the College of Law. And while from 1910 through 1915 he frequently admitted applicants who did not qualify under the school's published admission criteria, it remains unclear whether his actions were done to augment tuition revenues or just because he simply liked an applicant. Regardless, maintenance, let alone improvement, of academic standards suffered.

Then there was the quality of the faculty matter. Under Forbes, Stetson's new faculty members (including at the College of Law) typically were appointed following consultations with the president and members of the faculty at the University of Chicago. When Stetson's affiliation with Chicago terminated in 1908, President Hulley no longer could turn to Chicago for input. From that point on, Hulley seems to have paid less attention to the academic qualifications of the law faculty.[595] Though there were exceptions, rarely did new instructors graduate from prestigious universities or well-known law schools, as had been the pattern under Forbes and Farrah.

It might be said that, as the faculty goes, so goes the College. As the late Stetson law school dean, W. Gary Vause, noted during the administration of Lincoln Hulley, "the quality of Stetson's law program was in a state of precipitous decline."[596] Historian Lycan extended this negative assessment tthroughout the University:

> [Hulley's] unwillingness to be concerned with what went on inside the classrooms and failure to appoint a dean in Liberal Arts [and in the College of Law after Farrah's departure for five years] led to a disastrous decline in standards. For more than a decade of decline he met all requests for improvements with sharp denials that anything was wrong, and by grandiloquent statements about "Stetson's high and rising standards."[597]

---

594. *Id.* (citing Ltr. from Lincoln Hulley to Thomas B. Dowds of Palatka, Fla. (Jan. 2, 1923) (on file at Stetson U. Archives, DeLand, Fla, in *General Correspondence Stetson University*, *supra* n. ____, at vol. 84, 58a)).

595. W. Gary Vause, *Centennial History of the Stetson University College of Law* 59 (unfinished ms. 2003) (on file in Stetson U. College of L., Gulfport, Fla.) [hereinafter Vause, *Centennial History*]. The late Dean Vause drafted the manuscript in preparation for this book.

596. *Id.*

597. Lycan, *History of Stetson, supra* n. 109, at 234–235.

Despite Hulley's self-serving academic hype, both Stetson University's and its College of Law's academic reputations became suspect to many outside the University. Hulley, however, would hear none of it. In his 1922 Annual Report to the University's Board of Trustees, he stated that the Chief Justice of Florida's Supreme Court had been told that the Stetson law school "had gone to smash."[598] In anger, Hulley declared that whomever had first uttered that allegation "is an enemy of the College."[599] In the same report, Hulley wrote that upon his becoming a member of the Florida State Senate (while serving concurrently as Stetson's President), he refuted "false" statements about Stetson that he heard there.[600]

Hulley's disregard for academic quality and consequent impact on the University's reputation is difficult to understand, given his own academic success and prior experience in higher education. After attaining a Master's degree from Harvard University, Hulley associated with a well-respected university, Bucknell. As described earlier, in 1904, University of Chicago President William Harper recommended to Stetson's Board of Trustees that Hulley was well qualified for the presidency.[601] A recognized scholar in Semitic languages, Hulley had studied at the University of Chicago, earning a Ph.D. degree in Philosophy. He was extremely intelligent, had a "prodigious memory," and, it was said, could recite any Psalm in the *Bible* by referring to its number.[602] University archivist Olga Bowen wrote that Hulley could recite from memory the entire Gospel of Mark, as well as portions of the other Gospels.[603] Moreover, during his presidency, Hulley, though he never took any formal classes in law school, read law on his own and, for seven years (1906–1913), taught a course—elementary law—at the law school.[604]

Then why did Hulley fail in the critical realm of academic standards? Perhaps his ambitions, ego, and somewhat narcissistic personality got in the way. Previous Stetson University historians describe Hulley as "an aggressive man," "quick to anger," who "brooked no interference," "an autocrat," who "rarely called faculty meetings," and one who "did not accept kindly any suggestions as the operation of, or [academic] requirements at, Stetson."[605] Add to the mix

598. Lincoln Hulley, *Annual Report to the Board of Trustees of John B. Stetson University* 8 (Feb. 1, 1922) (on file at Stetson U. Archives, DeLand, Fla.).

599. *Id.*

600. *Id.*

601. *See supra* n. 527 and accompanying text.

602. Bowen, *supra* n. 524, at 3–4.

603. *Id.* at 4.

604. *Id.* at 9–10.

605. Bowen, *supra* n. 524, at 14, 16–18.

his distrust of faculty, especially those who did not agree with him, and a strong-willed and isolated autocrat emerges. During his tenure as Stetson's President, and throughout his two periods as de facto law dean, Lincoln Hulley ruled the administration and faculty with an "iron hand."[606] He "wanted to do everything himself."[607]

Thus, his insistence on micro-managing, while continually engaging in time-consuming activities off campus, was a major shortcoming, perhaps diverting his attention to academic matters. During his Stetson presidency, Hulley was elected to the Florida Legislature, serving as a state senator from 1918 through 1922.[608] Moreover, during his membership in the Florida Senate, Hulley ran for governor of Florida (but lost) after running a "one man election campaign."[609]

In addition to his political activities, Hulley sought and often attained positions of power and influence in a variety of organizations outside the University. In 1907, he began publishing a weekly newspaper, the *Gospel Herald,* setting forth his views on the Florida Baptist-Stetson University relationship, particularly writing on why he felt the University should be under the exclusive control of its trustees.[610]

In 1910, Hulley was appointed vice-president of the American Baptist Society, and in the same year was made a trustee of his alma mater, Bucknell University.[611] In 1917, he was elected president of the Florida Education Association,[612] followed in 1922 by his election to the board of trustees of Croger Theological Seminary.[613] Later, he founded the DeLand Rotary Club, becoming its first president in 1927.[614] Moreover, throughout his thirty years of leading Stetson University, Hulley routinely prepared and delivered lectures on scores of diverse topics across the country, usually for compensation.

If these activities beyond managing the University were not enough, Hulley authored scores of poems and forty-two plays.[615] Lycan underscores that

606. Vause, *Centennial History, supra* n. 595 at 59.

607. Lycan, *History of Stetson, supra* n. 109, at 111.

608. Vause, *Centennial History, supra* n. 595, at 11.

609. *Id.* at 14. Years earlier, President Hulley worked in the successful gubernatorial campaign of Doyle E. Carlton (a graduate from Stetson University, though not from its law school). Lycan, *supra* n. 109, at 249.

610. Bowen, *supra* n. 524, at 8.

611. *Id.* at 12

612. *Id.* at 11.

613. *Id.* at 12.

614. *Id.* at 14.

615. *Id.* at 18.

Dean Richmond Rasco

Hulley considered himself a highly talented writer and that he spent a "large portion of his time composing poetry, lullabies, hymns, and dramatic plays."[616] In an interview conducted by University archivist Olga Bowen, he proclaimed: "My plays are better than Shakespeare's."[617] On some occasions, Hulley would invite law students to be actors in his great works.[618]

Clearly, Hulley always enjoyed a stream of admirers, though he had outspoken detractors as well. One was Professor Richmond Rasco, who became dean of Stetson's College of Law during Hulley's presidency.[619] But before developing that story, one other major disruption involving Hulley is discussed—the Helen Hunt incident.

b. Helen Hunt

As noted previously, when it came to governance of the University, Lincoln Hulley wanted total control. Thus, when the "men" of Stetson (presumably including law students) began a self-governing organization, the president was displeased. He wrote Stetson's trustees that student governance "is a thing I never believed in."[620] Two years later, Hulley again wrote the trustees, this time

---

616. Lycan, *History of Stetson, supra* n. 109, at 231.

617. *Id.* at 232.

618. *Id.*

619. *See infra* nn. 708–20 and accompanying text.

620. Lincoln Hulley, *The Annual Report on John B. Stetson University to the Trustees* 2 (Feb. 15, 1923) (on file at Stetson U. Archives, DeLand, Fla.).

noting that the desire for student governance had spread to the women. He said: "The question here and elsewhere has been [s]hall young women have [student self-government]?"[621]

Besides student self-governance, Hulley also despised what he perceived as student disloyalty and lack of respect. He claimed: "There is an assertion [by students] of liberty, which borders on license. It is hard to restrain the students of today. [They display] a growing repugnance to obedience and [they declare they have] rights far beyond anything we have ever seen."[622] Hulley especially had little empathy with women students.

In a widely publicized incident, Hulley expelled a young female student from the University. His action eventually resulted in him and the University being embroiled in litigation for eighteen years, involving two lawsuits, both reaching the Florida Supreme Court.[623] (Interestingly, the law of these cases remains valid today).[624]

In the spring of 1907, Helen Hunt was a fifteen-year-old student attending Stetson University's preparatory school and living in a campus dormitory on campus. After completing two years in the normal division, Hunt decided that she wanted to become an attorney, but it would not happen at Stetson.[625]

Though on prior occasions Hunt had engaged in "rowdy behavior," her actions on the evening of April 6—which took place during a Stetson Board of Trustees banquet—prompted President Hulley to react in dramatic fashion.[626] Hunt's "rowdiness," which one observer characterized as "bordering on insurrection,"[627] occurred in the hallway above the dining room of Chaudoin Hall, where Hulley and the Board of Trustees were at a banquet.[628] During dinner, Hunt, who lived on the second floor of Chaudoin Hall, ran through the hallways above, "jumped up and down, shouted, rang [cow] bells, and made other

621. Lincoln Hulley, *The President's Report for February 19, 1925, to the Board of Trustees, John B. Stetson University, DeLand, Fla.* 4 (Feb. 19, 1925) (on file at Stetson U. Archives, DeLand, Fla.).

622. Hulley, *supra* n. 620, at 2.

623. *See John B. Stetson U. v. Hunt*, 102 So. 637 (Fla. 1925); *Hulley v. Hunt*, 57 So. 607 (Fla. 1912).

624. Jane A. Dall, *Determining Duty in Collegiate Tort Litigation: Shifting Paradigms of the College-Student Relationship*, 29 J.C. & U.L. 485, 489 (2003). "A 1924 case, *John B. Stetson University v. Hunt*, affirmed the College's right to suspend a student for ringing cowbells in the hallways and subverting the discipline of the college." *Id.*

625. *Helen Hunt West*, in *Florida's Women Lawyers*, *supra* n. 479, at 12.

626. *John B. Stetson U.*, 102 So. at 639.

627. *Id.*

628. Lycan, *History of Stetson*, *supra* n. 109, at 153.

disturbances."[629] Hunt's disruptive behavior both embarrassed and incensed President Hulley, who "ordered the young lady to leave Stetson forthwith."[630]

Had Hulley expelled or only suspended the hyperactive student? That question became a pivotal issue in subsequent litigation. This issue, and the question of whether her ordered departure was done with malice, eventually went before the Florida Supreme Court. The controversy finally came to an end on January 21, 1925, eighteen years after Hunt's noisy disruption of the Trustee's banquet.[631]

Hunt's initial litigation had centered on her allegation that Hulley had defamed her by stating or implying to others that she had inappropriate relations with male students.[632] As to the annoying ringing of cowbells, Hunt's explanation was that her conduct had been a schoolgirl prank of the kind that frequently took place in the University's women dormitories.[633] Regarding her charge of defamation, Hunt proved to the satisfaction of a jury that Hulley had slandered her by making derogatory statements to several individuals (including a member of the Board of Trustees) about her character.[634] Thus, in her defamation action, Hunt prevailed in the trial court, and the jury awarded her $15,000 in damages. This award, however, was subsequently overturned by the Florida Supreme Court on the basis that the evidence was insufficient to establish the alleged defamation.[635]

In 1922, Hunt filed a second suit against Hulley and Stetson University, alleging "malicious expulsion by a learning institution."[636] Like her first suit's result, she prevailed at trial, obtaining a jury verdict for $25,000. But once again, the Florida Supreme Court overturned the award, holding that her dismissal was not predicated on malice. The Court added that its decision upheld the right of colleges and universities to maintain discipline within their institutions.[637] Though Hunt never returned to Stetson, she did graduate from Florida State College for Women in Tallahassee. She then studied law in the office of attorney Fred B. Noble of Jacksonville, after which she was admitted to The Florida Bar. She had reached her goal and had become a lawyer.[638] Given her persistence in asserting what she believed to be her legal rights, it is

---

629. *Id.*

630. *Id.*

631. *John B. Stetson U.*, 102 So. at 637. The Florida Supreme Court denied a rehearing of its December 20, 1924, decision on January 21, 1925.

632. *Hulley*, 57 So. at 608.

633. *Helen Hunt West, supra* n. 625, at 12.

634. *Hulley*, 57 So. at 608.

635. *Id.*

636. *John B. Stetson U.*, 102 So. at 639.

637. *Id.*

638. *Helen Hunt West, supra* n. 625, at 13.

not surprising that Hunt became a leading champion of women's causes in Florida.[639] She has been described as a "political activist, journalist, and lawyer."[640]

A postscript to the Hunt-Hulley episode: Years following the final Supreme Court decision denying her claims, by coincidence, Hunt ran into Hulley in Jacksonville. He invited her to dinner and offered her flowers.[641] She accepted. What was said at dinner is not known.

c. *Baptist Relations During the Hulley Era*

In 1907, a new chapter in the stormy relations between Stetson University and the Florida Baptist State Convention began. At a special meeting of the Convention's Board held in Lake City, its trustees decided to open a "decidedly sectarian" Baptist college, one that would be owned by "The Florida Baptist Convention."[642] The Convention named its new institution Columbia College, to be located at Lake City, Columbia County.[643] The new Baptist college competed with Stetson in attracting Baptist undergraduate students. It was said that the two institutions engaged in a "fierce rivalry,"[644] but not for long. According to Lycan, Columbia College was "a financial disaster from the beginning."[645] The final blow came after the United States entered World War I. Thereafter, Columbia lost both students and faculty, while at the same time expenses spiraled upward due to the war's inflationary impact.[646] In 1918, eleven years after opening, Columbia College closed. Though Hulley had maintained "warm" relations with Columbia, the news of its closure pleased him: "I am happy to say that the sky looks brighter ... Columbia has failed."[647]

Dr. Henry Tribble, a Baptist Minister who had served as president of the Rawlings Institute, a preparatory school for girls in Charlottesville, Virginia, was one of Columbia College's three presidents during its brief existence.[648] Tribble and his wife, Estelle Carlton, raised nine children. Their second child,

---

639. *Id.*

640. *Id.*

641. Lycan, *History of Stetson, supra* n. 109, at 154 (citing interview with Olga Bowen (Nov. 17, 1977)).

642. Gordis, *supra* n. 105, at 24.

643. *Id.* at 25.

644. Lycan, *History of Stetson, supra* n. 109, at 189.

645. *Id.* at 194.

646. *Id.* at 198.

647. Gordis, *supra* n. 105, at 6.

648. James E. Tribble, *The Life and Times of Dean Lewis H. Tribble,* 30 Stetson L. Rev. 19, 20 (2000).

Dean Lewis Tribble

Lewis Herndon Tribble, was born in 1891. Lewis Tribble graduated from Stetson's College of Law in 1915, and a decade later become its third dean.[649]

Following Columbia's demise, Florida Baptists returned to the task of forging stronger ties with Stetson.[650] Negotiations ensued, and an agreement between the Convention and the University was executed by Lincoln Hulley for the University, and by S.B. Rogers, Secretary of the State Board of Baptist Missions for the Convention.[651] The new consensus became known as the "Hulley-Rogers Agreement of 1919."[652] The Convention, Lincoln Hulley, and Stetson's Board of Trustees all welcomed the new accords.[653]

For several years, Florida's Baptists opened their pocketbooks to Stetson University, though less so than had been anticipated at the execution of the Hulley-Rogers Agreement.[654] Nonetheless, in 1925, Baptists gave Stetson University $150,000, the largest single donation that the University had received to that date.[655] The gift, even though said to be "not nearly enough to place Stetson back in an easy financial condition," was welcomed. Stetson historian

649. *Id.* at 26–34. His father, Henry Tribble, had died earlier in an automobile accident in February 1912. *Id.* at 27.

650. Gordis, *supra* n. 105, at 201–202.

651. *Id.* at 202.

652. *Id.*

653. *Id.*

654. *Id.* at 204–205.

655. *Id.* at 205.

Gordis notes, "[O]ne wonders how the University would have survived without it."[656]

4.3 New Faculty Members; A New Dean

a. Faculty Hires: Richmond Rasco—The Next Dean

With support from Dean Farrah, in 1908 Hulley appointed Harry R. Trusler[657] to the law faculty. Trusler came to Stetson having earned his law degree from the University of Michigan, the fourth to have done so.[658] Trusler wrote Hulley conveying his gratefulness for the appointment, and added, "I am indeed glad to learn that I will find Michigan men in the work, and trust that I will do my work as a Michigan man should do it."[659] One year later, however, Trusler left with Farrah for the new UF law school.

To fill the vacuum caused by the departures, Hulley appointed Richmond Austin Rasco to the Stetson law faculty.[660] Rasco was the first native southerner to be appointed a Stetson law professor. Born in Newton, Mississippi, Richmond Rasco studied at Dickinson Normal School in Tennessee, where he received a Bachelor of Science degree in 1895.[661] He later earned an LL.B. degree from Southern Normal University in Huntington, Tennessee,[662] followed by an M.A. degree from Texas Normal University.[663]

Besides Rasco, Hulley also hired Fred Botts, a 1909 graduate of Stetson's College of Law who had earned a B.S. degree from Stetson,[664] but he remained only one year on the faculty, leaving to practice law in Miami. When Rasco and Botts joined the faculty, Judge Egford Bly and Professor G. Prentice Car-

---

656. *Id.* For a comprehensive discussion of the relationship between Stetson University and the Florida Baptists, see Garwood, *supra* n. 140; *see* also Rosser, *supra* n. 140.

657. From 1901 until Dean Farrah left Stetson College of Law, it appears that he brought all faculty prospects to President John Forbes, and later to President Lincoln Hulley's attention.

658. The comparatively large number of Michigan law school graduates on the Stetson faculty began, of course, with Dean Farrah's appointment by Stetson University President John Forbes.

659. Ltr. from Harry R. Trusler to Lincoln Hulley, *Appointment to the Stetson Faculty* (May 18, 1908) (copy on file at the Stetson U. Archives, DeLand, Fla.).

660. Bowen, *supra* n. 455, at 107.

661. *Id.*

662. *Id.* at 108.

663. *Id.*

664. *Alumni of the Law School*, in John B. Stetson U., *Annual Announcement 1914–1915*, at 20 (1914) (copy on file at Stetson U. College of Law, Gulfport, Fla.).

son—a Stetson undergraduate professor with no law training, but who had earned a Master's degree from Wesleyan University—were the other two members. In addition, Colonel W.H. Jewell, the mayor of Orlando and a practicing attorney who traveled back and forth to DeLand to teach Stetson's Practice Court course, was an adjunct, or part-time, faculty member.[665]

In 1910, Hulley appointed two recent Stetson law graduates as assistant professors: Dossie C. Hull and Roy V. Sellers. Each stayed briefly, Sellers leaving after one year, and Hull after two to become a partner in the DeLand firm of Hull, Landis & French.[666] Then, while serving as acting dean of the College of Law, Hulley in 1911 appointed to the law faculty Paul H. Dodge, holder of a Bachelor of Philosophy and a Juris Doctor degree from the University of Chicago. A specialist in English law, Dodge had studied at Oxford University.[667] He stayed only one year. Why four of Hulley's appointments remained on the faculty only one or two years is unclear. In similar fashion, law librarians came and went with frequency. J.I. Mitchell served one year; Frank N. Cullen, two years; and A.E. Roebuck, two years.[668]

By 1914, Hulley was beginning to turn over decanal responsibilities for the College of Law to Professor Richmond Rasco. Though still listed as a Professor of Law through spring 1913, Rasco's name first appears as "Acting Dean" in the law school's 1913–1914 Announcement.[669] Presumably, thereafter, Rasco added his input regarding faculty hiring.

His influence may be reflected in the hiring of Ralph Stanley Bauer, who came with solid credentials: a Bachelor of Arts degree from the University of Illinois; a Master's degree from the James Milikin University, and a Juris Doctor degree from the University of Chicago.[670] In addition to his strong academic background, Bauer was an experienced attorney and was admitted in both

---

665. *Faculty*, in John B. Stetson U. College of L., *Annual Announcement, 1909–1910* (1909) (copy on file at Stetson U. College of Law, Gulfport, Fla.). The faculty listing also included a "Professor [Fred] Botts," described as having had "a full course in Stetson in the College of Arts and Law," and the "Hon. Thomas M. Shackleford, LL.D., Associate Justice and formerly Chief Justice of the State." *Id.* In fact, Justice Shackleford did not teach on the faculty, but was said to have "addressed the graduating class in law at their commencement." *Id.*

666. Ltr. from Dossie C. Hull to J. Ollie Edmunds (n.d) (on file at Stetson U. Archives, DeLand, Fla.).

667. *Faculty* in John B. Stetson U. College of L., *supra* n. 665.

668. *Faculty*, in John B. Stetson U. College of L., *Annual Announcements*, *supra* n. 576.

669. *Faculty*, in John B. Stetson U. College of L., *Annual Announcement 1913–1914* (1913) (copy on file at Stetson U. College of L. Gulfport, Fla.).

670. *Id.*

Illinois and Montana, and had served on the law faculty at the College of Montana.[671]

Upon Rasco's suggestion, Hulley hired another highly credentialed law teacher to the faculty in 1916: Joseph Alexander Scarlett. A Stetson law school graduate, class of 1913, he had earned a Bachelor of Philosophy degree (Ph.B.) from Yale University.[672] Scarlett was later described as "one of the strong men of the Stetson [law] faculty."[673]

During this period, an aspiring law teacher wrote Hulley asking his advice about obtaining a position, either in practice, or, if possible, in law teaching.[674] The twenty-four-year-old inquirer was Lewis Herndon Tribble (the same person who six years later would join Stetson's law faculty, and later become dean).[675] He had graduated in Stetson's 1915 law class. In his letter, Tribble asked Hulley "to bear me in mind."[676] The president responded, "I wish I could do something for you," [but] "I shall keep you in mind, and, if anything turns up, I shall let you know."[677]

As the above exchange of letters illustrates, Hulley was not adverse to hiring recent Stetson law graduates to the faculty. He hired John D. Weir, a 1914 Stetson law graduate.[678] Weir transferred to Stetson after two years of law study at Indiana University.[679] (Incidentally, when Weir was hired, the College's enrollment consisted of fifty-six full-time and fifteen special, that is, non-degree-pursuing law students, making a total of seventy-one, at that time the largest in the school's history).[680] From 1909 through 1916, in addition to Weir, Hulley hired: Fred Botts and Dossie Hull, both of the class of 1909; Roy Sellers, class of 1911; and Joseph Scarlett, class of 1913. Of these five Stetson law graduates, by 1917 only Scarlett remained.[681]

---

671. *Id.*

672. *Faculty*, in John B. Stetson U. College of L., *Annual Announcement 1916–1917* (1916) (copy on file at Stetson U. College of L., Gulfport, Fla.).

673. *Id.*

674. Ltr. from Lewis H. Tribble to Lincoln Hulley (Jan. 10, 1916) (on file at Stetson U. Archives, DeLand, Fla.).

675. *See infra* nn. 747–751 and accompanying text.

676. *Supra* n. 674.

677. Ltr. from Lincoln Hulley to L.H. Tribble (Jan. 11, 1916) (on file at Stetson U. Archives, DeLand, Fla.).

678. *Faculty*, Stetson U. College of L., *Annual Announcement 1915–1916* (1915) (copy on file at Stetson U. Archives, DeLand, Fla.).

679. *Law School Flourishing This Year; Larger Than Ever*, Stetson Collegiate 1 (Oct. 31, 1913).

680. *Id.*

681. *Alumni of the School of Law*, *supra* n. 389, at 20–23.

Throughout the 1910–1920 decade, a Stetson undergraduate professor named Irving C. Stover (who held a Masters of Oratory degree) taught a course called "oratory and elocution,"[682] In an "Inter-Collegiate Contest in Oratory" among Southern and Midwest colleges, a Stetson law student under the tutelage of Stover won the prize.[683]

Another law faculty member during the 1915–1921 period was Major W.G.S. Lowe, described as having "endeared himself to students by his helpfulness and ready wit."[684] After America entered World War I, military drills were organized on Stetson's campus,[685] and Major Lowe led ninety "Stetson men" (which surely included law students) taking part in the drills.[686] Lowe continued to teach in the law school until 1921, when he resigned due to illness.[687]

b. A Different Personality, A Different Style

In contrast to President Lincoln Hulley's autocratic and aloof leadership style,[688] Dean Richmond Rasco's manner was laid back, soft spoken, and interactive with faculty and students alike. Students described him as "an outstanding teacher," one whom was "well liked."[689] A member of the law class of 1921, in expressing appreciation of Dean Rasco's efforts, wrote:

> [Dean Rasco] has labored with us ... has won our hearts by his personal sacrifice for our interests, and by his glowing smile and kindly interest and help in our troubles he has endeared himself in the memories of those who have come in contact with him.[690]

The Stetson 1915 yearbook describes Rasco as "unflagging in his efforts to build up the Law School, both in reputation and members."[691] In yet another reference to the respected dean, a student declared: "In the University no stronger department exists than the College of Law, which has been so care-

---

682. *Faculty*, *supra* n. 672.

683. *Id.*

684. *College of Law*, Oshzhzyi 65 (1921) (student yearbook, copy on file at Stetson U. College of L. Gulfport, Fla.).

685. Lycan, *History of Stetson, supra* n. 109, at 216.

686. *Id.*

687. *College of Law*, *supra* n. 684, at 65.

688. Tribble, *supra* n. 648, at 33.

689. Bowen, *supra* n. 455, at 108.

690. *College of Law*, *supra* n. 684, at 74. The author of the quotation was Adolphe Dressler, Jr., class of 1921.

691. *College of Law*, Oshzhzyi 57 (1915) (student yearbook, copy on file at Stetson U. College of L., Gulfport, Fla.).

fully brought to a high standard of efficiency under the direction of Dean Rasco."[692] Historian Lycan wrote, "[F]rom the beginning, Rasco was keen, innovative, popular, and successful."[693] In 1979, Lycan interviewed Stetson law school alumnus Henry V. Lofquist, who stated that "students of those earlier years, when looking back, waxed eloquent when describing Rasco's merits as a professor and his remarkably good influence on the students."[694]

In contrast to Hulley, Rasco was not satisfied with maintaining the status quo in the College of Law. From 1909 when he joined the faculty, through his deanship, Rasco sought to improve the law school's academic standards, teaching effectiveness and quality of student body. His most significant pedagogical contribution may have been his encouraging the faculty to adopt the casebook method of instruction.[695] In a letter to Hulley, Rasco wrote that "we are stressing the case system; yet we make considerable use of the problem method."[696]

During the 1910–1920 decade, the College of Law instituted "comprehensive exams" which students had to pass in order to graduate. These were in addition to two days set aside at the close of each term for examinations covering subjects just taken.[697] The law school's Annual Announcements stated that "the [term] examinations are in writing and are rigid and searching but are not final."[698] The "not final" referred to, of course, the requirement that at the conclusion of the student's senior (last) year of law study, she "must pass [a comprehensive] examination *in all subjects*" to be recommended for a degree.[699]

During the summers, Rasco traveled throughout Florida, recruiting students to come to Stetson's law school. His efforts succeeded, as the law school enrollment doubled between 1910 and 1915. The school's enrollment at the end of the 1914–1915 academic year totaled sixty—said to be the highest in its history—consisting of fifty-seven men and three women—Annie Joe Law, Marguerite Blocker, and Herberta Hathcock.[700] The graduating class had one woman, Law, and twenty-one men.[701] Not until after World War II would the

692. *College of Law*, Oshzhzyi 62 (1920) (student yearbook, copy on file at Stetson U. College of L., Gulfport, Fla.).

693. Lycan, *History of Stetson*, *supra* n. 109, at 179.

694. *Id.*

695. Ltr. from R.A. Rasco, Dean, Stetson College of Law to Lincoln Hulley, President, Stetson U. (Feb. 11, 1915) (on file at Stetson College of L., Gulfport, Fla.).

696. *Id.*

697. *Annual Announcement*, *supra* n. 576, at 14.

698. *Id.*

699. *Id.* (emphasis added.)

700. Stetson U. College of L., *supra* n. 691, at 57.

701. *Id.*

number of Stetson law students exceed this level. Not only in future success but also in quality did the Stetson law class of 1915 distinguish itself. Its graduated class included a future governor of the state—David Sholtz (Daytona Beach); a future justice of the Supreme Court of Florida—Elwyn Curtis Thomas (DeLand); and a man who would become the third dean of the College of Law—Lewis H. Tribble (Lake City).[702] These were heady times for the College of Law.

Then World War I intervened. Enrollment declined, faculty left, and the costs of running the University escalated.[703] As the number of students fell, so did the College's revenues. Lycan comments that World War I began a long-term downward trend for Stetson University.[704] He adds: "World War I dealt Stetson a blow ... Before the war, Stetson was relatively well-endowed. There were abundant funds ... [After] that war, Stetson [remained] poor, financially."[705]

4.4 Rasco's Deanship Ends Abruptly

President Hulley never enjoyed good relations with his faculty.[706] A few resented him deeply.[707] During the years immediately after World War I, the president's relations with the law faculty further deteriorated.[708] His interactions with Dean Rasco were especially tempestuous.[709] The president thought the law dean "wanted everything his way."[710] Rasco, in turn, "resented Hulley's constant interference."[711] At one point, Hulley wrote Rasco a curt memo "ordering him to see that the Courtroom was not to be used [by students] for studying in the evening" to save the University the cost of electricity.[712]

702. *Id.*, at 59, 62, 63, 67.

703. Vause, *Centennial History, supra* n. 595, at 309.

704. Lycan, *History of Stetson, supra* n. 109

705. *Id.* at 246.

706. *Id.* at 180.

707. Interview by Gilbert Lycan with Russell Brown, former Pres. of the Stetson U. Alumni Assn. (Dec. 1, 1977) (reported in Lycan, *supra* n. 109, at 185 n. 88).

708. Bowen, *supra* n. 455, at 16.

709. Vause, *Centennial History, supra* n. 595, at 310.

710. Lycan, *History of Stetson, supra* n. 109, at 242 (based on interview with Curtis Lowery, former Stetson U. professor (Dec. 29, 1977)).

711. *Id.* at 242.

712. *Id.*

This micro-management "was more than Dean Rasco could tolerate."[713] It became clear that Hulley would not allow him "to perform the normal duties as Dean."[714] The Hulley-Rasco dispute reached a climactic moment when, in frustration and anger, Rasco hurled an ink bottle at the president.[715] Though what specifically precipitated the flying-ink bottle attack is unclear, Lycan reports that "by a deft maneuver Hulley dodged the missile."[716] Rasco, however, could not dodge Hulley's response: a pink slip. With no hesitation, Hulley removed Rasco as dean of the College of Law, but allowed him to remain on the faculty.[717]

Upon learning of Rasco's demotion, students and alumni became outraged. The students were offended by Hulley's treatment of their admired dean.[718] Moreover, a group of Stetson law school alumni became so worked up that they sent former Stetson law school professor Fred Botts to see Stetson Trustee John B. Stetson, Jr. (son of John B. Stetson). Botts informed John Stetson of the group's displeasure with Hulley.[719] Then, in a candid letter to Hulley, Stetson wrote:

> What they wished was to present a united kick against your presidency in the University ... [They are] convinced that your incumbency is doing the institution harm and therefore would like to see you out ... Their feeling is entirely fomented by Dean Rasco who comes every year and to whom they give a dinner every year; they all think he is the greater man in the university.[720]

Of course, by the time John Stetson's letter reached Hulley, the latter had already removed Rasco as dean. But upon Hulley's learning of the Miami alumni's displeasure with his presidency, he became outraged, claiming that the law faculty had turned on him. Hulley wrote trustee Stetson that the "whole Law School faculty seems to be on strike," noting that the faculty had planned "an open demonstration against him but that he had prevented it and that he was going to 'act with resolution.'[721] Though the faculty did not go on

---

713. Vause, *Centennial History, supra* n. 595, at 309–10.

714. Lycan, *History of Stetson, supra* n. 109, at 242.

715. *Id.*

716. *Id.* (citing an interview with G.E. Gilliland (Dec. 30, 1977)).

717. *Id.*

718. *Id.* at 242 (citing interview with Olga Bowen on February 19, 1979, and interview with Henry Lofquist on October 17, 1979).

719. *Id.* at 243.

720. *Id.* (citing Ltr. from John B. Stetson Jr., Member, Stetson U. Bd. of Trustees to Lincoln Hulley (Mar. 4, 1922)).

721. *Id.*; *see also* Ltr. from Lincoln Hulley to John B. Stetson (Mar. 29, 1922) ("The whole law school Faculty seems to be on strike. But I am not going to budge.").

strike, Hulley wrote the Board of Trustees that "members of the [law] faculty were disloyal."[722]

Given alumni criticism of Hulley in contrast to their strong support of Rasco, the Stetson president decided to dismiss Rasco from the University. Rasco, however, had already chosen to leave. He accepted an offer to join the University of Florida law school faculty. It appeared that several Stetson law students "probably would go with him."[723] Sure enough, in spring 1922, Rasco moved to Gainesville, the same year, coincidentally, that Rasco's son, Russell A. Rasco, graduated from Stetson College of Law.[724]

A Stetson law student—Floyd Murphy—later opined that Dean Rasco's leaving was Stetson's College of Law loss and Florida's gain.[725] Adding insult to injury, four years after leaving Stetson to join the Florida law faculty, Richmond Rasco was invited to organize and become the founding dean of the University of Miami Law School,[726] serving as Miami's dean from 1926 until his death in 1931. His son, Russell A. Rasco, succeeded his father as Miami's dean. Russell Rasco graduated from Stetson Academy in 1915, earned a B.A. degree from Stetson in 1921, then his Stetson LL.B. degree in 1922.

Stetson historian Olga Bowen points out that Stetson's College of Law "was the mother of two law schools."[727] The founding law deans at both UF and Miami had come from the State's first law school, Stetson University College of Law.

722. Hulley, *supra* n. 571, at 3.

723. Lycan, *History of Stetson, supra* n. 109, at 242.

724. Vause, *Centennial History, supra* n. 595, at 310.

725. Lycan, *History of Stetson, supra* n. 109, at 243.

726. Bowen, *supra* n. 455, at 108.

727. *Id.*

CHAPTER FIVE

Attaining ABA Approval, AALS Accreditation — Dean Tribble

5.1 ABA and AALS Indirectly Regulate American Law Schools

In 1921, the American Bar Association (ABA) adopted standards to "approve" (that is, to accredit) law schools. From that year onward, the ABA promoted the standardization of American law schools, a process that exerted, and continues to exert, an enormous influence on the evolution and development of American legal education.[728] The net effect has been that law schools have, for the most part, become essentially alike regarding curricula, teaching methods, and requirements for graduation. Most importantly, the ABA accreditation process has caused the quality and standards of legal education to improve.

The ABA's oversight of the programs of America's law schools first began when the Association was founded at Saratoga Springs, New York, in 1878.[729] There, the ABA established a "Committee on Legal Education" (later renamed the "Section on Legal Education")[730] that, from the outset, promoted the position that formal, academic law school education was superior to law-office apprenticeships.[731] The ABA recognized that academic, in-school legal training was necessary to assure that competent and professional lawyers would be available for the public's needs. In 1879, the ABA Committee on Legal Edu-

728. Russell N. Sullivan, *Professional Organizations and Legal Education*, 4 J. Leg. Educ. 401, 403 (1952) [hereinafter Sullivan, *Professional Organizations*]. "It is impossible to measure or even estimate the effect which the activities of the principal national professional organizations have had on legal education in the United States." *Id.*

729. *Id; see also* Stevens, *supra* n. 196, at 27, 29, 38, 96–98.

730. Sullivan, *Professional Organizations*, *supra* n. 728, at 403.

731. *Reports of the American Bar Association* vol. 1, 16 (1878).

cation first drafted proposed regulations for law-school approval. The ABA urged the courts and the bars of each state to consider adopting its standards as prerequisites for bar admission.[732] Despite the ABA recommendations, twenty-five years would pass before they significantly impacted American law schools.

In 1890, a group of law professor members of the ABA spun off a new organization—the Association of American Law Schools (AALS).[733] The academics chose as president Harvard law professor James R. Taylor.[734] The AALS leadership desired to upgrade the quality of lawyer training in law schools and pursued this shared goal initially within the ABA's Section on Legal Education. The AALS over time, however, became more concerned with upgrading law schools' standards than focusing on the ABA's setting requirements for admission to practice. Thus, the AALS began to take its own path, and, to a degree, distance itself from the ABA.

Yet their respective objectives were complimentary, in that both organizations were concerned with upgrading the quality of legal education. To push law schools to emulate what ABA and AALS leaders considered to be an "elite" law school, the ABA promulgated standards for approval, while the AALS established minimum requirements for a school to be admitted into membership.[735]

During the early decades of the twentieth century, no state required an ABA applicant for admission to the bar be a graduate of a listed ABA "approved" school. Though the ABA recommended that law schools abide by their standards, not until the 1920s did it in effect mandate compliance for "approval." Furthermore, graduation from an ABA-approved law school became a prerequisite for a law school graduate to take a state's bar examination.[736]

Prior to 1921, the AALS's requirements for membership were more stringent than the ABA's standards for law school approval, but in that year the ABA adopted standards more rigorous than those of the AALS.[737] Thus, within

---

732. *Reports of the American Bar Association*, *supra* n. 422, at 27–28.

733. Warren A. Seavey, *The Association of American Law Schools in Retrospective*, 3 J. Leg. Educ. 153, 155 (1952).

734. *Id.*

735. *Id.* at 155.

736. Sullivan, *Professional Organizations*, *supra* n. 728, at 404–409.

737. Packer & Ehrlich, *New Directions*, *supra* n. 209, at 27. For a detailed listing of all American law schools in existence in 1921, including their founding dates (and in some instances their closing dates), *see generally* Alfred Z. Reed, *Training for the Public Profession of*

two years the AALS raised its requirements to match those of the ABA.[738] Thereafter, the two organizations worked side by side when it came to law school standards. Schools that had paid scant attention to the accrediting agencies, including Stetson, found it more difficult to ignore their growing power.[739]

Spearheading the drive for tougher ABA standards was Dean William Draper Lewis of the University of Pennsylvania Law School.[740] Upon Draper's motion, the ABA Section on Legal Education recommended that applicants for admission to the bar in any state should be limited *only* to graduates of approved law schools. The ABA standards prescribed that approved law schools had to require (1) a minimum of two years pre-law-school work; (2) a minimum of three years of full-time, or four years of part-time study; (3) an "adequate" law library; (4) a "sufficient" number of full-time law teachers; and (5) written examinations for all students prior to graduation.[741] With the ABA promulgating minimum academic standards, it took the first step necessary for its effective regulation of American legal education. The second step was both political and brilliant.

Understand that the ABA does not, and never has, set rules for admission to practice law in any state. Rather, the ABA promulgates and oversees compliance with its standards as part of its law-school "approval" process. Nonetheless, over time, the ABA successfully lobbied most states to adopt its law school standards by having the states require that only graduates of ABA "approved" law schools be eligible to sit for bar examinations.[742] The large ma-

---

Law: Historical Development and Principal Contemporary Problems of Legal Education in the United States with Some Account of Conditions in England and Canada (ABA 1921).

738. Stevens, *Law School*, *supra* n. 196, at 410.

739. Swygert, *supra* n. 80, at 123.

740. Sullivan, *Professional Organizations*, *supra* n. 728, at 410. One critic claims that in the 1920s, the principal goal of the ABA and AALS standards and regulations was to protect the "hegemony" of Anglo-Saxton Protestant culture." Jerold Auerbach, *Unequal Justice: Lawyers and Social Change in Modern America* 99 (Oxford U. Press. 1976).

741. Sullivan, *Professional Organizations*, *supra* n. 728, at 410.

742. The result has been that nearly all states (the major exception being California) require among their respective rules for admission, that applicants be a graduate of an ABA-approved law school prior to seeking admission. Then, to enforce its standards, the Section on Legal Education performs periodic site inspections of law schools. In the past, the ABA required law schools to hand over data on matters from the number of volumes in their law library to the salaries of the professors. The ABA approval process has produced many critics. Among them is Professor Harry First of New York University Law School, who argues that the ABA and AALS accreditation and inspection processes violate the Sherman Antitrust Act. *See* Harry First, *Competition in the Legal Education Industry (1)*, 53 N.Y.U. L.

jority of states did so. As a result, the "public profession" of law effectively became regulated not only by public authority—the courts—but also by two national private organizations: the American Bar Association and, to a lesser extent, the Association of American Law Schools.

After the ABA put its standards in place, in 1923 it issued its first list of approved law schools. Only thirty-eight of the then-149 law schools in existence (including those which were part-time and evening schools) received ABA approval.[743] The reason why a majority of law schools did not get ABA approval was because they failed to require at least two years of college-level work for admission.[744] Realizing ABA approval of law schools was becoming a requirement for admission of law graduates in most states, American law schools from 1923 onward upgraded their admission and other academic requirements to comply with ABA standards. As a result, within a decade the number of ABA-approved law schools doubled.[745]

Among the added schools on the ABA-approved list was Stetson University's College of Law. However, it had not been easy. Overcoming the obstacles, one man in particular made the difference: Lewis Herndon Tribble, who became the third dean of the Stetson University College of Law.

5.2 Lewis Herndon Tribble Takes Charge

Lewis Tribble, the man who led the College of Law from the latter half of the 1920s through the Great Depression, was a Stetson law school graduate, class of 1915. Prior to studying law, Tribble studied at the short-lived Columbia College, the Baptist institution where his father had served as president.[746] In 1922—the year following President Lincoln Hulley's removal of Richmond Rasco as dean—Hulley invited Tribble to become a member of the Stetson law faculty.[747] Previously, Tribble practiced law for seven years in his hometown of Lake City, Florida.[748] During his first year of practice, Tribble wrote President Hulley, hinting that he would like to be considered for a law-teach-

---

Rev. 311 (1978); and Harry First, *Competition in the Legal Education Industry (2): An Antitrust Analysis,* 54 N.Y.U. L. Rev. 1049 (1979).

743. Del Swords & Walwer, *supra* n. 214, at 41.

744. Albert J. Harno, *Legal Education in the United States* 96 (Brancroft-Whitney Co., 1953).

745. *Id.*

746. *See supra* nn. 648–649 and accompanying text.

747. Lycan, *History of Stetson, supra* n. 109, at 243.

748. *Id.*

ing job should one become available.[749] Though no openings existed at the time, Hulley never forgot Tribble's interest in the law school and, when one did arise, Hulley without hesitation hired him.

From 1922 through 1929, Tribble served as a member of the faculty, while Hulley, for the second time during his presidency of the University, took over the decanal duties of the law school, just as he had done after Dean Farrah left in 1909 until 1914, when Hulley named Richmond Rasco dean.[750] Tribble was not formally named dean of the College of Law until 1930, when, as will be explained below, Hulley had no choice but to grant Tribble the title of dean.[751]

Tribble's personality differed from that of Hulley's. While Hulley was narcissistic, quick to anger, and always wanting to be in charge of everything,[752] Tribble was "a mild-mannered gentleman,"[753] one who was "sincere," possessed a "keen sense of humor," and was "courteous and friendly" with all.[754] Despite differences in temperament, Tribble and Hulley worked well together, unlike the stormy relationship Hulley had had with Rasco. Nevertheless, the professor and the president each had different priorities.

Unlike Hulley, Tribble understood the significance of complying with the ABA standards for law school approval. Thus, he worked hard to raise the College of Law's academic requirements.[755] When Tribble became dean in 1930, the school had seventy-nine students,[756] but it did not require that an applicant have an undergraduate education to be admitted.[757] Then, Stetson law school's course of study was two years, but the ABA required three.[758] Due to Tribble, Hulley became aware of the higher ABA standards than those in place at Stetson. In March 1922, Hulley wrote several law schools, asking them to

749. *See supra* nn. 674–678 and accompanying text.

750. Vause, *Foundations for Excellence*, *supra* n. 308, at 313.

751. *See infra* nn. 779–780 and accompanying text.

752. *See supra* nn. 605–609 and accompanying text.

753. Lycan, *History of Stetson*, *supra* n. 109, at 245.

754. *Resolution of the Second Judicial Circuit for and in Leon County, Florida, on Behalf of the Tallahassee Bar Association in Honor of Louis Herndon Tribble* 5 (n.d.) (but said to be filed in the "Records of the Circuit Court in and for Leon County, Florida, as a permanent testimonial to Lewis Herndon Tribble to the legal profession."). This resolution appears as a handwritten six-page document and is located in the archives of the Stetson College of Law in Gulfport, Florida.

755. Lycan, *History of Stetson*, *supra* n. 109, at 243, 244.

756. Gordis, *supra* n. 105, at 62.

757. Lycan, *History of Stetson*, *supra* n. 109, at 244; Vause, *Centennial History*, *supra* n. 595, at 67.

758. Lycan, *History of Stetson*, *supra* n. 109, at 244.

describe their academic programs.[759] Based on the replies,[760] Hulley decided to increase the required length of Stetson's law program to three years.[761] This meant that more courses needed to be added to the curriculum and that additional faculty had to be hired.[762]

Believing that Stetson's adoption of a three-year course of study for an LL.B. degree would impress the AALS, Hulley asked the Association to admit Stetson College of Law into membership.[763] His effort, however, failed.[764] Among several "deficiencies" listed by the AALS, the most damaging was that the College continued to admit a large number of "special students" who did not meet the minimum two years of undergraduate college before entering law school.[765] In an effort to demonstrate good faith compliance with the AALS rules, Hulley in 1924 imposed a minimum one-year of undergraduate college as a prerequisite for an applicant's admission into law school.[766] Moreover, the one year had to be either in Stetson's College of Liberal Arts or in its School of Business Administration.[767]

This change, though an improvement, did not satisfy the AALS. Tribble understood that not only the AALS, but also the ABA, required a minimum of two years of college work for a school to be placed on the ABA "approved" list. Upon Tribble's persistence, Hulley finally consented to raising the College's requirement of pre-law study to two years, beginning with the 1927 academic year.[768] Given that the school's 1926 total enrollment was at a high—127—Tribble reasoned that raising the pre-law entrance requirement would have only a minor impact, even if the entering students were fewer in number.[769]

---

759. Ltrs. from Lincoln Hulley to nine school deans (U. Ala., U. Chi., Cornell, U. Mich., U. Tenn., U. Tex., U. Va., Wash. & Lee, and Yale) (Mar. 22, 1922) (on file in the Stetson U. Archives, Bell-duPont Lib., DeLand, Fla.).

760. Gordis, *supra* n. 105, at 62.

761. *Id.*

762. Bowen, *supra* n. 455, at 6.

763. Lycan, *History of Stetson, supra* n. 109, at 245 (citing an undated ltr. from Lincoln Hulley to Ralph W. Aigler, U. Mich. L. Sch., (n.d.) (on file at Stetson U. Archives, DeLand, Fla.)) *see also* Vause, *Foundations for Excellence, supra* n. 308, at 312.

764. The ABA requirements for law school approval went beyond the length of the law program and the prerequisite years in college. They included requirements regarding faculty, the law library, the course selection and content, and the teaching pedagogies. *See generally* Stevens, *Law School, supra* n. 196.

765. Lycan, *History of Stetson, supra* n. 109, at 245.

766. *Id.* at 244.

767. Bowen, *supra* n. 455, at 6.

768. Gordis, *supra* n. 105, at 62.

769. Vause, *Centennial History, supra* n. 595, at 311.

Though counseled and influenced by Tribble, Hulley made all final decisions regarding the College of Law.[770] Hulley's leadership notwithstanding, Stetson historians Bowen and Lycan each have concluded that Professor Tribble served as "unofficial head of the law school" during those years.[771]

5.3 ABA Approval and AALS Membership Achieved

In 1928, President Hulley for the second time sought the College of Law's admittance into the AALS. Concurrently, he petitioned the ABA Section on Legal Education for the school to be added to its list of approved schools.[772] To obtain AALS membership as well as ABA approval, the College had to undergo inspections by each agency. The requisite ABA inspection occurred in the fall of 1928; it "disclosed a sad state of affairs."[773]

Tribble had worked to improve the law school as best as he could, given Hulley's control, but the 1928 ABA inspection pointedly noted that the College had no "real" full-time dean.[774] In addition, the inspection found: the law library "seriously deficient"; faculty salaries "far too low"; the president "exercising too much control"; faculty teaching loads "too high"; and too many "special" students admitted (those without proper admission credentials).[775]

Will Shafroth came to Stetson's College of Law to conduct the inspection for the ABA. From Denver, Colorado, Shafroth served as the ABA Advisor to its Section of Legal Education.[776] Though he found Stetson's law school's facilities overall to be "adequate," as to the specific matter of low faculty salaries,

770. Lycan, *History of Stetson, supra* n. 109, at 243.

771. Bowen, *supra* n. 455, at 6; *see also* Lycan, *History of Stetson, supra* n. 109, at 243. "[Tribble] was considered the Dean, though he was not given that title for several years." *Id.* During the 1925–1926 academic year, Tribble was on leave at Yale University Law School pursing the LL.M. degree. *Id.*

772. Lycan, *History of Stetson, supra* n. 109, at 245.

773. Vause, *Centennial History, supra* n. 595, at 68. The actual 1928 ABA site inspection was not found, but is cited in Lycan, *History of Stetson, supra* n. 109, at 260 n. 71 ("Report, Rufus C. Harris," Dec. 15, 1930). Rufus Harris of Tulane University Law School was Secretary-Treasurer of the AALS. *See* Ltr. from Rufus C. Harris to Dean Lewis Tribble (Nov. 13, 1933) (Stetson U. Archives, DeLand, Fla.).

774. Lycan, *History of Stetson, supra* n. 109, at 245.

775. *Id.*

776. Stevens, *Law School, supra* n. 196, at 177. Shafroth later became chief administrative officer of the United States Courts. *See* United States of America *Administrative Office of the United States Courts*, U.S. Govt. Printing Off. (1957).

he proclaimed that Stetson "was almost at the foot of the list of American law schools."[777] Shafroth communicated his critical findings directly to Hulley.[778]

Following receipt of the ABA report, Hulley reluctantly conceded that the College of Law had to have a full-time dean. But he would not go the whole way, at least not yet. In early 1929, Hulley appointed Tribble to be "acting dean" only.[779] The following year, due to more pressure from the ABA, Hulley finally elevated Tribble to be Stetson's third dean of the College of Law, an office Tribble occupied until 1938 when he returned to the faculty.[780]

In response to other claimed deficiencies of the Stetson law school, Hulley provided each full-time law faculty member with a separate office; hired an additional full-time professor—M.S. McGregor—to reduce teaching loads of the existing professors; allocated increased funds to purchase library books; and hired a full-time law librarian.[781] The Stetson president then communicated these improvements to the ABA.[782]

By making these changes, Hulley and Tribble readied themselves for the next inspection, this one by the AALS.[783] Dean Harry Ferson of the University of Minnesota Law School conducted the inspection in February 1929.[784] Though the AALS still noted deficiencies in several areas, the College of Law was found "overall" to be in conformity with AALS standards. After the more favorable AALS report was sent to the ABA, the ABA in 1930 placed the Stetson College of Law on its "approved list" of American law schools as certified by the Section on Legal Education.[785] To appreciate the significance of ABA approval, consider that its Section on Legal Education reported that of 180 law schools in America, only seventy-seven were ABA approved.[786] Stetson's College of Law was one of them. This represented an important step forward in the College's history.

The year following ABA approval, the AALS considered admitting Stetson to its Association.[787] However, a serious snag developed. To be admitted to the

777. Lycan, *History of Stetson, supra* n. 109, at 245.

778. Ltr. from Will Shafroth to President Lincoln Hulley (June 6, 1930) (cited in Lycan, *History of Stetson, supra* n. 109, at 260 n. 74.

779. Vause, *Centennial History, supra* n. 595, at 68.

780. Bowen, *supra* n. 455, at 6.

781. Vause, *Centennial History, supra* n. 595, at 68.

782. Lycan, *History of Stetson, supra* n. 109, at 260 nn. 70, 72–74.

783. Vause, *Centennial History, supra* n. 595, at 112.

784. *Id.*

785. *See Annual Report of Legal Education,* in *Reports of the American Bar Association* (ABA 1930); *see also* Lycan, *History of Stetson, supra* n. 109, at 246.

786. *Reports of the American Bar Association* 609 (ABA 1931).

787. Lycan, *History of Stetson, supra* n. 109, at 246.

AALS, not only did a university's law school need ABA approval, the University also had to be accredited by its appropriate regional accrediting agency, in Stetson's case, by the Southern Association of Colleges and Secondary Schools, or "the Southern Association" (SA).[788] For years, Hulley had resisted joining the SA because he disliked its control over the academic standards of member schools.[789] Nonetheless, by October 1928, he could no longer ignore pressures to seek SA admittance.[790] The process turned out to be more difficult than he had expected, however, as it took four years for Stetson University to gain SA membership.[791]

Prior to the University attaining SA accreditation, however, the AALS learned that Stetson was not approved by the SA and, therefore, was not an accredited institution. Regional accreditation of the parent institution was one of the conditions for a law school to gain membership in the AALS. The problem, however, was that the SA would not admit Stetson University until the College was first admitted into the AALS—a "catch 22," can't win situation.[792]

Tribble telegrammed AALS Secretary-Treasurer Dean Rufus C. Harris of Tulane Law School in an attempt to resolve the dilemma. Tribble explained that Stetson University had been advised by the SA that the University would be accredited by the SA at its next meeting, *provided* the AALS would agree also to grant membership to the College of Law.[793] Given the assurance that the University would be granted SA approval, the AALS then granted Stetson's law school membership at its December 1931 meeting in Chicago.[794] Stetson historian Gilbert Lycan notes that the AALS vote to admit Stetson was, however, not unanimous, and that College officials were told that its membership was "strictly tentative."[795] Moreover, the AALS required the law school to undergo annual inspections rather than every several years as was customary.[796]

Hulley, nonetheless, was "deeply gratified" by the AALS action.[797] In his 1932 Report to the Trustees, he wrote:

788. *Id.* at 244.

789. *Id.*

790. *Id.*

791. *Id.*

792. *Id.*

793. Telegram from Dean Lewis H. Tribble to Dean Rufus C. Harris (Dec. 24, 1931) (on file at Stetson U. Archives, DeLand, Fla.); *see also* Telegram from Dean Lewis H. Tribble to President Lincoln Hulley (Dec. 24, 1931) (on file at Stetson U. Archives, DeLand, Fla.).

794. Lycan, *History of Stetson, supra* n. 109, at 244.

795. *Id.*

796. *Id.*

797. *Id.*

> The College [of Law] was admitted to membership in the Association of American Law Schools, an organization which has lifted its banner high, demanding that every college within its membership shall maintain the standards set by a ... committee of the Association ... Stetson was accounted worthy.[798]

In her 1969 unpublished history of the College of Law, Stetson historian Olga Bowen gives Dean Lewis Tribble credit for raising the academic standards of the law school and for meeting the requirements allowing it "to become fully accredited."[799]

5.4 Requirements for Admission to The Florida Bar

When the Stetson College of Law opened in 1900, its law graduates were not required to pass a bar examination for admittance to practice.[800] In 1907, Florida Senator Louis Massey wrote Hulley that the "Charter of Stetson University contains the provision that graduates of the law school shall be admitted to the bar upon presentation of their diplomas."[801] Massey advise Hulley of a bill pending before the Florida Legislature that would require all applicants for admission to practice in Florida (including Stetson's graduates) to take and pass a "general examination," either by "the Supreme Court, or by a Board of Law Examiners."[802]

Both President Hulley and Dean Farrah were concerned over the possible enactment of the proposal, since it would no longer permit Stetson graduates to be exempt from state examination. Despite opposition by Stetson's officials, the legislation passed. The new "Rule for Admission of Attorneys" provided:

> The first three days of every semi-annual term of this [Supreme] Court shall, if necessary, be devoted to the examination and admission of attorneys to practice law in the courts of Florida. Such examinations to be conducted in open court upon written or printed questions to be prepared by the court, the answers thereto to be in writing, and the court or

---

798. Memo. from Lincoln Hulley to Stetson U. Bd. of Trustees, *Report to the Board of Trustees, Stetson University* (1932).

799. Bowen, *supra* n. 455, at 6.

800. Lycan, *History of Stetson, supra* n. 109, at 244.

801. Ltr. from Louis Massey to President Lincoln Hulley (Apr. 20, 1907) (copy on file in Stetson U. Archives, DeLand, Fla.)

802. *Id.*

> any justice may supplement such written examination with oral questions from the bench.[803]

Though the Florida Supreme Court's rule did not require that a candidate for bar admission be a law school graduate, it did mandate that "applicants must have studied and familiarized themselves" with legal principles and sources from a list consisting of twenty-seven designated law treatises, the constitutions of the United States and Florida, judicial decisions interpreting the Florida Constitution, the State's general statutes, and its Rules of Practice.[804] The regulation stated that the Supreme Court's examinations would be based on this "prescribed course of study."[805] To pass the examination, an applicant must "answer with substantial accuracy at least seventy-five [percent] of the questions, written or oral."[806]

Despite Hulley's opposition to the new legislation and the Supreme Court's rule governing admissions, he understood that Stetson's College of Law graduates had to abide. Nonetheless, Farrah and Hulley believed that the new rule was vague. Hulley wrote the Court, asking it to clarify its rule by inquiring whether certain books that Stetson used were permissible and, therefore, included in the Court's list of required texts.[807] He also asked the Court to further define which Florida statutes were to be studied, or whether knowledge of all Florida statutes was required.[808] The Court's response, if any, to his questions has not been found.

Two years after the Court adopted its new rule for admission, Hulley mounted a new campaign to convince the Florida Legislature to change the bar admission requirements and to allow graduates of Florida law schools admittance without having to take a State examination.[809] In early 1909, he wrote to friends in the state legislature, including I.L. Farris, F.W. Sams, D.F. Pattishall, and George B. Selden, asking if they would channel a bill through the legislature that would exempt Stetson law graduates from examinations beyond those taken in law school.[810] Hulley pointed out that of thirty-five states

803. Fla. R. Admis. Attys. (Aug. 1907, as amended Nov. 17, 1908).

804. *Id.*

805. *Id.*

806. *Id.*

807. Vause, *supra* n. 595, at 61 (citing a Ltr. from Lincoln Hulley to Fla. Sup. Ct. (n.d.) (on file at Stetson U. Archives, DeLand, Fla.)).

808. *Id.*

809. Bowen, *supra* n. 455, at 150.

810. Ltr. from Lincoln Hulley to I.L. Farris (n.d.) (on file in Stetson U. Archives, DeLand, Fla.); Ltr. from Lincoln Hulley to F.W. Sams. D.F. Pattishall (n.d.) (on file in Stetson U. Archives, DeLand, Fla.); Ltr. from Lincoln Hulley to George B. Selden (n.d.) (on file in Stetson U. Archives, DeLand, Fla.)

having law schools, seventeen admitted their own state's graduates to the bar without a state examination.[811]

Hulley's lobbying of members of the Florida Legislature to enact a law granting a diploma privilege in Florida was successful. But it undoubtedly was also due in large measure to the State's 1909 decision to open its first public law school at the University of Florida (UF).[812] Soon after UF's law school commenced operations, the Florida Legislature reversed its position and passed legislation allowing graduates of Florida law schools to be licensed to practice law upon presentation of their LL.B. diplomas and satisfying the requirements of citizenship, character, and fitness.[813] In return, the Legislature granted the Florida Supreme Court additional regulatory powers to "determine the adequacy of the curriculum" and to determine which textbooks ought to be used at each of Florida's law schools.[814]

A few years later, in 1913, a new threat to the Florida diploma privilege arose. A bill was introduced in the Legislature that would require graduates of Florida's then-two law schools (Stetson and UF) to pass a state bar examination to be licensed.[815] President Hulley and President Murphree of the University of Florida joined together in soliciting friends in both the Florida Senate and House to defeat the bill.[816] The university presidents argued that, if enacted, the new law would encourage students to attend other law schools outside of Florida because there no longer would be a "home court advantage."[817] In addition, they suggested that if law students had to study for the state's bar examination during their last year of law school, they would not master those legal principles that were outside the scope of the state's examination.[818] The presidents' arguments and political influence succeeded. The

---

811. *Id.* This limited exemption from taking a state's bar examination is known as the "diploma privilege." At the time of this writing, 2005, the privilege continues only in Wisconsin, where graduates of its two law schools—Marquette University and the University of Wisconsin—are allowed to become members of the Wisconsin Bar without a state-administered examination. The diploma privilege began early in the genesis of American law schools, and from the beginning of this "special privilege," it was controversial. "The bar leadership was not pleased with the diploma privilege, which it felt took control of entry into the profession and away from practitioners and gave it to legal educators." Stevens, *Law School, supra* n. 196, at 27.

812. *See supra* nn. 546–550 and accompanying text.

813. Lycan, *History of Stetson, supra* n. 109, at 24.

814. *Id.*

815. Vause, *Centennial History, supra* n. 595, at 61–62.

816. Ltr. from Lincoln Hulley to A.A. Murphree, Pres., U. Fla. (May 16, 1913) (on file at Stetson U. Archives, DeLand, Fla.).

817. *Id.*

818. *Id.*

diploma privilege for Florida law school graduates remained in effect for the next thirty-eight years. Then in 1914, the Florida Supreme Court dispensed with its requirement that Florida law school graduates admitted under the diploma privilege still had to appear before the Court in Tallahassee to be licensed. Instead, if an applicant were a graduate of a Florida law school, he or she only needed to file an application, along with a copy of the LL.B. diploma, and pay an admission fee of five dollars.[819] The Supreme Court for the first time allowed diploma-privilege applicants to be sworn in by a judge or court clerk of any circuit in the state.[820]

The diploma privilege for Florida-based law school graduates remained in effect until 1951. From that point on, the Florida Supreme Court required that graduates of any accredited law school in America must be examined by the Florida Board of Bar Examiners, meaning, of course, that Florida's law school graduates no longer were given preferential treatment.[821] Not only did the Court's action remove the special privilege applicable only to Florida law school graduates, it also mandated that any graduates to be admitted to practice must graduate from an *accredited* law school. An accredited law school, of course, meant an *ABA-approved* law school.[822]

By 1951, the requirement that only graduates from ABA-approved schools may sit for a bar examination had become the norm for bar admission throughout most of America.[823] Hulley and Tribble had foreseen this development, and its prospect propelled their efforts to seek and ultimately obtain ABA approval in 1930, followed by AALS membership in 1931. It turned out to be none too soon.

In 1930, the ABA sponsored the formation of a new organization—the National Conference of Bar Examiners.[824] Will Shafroth, the same person who two years earlier had inspected Stetson's College of Law, headed the new body.[825] Due to Shafroth's efforts and the influence of the National Conference

---

819. Ltr. from M.H. Mabry, Clerk of the Fla. Sup. Ct. to Lincoln Hulley (May 22, 1914) (on file at Stetson U. Archives, DeLand, Fla.) (advising the Stetson president that the Court's Chief Justice directed that the change in the rule for admission be sent to Hulley).

820. *Id.*

821. Bowen, *supra* n. 455, at 5.

822. For the story of how ABA approval standards came about, *see supra* nn. 729–736 and accompanying text.

823. Stevens, *Law School, supra* n. 196, at 175–778. For a critical analysis of the bar examination phenomenon, see Leon Green, *Legal Education and Bar Admission,* 20 ABA J. (1934).

824. Stevens, *Law School, supra* n. 196, at 177.

825. *See supra* nn. 716–778 and accompanying text.

of Bar Examiners, most states required lawyer applicants to pass bar examinations for admittance to practice.

5.5 Stetson Law Students during the 1920s and 1930s

a. Great Depression and Falling Enrollments

Because of the 1926–1927 crash in real estate values, thereby ending Florida's land boom, the Great Depression impacted the state a few years before sweeping the rest of the country.[826] Its impact on Stetson University and the College of Law were soon felt: declining donations, especially from John B. Stetson, Jr.; lower investment returns on endowment funds; fewer students and their families being able to pay tuition; and smaller numbers of prospective applicants.[827]

Overall, the Great Depression wrecked havoc with higher education. By 1933, an estimated 1,500 institutions of higher learning had gone bankrupt or closed.[828] DeLand's economy also was hurting, not only due to the University's growing financial difficulties, but also because of a downturn in tourists.[829] In 1930, Hulley noted that the bank failures in Florida had "reached DeLand."[830] Alarmed, he wrote:

> [Stetson] University has a deposit of $6,661.88 locked up in the defunct bank ... The University was able to keep its head above water, but the very grave problem [is] what sort of an opening we can expect this Fall. The Mediterranean fly and the bank failures destroyed [the] ability to finance education ... This was reflected in our attendance this year.[831]

Throughout the state, land values sank, while prices for Florida timber and agricultural products dropped.[832] Many producers gave up and closed

826. Lycan, *History of Stetson, supra* n. 109, at 252.

827. *Id.* at 252, 254.

828. Vause, *Centennial History, supra* n. 595, at 72.

829. Lycan, *History of Stetson, supra* n. 109, at 279.

830. Memo. from Lincoln Hulley to Stetson U. Bd. of Trustees, *Report Made February 20, 1930 to the Board of Trustees of John B. Stetson University* (Feb. 20, 1930) (on file at Stetson U. Archives, DeLand, Fla.).

831. *Id.* at 3 (The total number of students enrolled in Stetson University for the 1929–1930 academic year was 430).

832. Lycan, *History of Stetson, supra* n. 109, at 252.

down.[833] The pattern was repeated throughout the country.[834] As for the College of Law, the effects were so bad at one point that President Hulley considered closing the school. Though, fortunately, it did not come to that, law faculty morale, as well as salaries, fell.[835] In a 1932 letter from Hulley to Tribble, the president wrote:

> *Dear Friend,*
> The Trustees direct me to notify you that owing to the loss of income during the summer, due to the depression, your salary, along with others, will be cut twenty-five percent.
>
> Respectfully,
> [signed, Lincoln Hulley].[836]

Fewer students, of course, meant less revenues for both the University and the College of Law. In 1926, the law school's enrollment was 127.[837] As the Great Depression took hold, enrollments began to fall, and fall fast. By the 1929–1930 academic year, the College's number dropped to forty-six.[838] Then, by 1933–1934, the law school's enrollment shrunk to forty-one.[839] In the following year, however, student enrollment rose to fifty-three, followed in 1935–1936 to fifty-five.[840] From that point, enrollment remained stable, averaging between fifty and fifty-five until the end of Tribble's deanship in 1938.[841] Amory Underhill, graduate of the class of 1936 (and later Chair of the College's Board of Overseers), recalled that only thirteen students were in his graduating law class.[842] Although the Depression caused Stetson's College of Law severe difficulties, it remained open while the students continued to study hard and play hard.

---

833. *Id.*

834. Beard & Beard, *supra* n. 6, at 452–462.

835. *See supra* nn. 774–775 and accompanying text.

836. Ltr. from Lincoln Hulley to L.H. Tribble (Sept. 19, 1932) (on file at Stetson U. Archives, DeLand, Fla.).

837. Vause, *Foundations for Excellence*, *supra* n. 308, at 311.

838. Memo. from Lincoln Hulley, *supra* n. 798, at 3.

839. Gordis, *supra* n. 105, at 62 (1946).

840. Memo. from William Sims Allen, Pres. Stetson U., to Stetson U. Bd. of Trustees, *Report of the President of John B. Stetson University to the Board of Trustees for the Year 1935–1936*, at 1 (1936) (on file at Stetson U. College of L., Gulfport, Fla.).

841. Memo. from William Sims Allen, Pres., Stetson U., to Stetson U. Bd. of Trustees, *Report of the President of John B. Stetson University to the Board of Trustees for the Year 1937–38*, at 1 (1938) (on file at Stetson U. College of L., Gulfport, Fla.).

842. Interview by Bruce R. Jacob with Amory Underhill (June 10, 1986) [hereinafter *Underhill Interview*].

b. Student Activities

(1) Law Fraternities Flourish

During the Depression years, students engaged in relatively few activities outside the classroom due to the grind of studying and the need to earn income to pay for tuition and expenses. The one major "escape" were law fraternities.

The first one to start at the College of Law was the David K. Brewer Chapter of Phi Alpha Delta (PAD), established on April 2, 1915.[843] Amory Underhill describes how he became active in the school's PAD fraternity:

> When I started law school [in 1933] they were about to jerk the charter on Phi Alpha Delta, which I knew was a good group ... [It] was only the only frat there at the time ... Dean Tribble pushed the panic button and called three or four of us in and said do you think you can do something about this ... And we did. Jack Phillips, Marvin Garrison, a couple of others, and myself.[844]

With Tribble's encouragement, Underhill attended a PAD convention in Chicago in 1934 and returned to Stetson with fresh ideas about organizing and running a law fraternity. Later, on campus, he met with representatives of the national Sigma Nu law fraternity, which wanted Stetson to start a local chapter. Underhill was not persuaded, even after having been informed that two members of the United States Supreme Court were honorary Sigma Nu members, and that unlike PAD, Sigma Nu had no initiation fee.[845]

After declining Sigma Nu's invitation, Underhill and his friends each paid a $25 initiation fee to become PAD members. In short order, he was elected PAD president and took charge. He instituted a visiting speaker program. Underhill was an acquaintance of former Stetson law professor Cary Landis, who then was Attorney General of Florida. Underhill invited Landis to come to DeLand to have "breakfast" with the PAD law students.[846] Landis did so, and thus began the tradition of the fraternity of inviting well-known people for breakfast at the College in DeLand.

In 1934, Stetson law students founded the College's second law fraternity—Sigma Nu. It, too, adopted PAD's "come-for-breakfast" invitations.[847] The fraternity-sponsored breakfasts usually took place off campus. When Attorney

843. *Local Chapter of Phi Alpha Delta Has Many Famous Alumni Members; David K. Brewer Chapter Famed for Jurists and Governors,* 3 Stetson Rptr. 8 (May 11, 1938)].

844. *Id.*

845. *Id.* at 8.

846. *Id.* at 9.

847. *Id.*

General Landis visited, the breakfast was held in DeLand's Eastwood Terrace Hotel.[848] In addition to the invited dignitaries, the fraternities asked the community's lawyers and Stetson's law faculty to attend.

Other speakers who came to fraternity functions during the 1930s included Professor Kenneth Sears of the University of Chicago Law School;[849] Edward G. Posniak of the Department of Justice (Washington, D.C.);[850] New York writer and criminologist Charles Francis Coe;[851] Francis P. Whitehair, prominent DeLand attorney, member of the Florida Board of Law Examiners, and former president of the Stetson Alumni Association;[852] and Egbert Rosecrans, who had been a lawyer for defendant Bruno Hauptmann, the man convicted of the baby Lindberg kidnapping and murder.[853] Rosecrans (whose sixteen-year-old daughter, Constance Rosecrans, was said to be the youngest pre-law student at Stetson), spoke at the Lexington Hotel in DeLand as part of a Sigma Nu fraternity function.[854]

Both the Phi Alpha Delta and Sigma Nu fraternities sought new members and held formal initiations each year.[855] Each also held special occasions for alumni members when they returned to the University's annual homecomings. On at least one occasion, Sigma Nu constructed a float for the homecoming parade.[856]

Among the more innovative fraternity proposals was PAD's plan to place each senior law student with a DeLand area attorney. The student would assist his or her lawyer in preparing pleadings and a brief of legal points relevant to an on-going case.[857] A supervising attorney would agree to serve as the student's "sponsor," and would then critique the neophyte's work. Finally, the student

---

848. *Id.*

849. *Sears Addresses Lawyers Tuesday, Will Speak on AAA Decision in PAD Room, Science Hall,* 1 Stetson Rptr. (n.p.) (Jan. 29, 1936).

850. *Posniak to Speak before Legal Frat,* 3 Stetson Rptr. (Dec. 8, 1937).

851. *P.A.D. to Initiate Renowned Writer: Charles Francis Coe Will Join the David J. Brewer Chapter,* 3 Stetson Rptr. (n.p) (Mar. 9, 1938).

852. *Legal Fraternity Installs Officers, Robert H. Gamble Leads Installation Services Here,* Stetson Rptr. (n.p.) (Apr. 27, 1938). Robert H. Gamble was a "prominent Jacksonville businessman and attorney." *Solomon Will Head Legal Fraternity,* 3 Stetson Reporter (n.p.) (Apr. 6, 1938).

853. *Egbert Rosecrans Tells Legal Frat of Famous Trial; State Used Robbery as Step to Murder Charge,* Stetson Rptr. (n.p.) (Feb. 19, 1936).

854. Vause, *Centennial History, supra* n. 595, at 79.

855. *See e.g., Hotel Putnam Scene of Initiation Banquet Legal Fraternity,* 1 Stetson Rptr. (n.p.) (Apr. 29, 1936); *Phi Alpha Delta Pledges Six; Legal Fraternities Announce Pledgings,* 2 Stetson Rptr. (n.p.) (Sept. 30, 1936).

856. *Phi Makes Plans for Parade,* 3 Stetson Rptr. 6 (Mar. 2, 1938).

857. *Law Frat Plans Student Practice: Senior P.A.D. Law Students Will Work with Attorneys,* 3 Stetson Rptr. 6 (Mar. 2, 1938).

would then "sit with his assigned counsel throughout the trial of a particular case."[858] Within two years of its conception, the plan was implemented.

(2) Trial Court—Murder in Downtown DeLand

Throughout Dean Tribble's era, Stetson's practice court (where students tried mock cases) continued. Stetson historian Gordis wrote: "Practice Court provided elaborate practical training paralleling the situation ... in actual legal practice."[859] The "practical training" on occasion was very "realistic." In 1937, students Perry Nichols and Harpo Haddock took opposite sides in a trial of a nuisance case involving the "blowing" of an oil well, scattering crude oil over a neighbor's land.[860] Another mock trial involved a breach of contract dispute. A real estate agent was not paid a commission after the principal sold the listed property to a buyer, a person whom the agent had earlier brought to the principal's attention. In this dispute, students Sidney Taylor and Philip "Chisel" Wright represented the opposing sides.[861] Another example involved a tort case where an alleged drunken driver crashed his automobile into the plaintiff's car. Stetson law students trying the case were Norman Abbott, Bob Powe, Pat Kelley, and Hughes Wilson.[862] Tribble assumed the role of judge (which he did at many student mock trials).[863] Then there was the infamous murder case.

Sidney Taylor, class of 1937, recalled years later the interesting facets of trial court involving mock-criminal cases.[864] A student who agreed to serve as the "sheriff" would roam the campus and "catch whoever happened to be there." Often those catched were ministerial or business students who would serve as jurors.[865] On occasion, a homicide would be acted out on the streets of DeLand, to the disgust of the town's police. Taylor described the circumstances of the murder case:

> [T]he big event was the murder case. [The students] pulled it off downtown ... There was a bunch of hollering and everything and then the sound of firing a pistol, a blank pistol and all. A sponge with catsup [was pushed against the victim's] head and the man fell down ... By that time

858. *Id.*

859. Gordis, *supra,* n. 105, at 62.

860. *Sid Taylor Wins in Contracts Case,* 2 Stetson Rptr. 3 (Apr. 28, 1937).

861. *Id.*

862. Francis Winters, *Moot Court Capers,* 3 Stetson Rptr. 5 (May 11, 1938).

863. *Id.*

864. Telephone Interview by Bruce R. Jacob with Sidney Taylor (June 1, 2001) [hereinafter Taylor Interview].

865. *Id.*

> the police were there ... From that time on the City told [the law students] not to pull off these stunts in the downtown area ... The last murder I remember was somebody coming out the door of the chapel ... Got hit with a bat there and never recovered.[866]

Taylor recalled that two students once took their participation in trial court too seriously. After the mock case had concluded, one student attorney asserted that opposing counsel had violated a court rule. Taylor goes on: "They had a fist fight over the [alleged] misconduct."[867] Occasional shenanigans notwithstanding, the trial court course (and its acted out dramas) was the students' most popular activity of their law school experience during the 1930s, just as it had been from the beginning of the College. In response to the question: "You actually tried cases, moot cases?" Taylor exclaimed: "[We] not only tried them, we made them!"[868]

(3) Legal Aid; Essay Contests; SBA; Politics

In 1938, Stetson law students Ralph Odum and Thomas Cobb, members of the Sigma Nu law fraternity, took the initiative and proposed a legal aid clinic be started at the College of Law.[869] Tribble agreed and implemented the suggestion. Consequently, a Stetson Legal Aid Clinic was established with the approval of the Ethics Committee of the Volusia County Bar Association[870] and its president, Thomas N. Tappy of Daytona.[871] The plan called for Stetson's senior law students to serve "as counsel for indigent persons who are not financially able to secure legal assistance."[872] Stetson law faculty members supervised the student attorneys, while a five-person Board of Directors—Tribble of the College of Law, the Clinic's faculty director, a Volusia County welfare officer, a practicing attorney, and a senior law student—oversaw the Clinic's operations.[873] The Board investigated and considered each case brought before it. The Clinic would take a case only if the Board members believed that the prospective client could obtain justice, avoid unnecessary litigation, and was otherwise unable to pay for legal assistance.[874]

---

866. *Id.* at 37.

867. *Id.* at 38.

868. *Id.* at 37.

869. *Legal Aid Clinic to Be Instituted Here,* 3 Stetson Rptr. 4 (June 1, 1938) [hereinafter *Legal Aid Clinic Instituted*].

870. Vause, *Centennial History, supra* n. 595, at 80.

871. *Legal Aid Clinic Instituted, supra* n. 869.

872. *Id.*

873. *Id.*

874. *Legal Aid Clinic,* 4 Stetson Rptr. (Sept. 21, 1938).

After law school commenced its Clinic, Florida's Attorney General Gibbs sanctioned student involvement, while two Florida Supreme Court Justices, Roy Chapman and Elwyn Thomas, commended Stetson for establishing a legal assistance program.[875] The Florida Board of Law Examiners also approved Stetson law school's legal aid program.[876]

Meanwhile, during the 1930s, Miami attorney D.H. Redfearn instituted writing competitions for students at each of Florida's law schools: Stetson, Florida, and Miami. Redfearn each year chose the topic and invited students from the schools to submit an essay on the assigned subject.[877] The school's winner received a cash award of fifteen dollars (later increased to twenty-five). In 1938, Stetson law students Mary Lou Baker and Tom Cobb tied for the winning essay on the topic "Divorce Traffic—Its Causes and Cure."[878]

Students not only competed in mock trials and writing contests, but they also created a self-governance system. For more than three decades after the College opened, law students did not have any governmental organization, their being considered part of the University's general student-government structure.[879] But in 1935, law students began to elect their own officers,[880] taking the first step toward establishing a student bar association, an objective that Stetson law students accomplished by the end of the decade.

Besides law fraternities and the student bar association, other student organizations included a University-wide debating club, as well as various political groups, one of the which was the Stetson University Young Democratic Club.[881] Meanwhile, law students daily attended religious observances. During the early decades of the College, all University students, including those studying law, had to attend chapel services. However, the law students did not sit as a group, as each law student was assigned a specific seat.[882]

Another student organization was the "Mystic Krewe," an honorary leader-

875. Vause, *Centennial History, supra* n. 595, at 80; *see also Attorney General Approves Legal Aid Clinic,* 4 Stetson Rptr. 1 (Mar. 1, 1939).

876. *Minutes of the Law Faculty* 1 (Jan. 5, 1939) (on file at Stetson U. College of L., Gulfport, Fla.).

877. *Baker and Cobb Split Law Prize, "Divorce Traffic" Is Subject for D.H. Redfearn Law Essays,* 3 Stetson Rptr. 1 (May 18, 1938).

878. *Id.*

879. *Lawyers Organize,* 1 Stetson Rptr. 1 (Oct. 25, 1935).

880. *Id.*

881. *Amory Underhill Heads Young Dems, Wongrey Vice-Pres.,* 1 Stetson Rptr. 3 (Mar. 25, 1936).

882. *Taylor Interview, supra* n. 864.

ship group organized in 1935.[883] Described as "the outstanding student organization on the campus in sponsoring activities that create school spirit and help achieve the ideals of the school," Mystic Krewe included several future state and community leaders.[884] Among the Stetson law students who established the University-promotive group was law student Perry Nichols,[885] who years later became a member of the College of Law Hall of Fame.

(4) People Say the Strangest Things (Part Two)

Every law school era, including the 1930s, has its humorous anecdotes. In criminal law class, Professor Paul Raymond presented a hypothetical involving a homicide committed "in the heat of passion." Raymond's hypothetical follows:

> [You are] off on a trip and came home unexpectedly and come into a darkened room with the fire flickering and find your wife and your best friend making love on the sofa and you grab a poker and beat him in the head until you kill him. What is your defense to that?[886]

Law student Jack Green replied to Raymond's hypothetical. Green argued that the crime should not be a capital offense because, under the circumstances, it did not justify executing a person "for some little thing like that."[887] Professor Raymond responded: "OK, let's change the facts a little bit; suppose it wasn't [in] a college town?" The student quickly reported, "Oh, that makes a difference."

Another law student in writing the history of his class reminisced about the first days at law school:

> We found much to our surprise that a swift left jab to the liver and a right hook to the jaw wasn't a knock-out, but a "Tort;" that a *fieri feci* wasn't a South African fruit, or that an easement wasn't a new brand of foot powder.[888]

Another story from class histories includes the following passage:

> Now that we have finished our prescribed law course and thereby have learned all the law to be learned, nothing now remains for us to do but to apply our legal knowledge and reap immense financial rewards. As we

883. *Krewe Initiates Campus Leaders; Year-Old Organization Has Helped Stetson Go Forward,* 1 Stetson Rptr. 1 (May 13, 1936).

884. *Id.*

885. *Taylor Interview, supra* n. 864.

886. *Id.* at 39.

887. *Id.*

888. *The Junior Law Class of 1920–21*; *College of Law*, Oshzhzyi, *supra* n. 684, at 73.

stand on the topmost pinnacle of success, we can define and discuss fully anything from an "Infamous Crime to the Rule in Shelly's case."[889]

Then, in analyzing the significance of *Blackstone's Commentaries on the Law,* a Stetson law student wrote:

> [Blackstone's] four-volume [edition] serves two purposes: first, to the law student it looks so unsurmountable that many give up in despair, hence, the noble profession is not crowded. Secondly, it is of value to the practicing attorney, [since] it impresses the client. Nothing is more impressive to the common or garden variety of client than to see four books of Blackstone reposing in a conspicuous place when he enters an attorney's office.[890]

Occasionally, a Stetson law student might try writing poetry, typically with mixed results. An example below, titled *LL.B's to Be,* appears in the school's 1937 yearbook.[891]

> Have you seen the learned Juniors
> Of the Law Departments Band?
> Have you heard them spreading knowledge
> Of the law across the land?
> Have you heard some of their sayings
> Of their questions day by day?
> How you embalm a turnip,
> How a cow absconds away.
> When the Dean asks a question,
> With the cutest little look,
> They just twist around and answer
> "Dean, that wasn't in my book."[892]

Sidney Taylor recalled a humorous incident involving Stetson law graduate Frank Ford, class of 1963, (who later for several years practiced law with Bruce Jacob).[893] According to Taylor, years after graduation he met Ford in DeLand, where the latter mentioned that he had sold some marginal-quality land to a

---

889. *Senior Law*; *College of Law*, Oshzhzyi 67 (1919) (student yearbook, on file Stetson U. Archives, DeLand, Fla.).

890. *Being a Short Lecture on Blackstone*; *College of Law*, Oshzhzyi 50 (1911) (student yearbook, on file at Stetson U. Archives, DeLand, Fla.).

891. *LL.B's to Be, College of Law*, Oshzhzyi 52 (1917) (student yearbook, on file at Stetson U. Archives, DeLand, Fla.).

892. *Id.*

893. *Taylor Interview*, *supra* n. 864.

buyer who had asked him whether it "was good fertile land." Taylor said that his classmate never lied, but that he knew how to respond: "Well," Ford said, "I saw a jackrabbit crossing it one day, but he was packing his lunch."[894]

c. Minority and Women Students

From its opening in 1900, Stetson's College of Law has always welcomed women. By 1930, thirty-six had attended the school. Though a few never completed their studies, by 1939, thirty-four women had earned Stetson law degrees.[895] During the school's first three decades, Stetson was the only law school in Florida to graduate women lawyers. Harvard Law School, on the other hand, did not admit women until 1950.[896] The University of Florida College of Law, which opened in 1909, did not permit women to apply until 1925, and even thereafter discouraged them from doing so before the first woman was admitted—Clara Backus Floyd[897]—who in 1933 became the first female law student to graduate from UF.[898] Miami, the other law school in Florida, in the 1930s, like Stetson, welcomed women from its opening in 1928, its first three women graduates receiving LL.B. degrees shortly thereafter.[899]

By the 1920s, women were applying to Stetson College of Law in increasing numbers. Of twenty-four admitted, nineteen during that decade earned a Stetson law degree.[900] One was Jane L. Phillips (Armstrong), class of 1920, who served in the United States Foreign Service for three decades in Cuba, Kenya, New Zealand, and the Philippines.[901] Another woman, Edith Meserve (Atkinson), Stetson law class of 1922, was elected a judge in Dade County. By doing so, Meserve was the first woman elected to a judgeship in Florida, the first woman graduate of a law school to become a judge in the State, and the first woman to graduate from the Stetson University College of Law to wear judicial robes.[902]

---

894. *Id.*

895. *See Florida's Women Lawyers, supra* n. 479, at 1–92. The statistics were compiled by the late W. Gary Vause, co-author of this volume.

896. Stevens, *Law School, supra* n. 196, at 84.

897. *Id.* at 58.

898. *Id.*

899. *Id.* at 45.

900. The authors counted the number of women admitted during the decade of the 1920s and also the number of women who graduated from the College of Law from University sources as well as from The Florida Bar publication reviewing the first 150 women lawyers in Florida. *See Florida's Women Lawyers, supra* n. 479, at 1–89.

901. *Id.* at 16.

902. *Id.* at 19, 20.

Speaking of firsts, the first woman to practice law in Palm Beach County was Stetson law graduate Helen S. Martin (Crabtree), class of 1922.[903] Interestingly, another woman graduate, Dr. Herberta Ann Hathcock Leonardy, one of two women in the 1926 Stetson law class, had previously earned a medical degree, but decided not to practice medicine. (Her family had earlier counseled her that a physician "was no job for a woman.")[904] Later, Leonardy became one of the country's leading parliamentarians and was president of the National Association of Parliamentarians.[905] She also authored several books on parliamentary law.[906]

The Stetson law class of 1927 included six women, a number not reached again until the 1970s. They were Laurine Lenore (Goffin), Mary Wakefield (Houston), Mary Anne Leddy, Lenea Stronberg (Adleheim), Zephyr Thorpe, and Charlotte Inez Farrington (Volger).[907] Farrington was among several from her class who became well known. Twenty years old when she received her Stetson LL.B. degree, Farrington later became a charter member of the National Organization for Women; she was known as the "Grandmother of the N.O.W. in Palm Beach County."[908] Florida attorney Wendy S. Loquasto, who edited a book on women lawyers in Florida, observes that Farrington (married name Vogler) "was among the 100,000 [people] who marched on Washington, D.C., in 1976 to support passage of the Equal Rights Amendment."[909] Charlotte Farrington-Vogler once declared: "God in His infinite wisdom gave the female as much brains as the male. There's no way you can keep the women of the world down now."[910]

The second Stetson woman graduate who become a jurist was Mada Burney Fraser (Babcock) (McLendon), class of 1932.[911] Elected a municipal judge of Lake Wales, Fraser served from 1938 until 1947.[912] She founded the Business and Professional Women's Club of Lake Wales. In 1989, Judge Fraser McLendon received the Stetson Lawyers' Association Ben C. Willard Memorial Award for her "outstanding service to the legal profession."[913] The judge died in 1999 at the age of eighty-nine.

---

903. *Id.* at 21.
904. *Id.* at 29, 30.
905. *Id.* at 31.
906. *Id.*
907. *Id.* at 37.
908. *Id.* at 39.
909. *Id.*
910. *Id.* at 39, 40.
911. *Id.* at 52.
912. *Id.* at 52, 53.
913. *Id.* at 53.

Catherine Stewart Howarth (Carter) graduated in the Stetson law class of 1934.[914] Her mother was Mary Stewart (Howarth), who in 1908, as noted earlier, was the first woman to graduate from the Stetson law school.[915] Catherine Howarth not only practiced law, she also managed Millard F. Caldwell's successful campaign to be Florida's governor. Among other commercial ventures, Howarth owned a marriage counseling business.[916]

Mother and daughter Stetson graduates did not always see eye to eye. In the 1970s, a dispute erupted over the family's property.[917] Stetson alumnus Sidney Taylor represented Mary Stewart and noted that it took twenty-nine days to try the case, followed by "years of appeals to the Florida Circuit and Supreme Courts."[918] After Mary Stewart's death, the dispute continued in probate.[919]

During the 1930s, several other women lawyers graduated from Stetson. Alma Oyama, class of 1937,[920] married her classmate, Doyle I. Carlton, brother of Vassar Carlton, and a cousin of Doyle E. Carlton, who in 1929 became governor of Florida.[921] Marjorie Hammer (DeShaw), class of l936, practiced law and remained in DeLand until her death.[922] In 1937, Mildred Ernestein Wilson earned her Stetson LL.B. degree.[923] Meanwhile, Mary Lou Baker received her Stetson law degree in 1938.[924] Baker became known as "a crusader for women's rights," who lobbied for passage in the Florida Legislature of the "Married Woman's Act" to remove legal disabilities of adult women in the state.[925] Though the proposed legislation was not enacted, grateful citizens elected Baker to represent Pinellas County in the Florida Legislature in 1942. She defeated the incumbent, Stanley Marshall of St. Petersburg.[926] One sad note from the 1930s concerns a woman law student named Helen Mae Christian of Jacksonville. She was to receive her law degree in June of 1937, but was

---

914. *Id.* at 66.

915. *See supra* nn. 496–500 and accompanying text.

916. *Florida's Women Lawyers, supra* n. 479, at 66–67.

917. *Taylor Interview, supra* n. 864.

918. *Id.*

919. *Id.* This may be Florida's example of a decades-long litigation over an estate which dominates Charles Dickens's novel *Bleak House*.

920. *Florida's Women Lawyers, supra* n. 479, at 88–89.

921. *Id.*

922. *Id.* at 73.

923. *Id.* at 86.

924. *Id.* at 87.

925. *Id.* at 88.

926. *Id.*

prevented from doing so because of "her unfortunate death" (the cause of which has not been learned).[927]

In sharp contrast with the experience of women, not one African-American graduated from a Florida-based law school during the 1920s or 1930s. Hispanic and Jewish students, on the other hand, were admitted and graduated from the state's law schools.[928]

5.6 Faculty and Alumni During the Tribble Era

a. Faculty

From the time Lewis Tribble joined the Stetson law faculty in 1915 until his leaving in 1938, the College of Law faculty was in continual flux with resignations and new appointments. One reason, of course, was the school's low faculty salaries.[929] Another reason, at least until Tribble became dean in 1930, was the autocratic style of President Hulley and his poor relations with several faculty members.

After Dean Tribble began to exert control in the 1930s, several strong faculty members were hired. One was Dr. J.J. Kindred, "a noted physician and psychiatrist" from New York City, a unique and long-remembered teacher in the school's history.[930] For several years, Kindred taught both medical jurisprudence and legal ethics at the College of Law.[931] At the same time, he owned three mental health hospitals in New York City.[932] In his medical jurisprudence class, Kindred emphasized the relationship of mental health problems to the law. Said to be an effective teacher, he was well-liked by his students.[933] Alumnus Sidney Taylor commented:

> He was a good one [law professor]. He had an M.D. from Edinburgh and something else from New York, a law degree, and had been a Congressman ... He was a good teacher on mental problems and medical ju-

927. Betty Lou Alexander, *Law School Has 29 Women Grads, Mrs. Howarth Was First to Receive Her Law Degree*, 3 Stetson Rptr. 2 (Dec. 8, 1937).

928. *Taylor Interview*, *supra* n. 864.

929. *See supra* nn. 774–775 and accompanying text.

930. *Dr. J.J. Kindred Gives $1,000 for New Law Building*, 1 Stetson Rptr. 1 (May 13, 1936) [hereinafter *Dr. Kindred Gives*].

931. *Taylor Interview*, *supra* n. 864.

932. *Id.*

933. *Id.*

> risprudence ... He was well-to-do. He was retired and taught during that Depression period.[934]

Kindred was a New York Congressman.[935] Though he never practiced law, after retiring from medical practice he spent winters in DeLand, and that is how he learned about Stetson's law school.[936] Alumnus Amory Underhill recalls Dr. Kindred as an energetic teacher,[937] one who in legal ethics course routinely engaged outside speakers to address students on ethical and moral issues of law practice.[938] One was Florida Circuit Judge Herbert B. Frederick. In lecturing to Stetson law students, Judge Frederick stressed that the first duty of a lawyer was to the court, and their second duty was to one's client.[939]

Besides instructing law courses, Kindred was a strong supporter of the College of Law. Jumping briefly ahead to the mid-1930s, the ABA put pressure on Stetson University to either expand its existing law school facilities, or to build a new building. The then-University President, William Sims Allen, put together a plan to raise funds for a new building. Among the first persons to join the campaign was Dr. Kindred, who pledged $1,000.[940] In thanking Kindred for his gift, Allen said, "The building proposed will give the law college twice its present capacity."[941] However, it did not happen. The new law building was predicated upon Stetson obtaining sufficient financial resources from alumni, but the efforts proved unsuccessful. Thus, a new law school facility at DeLand never materialized.

Though Kindred held seven earned degrees, Paul Everett Raymond, another new faculty member during the Tribble era, was a close second with four earned and two honorary.[942] Joining the law faculty in 1933, Raymond served one academic year, left for a year, then returned for another year, until he was offered a position in 1936 in Washington, D.C. Raymond returned to Stetson in 1938 as the successor to Lewis Tribble as dean of Stetson College of Law.[943]

934. *Id.*

935. *Dr. Kindred Gives, supra* n. 930, at 1.

936. *Taylor Interview, supra* n. 864.

937. *Id.*

938. *Judge Frederick Speaks of Ethics to Law Students,* 1 Stetson Rptr. 1 (Mar. 11, 1936).

939. *Id.*

940. *Dr. Kindred Gives, supra* n. 930, at 1.

941. *Id.*

942. Professor Raymond in 1938 was appointed Dean of the College of Law, and his background and degree will be discussed subsequently in the text. *See infra* n. 1062–1077 and accompanying text.

943. Bowen, *supra* n. 455, at 7.

Dean Paul E. Raymond

As a professor (and later as dean), Paul Raymond was greatly admired by students and the University's administration. He taught contracts, common law pleading, and real property.[944] Amory Underhill recalled Raymond as being "very kind, and a good professor."[945] Sidney Taylor recalled that Raymond was an "excellent teacher."[946]

Though Stetson's law faculty members rarely researched or authored scholarly publications during the 1920s and 1930s, Raymond became the exception. In 1936, his article "The Origin and Rise of Moral Liability in Anglo-Saxon Law" was published in the *Oregon Law Review.*[947] This article is the first authored by a Stetson law professor published in a student-edited law review. *The Stetson Reporter* described the piece:

> Dr. Raymond presents the causes and results of the growth of the moral idea, tracing it from the Bible to the end of the Anglo-Saxon period about 11 A.D. He points out that in ... Anglo-Saxon laws the purpose of the law was similar to all primitive law, to secure order among the people.[948]

944. *Taylor Interview, supra* n. 864.

945. *Underhill Interview, supra* n. 842.

946. *Taylor Interview, supra* n. 864.

947. Paul E. Raymond, *The Origin and Rise of Moral Liability in Anglo-Saxon Criminal Law,* 15 Or. L. Rev. 93 (1936)

948. *Leading Article in Law Paper Written by Paul Raymond; Treatise on Moral Liability in Criminal Law Is Featured,* 1 Stetson Rptr. 1 (Apr. 18, 1936).

In the article, Raymond explained that at the time of "primitive law," the "upper-most aim of man was to wreak vengeance upon those who injured him."[949] Therefore, Raymond pointed out, the immediate object of law was "to regulate private war."[950]

Other Stetson law professors of the 1920s and 1930s included Jacob A. Carpenter, Dr. Jennis W. Futch, Henry S. Jacobs, and Harvey Jernigan.[951] Three of these professors—Futch, Jacobs, and Carpenter—later were involuntarily dismissed by President Allen. As discussed later,[952] their terminations created an accreditation problem for the College taking years to resolve.

Jennis Futch held dual roles in the law school, not only teaching classes, but also during the 1930s serving as the law school's librarian.[953] In 1936, he became active in the AALS when Professor George Bogert, of the University of Chicago and President of the AALS,[954] appointed him to an AALS "Committee of Cooperation."[955] The committee consisted of seven law faculty representatives from various law schools and seven representatives of the American Association of Law Librarians. Futch was subsequently re-appointed to the committee, this time by Professor Bernita J. Long, then President of the American Association of Law Librarians.[956]

After William Sims Allen became Stetson University's third president, he scrutinized the law faculty more closely than had his predecessor, Lincoln Hulley. In 1937, Allen drafted a statement on the hiring of faculty members.[957] It stated:

> Four qualifications are absolutely essential for anyone who teaches in John B. Stetson University. (1) He must have high scholarship. (2) He must be an active working Christian. (3) He must be a good teacher. (4)

949. *Id.*

950. *Id.*

951. *See generally* the collected oral interviews of Stetson U. College of L. Alumni (on file at Stetson U. College of L., Gulfport, Fla.).

952. *See infra* nn. 1018–1039 and accompanying text.

953. *Two Law Professors Chosen for National Committee; Association of American Law Schools Chooses Futch, Tribble; Recognize Stetson*, 1 Stetson Rptr. 1 (Mar. 4, 1936) [hereinafter *Two Law Professors*].

954. *Id.*

955. *Id.*

956. *Member of Law Faculty Honored,* 3 Stetson Rptr. 2 (Dec. 8, 1937). AALS President Professor Bogert appointed Stetson College of Law Dean Lewis Tribble to the AALS Committee on Legal Literature. *Two Law Professors, supra* n. 953, at 1.

957. William Sims Allen, *Report of the President of John B. Stetson University to the Board of Trustees for the Year 1937, 1938*, at 3 (Feb. 17, 1938).

> He must have common sense. If I added a fifth, it would be that he must love young people.[958]

Though the majority of the College of Law faculty during the 1920s and 1930s met Allen's criteria, a few did not. In any event, several high-achieving alumni of the College graduated during that period.

b. Prominent Law Alumni

By the end of Tribble's decanal tenure in 1938, Stetson College of Law had produced more than its share of prominent and influential citizens. Marion Rowe, class of 1910, was a Circuit Judge in DeLand in the 1930s.[959] Murray Sams (class of 1910, and father of Murray Sams, Jr., class of 1950) "excelled as state attorney in DeLand as had Millard Smith, class of 1919, in Titusville."[960] Sams was described as "one of the great trial lawyers in Florida."[961] Louis Strum, class of 1912,[962] developed strong oratorical skills participating in the law school's Kent Club debates.[963] He practiced law in Jacksonville, later becoming its city attorney. In 1925, Strum was appointed to the Florida Supreme Court, a position he held until 1931, where for a time he served as chief justice.[964] In 1933, Strum was awarded an honorary LL.D. degree from Stetson University. Subsequently, he was appointed United States District Judge for the Southern District of Florida, where he served twenty years through 1950, when he was elevated to the United States Court of Appeals.[965] In 1951, the distinguished jurist was honored at the Golden Jubilee of the founding of the Stetson University College of Law.[966]

Stetson's first law school graduate who became a governor of Florida was David Sholtz, class of 1915.[967] However, the first Stetson undergraduate to win the governor's post was Doyle E. Carlton, a 1909 Bachelor of Arts graduate.

---

958. *Id.*

959. Vause, *Centennial History, supra* n. 595, at 81 (citing the DeLand Sun newspaper on Sept. 9, 1931).

960. *Id.* at 81.

961. Underhill Interview, *supra* n. 842.

962. *Law School Grads Earn Distinction, Stetson Alumni Gain Honors on Bench, at Bar, Abroad*, 3 Stetson Reporter 6 (Nov. 10, 1937) [hereinafter *Law School Grads*].

963. *Id.* at 6.

964. *Id.*

965. *To Honor Alumnus,* 14 Stetson Rptr. 30, 1 (May 25, 1951).

966. *Id.*

967. *Law School Grads, supra* n. 962, at 6; *see also Dean Tribble, DeLand Sun* (Sept. 9, 1931) (located in Dean Tribble's faculty file, Stetson U. Archives, DeLand, Fla.).

Judge Louis Strum

Elected Florida's governor in 1929, that same year Carlton was awarded a Stetson honorary LL.D. degree.[968]

Governor David Sholtz came to the Stetson College of Law by way of Yale University, where he had taken undergraduate studies. At Stetson, Sholtz was instrumental in establishing the David Brewer Chapter of Phi Alpha Delta law fraternity, and is considered "the father" of Stetson's PAD.[969] Two years after earning his law degree, he was elected to the Florida Legislature. From 1919 to 1921, he was a prosecuting attorney for Florida's Seventh Judicial District. He later became a municipal judge in Daytona Beach.[970] Sholz was elected Governor of Florida in 1933 on his second try, having lost an earlier bid in 1931.[971]

Among Stetson's better known early law alumni was Bert Fish, mentioned earlier, president of Stetson's first graduating law class. Besides practicing law, Fish served as superintendent of Volusia County Schools, a criminal court judge, and a United States Minister to three nations.[972] Other early Stetson law alumni who became well known included Judge J.E. Peacock;[973] Amory Underhill, a respected Washington, D.C., attorney and for several years, Chair of

968. *See generally* Bowen, *supra* n. 455.
969. Vause, *Centennial History, supra* n. 595, at 82.
970. *Law School Grads, supra* n. 962, at 6.
971. *Id.*
972. *Id.*
973. Vause, *Centennial History, supra* n. 595, at 81.

Alumnus Francis Whitehair

the Stetson College of Law Board of Overseers;[974] and Francis P. Whitehair, class of 1926, described by one classmate as "very dynamic, a good lawyer, good football player, good basketball player, good golfer, and [who] looked like Clark Gable."[975] He was only twenty years old when he graduated from Stetson's College of Law and joined the DeLand firm of Landis, Fish & Hull.[976] Later, Whitechair was appointed general counsel to the federal Economic Stabilization Agency in Washington, D.C. (which oversaw rationing during World War II).[977] Whitehair unsuccessfully ran for governor of Florida in 1939, but then was appointed as special assistant to United States Attorney General Homer Cummings. Following World War II, he became Undersecretary of the Navy.[978]

Francis Whitehair was a president of the Stetson Alumni Association and was a strong supporter of the College of Law. In 1950, he offered a cash prize for the best student-authored essay pertaining to an important political issue.[979] Whitehair, along with Stetson classmate Judge Louis Strum, were awarded Stetson University's Distinguished Service Citation at the College of

974. *See infra* nn. 2043–2044 and accompanying text.

975. *Underhill Interview, supra n.* 842.

976. *Whitechair Addresses Graduates,* 15 Stetson Rptr. 1, 2 (Jan. 18, 1952).

977. *Stetson Law Graduate Is ESA General Counsel*, 64 Stetson Rptr. 1 (Jan. 5, 1951).

978. *Whitechair Addresses Graduates, supra* n. 976, at 2.

979. *Id.*

Law's fiftieth anniversary in 1950.[980] Two years later, Stetson bestowed Whitehair an honorary LL.D. degree.

Frank Wideman was yet another widely known law alumnus of the times. A 1914 graduate, he was appointed an Assistant United States Attorney General.[981] An active politician, Wideman was a delegate at various Democratic National Conventions. His public responsibilities included his serving as a member of the Florida State Board of Control. It is said that Wideman honed his argumentative skills while a law student at Stetson, where he had represented the law school in national oratorical debates.[982]

"Little Joe" Hendricks was another politically successful Stetson lawyer. Four years after earning his Stetson LL.B. degree in 1934, Hendricks was elected to the United States Congress from the Fifth Congressional District of Florida.[983] Born in 1903 in Lake Butler, Florida, "Little Joe" (as he was called) was thirty-seven when he took his House seat in January 1938. The major issue confronting Congress at that time was the rising sentiment across the country to ban America from entering foreign wars (unless defensive).[984] By 1938, Hitler's troops already were pushing into parts of Europe. Congressman Hendricks campaigned in favor of what were then known as "neutrality bills."[985]

Another Stetson lawyer "on the Hill" was United States Congressman Albert W. Johnson, who served as a member of the House of Representatives from 1963 through 1977. Johnson, who graduated from Stetson's College of Law in 1938, was a native Pennsylvanian.[986] He had attended the Wharton School of the University of Pennsylvania. After graduating from Stetson, Johnson returned to his home state to practice, where he ran for the Pennsylvania House of Representatives and won.[987] Earlier, Johnson had served in the Pennsylvania State Senate for sixteen years before being elected to the United States Congress.[988]

Early Stetson lawyers were also elected to the Florida Legislature, including Robert Anderson, class of 1913. Anderson was president of the Florida Bar As-

---

980. *Id.; see also To Honor Alumnus, supra* n. 965, at 2.

981. Vause, *Centennial History, supra* n. 595, at 81.

982. *Id.*

983. *Son of Stetson—Hendricks—Takes Congress Place; "Little Joe" Assumes High Office in Nation's Capital,* 2 Stetson Rptr. 1 (Jan. 6, 1938).

984. *Id.*

985. *Id.*

986. Planet Smethport, *Home of Albert W. Johnson, Member of U.S. Congress, 1963–1977,* www.smethport.org/franklinstreet/richmond.409/richmond.htm (accessed May 14, 2004).

987. *Id.*

988. *Id.*

sociation while serving as a member of the Florida House of Representatives.[989] He had been general counsel for the East Coast Railroad and was a legal advisor to its owner, Henry Flagler. In later years, Anderson represented Flagler's estate.[990] Anderson later served as Chairman of the Florida State Board of Bar Examiners.

Besides Congressman Anderson, three other 1930s' Stetson law graduates served in the Florida Legislature: Senator E. William Gautier, class of 1932; Representative James H. Sweeny, Jr., class of 1931; and Representative Wilber H. Boyd.[991]

In the field of legal education, Russell A. Rasco, law class of 1921 (the son of Stetson's second law dean, Richmond A. Rasco), succeeded his father in 1933 to become the second dean of Miami University School of Law,[992] while J. Ollie Edmunds, a 1928 graduate of the Stetson College of Law, became president of Stetson University in 1948 at a point when the University and the College of Law were facing financially challenging times.[993] During his presidency, Edmunds supported and, with the trustees approval, authorized the College of Law's move to Gulfport in 1954.[994] After receiving his LL.B. and practicing law in Jacksonville, Edmunds became a prominent judge. Named a Trustee of Stetson University in 1933,[995] Edmunds was instrumental to the law school's subsequent development.[996]

5.7 Change in Administrations: Allen and Raymond Take Over

a. William Sims Allen Becomes President

Stetson University President Lincoln Hulley died in 1934 at the age of sixty-nine, one day after suffering a heart attack.[997] He had had poor health for more than a year.[998] Historian Lycan describes Hulley's end: "He was lovingly at-

---

989. Vause, *Centennial History, supra* n. 595, at 81.

990. *Id.*

991. W. Gary Vause, "*Prominent*" *Stetson Law Graduates* (n.d.) (handwritten notes on file at Stetson U. College of L., Gulfport, Fla.).

992. *See supra* nn. 725–727 and accompanying text.

993. Gordis, *supra* n. 105, at 66.

994. *Id.*

995. *Id.*

996. *See infra* nn. 1495–1509 and accompanying text.

997. Lycan, *History of Stetson, supra* n. 109, at 257–258.

998. *Id.* at 257.

tended during the night and until noon the next day, January 20, 1934, when the great man breathed his last breath."[999] Historian Gordis notes that Hulley's death "was a profound shock to all who were interested in the University. For thirty years he had efficiently piloted the Stetson ship, at first over somewhat stormy waters."[1000] For eleven of those thirty years, Hulley not only headed the University, he also ran the College of Law as a de facto dean.

Following Hulley's death, a Stetson College of Liberal Arts professor, Charles Sherwood Farris, was named acting president until a permanent successor would be hired.[1001] The Board of Trustees, with John B. Stetson, Jr., as chair, undertook a search, one that culminated in the appointment of William Sims Allen as the third president of Stetson University.[1002] Allen took office on September 1, 1934.[1003] Born in Texas in 1888, Allen graduated with an A.B. degree in 1912 from Baylor University (reputed to be the oldest Baptist-related college in America), and then from Columbia University in New York City in 1915 with an M.A. degree. After teaching ROTC at Baylor during World War I, Allen earned a Ph.D. degree in 1923 in school administration from Columbia University.[1004] He returned to Baylor, where he served, in succession, as professor of Latin, dean of the College of Arts and Sciences, acting president, and, until called to the presidency of Stetson University in 1934, vice president, dean, and chairman of the Baylor School of Education. He was well known not only in the Baptist world of higher education, but also by leading Southern educators of various backgrounds.[1005]

Allen enthusiastically began his new duties as Stetson's president. Immediately, he confronted the University's severe economic problems. Soon thereafter, he precipitated a crisis at Stetson's College of Law involving his dismissal of three faculty members. When Allen arrived at Stetson University in 1934, the Great Depression was exerting an impact. Students and revenues had declined. Both earnings and value of the University's endowment had diminished, while donations had fallen. The only significant contribution in the year 1934—$2,100—came from the Florida Baptist Convention.[1006] Consequently, the University had to cut faculty salaries throughout the University, including

999. *Id.* at 258.

1000. Gordis, *supra* n. 105, at 69.

1001. Lycan, *History of Stetson, supra* n. 109, at 265.

1002. Olga Bowen, *William Sims Allen* 1 (unpublished ms. 1967) (on file in the Stetson U. Archives, DeLand, Fla.).

1003. *Id.*

1004. *Id.*

1005. *Id.* at 2–3.

1006. Lycan, *History of Stetson, supra* n. 109, at 266.

those at the law school, a situation which did not go unnoticed by the ABA and AALS accrediting agencies.[1007]

b. Faculty Dismissals: A Bitter Battle with AAUP and AALS

Two years after the law school gained membership in the AALS, and three years after it became approved by the ABA, these agencies again came down hard on the College of Law.[1008] According to University records made available to AALS inspectors, no law student had ever been dropped for academic deficiency.[1009] Not surprisingly, this apparent lack of standards was a major concern to the AALS, which also chided the school over its low law faculty salaries and inadequate law library.[1010] Not for the first time, Stetson's College of Law's future seemed in jeopardy.[1011]

The AALS had earlier adopted a rule that $10,000 minimum must be expended every five years to keep a law library current in terms of the books and periodicals felt necessary for a working law school library.[1012] Stetson's law library was found to be seriously deficient both as to its collection and as to annual shortfalls in its expenditures on new materials.

Upon learning of the school's "deplorable conditions," Allen became dismayed, so much so that he considered "dropping the College of Law."[1013] Years later, Stetson University Chancellor Pope Duncan wrote that Allen had confided, "You know, when I came here, you couldn't believe what a rundown institution [the College of Law] was."[1014] Lycan notes that Allen decided to "make a hard try at bringing up the law school's standards so it would again be a respectable institution."[1015]

Despite the findings of serious deficiencies at the school during the 1934 AALS inspection, the agency assured the school that no action would be taken before it came back two years later to reinspect the school. This time, the AALS found even more problems, noting that the law school had too few pro-

---

1007. *Id.*

1008. Ltr. from Ruffus Harris to Dean Louis Tribble (Nov. 14, 1933) (on file in Stetson U. Archives, DeLand, Fla.).

1009. Lycan, *History of Stetson, supra* n. 109, at 295.

1010. *Id.* at 295–296.

1011. Vause, *Centennial History, supra* n. 595, at 75.

1012. Lycan, *History of Stetson, supra* n. 109, at 295.

1013. *Id.* (citing a quotation from Stetson law professor Jacob A. Carpenter found at 25 Am. Assn. U. Profs Bull. 383 (1939)).

1014. Pope A. Duncan, *Leaders of Stetson: Dr. Paul Raymond* 4 (n.p.) (Dec. 28, 1990) (on file in the Stetson U. Archives, DeLand, Fla.).

1015. Lycan, *History of Stetson, supra* n. 109, at 296.

fessors for the students' instructional needs. The Association threatened to suspend the Stetson College of Law from AALS membership unless several improvements—including the hiring of more professors—were forthcoming.[1016] Cognizant of the gravity of the situation, Tribble and Allen asked the AALS to hold off for one year to allow the College to make changes. The agency agreed.[1017]

During that year, Allen proceeded to analyze "the problem with the law school." He became convinced that "the only way to improve it was to replace three of the professors, Jacob A. Carpenter, Jennis W. Futch, and Henry S. Jacobs."[1018] Lycan describes the situation:

> [Allen] called in Dean Tribble and laid out the problem ... [Tribble] agreed that the three men were poor teachers and should be replaced. Personal friendships, [Tribble] said, had kept him from recommending dismissal earlier. Allen [however] thought this proved [Tribble's] "inefficiency as dean" though [Allen] knew [Tribble] was a good teacher.[1019]

Professor Paul E. Raymond (soon to become Tribble's successor as dean) said years later that the three professors "were such poor teachers that if a bar exam had been required at that time, very few of the Stetson law graduates would have passed."[1020] Allen told Raymond that his predecessor—President Hulley—had allowed the law faculty "to go to pot," and that Dean Tribble's hands were tied because "Stetson was a one man institution and that one man was Hulley," adding that the "three members of the small faculty should never have been teaching."[1021] Having convinced himself of their ineptitude, Allen in spring 1938 unilaterally dismissed professors Carpenter, Futch, and Jacobs.

The three fallen professors appealed their abrupt terminations to both the American Association of University Professors (AAUP), and to the Associa-

---

1016. *Id.*

1017. Ltr. from William Sims Allen to H.W. Arant, Secretary, AALS (Feb. 22, 1937) (on file in the Stetson U. Archives, Deland, Fla.); Ltr. from H.W. Arant to William Sims Allen (Mar. 1, 1937) (on file in the Stetson U. Archives, Deland, Fla.).

1018. Lycan, *History of Stetson, supra* n. 109, at 296.

1019. *Id.* (citing Ltr. from William Sims Allen to Ralph E. Hempstead, Secretary, AALS (Apr. 12, 1937) (on file at Stetson U. College of L., Gulfport, Fla.)).

1020. *Id.* ("Every member of the senior law class [back] in 1926 had signed a petition to President Hulley requesting removal of Futch on the grounds that he was such a poor teacher."); *see also* Vause, *Centennial History, supra* n. 595, at 75–76; Lycan, *History of Stetson, supra* n. 109, at 296.

1021. Duncan, *supra* n. 1014, at 3.

tion of American Law Schools (AALS).[1022] As a result, "a furious battle [between Stetson and the two agencies] broke out."[1023] The AAUP and AALS appointed a joint committee to investigate the fired instructors' charges of improper dismissal. Under the auspices of the AAUP, the joint committee was headed by Harvard University law professor James A. McLaughlin. The other two committee members were University of Alabama professor William M. Hepburn and Duke University law professor Lon Fuller.[1024]

The AAUP committee conducted lengthy hearings and took evidence from not only the three dismissed professors, but also from their friends as well as two Stetson trustees. Allen, however, refused to take part, proclaiming that only the Stetson Board of Trustees and the President of the University [himself] had authority over the hiring or firing of teachers, and that their authority was not to be "dictated by a teachers' union."[1025]

The final AAUP report, which exceeded one hundred pages, found that Stetson University had violated AAUP standards for dismissing tenured faculty members by, first, failing to afford the professors a hearing and, second, by not giving the long-serving Stetson faculty members a required one-year minimum notice before their terminations took effect. The report, however, did not consider whether the three fired professors were competent, the only issue Allen believed was important.[1026]

Despite the damaging AAUP findings, President Allen did not take them seriously until the AALS notified the University that it must either restore the dismissed professors to their former positions with back pay, or make a financial settlement satisfactory to them.[1027] Failure to do so, the AALS warned, would cause Stetson's College of Law to be expelled or, at a minimum, suspended from membership in the AALS. The threats notwithstanding, Allen re-

1022. Vause, *Centennial History, supra* n. 595, at 76.

1023. Lycan, *History of Stetson, supra* n. 109, at 296.

1024. *Id.* Professor Fuller became a legendary Harvard Law School professor and scholar who taught both contracts and jurisprudence. *See also* correspondence between Professor McLaughlin and President Allen in 1938–1939 (on file in the Stetson U. Archives, DeLand, Fla.).

1025. Ltr. from William Sims Allen to Judge O.K. Reaves, member, Stetson U. Bd. of Trustees (Feb. 4, 1939) (on file at Stetson U. College of L., Gulfport, Fla.).

1026. Vause, *Centennial History, supra* n. 595, at 76 (citing correspondence between then-Stetson Trustee Judge J. Ollie Edmunds and Professor James McLaughlin, chairman of the AAUP investigating committee from November to December 1938.).

1027. Lycan, *History of Stetson, supra* n. 109, at 297. Lycan describes a letter from Dr. Wilbur H. Cherry, president of the AALS, to President Allen as the ultimatum to the University. *Id.*

fused to comply with the AALS demands, much to the disbelief of Stetson University Board of Trustees Chairman John B. Stetson, Jr.[1028] A battle quickly ensued between Allen and the son of the University's namesake.[1029] At a Board of Trustees meeting in February 1939—which Lycan describes as "one of the most important ever held"[1030]—a "special" committee was formed; its mission: to negotiate a settlement of the University's dispute with the AALS.

Allen, however, was not pleased, and insisted that the committee be under his control. Stetson, on the other hand, protested that the committee was created by the Board; therefore, he held out that it had to be under the Board's authority. In reaction, Allen threatened to resign as University president (though he did not do so).[1031]

Believing the future of the College of Law was at stake, the majority of trustees sided with John B. Stetson, Jr., and directed the committee—President Allen, Doyle Carlton, Bryan Jennings, J. Ollie Edmunds, and O.K. Reaves (chairman)—should negotiate the best arrangement possible with the AALS to settle the dispute, and then report back to the Board.[1032] But the Board emphasized that two conditions were non-negotiable: first, despite suggestions by Harvard Professor McLaughlin, Allen must remain in office and, second, that the three former professors must not be rehired under any circumstances.[1033] With these guidelines, Board Chairman Stetson persuaded AALS Chairman Wilbur H. Cherry to have Stetson Trustee O.K. Reaves meet with the Association's executive committee to negotiate a resolution of the conflict. No agreement, however, resulted.[1034]

At a June 5, 1939, meeting of the Trustees, members Edmunds, Reaves, Jennings, and Board Chairman Stetson urged the full Board to "pay [the fired

1028. *Id.*

1029. Vause, *Centennial History, supra* n. 595, at 77.

1030. Lycan, *History of Stetson, supra* n. 109, at 298.

1031. Though the minutes of the Board of Trustees meeting for February 16, 1939, "in line with the usual policy of concealment" only curtly refers to the special committee, the meeting was transcribed and a fifty-two page stenographic report of the proceedings has survived and is located in the Archives of Stetson University in DeLand. Lycan, *History of Stetson, supra* n. 109, at 298, 320 n. 68.

1032. *Id.*

1033. *See* Ltr. from James A. McLaughlin to Judge J. Ollie Edmunds, (Dec. 19, 1939) (on file in the Stetson U. Archives, DeLand, Fla). "In view of unreserved frankness that I adopted with you, I am a little bit puzzled by some indirect hearsay that comes to me. My associate, Mr. Fuller, has it that you at once communicated to President Allen that I said that he lied to me and he ought to be fired. I did not estimate that you would do just that." *Id.*

1034. Lycan, *History of Stetson, supra* n. 109, at 299–300.

professors] and forget it."[1035] The majority, however, refused "to cave in," rather granting Allen continuing authority to negotiate with the AALS. Nothing, however, came out of this last-ditch effort. Having had enough of what seemed to be a run around, the AALS suspended Stetson's membership in its organization.[1036]

The school's suspension came as a shock to Allen, because he then realized that there was no way to resolve the AALS action unless the University settled with the dismissed law professors. Turning an about face, Allen persuaded the Board to authorize the University to pay each of the fired professors a one-year salary. The Board did so, and the dismissed professors and Stetson University finally reached what lawyers called an accord and satisfaction.

Even though the long conflict with the AALS drew to a close in November 1939, one month later the AAUP put the College of Law on its list of "censured administrations."[1037] The Association President, Professor Wilbur H. Cherry, telegraphed Allen:

> Having received notification of adjustment specified in our telegram of November third, I hereby announce termination of suspension of Stetson University College of Law. Stop. Executive Committee will report facts of case to annual meeting of Association and recommend that no further action be taken.[1038]

Henry Jacobs, one of the three dismissed Stetson professors, was quoted in the *Orlando Sentinel* as saying that the suspension of the College of Law "was lifted after the University had acceded to the minimum demands of the AALS."[1039]

c. Paul E. Raymond Succeeds Lewis Tribble as Dean

Part of the fallout resulting from Allen's dismissal of the three professors was Lewis Tribble being asked to resign the deanship of the Stetson College of Law. Tribble's replacement was Professor Paul Everett Raymond. To Tribble, his ouster had to be humiliating. After all, he had devoted nearly two decades to the betterment of the Stetson law school. He was admired by students, one declaring that "no other person in the history of the entire University was more liked and

---

1035. *Id.* at 300.

1036. *Id.*

1037. *Id.* at 301.

1038. *Id.*

1039. *College of Law Regains Standing,* 4 Stetson Rptr. 1 (Nov. 11, 1939) (quoting a story in the *Orlando Sentinel*).

honored than Dean Tribble."[1040] Another well-known Stetson law graduate of the Tribble era, Perry Nichols, has said that he "credited his survival and ultimate graduation [in law school] largely to Dean Tribble's patient prodding and encouragement."[1041] Lewis Tribble without question was a humane and compassionate man who cared for both students and faculty colleagues. Ironically, this may have been his downfall. Given Tribble's affability and "sympathetic" nature, he likely was reluctant to fire three friends on the faculty, even though some believed the three were "substandard professors." Tribble, moreover, was unsure that competent replacements could be found during "these hard economic times."[1042]

Nonetheless, Allen lost confidence in his law dean, and in May 1938 asked Tribble to relinquish the deanship of the Stetson College of Law. In short order, Allen offered Raymond the deanship.[1043] Years later, Raymond described the transfer in decanal leadership:

> I was offered the deanship ... when I was thirty-four ... Dean Lewis H. Tribble was a good friend. The [poor] situation [of the law school] was not his fault, and he deserved credit for keeping the law school open during the depression years. He did this by retaining teachers beyond normal retirement who were willing to serve on low salaries and by skimping on the library and other matters.
>
> When President Allen asked me to accept the deanship, he was no doubt motivated by a recent, highly critical report from the [ABA] Inspection Committee. He was determined either to improve the school or let it die .... President Allen agreed to allow me to replace most of the faculty and upgrade the library. Dean Tribble urged me to accept and I wanted him to remain on the faculty.[1044]

Tribble's son, James E. Tribble, notes, "Surely [my father] was deeply hurt when the University with which he had been so long and closely identified replaced him as head of the law school."[1045] James Tribble writes that his father came to believe that his friend, Paul Raymond, "had undermined him and sought the deanship," but Raymond later denied that that was the case.[1046] Stetson University Chancellor Pope Duncan recalled that Tribble had told Ray-

1040. *Dean Tribble Leaves Stetson,* 5 Stetson Rptr. 1 (Sept. 13, 1939).

1041. Tribble, *supra* n. 648, at 42.

1042. *Id.* at 40.

1043. Vause, *Centennial History, supra* n. 595, at 302.

1044. Paul E. Raymond, *"A Labor of Love": A Final Interview with Dean Paul E. Raymond,* 30 Stetson L. Rev. 57, 57 (2000).

1045. Tribble, *supra* n. 648, at 44.

1046. Raymond, *supra* n. 1044, at 58.

mond that it would be best if he, his friend, was dean "than somebody else."[1047] Tribble, however, changed his mind. His son remembered that although his father continued to have close associations with Stetson people throughout the remaining years of his life (especially with the dean's former student Ollie Edmunds, after the latter had become Stetson's president), Lewis Tribble's social contacts with Paul Raymond "were less frequent than before [the change of deans]."[1048] Justified or not, leadership of Stetson's College of Law passed between two men who at one point enjoyed a close friendship.

Tribble remained on the faculty for one year more, leaving in 1939 to accept a position as head of a newly created statutory-revision section of the office of the Florida Attorney General.[1049] George Gibbs, Florida Attorney General, extended the offer, and Tribble accepted, taking responsibility for a "continuous statutory revision" of Florida's biennial sessions laws.[1050] After completing the revision in 1941, Tribble worked as an attorney in the office of the State Comptroller, becoming General Counsel from 1949 until his death from a massive heart attack on December 7, 1963.

Lewis Herndon Tribble was seventy-three when he died. He had served on the faculty of the Stetson College of Law for seventeen years (1922–1939), twelve as the College's dean or acting dean. Tribble contributed to the College of Law in multiple ways, yet his greatest significance had to be his tireless and ultimately successful efforts in gaining ABA approval and AALS membership for the College at a time when the majority of America's law schools had not been able to do so. In 1958, Lewis Herndon Tribble was honored with the Stetson University Distinguished Service Award. Stetson University President J. Ollie Edmunds, his former student, presented the citation to Tribble. The citation reads in part: "For many years [as] the Dean of Stetson's Law School, you worked successfully to raise its professional standards and to secure its national recognition."[1051] When Tribble left Stetson in 1939, the student newspaper editorialized:

> The law school has lost one of the most beloved friends—Dean Tribble. Perhaps no other professor in the history of the entire University was more liked and honored. He was renowned for his wit and his characteristic laugh, which he so frequently used. Dean Tribble always had time to stop and talk with the "boys" no matter how urgent the business should be that was calling him. He will remain in the hearts of the stu-

1047. Duncan, *supra* n. 1014, at 4.
1048. Tribble, *supra* n. 648, at 44.
1049. *Id.*
1050. *Id.* at 45.
1051. Tribble, *supra* n. 648, at 53.

> dents and the faculty as the father of the Stetson law school and as a true gentleman.[1052]

Tribble was a good person, a good educator, and, for the most part, a good dean. In 2004, he became one of the original inductees into the Stetson University College of Law Hall of Fame.

1052. *Legal Language,* 5 Stetson Law. 2 (Sept. 13, 1939).

CHAPTER SIX

The Long Winter: Depression and WWII—Deans Raymond, Lambert, and Howes

6.1 The Long Winter

The difficult times began with the Great Depression, then the threat of war, followed by Pearl Harbor, World War II, the spread and fear of Communism, and finally the Korean War. But after two decades of adversities, America emerged into the springtime of "the fabulous fifties."

The country's hard times were reflected in the life of Stetson University and its College of Law as well. Severely limited financially by the depression, then by the exodus of students and faculty who entered military service in the fight against fascism, the College of Law—more so than the University—struggled throughout most of the 1930s and 1940s. For three years during World War II, the College was forced to close for lack of students. And when the school did reopen after the war, it was flooded with students using their G.I. higher education benefits. Nonetheless, the College confronted a possible loss of its accreditation, primarily due to its then horrendous facilities—a crumbling building on an abandoned military base on the outskirts of DeLand. Visionary leaders of both the University and College realized that the school's survival required a new home, preferably in a larger metropolitan area. Many within the law school saw relocation of the College of Law as the only road for survival.

Even the fear and threat of Communism affected Stetson University, albeit in an indirect manner. The American Communist Party had its beginning during the 1930s, many joining believing that capitalism had led the country into the Great Depression.[1053] Over time, the American Communist Party at-

1053. For a detailed description of these events, *see* Whittaker Chambers, *Witness Whittaker Chambers* 57 (Random House, Inc. 1952).

tempted to place party members into influential government positions. Two Communist agents who held high positions in the party and were involved in Communist infiltration effort were Whittaker Chambers and Alger Hiss.[1054]

Chambers, however, in the latter part of the 1930s broke from the American Communist Party and became a fugitive from its rigid control. Chambers wrote that after becoming a party member, one could not leave, and if he did, he would be tracked down by KGB-like agents. The "fugitives" often were not heard of again.[1055] Chambers ultimately cooperated with the Federal Bureau of Investigation in identifying party leaders operating in the United States. For two years, he was "in furtive isolation," on the run from his former co-conspirators.[1056] Fluent in German French, as well as English, during his hiding from the Communist party officials Chambers secretly translated books for a New York City publisher. At one point, fearing he had been spotted by party agents in Baltimore, Chambers relocated his family to Florida because "many transits go to Florida," and "new arrivals make no stir."[1057] His decision to move to Florida was predicated upon finding a quiet place where he could carry on translating books and where no one would likely take notice of him. In his autobiography, *Witness*, Chambers wrote: "If I could find a library nearby, I could do whatever research was necessary for the translation."[1058]

He succeeded in his search. Chambers and his family moved into a small bungalow beside the ocean in Daytona Beach. He found the place to work he was hoping for—the Stetson University Library. He wrote:

> In nearby DeLand, I found the library of Stetson College [sic] a friendly and helpful heaven. The fugitive from the Communist Party often sat, on a sweltering afternoon, among the spooning coeds, doing his research into the blood and iron policies of Bismarck and the gaudy follies of the man whom he called the Sphinx without a secret—Napoleon III.[1059]

In time, Whittaker Chambers' testimony resulted in the conviction of one who was said to be a top agent of the American Communist Party—Alger Hiss.[1060] Though the identity of Chambers' presence at Stetson was apparently unknown by anyone connected with Stetson for decades, this bit of historical lore

1054. *Id.*
1055. *Id.*
1056. *Id.*
1057. *Id.* at 56–57.
1058. *Id.*
1059. *Id.* at 58.
1060. *Id.* at 257.

became known after a person familiar with the University brought it to the attention of one of the co-authors of this work.[1061]

Despite depression, war, and even unbeknown infiltration by a former Communist spy, Stetson University and its College of Law found its way through the historical maze. But it did so only because of a few outstanding leaders. One was Paul Everett Raymond.

6.2 Dean Paul Everett Raymond, 1938–1941

a. Strong Qualifications

Paul Raymond was born on June 22, 1904, a few months after Orville Wright flew the first heavier-than-air propelled airplane at Kitty Hawk, North Carolina. Raymond grew up on a farm near Cedar Rapids, Iowa, where from a young age, he desired to become an engineer.[1062] Graduating from high school at fifteen, he entered Stanford University to study engineering.[1063] World War I, however, soon intervened, and after one year in Palo Alto, his parents could no longer pay Stanford's tuition. Raymond returned to Iowa to work on the family farm.

Then, in 1923, Raymond returned to college, this time to Coe College in Iowa, a few miles from his family home.[1064] After earning an undergraduate degree in mathematics in 1927, Raymond entered the University of Iowa Law School. There, he graduated first in his class and earned membership into the academic-honors society, the Order of the Coif.[1065] He also served as editor in chief of the *Iowa Law Review.* His outstanding record at Iowa gained him a scholarship to the Harvard Law School.[1066]

In the two years Raymond was at Harvard, he earned a Master's of law degree (LL.M.) in 1931, followed by a Doctor of Jurisprudence degree (S.J.D.) in 1932.[1067] At Harvard, Raymond honed his scholarly skills. Soon he authored

---

1061. Gregory Swygert, son of one of the co-authors of this volume, became aware of the Chambers's Stetson connection from a friend who had read Chambers's autobiography in the spring of 2004.

1062. Duncan, *supra* n. 1014, at 1.

1063. *Id.*

1064. *Id.*

1065. *Id.*

1066. *Dr. Paul Raymond Returns to Take Up Duties of Law Dean,* DeLand Sun. News 1 (Aug. 9, 1938) [hereinafter *Raymond Returns*].

1067. Lycan, *supra* n. 109, at 301.

scholarly articles published in the *Georgetown*, *Iowa*, and *Oregon* law reviews.[1068]

Former president and Stetson University chancellor Pope Duncan[1069] recalled that Raymond received offers from several New York City law firms and law schools.[1070] One of the schools was Stetson College of Law. Raymond accepted Stetson's offer, though the law teaching position paid only $1,500 a year, considerably less than Raymond would have made had he joined a New York City law firm.[1071] Though pleased by his decision, a few months after coming to the Stetson law school, however, Raymond began to have second thoughts. Duncan explains:

> [Raymond] enjoyed his [one year experience on the law faculty], but he had come to believe that the Stetson law school did not have much of a future. Dean Wayne Morris of the University of Oregon Law School offered him a much better salary [than Stetson's] and he took it.[1072]

Fortunately, Stetson enticed Raymond to return to the College of Law after being at Oregon law school for one year. Raymond not only missed Florida, but also appreciated Stetson's financial inducement to rejoin the faculty.[1073] For the second time, Raymond remained only one academic year, 1935–1936, as he accepted an invitation to go to Washington, D.C., as an assistant to the Attorney General of the United States. There, he studied, analyzed, and served as an associate editor of a detailed report on state parole and probation systems operating in the United States.[1074] Wayne Morris, who two years earlier had persuaded Raymond to join the faculty at Oregon law school, had since been elected to the United States Senate. Senator Morris knew several people in the U.S. Attorney General's Office and was aware that the Attorney General was seeking a highly qualified legal scholar to research the states' various parole systems. Morris suggested Paul Raymond for the position.[1075]

Raymond accepted the appointment, but only after President Hulley granted him a two-year leave of absence. During Raymond's stay in Washington, he not

1068. *Raymond Returns*, *supra* n. 1066, at 3.

1069. Duncan, *supra* n. 1014, at 3.

1070. *Id.*

1071. *Id.*

1072. *Id.* When Dean Tribble told President Hulley that Raymond was leaving Stetson, Hulley only said: "He has one of my golf books." *Id.*

1073. *Id.*

1074. *Raymond Prepares Volume Dealing with Parole Problems of Nation,* 3 Stetson Reporter 4 (Oct. 13, 1937) [hereinafter *Raymond Prepares Volume*].

1075. Vause, *Manuscript, supra* n. 595, at 83.

only researched the various parole programs in the United States, but he also co-authored a three-volume work (published by the U.S. Department of Justice) detailing the extent and variety of these programs.[1076] The study found that though a few states had sophisticated, well-developed parole regulations, many, including Florida, had failed to adopt any parole program.[1077]

b. Raymond Raises Academic Standards

After completing his Washington work, Paul Raymond returned to the Stetson law faculty. In May 1938, Stetson University President William Sims Allen offered thirty-four-year-old Paul Raymond the deanship of Stetson College of Law.[1078] Though he took the job, years later Raymond commented that he "was very hesitant about accepting the responsibility," knowing the "poor condition of the law school."[1079]

A sports fan, Raymond had to be pleased with the University's football team. During Raymond's first year as dean, Stetson University defeated the University of Florida 16 to 14 in football, the first time Stetson had done so in the twenty-nine years they had played each other.[1080] Stetson Historian Bowen writes that Stetson's win "ended the competition in football between the two schools."[1081]

Meanwhile, in President Allen's annual reports to the University Board of Trustees, he included assessments of the College of Law, one noting that during Raymond's first two years as dean, the academic standards of the College of Law had risen significantly.[1082] Beginning with the 1939–1940 academic year, law school applicants had to either have an undergraduate degree, or had taken three years of college work which, when then combined with three years of law school, was called the "three-three" program.[1083] Despite the more rigid policy, Raymond realized there was a downside to raising admissions standards, causing the size of the entering class to be smaller. Still, he realized that "at the same time, [higher standards] have raised the quality of the entering student."[1084]

1076. *Id.*

1077. *Id.* at 83–84.

1078. *Raymond Prepares Volume*, *supra* n. 1074, at 57.

1079. *Id.*

1080. Bowen, *supra* n. 455, at 125.

1081. *Id.*

1082. Paul E. Raymond, *The College of Law*, in W.S. Allen, Pres., Stetson U., to Stetson U. Bd. of Trustees, *Report of the President of John B. Stetson University to the Board of Directors for the Year 1939–1940*, at 9 (Feb. 15, 1940) (on file at the Stetson U. Archives, DeLand, Fla.) [hereinafter Raymond, *1939–1940 Report*].

1083. *Id.*

1084. *Id.*

Not only did Raymond raise admission standards, he also made the law program more rigorous. Beginning in spring 1940, for the first time in the College's history it required students to attend classes six days a week. Raymond explained that the change was made "to obtain a higher quality of professional study."[1085] Though only morning classes were held, students (not surprisingly) were quite unhappy with the six-day class schedule. Reportedly, they voiced their concerns about the impact these classes would have on their Friday evening parties (or vice versa). Other students argued that Saturday classes would make it more difficult to travel home for weekends and to work to make money.[1086] One student, in commenting on Saturday classes, wrote: "A shadow of gloom has been cast upon the austere halls of the Law School ... we refer to Saturday classes next semester."[1087]

Not dissuaded by such student protestations, Raymond remained adamant, reminding students that it was their duty to acquire as much legal knowledge as possible during their three years of legal study.[1088] A newspaper account said that the "dean and faculty believed the six-day schedule was essential" for the school.[1089] In response to the students' specific concern about the impact on their weekend partying, Raymond retorted, "It seems evident that a mature student will have little difficulty in fitting a social evening into his schedule if he makes sufficient use of the time available for studying."[1090] Issue decided. Now, how about a summer program?

In the summer of 1939, UF and Stetson law schools jointly held a summer school session in which students from both schools took classes.[1091] Raymond reported that the combined program was a success and indicated it would be repeated the following summer.[1092] However, that did not happen. Rather, Stetson's College of Law held its own six-week summer session in 1940, offering nine courses from which interested students could choose.[1093] After America's entry into World War II, the law school's summer school enrollment fell. Nonetheless, in the summer of 1942, the school offered a special program in

---

1085. *Id.*

1086. *Lawyers to Have Six-Day Week Second Semester,* 5 Stetson Rptr. 1 (Jan. 17, 1940) [hereinafter *Six-Day Week*].

1087. *Legal Talk,* 5 Stetson Rptr. 3 (Jan. 17, 1940).

1088. *Six-Day Week, supra* n. 1086, at 1.

1089. *Id.*

1090. *Id.*

1091. Raymond, *1939–1940 Report, supra* n. 1082, at 10.

1092. *Id.*

1093. *Law Summer School Offers Nine Courses,* 5 Stetson Rptr. 4 (May 22, 1940.)

military and constitutional law, described as one "of value to young men and women preparatory to actual service in military affairs."[1094]

When it came to the curriculum during Raymond's deanship, "innovative" is the appropriate adjective. In line with what began at Columbia University's law school around 1915, Harvard shortly thereafter, and Yale from the mid 1920s forward,[1095] Stetson's College of Law introduced "more non-legal materials" into the curriculum "to better train the young lawyer for his citizenship responsibilities."[1096] Perhaps anticipating by four decades the significance of law and economics—one that gained momentum from the 1980s onward in American legal education—certain Stetson faculty members espoused that students, prior to coming to law school, should receive the "highest quality of instruction in the field of economics."[1097] The faculty, beginning with the 1939–1940 academic year, introduced two "perspective courses" well before many other law schools did so: a comparative law course called "The Development of the Law," and a course on "International Law."[1098]

Because he believed the College of Law lacked academic rigor, Raymond made remedying this perceived deficiency a high priority. Both Raymond and Allen were concerned about the school's low standards for student retention, partly but not entirely due to the ABA and AALS. Allen reported that according to records from the school's registrar's office, not a single law student "had ever been dropped from the school because of poor scholarship" through the academic year 1937–1938.[1099] During Raymond's first year as dean, he noted in his annual report to the president that many students "had no aptitude for the legal profession."[1100] The faculty supported Raymond's efforts to raise the standards for student retention. In his 1940–1941 report to Allen, Raymond commented that the "principle objective of the law faculty has been to improve scholarship standards in the law school ... [believing] that a law school with a high reputation for scholarship would contribute more to the University and more to the State than would a low grade law school with a free and

1094. *College of Law Summer Program Given; Military and Constitutional Law Will Be Stressed,* 7 Stetson Rptr. 1 (May 6, 1942).

1095. *See e.g.* James Vescovi, *A Survey of Columbia Law School's Expanding Curriculum,* Columbia L. Sch. Rpt. 9, 12 (Spring 2003); *see also* Herman Oliphant, *Summary of the Studies of the Legal Education by the Faculty of Law of Columbia University* (Colum. U. 1938).

1096. Duncan, *supra* n. 1014, at 9.

1097. *Id.*

1098. *Id.*

1099. *Id.*

1100. *Id.*

easy path to the Florida Bar."[1101] With candor, Raymond commented that "it will be sometime yet before we can state that the students are doing the same quality of work as is being done in first class law schools."[1102]

During the 1940–1941 academic year, Raymond and the faculty continued in their combined effort to raise the academic quality at the College of Law, though this turned out to be the last year in which the standards rose until after World War II. A joint faculty-student bar association report on the College of Law curriculum proposed that a new course, titled "Practice in Legal Argumentation," be adopted.[1103] Under the proposal, the course would replace the student Law Clubs' competitions.[1104] Weekly sessions in the skills of making legal arguments would be held, giving "students training that is much needed and which is not available at any other school."[1105] Professors Wilson and Lambert proposed the new program, which called for students to be assigned problems related to their class work, and then to have them argue both sides of the issues in weekly sessions.[1106] The faculty backed the plan, since all students would have to participate and, thereby, reap benefits.[1107]

As regards faculty scholarship, Raymond urged his colleagues to research and write. In the spring of 1939, he requested that each faculty member "submit a list of articles and book reviews" published during the 1938–1939 academic year.[1108] (The list has not been found).

c. Raymond Begins Annual Law Days

Among Raymond's important innovations was his instituting annual law-day programs, which brought leading jurists and lawyers to campus. The first annual "Stetson Law School Day" took place on May 6, 1939.[1109]

1101. Paul E. Raymond, *The College of Law,* in memo. from W.S. Allen, Pres., Stetson U., to Stetson U. Bd. of Trustees, *Report of the President of John B. Stetson University to the Board of Trustees for the Year 1940–1941,* at 10 (Feb. 20, 1941) (on file at the Stetson U. Archives, DeLand, Fla.) [hereinafter Raymond, *1940–1941 Report*].

1102. Duncan, *supra* n. 1014, at 9.

1103. *Id.* at 7.

1104. *Id.*

1105. *Id.*

1106. *Minutes of the Law Faculty* 1 (Nov. 7, 1940) (on file at Stetson U. Archives, DeLand, Fla.).

1107. *Id.*

1108. *Minutes of the Meeting of the Law Faculty* 1 (May 25, 1939) (on file at Stetson U. Archives, DeLand, Fla.).

1109. *Law School Day Is Saturday May 6; Dean Paul Raymond Announces Program of Events; Law Club Competition Finals Will Be Held in Stover Little Theatre; Supreme Court Justices Will Preside,* 4 Stetson Rptr.1 (May 3, 1939).

Highlighting the day was the final oral arguments in the Law Club competitions before three sitting justices of the Supreme Court of Florida: Justices Roy F. Chapman, Elwyn Thomas (both Stetson College of Law graduates), and Rivers Buford.[1110] Students Tom Cobb, Elwyn Middleton, Grady Crawford, and Rodney Durrance argued the merits of the case.[1111] Rodney Durrance, after graduating in 1939 from the law school, became "the first man from Stetson to be elected as research assistant to the Supreme Court of Florida."[1112]

The first law day included a symposium on public law, with J.J. Taylor of the Florida Department of Agriculture speaking on administrative adjudication; Ray C. Brown, labor law specialist from Tampa, discussing collective bargaining agreements; and D.H. Redfearn, President of the Florida State Bar Association, analyzing the taxation of decedents' estates.[1113] In the evening, alumni, guests, faculty, and students attended a "Barristers Banquet." Fred Botts, Stetson law graduate of 1911 who had become a Miami judge, served as toastmaster. After-dinner speakers included Joseph Scarlett, president of the Volusia County Bar Association; Neil Ferguson, chairman of the Florida Board of Law Examiners; Judge Millard B. Smith; Judge Herbert Frederick; Francis Whitehair; and Stetson President William Sims Allen.[1114] Raymond reported afterwards that "the alumni reaction to the affair was so favorable that plans are now being made for [another]."[1115]

1110. *Proceedings of the First Annual Law School Day,* 4 Stetson Rptr. 1 (May 10, 1939).

> Sitting *pro tempore* as Justices of the Supreme Court of John B. Stetson University, the Law Club Competition Finals were judged by Supreme Court Justice Roy F. Chapman, and Circuit Court Judges Herbert Frederick and Frank V. Smith. Arguing for the Plaintiff were Tom Cobb and Elwyn Middleton, while Grady Crawford and Rodney Durrance argued for the Defendant in a case involving the right of an automobile guest to recover from a service station operator for injuries caused by his negligent replacement of a wheel.... After a decision for the defense was rendered, Justice Elwyn Thomas presented copies of Black's Law Dictionary to the winning attorneys, Crawford and Durrance and Justice Roy Chapman presented to the attorneys for the Plaintiff, Cobb and Middleton at the banquet following the competition.

Id.

1111. *Id.*

1112. *Last Year Law School Grads Succeed in Chosen Field,* 5 Stetson Rptr. 6 (Sept. 13, 1939).

1113. Lycan, *History of Stetson, supra* n. 109, at 302.

1114. *Id.*

1115. Duncan, *supra* n. 1014, at 10.

The second annual Stetson Law Day was held on April 6, 1940.[1116] It took place in conjunction with the silver anniversary of the David Brewer Chapter of the Phi Alpha Delta law fraternity.[1117] The special day, like in the previous year, included student moot court arguments before three justices of the Florida Supreme Court.[1118] George A. McNulty of the United States Department of Labor gave the principal address in the afternoon. The day ended with the traditional banquet, which was said to have drawn "a large number of the alumni."[1119]

The third and final Stetson Law Day under Raymond until after WWII included Francis Biddle, Solicitor General of the United States, as the scheduled keynote speaker.[1120] A former United States Appeals Court judge, Biddle

---

1116. See, *Proceedings of the Second Annual Law Day,* 5 Stetson Reporter 1, 1–36 (Apr. 6, 1940), stating:

> The Second Annual Law Day Program, held on April 6, 1940, featured an address by George McNulty, general counsel of the Wage Hour Division of the Federal Department of Labor. Speaking on "The Administration of the Wage Hour Law." Mr. McNulty espoused the Act's success in raising the minimum wage from 25 cents an hour, or $11 for a 44-hour week, in 1938 to 30 cents an hour, or $12.60 per week based on a 42-hour week in October 1939. Mr. McNulty was followed by G. L. Reeves, an attorney from Tampa who discussed the adverse impact the implementation of the Wages and Hours Laws had on the Citrus industry in Florida. Mr. M. L. Fleishel, president of Putnam Lumber Company in Jacksonville, then discussed the adverse impact the Act had on the lumber industry."
> *Id.*

1117. Vause, *Centennial History, supra* n. 595, at 90.

1118. *Proceedings of the Second Annual Law School Day, supra* n. 1116, which explained,

> During the Barrister's Banquet, Joseph Scarlett, President of the Volusia County Bar Association, addressed the issue of ethics in lawyering in "The Local Bar Association and the Law School. Circuit Court Judge Millard B. Smith, speaking as "An Alumnus Looks at the Law School," related his memories of Stetson, presenting his evidence of its success: "Exhibit No. 1-Two Supreme Court Judges, Exhibit No. 2-Two Ex-Governors, Exhibit No. 3-Federal judge, numerous Circuit judges, a whole host of county Judges and a few good lawyers." Florida Supreme Court Justice Rivers Buford also addressed the gathering, presenting "The Supreme Court Looks at the Law School." Students presented their "Look at the Law School," recreating their most amusing memories. President Allen presented the administration's viewpoint in his soliloquy on "The University and the Law School." Prizes were also awarded during the banquet. Francis Whitehair awarded the Freshman Law Club Prizes, Judge Herbert Frederick awarded the Junior Law Club Prizes and Justices Roy Chapman and Elwyn Thomas awarded the Senior Law Club Prizes.

Id.

1119. Duncan, *supra* n. 1014, at 8.

1120. *Francis Biddle to Speak on Third Law School Day,* 6 Stetson Rptr. 1 (Mar. 12, 1941).

spoke on legal control on "subversive activities in the United States." The theme for the third Law Day was "National Defense."[1121] In addition to Biddle's address, per custom, Stetson law students argued a mock appeal before distinguished jurists. Pleased with the events, Raymond described the purpose of the annual law days was "to allow alumni and students of the Law School to reconvene once a year to discuss problems pertinent to the legal profession."[1122]

The 1941 Stetson Law Day was the last under the Raymond administration. In less than a year, Dean Raymond would be gone, the United States would be fully engaged in World War II, and Stetson's law faculty and students would be leaving (or had already left) to go off to war. Moreover, officials of Stetson University College of Law would be confronting the realities of the war and the possible closure of the school, at least for the duration of the conflict.[1123]

d. Student Activities: 1938–1942

Throughout the Raymond decanal period, law students kept busy. In the fall of 1938, students formed the Stetson Law Student Association (later renamed the Student Bar Association).[1124] An announcement proclaimed that the student organization came about "with the purpose of insuring a closer bond between the faculty and students and to advocate the welfare of the school."[1125] The members elected Tom Cobb the organization's first president; Edwin Middleton, vice-president; John Cherry, secretary; and Dick Sauls, treasurer.[1126] The Stetson University student-body president (and law student), the presidents of Phi Alpha Delta and Sigma Nu law fraternities, and the presidents of the three law classes together drew up the constitution and the bylaws for the new organization.[1127] Several students discussed the challenges and opportunities of the new student association. A "Silver-Tongued Orator from the Florida Flatwoods" named William Ward Hunter evoked "cheers of glee from the audience" in response to his suggestions.[1128] Other discussants included "Blind" Tom Kirkland, "Cassanova" MacMillan, and Ed "Sully" Mason.[1129]

1121. *Id.*
1122. *Id.*
1123. *See infra* nn. 1237–1250 and accompanying text.
1124. *Law Association Formed Wednesday,* 4 Stetson Rptr. 1 (Oct. 12, 1938).
1125. *Id.*
1126. *Id.*
1127. *Id.*
1128. Vause, *Centennial History, supra* n. 595 at 87.
1129. *Id.*

In the fall of 1939, third-year law student John Cherry became the second president of the Stetson Law School Association. Other officers were Tom Kirkland, vice-president; Dick Sauls, secretary; and Wallace Smith, treasurer.[1130] The 1940 officers consisted of Dick Sauls of West Palm Beach, president; Tom Watson of Orlando, vice-president; Harold Clark of Jacksonville, secretary; and Gadi Lawton of Orlando, treasurer.[1131]

In addition to social and student government activities, law students were encouraged by the law faculty to respond to an invitation from the *Florida Bar Journal* to write case comments for possible publication in its periodical. The *Journal* invited law students at Florida and Miami law schools as well to submit articles.[1132] Professor Wilson advised the Stetson law student contributors who contributed seven comments to the *Journal* in the fall of 1939.[1133] All were published.[1134]

From 1936 onward, the College of Law awarded various prizes to graduating students. These included scholarship keys, awards from Phi Alpha Delta and from Sigma Nu law fraternities, a set of *Florida Reports* for the student having the highest scholastic average, the Athenian prize of $25 for the best debater in the class, and various book awards for course honors.[1135]

Stetson law students for several decades were required, like all Stetson University students, to attend chapel on the DeLand campus. But during Raymond's administration, the faculty approved a motion submitted by the dean which provided:

> Exempting first year law students who do not hold a bachelor's degree, chapel attendance by law students is optional. In case a student who must

---

1130. *Cherry Is Chosen Law Group Proxy,* 5 Stetson Rptr. 1 (Sept. 27, 1939).

1131. Vause, *Centennial History, supra* n. 595.

1132. *See generally* Raymond, *supra* n. 1101, at 8.

1133. *Seven Law Students Contribute to Bar Journal; Students Write Case Comments for Magazine,* 5 Stetson Rptr.6 (Nov. 15, 1939). The students and their comments were Harold A. Boire, *Conflicts of Law: Full Faith and Credit for Workmen's Compensation*; Carol O. Teague, *Mortgages: Pledges, Venue, and Waiver of Security by Personal Suit*; Lawrence DeShaw, *Validity of Unrecorded Trust Receipts against Third Parties*; E.M. Ferguson, *Wood Pulp Mill as Public Nuisance*; Harry T. Newett, *Constitutional Law: Validity of Municipal Restrictions on Rights of Free Speech and Assembly*; J.E. Clouts, *Constitutional Law: Validity of Grower's Cost Guarantee*; and Hal P. Dekle, *Dower: Operation of Stepmother Clause. Id.*

1134. *Id.*

1135. *Prizes and Awards, John B. Stetson Commencement 1939 Graduation Exercises* (n.p.) (June 6, 1938) (pamphlet on file at Stetson U. Archives, DeLand, Fla.).

> attend chapel is absent therefrom an unreasonable amount, the faculty will take such action as is appropriate.[1136]

Then there was the matter of study aids. Faculty minutes of the period reveal that law students were using so-called "canned briefs."[1137] (The topic is noteworthy since this concern continues through the present). The faculty considered various alternatives to discourage students from using canned briefs. Finding no quick and easy solution, they suggested that Raymond discuss the matter with officers of the Student Bar Association to try to discourage the practice.[1138] The "problem" persisted.

Faculty minutes of an October 1941 meeting reveals another student problem: sleeping in class. The distracting lack of attention pertained to one student in particular.[1139] As to that individual, "it was finally suggested that [his dozing] be investigated whether or not the practice was volitional and remedial, or involuntary."[1140]

Finally, in a weekly column in *The Stetson Reporter* titled "Legal Language," a student using the pseudonym "Usca," reported that, "A bill to plow under every third lawyer in Florida to relieve the congestion in that profession was before a [Florida] legislative committee. [The author of the bill] advocated two plowings per year by means similar to those used in crop control. The bill was referred to the House Committee on Livestock."[1141] In yet another column, with similar tongue-in-cheek, the student wrote: "With the exception of a few expulsions, a fire in the library, and a window being kicked out, last week was a rather quiet one in the law school."[1142]

e. Relocation to Jacksonville?

Dean Raymond and the faculty believed that the school's evidence course needed to be improved. Raymond wrote:

1136. *Minutes of Special Meeting of the Law Faculty of the John B. Stetson College of Law*, 1 (Apr. 28, 1940) (on file at Stetson U. Archives, DeLand, Fla.).

1137. *Minutes of the Regular Meeting of the Law Faculty of the John B. Stetson College of Law* 2 (Sept. 21, 1939) (on file at Stetson U. Archives, DeLand, Fla.).

1138. *Id.*

1139. *Minutes of the Regular Meeting of the Law Faculty, John B. Stetson College of Law* 1 (Oct. 29, 1941) (on file at Stetson U. Archives, DeLand, Fla.).

1140. *Id.*

1141. *Legal Language*, 4 Stetson Rptr. 3 (May 24, 1939).

1142. *Legal Language*, 4 Stetson Rptr. 5 (Nov. 19, 1938).

> Almost everyone who has taken a course in Evidence as a student or who has taught the course has been dissatisfied with it. Evidence is a course which must be presented, partially at least, by laboratory methods ... *Adequate facilities* are not presently available for the proper presentation of this course.[1143]

Raymond knew the College of Law had inadequate facilities as soon as he joined the faculty. In a report to President Allen, Raymond pointed out that, following the 1940 inspection of the College of Law by the AALS and ABA, the inspectors emphasized that "the greatest immediate need of the school is a building of its own. The sharing of a building with [undergraduate] academic students necessarily interferes with the professional attitude of the [law] students."[1144] These findings were authored by Dean F.G. Ribble of the University of Virginia Law School, a member of the AALS executive committee, who headed the on-site inspection.[1145] Though Raymond considered the report overall to be "thoroughly favorable," Ribble in the AALS report noted that the school's facilities "limit the possibilities for research on the part of the faculty ... and students."[1146] Ribble added that "It would be manifestly desirable to increase the library."[1147] This meant not only the size of the collection, but also the size of the physical plant for housing the collection and for the staff offices and space for processing the library's materials.

Besides Raymond, Allen too understood the need for a new law school building. The third floor of the school's quarters wasn't strong enough to hold the weight of the books. In a report to the Board of Trustees, Allen proposed that a new law school building be added to the DeLand campus, noting that it would add prestige to the law school and free up space in Flagler Hall for the Liberal Arts College.[1148] But not every Board member wanted a new facility in DeLand. One member, in particular, had other ideas: J. Ollie Edmunds.

Edmunds graduated from the Stetson College of Law in 1928, and later became a judge for Duval County (Jacksonville).[1149] Edmunds later served as president of the Stetson University Alumni Association and was elected to the

---

1143. Assn. of Am. L. Schs., *Report on Stetson University College of Law* 8 (unpublished ms. 1940) (on file at Stetson U. Archives, DeLand, Fla.).

1144. *Id.* at 7.

1145. *Id.* at 6.

1146. *Id.* at 7.

1147. *Id.*

1148. Lycan, *History of Stetson, supra* n. 109, at 285.

1149. Gordis, *supra* n. 105, at 66.

Stetson University Board of Trustees in 1933. As a trustee, he attended his first board meeting in February 1934,[1150] and four years later served as Chair of the Board's Finance Committee. At the February 15, 1939, meeting of the Trustees,[1151] Edmunds suggested that Stetson College of Law move to the "Gate Way" city—Jacksonville.[1152] He told the Trustees that several Jacksonville organizations supported the move, so much so, that they would raise money to construct a building in a good location so as "to relieve the University of all further expenses ... in connection with it."[1153] This, Edmunds reasoned, meant that the University would save between $10,000 to $15,000 per year, an amount within the range of the College's annual operation's deficit over the past several years.[1154]

> Historian Lycan details the reactions to Edmunds' proposal: Mr. [John B.] Stetson [Jr.] spoke strongly for the move ... [Trustee] Jennings spoke for the move stating: "The City of Jacksonville will give us any amount of money that we want." Further, he said the trustees should also consider establishing a medical school in Jacksonville.[1155]

1150. Lycan, *History of Stetson, supra* n. 109, at 269. Lycan wrote that when Edmunds was elected to the Board of Trustees, "nobody loved Stetson more deeply." *Id.*

1151. *Id.* at 303.

1152. *Id; see also Editorial; Law School to Jacksonville May Not Be a Catastrophe,* 5 Stetson Rptr. 2 (Feb. 21, 1940).

1153. Lycan, *History of Stetson, supra* n. 109, at 303.

1154. *Id.*

1155. *Id.* At our annual meeting on February 15, 1940, President W.S. Allen reported to this board:

> The Jacksonville Bar Association by unanimous vote some months ago invited the Trustees of John B. Stetson University to move the College of Law to Jacksonville. The Bar Association was joined in this invitation by the Mayor and the Council of Jacksonville, as well as by the Board of Governors of the Chamber of Commerce. A Committee representing the organizations stated that if the trustees would move the college of law to Jacksonville, the City of Jacksonville would furnish a worthy building to house the law school and take care of the expenses of the law library ...
>
> Naturally, there will be some sentiment against moving the College of Law to Jacksonville. Personally, I prefer to see it remain on the campus with the main institution, if adequate facilities could be provided. However, the ultimate good of the college and of the entire institution must be considered.
>
> Accordingly, I recommend that, provided the City of Jacksonville will furnish an adequate building, properly equipped including lights, water, and heat, and an annual cash appropriation for the library for a minimum of ten years, and such other items that the Board may deem wise, that the College of Law be moved to Jacksonville and that a Committee of the Board of Trustees, with the President

Despite the support of influential Board members, DeLand's civic organizations and the local *Sun News* came out "so strongly against moving the College of Law that the trustees hesitated."[1156] Over the next several months, as the relocation proposal simmered, additional voices in opposition to the proposed move surfaced, especially from DeLand residents, and from Stetson law alumni, faculty, students, and staff. The proposal appeared to be sinking. Then, in January 1940, the Jacksonville Bar Association formally invited the University to move the College of Law to its city.[1157] The Association, together with Stetson law alumni from Jacksonville, submitted a proposal that included a plan to donate a suitable building within the city to the College.[1158]

In response to the bid, the Board Trustees created a committee to study the Jacksonville proposal, as well as the entire issue of possibly moving the law school out of DeLand.[1159] In addition to President Allen, the committee consisted of three University Trustees: former Governor Doyle E. Carlton; S. Bryan Jennings; and J. Ollie Edmunds, who served as chair. Three of the four committee members strongly supported the move. Only Governor Carlton considered the move a bad idea.[1160] Minutes of the Board's February 1940 meeting reveal that the members extensively debated the move.[1161]

Following the Board's February 1940 meeting, the student newspaper, *The Stetson Reporter*, reprinted an earlier editorial published in the DeLand *Sun*

> of the University and the Dean of the College of Law, be appointed to work out details in this matter.

Memo. from J. Ollie Edmunds, Pres., Stetson U., to Stetson U. Bd. of Trustees, *Report of the President of John B. Stetson University, Calendar Year 1952*, at 1 (Feb. 19, 1953) (on file at the Stetson U. Archives, DeLand, Fla.).

Upon receiving this special report from the President, Governor Doyle Carlton, Judge O. K. Reaves, S. Bryan Jennings, and J. Ollie Edmunds, Chairman, were appointed to "meet with the officials of the City of Jacksonville to study the invitation of the Jacksonville Bar Association and report to this Board at its next meeting." *Id.*

1156. Lycan, *supra* n. 109, at 303. Lycan cited editorials and articles in the DeLand *Sun News* without specific reference to document the extent of the local opposition to the proposed relocation of the College. *Id.* at 320 nn. 85–86.

1157. *Trustee Committee Holds Key to Future of Law School; Board Discusses Plans at Annual Meeting to Move College of Law,* 5 Stetson Rptr. 1 (Feb. 21, 1940) [hereinafter *Trustee Committee*].

1158. *Id.*

1159. *Id.*

1160. *Minutes of the Board of Trustees Meeting, John B. Stetson University* 1–2 (Feb. 15, 1940) (on file at the Stetson U. Archives, DeLand, Fla.).

1161. *Id.*

News, on June 10, 1939, titled: "Law School to Jacksonville May Not Be a Catastrophe."[1162] The editorialist declared:

> Opinions, naturally, are divided on the move [of the law school to DeLand]. There are those who believe it would be the ruin of Stetson [University] as a DeLand institution. Others feel that it would eventually benefit the local school.
>
> We hear it from some source that Jacksonville is going to have a law school of some sort. Miami has a law school. Tampa has a comparatively young [Tampa] university, and Jacksonville isn't going to be left out in the cold. If Stetson's law school doesn't go to Jacksonville, then some other [law school] will locate there ... That won't do Stetson any particular good.[1163]

The editorial opined that Jacksonville area law students presently going to UF's law school in Gainesville would likely go the Stetson law school should it relocate to Jacksonville.[1164]

As the discussions continued, the intensifying military conflicts in Europe and in the Pacific began to divert attention to the increasing likelihood of the United States becoming involved. After the bombing of Pearl Harbor on December 7, 1941, all concerns and priorities changed. No new University buildings could be built unless they were connected to the nation's military efforts.[1165] As America's involvement in World War II rose, issues such as relocation of a small law school became irrelevant. The Jacksonville Bar Association proposal was an early casualty of the country's darkening of hope and the setting aside of business as usual. Of course, WWII did eventually come to an end. Then, opportunities for relocating the Stetson College of Law would once again be considered and acted on. But for a few years, war took the entire stage.

f. Clouds of War: Faculty Turnover

During the nearly four-year deanship of Paul Raymond, followed by the one-year deanship of Roy Howes, the law faculty members came and went with rapidity. As the world sped toward war, many left either to go to Washington to assist the government's war efforts, or to join American military services. A few resigned to go to other law schools, presumably attracted to higher salaries. Students also left to join the armed forces, many voluntarily, others

1162. *Trustee Committee, supra* n. 1157, at 2.

1163. *Id.*

1164. *Id.*

1165. Lycan, *History of Stetson, supra* n. 109, at 303.

after receiving slips of paper with the Commander in Chief's signature delivered by way of the Selective Service System.

Just prior to Paul Raymond becoming dean in the fall of 1938, Professors J.A. Carpenter, J.W. Futch, and H.S. Jacobs left the law faculty.[1166] Holding over from the Tribble administration was Professor Henry J. Fox, as well as former dean Lewis H. Tribble himself.[1167] Raymond replaced Carpenter, Futch, and Jacobs by adding Claude Hilling Brown, James Jefferson Lenoir, and James Robert Wilson to the faculty.[1168] Brown had a J.S.D. degree from Yale Law School, and a LL.B. degree from Drake University. Stetson law students considered Brown an excellent teacher.[1169] Lenoir held the LL.M. degree from Columbia Law School, and a Ph.D. from the University in Illinois, as well as a B.A. degree from the University of Mississippi.[1170] Raymond's third initial appointment—James Wilson—had a Jur.Sc.D. degree from Columbia University, as well as an A.B. and a LL.B. degree from the University of Iowa.[1171]

Soon, Raymond added two additional instructors: visiting professor Leonard J. Curtis from the University of Chicago, and Lemuel Allan Haslup (later to become a dean of the College of Law). Professor Curtis taught a course in equity. He had earned a juris doctor (J.D.) degree from the University of Chicago and had taught on the law faculties at both the University of Wisconsin and the University of Arizona.[1172]

Haslup was a retired officer of the United States Marine Corps. After earning an A.B. degree from the University of Maryland in 1934, he received his LL.B. degree from George Washington University, and was a member of the District of Columbia Bar.[1173] In addition, the year Haslup came to Stetson as a visiting lecturer in law, he was admitted to practice before the United States Supreme Court.[1174]

1166. Paul E. Raymond, *The College of Law,* in Memo. from W.S. Allen, Pres., Stetson U., to Stetson U. Bd. of Trustees, *Report to the President of John B. Stetson University to the Board of Trustees 1938–1939,* at 14 (Feb. 16, 1939) (on file at the Stetson U. Archives, DeLand, Fla.) [hereinafter *1938–1939 Report*].

1167. *Raymond Returns, supra* n. 1066, at 1.

1168. Duncan, *supra* n. 1014, at 15.

1169. *Id.*

1170. *Id.*

1171. *Id.*

1172. *Professor Curtis Will Teach Law,* 4 Stetson Rptr. 3 (Feb. 8, 1939).

1173. *People You Should Know, Dean Lemuel Allen Haslup* (n.d.) (clipping from unidentified newspaper) (on file in Faculty File, Stetson U. College of L., Gulfport, Fla.); *see also* Duncan, *supra* n. 1014, at 14.

1174. Duncan, *supra* n. 1014, at 14.

Dean Lemuel A. Haslup

At the end of the 1938–1939 academic year, Tribble resigned from the faculty and was replaced by Henry J. Fox, a practicing lawyer from Washington, D.C. Fox had taught law for one year at the University of Kentucky[1175] and was well qualified for his position. He had earned both the A.B. and LL.B. degrees from the University of Wisconsin, then went on to earn an LL.M. from Harvard Law School in 1936.[1176] The following year, Fox earned the S.J.D. degree from the University of Wisconsin.[1177]

By the spring of 1940, Stetson's law faculty consisted of Dean Raymond and professors Brown, Curtis, Lenoir, Wilson, and Fox, along with instructor Neil Jackson (whom Raymond hired a few months earlier). In the following fall, with full faculty support, Raymond hired Thomas F. Lambert as an instructor in law to take Professor Curtis' place, who had resigned the previous spring.[1178] Though young, Lambert possessed outstanding academic credentials. After receiving an A.B. degree from the University of California, he was awarded a coveted Rhodes Scholarship to Oxford University.[1179] After he had studied jurisprudence and civil law over a three-year period, he graduated from Oxford with an LL.B. degree with honors in 1939.[1180] The following year, Lambert enrolled in Yale Law School with a Sterling Fellowship. At Yale, he completed the

1175. *1938–1939 Report*, *supra* n. 1166, at 8; *see also* Paul E. Raymond, *Special Meeting of the Law Faculty* 1 (Minutes, Aug. 3, 1939) (on file at Stetson U. Archives in DeLand, Fla.).

1176. *1938–1939 Report*, *supra* n. 1166, at 8.

1177. *Id.*; *see also Outstanding Man Added to Faculty of Law School; Appointment Follows Resignation of Professor Tribble,* 5 Stetson Rptr. 6 (Sept. 13, 1939).

1178. Duncan, *supra* n. 1014, at 2; *see also* Paul Raymond, *Minutes of a Special Meeting of the Law Faculty* 1 (Aug. 13, 1940) (on file at Stetson U. Archives, DeLand, Flas).

1179. Joy Reese, *Thomas Lambert Is Talented New Law Professor, Rhodes Scholar Comes to DeLand from California,* 6 Stetson Rptr. 1 (Sept. 11, 1940).

1180. *Id.*

Dean Thomas F. Lambert

S.J.D.—the highest degree in law.[1181] The young Lambert, of course, did not know when he graduated from Yale that in only two years he would be thrust into the dean's position of the Stetson University College of Law in DeLand, Florida, twelve hundred miles south of New Haven, Connecticut.

To the surprise of many at the University, in the summer of 1941, Raymond resigned from his deanship of the College of Law to become Assistant Attorney General of the State of Florida.[1182] President Allen asked Lambert—then only twenty-six years old—to serve as acting dean of the Stetson College of Law.[1183] The natural question is, why Lambert? Why was such a young faculty member, holding the lowest teaching rank of instructor, a person having no prior law teaching experience, appointed acting dean? One reason may have been Allen's recognition of Lambert's "brilliant record as a scholar."[1184] Another explanation may be that by the fall of 1941 several other faculty members had resigned, including professors Brown, Lenoir, Wilson, Fox, and Jackson. They

1181. *Id.*

1182. Lycan, *History of Stetson, supra* n. 109, at 302.

1183. *Garwood Appointed New Dean, Lambert Will Head Law School; Outstanding Men Replace Davis and Raymond. Former Dean Raymond Will Be Assistant Attorney General,* 7 Stetson Rprt. 1 (Sept. 18, 1941) [hereinafter *Garwood Appointed New Dean*]; *see also* Memo. from W.S Allen, Pres., Stetson U., to Stetson U. Bd. of Trustees, *Report of the President of John B. Stetson University to the Board of Trustees for the Year 1941–1942,* at 1 (Feb. 19, 1942) (on file at Stetson U. Archives, DeLand, Fla.) [hereinafter *1941–1942 Report*].

1184. *1941–1942 Report, supra* n. 1183, at 1.

Dean Roy Howes

left for various reasons: better positions, more money, and in part in response to the rise of totalitarianism and war in the South Pacific and in Europe.

These were anxious times. America was not yet out of its Great Depression. As the clouds of war were gathering, many foresaw that the ominous arms of "Europe's war" would reach out further and soon ensnare America. But the College of Law continued to operate. The departure of several highly qualified faculty members necessitated, of course, that the law school hire several replacements, and add them quickly. Allen responded and signed letters of appointment. The new brigade included Roy Frances Howes, William Grey Loehr, and J. Richard McClure, who all joined the faculty in the fall of 1941.[1185]

Like Lambert, Roy Howes came with top-notch credentials.[1186] A native New Yorker, Roy Howes had earned an A.B. from Clark College, an M.A. from Stanford University, an LL.B. from Cornell University, and an S.J.D. from New York University.[1187] In contrast, Richard McClure, a native Mississippian, received all his degrees—A.B., LL.B., and M.A.—from the University of Mississippi.[1188]

1185. Thomas F. Lambert, Jr., *Minutes of the Meeting of the Faculty of the College of Law* 1 (Sept. 17. 1941) (on file at Stetson U. Archives, DeLand, Fla.).

1186. *Many New Faculty Members Appointed, Three New Men on Law School Staff*, 7 Stetson Rptr. 4 (Sept. 17, 1941).

1187. *Id.*

1188. *Id.*

Finally, William Loehr, from Warsaw, Indiana, held both A.B. and LL.B. degrees from Indiana University and had done graduate work at Harvard Law School. Loehr also had real-world experience for two decades prior to joining Stetson's law faculty both as a judge and as a practicing lawyer.[1189]

Despite these new appointments, the Stetson law faculty continued to come and go. Allen appointed Vernon W. Turner, a recent Stetson law graduate, to the faculty. Meanwhile, several of the recently hired professors left. McClure resigned one semester after his appointment. He was replaced in the spring of 1942 by Colonel Frank W. Halliday, both a Dartmouth College and Stetson College of Law graduate who had served in the Judge Advocate's Fourth Army's Corps. Moreover, Halliday had taught constitutional law for five years at West Point.[1190] Allen's other 1942 appointment went to another recent Stetson law graduate—Neil S. Jackson.[1191]

Finally, in the fall of 1942, Erich Saxl was added to the faculty, who was touted as "a highly successful lawyer and judge" from Vienna, Austria. Saxl came to America in 1939 from his native country to escape Hitler and Nazism. He chose to study American law at Stetson's law school. Following two-and-one-half years of study, he graduated from the College of Law in 1942.[1192] Immediately, Allen asked Saxl to teach a course in international trade law, his area of expertise. Saxl co-authored what was described as "the standard work on Trade Regulation under the Austrian Republic."[1193]

Despite the churning of faculty, several Stetson professors were solid teachers who made contributions to the legal profession during this turbulent period. For example, Professor Brown was in charge of the Stetson Legal Aid Clinic that benefitted area indigents, though relatively few in number.[1194] Professor Wilson was active in the AALS Roundtable on labor law, Dean Raymond served on the AALS Council. Professors Brown and Fox spoke at the Tenth Judicial Circuit Institute of the Florida Bar Association.[1195] Professor Wilson di-

---

1189. *Id.*

1190. *Lambert Resigns Deanship for Board of Economic Warfare Job,* 7 Stetson Rptr. 1 (Feb. 4, 1942) [hereinafter *Lambert Resigns Deanship*]; *see also* Ltr. from R.F. Howes, Prof., Stetson U. College of L., to Dr. Bernard C. Gavit, Sec., Assn. of Am. L. Schs. 1 (July 11, 1942) (on file in the Stetson U. Archives, Deland, Fla.).

1191. *Lambert Resigns Deanship, supra* n. 1190, at 1.

1192. *John B. Stetson University Commencement 1942; Graduation Exercises* 1 (June 1, 1942) (program, on file in the Stetson U. Archives, Deland, Fla.).

1193. *Austrian Law Scholar Engaged as Lecturer at College of Law* 4, 8 Stetson Rptr. (Sept. 23, 1942).

1194. Duncan, *supra* n. 1014, at 9.

1195. *Id.* at 10.

rected the law club competitions,[1196] Professor Lenoir addressed the annual meeting of the Southern Political Science Association on the topic "Judicial Control of Administrative Agencies," and Professor Fox drafted proposed legislation for the Wisconsin Legislature.[1197] Meanwhile, Raymond was active, serving as chairman of the Legislative Committee of the Florida Probation Association, chairman of the State Committee on Public Affairs, and as a member of the State Crime Prevention Committee.[1198]

Raymond's practice was to "accept practically every invitation to speak in public" to promote the University and the College of Law. In one year alone, he spoke at public gatherings in cities including Jacksonville, Daytona, Tallahassee, Sanford, Miami, and at the Florida State Bar annual meeting in Bellair.[1199]

During his deanship, Raymond replaced head law librarian Oveda Cheatham with O. C. Taylor, thereby satisfying one of the complaints the AALS had raised with the College—the absence of a "qualified librarian whose principal activities are devoted to the development and maintenance of an effective library service."[1200] Moreover, Raymond raised the funds necessary to bring the law library's collection in line with AALS and ABA expectations. When Raymond became dean, the law library had approximately 10,000 volumes. By the time he left in 1941, the library's volume count had risen to "13,500 books by actual count."[1201] Raymond noted that the AALS inspector was "especially pleased with the manner in which Mrs. Taylor [was] supervising the law library."[1202]

In contrast with his predecessors, Raymond throughout his deanship held bi-weekly meetings with the faculty to discuss ways to improve the law school, not merely to consider "housekeeping" items such as student petitions.[1203] Serving as a role model for his colleagues, Raymond attended local, state, and national conferences. In addition, he urged his faculty colleagues to participate in national AALS meetings and to attend conferences and programs of the Florida State Bar Association.[1204] In November 1939, Raymond reported that five Col-

1196. *Wilson Will Change Law Club Procedure,* 4 Stetson Rptr. 3 (May 31, 1939).

1197. Aubrey Vincent, *Trial and Error,* 6 Stetson Rptr. 25 (Mar. 19, 1941).

1198. Duncan, *supra* n. 1014, at 9–10.

1199. *Id.* at 10.

1200. *Id.* at 7, 8.

1201. *Id.* at 7.

1202. *Id.*

1203. *Minutes of the Law Faculty, September 29, 1938,* at 1 (Sept. 29, 1938) (on file at Stetson U. Archives, DeLand, Fla.).

1204. *See e.g. Legal Language, supra* n. 1141. Dean Raymond and Dr. Wilson attended the Florida State Bar Association meeting where Wilson addressed the gathering on the subject, "Continuous Code Revision." *Id.*

lege of Law members attended the AALS annual meeting in Chicago.[1205] In his report to Allen, Raymond said that for two years in a row "the law staff is attending all county and state bar association meetings."[1206] One example: Raymond, along with Brown, Wilson, Lenoir, and Haslup were present at the Florida State Bar Association's 1938 annual meeting in Gainesville.[1207]

The law faculty's teaching and scholarship—characteristic during the Raymond period—on occasion was interrupted by some mirth. At a student-sponsored banquet, the faculty sang songs to the assembled law students. According to a story in *The Stetson Reporter*:

> A hilarious highlight of the evening was the "Law Professors Sextet," composed of professors Tribble, Wilson, Curtis, Lenoir, Brown, and Dean Raymond. They sang appropriate words to the tune of "Smiles." The whole group then joined in singing law school songs. Everyone was enthusiastic about the good time they had.[1208]

The banquet was the culmination of the student Law Clubs competitions for the 1938–1939 academic year. The losing Thomas Club put on the dinner for the winning Chapmans Club in celebration of the latter's victory in the competition, held at the University Commons.[1209]

g. Raymond's Importance to Law School

Raymond's accomplishments went beyond those noted above. For one thing, after becoming dean, he re-organized the law library following its receipt of "a valuable gift" from William Hull Ellis, chief justice of the Florida Supreme Court.[1210] For another, Raymond promoted mock appellate arguments among law students by encouraging them to form two "law clubs."[1211] The students did so and named their competing clubs the Chapman and the Thomas "law clubs."[1212] Near the end of each academic year, the students who

---

1205. Duncan, *supra* n. 1014, at 9.

1206. *Id.*

1207. *Law Professors Attend Groups,* 4 Stetson Rptr. 3 (Dec. 14, 1938).

1208. *Thomas Law Club Fetes Chapmans; Advisors Dekle, Kirkland to Speak; Law Profs. Sextet Is the Highlight,* 4 Stetson Rptr. 2 (May 3, 1939).

1209. *Id.*

1210. *College of Law Revamped: Law Library Has Many Changes* 4 Stetson Rptr. 8 (Sept. 21, 1938).

1211. *Law School Competitions Are Part of Re-Modeled School,* 4 Stetson Rptr. 8 (Sept. 21, 1938).

1212. *See e.g. Proceeding of the First Annual Law School Day, supra* n. 1110, at 5; *Proceedings of the Second Annual Law Day, supra* n. 1116, at 3.

had performed best during the school year were assigned to argue one last case for the championship, usually before one or more members of the Florida Supreme Court.[1213] By 1941, however, Raymond had done away with the Law Clubs and their annual competitions.[1214] He and the faculty believed that the system was deficient in that only the first-year winners were eligible to argue mock cases during second and third-year competitions. In contrast, a new program allowed all law students to continue to have opportunities to participate in moot court through their third year of law school.[1215] Professors Wilson and Lambert organized and administered the new program.[1216]

During his deanship, Raymond assisted and supported the Stetson student Legal Aid Clinic from its beginning in 1938. In 1940, however, Allen noted that though "the Legal Aid Clinic is doing good work ... there are not enough cases referred to it." He added: "This is no doubt due to the [small] size of the [DeLand] community."[1217] The following year, Allen commented that it was "unfortunate that more cases are not available to the Clinic, since it provides excellent practical training for the student."[1218]

An anonymous law student—who authored a weekly column called "Legal Language" in *The Stetson Reporter*—dryly opined that the purpose of the legal aid clinic was "to give legal assistance to indigent persons, which included me."[1219] But the issue of indigent legal aid became moot, and Stetson's Legal Aid Clinic closed its doors following the United States entry into World War II, not only due to the paucity of indigents eligible for legal services, but also due to the impact of the war on Stetson University's enrollment, especially at its College of Law.

As stated earlier, Paul Raymond resigned in the summer of 1941 to become an assistant Attorney General for the State of Florida.[1220] A few months following the Japanese bombing of Pearl Harbor, he left that post to enlist into the United States Navy, where he spent four years as an intelligence officer.[1221] His service included checking the security of Naval bases in the Caribbean,

---

1213. *See e.g Legal Bigs Here for Law School Day; State Supreme Court Justices Will Hear Law Club Finals,* 6 Stetson Rptr. 1 (Apr. 30, 1941).

1214. *New Argument Plan Provides Practice for Law Students; Unique System Takes Place of Law Club Competition,* 6 Stetson Rptr. 1 (Mar. 12, 1941).

1215. *Id.*

1216. *Id.*

1217. *1939–1940 Report, supra* n. 1082, at 9.

1218. *1940–1941 Report, supra* n. 1101, at 8.

1219. *Legal Language, supra* n. 1141, at 7.

1220. *See supra* nn. 1122–1123 and accompanying text.

1221. Duncan, *supra* n. 1014, at 1–7.

where the United States was losing a large number of ships to the German submarine fleet. Subsequently, he was sent to oversee the Operation Intelligence School in New York.[1222]

After the war, Raymond entered private law in Daytona Beach, establishing what was described as a highly successful law firm.[1223] Throughout his practice, he also actively participated in civic ventures. In 1976, Stetson University President Pope Duncan appointed Paul Raymond the General Counsel of Stetson University during Richard T. Dillon's deanship of the College of Law.[1224] Raymond stayed on as the University's General Counsel until he resigned in 1986.[1225]

In summarizing Raymond's significance as dean of the Stetson University College of Law, W. Gary Vause wrote in 2002:[1226]

> The three years that Mr. Raymond served as Dean of the College of Law (1938–1941) were critical years in the life of the law school. He arrived to find the school neglected by the University administration, underfunded, and in continuing jeopardy of losing its accreditation ... He later would describe his three years as Stetson's law dean as "the most hectic of my long life."[1227]

In later years, as general counsel of the University, Raymond's professional counsel in obtaining funds from the $7 million plus Rosa estate for the University and College of Law was noteworthy, a story related subsequently.[1228] Stetson University honored Paul Raymond with an honorary doctors of laws degree.[1229]

During the summer of 1999, Paul Raymond, then ninety-five years old and in failing health, himself recollected his years at the Stetson law school in an interview with editors of the *Stetson Law Review*.[1230] Three months later, on December 3, 1999, Raymond died. His remembrances were published posthumously in the Centennial Celebration Symposium of the *Stetson Law Review*.[1231] In response to the question of how he was able to raise academic standards at the College of Law, he stated:

1222. *Id.*

1223. *Id.*

1224. *Id.*

1225. *Id.*

1226. Vause, *History of Stetson, supra* n. 109, at 84.

1227. *Id.* (citing Ltr. from Paul E. Raymond to W. Gary Vause (July 24, 1999) (on file in Stetson U. College of L., Gulfport, Fla.)).

1228. *See infra* nn. 2660–2670 and accompanying text.

1229. Raymond, *supra* n. 1044, at 57–67.

1230. *Id.*

1231. *Id.* at 59.

> We employed younger, better educated, and more energetic professors. The library was updated. The curriculum was enriched. Class assignments were more rigid [as were] examinations and grading ... Students were soon impressed with the fact that registration in the law school was no longer an easy ticket to practice via the diploma privilege. [On the other hand], neither faculty nor funding were available for a law review.[1232]

Former University President and Chancellor Pope A. Duncan observed that Paul Raymond's "career brought him many honors," including a Stetson honorary doctor of laws degree that Raymond described as "one of the most significant" recognitions he had ever received.[1233] Throughout his three-and-one-half years as Dean of Stetson University College of Law, Raymond pushed the school forward in spite of severe financial restraints.[1234] Once, Dean Raymond wrote the Board of Trustees that "doubtless no other accredited law school in the United States is operating under as limited budget as this one."[1235]

6.3 World War II; Deans Lambert and Howes

a. Impact of the Coming War

After Dean Raymond left in the summer of 1941, President Allen appointed Thomas Lambert acting dean of Stetson College of Law. Only twenty-six years of age, Lambert was said to be the youngest law school dean in the country.[1236] Upon taking office, the youthful but talented Lambert confronted a serious problem—a precipitous decline in the law school's enrollment.[1237]

More than a year before the Japanese attack on Pearl Harbor, all males in the country between the ages of twenty-one and thirty-six were required to register with the United States Selective Service for possible induction into U.S. military service.[1238] In line with this mandate, male students of the Stetson College of Law went to the DeLand High School gymnasium on October 16, 1940, to register for the draft. There, the Volusia County Selective Service Board issued a draft

1232. *Id.* at 61–62.

1233. *Id.*

1234. Raymond, *1940–1941 Report, supra* n. 1101, at 9

1235. *Id.*

1236. *Garwood Appointed New Dean, supra* n. 1183, at 1.

1237. As to the University's decline in enrollment, see Bowen, *supra* n. 455, at 129.

1238. *Mandatory Registration Today at High School Gymnasium; Every Male Student between 21 and 36 Required to Sign Up*, 6 Stetson Rptr. 1 (Oct. 16, 1940).

card to each of the students.[1239] By this time, the Selective Service offered no exemptions except for health reasons or those whose jobs were related to war preparations.[1240] One month after the Japanese attack on Pearl Harbor, Dean Lambert and a large number of Stetson's law students, upon the request of the Volusia County Draft Board, went to Orlando to take the Army physical examination.[1241]

Three years earlier, in the spring of 1939, Stetson University's enrollment had reached an all-time high of 876 students.[1242] At the start of the 1939–1940 academic year, forty-five students enrolled in the College of Law.[1243] The following fall, the number fell to thirty-five.[1244] In the fall of 1941, the number of Stetson's law students was twenty-one.[1245] Then, after Pearl Harbor and the draft going into effect, only seventeen law students enrolled in the fall of 1942. Of the seventeen, only twelve were paying tuition.[1246] President Allen predicted that "practically all [of these seventeen] will be in the nation's service before next fall,"[1247] adding that the "university is faced with the probability of having no law students at all in September 1943 and for the duration of the war."[1248] He was right.

But not only did enrollment suffer as war approached, so did the academic standards of the College of Law. In the fall of 1941, with the approval of the newly appointed acting dean, Thomas Lambert, the University agreed to reduce the requirements for admission to the law school by lowering the three-year requirement for academic pre-law study to two years.[1249] Lambert hoped "the plan [might] bring more students."[1250] It didn't. Student enrollment continued to fall as faculty members continued to leave—both developments consequent to America's increasing support of the Allies' efforts to defeat Hitler's armies marching across Europe.

1239. *Id.*

1240. *Id.*

1241. Aubrey Vincent, *Trial and Error,* 7 Stetson Rptr. 7 (Jan. 21, 1942).

1242. *Enrollment Reaches All-Time High Here,* 5 Stetson Rptr. 1, (Feb. 15, 1939); *see also 1938–1939 Report, supra* n. 1166 (Feb. 16, 1939).

1243. *1938–1939 Report, supra* n. 1166, at 1.

1244. *1940–1941 Report, supra* n. 1101, at 1

1245. *1941–1942 Report, supra* n. 1183, at 1

1246. Vause, *Centennial History, supra* n. 595, at 100.

1247. W.S. Allen, Pres., Stetson U., *Report of the President of John B. Stetson University to the Board of Trustees 1942–1943,* at 4 (Feb. 18, 1943) (on file at Stetson U. Archives, DeLand, Fla.).

1248. *Id.* at 5.

1249. *1941–1942 Report, supra* 1183, at 4.

1250. *Id.*

The first to leave was the recently appointed law school acting dean, Thomas Lambert[1251] (successor to Paul Raymond, who a few months earlier had resigned to enter public service).[1252] Eleven months after being appointed acting dean, Lambert himself left Stetson to serve on the general counsel staff of the "Board of Economic Warfare" in Washington, D.C.[1253] Reportedly, Lambert entered the Columbia School of Military Government for a program that trained Army personnel to administer occupied enemy territories.[1254] The Navy subsequently commissioned Lambert an ensign; he became part of the Allied Normandy invasion of France.[1255] Following the war, Lambert served as trial counsel at the International Military Tribunal at Nuremberg, working with Justice Robert H. Jackson.[1256] There, he would encounter a future dean of the Stetson College of Law, Justice Harold Sebring.[1257] In later years, Thomas Lambert served as Executive Director of the American Trial Lawyers Association, headquartered in Cambridge, Massachusetts.[1258]

During this period, America's disgust with Hitler's military invasions in Europe intensified, as did its appetite for war. The same was true at Stetson's College of Law. In a 1940 column in the Stetson University student newspaper, a law student declared:

> As this column is being written, men are giving their lives for that intangible thing called "liberty." 3,000 miles across the Atlantic ... the Allies and the Germans are locked in deadly combat ... All of us echo President [Roosevelt's] words when he said, "Our ideal is peace ... We stand ready to give even our lives ... for our American liberties."[1259]

Also in 1940, Lambert had extemporaneously addressed law students on the patriotic duty of all citizens to defend sacred freedom from tyrants like Hitler and on the importance of fighting to defend liberty. A law student reacted to the exhortation as follows:

1251. Dean Thomas Lambert's eleven-month deanship is the shortest in the school's history.

1252. *See supra* n. 1182–1183 and accompanying text.

1253. *Lambert Resigns Deanship*, *supra* n. 1190, at 1.

1254. Vause, *Centennial History, supra* n. 595, at 98.

1255. *Id.*

1256. *Id.*

1257. *See infra* Chapter 9.

1258. Bruce Jacob, *Memorandum to File on History of the Law School, Re. Acting Dean Tom Lambert* 1 (unpublished ms. July 27, 1987) (on file in the Stetson U. College of L., Gulfport, Fla.).

1259. *Legal Language,* 5 Stetson Rptr. 4 (May 22, 1940).

> [Lambert] made one of the most inspiring talks ... that it has even been this writer's privilege to attend ... [The] theme should be sent to every law student, lawyer, and judge in the land.[1260]

At the April 1941 meeting of the Florida Bar Association in Tampa, its members "voted to do all in their power to defeat Hitlerism, and not to just defend this country from totalitarian ideologies."[1261] Dean Raymond reacted: "The vote was a remarkable indication for the temper of the times."[1262] That meeting held other significance for the College of Law. Besides Paul Raymond, two additional Stetson law school representatives were in attendance—Robert Milan of Jacksonville and G. Harris Drew, both alumni of the College of Law. At the 1941 meeting, Milan was elected President of the Florida Bar Association, and Drew, President of the Stetson University Alumni Association, met with the College of Law alumni who attended the bar convention.[1263] At the caucus, Drew asked three Stetson law alumni to work with the school in organizing a law school alumni association: Walter E. Smith of Orlando, D.C. Hull of DeLand, and Tom Henderson of Holly Hill.[1264]

Meanwhile, as America's entry into World War II drew nearer, the University found itself with less funds to operate, due to fewer gifts coming in and a large drop in tuition revenues because of a declining enrollment. Financial problems were even graver at the College of Law, where a higher percentage of its students (predominantly male and older) were either volunteering or being drafted into military service.

Aware of the drop in law school tuition, President Allen directed the College of Law to purchase no more books for the law library until further notice.[1265] Moreover, the minutes of faculty meetings from 1942 through April 1943 reveal that the law school's future of the school seemed bleak.[1266] The assessment was correct. It was acknowledged that "for several years, the Law School had been operating under a deficit."[1267] Then, ominously, the minutes added:

1260. Mac Ferguson, *Legal Language,* 6 Stetson Rptr. 4 (Oct. 30, 1940).

1261. Sylva Landress, *Bar Association Names R. Milan Pres. at Meet; New Head Is Stetson Alumnus; Stress Public Duty in Crisis,* 6 Stetson Rptr. 1 (Apr. 2, 1941).

1262. *Id.*

1263. *Id.*

1264. *Id.*

1265. Ltr. from W.S. Allen, Pres., to R.F. Howes, Dean, Stetson U. College of L. (Mar. 7, 1942) (on file in Stetson U. Archives, DeLand, Fla.).

1266. *Minutes of Special Meeting of Faculty of Stetson College of Law* 1 (Mar. 17, 1943) (on file in Stetson U. Archives, DeLand, Fla.) [hereinafter *Minutes of 1943 Meeting*].

1267. *Id.*

> With the lowering of draft age to 18 years, however, another problem had been raised, and it seems quite impossible to continue, irrespective of operating expenses, because of lack of students.[1268]

In its forty-third year of continuous operation, Stetson University College of Law was on the verge of closure.

b. Roy F. Howes—A Dean without Portfolio (1943–1946)

Despite the war, the entering first-year law class in the fall of 1942 was larger than it had been in previous years. Four women were among the thirteen entrants: Delphene Converston, Doris Hampton, Marion Merrill, and Betty Smith. A student-authored article described them as "four co-eds, the largest contingent of femininity ever to enter legal study in one year."[1269] Despite the comparative large number of first-year students, only four upper class students enrolled (while only twelve of the seventeen overall were paying tuition), and only five faculty members remained. In January of 1943, three of the students graduated.[1270] A crisis was at hand.

Believing no other option existed, in March, the Stetson University Board of Trustees directed the closing of the College of Law, effective at the end of the current semester, May 1943.[1271] A memorandum described the Board's action:

> A record is here made of the action of the Board of Trustees ... in voting to suspend classes in the College of Law during the academic year 1943–1944 ... A Special Committee of the Board was constituted, consisting of Judge O.K. Reaves, Judge I. Ollie Edmunds, and honorable Doyle E. Carlton to canvass the situation and determine when and where the College should resume regular sessions.[1272]

President Allen said that the closure was ordered by the Trustees, given "the prospect of a complete shortage of young men studying for law degrees."[1273] Allen added that everything would be done to retain the framework of the law

---

1268. *Id.*

1269. *College of Law Invaded by Girls; Four Co-Eds Register for Legal Study Here,* 8 Stetson Rptr. 3 (Oct. 7, 1943) (on file in Stetson U. Archives, DeLand, Fla.).

1270. *Dr. Howes Challenges Grads to Carry Out Stetson Ideals,* 8 Stetson Rptr. 1 (Feb. 3, 1943) (on file in Stetson U. Archives, DeLand, Fla.).

1271. Memo. from R.F. Howes, Dean, Stetson U. College of Law (Mar.1, 1943) (on file in Stetson U. Archives, DeLand, Fla.).

1272. *Id; see also* Lycan, *History of Stetson, supra* n. 109, at 303–304.

1273. *Law Classes Suspend for 43–44 Session, Board Calls Effects of War Disastrous to Enrollment,* 8 Stetson Rptr. 1 (Feb. 24, 1943) [hereinafter *Law Classes Suspend*].

school so that "the lawyers' training program will be resumed by Stetson just as soon as war conditions are relieved," so that "young men may again return."[1274]

Allen told Howes to inform the law faculty. At a March 17, 1943, meeting, the dean explained the combined deteriorating financial condition of the University and the lowering of the draft age to eighteen required the temporary closing of the College of Law.[1275] Howes floated the idea that the school might be able to remain open if it were to solicit law alumni to subsidize the College at the rate of $10,000 per year, but the faculty rejected the idea, given an earlier lack of alumni support to fund the library's purchase of needed books.[1276] At the meeting, faculty members expressed concern that if the law school were to be temporarily closed, it might result in its "permanent disbandment."[1277] Allen assured them that was not the University's intention.

After notifying the AALS of the law school's pending closure, Allen released the entire law faculty as of June 1943, with the exception Roy F. Howes, who a few months earlier had been named dean after Lambert's departure. Howes turned out to be a law dean without a law school.[1278]

Born in Troy, New York, in 1887, Roy Francis Howes was the son of a Baptist minister.[1279] He held five earned degrees, including an LL.B. from Stetson's College of Law (class of 1918). In addition, he had an A.B. degree from Clark College (1910), an A.M. in history from Stanford University (1912), a second LL.B. degree from Cornell Law School (1926), and a J.S.D. degree from New York University (1931).[1280] Prior to being appointed to the Stetson law faculty, Howes had taught on the faculties at five other colleges or universities: history at Whittier College, DePauw University, Bucknell University, and Alfred University; and law at the University of Miami Law School.[1281]

Howes in actuality served as the law school dean for only one year—1942–1943—though his name appears as dean until he was replaced by Lamuel A. Haslup in 1946. During the time the law school was closed, 1943–1946, Howes was assigned to teach constitutional law in the Stetson University's undergraduate college.[1282] When the law school reopened in the fall

1274. *Id.* at 3.

1275. *Minutes of 1943 Meeting, supra* n. 1266, at 1.

1276. *Id.*

1277. *Id.*

1278. *Law Classes Suspend, supra* n. 1273, at 3.

1279. *Stetson University Biographical and Professional Information* 1 (unpublished ms. Mar. 1, 1955) (on file in Stetson U. Archives, DeLand, Fla.).

1280. *Id.* at 2.

1281. *Id.*

1282. *Bowen, supra* n. 455, at 7.

of 1946, Allen appointed Haslup to be Howes' replacement, an event Howes had not anticipated.[1283] A Stetson alumnus, William Maness (class of 1948), who, while in law school, lived with Howes' family for a brief period, disclosed that Dean Howes was "hurt" by his not being reappointed dean.[1284] He was a proud man who had worked hard to improve the College of Law. His students, in any event, long remembered Roy Howes, who remained on the faculty into the 1950s.

1283. Ltr. from William H. Maness, Stetson U. College of L. alumnus, to W. Gary Vause, Dean, Stetson U. College of L. 1–2 (Apr. 5, 1999) (on file in Stetson U. College of L., Gulfport, Fla.).

1284. *Id.*

CHAPTER SEVEN

Survival at Naval Air Base Is Problematic—Dean Haslup and President Edmunds Tangle

7.1 L.A. Haslup's Deanship—The Naval Air Station (1946–1953)

a. Colonel Lemuel Allen Haslup

Lemuel Allen Haslup became the seventh dean of the Stetson College of Law upon its reopening following WWII.[1285] After earning a B.S. degree from the University of Maryland in 1917, he entered the United States Marine Corps, serving in Guam, China, and Nicaragua.[1286] While in the Corps, Haslup earned an LL.B. degree in 1934 from George Washington University.[1287] After he mustered out in 1938 with the rank of Captain, Haslup joined Stetson's law faculty as a lecturer in law for only one year,[1288] leaving to teach at the University of Miami Law School.[1289]

With the outbreak of WWII, Haslup re-enlisted in the Marine Corps and was assigned to the Navy Department's Judge Advocate General's staff, until he left the Navy in 1945 as a Lieutenant Colonel.[1290] After spending a short time on the George Washington law faculty, he returned to Stetson. In short order, President Allen appointed Haslup in the summer of 1946 to be dean of

1285. *Lemuel A. Haslup, Faculty File* (n.d.) (on file at Stetson U. Archives, DeLand, Fla.) [hereinafter *Haslup Faculty File*].

1286. *Id.*

1287. *Id.*

1288. *Id.*

1289. Gordis, *supra* n. 105, at 90–91.

1290. *Haslup Faculty File, supra* n. 1285.

the law school, a post he held for seven years until he died in 1953.[1291] At Stetson, students respected Dean Haslup; so did the faculty. He also was a productive scholar.[1292] His dealings with President Allen, however, were troublesome.[1293]

Haslup re-established the annual Law Day tradition that had been inaugurated by Dean Thomas Lambert ten years earlier, but that had ended with America's involvement in WWII.[1294] Haslup wrote the alumni:

> [Law Day] was planned as a culmination of a series of inter-club competitions between the two law clubs which are named for illustrious alumni—the Honorable Roy H. Chapman and the Honorable Elwyn Thomas, Justices of the Supreme Court of Florida.[1295]

The May 1950 Law Day was a special occasion. In addition to the traditional student arguments before members of the Florida Supreme Court, the occasion was used to commemorate the College of Law's fiftieth anniversary of its founding.[1296] Stetson law alumnus and Florida Supreme Court Justice Louis Strum, class of 1912 (subsequently appointed to the United States Court of Appeals), took part, as did Florida Supreme Court justices Harold Sebring and Roy Chapman, Stetson law class of 1909.[1297] Several prominent Stetson law school alumni also spoke, including C. Robert Burns, class of 1934, the banquet's toastmaster.[1298]

Beginning with 1951 Law Day, the College added a "Legal Institute," where noted attorneys lectured on specific areas of law practice.[1299] The Volusia County Bar Association cooperated with the law school in putting together these institutes (which represent the first continuing legal education programs

---

1291. Bowen, *supra* n. 455, at 7–8.

1292. *See e.g.* J. Blanford Taylor, *Press Release* (1950) (It announced that Haslup was the author of the "leading article in the University of Florida Law Review for the summer, 1950.... The title of the article is Divisible Divorce.").

1293. Haslups was especially frustrated because Allen would not allow him to make any significant decisions at the law school.

1294. Letter from L.A. Haslup to the Law Alumni of the John B. Stetson University 2 (Oct. 31, 1949) (on file at Stetson U. Archives, DeLand, Fla.) [hereinafter Haslup, *Alumni*].

1295. *Id.*

1296. *Stetson Law School Celebrating 50th Anniversary This Year; Justices Here,* 63 Stetson Reporter 2 (Apr. 28, 1950) [hereinafter *Celebrating 50th Anniversary*].

1297. Vause, *Centennial History, supra* n. 595, at 109–110.

1298. *Celebrating 50th Anniversary, supra* n. 1296, at 2.

1299. *Second Annual Legal Institute and Law Day Activities Are Planned for Tomorrow at 2 p.m.,* 65 Stetson Law. 1 (Apr. 25, 1952).

Supreme Court Justices Roy Chapman, E. Harris Drew and Elwyn Thomas, below

sponsored by Stetson).[1300] At the evening's "Barrister's Banquet," former Stetson law dean Paul Raymond spoke on the origins and purpose of the Stetson Law Day.[1301]

1300. *Id.*
1301. *Id.*

b. The College Reopens

As noted above, with the war's end, the Stetson Board of Trustees voted to reopen the College of Law. In announcing the decision, President Allen stated: "We are determined to have a law school of even greater distinction than past years."[1302] Allen, of course, was aware that veterans were entering America's colleges in record numbers, in part due to the G. I. Bill of Rights, a law enacted by Congress and signed by President Roosevelt.[1303]

The G.I. Bill's benefits for veterans impacted the enrollments of America's law schools. Nationally, law students swelled from 6,422 in the fall of 1944 to 51,015 in the fall of 1947.[1304] Proportionally, the increase in law students was greater at Stetson than the nation as a whole, going from fourteen in the spring of 1943 to 262 in the fall of 1948.[1305]

When the College of Law reopened in September 1946, sixty-four new students, mostly veterans, enrolled.[1306] The following fall, the entering class rose to an "all-time high" of 167,[1307] followed by an even larger enrollment in 1948.[1308] Haslup reported that the increase that year in the number of first-year students was the greatest in the school's history.[1309] In February 1947, Allen and Haslup, "in response to popular demand of an all-time record number of students," announced that the College of Law was inaugurating a summer session to accommodate the higher enrollment, largely WWII veterans who tended to be older and more mature than those who entered directly from college.[1310] The non-veterans had to have a minimum three-years of undergraduate education for admittance, but veterans could enter with two years, the third year being waived due to their "life experi-

1302. William Sims Allen, *Report of the President of John B. Stetson University to the Board of Trustees for the Year 1945–1946*, at 7 (Feb. 21, 1946) (on file at Stetson U. Archives, DeLand, Fla.).

1303. Pub. L. No. 78-346 (June 22, 1944). The enabling legislation was officially known as the Servicemen Readjustment Act of 1944.

1304. Stevens, *Law School*, *supra* n. 196, at 205.

1305. J. Ollie Edmunds, *Report of the John B. Stetson University, DeLand Florida, to the Trustees* app. 1 (Sept. 1, 1949).

1306. William S. Allen, *Report of the President of John B. Stetson to the Board of Trustees for the Year 1946–1947*, at 2 (Feb. 20, 1947) (on file at Stetson U. Archives, DeLand, Fla.).

1307. L.A. Haslup, *Letter to the Law Alumni of the John B. Stetson University* 1 (Oct. 25, 1947) (on file at Stetson U. Archives, DeLand, Fla.).

1308. *Law School Enrollment Reaches All-Time High*, 12 Stetson Rptr. 6 (Oct. 1, 1947).

1309. *Legal Language*, 12 Stetson Rptr. 8 (Oct. 22, 1947).

1310. *Stetson Law School Announces Plans for Summer Enrollment*, 11 Stetson Rptr. 6 (Feb. 14, 1947).

Law Students (Veterans of World War II) at Naval Barracks

ences."[1311] One problem arose, however: Many veterans were married and needed living accommodations, but locating sufficient housing became a difficult task. Many found they had to live in trailers or at great distances from campus.[1312]

Meanwhile, student parties flourished. Following the war, dancing—especially the "bebop"—became the rage. Frequently, law students held their dance parties at the former Air Station campus, though this conflicted with the "no dancing rule" of the Florida Baptist Convention, a rule that Stetson University had adopted. Learning that the prohibition was being ignored, Florida Baptists complained to Haslup and other University officials. Thereafter, the dean directed law students to hold dances off campus and with little public fanfare.[1313]

c. *Move to the Naval Air Base*

At the close of the WWII, the law school was ill prepared to accommodate the sudden increase in students. During the war, when the school was closed, the University converted Elizabeth Hall to general classrooms, though the law

1311. Vause, *Centennial History*, *supra* n. 595, at 105 (citing interview by Todd Richardson with Judge Uriel Blount, Jr. (Oct. 9, 1986)).

1312. *Id.*

1313. *Id.*

library stacks remained.[1314] Then, when the school reopened, the College of Law moved into the Science Building across from Elizabeth Hall.

About that time, President Allen hired Ray Jordan to be the law school's librarian. She accepted and remained in the post for eight years.[1315] Upon arriving in the fall of 1946, Jordan found the library collection in complete disarray. Moreover, the weight of the books were too heavy a load on the third floor of Elizabeth Hall, a condition Jordan described (in understatement) as "terrible."[1316]

The library sinking and the enrollment expanding, Allen scurried to find new facilities. The best he could find was a deactivated Naval Air Station three miles northeast of the University's campus.[1317] After leasing the deactivated base, in 1947 Allen announced that the College of Law would move to the Naval Station.[1318] Facilities included an administration building, gymnasium, and two buildings that had served as officers' living quarters.[1319]

In late May of 1947, the law school moved to its new quarters. Librarian Jordan describes how the library's books were transferred:

> I moved the library in orange crates, and I labeled them all. I had a system and I got out there and told them what shelving we needed and my system, you know, everything works except when it didn't. It would have been beautiful if the University had paid any attention and had built the shelves I told them we needed, but they wouldn't do it, so we filled up the shelves and I'd call them and told them we needed more shelves.[1320]

Inadequate shelving, however, was not the only problem. When the school opened in September, the classrooms had no chairs. Jordan remembered that one of the professors, Roy Howes, after informing his students that "we are holding class," told them to sit on the fire escape, while he lectured from the bottom rung.[1321]

Given the cramped conditions students encountered in Flagler Hall the previous year, they—and the faculty—welcomed the spacious environs of the

1314. *Id.* at 102.

1315. Interview by Ray Jordan with Bruce Jacob 2 (Oct. 21, 1985) (on file at Stetson U. College of Law, Gulfport, Fla.) [hereinafter *Jordan Interview*].

1316. *Id.* at 4; *see also* interview by Todd Richardson with Ray Jordan 3 (Oct. 9, 1986) (on file at Stetson U. College of Law, Gulfport, Fla.).

1317. Haslup, *Alumni*, *supra* n. 1294, at 1.

1318. *Law School to Move to Air Base,* 11 Stetson Rptr. 3 (May 26, 1947).

1319. *Id.*

1320. *Jordan Interview*, *supra* n. 1315, at 5.

1321. *Id.*

Naval Air Station, the furniture problem notwithstanding. The buildings, however, had not been well constructed, were not air conditioned, and needed major repairs.[1322] (The Naval Air base had been hurriedly built).

De-emphasizing these shortcomings, Haslup described the law school's new home as being adequate to accommodate an expanded library, larger classrooms, offices for teachers, a student lounge, and "fraternity rooms and a student-operated canteen and coffee shop."[1323] He added that the administration building was large enough for an "equipped moot court room suitable for both a lecture hall and a meeting place for the law clubs."[1324]

The base's former "Bachelor's Officers Quarters" (B.O.Q.s) served as dormitories for law students.[1325] Meanwhile, busses "shuttled students between the base and the DeLand campus."[1326] Married students, for the most part, lived off campus, especially in a trailer park near the base.[1327] One married veteran who resided in the trailer park was Judge Lloyd Hughes, class of 1949, who later served as a circuit judge in Lake County, Illinois, for twenty-seven years.[1328] His widow, Ann Hughes-Johnson, described their living arrangements: "The trailers were stationary and had two sides that folded out into a living room and bedroom, very small and bad," adding that "washroom facilities were outside the trailers in a common area."[1329]

Though married student housing was inadequate, the Naval Air Station campus was worse, according to an alumnus of the period, Judge Melvin Orfinger (later appointed a 4th District Court of Appeal Judge by Florida Governor Rubin Askew).[1330] In an interview, Judge Orfinger said that the best word to describe the law school Naval Base facilities was "primitive."[1331] It turned out that the ABA agreed. Haslup and a new University president would have no choice but to confront the problem.

Following the death of President Allen in 1947, the Stetson Board of Trustees appointed J. Ollie Edmunds, a graduate of Stetson's law school, as the

1322. *Id.* at 6.

1323. Haslup, *Alumni*, *supra* n. 1294, at 1.

1324. *Id.*

1325. Bowen, *supra* n. 455, at 8.

1326. *Id.*

1327. Memo. from Ann Hughes-Johnson to Assoc. Dean W. Gary Vause 1 (Mar. 30, 1999) (on file in Stetson U. College of L., Gulfport, Fla.).

1328. *Id.* at 2.

1329. *Id.*

1330. Interview by Dotti Bressi and Darlene Kelly with Judge Melvin Orfinger 1, 2 (n.d.) (on file at Stetson U. College of L., Gulfport, Fla.) [hereinafter Orfinger Interview].

1331. *Id.* at 16.

President J. Ollie Edmunds

University's president.[1332] One of Edmunds' first acts was asking Haslup to report on the conditions of the school's Naval Air Station campus.[1333] To prepare a response, Haslup appointed Professor Charles Henderson to head a committee to assess the facilities and to make recommendations for improvements. The committee's report listed seven areas in need of repairs.[1334] Henderson indicated that law students could perform several of the tasks over the summer.[1335] The report catalogued thirty-four "rotten places" in the weather boarding, "rotten" boards [in] the steps, "dilapidated" wooden awnings, and a building with a "decidedly unattractive appearance that could use a coat of paint."[1336]

Haslup mentioned an additional concern: the need for "adequate lighting" for both the library and an auxiliary reading room.[1337] He wrote the president: "If it is the intention of the University to continue the operation of the law school, I suggest sealing the ... entire second floor of this building.[1338] Ac-

1332. *See supra* Ch. 8.

1333. *See* Ltr. from Dean L.A. Haslup to President J. Ollie Edmunds (Aug. 4, 1948) (on file at Stetson U. Archives, DeLand, Fla.) [hereinafter *Haslup Letter to Edmunds*].

1334. *See* Ltr. from Charles Tom Henderson to Dean L.A. Haslup 1–2 (Aug. 2, 1948) (on file at Stetson U. Archives, DeLand, Fla.).

1335. *Id.* at 1.

1336. *Id.*

1337. *Haslup Letter to Edmunds, supra* n. 1333.

1338. *Id.*

cording to alumni accounts of the period, the building was cold in the winter, hot in the summer, and let rain in year round.[1339]

Despite these problems, the school's Naval base campus initially pleased the ABA and the AALS. Bernard C. Gavit, Executive Director of the AALS, wrote Dean Haslup in January 1947 that the accreditation committee "regards with favor the ... acquisition of the Naval Training Station [sic] building for law school use. Clearly this building will provide adequate facilities for the school."[1340] But not for long. When the ABA/AALS inspectors came back in 1951, they assessed the law school's facilities to be woefully inadequate, putting Stetson College of Law into another accreditation crisis.[1341] The story follows.

Cecil Bailey (later to become one of the initial members of the Stetson College of Law's Board of Overseers)[1342] told Dean Bruce Jacob in a 1986 interview that when he looked back at the school's move to the former Naval Air Station, it seemed to him as if that school was "put out to pasture in the wayward; I think that was a major tragedy for the law school."[1343] Bailey added:

> The law school almost faded out of the picture entirely while it was there, and it was touch and go for a long time as to whether it would survive or whether it wouldn't.... It was stuck out there on the highway to Daytona Beach.... Its attendance [in the late 1940s and early 1950s] dwindled and its faculty had a rough time of it.... I am surprised they were able to keep any faculty at all.[1344]

Bailey's observations were accurate.

d. Haslup's Faculty

When the law school reopened in 1946, the full-time faculty consisted of professors Roy F. Howes, Charles Tom Henderson, William F. Schulz and Dean Haslup.[1345] Howes remained on the faculty after serving as the titular dean dur-

---

1339. *See Fiftieth Anniversary of the Stetson University College of Law Move to Gulfport, Florida, Banquet Dinner* (Sept. 2004) (videotapes) (on file at the Stetson U. College of L., Gulfport, Fla.).

1340. Ltr. from Bernard C. Gavit to Dean L.A. Haslup (Jan. 17, 1947) (on file in Stetson U. Archives, Deland, Fla.); *see also* Ltr. from Dean H.A. Haslup to Dean Bernard C. Gavit 1–2 (Feb. 7, 1947) (on file in Stetson U. Archives, Deland, Fla.).

1341. *See infra* nn. 1526–1555 and accompanying text.

1342. Interview by Bruce Jacob with Cecil Bailey 17 (Jan. 13, 1986) (on file at Stetson U. College of L., Gulfport, Fla.).

1343. *Id.*

1344. *Id.* at 8.

1345. Haslup, *Alumni*, *supra* n. 1294, at 1.

ing the war. Schulz, who had earned both B.S. and LL.B. degrees from Stetson,[1346] was described as a "versatile Stetson alumnus."[1347] Well, not in education—Schulz remained on the Stetson law faculty for one year.[1348]

With Haslup's input, in 1946 Allen added three part-time instructors. One was Leonard A. Curtis, who was ninety-one years old, and who had taught full time on the Stetson faculty from 1937 until the school closed in 1943.[1349] Other part-time teachers were Arthus W. Mitchell and Neill S. Jackson.[1350] Meanwhile, the law librarian, Ray Jordan, continued in her position.[1351] New blood came in the fall of 1947, when Earl Casper Arnold and J. William Norman joined the full-time faculty. Arnold was a retired law professor and dean emeritus of the Vanderbilt University School of Law.[1352] He served on the Executive Committee of the AALS. Norman received an LL.B. degree from the University of Florida and an LL.M. degree from Harvard Law School, and had served in the Navy.[1353]

During this period, Stetson faculty were paid little. Haslup's salary was $4,000, and the professors received about $3,000 each, while the one woman, Librarian Jordan, received $1,800.[1354] At the same time, the annual budget for the library was $2,500 and the law school's total budget for the 1946–1947 year totaled $20,000.[1355] She was the daughter of a DeLand lawyer, and was very popular with both students and faculty. The *Barrister's Bar*, a column authored by a law student in the weekly *Stetson Reporter*, once was dedicated to Jordan. Law student John Mattingly wrote, "For the students and the faculty of the Law School, I wish to extend a bouquet of thanks to the charming and gracious Law Librarian—Ray Jordan."[1356]

During Haslup's deanship—just like before WWII—faculty members came and left frequently. Consider that following one year at Stetson, William Schulz left and soon joined the faculty at the University of Pittsburgh. Meanwhile, Charles Henderson left to become Assistant Attorney General of Florida, in charge of statutory revision; James Norman resigned to practice law in West

1346. Gordis, *supra* n. 105 at 67.

1347. *Id.*

1348. *Id.*

1349. Vause, *Centennial History*, *supra* n. 595, at 106.

1350. Haslup, *Alumni*, *supra* n. 1294, at 1.

1351. *Id.*

1352. *Id.*

1353. *Id.*

1354. W.S. Allen, *Report of the John B. Stetson University to the Board of Trustees* app. (Feb. 7, 1927) (on file at Stetson U. College of L., Gulfport, Fla.).

1355. *Id.*

1356. John Mattingly, *Barrister's Bar*, 67 Stetson Rptr. (n.p.) (Nov. 6, 1953).

Palm Beach; and Earl Arnold, the former Vanderbilt law dean, returned to Tennessee for health reasons.[1357] Their replacements were Alvin E. Evans, Dean Emeritus of the University of Kentucky Law School; Frank H. Randall, Professor Emeritus, also of the University of Kentucky; and Ben F. Johnson, Jr., a visitor during the summer of 1948, on leave from Emory Law School.[1358] In addition to the visitors, new faculty members during the 1946–1950 period included: Harvey J. Jernigan; William R. Arthur, who had retired from teaching; Clifford W. Crandall, a law professor at the University of Florida Law School for thirty-six years; James R. Richardson, LL.B., University of Kentucky and a former assistant state attorney general; and William J. Lemmon, LL.B., University of Florida, LL.M., Duke University.[1359] Two other professors hired in the early 1950s were John Thomas Pearson and Harvey Jernigan.[1360] Pearson was a graduate of the University of Kansas (LL.B., 1916) and George Washington University (LL.M., 1934), and had worked several years in the office of the Solicitor General of the United States, then as an officer in the Judge Advocate General's Department of the United States Army during WWII.[1361] Jernigan was an undergraduate of Stetson University who had received his LL.B. degree from the University of Florida.[1362]

e. Professor Roy Howes

Alumni of the College of Law from 1947 through 1956 seem to recall one professor more than any other: Roy Howes.[1363] Many describe him as the most demanding and most serious of their professors. It is the demanding characteristic most of his former students remember best.

Alumnus Cliff B. Gosney, Jr., class of 1952, comments that Roy Howes was his "toughest professor."[1364] Though admiring his intellect, Gosney notes that Howes was a "tough grader" who "did not particularly care for me," adding

---

1357. Haslup, *Alumni, supra* n. 1294, at 1.

1358. *Id.*

1359. *Id.*

1360. *Pearson Continues on Law Faculty,* 66 Stetson Rptr. 5 (Aug. 29, 1952).

1361. *Id.*

1362. *Id.*

1363. The statement is based on two sets of evidence: first, the number of oral interviews (later transcribed) of alumni of that period; and second, remarks made by several alumni present at the fiftieth anniversary banquet of the College of Law moving to Gulfport, Florida, in September 2004, a video tape of which is available at Stetson College of Law.

1364. Ltr. from Cliff B. Gosney, Jr., to W. Gary Vause 1 (Apr. 2, 1999) (on file at Stetson U. College of L., Gulfport, Fla.) [hereinafter *Gosney Letter*].

that Howes could not visualize me being a lawyer."[1365] With candor, insight, and a bit of humor, Gosney continues:

> [Howes'] favorites usually sat in the front two rows and, unfortunately, one of his few fallacies was to show grade preferences to these individuals. Ironically, those of us [who sat in the back], generally speaking, were more successful than [Howes'] front-row favorites.... I know of at least "two most likely to succeed" [students] that ultimately ended up at Rayford Prison, not as wardens, but as inmates."[1366]

Then, there was a problem regarding examinations. Dean Emeritus Bruce Jacob believes that Howes "took many of his questions from old exams."[1367] But a more serious problem arose. Jacob writes:

> The old exams were floating around and could be bought. A small group of us went to him and told him that his old exams were [available to students] and to please use new questions for Constitutional Law.... Some students had as many as fourteen old exams and had every question ahead of time. I refused to buy the old exams and I got a B [grade].[1368]

Jacob, however, adds there were students who did not share his negative opinion of Howes.[1369] Actually, there were many. One was a fellow Stetson dean emeritus, Richard Dillon. Dillon describes Howes as one of "the strongest teachers" of the period.[1370] He set very high standards and demanded students meet them.[1371] Stetson law alumnus Judge Melvin Orfinger, class of 1948, agrees that Howes was tough in grading students, but adds opinions about Howes changed. Orfinger explains, "Most of us came to realize how good he was *after* we graduated.[1372] He had done more for us," Judge Orfinger concluded, "than what we had originally thought."[1373]

1365. *Id.*

1366. *Id.* at 1, 2.

1367. Memo. from Bruce Jacob to Michael Swygert 1 (Feb. 10, 2004) (on file at Stetson U. College of L., Gulfport, Fla.).

1368. *Id.*

1369. *Id.*

1370. W. Gary Vause, *Milestones in Stetson Law School History—The Dillon Years*, 30 Stetson Law. 22, 23 (Fall 1990) [hereinafter Vause, *Milestones*].

1371. *Id.* at 23.

1372. *Orfinger Interview*, *supra* n. 1330, at 11 (emphasis added).

1373. *Id.* A well-remembered Stetson law professor during the 1970s through the 1990s—Calvin Kuenzel—is similarly described by many of his former students as their best professor from whom they learned the most, but rarely, however, did any of them think so while taking his required contracts course. The story of the Professor Kuenzel—de-

Other students who admired Howes include alumnus John Wood (who, prior to law school, had been a prisoner of war in Japan).[1374] He describes Howes as "extraordinary," noting that "he was a great constitutional scholar."[1375] Wood recalls that because Howes was considered "a bit liberal" in teaching constitutional law, the law school removed him from instructing that course.[1376] (Howes, Wood explains, looked at the Constitution "like judges look at it now, as an elastic document.")[1377] Wood was disappointed when he learned Howes was not listed as the instructor in constitutional law. Wood approached Howes and asked: "[I]s there some reason you don't want to teach constitutional law?" Howes replied: "[T]hey won't let me."

A classmate of John Wood, Elsie Merit (later Elsie M. O'Laughlin), on the other hand, recalls Howes in a far different manner. She describes Howes as her "least favorite professor," adding "after taking his contracts course, I didn't sign up for any of his other classes."[1378] Merit believes that Howes didn't like women in law school.[1379] Asked by Haslup to work part-time for Howes, Merit initially refused, but finally agreed after Howes consented to her demand that she did not "take constitutional law" from him. She only then worked for him, despite serious reservations.[1380]

On the basis of alumni recollections, it seems that professor Roy Howes was a complex, demanding, rigorous, and thought-provoking professor—one that former students do not forget. Once he shared with students a humorous and creative piece,[1381] a poem authored by two famous law professors—William Prosser and Karl Llewellyn.[1382]

---

scribed "as a legend in his own time"—is set out in a subsequent chapter of this history. *See infra* Ch. 10.

1374. *See infra* nn. 1456–1473 and accompanying text.

1375. Interview by Carrie Lambeth with John Wood 6 (July 18, 2001) (on file at Stetson U. College of L., Gulfport, Fla.).

1376. *Id.*

1377. *Id.*

1378. Interview by Maria Guerrero, Student, with Elsie M. O'Laughlin 7 (Nov. 2, 2001) [hereinafter *O'Laughlin Interview*].

1379. *Id.* at 3.

1380. *Id.* at 7.

1381. *Oral History Interview by Michael Swygert with Richard Dillon* (Dec. 29, 2004) (on file at Stetson U. College of L., Gulfport, Fla.).

1382. William Prosser & Karl Llewellyn, *Non-Negotiable You* (reprinted as *Embrace Me, Non-Negotiable You*, Prelude 2 (Sept. 30, 1977)).

NON-NEGOTIABLE YOU
I study law
With the proper awe.
  I'm an earnest sort of lad;
But I've got a flair
For a lady fair
  Who's no way to be had;
She won't be hugged and she won't be kissed
  Though I've tried to be empiric;
So I sing to the girl who CAN resist
  This legalistic lyric:
You're the note
That's got my goat,
  Non-Negotiable you
You've got class
That I can't pass,
  Non-Negotiable you.
You've the only form that I endorse.
I've not used fraud and I've not used force,
And I want to be your holder in due course,
  Cause you're due!
You're the Jill
That fills the bill,
  Non-Negotiable you.
You've set the date
And payment's late,
  Non-Negotiable you.
Another slip wants me for a taker,
Her sum is certain, but I'd still forsake her
To be your own accommodation maker,
  Non-Negotiable you.[1383]

f. Students—Active and Inventive

Following the war, returning veterans contributed to student activities in varied and inventive ways. They tried to open a bookstore, proposed establishing a student trust fund, requested that students evaluate their professors, started a new law fraternity, established a student Honor Court, re-instituted

1383. *Id.*

the "law clubs," and, of course, held dances off campus, out of sight and mind of members of the Florida Baptist Convention.[1384]

(1) Student Entrepreneurs

In the spring of 1948, members of the Stetson Student Bar Association (SBA) put together a plan whereby it would "own and operate a law school bookstore."[1385] The purpose was to aid students "obtain text and casebooks at a reasonable cost that would allow the SBA to use the profits to purchase second-hand law books for resale."[1386] By July 1948, the SBA had collected 146 signatures on a petition they sent to Dean Haslup in which they asked to go forward with their bookstore entrepreneurship,[1387] but it did not happen. Despite Haslup's endorsement, the day after President Edmunds received the petition, he rejected it in a one sentence memorandum to Haslup.[1388] Not one to easily give up, Haslup sent a return letter to "Judge Edmunds" (the manner in which Haslup addressed the president) stating:[1389]

> [Your memorandum] leaves me in the position of the fabled mule whose owner attempted to teach [the animal] to live without eating. Unfortunately, as soon as the educational process was complete the mule died.[1390]

Haslup was determined that something had to be done about the problem of expensive law books students could ill afford. He proposed that the school operate a bookstore under the management of librarian Ray Jordan, one that would attempt to buy books from publishers at discounted prices.[1391] Edmunds eventually gave in, but insisted that the control of the bookstore be under the University's administration, not the law school's.[1392]

1384. It was the policy of the Florida Baptist Convention that student dances could not be held on Stetson's campus, a policy the University followed.

1385. Ltr. from One-Hundred Forty-Six Signed Student-Petitioners to Dean L.A. Haslup 1 (July 20, 1948) (one-page petition, three pages of signatures on file at Stetson U. Archives, DeLand, Fla.).

1386. *Id.*

1387. *Id.*

1388. Memo. from J. Ollie Edmunds to Dean L.A. Haslup (July 23, 1948) (on file at Stetson U. Archives, DeLand, Fla.).

1389. Ltr. from Dean L.A. Haslup to President J. Ollie Edmunds (July 30, 1948) (on file at Stetson U. Archives, DeLand, Fla.).

1390. *Id.* at 1.

1391. *Id.* at 1–2.

1392. *See* Memo. from J. Ollie Edmunds to Dean Haslup (Aug. 1948) (on file at Stetson U. Archives, DeLand, Fla.).

(2) Student Honor Court

The first evidence of the law school instituting a student honor program appears in the 1948 John B. Stetson University Bulletin.[1393] Under the heading, "The Honor System," the bulletin describes the students' responsibilities:

> The students of the College of Law ... being determined to uphold a high standard of professional ethics, have adopted an Honor System as an integral part of their student government. The essence of the Honor System is that every student is accepted as a person of honesty and thoughtfulness, and that each student has as an individual responsibility for self discipline, self-respect and the building of deep appreciation for professional ethics.[1394]

It was clear that every law student was required to learn and follow the dictates of the "Honor Code," one which demanded honesty, yet was based on the student's voluntary compliance.[1395] The catalog entry continues:

> After having of his own free will enrolled himself as a member of the student body and the Honor System, he is thereafter bound by the provisions of the Honor Code ... *Examinations are conducted* without surveillance of the instructors or monitors. Each student signs a pledge that he has neither given nor received aid in the course of his examination.[1396]

The Honor Code also made a student's failure to report another student's violation itself an infraction.[1397] An "Honor Court," composed entirely of students, administered the Code. The Court held hearings and made recommendations for appropriate discipline that might include a violator's "involuntary withdrawal from school."[1398] Any student brought before the Honor Court had "the right to be heard, present evidence, and be represented by counsel."[1399] In addition, the findings of the Court were "reviewable by the law school administration."[1400]

1393. *College of Law, The Honor System,* 48 John B. Stetson U. Bull. (Ann. Catalogue) 120–121 (Apr. 1948) (on file at Stetson U. Archives, DeLand, Fla.) [hereinafter *Honor System*].

1394. *Id.* at 120.

1395. *Id.*

1396. *Id.* (emphasis added).

1397. *Id.*

1398. *Id.* at 121.

1399. *Id.*

1400. *Id.*

Though several references to the Honor Court have been found, no specific document explaining how or when it began has been located. Faculty minutes and reports in the University student newspaper—*The Stetson Reporter*—often contained references to the school's Honor Court.[1401] A story in the *DeLand Sun News* reported that the Stetson Honor Court was "responsible for administration of the honor system in Stetson's College of Law," but added that the Honor Court "is not a busy court."[1402] Nonetheless, the *DeLand Sun News* commented that election to the Honor Court "is considered a high honor."[1403] And it was. Stetson's Honor Court consisted of seven associate justices, two elected from each of the three classes, and a chief justice from the third-year class.[1404] A description of the honor system in the student newspaper stated:

> As all of the law students know ... we are governed more or less by a code of ethics, insofar as our examinations are concerned, and these ethics or standard of conduct are enforced by the honor court. In other words, the law students are governed by their fellow law students. Offenses that the honor court are mainly concerned about are cheating during exams and encroachments on the rights of the other students, which is what cheating amounts to.[1405]

A Stetson law student wanted to add a new offense to the list of Code violations: "ear-banging."[1406] Ear-banging was described as a student's "excessive use and abuse of the privilege of academic inquiry after classes" to the "detriment of their fellow students, [that may] amount to as nearly as great an offense as cheating during exams."[1407]

Early officers of the Stetson College of Law Honor Court included Chief Justice Perry Penland and Associate Justices Rondo Sullivan, James Darby, Irving Felder, Glen Martin, Lloyd Mosley, and Andrew Kay.[1408] Throughout the Haslup deanship, the student Honor Court continued to function.[1409]

1401. *See e.g.* Fred Hope, *Law Briefs,* 13 Stetson Rptr. (n.p.) (Oct. 28, 1949).

1402. *Honor Court,* DeLand Sun News 8 (Nov. 11, 1949) (on file at Stetson U. Archives, DeLand, Fla.).

1403. *Id.*

1404. *Id.*

1405. Hope, *Law Briefs, supra* n. 1401, at 8.

1406. *Id.*

1407. *Id.*

1408. *Id.; see also Honor System, supra* n. 1393, at 8.

1409. John Mattingly, *Barrister's Bar,* 67 Stetson Rptr. (Oct. 16, 1953).

(3) The Faculty Considers a Student Law Review

Haslup was aware that many law schools sponsored student-edited law reviews, a phenomena that had its origin in 1875 at the Albany Law School of Union University.[1410] The Stetson faculty and students also had heard about student law reviews at other schools.[1411] Haslup understood the benefits of a student-edited journal, including its value for developing legal research and "creative writing [skills] in the field of law."[1412] He also knew that "law review men are given priority in employment after graduation."[1413]

In spite of these benefits, Haslup declared "it would be unwise for our law school to undertake the publication of a law review."[1414] In defending his decision, he noted that the field was already "overcrowded" with reviews, and that "an attempted entry at this late date ... is a venture attended by considerable hazard."[1415] In lieu of publishing a law review, the dean suggested that a faculty committee assist students in writing a series of legal "handbooks."[1416] However, no student-written handbooks have been found.

(4) Student Concerns and Activities

With nearly 300 law students enrolled in 1948, many soon to graduate, Haslup considered setting up a placement service, but this too did not happen because no one knew how to go about doing it, and because, in any event, funds were not available to hire a placement director.[1417] Regarding a matter of less significance, however, students got one thing they had asked for. The University gave permission to the law school to start a coffee shop on the premises.[1418]

Meanwhile, traditional student activities continued at full throttle. Post-war Stetson law students, as had their predecessors, found practice court especially to their liking. Though not immediately re-established when the school reopened in 1946, practice court trials were soon taking place by the end of the

1410. Swygert & Bruce, *supra* n. 467, at 763–778.

1411. Haslup, *Alumni, supra* n. 1294.

1412. *Id.*

1413. *Id.*

1414. *Id.*

1415. *Id.*

1416. *Id.*

1417. L.A. Haslup, *Annual Report of the College of Law for the Academic Year 1948–49,* at 3 (1949) (on file at Stetson U. Archives, DeLand, Fla.) [hereinafter Haslup, *1948–1949 Report*].

1418. *Id.*

1940s.[1419] Visitors would assist. In one instance, a DeLand attorney lectured to a Practice Court class on trial procedures.[1420] In commenting on the lecture, a Stetson student noted that without knowledge of the practical aspects of the law, "the young lawyer would starve before he won a case."[1421]

Until the college relocated in 1954, practice court trials had been held in the Volusia County Courtroom.[1422] There, in 1953, students participated in seven mock cases, including two homicide trials. These were conducted "under normal conditions, including witnesses, jury, and judge," and the public was invited to attend.[1423] One of the more interesting homicide cases was the subject of a story in the student newspaper:

> Approximately 350 or 400 persons filed into [Volusia] County Court last Monday to hear the mock murder trial of Florida versus James Sheldon, accused of first degree murder in the practice trial of Stetson law school. The spectators went "wild" with applause when the jury after deliberating 20 minutes handed down a verdict of "Not guilty."[1424]

Students also continued the tradition of participating in appellate competitions. At an argument held in March 1954, only months prior to the law school's move to Gulfport, for the first time a woman presided as "justice" over the "Supreme Court of Stetson University."[1425] Her name was Carmelita B. Tartari, Esquire, and she practiced law in DeLand.[1426] At that time in the school's history, appellate arguments, unlike student trials, were conducted in a special room on the base of the Naval Air Station.[1427]

In addition to taking part in academic endeavors outside the classroom, students were involved in several social and quasi-professional organizations. Haslup especially encouraged students to join the SBA (even though dues were a "steep" $1.50 per year).[1428] The SBA often invited guest speakers to address its members, as frequently as once per week.[1429] The SBA activities in the early

---

1419. Interview by Michael I. Swygert with Judge Melvin Orfinger Interview (n.d.) (circa 2000) (17 pgs. transcribed, on filed at Stetson U. College of L., Gulfport, Fla).

1420. John Mattingly, *Barrister's Bar,* 67 Stetson Rptr. 1 (Oct. 23, 1953).

1421. *Id.*

1422. *Law School Sets Seven Moot Trials,* 67 Stetson Rptr. 7 (Oct. 30, 1953).

1423. *Id.*

1424. *"Not Guilty" Is Verdict in Law School Trial,* 65 Stetson Law. 3 (Nov. 16, 1951).

1425. *Woman Presides over Law Court,* 67 Stetson Rptr. 7 (Mar. 19, 1954).

1426. *Id.*

1427. *Id.*

1428. Haslup, *1948–1949 Annual Report, supra* n. 1417, at 3.

1429. *Id.*

1950s were led by the organization's presidents, including Jerry Arnowitt and Bill Singleton.[1430]

In the fall of 1947, a chapter of Phi Delta Phi was established at the law school. It was known as the Cardozo Inn.[1431] Its original officers were Donald Butler, magister; William Dicous, secretary; Robert Freeman, treasurer; and Arthur Spalding, historian.[1432] Meanwhile, Phi Alpha Delta's David J. Brewer Chapter instituted a "Legal Forum," bringing guests who talked about the practice of law.[1433] Topics and speakers included "Starting the Practice of Law" (James H. Sweeney), and "The Working of the Municipal Court" (Judge Lewis Schott).[1434] In 1949, Phi Alpha Delta's members traveled to Tallahassee to attend five appellate arguments before the Florida Supreme Court. A fraternity member explained: "[I]f we know something about the practical side of jurisprudence as distinguished from the scholastic, we can better serve our client."[1435] In Tallahassee, the students met with Attorney General Richard Ervin, Assistant Attorney General Murray Sams, Jr., (a Stetson law graduate), and former Stetson law dean Lewis Tribble (who was then counsel for the State of Florida Comptroller).[1436]

During the early years of Haslup's deanship, a third law fraternity at the school—the Fuller Warren Chapter of Delta Theta Phi—was started.[1437] The dean announced the installation of the new fraternity in a 1948 letter to alumni, noting that "three of the leading national legal fraternities now have active organizations at the school."[1438] In May 1950, the young Delta Theta Phi fraternity held its first "Founders Day Banquet" at the Sheraton Plaza Hotel in Daytona Beach.[1439] Besides fraternities, law students participated in the University-wide Student Christian Association and Westminster Fellowship.[1440] One law student, Ernie Breed, served in 1951 as president of the Student Christian Association.[1441]

1430. Hope, *supra* n. 1401, at 8.

1431. *See* 12 Stetson Rptr. 1, 5 (Jan. 30, 1948).

1432. *Id.*

1433. *Legal Forum*, 11 Stetson Rptr. 1, 7 (Apr. 1, 1947).

1434. *Id.; see also* 12 Stetson Rptr. 1, 6 (Oct. 29, 1947).

1435. Ltr from Joseph A. Peel, Jr., President of PAD, to J. Ollie Edmunds, Pres. Stetson U. 1 (Feb. 2, 1949) (on file at Stetson U. Archives, DeLand, Fla.).

1436. *Phi Alpha Delta Legal Frat Tours Tallahassee; Hears Court Arguments,* 13 Stetson Rptr. 2 (May 19, 1950).

1437. Haslup, *1948–1949 Report, supra* n. 1417, at 4.

1438. Haslup, *Alumni, supra* n. 1294.

1439. *Delta Theta Phi Installs Officers; Leeds New Dean,* 13 Stetson Rptr. 2 (May 19, 1950).

1440. Jerry Fine, *The Barrister's Bar,* 65 Stetson Rptr. 2 (Dec. 7, 1951).

1441. *Id.*

Contrary to the situation in existence before Lambert became dean,[1442] by the end of the 1940s, the law school's academic attrition rate had dramatically changed, evidencing a more rigorous and demanding academic program. In the fall of 1949, fifty-three out of 216 Stetson law students were on academic probation. At the same time, only nineteen were on either the dean's list (six) or on honor roll (thirteen).[1443] Many students voluntarily or involuntarily withdrew on account of their academic deficiencies. One student wrote in *The Stetson Reporter* that, though some faculty believed law school grades were too high, the number of students on probation and not returning proved that everyone in law school [was] not getting high grades.[1444]

(5) Admission Standards; Grading; Teacher Evaluations

In 1949, the Council on Legal Education[1445] of the ABA Section on Legal Education urged that the recommended three years of pre-law studies for admission to ABA-approved schools become mandatory, starting with the 1952–1953 academic year.[1446] Dean Haslup informed the faculty of the stricter ABA requirement.[1447] Prior to WWII, the three-year prerequisite had been in effect at Stetson, but the ABA lowered it to two years after the war's onset.[1448] In light of the ABA requirement, the Stetson faculty reestablished the three-year pre-law condition to begin in the fall of 1950.[1449]

Stetson's faculty imposed an even higher entrance requirement to take effect in the fall of 1952. To be admitted, an applicant had to have an undergraduate degree,[1450] the exceptions limited to veterans who could still be admitted with three-year's undergraduate work, and Stetson's undergraduate students who had completed three years of college under what was called Stetson's "three-three program."[1451]

1442. Fred Hope, *Law Briefs,* 13 Stetson Rptr. 4 (Apr. 21, 1950).

1443. *Id.*

1444. *Id.*

1445. Stevens, *Law School, supra* n. 196, at 114.

1446. *Id.*

1447. *Minutes of the Law Faculty Meeting* (Oct. 5, 1949) (on file at Stetson U. Archives, DeLand, Fla.).

1448. In recognition of the huge impact World War II would have on law school enrollments, it rolled back the three-year, pre-law requirement in the hope law schools could stay open.

1449. *Law Briefs* 13 Stetson Rptr. 4 (Apr. 14, 1950).

1450. *Minutes of the Law Faculty Meeting* (Oct. 25, 1950) (on file at Stetson U. Archives, DeLand, Fla.).

1451. *Id.*

During the period when the law school was implementing higher admission standards, Stetson's law students began to agitate the dean and faculty to be permitted "to grade the instructors."[1452] Students were increasingly becoming unhappy with "D" and lower grades and demanded to evaluate their teachers' performance.[1453] Fred Hope, who wrote a weekly column in *The Stetson Reporter* titled "Legal Briefs," opined on the other side of the issue, writing that "the grading of instructors would result in chaos," adding that "every instructor is presumed to be capable until proven otherwise."[1454] This student commentator was not alone in opposing student evaluations; not surprisingly, he was joined by the majority of the faculty. Haslup noted the students' teacher-evaluation proposal at a faculty meeting. The minutes reflect the faculty consensus:

> The matter of calling upon students to participate in the rating of instructors ... was raised. The consensus of opinion seems to have been that no useful purpose would be achieved.... If it is necessary to have student evaluations of instructors, a questionnaire should be mailed only to such students as have already graduated.[1455]

The students' request to evaluate their professors, though unsuccessful, is significant, as it reflected the beginning of what might be called "student activism" at the College. Also throw in the students' desire to own and manage a bookstore, their institution of an honor system, and their expressing concerns about grades, it is apparent that the post-war generation of students was different than its predecessors. The cause in part had to relate to WWII, and that generation's participation in it. The war changed the world and it changed the young people who fought in it. Veterans came back to school more mature, independent, and, to a degree, more cynical than were previous generations of law students, even those who had survived WWI and the Great Depression.

(6) Alumnus John Wood: Prisoner of War

Despite the poor physical facilities at the former Naval Air Station, the Stetson students who earned their law degrees in an environment something less than the Ritz excelled in the legal profession. One graduate, John Wood, became a highly respected attorney in Sarasota. But then, he had attained hero-

1452. Fred Hope, *Legal Briefs*, 13 Stetson Lawyer 5 (Jan. 20, 1950).

1453. *Id.*

1454. *Id.*

1455. *Minutes Faculty Meeting* (Jan. 25, 1950) (on file at Stetson U. Archives, DeLand, Fla.).

status even before he entered Stetson law school.[1456] Wood was born in 1920 in Panama, Central America, where his father spent ten years helping to build the Panama Canal.[1457] He was attending St. Mary College in Shreveport, Louisiana, when World War II broke out. After joining the Army, he was sent to the Philippines in 1941. Wood explains what happened:

> The Japanese took the Philippiness. The same day they bombed Pearl Harbor, they bombed me [as part of U.S. forces] in Manilla. We fought [them] for four months, and then we had to surrender.[1458]

There is much more to the story. As told by the Public Broadcast Service in the "Douglas MacArthur" segment of its *American Experience* series, during the summer of 1941 imperial Japan launched invasions of its Pacific neighbors.[1459] America sent thousands of troops to the Philippines—one was John Wood—to help protect the archipelago from possible Japanese attack. Then, like Pearl Harbor, Japan bombed the Philippine Islands on December 7 and 8, 1941.[1460] In doing so, they destroyed America's fleet of B-17 aircraft sitting on the ground at Clark Field, and commenced their invasion of the Philippine Islands.[1461]

With air, artillery, and heavy armored support, Japanese troops advanced on 70,000 American and Filipino defenders who had no air, and little artillery support.[1462] General Douglas MacArthur commanded the American forces, which had to draw back in the face of the overpowering Japanese military advantage. The Japanese "quickly shredded MacArthur's army."[1463] Pursuant to a pre-invasion scenario called "War Plan Orange," American and Filipino forces retreated into the Bataan peninsula.[1464] Soon, they were cut off by Japanese forces. As their food rations ran out and health deteriorated, their chances of warding off the Japanese evaporated.

MacArthur had by then left for Australia, and General Jonathan Wainwright had taken over the Philippine command. Wainright's field commander was

---

1456. Interview by Carrie Lambeth with John Wood, 1 (July 19, 2001) (on file at Stetson U. College of L., Gulfport, Fla.) [hereinafter *Wood Interview*].

1457. *Id.*

1458. *Id.* at 4.

1459. Pub. Broad. Serv., WGBH Educational Foundation 1999, *The American Experience: MacArthur, the Siege of Bataan* 1, www.pbs.org/wgbh/amex/macarthur/sfeature/bataan_siege.html (accessed Jan. 14, 2004).

1460. *Id.*

1461. *Id.*

1462. *Id.*

1463. *Id.*

1464. *Id.*

General Edward King.[1465] Seeing no alternative, on April 9, 1942, General King signed surrender papers ending the Japanese siege. It was "the largest American army in history to surrender."[1466] The worst was still to come.

The terror began as American and Filipino prisoners of war were "harshly beaten and killed for the slightest or no reason at all."[1467] The day after the surrender—April 10—the Japanese army forced thousands of POWs to march sixty miles from Mariveles to Camp O'Donnell through a malaria-infested jungle under scorching heat and humidity, and with little water and no food.[1468] Those POWs who fell behind "were executed."[1469] The forced movement of POWs became known as the "Bataan Death March." Thousands of captured soldiers and civilians died along the way.[1470] Among the survivors of the ordeal was John Wood. He tells of his POW experience:

> I was on the [Bataan Death March] as a prisoner of war. Then I served forty-two months as a Japanese prisoner of war and wound up in Japan.... [I was sent to] work camps [and they] were very brutal. They had me working in a copper mine in Japan for forty-two months.... I was in the Japanese prison camp for a long time.... General Jonathan Wainwright took over command when MacArthur left.... He became a prisoner along with me and others.[1471]

Though General Wainwright and Wood never met in the Japanese prison camps, they did meet years later, when Wood graduated from Stetson University College of Law. As Wood explains, "When I graduated [in 1951] from law school, [President] J. Ollie Edmunds had General Wainwright down as a principal speaker and [Wainwright] gave me my diploma, and there is a picture to prove it!"[1472] Indeed! Besides General Wainwright and graduate John Wood, the other people in the photograph are Stetson University President J. Ollie Edmunds, College of Law Dean Tom Lambert, and the Philippine Ambassador to the United States.

1465. Pub. Broad. Serv., *Capture and Death March* 1, www.pbs.org/wgbh/amex/macarthur/sfeature/bataan_capture.html (accessed Jan. 14, 2005).

1466. *Id.*

1467. *Bataan Death March* 3 (accessible at http://history.acusd.edu/gen/st/~ehimchak/death_march.html).

1468. *Id.*

1469. *Id.*

1470. *History: The Bataan Memorial Death March* 1, www.bataanmarch.com/history.htm (accessed on Jan. 14, 2005).

1471. *Wood Interview, supra* n. 1456, at 4, 5, 9.

1472. *Id.* at 9.

President J. Ollie Edmunds and War Hero John Wood

Following graduation from Stetson's College of Law, Wood practiced law in Sarasota with his law partner and Stetson law school classmate, John Scheb. Both became judges, Scheb serving on the Florida Second Circuit Court of Appeal (and, after retirement, an appointed Distinguished Professorial Lecturer at the law school), and Wood serving as a Sarasota Municipal Judge.[1473]

Judge John Wood

1473. *Id.* at 8.

(7) Other Alumni from the Lambert and Haslup Years

According to a story written by James A. Jones in *The Bradenton Herald*, a Stetson law graduate—Janna Tucker—was one of the first women in Florida to enter the armed services.[1474] Shortly after the United States organized the Women's Army Auxiliary Corps (WAAC) in May 1942, Janna Tucker enlisted as a private in WAAC (later changed to WAC, Women's Army Corps).[1475] Following basic training at Fort Des Moines, Iowa, the Army trained Tucker to operate and repair radios.[1476] Reporter Jones notes that in 1945 Tucker moved from the WAC to the Air Force, where she used her legal knowledge acquired at Stetson as a staff member of the Judge Advocate General's Corps. She retired from the Air Force in 1964 after nearly twenty-two years of active duty.[1477]

While Tucker was never in an actual fighting situation, another notable student—Jack Graves—reportedly was, although his was a different kind of fighting. It is said that Graves was a prizefighter before entering Stetson law school in the fall of 1949.[1478] *The Stetson Reporter* columnist Fred Hope, a law student, wrote that Graves had "a vicious right hook."[1479] Hope added:

> Realizing his potentialities, I became his assistant manager under his regular manager [law student] Bill Whitaker. Bill and I have gotten together and mapped out a plan of conquest for our protege.... We plan on challenging [student] Ray Robinson, the welter king.[1480]

Another interesting student of the era was Elsie Merit.[1481] One of three women in the first law class to enter after the war, Merit married fellow law student "Red" O'Laughlin, and both received LL.B. degrees in 1948.[1482] In marrying Red, she knew that she had made a good choice, pointing out: "I wasn't going to marry a dumb bunny that couldn't get through law school."[1483] Despite Merit's marriage, Stetson's dean of women demanded that she live in a women's dormitory. Bristling, Merit told the dean: "If I have to live in the dor-

---

1474. James A. Jones, Jr., *Former WAC Ties for Most Time in Military*, Bradenton Herald Local Sec. 1 (Aug. 17, 2003).

1475. *Id.*

1476. *Id.*

1477. *Id.*

1478. Fred Hope, *Law Briefs*, 63 Stetson Rptr. 4 (Feb. 3, 1950).

1479. *Id.*

1480. *Id.*

1481. *See supra* nn. 1378–1381 and accompanying text.

1482. *O'Laughlin Interview*, *supra* n. 1378, at 4.

1483. *Id.*

mitory, then I don't go to law school. It's as simple as that."[1484] She remained in law school.[1485] During the period Merit attended Stetson law school, the University dean of women was in charge of all women law students. The University catalog stated:

> The Dean of Women is the advisor and administrative officer for matters pertaining to the life and social activities of women students in *all* departments of the University [including the Law school].... All women students must have their living arrangements approved by her.[1486]

Then there is the story of law student Cliff Gosney, class of 1952, who with hyperbola claimed he saved the law school from burning down.[1487] During the period when the school was at the Naval Air Station, one evening Gosney walked into the two-story, all wooden, Naval officers' barracks that had been converted to apartments.[1488] Once inside, Gosney walked into the men's washroom; there he discovered a fire in a large trash can.[1489] Realizing the building was in jeopardy, Gosney frantically extinguished the flames. He commented years later, "I saved the building from burning down.... A few minutes later, the whole building would have gone up in smoke."[1490]

While there are far too many other successful and prominent law graduates from the 1938 through 1953 period to name all, a few included Robert Milan, a Jacksonville attorney and former president of the Florida Bar Association; Florida District Court of Appeals Judge T. Frank Hobson; Congressman and later Florida Supreme Court Justice Fred Karl; Florida Senators Douglas Senstrom and Thomas Cobb; Assistant Florida Attorney General Ralph Odom; Florida State Comptroller Fred Dickinson; prosecutor and later litigator Murray Sams, Jr., (the son of another prominent Stetson law graduate, Murray Sams, Sr., class of 1910); and scores of judges, including Fred Scheb, William

1484. *Id.* at 11.

1485. *Id.* In her 2001 interview, Merit-O'Laughlin discussed that when she practiced law, legal fees were modest compared to today's. She said that back then, a lawyer would charge $50 for a divorce. Today, she said, she knew someone who had obtained an uncontested divorce for $1,500, but then had another problem—"she stabbed her boyfriend." Merit then said that the lawyer has charged $7,000 for the divorce. "Can you believe that?" She did not say how much the stabbing defense cost. *Id.*

1486. *College of Law*, 49 John B. Stetson U. Bull. 2, 119 (Apr. 1949) (emphasis added).

1487. *See supra* nn. 1364–1366 and accompanying text.

1488. Gosney Letter, *supra* n. 1364, at 2.

1489. *Id.*

1490. *Id.*

Blunt, John Wood, V. Williams, Frank Hobson, Sr. (a jurist on the Florida Supreme Court, and his son, Frank Hopson, Jr., a member of the Second District Court of Appeals), and Melvin Orfinger (who sat on both Florida's Fourth and, later, Fifth District Court of Appeals).[1491]

g. President J. Ollie Edmunds and Dean L.A. Haslup

(1) The Judge from Jacksonville

In September 1947, in ill health, William Sims Allen resigned as the president of Stetson University.[1492] Allen and his wife retired in San Antonio, Texas.[1493] On June 1, 1951, the admired third president of the University and strong supporter of the College of Law, died. Historian Lycan appraised Allen as "a great man" who pushed the University forward.[1494]

Allen's successor was a member of the University's Board of Trustees, a successful Jacksonville judge, attorney, and religious leader, John "J." Ollie Edmunds, Sr.[1495] Edmunds was the first graduate of both Stetson University and the College of Law to become president of the University. By the end of his career, Edmunds held four degrees from Stetson: B.A. (1925), M.A. (1927), LL.B (1928), and LL.D. (hon.) (1943).[1496]

In 1931, Governor Doyle Carlton appointed Edmunds—then twenty-seven—County Judge for Duval County.[1497] He served thirteen years in that post.[1498] During this period, Edmunds was president of the Stetson Alumni Association for three years and, in 1934, became a member of the Stetson University Board of Trustees.[1499] After serving three consecutive terms as Duval County Judge, Edmunds retired from the bench in 1944 to seek the Democratic nomination in Florida to be a United States Senator in an attempt to unseat the incumbent, Claude Pepper. Edmunds lost his bid and returned to practicing law in Jacksonville.[1500]

1491. The above list was compiled from several sources located in the College of Law files.

1492. Ltr. from W.S. Allen to the John B. Stetson U. Bd. of Trustees 1, (Sept. 19, 1947) (on file at Stetson U. Archives, DeLand, Fla.); *see also* Lycan, *supra* n. 109, at 317–318).

1493. Lycan, *History of Stetson, supra* n. 109, at 318.

1494. *Id.*

1495. Gordis, *supra* n. 105, at 116.

1496. *Id.; see also* Lycan, *History of Stetson, supra* n. 109, at 330.

1497. Lycan, *History of Stetson, supra* n. 109, at 330.

1498. *Id.*

1499. *Id.*

1500. *Id.* at 330–31.

According to Cecil Bailey, a fellow Jacksonville lawyer and close friend of Edmunds, the judge was involved in the probate and administration of the wealthy duPont family estate.[1501] Bailey speculated that Stetson's trustees selected Edmunds to be president of the University because of Edmund's "contacts with men and organizations that might furnish some much needed funds for the University." If so, his connection with the duPont estate could be very strategic.[1502] Bailey substantiates his claim by noting the Stetson trustees overlooked the fact that Edmunds was not a Baptist minister, the first time a Stetson University president had not been.[1503]

Whatever the case may be, J. Ollie Edmunds was elected by the Stetson Board of Trustees to be the University's fourth president. Historian Gordis wrote that Edmund's election was "met with unanimous enthusiasm."[1504] Following his 1947 appointment, Edmunds took nine months to close his law practice before assuming his new duties in January 1948.[1505] During the interim, University Dean Harry C. Greenwood served as acting president,[1506] one whom historian Olga Bowen described as "not outstanding."[1507]

Then, on January 1, 1948, J. Ollie Edmunds assumed full responsibilities of overseeing the first private university and law school in Florida. He remained in office for nineteen years, retiring in 1967.[1508] During that period, Edmunds worked with three deans of the College of Law—Lemuel Haslup, Charles Hilkey, and Harold Sebring, not always in harmonious fashion.

(2) Tensions Rise between Edmunds and Haslup

Less than four months after Edmunds became president, he and Dean Haslup were in sharp disagreement regarding the College of Law. In a joint letter to Edmunds and Haslup, University Dean William Hugh McEniry, Jr.

1501. Interview by Bruce Jacob with Cecil Bailey 9 (Jan. 13, 1986).

1502. *Id.*

1503. *Id.*

1504. Gordis, *supra* n. 105, at 116.

1505. Bowen, *supra* n. 455, at 139.

1506. Lycan, *History of Stetson, supra* n. 109, at 325.

1507. Bowen, *supra* n. 455, at 140. Greenwood eventually retired from the University in 1958. For the next two years, he researched and authored a book titled *Stetson University and the Florida Baptists.* It chronicled the history of the troubled relationship between the Florida Baptist Convention and the University from 1885 though 1960. The Southern Baptist Historical Society subsequently published the book after it had been edited by Stetson professor Edward A. Jones, Jr. (who was secretary-treasurer of the Society). *Id.* at 141.

1508. Lycan, *History of Stetson, supra* n. 109, at 416.

recommended that the two meet "to discuss the points of friction arising between the College of Law and the rest of the University."[1509] It was said that the law school and the University disagreed over whether the law school could maintain its own applications and records rather than their being processed and held in the University registrar's office; whether the rules for academic probation pertaining to law students should be separate from those for applying to undergraduate students; whether law student rules of conduct should be administered by the law school rather than by the University; and whether *"the autonomy of the Law School, within the larger framework of the University, should be recognized and promoted as far as can be done without removing the Law School from the final control of the University."*[1510] This last issue was the most significant, and embodied all other disagreements between the University's central administration and the College of Law's dean and faculty.

McEniry's letter made it clear that the law school was urging major changes to the existing relationship between itself and the University.[1511] Haslup and McEniry suggested to Edmunds that "a conference be held at your convenience to consider" the issues.[1512] Nothing came of it, however, and Haslup's hopes were dashed when Edmunds did not budge in expanding the autonomy of the College of Law.

One example of Edmunds' pattern of rejecting Haslup's requests concerned admissions. With the backing of the law faculty, Haslup requested that law school admissions no longer be within the total province of the University Committee on Admissions.[1513] Earlier, the University-wide Committee of Administration notified Edmunds that a majority of its members believed University policy required the committee to continue the practice whereby all applicants to the University, including to the law school, must be processed through the University Admissions Committee, which has "*the final decision concerning any applicant.*"[1514] Edmunds agreed.

Not at all pleased, Haslup sent an eight-page typed letter to Edmunds expressing not only displeasure with the president's decision, but also pointing out that the standards of admission applied by the University differed in ma-

---

1509. Ltr. from Wm. Hugh McEniry, Jr., and Lemuel A. Haslup to Dr. J. Ollie Edmunds and Dr. H.C. Garwood (Apr. 27, 1948) (on file at Stetson U. Archives, DeLand, Fla.).

1510. *Id.* at 1, 2 (emphasis added).

1511. *Id.*

1512. *Id.*

1513. Ltr. from Dean L.A. Haslup to Pres. J. Ollie Edmunds (Nov. 19, 1949) [hereinafter *1949 Haslup Letter*].

1514. Memo. from Comm. on Admiss. to J. Ollie Edmunds (Sept. 27, 1949) (emphasis added).

terial respects from those required by the College of Law.[1515] Haslup's anxiety with Edmunds came crisply through the spaces between his words when he quoted a resolution the law school faculty had unanimously passed ten years earlier, one that declared that the faculty of the College of Law may "adopt rules governing the College of Law although varying from rules governing the College of Liberal Arts."[1516] Haslup caustically added, "It was with this in mind that I accepted the deanship of the Stetson Law School at the invitation of President Allen."[1517]

In an effort to make Edmunds aware of relevant ABA and AALS policies, Haslup described the agencies' standards and rules requiring a high degree of law school autonomy in the governance of its internal operation. Haslup emphasized that under ABA and AALS policies, "the primary responsibility for the admissions policies of law schools should be vested in the dean of the law school and the law faculty."[1518] Haslup concluded his letter to Edmunds by adding:

> I consider it absolutely essential to the welfare of the Law School, and therefore necessary to the general welfare of the University as a whole, that matters pertaining to [admission and] graduation of lawyers be left to the discretion of the Law Faculty.[1519]

Despite Haslup's arguments and emotive plea, Edmunds quickly and curtly again denied the dean's entreaties. In his characteristic brief style in an unsigned memorandum, the president wrote:

> I have carefully read your [Haslup's] request for reconsideration of my approval of the decision of the Committee on Admissions, dated September 27, 1949, but I am still of the opinion that the Committee has stated a wise one.[1520]

Similar exchanges between Edmunds and Haslup appear in the College of Law records. The exchanges follow a pattern: Haslup makes requests; then Edmunds rejects them with little or no explanation. Another example concerns faculty salaries. After Edmunds had rejected Haslup's recommendation that

1515. *1949 Haslup Letter*, *supra* n. 1513, at 1.

1516. *Id.*

1517. *Id.*

1518. *Id.* at 3.

1519. *Id.* at 8.

1520. Memo. from J. Ollie Edmunds to Dean Haslup (Nov. 30, 1949) [hereinafter *Edmunds-Haslup Memo*] (on file at Stetson U. archives, DeLand, Fla.).

the law faculty salaries had to be raised, Haslup sent the president two surveys of law school compensation that revealed that "the differential in salaries paid to law teachers here and in other schools materially affects the results of our efforts to keep qualified teachers here."[1521] Edmunds still did not budge. Salaries stayed put, but several faculty did not.

The pattern was the same regarding many less significant issues. The dean wanted the school to adopt its own academic calendar, one that would be in line with ABA requirements on length of semesters, and thus be accommodative to the College of Law. Edmunds said no, stating "that the many complications that would be involved in having two separate [calendars], I believe, make the adoption [of Haslup's] proposal inadvisable."[1522] Another of Haslup's requests rejected by Edmunds was one that sought permission for the school to adopt a semester plan rather than be under the University's quarter system. Haslup wrote Edmunds, "The opinion of the faculty of the College of Law is unanimous that the semester system should be adopted."[1523] The president replied, "I do not believe that it would be for the best interest of the University."[1524] Edmunds' unwillingness to change the status quo at the law school only changed after the ABA and AALS inspected the College of Law in 1951. The ABA inspector found a near complete absence of law school autonomy in managing its affairs, among other deficiencies.[1525] The details follow.

h. A Critical 1951 ABA and AALS Inspection

The earlier 1947 ABA/AALS inspection of Stetson's law school caused the AALS to put the school on notice that because its dilapidated former Naval Air Station barracks were unsuitable—unless the situation was remedied within a reasonable time—the College of Law would be suspended from membership in the AALS.[1526] The seriousness of the situation should not have been ignored, yet it was—for four years. At that point, the law school's con-

1521. L.A. Haslup, *Supplemental Annual Report of the College of Law for the Academic Year 1948–1949 to the President of the University* (Jan. 15, 1949) (on file at Stetson U. Archives, DeLand, Fla.).

1522. *Id.*

1523. Ltr. from L.A. Haslup to President John B. Stetson (Oct. 17, 1949) (on file at Stetson U. Archives, DeLand, Fla.).

1524. *Edmunds-Haslup Memo, supra* n. 1520.

1525. *See infra* nn. 1546–1550 and accompanying text.

1526. *See supra* nn. 1340–1344 and accompanying text; *see also* Vause, *Centennial History, supra* n. 595, at 112.

tinued existence came into jeopardy, this time after the ABA in 1951 issued a highly critical report on the problems of the law school.[1527]

Conducting an on-site inspection assessment of the school was the Advisor to the ABA Section on Legal Education, Dean John G. Hervey.[1528] After inspecting the school's Naval Air Station facilities, Hervey found that the physical plant could not be regarded as "even reasonably adequate."[1529] The classrooms and other facilities were "not attractive, needs repainting badly on the outside, and a good cleaning on the inside," adding that "the lighting was poor." He described the furnishings as "a rag-tag collection of odds and ends, neither comfortable nor serviceable in some cases."[1530]

Turning to the library, Hervey found it to be "no more than adequate," commenting that the ceiling was so low, that noise from the upstairs classrooms could be heard by students studying in the library below.[1531] But there was an even more serious problem—law books and walls had been severely damaged by leaks from heavy rains.[1532] Alumnus David Kadyk, class of 1951, recalls that during storms, "wind-driven rain penetrated [into the interior] between the outer wood framing of the building."[1533] Then there was the lack of sufficient housing facilities for students, and the absence of a frequent bus service from DeLand to the campus, thus requiring students to hitchhike.[1534]

Professor Hervey also addressed the school's finances. Though finding that the school's revenues exceeded expenditures, he pointedly noted that the University had been siphoning off up to fifty percent of the school's positive cash flow each year, resulting in "inadequate financial support of the school."[1535]

The report included the following table:

1527. *See* John G. Hervey, *Inspection Report: John B. Stetson University College of Law* (May 7, 1951) (copy on file at Stetson U. College of L., Gulfport, Fla.) [hereinafter Hervey, *1951 Inspection Report*].

1528. J. Ollie Edmunds, *The President's Report to the Trustees, Stetson University, DeLand, Florida* 14 (Feb. 19, 1953) [hereinafter Edmunds, *1953 Report*].

1529. Hervey, *1951 Inspection Report, supra* n. 1527, at 2.

1530. *Id.*

1531. *Id.* at 3.

1532. *Id.*

1533. Ltr. from David J. Kadyk to Dean W. Gary Vause 1 (Apr. 6, 1999) (on file at Stetson U. College of L., Gulfport, Fla.).

1534. *Id.*

1535. *Id.* at 4.

Stetson Law School—Income and Expenditures (1947–1950)

Year	Income	Expenditures
1947–48	$80,224.72	$39,853.99
1948–49	$107,640.00	$60,864.96
1949–50	$112,624.23	$59,296.56

Hervey was displeased by the figures. After talking with both Edmunds and Haslup, the ABA inspector concluded that the law school had no control over its budget. Haslup had not even been given copies of the school's budget, nor was he aware of how much money the University allocated to the law library or paid to the law faculty members.[1536] In his conversation with Edmunds, Hervey candidly expressed his dismay over the school's budgetary problems.[1537] He later wrote, "Suffice it to say that the budget arrangement is unusual and the excess of income over expenditures *smacks of exploitation of the law school to support other divisions of the University*."[1538] He added: "no relief was promised" by Edmunds.

The report then turned to issues of autonomy. Hervey wondered why law school admission requirements were fixed by the University and not by the law school.[1539] He noted this arrangement "caused difficulties and irritations,"[1540] given that the dean of the University's College of Liberal Arts was effectively in charge.[1541] Hervey further underscored the law school's lack of autonomy (and the University's contempt for the ABA approval process) by citing a letter from Edmunds to the school's law librarian, instructing her (Ray Jordan) "to spend only such amount as is necessary to retain accreditation."[1542] If this were not enough, Hervey discovered that law students' dismissals and re-admissions were determined by a University committee of which only Dean Haslup represented the law school. Moreover, whenever Haslup disagreed with other University committee members, Edmunds charged the law school dean with being "non-cooperative."[1543]

Other deficiencies related to the law faculty. Not only were their salaries uniformly low in Hervey's opinion, their average age was too high, taking note,

1536. *Id.*
1537. Vause, *Centennial History, supra* n. 595, at 115.
1538. Hervey, *1951 Inspection Report, supra* n. 1527, at 4 (emphasis added.).
1539. *Id.*
1540. *Id.* at 5.
1541. *Id.*
1542. *Id.*
1543. *Id.* at 7.

for example, that Professor Crandall was seventy-seven, and Professor Curtis eighty-four. To compound the situation, faculty morale was low, as evidenced by the high turnover of professors.[1544] At the time of Hervey's visit, two of the full-time professors had accepted offers to go to other schools, while other faculty members had said that they would leave Stetson if they could find other teaching positions.[1545]

Dean Hervey found the pervasive and serious problems at the Stetson College of Law to be "inexcusable," and he placed the responsibility squarely on President Edmunds.[1546] Noting that the president himself was a law school graduate and had a successful law practice in Jacksonville before assuming the presidency of Stetson University, Hervey noted the irony:

> He should know what is required for a law school. Nevertheless, the law school has been treated as a step child, as it were, and President Edmunds seems to have resented the repeated requests of the law Dean for adequate funds, budget, autonomy, etc., to such extent that a change is imminent. The situation is serious and the *future of the school hangs in balance without any doubt.*[1547]

Hervey even expressed suspicions over the president's intentions:

> President Edmunds only recently suggested to the Dean of the Law School in writing that the University Dean of Administration, who is really an administrative vice president, (commonly referred to in many institutions as a "hatchet man") administered the school this summer on the excuse that the law Dean's health is not good.[1548]

Given his grave assessment of the future of the Stetson College of Law, Hervey recommended that the Council on Legal Education of the ABA Section on Legal Education require a re-inspection of the Stetson College of Law the following year, 1952.[1549] After studying Hervey's findings, the Council agreed that a re-inspection take place in 1952.[1550]

As expected, Edmunds was not pleased with the 1951 ABA Inspection Report. Making matters worse, he was directed to appear before the Council on

1544. *Id.* at 6.
1545. *Id.*
1546. *Id.*
1547. *Id.* at 6–7 (emphasis added).
1548. *Id.* at 8–9; *see also* Vause, *Centennial History, supra* n. 595, at 119.
1549. *Id.* at 119.
1550. *Id.*

Legal Education of the ABA Section on Legal Education in New York City.[1551] He went. Following the meeting, Edmunds wrote that he had been "advised by Dean Hervey" of the Council's decision:

> After full consideration, the Council regarded the approved status of your law school as precarious and members of the Council expressed themselves quite frankly as of the opinion that the deficiencies in your school for a period of years and the tenor of the conversation of the meeting in New York was that no deficiency should be permitted beyond September 1952.[1552]

Rightfully alarmed by the Council's warning, Edmunds believed that the issues raised by the ABA "should be studied by a larger group."[1553] He appointed a committee of law alumni and local citizens to work with the University Committee on Administration to study and make recommendations regarding building new law school facilities in DeLand, or relocating it to another community.[1554] This was the first step signaling possible relocation since he, Edmunds, had first broached the idea in 1939.[1555]

i. 1952 Reinspection: Is Relocation the Answer?

Following receipt of the 1951 ABA inspection report, Edmunds authorized $9,000 be spent on sprucing up the law school, specifically, by painting the buildings inside and out, purchasing new tables, chairs, and light fixtures for the library, and equipping faculty offices with new furniture and filing cabinets."[1556] In addition, he increased both the dean's and faculty salaries.[1557] Moreover, in reversal of University policies he had upheld from 1948 through 1951, Edmunds authorized the dean and law faculty to make decisions on law school admissions, dismissals, and academic standards for retention and graduation.[1558]

Dean Hervey returned to the Stetson University campus on March 20, 1952, to conduct the school's reinspection.[1559] In his 1952 report, Hervey chronicled

---

1551. Edmunds, *1953 Report*, *supra* n. 1528.

1552. *Id.*

1553. *Id.*

1554. *Id.*

1555. *See supra* nn. 1152–1165 and accompanying text.

1556. *Id.*

1557. *Id.* at 120.

1558. *Id.* at 121.

1559. John G. Hervey, *Inspection Report, John B. Stetson University College of Law, DeLand Florida,* 1 (Apr. 4, 1952) (copy on file at the College of L.) [hereinafter Hervey, *1952 Inspection Report*].

all the improvements that had occurred at the law school since his visit the year before.[1560] Not only did he find the facilities to be "adequate," he also found that there existed a "dignified, professional atmosphere about the place which definitely was lacking a year ago."[1561]

Nonetheless, Hervey's 1952 Inspection Report was in certain respects more critical than the previous year's assessment. Despite small increases in faculty compensation, faculty morale remained low, and the high rate of faculty turnover continued, a level Hervey described as having exceeding that "of any [ABA] approved law school in the country."[1562] Again he pointed to the advanced age of many of the professors who remained, noting that three had joined the Stetson faculty after retiring from other law schools.[1563]

On a more positive note, Hervey did find that the faculty had been granted a measure of autonomy in setting academic standards, yet he expressed reservations about the University's motives.[1564] He wrote: "But this [control over the law school's affairs] must be watched. Past history is not favorable to a continuation of present policy."[1565] To lend credence to this cautionary statement, Hervey found that the faculty and Haslup continued to be left out of important decisions affecting the school. For example, when Edmunds appointed a committee to study possible relocation of the law school,[1566] he never told Haslup their names until the day of the 1952 inspection."[1567] Hervey criticized President Edmunds for his veil of secrecy, writing:

> One would think that he [Edmunds] would take the law faculty into greater confidence and manifest a greater interest. [Edmunds] has visited the law school only once since he became President in 1948 [four years earlier].[1568]

Hervey added that he had not found any law school placing a greater emphasis on its past history rather than looking to the future than Stetson.[1569] His advice was that "Stetson should be up and at it in doing something for today and the future. The spirit is willing but the flesh is truly weak on that

1560. *Id.*
1561. *Id.* at 2.
1562. *Id.*
1563. *Id.* at 6.
1564. Vause, *Centennial History, supra* n. 595, at 121.
1565. Hervey, *1952 Inspection Report, supra* n. 1559, at 3.
1566. *See infra* nn. 1606–1613 and accompanying text.
1567. Hervey, *1952 Inspection Report, supra* n. 1559, at 4.
1568. *Id.* at 5.
1569. Vause, *Centennial History, supra* n. 595, at 122.

score."[1570] The ABA inspector concluded his 1952 report on a pessimistic note, speculating that Haslup would not succeed in getting favorable responses to his demands to improve the law school. It seemed clear that the University would not act unless pressure came from the outside. Hervey recommended that the ABA Council on Legal Education must continue to exert that pressure.[1571] It did so. It advised that for Stetson College of Law to remain accredited, the University administration had to take several actions:

1. Concede the professional status of the College of Law;
2 Recognize the school cannot be operated at a profit;
3. Establish stability in faculty personnel;
4. Formulate a distinctive program of legal education; and
5. Construct a building commensurate with the needs of the law school.[1572]

Of these, the most critical were giving the law school more autonomy and constructing, or purchasing, adequate physical facilities—the same key issues which had been raised the year earlier. By the time the 1952 Inspection Report came down, the University was already giving serious consideration to relocating the College of Law. Though many said absolutely not, in time nearly all the University's trustees favored relocation.[1573]

1570. Hervey, *1952 Inspection Report, supra* n. 1559, at 5.

1571. *Id.* at 7.

1572. *Id.*

1573. *See infra* nn. 1614–1615 and accompanying text.

CHAPTER EIGHT

Relocation to Gulfport — Dean Hilkey

8.1 A Law School in Crisis

Not only did the ABA's 1951 and 1952 Inspections Reports put the future of Stetson's College of Law in question, so did the school's declining number of students and deteriorating finances. When the school reopened after World War II, only eighty-three students matriculated. The following year, the number shot up to 200, then to a record 315 students in the 1948–1949 academic year.[1574] But that was the peak enrollment, as it fell precipitously over the next several years. The table on the next page reflects the roller-coaster fluctuations.[1575]

In 1953, Edmunds advised the trustees that the post-war "bulge period" of after the end of World War II veterans had ended.[1576] The decline in enrollment, he said, was compounded because the country "faced a partial mobilization caused by the Korean conflict."[1577] The so-called "Police Action" by United Nations forces (mainly Americans) against Communist North Korea (and later China) had begun just five years after World War II.[1578] Edmunds warned that the combined impact of fewer veterans and the Korean mobilization "has threatened the very existence of many independent and church-related colleges

1574. J. Ollie Edmunds, *1951–1952 Report of the President of Stetson University to the Trustees, Enrollment Summary* app. (Feb. 21, 1952) (on file at Stetson U. Archives, DeLand, Fla.) [hereinafter Edmunds, *1951–1952 Report*]

1575. In comparison, Stetson law school's average enrollment for its forty pre-war years was fifty-three. *See* J. Ollie Edmunds, *1952–1953 Report of the President of Stetson University to the Trustees, Enrollment Summary* 14 (1953) (on file at Stetson U. Archives, DeLand, Fla.). [hereinafter Edmunds, *1952–1953 Report*].

1576. *Id.* at 1.

1577. *Id.*

1578. On a national basis, the onset of the Korean War had very little impact on law school enrollments in contrast to World War II. *See* Stevens, *Law School, supra* n. 196, 205–16.

RISE AND FALL IN LAW SCHOOL ENROLLMENT

Academic Year	*Enrollment*	*Reason for Enrollment Fluctuation(s)*
1940–1941	36	America prepares for war
1941–1942	22	America enters WWII
1942–1943	16	Last year before law school closes
1943–1946	0	School closed for duration of war
1946–1947	83	College reopens
1947–1948	200	Post-war bulge of veterans begins
1948–1949	315	Peak in enrollment
1949–1950	309	Fall off in first-year enrollment
1950–1951	229	Major decline in veterans
1951–1952	156	Veteran bulge ends; Korean Conflict starts
1952–1953	107	Korean mobilization
1953–1954	79	Law school's last year in DeLand

and universities."[1579] He underscored that the University's decline in students had been more severe than at other colleges.[1580] Moreover, the decline had adversely affected the College of Law to a greater extent than it had the undergraduate school. Haslup added that the national decline in law school enrollment from 1948 through 1951 averaged nineteen percent, while at Stetson law school the number was "nearly fifty percent."[1581] Meanwhile, another statistical comparison—which had to alarm the president and trustees even more—revealed that law school enrollment at the University of Miami law school "had *increased* from 763 to 1,175, or approximately fifty-four percent."[1582]

Haslup reported:[1583]

> [T]hese figures seemingly support a belief long held by the writer that *it is only with difficulty that privately supported law schools may be successfully operated in smaller communities.* A survey of American Bar Association approved schools discloses that with a very few isolated exceptions, the suc-

1579. Edmunds, *1952–1953 Report, supra* n. 1575, at 1.

1580. *Id.*

1581. L.A. Haslup, *Report to the President of Stetson University* (quoted in Edmunds, *1951 Inspection Report, supra* n. 1527, at 8); *see also* Stevens, *Law School, supra* n. 196, at 205, 206. "World War II veterans *temporarily* swelled the depleted ranks of law students." Stevens, *Law School, supra* n. 196, at 205, 206 (emphasis added).

1582. Haslup, *supra* n. 1581, at 9 (emphasis in original).

1583. *Id.*

> cessful law schools, other than tax-supported schools, are either located in a large metropolis or ... [in] a relatively densely populated area.[1584]

During the "veterans' bulge"—1947 through 1950—the College of Law brought in substantially greater revenues than the University allowed the school to retain, a situation that needled the ABA's Council on Legal Education.[1585] The excess revenue "problem," however, soon evaporated, as smaller enrollments turned the period of surpluses into one of deficits.

To meet the "financial emergency" brought on by the reduction in students, Edmunds reduced the size of the teaching staff.[1586] Hervey and Edmunds agreed that the law school was operating at a loss, though they differed widely over the amount.[1587] From 1952 through 1955, the school's deficits grew. Prior to the 1947–1950 surpluses, the school was in financial difficulty every year since its founding,[1588] prompting Edmunds to comment that, except for the years right after World War II, "the law school has always operated at a deficit."[1589]

Thus, with unexpected rapidity, the post-war conditions of overcrowding and surpluses became replaced by smaller enrollments and deficits. At the same time, the ABA's concerns about the school's dilapidated quarters, inadequate library, low faculty salaries, and insufficient autonomy continued. In short, the University's president, dean of the law school, and board of trustees came to understand that, given the crisis at hand, something had to be done or the law school faced closure.

8.2 The Decision to Relocate the College of Law

a. A Difficult and Contentious Process

As noted earlier, in 1939 the Jacksonville Bar Association invited Stetson University to move its law school from the DeLand campus to Jacksonville.[1590]

1584. *Id.* (emphasis added).

1585. *See supra* n. 1538 and accompanying text.

1586. J. Ollie Edmunds, *Report of the President of John B. Stetson University, Calendar Year 1950, Report to the Trustees* (Feb. 15, 1951) (on file at Stetson U. Archives, DeLand, Fla.).

1587. Hervey, *1952 Inspection Report, supra* n. 1559, at 4–5; *see also* Vause, *Centennial History, supra* n. 595, at 121–122.

1588. Ltr. from Stetson University President W.S. Allen to Dean L. Haslup (Mar. 6, 1947) (cited in Lycan, *History of Stetson, supra* n. 109, at 361).

1589. *See supra* n. 1575 and accompanying text.

1590. *See supra* nn. 1152–1160 and accompanying text.

Edmunds, then a Jacksonville judge and Stetson University trustee, brought the Jacksonville proposal before the Board.[1591] Though rejecting the offer, the University did begin to consider the possible relocation of the law school, but not for long. Soon, the immediate issue was no longer relocation, it was survival—as the College of Law experienced the financial impact of World War II. In January 1944, the Florida Baptist Convention initiated a joint campaign with the University to raise $1,000,000.[1592] The Convention assigned a $50,000 quota "to the people of DeLand."[1593]

Near the war's end, the question came up again. Edmunds called a special meeting of the Board of Trustees for April 18, 1944, to consider whether the law school, whenever it reopened, should remain in DeLand or be moved to Jacksonville.[1594] Edmunds invited town representatives to attend the Board meeting,[1595] at which DeLand Mayor Leo Fugle spoke in opposition to any move and "expressed the hope that the law school would remain in DeLand."[1596] Other speakers echoed Fugle's sentiment. The meeting ended inconclusively, with the University Trustees unanimously passing a resolution that the University at that time "take no official action regarding the removal of its Law School from DeLand."[1597]

By the Board's dodging the issue, DeLand residents remained hopeful that the school would stay put, especially if a new facility could be financed. The town's leaders requested that the $50,000 which the Baptists had asked the town to raise in the Convention's $1,000,000 campaign for Stetson be allocated for a new law school.[1598] Subsequently, "the people of DeLand" together with "College faculty members and all of the churches of the City," raised a combined total of $29,134.81, which the University held as "trust funds earmarked for a law building in the City."[1599] As a consequence, the University's thinking about relocating the law school lessened in counterpoint with a growing interest in constructing a new building in DeLand, an outcome most alumni and local residents clearly supported. One such person was Hilda Towse, referred to as a "prominent citizen" of the community, who wrote the

---

1591. *Id.*

1592. Vause, *Centennial History, supra* n. 595, at 361.

1593. Edmunds, *1952–1953 Report, supra* n. 1575, at 13.

1594. *Id.* at 13 (quoting from *The John B. Stetson University Board of Trustees Meeting* (Jan. 8, 1944) (on file at Stetson U. Archives, DeLand, Fla.).

1595. *Id.*

1596. *Id.*

1597. *Id.*

1598. *Id.*

1599. *Id.* at 13–14.

DeLand *Sun News* imploring residents to use "thought and effort" to keep the law school in town.[1600] Meanwhile, Edmunds, who earlier believed the law school should be moved to Jacksonville, changed his mind and assumed it would be better to keep the College in DeLand.[1601] He enlisted Florida Governor and Stetson law school graduate David Sholtz to travel with him throughout the state in an effort to obtain private donations for a new school building in DeLand.

In spite of the sentiment for the law school to stay home, the question of relocation as a guarantee of the school's survival resurfaced. This alternative especially came to the forefront following the ABA's critical 1951 and 1952 inspections.[1602] Warned by the ABA back in 1947 of the poor conditions at the Naval Air Station, the University then reacted by taking only cosmetic measures, and for a time that was enough.[1603] But the University could not ignore the ABA's 1951 and 1952 warnings of loss of accreditation, given the overwhelmingly inadequate facilities of the College of Law.[1604] The Board had little choice but to act quickly, in response to the ABA's declaration that "no deficiency should be permitted beyond September 1952."[1605]

After the ABA 1952 warning, Edmunds called for creation of a "Special Law Alumni Committee" of prominent graduates to study "the future of the Law School of John B. Stetson University."[1606] He directed the committee to make recommendations related to the school's survival, and then to report back to the Board of Trustees' Committee on Administration—the group that managed the University.[1607] The committee members consisted of United States Circuit Court of Appeals Judge Louie W. Strum, chair;[1608] three Stetson law graduates on the Florida Supreme Court—Justice Elwyn Thomas (Tallahassee), Justice E. Harris Drew (West Palm Beach), and Justice Roy Chapman (Jacksonville);[1609] Judge O.K. Reeves (Tampa); Judge Frank Smith (Orlando); Charles Tom Henderson (Tallahassee); J.O. Simmons (Miami); D.C. Hull (De-

1600. *Lycan,, History of Stetson, supra* n. 109, at 360.

1601. *Id.*

1602. *See supra* nn. 1556–1561 and accompanying text.

1603. *See supra* n. 1331–1344 and accompanying text.

1604. *See supra* n. 1526–1573 and accompanying text.

1605. Edmunds, *1952–1953 Report, supra* n. 1575, at 14.

1606. *Id.*

1607. *Id.*

1608. *Minutes of the Committee on Administration of the Board of Trustees,* 1 (Oct. 3, 1952) (on file at Stetson U. Archives, DeLand, Fla.) [hereinafter *Minutes Oct. 3, 1952*].

1609. *Relocation: The Law School,* 66 Stetson Rptr. 1, 2 (May 1, 1953) [hereinafter *Relocation*].

Land); S. Bryan Jennings (Tampa); Cecil C. Bailey (Jacksonville); Arthur Milan (Jacksonville); and former Florida Governor Doyle E. Carlton, the only member who was not a Stetson law school alumnus (though a graduate of Stetson's College of Arts and Sciences).[1610]

The Special Committee of Law Alumni on the Future of the Law School met on May 17, 1952, in Jacksonville.[1611] After discussing the school's crisis, the committee drafted a resolution calling for immediate action:

> We recommend to the Board of Trustees that in the interest of enlarging and expending [sic] the Law School, planning its future and extending its service to the public, the School be made the nucleus of a planned Law Center, *to be located in one of the metropolitan areas of Florida* ... and [that] the Board at an early meeting approve such a move in principle and invite proposals from our various metropolitan areas which may be offered as an inducement for its [re] location.[1612]

The vote was unanimous with one exception—attorney D.C. Hull of DeLand, who strongly opposed the law school leaving Volusia County.[1613]

After receiving the Committee's proposal, Edmunds asked the Board's Trustee's Committee on Administration to decide whether to accept it.[1614] Following "considerable discussion," it did so and recommended moving the law school out of DeLand.[1615] The trustees called for the resolution to "be made public" and for Edmunds to "bring the recommendation to the attention of officers of state and local bar associations, and to each graduate of the Stetson Law School."[1616]

In early November 1952, Edmunds publicly announced the Board's intention of moving the law school out of DeLand.[1617] A little later, on December 18, Edmunds contacted the president of the DeLand Chamber of Commerce, explaining that the Chamber's members must understand that it was imperative that the University "take pertinent actions regarding the law school.[1618]

1610. *Id; see also* Edmunds, *1952–1953 Report, supra* n. 1575, at 14.

1611. *Minutes Oct. 3, 1952, supra* n. 1608, at 1.

1612. *Id.*

1613. *Id.*

1614. *Relocation, supra* n. 1609, at 2.

1615. *Id.*

1616. *Minutes Oct. 3, 1952, supra* n. 1608, at 1.

1617. Edmunds, *1952–1953 Report, supra* n. 1575, at 14, 15; *see also Relocation, supra* n. 1609, at 1.

1618. *Id.*

Edmunds pointed out that the trustees were under a "heavy responsibility to the Bar of Florida and to the law graduates of the University to keep the Stetson Law School in existence, even though it might be necessary to transport it in order to save it."[1619]

b. Florida Cities Compete for the Law School

On February 19, 1953, the Board of Trustees met in DeLand for its annual meeting. One month earlier, President Edmunds had mailed a communication titled "A Frank Statement to Stetson Law Alumni," advising them that the law school's survival was in question, and that one solution was finding a new home for the school in a large metropolitan area as soon as possible.[1620] Edmunds reported at the trustees' February 1953 meeting that he had received thirty-six replies to his January letter.[1621] One response from a group of alumni in Tallahassee expressed strong interest in the school relocating to their city, but contained no specific proposal.[1622] But that was not the case for other communities in the state. Attending the Board's February meeting were representatives from four cities to present proposals for the school's relocation. Edmunds told the trustees:

> I am advised that representatives from the City of DeLand, City of Tampa, City of Jacksonville, and City of Tallahassee, and perhaps others are in DeLand today [February 19, 1953] and desire to make statements to this Board about the problem [of the law school's survival].[1623]

The competition of Florida cities to be the future home of the Stetson University College of Law was off to a fast start. First to speak were representatives from DeLand. Stetson University historian Gilbert Lycan describes the burden confronting local interests in convincing the trustees to leave the law school in its home city:

> Clearly, if the College of Law was to be saved from moving away, the people of DeLand must save it. Hope from all other sources had dissolved. [Local attorney] Sidney Taylor, speaking for the alumni, especially those living in DeLand, and Earl Brown, [of the] Chamber of Commerce, ap-

1619. *Id.*
1620. Edmunds, *1952–1953 Report, supra* n. 1575, at 15.
1621. *Id.*
1622. *See* Bowen, *supra* n. 455, at 8.
1623. *Id.*

> peared before the trustees ... and gave powerful arguments in favor of keeping the Law College in DeLand.[1624]

Representing local business interests, Brown reminded the trustees about DeLand's cultural opportunities, and especially emphasized the citizens' and merchants' intention to assist the law school to remain in the community.[1625] Taylor assured the trustees that DeLand's citizens and businesses would raise between $100,000 to $150,000 (including $30,000 previously donated) to keep the school at is birthplace.[1626] According to Lycan, the plan envisioned using donated funds to purchase an abandoned hospital building "on North Stone Street," and then to pay for two additional wings to be built "to house classrooms, the law library, and a courtroom."[1627] Taylor accompanied the offer of promised donations for a new facility with "the most emphatic promises of continued financial support" to follow.

Taylor's assurances notwithstanding, he could not guarantee that the monies would be raised.[1628] It is not surprising, therefore, that the trustees were not persuaded by Taylor's promises of hoped for financial support, not knowing what amount might be raised, or, for that matter, what a new law school facility in DeLand might cost. Lycan writes: "Taylor pled with the Board to tell him just how large a donation DeLand would have to make to hold the Law School."[1629] The Board said nothing in response to his plea.[1630]

Though Taylor's financial offers seemed unachievable to the trustees, he did make some telling points that surely struck many ears as relevant. For one thing, he suggested that "potential young lawyers needed the Christian atmosphere of the Stetson campus" as well as the cultural advantages of the University and its law school. Each would "stimulate the other intellectually," he added.[1631] Taylor, however, failed to provide viable solutions to the school's precarious financial situation and accreditation uncertainties.

One of the stronger supporters for relocation, trustee Rev. C.H. Boltan (of Avon Park), countered Taylor's presentation by suggesting that a new location

---

1624. Lycan, *History of Stetson, supra* n. 109, at 361.

1625. Vause, *Centennial History, supra* n. 595, at 126.

1626. Lycan, *History of Stetson, supra* n. 109, at 361.

1627. *Id.* at 362 (citing a newspaper article in the *DeLand Sun News,* dated February 20, 1953).

1628. *Id.*

1629. *Id.*

1630. *Id.*

1631. *Id.*

for the College of Law would help the school become "entirely self-supporting," adding that the University would also benefit since the law school's annual deficits would end, thus allowing more money to be directed to the Liberal Arts, Music, and Business colleges.[1632]

Representatives from Tampa spoke next to the assembled trustees, led by attorney James M. McEwan.[1633] McEwan underscored advantages he believed the City of Tampa offered Stetson law school: a more populous community; greater opportunities for part-time student employment; the likelihood of a significantly larger student body; numerous venues for clinical work; access to state and federal courts within the city; and the availability of a large number of lawyers to serve as part-time instructors at the school.[1634] Another strong supporter of the law school moving to Tampa was former Stetson law dean Richmond Rasco (then dean of the Miami University Law School). Dean Rasco sent a telegram to the Stetson trustees noting the strategic advantages a Tampa location would have for the future of Stetson College of Law.[1635]

After proponents for DeLand and Tampa finished their presentations to the Board, it was Jacksonville's turn. Judge McKenney J. Davis represented the city, but was not present at the meeting.[1636] Davis, however, previously had authorized Edmunds to inform the trustees that Jacksonville's earlier proposal to relocate to that city was still on the table, and that in due course, additional details would be forwarded.[1637]

At the end of the presentations, the trustees discussed the three proposals.[1638] Making no immediate decision, the Board asked Edmunds to appoint a "Special Committee of Trustees" to study the offers.[1639] The Board directed the committee to explore the potential of each Florida city that had expressed, *or might express*, an interest in becoming the future home of the Stetson College of Law.[1640] Serving on the special committee were Rev. C.B. Bolton, chair; Thomas Hansen (Ft. Lauderdale); J.J. Cater (West Palm Beach); Walter Mann (New York

---

1632. *Id.*

1633. Vause, *Centennial History, supra* n. 595, at 126.

1634. *Id.*

1635. *Id.*

1636. *Relocation, supra* n. 1609, at 2.

1637. *Id.*

1638. Vause, *Centennial History, supra* n. 595, at 362.

1639. *Minutes, Adjourned Meeting of Board of Stetson University* 1, 2 (Nov. 13, 1953) (on file at Stetson U. Archives, DeLand, Fla.) [hereinafter *Minutes Nov. 13, 1953*].

1640. Vause, *Centennial History, supra* n. 595, at 127, (emphasis added.)

City);[1641] and Earl H. Gaston (Pensacola).[1642] Edmunds announced that "[T]he trustees are aware of the University's responsibility to The Florida Bar, not only to students but [also] to the practicing attorneys."[1643] He said that a decision should be reached within sixty days on the school's future location.[1644]

On April 30, 1953, the trustees committee studying the relocation of the Law School issued an interim report—after meeting at different locations throughout the state, including Hollywood, at the annual meeting of The Florida Bar—to Stetson's entire Board of Trustees.[1645] The report began by recognizing that the University's charter needed to be amended should the law school be moved anywhere other than Jacksonville, the one place the original charter permitted the school to relocate to.[1646] In response, the Board authorized University attorneys to petition the State Legislature to amend the charter, thereby allowing the school to relocate.[1647] The Legislature quickly did so.[1648] The amended charter provided that the Stetson University Board of Trustees, by a two-thirds vote, could move and operate the College of Law within the state at "some place other than DeLand."[1649] Guaranteeing that wherever the school relocated the University's authority over the College of Law would continue, the trustees had the charter amended so that the law school would "be and ever remain under the absolute control of the Trustees of Stetson University."[1650]

The historic decision was ready to be announced. On May 1, 1953, the University Board of Trustees unanimously agreed that the College of Law would not stay in DeLand, but rather would be relocated to a metropolitan area, most likely Jacksonville or Tampa.[1651] In announcing the Board's action, Edmunds made it clear that the trustees were convinced that relocation was in the best long-term interests for both the law school and for legal education in Florida.[1652] The president pointed out that Stetson law school was "one of the

---

1641. *See Minutes Nov. 13, 1953, supra* n. 1639, at 3 (summarizing the decisional process).

1642. *Id.*

1643. *Allow Sixty Days for Law Decision,* 66 Stetson Rptr. 3 (Feb. 27, 1953).

1644. *Id.*

1645. *Minutes of the Board of Trustees of the John B. Stetson University, Annual Meeting, DeLand, Florida* 1–5 (Apr. 30, 1953) [hereinafter *Minutes Apr. 30, 1953*].

1646. *See supra* nn. 257–258 and accompanying text.

1647. *Id.*

1648. Lycan, *History of Stetson, supra* n. 109, at 363.

1649. Laws of Florida 1953, Ch. 28, 704 (June 15, 1953).

1650. *Minutes Apr. 30, 1953, supra* n. 1645.

1651. *Trustees Agree to Move Law School,* 66 Stetson Rptr.1 (May 1, 1953).

1652. *Id.*

few privately supported law schools accredited by the American Bar Association which is operated in a community as small as DeLand."[1653] Before a final decision as to when the school would be moved was made, Edmunds explained, a committee of the trustees charged with comparing the offers of relocation to various cities would issue a report to the Board, setting out the specifics of each proposal, and would then recommend which offer should be accepted.[1654]

At the close of business on May 1, Stetson's Board agreed to reconvene when a final report from the trustees committee on relocation was completed.[1655] In the interim, a new—and unexpected—competitor for the College of Law emerged.

c. St. Petersburg (and Gulfport) Come to the Table

When the Board reconvened on November 13, 1953, it did so in the office of President Edmunds.[1656] Though only eight members were present, nine who were absent had earlier sent Edmunds their proxies (including Board Chairman Colonel F.W. Bailey; New York Trustee Walter Mann; and former Florida Governor Doyle E. Carlton).[1657] Three absent members had not sent proxies. The purpose of the meeting was to hear the report of the committee of trustees setting out the details of each proposal for relocation.

Having visited all the properties offered and after "due and prayerful consideration," the members of the special committee—Walter Mann, Thomas Hansen, J.J. Carter, Earl Gaston, and C.H. Bolton—had reached a conclusion, one that would come as a surprise to many of those assembled.[1658] But first, they reported on the specific offers from the three finalists: Tampa, Jacksonville, and, for the first time, St. Petersburg. The Tampa offer (as summarized) follows:

> **Tampa's Proposal**
>
> The City of Tampa offers a tract of land on Davis Island, and the Board of County Commissioners of Hillsborough County offers approximately $75,000 for the purpose of constructing a building. The lands to be acquired from the City of Tampa would be owned by the Hillsborough

1653. *Id.*
1654. *Id.*
1655. *Nov. 13, 1953 Minutes*, *supra* n. 1639, at 1.
1656. *Id.*
1657. *Id.*
1658. *Id.* at 2, 3.

County Law Center Authority and long-term leases would be made to Stetson University.[1659]

Jacksonville's proposal was considered next. It was more detailed than it had been previously. A summary follows:

Jacksonville's Proposal

The City of Jacksonville owns a building situate [sic] at 311 West Duval Street, which was erected approximately twenty-five years ago by the Jacksonville Chamber of Commerce ... The [City of Jacksonville] has assured the Federal Communications Commission that a portion of this building will be available for use as a television broadcasting building, [the remainder] to be leased to Stetson University for a period of ten years at $1.00 per year with the right of renewal for an additional ten-year period at the same rental with a twenty-year option to purchase the premises at a price of $180,000. [Moreover], the City further proposes that the $8,000 to $10,000 rental from [the television station] shall be income to the University during the rental period.[1660]

Jacksonville's proposal included the City's assurance that during each of the first two years of the lease, it would expend "not less than $25,000 in renovations and improvements."[1661] The building offered was the vacated Chamber of Commerce structure across the street from the Jacksonville federal court house.[1662] The most outspoken advocate for the school moving to Jacksonville was Cecil Bailey, an alumnus who later became chair of the College of Law Board of Overseers.[1663] Years later, Bailey recalled that, "I worked hard for [relocation to Jacksonville] and had the strong support of the city administration to bring it here."[1664] Looking back, Bailey confessed: "[W]e didn't win ... that's one battle that I'm really glad we lost."[1665]

In 1953, however, Bailey and others believed that the building Jacksonville offered was "adequate for classroom purposes, but no facilities are presently available for dormitories."[1666] The lack of dormitories turned out to be a sig-

---

1659. *Id.* at 1. (The Board's Nov. 13, 1953 Minutes include the special committee's "Report to the Board of Trustees" in its entirety.).

1660. *Id.* at 1, 2.

1661. *Id.* at 2.

1662. Interview by Bruce Jacob with Cecil Bailey 10, 11 (Jan. 13, 1986) (on file at Stetson U. College of L., Gulfport, Fla.) [hereinafter *Bailey Interview*].

1663. *Id.* at 10, 11.

1664. *Id.* at 11.

1665. *Id.*

1666. *Id.*

nificant consideration after another proposal had come in from citizens of St. Petersburg, Florida.

Serendipity is a significant catalyst for change in the lives of both people and institutions. During the window of time when Stetson University was searching for a new location for its law school, a large property with unique buildings came into foreclosure.[1667] Located in Gulfport, Florida—a small community adjacent to St. Petersburg—the property featured several attributes. One was the prospect for living quarters, consisting of dormitory rooms from a defunct military academy. Prior to the academy's occupation, the property had been a posh resort complex at the height of the "roaring twenties," during a Florida land boom.[1668] This historical property with a remarkable past became the basis for an offer from the St. Petersburg group. A summary of the proposal follows:

> **St. Petersburg's Proposal**
>
> Citizens of St. Petersburg have offered to raise from private sources $50,000 in cash and $50,000 in bona fide pledges, payable during 1954 and to apply this toward a $200,000 purchase price of the Florida Military Property located in the City of Gulfport, Florida, now owned by the Union Trust Company.[1669]
>
> This property consists of a group of one, two, and three story buildings on a beautifully landscaped ten acre tract of land on the edge of St. Petersburg. It includes a dining hall, modern kitchen facilities, and 100 bedrooms, each with a private or connecting bath, together with a number of classrooms which [had been] used by the Florida Military Academy and which could be remodeled into larger classrooms.[1670]

d. St. Petersburg/Gulfport Is the Winner

Following its report, the special committee made its recommendation after suggesting that representatives of Tampa and Jacksonville "be informed that their offers as given were not acceptable."[1671] It then offered the following proposal to the assembled trustees:

1667. *See* Ltr. from W.F. Davenport, Jr., to Assoc. Dean W. Gary Vause 2 (Apr. 5, 1999). Mr. Davenport, a Stetson law school graduate of 1950, was one of the lawyers that had represented the bank that had acquired the property in foreclosure, the Union Trust Company of St. Petersburg. *Id.*

1668. *See supra* nn. 1757–1779 and accompanying text.

1669. *Minutes Nov. 13, 1953, supra* n 1639, at 2.

1670. *Id.*

1671. *Id.*

Recommendation

> [T]he Committee representing the City of St. Petersburg be advised that this Committee looks with favor upon their proposal, [provided the] cash and proposals are presented to the University [by] December 31, 1953, and if the Union Trust Company will accept a note and mortgage restricted to the Gulfport property ... and if St. Petersburg [committee members] pledge their continuing interest and support in making the Stetson University Law Center in St. Petersburg one of the most outstanding in the nation, [then] President J. Ollie Edmunds and the officers of the Board be authorized to carry through negotiations with the St. Petersburg group and acquire said property at the earliest date possible.[1672]

The full Board unanimously approved the committee's recommendation.[1673] It was agreed that as soon as details were finalized, the Trustees Committee on Administration would execute the sale and acquire the Gulfport property for Stetson University.

Carroll R. Runyon, alumnus of the College of Law, had spearheaded the St. Petersburg proposal.[1674] Other significant backers included William "Bill" J. Clapp, president of Florida Power Company,[1675] and legendary baseball promoter Al Lang, who "helped finance the moving of Stetson's College of Law to St. Petersburg."[1676] Pinellas County citizens involved included Robert Guthrie, businessman; R.J. McCutcheon, Jr., real state and insurance; T.G. Mixon, President of City Bank and Trust Company; Jack White, Pinellas County Judge; and John Rowe, '40, Clearwater attorney.[1677] Edmunds also brought his daughter Jane with him. She recalls running through the weeds. She went on to become a trustee.

President Edmunds decided to see for himself what the abandoned Florida Military Academy property looked like, and with his son drove from DeLand to Gulfport.[1678] What greeted them was an "overgrown campus with weeds and

---

1672. *Id.* at 3.

1673. Vause, *Centennial History, supra* n. 595, at 128.

1674. H.L. Sebring, *Stetson University College of Law* 2 (Feb. 1968) (a twenty-two page typed summary of the history of the Stetson University College of Law on file at the Stetson U. College of L., Gulfport, Fla.).

1675. Vause, *Centennial History, supra* n. 595, at 128.

1676. Bill Beck, *He Gave to Florida: Spring Baseball; A Billion Dollar Industry* 39 (n.d.) (newspaper clipping, on file at Stetson U. College of L., Gulfport, Fla).

1677. *Runyon's Death Recalls Local Bid for Stetson*, 2 Stetson Lawyer 1 (May 1968)

1678. Bruce Jacob, *My Recollections What It Was Like to Be a Stetson Law Student and Graduate; The Move of the Law School to Gulfport* 1 (Sept. 1, 1999) (on file at the Stetson U. College of L., Gulfport, Fla.) [hereinafter Jacob, *Recollections*].

President William J. Clapp

buildings—vacant for nearly three years—which were in disrepair and vandalized, all the windows having been broken."[1679] Yet, despite the obvious need for substantial renovations, Edmunds knew immediately that these facilities "would be the perfect place for the law school,"[1680] though prior to his Gulfport trip, he had favored Jacksonville's proposal.[1681]

e. The Decision Is Made

Under direction from Edmunds and the Trustees Committee on Administration, attorneys worked out details of the purchase from Union Trust Company. On December 3, 1953, in the Directors' room of Barnett National Bank, Edmunds presented his report to the trustees:[1682]

> [T]he group in St. Petersburg now has $59,000 in cash in the bank and has more than enough additional pledges (payable in 1954) to make up the promised $100,000;
> [T]he Avalon Foundation has contributed $50,000 to the University to be used by the Trustees in re-locating the law school; Charles E. Merrill has contributed $17,500 toward the re-location of the law school;

1679. *Id.*

1680. *Id.*

1681. Lycan, *History of Stetson*, *supra* n. 109, at 363.

1682. *Minutes of Special Meeting of Committee on Administration of the Board of Trustees* 1 (Dec. 3, 1953) (on file at Stetson U. College L., Gulfport, Fla).

> [T]he Union Trust Company has agreed to accept for the property $35,000 cash and a note of the University in the amount of $165,000 … secured by a mortgage;
> [T]hat Lester L. Krauss, member of the American Institute of Accountants, and approved FHA appraiser for lending institutions, … has furnished the University with a documented appraisal showing that the [Gulfport] property … has a replacement value in his opinion of $1,056,000.[1683]

Thereupon, the Trustees Committee on Administration passed a historic resolution:

> NOW THEREFORE BE IT RESOLVED, that John B. Stetson University do purchase of and from said Union Trust Company that certain real estate and personal property located in Pinellas County, Florida … together with the buildings and improvements thereon … that the total purchase price shall be in the sum of Two Hundred Thousand Dollars ($200,000).[1684]

The $200,000 price consisted of $35,000 cash and a purchase money mortgage of $165,000. F.N.K. Bailey, the Board's president, and L.A. Perkins, the Board's secretary, executed the note and mortgage on behalf of the University.[1685] The mortgage was payable over a ten-year period, with annual installments of $16,500.[1686] At the same time, the University purchased four vacant lots south of the Gulfport campus for $8,000, and a house and lot at 6114 Twelfth Avenue South for $7,500, the latter to be the residence for the College's "Superintendent of Maintenance and Grounds."[1687] These properties were separately financed.[1688]

By putting only $38,000 down for the properties, and in light of $157,500 in gifts and pledges, the University ended up with a surplus of about $120,000, but not for long.[1689] As a new Stetson law dean—Harold Sebring—would soon discover: "to make the buildings fit for occupancy, extensive renovations and repairs had to be made at a cost of $105,000."[1690]

1683. *Id.* at 2.

1684. *Id.* at 2, 3.

1685. *Id.* at 3; *see also* Harold L. Sebring, *A Few Facts About the College of Law, Acquisition of Property* 2 (Feb. 20, 1957) (twelve-page report distributed to the newly appointed members of the Board of Overseers, along with five appendices; on file at Stetson U. College of L., Gulfport, Fla.) [hereinafter Sebring, *Facts.*]

1686. Sebring, *Facts, supra* n. 1685, at 2.

1687. *Id.*

1688. *Id.*

1689. *Id.*

1690. *Id.*

f. Reaction

Reaction to the now fait accompli was mixed. While St. Petersburg's proponents naturally were delighted, Jacksonville's supporters were disappointed and, at least a few, angry.[1691] But the most vociferous and "recriminatory reactions" came from DeLand.[1692] An editorial titled "The End of an Era" in the *Sun News,* commented: "It was a David and Goliath battle from the start. Money talks. And the big money wasn't here."[1693] Alumnus Cecil Bailey recollected that, "a lot of people were strongly opposed to seeing the law school removed,"[1694] while alumnus Amory Underhill remembered that there was "much resistence" to the move from folks in DeLand.[1695] Similarly, Dean Emeritus Bruce Jacob recalled that many alumni of that era remained angry for years after the law school left Deland.[1696]

Throughout Volusia County it had been assumed that Edmunds would move the law school to Jacksonville, after which he would relinquish the University's presidency and become dean of the relocated College of Law.[1697] Years later, Edmunds in an interview remarked: "When we decided to move the law school from DeLand, I lost all my friends in DeLand. When we decided not to go to Jacksonville, I lost all my friends in Jacksonville."[1698] Meanwhile, a rumor circulated among alumni that the City of St. Petersburg had given the Gulfport property and buildings to Stetson at no cost.[1699] This, of course, was false.

In any event, the outrage in DeLand at the time was real. In emotive and sarcastic language, one writer wrote Edmunds that the president had never done anything good for the University, predicting that the schools of business, art, and music would soon be relocated as well, thereby "leaving only a nice girls seminary for the remote and secluded quiet of our pastoral little setting."[1700]

In contrast to DeLand's reaction, St. Petersburg's and Gulfport's citizens were enthusiastic over the law school moving to Pinellas County. As for the

---

1691. Vause, *Centennial History, supra* n. 595, at 363.

1692. *Id.*

1693. *End of an Era,* Sun News 1 (Feb. 20, 1954).

1694. *Bailey Interview, supra* n. 1662, at 11.

1695. *Underhill Interview, supra* n. 842, at 118.

1696. Memo. from Bruce Jacob to Michael Swygert 1 (Apr. 26, 2004) (on file at Stetson U. College of L., Gulfport, Fla.) [hereinafter *Jacob Memo*].

1697. Lycan, *History of Stetson, supra* n. 109, at 363.

1698. *Id.* Lycan cites the interview of J. Ollie Edmunds. *Id.* at 383 n. 54.

1699. *Jacob Memo, supra* n. 1696, at 1.

1700. Ltr. from Innes Henry to J. Ollie Edmunds (Feb. 28, 1954) (on file in Stetson U. Archives, DeLand, Fla.).

Stetson University College of Law, its relocation was about to happen. Interestingly, it would not occur under a law school dean who had been minimally involved—Lemuel Haslup.

8.3 A Change in Deanship: Hilkey Succeeds Haslup

On August 9, 1953, Dean Lemuel A. Haslup unexpectedly died.[1701] His death came at an inopportune time, the school's relocation only months away. Edmunds was faced with the challenge of finding someone to lead the College of Law just after the decision to relocate had been made—a critical period in the school's history. One week after Haslup's death, Edmunds, having few options, named Charles J. Hilkey acting dean.[1702] Hilkey was seventy-four years old. He had previously served a combined twenty-six years as dean at two law schools—Drake and Emory. After retiring as dean, he joined Stetson's law faculty in 1951 as a visiting professor of law.[1703] Hilkey was dean of the Emory University law school from 1925 through 1948.[1704] His academic credentials were outstanding, earning five degrees, including a Ph.D. from Columbia University and a S.J.D. from Harvard Law School.[1705] He also earned an A.B. degree from College of Emporia (Kansas), an M.A. from University of Kansas, and a J.D. degree from University of Michigan Law School,[1706] where he served on the law review.[1707]

Prior to being dean at Emory, Hilkey taught at Dartmouth College, then at Drake Law School, where he also served as dean.[1708] He authored four books, including one still in use today: *Legal Development in Colonial Massachusetts.*[1709] Hilkey also wrote *History of the Supreme Court of Georgia* and co-authored *The Constitution of Georgia: Cases and Comments*, the latter published in 1952, a few months after he had joined the Stetson law faculty.[1710]

1701. Lycan, *History of Stetson, supra* n. 109, at 364.

1702. *Id.*

1703. *Stetson Law Prof Co-Author of Book*, 65 Stetson Rptr. 3 (Apr. 18, 1952).

1704. *College of Law Adds C.J. Hilkey to '51 Staff*, 65 Stetson Rptr. 4 (Oct. 26, 1951).

1705. Vause, *Foundations for Excellence, supra* n. 308, at 320.

1706. J. Blanford Taylor, *News Release* (Apr., 1952) (on file at Stetson U. Archives, DeLand, Fla.).

1707. J. Blanford Taylor, *News Release*, 1 (Oct. 1951) (on file at Stetson U. Archives, DeLand, Fla.).

1708. *Id.*

1709. *Id.* at 2. Professor Michael Swygert, an Author of this work, looked up his name on Google.com and found numerous references to this historical work.

1710. *Stetson Law Professor Co-Author, Book, supra* n. 1703.

Dean Charles J. Hilkey

When Edmunds offered Hilkey the position of acting dean, the latter was reluctant to accept, but Edmunds persuaded him with the understanding that a permanent dean would be hired as quickly as possible.[1711] A University news release stated that Hilkey's appointment "gave Dr. Edmunds and the trustees a year to select an outstanding legal authority to head the College when it opens in either Tampa or Jacksonville in September 1954."[1712]

Little evidence has been found that Hilkey did anything significant as dean other than serve as caretaker. He did not have a secretary,[1713] and at the same time he functioned as Stetson's acting dean, he served as a hearing commissioner for the National Production Authority of the U.S. Department of Commerce.[1714] At least once, he went to Miami to hear cases, an event suggesting that he may have been away from the law school with some regularity.[1715] Despite Hilkey's apparent inattention as an administrator, students remember him as a "good" and "excellent" teacher. One is Stetson law school Dean Emer-

1711. Lycan, *History of Stetson, supra* n. 109, at 364–365.

1712. J. Blanford Taylor, *Stetson News Bureau for Release Sunday*, 1 (Aug. 14, 1953) (on file at Stetson U. Archives, DeLand, Fla.).

1713. Telephone Interview by Michael Swygert, Prof. Emeritus, Stetson U. College of L., with Richard T. Dillon, Dean Emeritus, Stetson U. College of L. (Jan. 27, 2005) [hereinafter *Dillon Interview*].

1714. *Stetson Law Professor Charles Hilkey Holds Prominent Government Position*, 66 Stetson Rptr. 6 (Mar. 6, 1953).

1715. *Id.*

itus Richard T. Dillon, who has "fond recollections about learning property law in Hilkey's class."[1716]

Not everyone, however, liked the man. Ray Jordan, the law librarian in DeLand for several years, felt that Hilkey was "egotistical" and "had a way of twisting things that annoyed me to death."[1717] She added that Professor Howes referred to Hilkey as "the old goat," noting that the two "could not stand each other."[1718] The animosity may have developed when Howes, who had been dean before the school reopened after the war, took offense after Edmunds appointed Hilkey dean rather than Howes.

Nevertheless, Acting Dean Charles J. Hilkey's impact on the development of the Stetson College of Law was minimal. His marginality is suggested by Edmund's statement in a 1954 report to the University trustees: "The critical need of the Law School is for a Dean."[1719] One thing is clear: throughout the long process of deciding whether and where to relocate the law school, Hilkey played no part, as Edmunds and the trustees oversaw the entire process. In fairness to Hilkey, it should be remembered that he had not wanted to be acting dean and had been assured a successor would be hired.

Hilkey remained acting dean for an additional year after the school moved to Gulfport. During this period, Edmunds assigned Elkanah Hulley, a contractor as well as a University trustee and a nephew of former University President Lincoln Hulley, to oversee the repairs and refurbishment of the facilities.[1720] The Board named Hulley the "resident trustee" for the College of Law. Thereafter, he moved to St. Petersburg to prepare the property for the school's opening, only a few months away.

Meanwhile, excitement among law students in DeLand was growing. After their December 1953 examinations, they caravanned to St. Petersburg to assess their new "home."[1721] And what a home it was—a former resort hotel complex, one where the rich and famous had vacationed in the 1920s, and where Babe Ruth and other notables had stayed.[1722] The story of the posh hotel and the military academy that succeeded it follows.

1716. *Dillon Interview, supra* n. 1713.

1717. *Jordan Interview, supra* n. 1315, at 9.

1718. *Id.*

1719. J. Ollie Edmunds, *Report of the President of Stetson University, Calendar Year 1953*, at 9 (Feb. 18, 1954).

1720. Vause, *Centennial History, supra* n. 595, at 130.

1721. *Id.*

1722. *Id.*

CHAPTER NINE

The New Home—Former Rolyat Hotel, Florida Military Academy

9.1 Disston City, Bonafacio, Veteran City, and Gulfport

In 1867, James and Rebecca Barnett settled along the shore of Boca Ciega Bay on the west-central coast of Florida. One Florida historian named the area "Barnett's Bluff."[1723] Two decades later, Hamilton Disston, a northern investor, acquired the property as part of a one-million acre purchase from the State in 1881. He bought the land for twenty-five cents an acre.[1724] The entrepreneur then set out to develop a new community, one he called "Disston City."[1725]

According to historian Lynne Brown, Disston City subsequently became known by two other names, "Bonafacio" (smiling face), and later, "Veteran City."[1726] Veteran City was the community's name in 1905 when it was linked by a trolley line to nearby St. Petersburg.[1727] Catherine Hickman, founder of the Gulfport Historical Society,[1728] notes that the name Veteran City was

---

1723. Lynne S. Brown, *Gulfport, Florida* 10 (Arcadia Publg. 1999).

1724. Vance, *supra* n. 70, at 1–10.

1725. *Id.*

1726. *See* Brown, *supra* n. 1723, at 15.

1727. *Id.*

1728. *Id.* The City of Gulfport, Florida, is fortunate to have several persons who have researched and written about the history of the community. Besides Catherine A. Hickman, who first wrote about its history, most prominent is Lynne S. Brown. *See supra* n. 1723 and accompanying text. Brown authored a published history of Gulfport in 2004. Still another important contributor is Claudette Dean. Tom Carney has written about Gulfport during the early 1920s. *See infra* n. 1737 and accompanying text. Meanwhile, historian Raymond Arsenault included a brief section on Gulfport's colorful past in his published treatise on the history of St. Petersburg. *See infra* n. 1736 and accompanying text. Many Gulfport citizens have taken an active part in researching the history of their city. One has been Stetson University College of Law Staff Librarian Mary Stull.

changed to "Gulfport" after the village was incorporated in 1910.[1729] Though Gulfport's population remained small for fifteen years after its founding, the residential community grew rapidly during Florida's 1920 land boom. Between 1923 and 1928, developers constructed more than 300 new homes and buildings.[1730]

One developer was Alvah Curtis Roebuck. On September 16, 1893, Roebuck and Richard W. Sears of Chicago formed Sears, Roebuck and Company,[1731] the same Roebuck who in 1925 began to construct homes in a subdivision named "Roebuck Park," as reported by Scott Taylor Hartzell, history correspondent to the *St. Petersburg Times.*[1732] Gulfport historian Claudette Dean adds that Roebuck lost his Gulfport investment within a few years, following the 1927 Florida land bust, including a few of his still-standing Sears' "catalog houses" in other parts of the country.[1733] Yet, except during World War II, the small, predominately residential Gulfport community continued to grow. In 2005, Gulfport's population hovered around 12,000 and was continuing to increase, primarily due to new condominium developments.[1734]

9.2 "Handsome" Jack Taylor Develops Pasadena-on-the-Gulf

Hamilton Disston and Alvah Roebuck notwithstanding, the most flamboyant, mysterious, "handsome" developer to arrive in Gulfport was I.M. Jack Taylor.[1735] Described as a "mysterious Gatsby-like character," "Handsome Jack," as he came to be called, appears to have been born in New Hampshire in 1876 with the name Ivan Marshall Taylor from a family lineage of Eastern Europeans.[1736]

Taylor was extravagant in everything he did—from building a grand and lavish hotel, to promoting money-making schemes, and courting and marry-

1729. Vause, *Centennial History, supra* n. 595, 132.

1730. Scott Taylor Hartzell, *Gulfport Owes It All to Catalog Mogul Roebuck,* St. Pete. Times Neighborhood Sec. 2 (Feb. 18, 2004).

1731. *Id.*

1732. *Id.*

1733. *Id.* (quoting Gulfport historian Claudette Dean).

1734. *See* Brown, *supra* n. 1723, at 3.

1735. Hirshberg, *supra* n. 23, at 20–23.

1736. Raymond Arsenault, *St. Petersburg and the Florida Dream: 1888–1950*, at 202 (Donning Co. 1988).

ing what some say were rich socialites. His first wife may have been "Maggie" Cunningham (daughter of a New York family "worth several fortunes"),[1737] but this is not clear.[1738] After his first wife divorced him, Taylor married another wealthy and socially prominent woman—Evelyn duPont.[1739] She likely knew little about her new husband's past.

Jack Taylor arrived in Gulfport in 1921 after a major hurricane had struck the Tampa Bay region. He had recently returned to the United States after leaving the country, reportedly to escape prosecution for a fraudulent stock swindle he had perpetrated on investors.[1740] Historian Raymond Arsenault describes what happened:

> [H]e enjoyed a successful career as an investment banker in Boston and New York, before an ill-fated stock promotion scheme involving a venture called the East Coast Fisheries drove him to Europe. After a three-year exile, during which he was able to elude both angry investors and law enforcement officers, he returned to the United States.[1741]

Thus, it is not surprising that Taylor was dubbed "a master con-man."[1742] Among the defrauded investors was his first wife. Upon learning of being duped, she quickly bid Taylor *adieu.*

Though lacking forthrightness, handsome Jack exuded charm. Many considered him handsome, and his photographs bear that out. He was tall, slender, had a characteristic pencil moustache, and was described as "an always good looking man."[1743] The renowned American golf professional of that era, Walter Hagen—who had come to the Pasadena Country Club at Taylor's request to be its resident pro and president[1744]—described Handsome Jack as a "work of art," a man who was "well over six feet tall with an unruly mass of thick curly hair, [and who] wore a green coat which hung to his knees, jodhpurs, and boots. [Taylor] drove around his property in a Minerva automobile of extreme design, complete with a chauffeur in eye-catching livery."[1745]

1737. Tom Carney, *The Downfall of Handsome Jack,* 1 Old Pinellas Press 2, 2–4, (1992).

1738. Ltr. from Lynne Brown, Gulfport, Fla. Historian, to Michael I. Swygert, Prof. Emeritus, Stetson U. College of L. (Aug. 2005) (on file with co-author Michael I. Swygert) [hereinafter *Brown Letter*].

1739. Carney, *supra* n. 1737, at 3.

1740. *Id.* at 5.

1741. Asenault, *supra* n. 1736, at 202.

1742. Carney, *supra* n. 1737, at 4.

1743. *Id.* at 5.

1744. Walter Hagen, *The Walter Hagen Story* 118–122 (Simon & Schuster 1956).

1745. *Id.*

Just prior to the "Florida Boom" of the 1920s, a hurricane in 1921 ravaged large areas of the state, with the Tampa Bay region and St. Petersburg area especially hard hit.[1746] Taylor viewed the damage "after the worst storm the city had ever experienced," and considered "the debris-strewn city" as an investment opportunity.[1747] Without hesitating, he began to acquire property.[1748] With "two partners, Fred Aulsbrook and Innes Henry," Taylor bought 600 acres of land then known as "Davista,"[1749] agreeing to pay $5,000 down on a purchase price of $195,000.[1750]

One account of the closing describes Taylor turning to his wife, Evelyn duPont, and asking her for the $5,000 cash. She supposedly "extracted a $10,000 bill from her stocking." Since the sellers did not have change for the $10,000 bill, the buyers postponed the sale for one day.[1751] St. Petersburg historian Arsenault tells virtually the same story. He writes that a real estate salesman "spread the rumor (apparently true) that Evelyn had sealed the deal by rolling down her stockings to produce a ten-thousand dollar bill."[1752]

Taylor and his partners began to develop their newly acquired properties. Taylor oversaw the building of what he wanted to become an "opulent" new community, directing the project from his office in a private railroad car.[1753] The end result was an expansive subdivision, one described as having "[b]eautiful parks, tree-lined boulevards, Mediterranean Revival mansions, [and] a championship-quality golf course and country club."[1754] Taylor named it

---

1746. Hamilton Dunn, *Photouring Florida, Stetson University's College of Law: It's Taylor Spelled Backwards* (undated newspaper clipping, likely from Tampa Bay area newspaper circa 1954–1955) (on file in Stetson U. College of L., Gulfport, Fla.).

1747. *Id.*

1748. *Id.*

1749. Hirshberg, *supra* n. 23, at 22.

1750. *Id.* at 22. Recall that Hamilton Disston originally had paid twenty-five cents an acre for these and other properties in 1841. *See* Vance, *supra* n. 70.

1751. Hirshberg, *supra* n. 23, at 22.

1752. Arsenault, *supra* n. 1736, at 203. Jack Taylor was able to acquire the property with the small down payment of only $5,000, despite the fact that his own financial backing was "shaky at best." Additionally, wife Evelyn's family "had all but disowned their daughter after her marriage" to Taylor. *Id.* Nonetheless, Taylor "never missed an opportunity to remind people that was he married to a DuPont." *Id.*

1753. *Id.*

1754. *Building Begun on Hotel Rolyat,* 1 Pasadena Progress 1 (Nov. 2, 1924) [hereinafter *Building Begun*]. This community news flyer was in fact an advertising promotional brochure in the form of a newspaper. It had five columns with various headlined articles, and consisted of four large, newspaper-size pages. Under its bold-face twenty-eight point title, "PASADENA PROGRESS," appears a subheadline stating: "PASADENA-ON-THE-

"Pasadena-on-the-Gulf," later renamed "Pasadena Estates." This development included portions of what today is known as South Pasadena and much of Gulfport.[1755]

Though accomplishing his dream of developing a high-scale country club bordered by an upscale residential community, Jack Taylor wanted more. He knew that the 1920s hotel boom in Pinellas County was gaining momentum.[1756] Recognizing the potential for the Pasadena-on-the-Gulf community to attract tourists, Taylor began to make plans for a lavish hotel, envisioning a resort that would attract guests, especially from the populous northeastern states. What could do this better, he thought, than an architecturally distinctive edifice?

GULF—FLORIDA'S OUTSTANDING DEVELOPMENT." *Id.* The semi-annual, free brochure was published by Pasadena Estates, Inc., of St. Petersburg, Florida. *See* 3 Suniland: The Magazine of Florida 112 (Nov. 3, 1925) (published monthly by the Peninsular Publishing Co. of Tampa, Fla.).

1755. Brown Letter, *supra* n. 1738.

1756. William D. Slicker, *The Building Boom in St. Petersburg: A Photographic Essay*, 11 Tampa Bay History 22 (Fall/Winter 1989) (on file at the library of the U. of S. Fla.) (available at www.lib.usf.edu/ldsu/digitalcollections/T06/journal/v11n2_89_22pdf). Slicker notes that the St. Petersburg boom occurred primarily between the years 1922 and 1926. *Id.* He includes the following hotels:

Ponce De Leon, *First Street and Central Avenue (1922);*
Mason Hotel, *First Avenue North and Fourth Street (1923);*
Pheil Hotel *(later, Madison Hotel), Central Avenue (1923);*
Suwannee Hotel, *First Avenue North and Fifth Street (1923);*
Soreno Hotel, *Beach Drive (1924);*
Dennis Hotel, *First Avenue across from Williams Park (1925);*
Jungle Country Club Hotel, *Park Street, Fifth Avenue North (1925);*
Vinoy Park Hotel, *Beach Drive (1925);*
Pennsylvania Hotel, *Third Avenue North and Fourth Street (1925);*
Rolyat Hotel, *Gulf Boulevard, Gulfport (1926);*
Don CeSar Hotel, *Pass-a-Grille Beach (1927).*

Id. *at 4–17.*

Also constructed during the 1920s were the Gandy Bridge (1922); the St. Petersburg Coliseum (1924); and the original "Million Dollar Pier" (1926), replaced in 1972. *Id.*; *see also* Arsenault, *supra* n. 1736; Walter P. Fuller, *St. Petersburg and Its People* (Great Outdoors Publg. Co. 1972); Karl H. Grismer, *The Story of St. Petersburg, Florida* (P.K. Smith 1948); Scott Taylor Hartzell, *Jungle Sparkled as 1925 Hotel Boom's Crown Gem*, St. Pete. Times, S. Pinellas Sec. 1 (Apr. 11, 2001).

Rolyat Hotel

9.3 The Rolyat Hotel Is Designed as a Medieval City

Consequently, Jack Taylor decided to place in the middle of his community a "splendid" hotel, one that would be "his pride and joy."[1757] He planned to build the resort in the Country Club segment of Pasadena Estates, a short distance from the championship golf course.[1758] His vacation oasis would consist of architecturally unique buildings, each lavishly furnished, and set amidst tropical gardens located on eleven acres of prime real estate, "twenty-five feet above sea level [with] an extensive view of Boca Ciega Bay."[1759] The land's elevation above sea level was important, given the likelihood of future hurricanes striking Florida's west coast.

Taylor wanted the hotel's style to be designed in accordance with a "Spanish conception."[1760] After soliciting various architects, Walker & Weeks of Cleveland, Ohio, apparently responded to his invitation.[1761] The firm proceeded to draw plans for "a large luxurious resort hotel in St. Petersburg called 'El Pasadena.'"[1762]

1757. *Building Begun, supra* n. 1754, at 1, 145.

1758. *Id.*

1759. *Id.*

1760. *Id.*

1761. Ltr. from Eric Johannesen, Preservation Officer, W. Res. Historical Socy., Cleveland, Ohio, to "Dean of the College of Law, Stetson University" (Oct. 7, 1989) (responded to by a letter from Stetson College of Law Dean Bruce R. Jacob dated Nov. 1, 1989) (both letters on file in the Stetson U. College of L., Gulfport, Fla.).

1762. *Id.* The 1923 architectural drawings for the El Pasadena are preserved at the Western Reserve Historical Society in Cleveland.

However, the architectural firm that ultimately won Taylor's approval was Kiehnel & Elliott of Miami, Florida.[1763] The architects in one document claimed to be "nationally famous."[1764] To fulfill Taylor's desire for a Mediterranean Revival-style Spanish hostelry, the Miami architects drew up the hotel's plans "after extensive travel and first hand observations in California and Spain."[1765]

Within two years after the plans were drawn, the several buildings, fountains, towers, and arcades comprising the hotel complex were built at "top-speed."[1766] Jack Taylor named the completed complex the "Rolyat," his last name spelled backwards. Though not easy to pronounce or remember, subsequent owners did not change the hotel's name.

The firm of George A. Fuller Construction Company of New York City served as the general contractor to construct the facilities.[1767] The selection of Fuller Company was described as "a guarantee of all that is best in construction from foundation to roof."[1768] Time proved the assertion correct. (In clearing land and in completing necessary excavations, Fuller used heavy equipment manufactured by International Harvester Company, which placed advertisements in national publications showing its machines working at the Gulfport site.[1769]

The construction proceeded on schedule without serious obstacles. On New Year's Eve 1925, a festive gathering of the dignitaries partied at the new Rolyat Hotel. The future home of the Stetson University College of Law officially opened for guests the next day, January 1, 1926.[1770]

9.4 The Rolyat Called an "Architectural Gem"

As 1925 came to an end, the *Pasadena Progress*, the newspaper of the Pasadena-on-the Gulf development, in exuberant prose, proclaimed:

1763. *Building Begun, supra* n. 1754.

1764. *Description of Construction of Hotel Rolyat Now Stetson University College of Law* 1 (undated typed document with no author indicated, but providing in more detail the actual construction of the hotel than found in any other source) (on file at Stetson U. College of L., Gulfport, Fla.).

1765. *Building Begun, supra* n. 1754, at 1.

1766. *Id.*

1767. *Id.*

1768. *Id.* For example, the Harvester Company placed a full-page advertisement in the *Saturday Evening Post* featuring their earth-moving machines working at the site of the future Rolyat Hotel). Lynne Brown, *Notes on the Rolyat Hotel* (unpublished ms. 2004) (on file at Stetson U. College of L., Gulfport, Fla.).

1769. *Id.*

1770. *Id.*

> Inspected by thousands of interested and critical observers since its opening last month, the Rolyat has been conceded by all to be fully-deserving of the title of "America's Most Distinctive Hotel."[1771]

Another description of the Rolyat—still accurate today as pertaining to the Gulfport campus of the Stetson College of Law—follows:

> [The Rolyat] is a rambling group of buildings around a large court or, as the Spanish call it, "plaza mayor" resembling a medieval Spanish settlement with towers, turrets, balconies, open staircases, and an arcade passing all around the picturesque little town, having a total length of about eleven hundred feet. This type of unique hotel grouping is ... the only one of its kind in the country and perhaps in the whole world.... The main tower ... resembles the Golden Tower of Seville. The main entrance from the "Plaza Mayor" [has] a striking entrance similar to one in Cordoba. Adjoining this are masonry arches and wooden balconies as beautiful as those in Patio or the Casa Moresco in Ronda, and the Casa del Chapiz in Granada. All woodwork is of solid [cypress] timbers colored and antiqued. The exterior stucco has the appearance of an old Spanish wall in many colors. The interiors of all principal [public] rooms have the appearance of old Spanish monasteries or colleges, with wooden trusses having ornamental bands—and the wooden timbers are brilliantly decorated with many colors on Medieval lines.[1772]

Finally, another early depiction of the hotel, portions of which Stetson's College of Law still includes in an information brochure of campus architecture, follows:

> THE ROLYAT is a picturesque re-creation of a Spanish walled settlement of the feudal ages.... The group of buildings encloses a great court, the *Plaza Mayor* [where today law school graduations take place].... It contains a [wishing] well and two large fountains of colorful design in imported hand-made antique tile.
>
> The main entrance to the *Plaza* is a reproduction of the entrance to the old *Alcantara* Bridge at Toledo, Spain. The lobby is built in the form of a

1771. *Rolyat Pronounced Architectural Gem; Pasadena's Highly Picturesque Spanish Hostelry Is Acclaimed as a Distinct Addition to the Fine Show Places of the Country*, 2 Pasadena Progress 1 (Nov. 5, 1925).

1772. *Pasadena-on-the-Gulf, Florida's $100,000,000 Development—"A Slice of Old Spain"* 2 (a several page—though not paginated—printed and undated document [presumably a Pasadena-on-the-Gulf promotional brochure], probably issued by the development's owners in 1926 or 1927) (on file at Stetson U. College of L., Gulfport, Fla.).

> cloistered monastery chapel. The dining room is similar in form and size to the nave, or central portion, of a cathedral.
>
> The great doorways from the lobby to the dining room are of a design inspired by the monastery doors separating the living quarters from the patio of the house of *el Greco,* Spain's most celebrated painter. The huge fireplace in the lounge [today it is called the Mann Lounge] is a slightly modified reproduction of *Greco's* favorite fireplace. The floor tiles are very old, presumably dating from about 700 A.D., during the Roman occupation of Spain.
>
> The roof tiles have been brought from monasteries and other structures from Spain and are about 400 years old. The quaint outside stairways which form a picturesque feature of the *Plaza* are similar to those found in old Spanish palaces....
>
> The circular tower, known as the *Granary Tower,* is of the type which was used in times of peace for the storage of grain, and in war as a point of defense. The numerous loggias, colonnades and cloistered arcades with their broad low arches, are just like those seen in monasteries, nunneries, and many massive old buildings of Spain.
>
> The three great vases, or *Talaveras* (so-called from the name of the Spanish city of their origin), were made especially for the Brazilian exposition. These are the only ones of their kind in the world owned privately, the remaining six [then in existence] being the property of national museums.[1773]

The above claims regarding the hotel's architecture and references to specific buildings, bridges, and towers in Spain have not in all regards been verified, but neither have any knowingly been disputed. The likely descriptions were written by the Rolyat's architects, who had drawn the plans for the singularly designed hotel with its Spanish and Moorish Mediterranean-Revival motif. That architectural style has been described as an example of that architectural style in vogue in Florida during the 1920s.

Regarding the hotel's furnishings, a New Yorker named John Wanamaker supplied interior furniture and accessories at a cost of a quarter of a million dollars.[1774] The wife of the Roylat's manager at the time it closed in 1932—Elizabeth Worth—revealed years later that she possessed two lovely dinner plates with the following inscription: "made especially for the Rolyat Hotel by John Wanamaker." She further described them as "gilt-edged with a picture in

1773. *Id.* (specifically, the article *Some Interesting Features of the Rolyat*); *see also* Stetson U. College of L., *Campus Tour, Stop One: Plaza Mayor,* www.law.stetson.edu/general/tour/a.asp.

1774. Dunn, *supra* n. 1746.

the center of a ship and a buccaneer-looking fellow."[1775] Worth gave pieces of the Rolyat china to her daughter, who in turn sold them to Dean Bruce Jacob for $2,000, who then gave them to the law school.[1776] Today, they are on display at the College of Law's library in Gulfport, Florida.

People who stayed in Gulfport's distinctive resort hotel, with its flashy interior, were impressed. One visitor was a world-class golf champion, Walter Hagen.[1777] Hagen wrote in his autobiography that "Jack Taylor's Rolyat Hotel was the most magnificent and luxurious hostelry constructed in the booming twenties."[1778] The consensus was that the Rolyat was, indeed, "a gem—unlike anything seen heretofore in this part of the world."[1779]

9.5 The Rich and the Famous Come (But Not for Long)

On New Year's Eve, December 31, 1925—the Rolyat's opening night—the main fountain in the *Plaza Mayor* was "filled with champagne" while "guests lingered leisurely in the tropically landscaped grounds" and inside the lavish lounge, dining room, and lobby of the hotel. The inaugural evening party was said to be "the talk of St. Petersburg for months afterwards."[1780]

During the Rolyat's brief existence, it attracted numerous "celebrities," including the son of Calvin Coolidge and his family, "opera prima donna Frieda Hempel, and the ubiquitous Babe Ruth."[1781] Besides the "Babe," other professional baseball players such as Jimmy Fox, Mickey Cochrane, Rube Marquard, and Cy Perkins came.[1782] Also coming to the Pasadena Estates Golf and Country Club to play with the champion golf pro Hagen were several other top-rated professional golfers, including Chick Evan, Gene Sarazen, Jock Hutchin-

---

1775. Ltr. from Mrs. Robert S. (Geraldine G.) Salisbury to Bruce R. Jacob, Dean, Stetson U. College of Law 2–3 (June 6, 1983) (on file at Stetson U. College of L., Gulfport, Fla.).

1776. Jacob July 10 Ltr., *supra* n. 393.

1777. Bob Harig, *Hagen's Approach: Be a Real Swinger,* St. Pete. Times C-1 (Aug. 14, 1989). Walter Hagen was hired by Jack Taylor to be president of the Pasadena Golf and Country Club (part of Pasadena-on-the-Gulf) in 1924. *Id.* at 2. Hagen signed a three-year contract under which he spent four winter months each year as the Club's professional golfer and president for $30,000 a year. *Id.* During his Florida stays, Hagen lived at the Rolyat Hotel. *Id.*

1778. Hagen, *supra* n. 1744, at 120.

1779. *See The Rolyat* 7 (1926) (promotional brochure) (on file at Stetson U. College of L., Gulfport, Fla.).

1780. Carney, *supra* n. 1737, at 7.

1781. Hagen, *supra* n. 1744, at 121.

1782. Hirshberg, *supra* n. 23, at 22.

son, Joe Kirkwood, Laurie Ayton, Bob MacDonald, and Bobby Jones.[1783] Presumably some, if not all, stayed at the Rolyat.

The hotel's first year of operation was a success, as reflected by its hosting members of the rich and famous. The following year, 1927, however, the Florida land boom came to an abrupt end. The Rolyat struggled, the gilded guests being substantially fewer. During its three-month season, nothing noteworthy at the resort apparently took place.[1784]

Then, the situation turned more positive, but only after a new director took over operations of the hotel.[1785] The Rolyat's new management also owned and ran the Soreno Hotel in downtown St. Petersburg.[1786] Whether due to more effective management or other reasons, during the winter of 1928 the Rolyat enjoyed a splendid season, so much so that overflow guests were offered rooms at the Soreno.[1787] Highlighting the Rolyat's year was the engagement party for Calvin Coolidge's son, who was married to Florence Trumbell, daughter of the Connecticut Governor.[1788]

During those relatively good times, in sharp contrast Jack Taylor's financial house of cards was collapsing.[1789] Despite an overflow of patrons, the money did not roll in. In 1928, Soren Lund leased the Rolyat property after the George Fuller construction company foreclosed on the hotel and golf course.[1790] Though guests continued coming to the Rolyat through the 1929 season, its debts multiplied.[1791] John Wanamaker, who had supplied the hotel's deluxe furnishings four years earlier, sued for the quarter of a million dollars the Rolyat still owed him.[1792] Facing mounting debts, in December 1929, the Rolyat was sold to the Hugh Jay Fuller Company of New York.[1793]

1783. Hagen, *supra* n. 1744, at 123; *see also The Rolyat, supra* n. 1779, at 13. The golfers played on what was described as an "eighteen-hole, champion course, laid out by Walter Hagen, president of the club, in collaboration with Wayne E. Stiles and John Van Kleek, among the foremost golf course builders in America." *Id.*

1784. Historian Lynne Brown has commented that the Rolyat "seemed to drop out of sight" in 1927, noting that not a single reference to it was made in the local press that year. *See* Brown, *supra* n. 1723.

1785. *Id.*

1786. *Id.*

1787. *Id.*

1788. *Brown Letter, supra* n. 1738.

1789. Carney, *supra* n. 1737.

1790. *Brown Letter, supra* n. 1738.

1791. Brown, *supra* n. 1723.

1792. *Id.*

1793. Brown, *supra* n. 1723.

To increase the hotel's attractiveness, Fuller added a pool prior to the hotel's 1930 season opening. The season was a success, with regard to the number of guests.[1794] At one point, Fox's "Movie Tone Reels" shot a newsreel at the Rolyat, thereby enabling "moving pictures" of the resort to be portrayed on movie screens throughout the country.[1795] At the end of the season, given the intensifying effects of the Great Depression, the hotel's ownership once again changed hands.[1796] Two brothers, Walter and William Mendels, who were part of the Flynn Consortium, purchased the Rolyat.[1797]

To continue to attract visitors from the northeast to the hotel, the Mendels brothers placed small classified advertisements under the heading of "Florida" in *The New York Times* newspaper during late 1929 and early 1930.[1798] But *The Times*' ads did not work. Under management of the Mendels, the 1931 season was a financial disaster, even though the year had begun with a dinner and open house for 200 guests.[1799] The nation's depression was deepening, as hundreds of banks failed and unemployment rose to record highs.[1800] Meanwhile, many among America's "gilded aristocracy" who had frequented the Rolyat, increasingly were experiencing the distress of severe and, in some cases, total financial loss.

In the wake of widespread financial hardship, the Rolyat's days as a hotel became numbered. Before the final day came, however, the Royalt hosted one more significant event—Babe Ruth's signing of a lucrative major league baseball contract.

9.6 The "Babe" Makes History at the Rolyat

"Babe" Ruth was born on February 6, 1895, in Baltimore, Maryland.[1801] George Herman Ruth, Jr., his real name, was one of eight children of whom

---

1794. *Id.*

1795. *Id.*

1796. *Id.*

1797. *Brown Letter, supra* n. 1738

1798. *See e.g. The Rolyat Hotel, St. Petersburg, Florida,* N.Y. Times Classified Ad Section (n.p.) (Dec. 24, 1929). Reportedly seven classified ads for the Rolyat appeared in *The New York Times*, the last being on March 11, 1930. *Id.*

1799. Brown, *supra* n. 1723.

1800. *See generally* David M. Kennedy, *The American People in the Great Depression: Freedom from Fear,* in *Oxford History of the United States* 9 (Oxford U. Press 2003).

1801. BabeRuth.com, *Biography*, www.baberuth.com/flash/about/biograph.html (accessed Dec. 30, 2004) [hereinafter *Babe Biography*].

only he and a sister survived infancy.[1802] At the age of seven, his parents placed him in a Catholic "reformatory and orphanage."[1803] Ruth acknowledged that he was "a bum when I was a kid."[1804] In a feature story on his life, *St. Petersburg Times* staff writer Jeff Klinkenberg wrote that Babe was "[a] habitual truant."[1805]

At nineteen, Ruth put truancy behind him and began his fabled baseball career, joining the Baltimore Orioles, then a minor league team owned by the Boston Red Sox.[1806] Within months, he was elevated to the major league Boston Red Sox team.[1807] According to one account, Ruth got the nickname "Babe" by his new Red Sox teammates due to what they considered the youth's "baby face."[1808] Klinkenberg, on the other hand, offers a different explanation: Red Sox players named Ruth "Babe" because "of his naiveté *off* the field."[1809]

On the field, however, the "Babe" proved he was to be taken seriously. At twenty-one, he pitched his first World Series game for the Red Sox, a complete game lasting fourteen innings that the Sox won 2–1. His performance "stands as the longest complete game in World Series History."[1810] After being traded to the New York Yankees, he continued to make baseball history by, for example, hitting sixty home runs during the 1927 season.[1811]

Babe spent several springs in St. Petersburg and Gulfport preparing for upcoming seasons. Ruth's first spring training appearance in the Tampa Bay area occurred during February and March 1925; his last was in1934.[1812] In all, the "Babe" spent ten spring training camps practicing at the Huggins-Stengel Field in St. Petersburg.[1813]

But like many Americans, the "Babe" also experienced the effects of the events that shook the nation in the early 1930s. In 1932, the New York Stock Exchange fell to its lowest level of the century, losing roughly ninety percent

---

1802. *Id.*

1803. *Id.*

1804. Jeff Klinkenberg, *Thanks Babe*, St. Pete. Times E1 (Mar. 21, 2004) (available at www.sptimes.com).

1805. *Id.*

1806. *Babe Biography*, *supra* n. 1801.

1807. *Id.*

1808. *Id.*

1809. Klinkenberg, *supra* n. 1804, at E1 (emphasis added).

1810. *Babe Biography*, *supra* n. 1801.

1811. *Id.*

1812. Klinkenberg, *supra* n. 1804 at E1.

1813. *Id.*

of its 1929 peak value.[1814] That same year, bank failures rose to their highest level.[1815] Not coincidentally, in 1932, the Rolyat Hotel had its seventh and final opening, after which it went out of business.[1816] Not only were millions of people unemployed, those who had jobs often were forced to take cuts in pay. George Herman Ruth, Jr., was not an exception.[1817] In 1932, he signed a contract lowering his previous year's salary before reporters, photographers, and newsreel cameramen from around the country in the lounge of the Rolyat Hotel. One who witnessed the signing was a sports reporter for *The New York Times*, William Brandt.[1818] The signing took place at a table next to the Rolyat's stone fireplace. Nearby, three large and beautiful Talaveras, five-feet tall, rare ceramic vases, stood in blue and white splendor.[1819] Today, the Mann Lounge of the Stetson College of Law, along with two of the Talaveras continue to awaken nostalgic feelings of an earlier era.[1820]

Brandt's story of Babe Ruth's contract signing was published in *The New York Times* on March 17, 1932.[1821] Under the headline *"Home-Run Ace Takes a $5,000 Salary Cut,"* the story relates how Ruth and the New York Yankees came to terms. A few minutes after the signing, a "staged" second signing was held outside in the Rolyat's Plaza Mayor because newsreel cameramen needed sunlight.[1822] Under the subheadline of "*Setting Is Appropriate*," Brandt described the event: "The setting befitted so important an episode in the career of the great orphan boy who grew up to make a million dollars."[1823] After the signing, Ruth, his wife, and Ruppert adjourned to the hotel with its "subtropical garden background."[1824] "The crowning touch, characteristic of the Babe's

1814. *See* John Kenneth Galbraith, *The Great Crash, 1929* (7th ed., Houghton Mifflin Co. 1997).

1815. *Id.*

1816. Brown, *supra* n. 1723.

1817. Tom Zucco, *Outstanding in His Field; Part of Babe Ruth's Legacy Lives in St. Petersburg,* St. Pete. Times D4 (Mar. 2, 1998).

1818. *See e.g.* William E. Brandt, *Home Run Ace Takes $5,000 Salary Cut; Accepts a Compromise Offer after Brief Conference with Ruppert in Camp: Movies Record Signing,* N.Y. Times § 1, 26 (Mar. 17, 1932).

1819. *See Interesting Features of the Rolyat, supra* n. 1773. Today, there are two talaveras vases in Stetson College of Law's Mann lounge. They contribute to the ambience of the lounge, one conjuring up images of a medieval inn.

1820. Most Stetson law students preparing for class in the Lounge today are likely unaware that Babe Ruth, the most famous baseball player in history, made history there.

1821. Brandt, *supra* n. 1818, at 26.

1822. *Id.*

1823. *Id.*

1824. *Id.*

background," Brand wrote, "came when he and Mrs. Ruth and Rupert lined up at the Spanish wishing well."[1825]

There, Ruth, his wife, and Ruppert each made a wish and tossed a silver half dollar into the well. Ruth wished that the Yankees would win the American League pennant in 1932, so that he could participate in his tenth World Series. Claire Ruth wished for many more contracts for her husband to sign. Ruppert then wished he could have the coins on the floor of the well, so that he could purchase another minor league club. After tossing his silver half dollar into the well, Ruth declared: "There goes some of this year's contract."[1826]

During Ruth's spring seasons in St. Petersburg, he often played golf with Walter Hagen, then president of the Pasadena Golf and Country Club, adjacent to the Rolyat.[1827] Though Yankee manager Joe McCarthy prohibited Yankee players from playing golf during spring training, Hagen has written that "a number of the fellows sneaked over for bootleg games."[1828] Ruth was one.

When in St. Petersburg, Ruth resided in various places. According to *St. Petersburg Times* writer Jeff Klinkenberg, they included a home in Northeast St. Petersburg, the Princess Martha Hotel, the Hotel Dennis, the Jungle Club Hotel, the Flori-de-Leon, and the Don CeSar on the beach.[1829] A rumor that Ruth owned a home in Gulfport near the Rolyat hotel is not true,[1830] though he did own two lots on 10th Avenue.[1831] On the other hand, the story that Ruth dined frequently in the Rolyat dining room seems more credible, as it was across the street from the golf course where he frequently played.[1832]

1825. *Id.* The colorful, handmade imported Spanish-tiled well added a unique setting along with the semi-tropical atmosphere for the picture version.

1826. *Id.*

1827. Hagen, *supra* n. 1744, at 121. Hagen noted that "Babe Ruth and I played many rounds [of golf] together," adding that the Babe did not play well through an eighteen-hole match. *Id.*

1828. *Id.*

1829. Klinkenberg, *supra* n. 1804, at E1.

1830. *Brown Letter, supra* n. 1738; *see also* William Moriaty, *Book Review*, 4 La Floridiana 6 (Feb. 3–9, 2003) (reviewing Dan Allison, *On the Whispering Wind* (Writers Club Press 2002).

1831. *Brown Letter, supra* n. 1738.

1832. Ruth and his second wife, actress and model Claire Hodgson, also stayed at the Rolyat. Ruth's first wife was Helen Woodford whom he married in 1914 when she was fourteen. *Babe Biography, supra* n. 1801, at 3. They separated in 1925. *Id.* Helen subsequently died in a house fire in 1929. *Id.*

9.7 Rolyat Hotel Closes; Florida Military Academy Opens

The Rolyat's final year was climatic. In addition to the March visit and contract signing of Babe Ruth, the hotel's managers on Valentine's Day held a gala costume party.[1833] According to Gulfport historian Brown, the fete was touted as the "Beaux Arts Ball."[1834] More than 600 guests attended; most came dressed as movie stars.

Despite the gala's success, the Rolyat's end was only weeks away. The hotel's final social function took place on March 26, 1932.[1835] By the end of April, the grand hotel was history. Though guests assumed the Rolyat would open for another season in 1933, that did not happen. Rather, the hotel's owners, the Mendels brothers, announced that the hotel was "permanently" closed.[1836] Like other grand Florida resorts, the unique Mediterranean Revival hotel in Gulfport had become another casualty of the Florida land bust and the Great Depression.[1837]

When the Rolyat finally closed for good, Walter and William Mendels were its owners.[1838] Despite the hotel's heavy debts, the brothers did not sell the property. Instead, they purchased a boys' school—the Florida Military Academy (FMA)—located in Duval County near Jacksonville in a community

1833. Brown, *supra* n. 1723.

1834. *Id.*

1835. *Id.*

1836. *Id.*

1837. *See* Scott Taylor Hartzell, *Jungle Sparkled as 1925 Hotel Boom's Crown Gem,* St. Pete. Times, S. Pinellas News Sec. (Apr. 11, 2001) (available at www.sptimes.com/News/041101/news_pf/SouthPinellas/Jungle).

Meanwhile, the man who started it all—"Handsome" Jack Taylor—had reportedly been long gone, having "quickly slipped out of town, carefully avoiding unpaid creditors and abandoned employees in the fall of 1926." Arsenault, *supra* n. 1736, at 203. "Taylor reappeared in New York, no longer married to Evelyn [DuPont]." *Id.* One account claimed that Taylor "disappeared on a ship headed for Europe." *Id.*

Although it remains uncertain whether or not Taylor ever returned to Gulfport, one report tells how he came back to his former Rolyat Hotel for a nostalgic look. *Id.* Thomas Lawson, a Stetson College of Law custodian during a night shift in 1956, "noticed an old distinguished man standing in the shadows." Carney, *supra* n. 1737, at 4. The stranger said he knew the "building's history," and mentioned that he had attended "glorious parties," adding that he had known "Babe Ruth and other famous people." *Id.* Some time later, Thomas Lawson saw a picture of Jack Taylor in an article describing the history of the Rolyat Hotel. Lawson exclaimed that the image looked "exactly like the old stranger." *Id.*

1838. *Supra* n. 1723 and accompanying text.

called Green Cove Springs, and began preparations to move it to what had been the Rolyat.[1839]

Initially called the Florida Military and Naval Academy, the private institution—founded in 1908 by Colonel George W. Hulvey—was Florida's first military school.[1840] The Academy was originally located in Jacksonville, but later moved to the Magnolia Springs Hotel in Green Cove Springs. In 1925, the school relocated to Jacksonville into the former San Jose Hotel, where it remained until the Mendels acquired the boys' school.[1841]

Perceiving that the economically stricken school might provide a financial opportunity for their former Rolyat Hotel, the Mendels brothers purchased the Academy "lock, stock, and barrel" in October 1932,[1842] one month before the public announcement of the Rolyat's closing.[1843] The Academy was in bankruptcy and the Mendels reportedly bought it for ten cents on the dollar.[1844]

St. Petersburg lawyer Joseph W. Bradham, Jr., a graduate and later legal counsel of the Academy after its relocation to Gulfport, tells what happened next:

> The Commandant of the Florida Military Academy, Colonel Burnell V. Bryant (U.S. Army), loaded the 200 plus cadets on a train and transported them to a small railroad station near 64th Street and 3rd Avenue South in Pasadena, adjacent to Gulfport. Colonel Bryant unloaded the troops and marched them to their new barracks, which had been the luxurious Rolyat Hotel.[1845]

1839. Joseph W. Bradham, Jr., *Select History, Florida Military Academy Transition to Stetson University College of Law* 1 (two-page typed document attached to a handwritten letter from Mr. Bradham to Professor Michael Swygert, dated August 8, 2004) (on file with author).

1840. Fla. Mil. Acad., *1933 Commencement Exercises* 1 (brochure, on file at Stetson U. College of L., Gulfport, Fla.).

1841. *Id.*

1842. Elizabeth B. Worth, *History of Frank Worth* (May 24, 1983) (one-page typed ms. on file at Stetson U. College of L., Gulfport, Fla.) (originally included in letter from Mrs. Robert S. Salisbury to Bruce Jacob, Dean, Stetson U. College of L. (June 6, 1983)). Frank Worth was hired by the Mendels brothers to manage the Rolyat Hotel, however, by the time he arrived in September 1932, the brothers had decided to close the hotel, but they kept Worth to serve as the Quartermaster of the Florida Military Academy for two years. *Id.*

1843. *Id.*

1844. *Id.*

1845. Bradham, *supra* n. 1839 at 1.

The move was accomplished quickly as, "over a weekend, the entire personnel and equipment of the Academy were moved to St. Petersburg and housed in the almost palatial quarters of the Rolyat."[1846]

As the Academy's new owners, Walter Mendels named himself president of the Academy, and his brother William L. Mendels, treasurer.[1847] Interestingly, after the purchase, the Mendels brothers each "acquired a military title," though apparently neither had ever served in the military.[1848] Walter Mendels gave himself the additional title of "Colonel," while William took the rank of "Major."[1849] Among the cadets, Major Mendels was referred to as "Uncle Bill."[1850] The cadets dedicated their 1948 yearbook to the "Major" with the inscription, "Known as Uncle Bill, his tireless interest in the activities of all the cadets leaves him as one of the figures the seniors will long remember."[1851]

The properties of the Academy grew in 1937 when the Mendels purchased land for a "Beach Recreation Center."[1852] The undeveloped property was located on Sunset Beach of Treasure Island, between the Gulf of Mexico and Boca Ciega Bay.[1853] Two miles from the Gulfport campus, the Center in time

---

1846. *Florida—Tampa And Its Neighbors* (unpublished, undated two-page printed document circa mid-1930s) (on file in the Stetson U. College of L., Gulfport, Fla.).

1847. Telephone interview with Joseph W. Bradham, Jr., Fla. Mil. Acad. graduate (Oct. 4, 2004) [hereinafter *Bradham Interview*].

1848. *Id.*

1849. *Id.*

1850. *The Dugout of 1948*, at i (Fla. Mil. Acad. 1948) (approximately 149 unnumbered pages, except for advertisements at end. *The Dugout* was the annual yearbook of the Florida Military Academy.

1851. *Id.*

1852. *Bath Houses to Be Erected; Cadets to Use New Treasure Island Center for Beach, Aquatic Activities,* (May 2, 1937) (according to a written notation on the top of the reproduced copy of the story) (a news story in what was likely either the *St. Petersburg Times*, or the *Evening Independent* (on file at Stetson U. College of L., Gulfport, Fla.) [hereinafter *Bath Houses*]. On the same page, there is a five-column wide, one half-page "announcement of the planned for center" apparently placed by the Florida Military Academy. The display advertisement includes in large type the following language: "AND NOW ... Continuing the all-round development of the facilities of the Academy, Colonel Walter B. Mendes, President, *Announces* the Beach Recreation Center of the FLORIDA MILITARY ACADEMY at SUNSET BEACH, TREASURE ISLAND 'On the Gulf of Mexico.'" *Id.* In addition there is a drawing of the proposed buildings laid out on the site. *Id.* The 1939 FMA catalog includes a map of "Gulfport and St. Petersburg" that indicated where the Florida Military Academy is located on Gulfport Blvd., and where the F.M.A. Beach Center is located.

1853. *Id.*

consisted of a lodge, boat house, and four small bath houses, all designed to be used for cadets' "beach and aquatic activities."[1854]

The recreation center was used extensively by the cadets. A 1939 promotion of the center says:

> Some of the most enjoyable and memorable hours of a cadet's life at the Academy are those spent at our Beach Recreation Center located on Treasure Island, only two miles from the Academy.... On the [Boca Ciega] Bay side, cadets may enjoy boating and fishing, while swimming and beach games are prevalent on the Gulf side. Our cadets go to the beach almost every afternoon.... Transportation is provided in our own fleet of buses.[1855]

In addition to swimming, the Academy offered horseback riding, football, track, baseball, boxing, and tennis.[1856] Moreover, the FMA encouraged "the boys" to attend Camp Cedar-Pines over the summers. It was located in Pine Creek Gorge, near Harrisburg, Pennsylvania.[1857] Tuition for an entire school year (excluding summer) was $975. In addition, there were extra fees for "equitation," (fifteen dollars), "dancing," (fifteen dollars), and "cadet membership in the Pasadena Golf Club," (twenty-five dollars).[1858]

A 1939 FMA catalog included instructions on how to reach the Academy in Gulfport:

> Tickets may be purchased to the Florida Military Academy station on the Seaboard Air Line Railroad, or to St. Petersburg, Florida, via Atlantic Coast Line Railroad. Several steamship lines from New York, Havana, and other points dock at Port Tampa, twenty miles distant from St. Petersburg, and the Florida Motor Lines operate on convenient schedules between the two cities.[1859]

1854. W.D. Berry Company constructed the facilities. Academy President Walter Mendels acquired the strip of land from Lex D. Herron in exchange for free tuition for Herron's son to attend the Academy. The Academy announced its acquisition on May 2, 1937. Ltr. from Joseph W. Bradham to Michael I. Swygert 1 (Oct. 7, 2004) (on file in Stetson U. College of L., Gulfport, Fla.).

1855. Fla. Mil. Acad., *An Accredited University Preparatory School, Reserve Officers Training Corp, College Entrance Board Examination Center, Designated as an Honor Military School by the U.S. War Department* (1939) (on file at the Stetson U. College of L., Gulfport, Fla.).

1856. *Id.*

1857. *Id.*

1858. *Id.*

1859. *Bath Houses*, *supra* n. 1852.

From the Florida Military Academy's relocation in Gulfport in 1932 through 1941, Colonel Burnell Bryant served as its commandant, though at times he was referred to as the superintendent.[1860] Born in Houlton, Maine, Bryant graduated from the New York Military Academy in 1923 and later from the University of New Hampshire. He became commandant of the Florida Military Academy when the school was located at Green Cove Springs.[1861]

The Mendels brothers advertised the Academy during the 1930s and 1940s in various venues. One was the classified section of *The New York Times.* Under the heading "schools," a two-inch by two-inch box contained a drawing of the school's replicated tower of Seville, beneath which appeared the heading, "Florida Military Academy."[1862] The language of the advertisement follows:

> One of America's outstanding military schools. The only resident military school in Florida with Junior R.O.T.C. unit. An accredited university preparatory school. Highest government rating. All branches of athletics, swimming pool. Limited enrollment. All inclusive rate $1,075. Address Colonel Walter Mendels, Pres., St. Petersburg, Fla.[1863]

Under the heading "Army Orders and Assignments," *The New York Times* listed appointments of military officers. Lt. Colonel Friedersdorff from Fort Bragg, North Carolina, for example, was ordered in 1936 "to the Florida Military Academy, St. Petersburg, Fla."[1864] On one occasion, a wedding of an FMA cadet—James Dayton Hedges of East Hampton, Long Island—made the society pages of *The Times.*[1865]

1860. *Bradham Interview, supra* n. 1847.

1861. After the United States entered World War II, Bryant reenlisted in the Army and for the next sixteen years served in various capacities. These included Chief of Operations and Training at Camp Zena, Japan, from 1953–1955; then Provost Marshall, Headquarters, First U.S. Army, Governors Island, New York, from 1955–1957. U. of Neb. *The University of New Hampshire Army and Air Force ROTC Hall of Fame, Colonel Burnell V. Bryant, U.S. Army,* www.unh/edu/army-rotc/AlumniPage/bryant.html.

1862. *Schools,* N.Y. Times Classified Sec. (Aug. 7, 1949) (on file at the Stetson U. College of L., Gulfport, Fla.). A virtual identical ad appears in other editions of *The N.Y. Times.*

1863. *Id.*

1864. *Army Orders and Assignments, Special* to The New York Times, N.Y. Times 30 (Aug. 20, 1935).

1865. *Muriel Mendels Bride; Former New Jersey Girl Is Wed in South to James D. Hedges,* N.Y. Times 22 (Feb. 16, 1934). At a subsequent date, *The Times* again recognized the Florida Military Academy, noting that the school "will be the scene of a ball on Friday night." *Along Florida's West Coast,* Special to The New York Times, N.Y. Times 22 (Feb. 16, 1936).

By the spring of 1948, the Academy had grown to twenty-seven faculty members and 177 students.[1866] Cadets and faculty lived on campus. About fifty percent of the students came from Florida, the remainder from eighteen other states, the District of Columbia, and Cuba.[1867]

The Academy's 1948 yearbook, *The Dugout,* included fourteen pages of advertisements from various community businesses, or "sponsors." One surely remembered by Stetson law students of the 1950s, 60s, and early 70s, who likely had frequented St. Petersburg's major attraction of that era, Webb's City (where mermaids swam in a large tank). The advertisement read:[1868]

Congratulations
J. E. "Doc" Webb
and the
more than 850 employees of
WEBB'S CITY
Home of the World's Most Unusual Drugstore

In the fall of 2004, one of FMA's former teachers—John. H. Cook from Freehold, New Jersey—visited the Stetson College of Law Gulfport Cam-

---

1866. *The Dugout of 1948, supra* n. 1850.

1867. The states were New York, New Jersey, Connecticut, Massachusetts, Pennsylvania, Ohio, Illinois, Wisconsin, Michigan, Minnesota, Virginia, West Virginia, Alabama, Georgia, North Carolina, Kentucky, Tennessee, and California. *Id.*

FMA was divided into two "schools." The senior school consisted of the four upper grades, eighth through twelfth. In 1948, seventy-seven students attended, consisting of thirty seniors (12th grade), nineteen juniors (11th grade), eighteen sophomores (10th grade), and thirty freshman (9th grade). In addition, three post-graduate students studied in the senior division. In the junior school—grades one through eight—ninety-seven students were in attendance.

Faculty members came from all parts of the country. They had studied at universities including Alabama, Olgelthorpe, Florida Southern, Case, Lehigh, Monrovia, Colgate, Maine, Pennsylvania, U.S. Military Academy, Niagara, Emory, Evansville, and Columbia University. One instructor—Lt. Frank R. Arnold—had earned an LL.B. degree from Brooklyn Law School.

In 1948, Colonel Walter Mendels was FMA's President; Major William Mendels, Treasurer; and Lt. Colonel Paul Bauder, Headmaster. Senior Cadet William F. Casler was the students' Commandant. "Bill" Casler later graduated from the Stetson College of Law, having earlier become a veterinarian. For years, he practiced both veterinary medicine and law in adjacent offices on St. Petersburg Beach.

1868. *Id.* at 139.

pus.[1869] In a conversation with Brandi Palmer, a staff member of the law school, Cook affirmed that most Academy faculty and students lived on the campus during the late 1930s. Cook mentioned that he was paid $75 a month as a physics teacher.[1870] During his 2004 Stetson campus visit, Cook was delighted to see that trophies, uniforms, and other memorabilia from the Academy had been preserved and were on display in Stetson's Great Hall.

Of interest: during World War II, the Academy cadets scratched their names on the central tower, many of which remain readable sixty years later.[1871] According to historian Lynne Brown, during WWII, the tower was used as a "plane spotting station," and was staffed by Gulfport citizens, "many of whom gave countless hours during the two years the project was in existence."[1872] One final note: Stetson law school Dean Emeritus Bruce Jacob believes the Academy's graduates included the baseball legend Al Rosen, and the son of the U.S. Supreme Court Associate Justice Hugo Black.[1873]

Two years after the Academy closed in 1951, Stetson University purchased the campus. The following year, the College of Law moved from DeLand to the former home of the Rolyat Hotel and, later, of the Florida Military Academy.

1869. E-mail from Brandi Palmer to Frank Klim, Davina Gould, and Aaron Reincheld, Stetson U. College of L. Communications Off. (Sept. 24, 2004) (forwarded to Dean Dickerson and Professor Swygert).

1870. *Id.*

1871. *Id.*

1872. *Brown Letter*, *supra* n. 1738.

1873. Conversation between Bruce R. Jacob, Dean Emeritus, Stetson U. College of L., and Michael I. Swygert, Prof. Emeritus, Stetson U. College of L. (Feb. 2005).

CHAPTER TEN

Rebuilding the Law School and Its Reputation — Dean Sebring

10.1 New Home in St. Petersburg

a. Law Center to Be Patterned after English Inns of Court

Having acquired the buildings and site of the former Rolyat Hotel, later, Florida Military Academy,[1874] Stetson University announced that the College of Law would move in the summer of 1954 to its Gulfport campus.[1875] President Edmunds stated that the college would become a law center where, "part of the full-time faculty will live with the students to carry out the Christian influence which has predominated the campus in DeLand since the founding of the University."[1876]

Edmunds' remarks were intended both to appease DeLand residents unhappy about the school being relocated across the state by praising the University's virtues, and to appeal to prospective law students. The school's officials envisioned a law center modeled along the lines of the English Inns of Court where judges, barristers, students, and prominent guests lived, ate, and worked together.[1877] Though an inns of court arrangement was implemented in 1955 by Dean Harold Sebring, the plan was conceived by President Edmunds, and announced a year before Sebring's arrival. An advertisement asserted that students "associate around the clock with experienced teachers who

---

1874. *See supra* nn. 1682–1690 and accompanying text.

1875. *New Million-Dollar Law School Site Is Patterned after English Legal Inns*, 67 Stetson Rptr. 1 (Dec. 11, 1953) [hereinafter *New Million Dollar Law School*].

1876. *Id.* at 5.

1877. *Id.* Though an article by Norman Gelman printed in the *St. Pete. Times* on September 29, 1957, claims the Inns of Court Idea was that of Harold Sebring, who became dean in 1955, news reports and University announcements in 1953 and 1954 indicate President Edmunds first espoused the Inns of Court plan for the College of Law.

not only teach them ... but also share with them the wisdom they have acquired in actual law practice."[1878]

Sebring emphasized that the Stetson College of Law had adopted a personalized, interactive law program. He wrote:

> Stetson College of Law [has] embarked upon a lawyer-training program patterned in concept after the historic Inns-of-Court System under which training for the Bar has been centered in England for more than seven centuries. [Stetson adopted] [t]his time-honored system of training law students by "osmosis" [which] retained the basic idea ... of maintaining close personal contact between embryo lawyers and eminent scholars, lawyers, and judges.[1879]

As grand as the plan was, the proclaimed "around the clock" association of law students with their professors did not happen. Students of Sebring's era, when asked, do not recall informal sessions or get togethers with members of the law faculty outside class.[1880] To the contrary, as revealed in later interviews, several remember many of their professors as being aloof. Moreover, none of the interviewees mentioned visiting professors in their campus residences.[1881]

Even though the reality of an English-like inns-of-court system did not occur, the goal of students living together on one campus, apart from other university students or the community at large, was realized. Sebring believed that legal education should be intense and interactive. To a significant degree, he succeeded. He and the faculty used seminars, legal clinics, moot court, and trial advocacy classes where students had greater opportunities to interact with faculty.[1882]

Though Sebring puffed up Stetson's inns-of-court program as resembling the English system, he did coin a phrase to describe the College of Law that did not overstate the matter: Stetson's College of Law, Sebring emphasized, was"*One of America's Most Interesting Law Schools.*"[1883]

1878. *New Million Dollar Law School*, *supra* n. 1875, at l.

1879. Harold Sebring, *Report on Stetson University College of Law* 8 (Dec. 1957) (on file in Stetson U. College of L., Gulfport, Fla.) [hereinafter Sebring, *1957 Report*].

1880. Dean Emeritus Bruce R. Jacob, Professor Emeritus Michael I. Swygert, and Associate Vice President Dotti Bressi, along with Stetson Law students, interviewed around ten alumni who graduated from Stetson University in the 1950s and 1960s, all of which have been transcribed and are in the files of Stetson University College of Law, Gulfport, Florida.

1881. *Id.*

1882. *See infra* nn. 2453–2455 and accompanying text.

1883. Harold L. Sebring, *Annual Report to Board of Overseers, Stetson University College of Law* (Jan. 1, 1959) [hereinafter Sebring, *1959 Overseers Report*]; *see also One of America's*

College Opens in Gulfport

b. Makeshift Facilities Allow School to Open

The school's new campus, as lovely as it was, presented Dean Hilkey, and subsequently Dean Sebring, with several problems. The first was relatively minor—moving the library collection and furnishings 150 miles from the Naval Air Station in DeLand to the former Rolyat Hotel and Florida Military Academy in Gulfport. Fortunately, the move went smoothly.

The second problem, however, was not as easily disposed—the serious deficiencies of the Gulfport facilities. Despite the original grandeur of the former hotel's rooms, they could not be used as living quarters in their rundown condition. Moreover, there were no offices for faculty nor classrooms for students.[1884] The only option was to renovate three temporary buildings.[1885] One

Most Interesting Law Schools (1956) (a twenty-four page advertising brochure containing mostly pictures of the Gulfport campus on file in Stetson U. College of L., Gulfport, Fla.).

1884. Vause, *Centennial History, supra* n. 595, at 146.

1885. Telephone Interview by Michael Swygert, Prof. Emeritus, Stetson U. College of L., with Richard T. Dillon, Dean Emeritus, Stetson U. College of L. (May 4, 2005) [hereinafter May 4 *Dillon Interview*].

was built during the Military Academy's occupancy. Under supervision of University Trustee Elkanah B. Hulley, a portion of the shoddily built temporary structure was cleaned out and divided into two classrooms and several library-carrel size faculty offices.[1886] Hulley completed the necessary renovation and clean-up prior to the opening of the Gulfport campus in September 1954.[1887]

Parallel to what became the renovated classroom building stood a smaller temporary structure (probably built by the Florida Military Academy) that Hulley decided to restore to hold the library's limited collection.[1888] The structure, consisting of several small cubicles, was located on the northeast side of the property. For years, students called this building the "stables" because it appeared to be where the military school housed its horses.[1889]

When moved from Deland to Gulfport in 1954, all the law books "fit into one moving van."[1890] Richard Dillon—a student in the first entering law class on the Gulfport campus—recalls that the school's 1954 law library was not only small, it was also in a deplorable state.[1891] The collection was inadequate, disorganized, and suffered from neglect, he said, and advance sheets and supplements were unsorted and piled into boxes.[1892]

Once renovated, the books and supplements could be stored and placed in the converted stacks building. The structure, however, was not large enough for chairs and tables for the students. Hulley rectified this problem by converting another building into a library reading room.[1893] Years later, this structure was moved to its present location and is known as Classroom "H."[1894] In 1957, it was converted into a courtroom.[1895]

To have the facilities functional in time for the school's opening in September 1954, the College of Law spent over $123,000, the bulk of which was

---

1886. Edmunds, *1952–1953 Report*, *supra* n. 1575, at 9.

1887. Lycan, *History of Stetson*, *supra* n. 109, at 364.

1888. Sebring, *1957 Report*, *supra* n. 1879, at 6–7; *see also Law School Moves*, 68 Stetson Rptr. 1 (Oct. 1, 1954).

1889. Jacob, *Recollections*, *supra* n. 1678.

1890. *Id.*

1891. Interview by W. Gary Vause of Richard T. Dillon, Dean Emeritus, Stetson U. College of L. (Oct. 24. 1986).

1892. *Id.*

1893. Vause, *Centennial History*, *supra* n. 595, at 146.

1894. *Id.*

1895. Jacob, *Recollections*, *supra* n. 1678, at 3; *see also* Note from Bruce Jacob, Dean Emeritus, Stetson U. College of L., to Michael Swygert, Prof. Emeritus, Stetson U. College of L. (Feb. 22, 2005) (on file at Stetson U. College of L., Gulfport, Fla.).

Classroom "H"

for the cleaning out and repair of the old hotel.[1896] Assisting Hulley in these efforts was Harold F. Archibald, whom Edmunds appointed to be business manager for the school in Gulfport.[1897] Though Hulley and Archibald had accomplished many campus improvements in a short time, they realized that far more needed to be done, including additional repairs to the hotel, new classrooms, new faculty offices, and a stand-alone large library facility. But those improvements would have to wait.

c. *Disgruntlement Continues in DeLand*

Meanwhile, citizens and University personnel back in DeLand continued to ask why the law school's move to Gulfport was necessary. Explaining the relocation, the chair of the University Board of Trustees, Rev. C. H. Bolton, was quoted in the DeLand *Sun News* to have said that the decision came down to revenues, which in turn were directly related to the number of students.[1898] Bolton said, "[T]o finance the operation of a law school in America that will meet [ABA] standards ... without endowment, a minimum enrollment of 150 students is required."[1899] He pointed out that while the average enrollment of ABA-approved law schools was 357, Stetson law school had only sixty-eight

---

1896. Harold L. Sebring, *A Five-Year Report of Progress; Stetson University College of Law, 1954–1959*, at 2 (July 28, 1959) (on file at Stetson U. College of Law, Gulfport, Fla.) [hereinafter Sebring, *Five-Year Report*].

1897. Lycan, *History of Stetson*, *supra* n. 109, at 364.

1898. J. Blanford Taylor, *News Release* 1, 2 (Dec. 5, 1953).

1899. *Id.* at 2.

students during its last year on the DeLand campus, adding that "moreover, there has been a decline in the Stetson law enrollment during each of the past five years."[1900] Bolton concluded his explanation:

> In my opinion, it would be difficult for anyone who has the welfare of the law school at heart—rather than civic pride or pleasant memories of past associations—to disagree with the wisdom of the board's decision ... Stetson is Florida's oldest law school; it must remain Florida's best."[1901]

The arguments were sound, but even if they did not persuade the resisters, the move was a *fait accompli.* More pressing was the need to find a new dean for the College of Law who had experience, vision, and leadership to actualize the potentialities of its new location in a growing metropolitan area on the west-central coast of a growing state.

10.2 Arrival of Harold J. "Tom" Sebring

a. Multifaceted Achiever

As acting dean, Charles J. Hilkey understood that he would be replaced as soon as President Edmunds could find "the right person" to be dean of the College of Law.[1902] Prior to the school's relocation, Edmunds told the trustees that the critical need of the law school was to find a permanent dean.[1903] Evidence suggests that Edmunds' first choice may not have been Justice Harold Sebring, but Edmunds' friend, Stetson law alumnus and later chair of the law school's campaign for a new law library, Florida Supreme Court Justice E. Harris Drew.[1904] But Edmunds did not appoint Justice Drew dean. Stetson graduate J. Ben Watkins believes that Drew did not wish to become Stetson's law dean at that point in his career, and recommended to Edmunds that he consider another member of the Florida Supreme Court, Justice Harold L. Se-

1900. *Id.*

1901. *Id.* at 6–7.

1902. Edmunds, *1952–1953 Report, supra* n. 1575, at 9.

1903. *Id.*

1904. Interview by Bruce R. Jacob, Dean, Stetson U. College of Law, with J. Ben Watkins, former member of Stetson U. College of L. Bd. of Overseers, (Oct. 21, 1999). The likelihood that Drew was Edmunds's first choice was also suggested during an interview with Richard T. Dillon, Dean Emeritus, Stetson U. College of Law (Jan. 29, 2004) [hereinafter *Jan. 29 Dillon Interview*].

Dean Harold Sebring

bring. In 1953, Justice Drew was an active member of the State's highest court and was said to be very close to Edmunds.[1905]

While Edmunds did not know Sebring well, the two soon became better acquainted due to Drew's intervention.[1906] Edmunds quickly became aware of Sebring's impeccable reputation and incredible background.[1907] The jurist was known throughout Florida, so much so, that he was once described by Stetson graduate Amory Underhill as "Mr. Florida."[1908] Bruce Jacob recalls a conversation he had with Edmunds in which the president said that he hired Sebring because the jurist had many influential friends and Edmunds "wanted those friends for Stetson."[1909] Underhill underscored the same point: "Everybody [in Florida] knew Judge Sebring."[1910] Less important, perhaps, but still a plus was the fact that Sebring was a Baptist.[1911]

Harold Sebring had a good education and excelled in virtually everything he undertook. He earned a B.S. degree in commerce from Kansas State Agri-

1905. Jacob, *Remembering Sebring*, *supra* n. 9, at 129.

1906. *Id.*

1907. *See* Norman Gelman, *To Stetson Law School Dean, Every New Job Has Been More Enticing Than the Last*, 74 St. Pete. Times 4, 5 (Sept. 29, 1957).

1908. Jacob, *Remembering Sebring*, *supra* n. 9, at 137.

1909. *Id.* at 138.

1910. *Underhill Interview*, *supra* n. 842, at 12.

1911. Gelman, *Every New Job*, *supra* n. 9, at 6.

Dana Foundation and Overseer President William Amory Underhill

cultural College (ultimately renamed Kansas State University).[1912] There, he took classes in architecture, engineering, and business administration.[1913] Years later, in 1928, Sebring earned an LL.B. degree from the University of Florida College of Law "while working there as head football [and] track, and boxing coach."[1914]

Though Sebring's grades may not always have been at the top of his class, his football teams usually were at the top of their league. Because of his singular achievements in various fields, Sebring in time was awarded honorary doctorate degrees from University of Kansas, Stetson University, University of Florida, and University of Tampa.[1915] These honors are well deserved in light of Sebring's career. Sebring was a farmhand in Kansas, a roustabout on oil rigs in the southwest, a rancher in Canada,[1916] a highly decorated combat soldier on the front lines in France during World War I,[1917] a record-breaking football player in college,[1918] the head football coach at the University of Florida (one

1912. Jacob, *Remembering Sebring, supra* n. 1905, at 80.

1913. Fla. Supr. Ct., *Justices of the Supreme Court, "The International Judge," Justice Harold L. Sebring*, www.flcourts.org/pubinfo/gallery/sebring.html (accessed Jun. 24, 2004).

1914. *Id.*

1915. Bowen, *History of Law School, supra* n. 455, at 9.

1916. Jacob, *Remembering Sebring, supra* n. 9, at 74–76.

1917. *Id.* at 76–79.

1918. *Id.* at 81–84.

of the winningest in the school's history),[1919] a college football referee,[1920] a successful practicing attorney in Jacksonville,[1921] a respected judge on Florida's Eighth Judicial Circuit,[1922] a justice and subsequently chief justice of the Florida Supreme Court,[1923] and a presidential-appointed judge on the international tribunal at the Nazi war crimes trials in Nuremberg, Germany.[1924]

When he was a law student, Bruce Jacob in 1959 introduced Dean Sebring to a group of lawyers and judges. Jacob told them they were about to meet "one of the most versatile figures in the history of our State."[1925] Jacob continued:

> I introduce to you, Tom Sebring, a former judge of the Nuremberg war crimes trials, former justice and chief justice of the Supreme Court of Florida, the dean of our law school, and former head football coach of the University of Florida.[1926]

In response to Jacob's final remark, the audience burst into laughter[1927] Though the football coach reference was true, the audience had not anticipated it.

When Harold Sebring came to Stetson in 1955 at the age of fifty-seven, he brought diverse experience along with mature wisdom. He approached his new challenge at Stetson with vigor, enthusiasm, and imagination and determination.[1928] However, only nine months after his arrival, his ambitions were interrupted by a heart attack, his second, which forced him to remain at home for a prolonged period of time. During this period, Professor William Morris and Business Manager Archibald more or less ran the school.[1929] But Sebring in time recovered and took charge.

Over the years, Sebring advanced the Stetson College of Law in several important areas, as recounted below. His tenure has been described as the "watershed era in the history of Stetson College of Law."[1930] During Sebring's deanship, the quality and the productivity of the faculty were upgraded; teaching became more demanding; academic standards were raised; several new buildings were

---

1919. *Id.* at 85–102; *see also* Vause, *Centennial History, supra* n. 595, at 134.
1920. Jacob, *Remembering Sebring, supra* n. 9, at 103.
1921. *Id.* at 103–04.
1922. *Id.* at 105.
1923. *Id.* at 106–07, 124–37.
1924. *Id.* at 108–14.
1925. *Id.* at 73.
1926. *Id.*
1927. *Id.*
1928. Vause, *Centennial History, supra* n. 595, at 135.
1929. *May 4 Dillon Interview, supra* n. 1885.
1930. Vause, *Centennial History, supra* n. 595, at 135.

completed, including a new library, classrooms, and administrative buildings; and the library's collection was greatly augmented, thereby making serious research possible. In addition, Sebring and certain key figures convinced the University Trustees and Edmunds to establish a board of overseers dedicated to improving the law school. They also persuaded the trustees to sanction the founding of an independent foundation designed to assure the institution's financial security. Of course, none of these accomplishments came easily. But Harold Sebring's background and broad life experience had taught Stetson's eighth dean to persevere.

b. Justice at Nuremberg

(1) Background

In 1945, Florida Supreme Court Justice Harold L. Sebring received a letter from President Harry S. Truman,[1931] which did not surprise him since, as in the case of other American judges selected to serve at Nuremberg, Sebring had been recommended by the War Department to serve on tribunals at the Nazi War Crime Trials in Germany.[1932] The judges were selected in part on geographical diversity (Justice Sebring represented the southeast of the United States) and, in part, on experience (fourteen of the judges, including Sebring, were or had been members of the highest court of their respective states).[1933]

According to the United States Chief Counsel at Nuremberg, Telford Taylor, the War Crime Trials grew out of discussions during World War II among representatives of those European countries then occupied by Germany—Belgium, Czechoslovakia, France, Greece, Luxemburg, the Netherlands, Norway, Poland, and Yugoslavia.[1934] These discussions prompted the United States, Soviet Union, France, and Great Britain to create an international tribunal to adjudicate war crimes at the end of the war.[1935] The agreement was called the London Charter agreement of August 8, 1945.[1936]

The first trial involved prosecution of twenty-four of the highest-ranking Nazi officials.[1937] While this trial was in process, the parties to the London

---

1931. Jacob, *Remembering Sebring*, *supra* n. 9, at 112.

1932. As to the process of selecting the Nuremberg judges, see Telford Taylor, *Final Report to the Secretary of the Army on the Nuremberg War Crimes Trial under Control Council Law No. 10*, at 156–157 (William S. Hein & Co. 1997) [hereinafter Taylor, *Final Report*].

1933. *See generally* Telford Taylor, *The Anatomy of the Nuremberg Trials: A Personal Memoir* (Knopf 1992).

1934. *Id.* at 4.

1935. Taylor, *Final Report*, *supra* n. 1932, at 238–240.

1936. *Id.*

1937. *See* Jacob, *Remembering Sebring*, *supra* n. 9, at 108.

Charter adopted Allied Control Council Law Number 10, authorizing additional war crime trials involving Third Reich "diplomats, doctors, lawyers, judges, businessmen, and military leaders."[1938] The accused were placed into groups based on occupation, then each group was separately prosecuted.[1939] One contingent consisted of administrators and officials carrying out Holocaust, the mass genocide of millions of children, women and men. This trial became known as "the Executioners Trial."[1940]

(2) The Doctors' Trial and Judge Sebring

Twenty-three additional defendants were prosecuted in what is called the "Doctors' Trial," also known as the "Medical Trial." The defendants—all physicians except three—were charged with crimes against humanity. In an opening statement, United States Chief of Counsel Telford Taylor accused the defendants of committing murders, tortures, and other atrocities in the name of medical science.[1941] The atrocities included performing medical experiments on concentration camp inmates and prisoners of war that killed or disabled the "objects" of those experiments.[1942] Two defendants were accused of murdering 112 Jews for the purpose of "completing a skeleton collection for the Reich University of Strasbourg." Other inhumane experiments involved freezing inmates, deliberately infecting them with deadly pathogens, injecting their bodies with phosphorus from incendiary bombs, and making them drink saltwater.[1943]

Sebring was one of three judges appointed to the Doctors' Trial tribunal, the other two being Justice Walter B. Beals of the Supreme Court of Washington (who served as the presiding judge) and Judge Johnson Crawford, a former district court jurist from Oklahoma. The trial was held in the Palace of Justice in Nuremberg.[1944] The Doctors' Trial case is titled *United States v. Karl Brandt, et al.*, Case 1.[1945] Karl Brandt was Adolph Hitler's private physi-

1938. Taylor, *Final Report*, *supra* n. 1932, at 159.

1939. *See Trials of War Criminals before the Nuremberg Military Tribunals under Control Council Law 10*, vol. 1 (Govt. Prtg. Off. 1950).

1940. Taylor, *Final Report*, *supra* n. 1932.

1941. *Id.*

1942. W. Paul Burman, *The First German War Crimes Trial: Chief Justice Walter B. Beals' Desk Notebook of the Doctors' Trial, Held in Nuremberg, Germany, December 1945 to August 1947*, 130–34 (Documentary Publications 1985).

1943. *Id.* at 131–32. For a compelling description of the Medical Trial, see Jacob, *Remembering Sebring*, *supra* n. 9, at 113–24.

1944. *Id.* at 93–94.

1945. *Id.*

cian and the Reich's general commissioner for medical and health matters.[1946] On August 19, 1947, Judges Sebring, Beals, and Crawford handed down their judgement in the Doctors' Trial.[1947] The judges wrote:

> Judged by any standard of proof, the record clearly shows the commission of war crimes and crimes against humanity substantially as alleged.... Criminal medical experiments on non-German nationals, ... including Jews and "asocial" persons were carried out on a large scale.[1948]

(3) The "Nuremberg Code"

The case of *United States v. Karl Brandt* remains a landmark decision that establishes the legal recognition of international human rights in medicine. It delineates for the first time "the rights of human subjects" in medical treatment and medical experimentation.[1949] The opinion contains what today is called "the Nuremberg Code," described as "the basic guide to the rights of research subjects."[1950] The standards enunciated by Judges Sebring, Beals, and Crawford in the Nuremberg Code have been restated several times, including in the Declaration of Helsinki, and in the American Medical Association's Ethical Guidelines for Clinical Investigation.[1951]

Though Sebring had taken part in enunciating an authoritative declaration of fundamental human rights, during his tenure at Stetson, he rarely talked about the horrific details of the case. On these occasions, Sebring talked to students about the inhumanity of the Nazis, showing them a few of the shocking images introduced at the Doctors' Trial.[1952] Dorothy Bishop, assistant registrar at the time, recalls that Sebring's Nuremberg experiences were

1946. Taylor, *Final Report*, *supra* n. 1932, at 77.

1947. Jacob, *Remember Sebring*, *supra* n. 9, at 121.

1948. Taylor, *Final Report*, *supra* n. 1932, at 165.

1949. Edward P. Richards, III, LSU L. Ctr.'s Med. & Pub. Health L., *The Nuremberg Code* http://biotech.law.lsu.edu/Books/aspen/Aspen-The-8.html (accessed June 21, 2004).

1950. *Id.*

1951. *Id.* For a listing of the minimum standards for conducting experiments on human beings enunciated in the Nuremberg Code, see Jacob, *Remembering Sebring*, *supra* n. 9, at 122–24.

1952. Bruce Jacob learned this fact from alumnus Joe Ann Taylor Van Gelder and relaid it to Professor Michael Swygert on April 25, 2005. Interview by Bruce Jacob, Dean Emeritus, Stetson U. College of Law of Joe Ann Taylor Van Gelder, Stetson U. alumnus (Apr. 25, 2005) (on file at Stetson U. College of L., Gulfport, Fla.).

"off-limits" as far as he was concerned.[1953] In the dean's office sat four large volumes containing Sebring's personal notes, partial transcripts, and photographs depicting the Nazis' grotesque medical experiments. Today, these volumes are located in the documents room of the College of Law Library in Gulfport, and are available to WWII historians and Holocaust researchers.[1954]

Nobel Prize Laureate and humanitarian Elie Wiesel has described the historical significance of the College's Nuremberg collection: "To visit the Nuremberg archives at Stetson University's College of Law is a moving experience ... Anyone dealing with the Second World War would benefit from seeing them."[1955] Wiesel noted that the collection "houses more than 100 volumes of court transcripts and personal papers. They represent an immense source of information and knowledge."[1956]

c. Sebring Resigns from the Court; Accepts Stetson's Offer

Edmunds announced on June 25, 1955, that Stetson had extended an offer to Justice Sebring to be dean of the College of Law.[1957] One week later, Sebring announced that he was resigning from the Florida Supreme Court and accepting Stetson's offer.[1958]

Though it was clear why Edmunds wanted Sebring, the evidence is mixed why Sebring resigned from the Supreme Court to come to Stetson. In 1954, the justice suffered a heart attack while on the court. His grandson, Harold L. Sebring III, said that his grandfather may have stepped down for health rea-

---

1953. Interview by Michael I. Swygert, Prof. Emeritus, Stetson U. College of L, with Dorothy Bishop, Asst. Dean's Sec. (Retired) 5 (May 17, 2004) (on file at Stetson U. College of L., Gulfport, Fla.) [hereinafter *Bishop Interview*].

1954. An example of the research value of the Sebring Nuremberg collection occurred in February 2004. A biographer of Telford Taylor (the war crimes trial Chief of Counsel), Professor Jonathan A. Bush of Columbia University visited Stetson's Law Library to study the papers of Justice Sebring, as well as those of Justice James T. Brand (who became a Stetson law professor at the invitation of Sebring after they both served as Nuremberg judges). In a letter to Dean Darby Dickerson and Librarian Madison Mosley, Professor Bush noted that he had found that the Sebring Nuremberg documents included several papers and documents that "had not been touched" by outside researches since the trials ended in 1947. *See* Ltr. from Jonathan A. Bush, Adjunct Prof., Columbia U., to Darby Dickerson, V.P. and Dean, Stetson U. College of L., and Madison Mosley, Libr., Stetson U. College of L. (Mar. 2, 2004) (on file at Stetson U. College of L., Gulfport, Fla.).

1955. *Nobel Laureate Visits Stetson*, 29 Fla. B. News 35 (May 15, 2002).

1956. *Id.*

1957. Jacob, *Remembering Sebring*, *supra* n. 9, at 137.

1958. Lowell Brandle, *Sebring Decides to Accept Post as Stetson Dean*, St. Peter. Times, sec. 1, 15 (July 2, 1955).

sons.[1959] Amory Underhill noted that given Justice Sebring's heart attack and his fast-paced career, the jurist may have "been tired."[1960] Sebring may have thought that a dean's life would be less stressful than that of a Supreme Court Justice.[1961]

On the other hand, another possible explanation comes from Hazel Clapp, the wife of College of Board Overseer William E. Clapp. She recalls Sebring told her that he accepted the deanship because "he loved working with young people."[1962] Sebring's son corroborated that reason, remembering that what his dad "really wanted to do was to teach."[1963] A dean of a law school, however, has little time for teaching.

10.3 Sebring's First Year

a. Faculty; Administrative Assistant, Mrs. Kay Eddy

During Sebring's first year as dean, his main concerns related to infrastructure, mission, and faculty. When he arrived in the fall of 1955, Sebring found the Gulfport campus "a shambles."[1964] Having taken classes in architecture at Kansas State University, Sebring possessed considerable architectural skills and talent.[1965] He was constantly searching for opportunities to put his talent to use at the College.[1966] Upon seeing the condition of the campus, he saw a welcome challenge.[1967]

According to Dean Emeritus Richard Dillon:

> Designing a new building or remodeling an old one stirred his passion to a greater degree than did most of the mundane decanal duties. The pleasure he received from orchestrating the campus makeover was surpassed only by the pleasure of his first love—teaching.[1968]

1959. Bruce R. Jacob, *Reflections and Memories of Justice Harold L. "Tom" Sebring and Justice E. Harris Drew* (Fla. Sup. Ct. Historical Socy. Nov. 2, 1990) (video recording) (copy on file at Stetson U. College of Law Library).

1960. *Underhill Interview*, *supra* n. 842, at 12.

1961. Jacob, *Remembering Sebring*, *supra* n. 9, at 138.

1962. *Id.* (citing Jacob conversation with Hazel Clapp, wife of Wm. E. Clapp, Board of Oversees, Stetson U. College of Law (early 1980s)).

1963. *Id.*

1964. Peter Kramer, *An Informal Visit with Mr. Sebring of Stetson*, St. Pete. Times 10, 10–11 (Nov. 28, 1965).

1965. Jacob, *Remembering Sebring*, *supra* n. 9, at 14.

1966. *May 4 Dillon Interview*, *supra* n. 1885.

1967. *Id.*

1968. *Id.*

Dean Sebring designed the reflection pool that is located today in the middle of the "horseshoe," the circular driveway between the former Charles A. Dana law library and the Eleonor Naylor Dana administration hall.[1969] Sebring's design consisted of squares representing the states.[1970] In addition, he had seven pedestals built to represent the seven justices of the Florida Supreme Court.[1971] The American flag stood at one end of the pool, while at the other rose the five different flags that have flown over Florida throughout its history.[1972] Sebring laid out the entrance to the school. Moreover, he designed the Crummer classroom building, the library, the Dana administration hall, and the Firestone apartment.[1973]

Though restoring the attractiveness of the campus was important to Sebring, of more significance was the law school's mission. After becoming dean in 1955, Sebring spoke about the objectives of Stetson College of Law:

> Stetson has not been, and never will be, satisfied to train students to become mere legal technicians. Its aim is to develop not just competent lawyers, but [also] lawyers imbued with high standards of character and integrity and a philosophy of Christian living that will accompany them wherever their legal pursuits may take them.[1974]

Among those listening to Dean Sebring's remarks was student Richard Dillon, a member of the first class on the Gulfport campus. At that point in time, neither Dillon nor Sebring could fathom that in thirteen years, Richard Dillon would succeed Harold Sebring as dean, but that is what happened.[1975]

Sebring's other initial concern was the composition and competence of the faculty he inherited. Moving with the College of Law when it relocated to Gulfport in 1954 were Dean Charles Hilkey and three DeLand law faculty members, Roy Howes, Louis Clay James (who later went to American University), and Harvey Jernigan (who had an LL.B. from Stetson, and an LL.M. from the

---

1969. Discussion between Michael I. Swygert, Prof. Emeritus, Stetson U. College of L. and Richard T. Dillon, Dean Emeritus, Stetson U. College of L. (Jan. 29, 2005) (hereinafter *Jan. 29 Dillon Discussion*].

1970. Jacob, *Recollections*, *supra* n. 1678, at 3.

1971. Vause, *Centennial History*, *supra* n. 595, at 147.

1972. *Id.*

1973. *May 4 Dillon Interview*, *supra* n. 1885.

1974. *Learning, Versatility Characterize Largest Faculty; Aim to Develop Lawyers, Not Legal Technicians. Says Dean*, 4 Stetson Law. 5 (Oct. 1960) [hereinafter *Learning, Versatility*] (an article quoting Sebring's 1955 opening remarks).

1975. *See infra* n. 2584 and accompanying text.

University of Illinois).[1976] In Gulfport, Hilkey hired a new full-time faculty member, C.W. Leaphart (former dean at University of Montana Law School),[1977] and appointed six part-time adjunct faculty members: Wm. Reece Smith of Tampa (future president of the American Bar Association and the American Bar Foundation); John J. Trenam (one of the founders of an esteemed Tampa law firm); Judge Victor O. Wehle (a judge who later became a full-time faculty member); Baya Harrison (a president of The Florida Bar); Harold Kooman; and Francis Nicholson.[1978]

Two years later, only one of the original five full-time faculty members remained—Professor Roy Howes. The four who left were replaced by professors Edwin Platt, William Morris, Burton Stevenson, and Jack Rappaport.[1979] Sebring had his own notions on how a law faculty should be composed. Over the next dozen years, he put together a radically different kind of faculty than had existed before at the College of Law, a subject addressed subsequently in this chapter.[1980]

The task of running every aspect of the law school was on Sebring's shoulders from the beginning. When he took over the deanship, there were no assistant dean, registrar, or director of admission. To lessen his administrative burden, in 1955 Sebring hired "Mrs. Kay Eddy [as] Registrar and Director of Admissions."[1981] She remained at the College of Law until she retired in October 1971 during Dean Richard Dillon's administration.[1982] Mrs. Eddy, as she was called, endeared herself to both faculty and students. She was an efficient, hard worker, dedicated to serving the College and all the members of the school community.

Before coming to Stetson, Eddy worked in Washington, D.C., as "the first employee in the first office established by the Railroad Act."[1983] A guest at the White House, at one point "she was asked to hire White House secretaries."[1984] Following her retirement, an article in the *Stetson Lawyer* noted that "through

1976. Charles Hilkey, *Report to President Edmunds* 5 (Oct. 1954) (on file at Stetson U. College of Law, Gulfport, Fla.)

1977. *Id.*

1978. *See infra* nn. 2236–2258 and accompanying text.

1979. Jacob, *Recollections*, *supra* n. 1678, at 6.

1980. *See infra* nn. 2236–2237 and accompanying text.

1981. Kay Eddy, *New Faces, Retirements Characterize 1971–1972,* 15 Stetson Law. 2 (Aug. 1972).

1982. *Id.*

1983. *Id.*

1984. *Id.*

Kay Eddy, Registrar

her hands passed every diploma given to a graduate of the College of Law in St. Petersburg."[1985] Dean Emeritus Richard Dillon remarked that "Mrs. Kay Eddy won the affection of every student who had contact with her."[1986]

b. Two Students

(1) Harvey Firestone III

In 1954, Harvey Firestone, Jr., President and Chief Executive Officer of the Firestone Rubber Company, of Akron, Ohio, contacted Governor Doyle Carlton, inquiring about which law school in Florida would be most suitable for his son, who was afflicted with cerebral palsy.[1987] Dean Hilkey wrote Firestone, touting the advantages of both the Stetson law program and the school's physical facilities.[1988] Admissions Counselor Georgiana Sheldon mailed information about Stetson to the Firestones. Soon after, the family notified the school that they had

---

1985. *Id.*

1986. Conversation between Michael I. Swygert, Prof. Emeritus, Stetson U. College of L., and Richard T. Dillon, Dean Emeritus, Stetson U. College of L. (July 25, 2005) [hereinafter *July 25 Dillon Conversation*].

1987. Ltr. from Charles J. Hilkey, Dean, Stetson U. College of L., to Harvey Firestone, Jr., (Jan. 6, 1955) (on file at Stetson U. College of Law, Gulfport, Fla.) [hereinafter *Hilkey, 1955 Letter*]; *see also* Jacob, *Recollections*, *supra* n. 1678 at 12.

1988. *Hilkey 1955 Letter*, *supra* n. 1987.

Benefactor Harvey Firestone, Jr.
(*Courtesy of Automotive Hall of Fame, Dearborn, Michigan*)

chosen Stetson for their handicapped son because it "meets all our requirements."[1989] In the fall of 1955, Harvey Firestone III began law school at Stetson.[1990]

Law student (and later professor) Everett Cushman tutored his classmate Firestone III.[1991] Cushman had earlier been Firestone's tutor at the University of Miami, when Firestone was in undergraduate school.[1992] At Stetson, Firestone took a lighter load than the other students. He received the LL.B. degree in 1959, ranked third in his class after Cushman and Bruce Jacob.[1993] At Firestone III's graduation, his father, Harvey Firestone, Jr., was the featured speaker.[1994]

Armed with his Stetson law degree, young Firestone III was prepared to confront his next challenge, the Florida Bar Examination. Because of Harvey's physical limitations, the Florida Board of Bar Examiners, through its Director James Tippen, called on Assistant Dean Richard Dillon to specially adminis-

---

1989. Ltr. from Gov. Doyle E. Carlton to Georgiana Sheldon, Dir. of Admissions, Stetson U. College of L. (Jan. 10, 1955) (on file at Stetson U. College of Law, Gulfport, Fla.).

1990. Bowen, *History of Law School*, *supra* n. 455, at 13.

1991. Jacob, *Recollections*, *supra* n. 1678, at 12.

1992. *May 4 Dillon Interview*, *supra* n. 1885.

1993. *Id.* Bruce Jacob recalls that during the Christmas Season, Firestone III gave a party in the courtyard of the school for the community's handicapped children.

1994. *Harvey Firestone, Jr., Is Commencement Speaker; Thirty-Six Graduates to Receive Degrees in Spring Exercises*, 2 Stetson Law. 1, 1 (Apr. 1959).

ter and proctor Firestone's bar examination when it was given in Miami, Florida, in March 1960.[1995] Dillon agreed. Harvey was capable of speaking for extended periods of time and could communicate quite effectively with someone familiar with his speech pattern, but he was unable to use his hands to type or otherwise write his answers.[1996]

During the examination, Harvey would read each question and then, after a reasonable time for thought and reflection, he would dictate his answer to Dillon. Dillon was directed by Tippen to act as a scrivener and record Firestone's every word verbatim in a standard examination blue book. Tippen adopted this procedure to maintain Harvey's anonymity throughout the grading process.[1997]

Young Firestone III passed his bar examination, though he never knew it. Only a few weeks after taking it, but before the results of the examination were announced, he died tragically as the result of a fall from a hotel balcony in Havana, Cuba, where he and several friends were vacationing.[1998] He left a wife, Beverly, and a baby daughter, Diane, both of whom were present fourteen years later for the dedication of the Harvey Firestone III Memorial Recreation Center in 1974 on the campus of Stetson College of Law.[1999]

Harvey Firestone III was admitted to the Florida Bar posthumously. An article in the Stetson Lawyer stated that Firestone's classmates "will remember his spirit and determination ... [traits that] enabled him to graduate third in his class and pass the Florida bar despite his physical handicaps."[2000]

Prior to his son's death, Harvey Firestone, Jr., reportedly gave $42,000 to the College of Law.[2001] These funds helped pay for a new classroom, a seminar room, two faculty offices, a suite for guests of the College (the Firestone apartment where Firestone III lived during law school), a modern courtroom, and renovation of an athletic center and a swimming pool (later renamed in honor of his deceased son, Harvey Firestone III).[2002] Harvey Firestone, Jr., continued

---

1995. *May 4 Dillon Interview*, *supra* n. 1885.

1996. *Id.*

1997. *Id.*

1998. *Id.*

1999. *See infra* nn. 2654–2658 and accompanying text.

2000. *Illinois Justices Establish Book Memorial to Harvey Firestone III*, 5 Stetson Law. 7 (Oct. 1961).

2001. J. Ollie Edmunds, *Annual Report of the President of Stetson University* 4–5 (1955) (on file at Stetson U. College of L., Gulfport, Fla.).

2002. *New Facilities Gift of Harvey Firestone, Jr.*, 4 Stetson Law. 6 (Oct. 1960); *see also* J. Ollie Edmunds, *Stetson University President's Annual Report to the Board of Trustees* 10 (Feb. 19, 1960).

to make substantial contributions to the College.[2003] Firestone's most unusual gift consisted of two magnificent Flemish tapestries representing a characteristic pastoral scene.[2004] Belonging to the "seventeenth century genre," they are regarded as examples of "the finest tapestries then being made anywhere in the world."[2005] One of two was hung in the Great Hall in 1961 and the other in the Mann Lounge.

(2) Joe Ann Taylor (Van Gelder)

President Edmunds and the Board of Trustees hoped that the law school's move to Gulfport would produce a larger student body. It did. The last year in DeLand (1953–1954), the school's enrollment was seventy-one.[2006] The first year in Gulfport (1954–1955), the number rose to ninety-four; then to 138 the following year, and to 148 in 1956. Within three years, the total number of law students on the new campus doubled from what it had been in the school's final year on the DeLand campus.[2007]

Six women were among the ninety-four students comprising the first student body on the Gulfport campus: Joe Ann Taylor, Carolyn Daniel, Clara Britton, "Mrs. Carl B. League," Erica Wagner, and Ann Longshore.[2008] In an article titled "Men, Men, More Men—And Stetson Gals Talk Taxes," a writer for the *St. Petersburg Times* described Joe Ann Taylor as a "blond model turned bookworm" from Tallahassee, and Carolyn Daniel as a "red haired" gal from Orlando.[2009]

In a letter she sent to the College of Law in 2004, Joe Ann (Taylor) Van Gelder recollected when she was the only woman student who lived in the rooms of the old Rolyat hotel, where men resided.[2010] She wrote: "I chuckled

---

2003. Bowen, *supra* n. 455, at 13.

2004. Firestone Tapestry Given to Stetson University College of Law (an undated copy of a two-page professional evaluation and assessment of the gift) (on file at Stetson U. College of L., Gulfport, Fla.).

2005. *Id.*

2006. J. Ollie Edmunds, *Annual Report of the President of Stetson University* 10 (1960) (on file at Stetson U. Archives, DeLand, Fla.).

2007. Vause, *Centennial History*, *supra* n. 595, at 142–143 (citing 1957 ABA Inspection Report of the Stetson University College of Law).

2008. Bette Orsini, *Men, Men, More Men, and Stetson Gals Talk Taxes*, St. Pete. Times E7 (Oct. 17, 1954).

2009. *Id.*

2010. Ltr. from Joe Ann Van Gelder, alumnus of Stetson U. College of L., to Frank Klim, Ex. Dir. of Commun. (July 10, 2004) (on file at Stetson U. College of L., Gulfport, Fla.) [hereinafter *Van Gelder Letter*].

when I thought how outraged DeLand officials might have been if they had known we had a co-ed dorm."[2011]

Taylor emphasized that she was "treated as an equal" by male students, but that "two older professors" were strongly prejudiced against women law students.[2012] She described an occurrence where, after a woman classmate responded to a professor's question, the professor retorted: "Miss [so and so], your explanation of this case and the pertinent points reminds me of a lovely meadow in which there is a very contented cow grazing—one who doesn't know a dandelion from the hay, and as a consequence consumes both as she remains silent."[2013] On another occasion, the same professor "informed" Taylor that the only reason she was in law school was "to find a husband."[2014] Finding a husband was not why she was in law school, of course, though after completing her first year, Taylor did drop out of school and got married.[2015] Within two years, she returned and graduated with the class of 1959.

Prior to her graduation, Sebring asked Taylor if she would edit a new publication for Stetson law alumni.[2016] She agreed.[2017] During the 1957–1958 academic year, she wrote and edited two issues, the first titled *Stetson's Lawyers' Report* (October 1957), and the second titled *Stetson Law News* (January 1958).[2018] Her name and title—"Mrs. Joe Ann Taylor, Editor," appears in each issue.[2019] In 1959, the publication was renamed the *Stetson Lawyer*, a title which continues today.[2020] That same year, Professor Everett Cushman succeeded Joe Ann Taylor as editor, a position he held for seventeen years.[2021] In selecting Taylor to be the paper's first editor, Sebring recognized her intellect, skills, and maturity (and perhaps, her family's friendship with his own).[2022]

2011. *Id.*

2012. *Id.* at 2.

2013. Joe Ann (Taylor) Van Gelder, *St. Patrick's Day* (1955) (a two-page attachment to *Van Gelder Letter*, *supra* n. 2010) (on file at the Stetson U. College of Law, Gulfport, Fla.).

2014. *Van Gelder Letter*, *supra* n. 2010, at 2.

2015. *Id.*

2016. *Jan. 29 Dillon Discussion*, *supra* n. 1969.

2017. *Van Gelder Letter*, *supra* n. 2010, at 2.

2018. *See* 1 Stetson Laws. Rptr. (Oct. 1957); 1 Stetson L. News (Jan. 1958).

2019. *Id.*

2020. *See* 2 Stetson Law. 3 (Apr. 1959).

2021. *See* 19 Stetson Law. 7 (Aug. 1976).

2022. Joe Ann Taylor Van Gelder, *Mid-Year Graduation* (1959) (an attachment to *Van Gelder Letter*, *supra* n. 2010) (on file at Stetson U. College of L., Gulfport, Fla.). Years earlier, Taylor had attended high school in Tallahassee with Sebring's son.

10.4 The Board of Overseers

a. Background

On September 14, 1955, two weeks after Sebring resigned from the Florida Supreme Court, ABA Consultant John Hervey wrote Sebring, saying how pleased he was that Sebring was the new dean of Stetson College of Law, and adding that this position presented Sebring a singular opportunity.[2023] Hervey declared that "the time is at hand when Stetson University College of Law can again be elevated to a position of primacy in Florida."[2024] Recall that, as an ABA inspector, Hervey had conducted the 1951 and 1953 inspections that led the ABA Council on Education to reconsider Stetson College of Law's accreditation status.[2025]

One issue still troubled the ABA after the move to Gulfport—the law school continued to be "managed" from DeLand rather than by the dean and faculty of the College of Law.[2026] Sebring's predecessor, Dean Haslup, had expressed that same concern to Edmunds a few years earlier.[2027] In his letter to Sebring, Hervey reiterated that the lack of autonomy issue was especially troublesome because the law school had no control over its budget.[2028]

After coming to the law school, Sebring became acquainted with its economic situation. Dean Hilkey, the previous year (1954–55), had spent all available law school funds on renovations.[2029] Despite the efforts of Hilkey and Business Manager Harold Archibald to economize, the school's financial well was dry when Sebring arrived on campus in the fall of 1955.[2030]

Sebring went to Edmunds seeking financial assistance, but he was rebuked. The president pointed out that the St. Petersburg citizens who had raised $150,000 to enable the University to purchase the Gulfport property had also pledged their continued financial support to the school.[2031] Unfortunately, the local support did not come close to what was needed. In short order, the friction that earlier had existed between Edmunds and deans Raymond, Haslup,

2023. Ltr. from John G. Hervey, ABA Consultant on Leg. Educ., to Harold L. Sebring, Dean, Stetson U. College of L. (Sept. 14, 1955) (on file at Stetson U. College of L., Gulfport, Fla.) [hereinafter *Hervey Letter*].

2024. *Id.*

2025. *See supra* nn. 1528–1550 and accompanying text.

2026. *Id.*

2027. *See supra* n. 1509–1517 and accompanying text.

2028. *Hervey Letter*, *supra* n. 2023.

2029. *See supra* nn. 1886–1892 and accompanying text.

2030. Vause, *Centennial History*, *supra* n. 595, at 136.

2031. Lycan, *History of Stetson*, *supra* n. 109, at 366.

Benefactor Walter Mann

and Hilkey, resurfaced, this time between Edmunds and Sebring. The points in contention, as before, centered on the inter-locking issues of autonomy and finances.[2032]

During Sebring's initial year as dean, the University contributed only $20,000 to the law school.[2033] Sebring was displeased. Historian Lycan describes the situation:

> Sebring, who so recently had stood alone at the top of the legal profession in Florida, was so vexed by [the financial] restraints that in 1956 he told his friends he was going to resign. In a five-hour conference with [University Trustee Walter Mann], Mann got his promise to remain if he could get *a board of overseers* to take over the operations of the College.[2034]

b. Walter Mann Persuades the President

Walter H. Mann, a member of the Stetson University Board of Trustees, was a New York City investor who had been associated with the Irving Trust Company and who served on the boards of several corporations.[2035] Mann became interested in the well-being of the College of Law. Even prior to the College's

2032. *Id.* at 366.

2033. *Id.*

2034. *Id.* at 368 (emphasis added).

2035. Walter Mann, *Winter Haven Pioneer, Receives Honorary Degree*, Winter Haven News 2 (May 23, 1973).

move to Gulfport, Mann became convinced that the school needed a higher level of autonomy from the University.[2036] Cecil Bailey recalls:

> Mann was always concerned that the DeLand campus would try to totally dominate the law school and would not allow it any high degree of independence. He was concerned about maintaining [the school's] independence ... and preserving its assets and financial independence in St. Petersburg.[2037]

Upon learning of Sebring's angst, Mann used his authority as a trustee to take up the "cudgels for the Law College against Edmunds."[2038] Mann was joined by another Board member who also supported greater autonomy for the school—Arthur N. Morris.[2039] Morris was the owner of Rock-Tenn, "a huge cardboard box manufacturing company" in Philadelphia, and was a devout "Christian who had trained to be a cleric and served as a lay minister."[2040]

After his visit with Sebring, Mann informed Edmunds about Sebring's intended resignation. Only the creation of a board of overseers that would have responsibility for the law school's operations would appease the dean.[2041] Edmunds did not react adversely to the suggestion, perhaps realizing that it might benefit him, since it could shift the law school's financial problems from University administrators in DeLand to the school's overseers in St. Petersburg. Thus, with the president's approval, he directed a resolution to the Trustees Committee on Administration.[2042]

c. *The Board of Overseers*

Prior to the Trustees annual meeting on February 21, 1957, the "deal" between Edmunds, Sebring, and the Trustees Committee on Administration was finalized. At the February 1957 Board meeting, the trustees passed a resolution formalizing the establishment of the Stetson College of Law Board of Overseers.[2043] The enabling language declared:

2036. *Bailey Interview*, *supra* n. 1662, at 15.

2037. *Id.*

2038. Lycan, *History of Stetson*, *supra* n. 109, at 366.

2039. *Id.*

2040. Jacob, *Remembering Sebring*, *supra* n. 9, at 146-47.

2041. Lycan, *History of Stetson*, *supra* n. 109, at 368.

2042. *See Annual Meeting of the John B. Stetson University Board of Trustees Minutes* 2 (Feb. 21, 1957) (on file at Stetson U. College of L., Gulfport, Fla.); *see also Amendment to the Minutes of Annual Meeting of Board of Trustees of John B. Stetson University* (Feb. 21, 1957) (on file at Stetson U. College of L., Gulfport, Fla.).

2043. *Id.*

> WHEREAS, it appears to the Board of Trustees that it is for the best interests of Stetson University and for its College of Law that a Board of Overseers should be created and given authority to supervise and direct the operations of the College of Law.
> THEREFORE, BE IT RESOLVED that there shall be ... created and established a permanent committee to be entitled the Board of Overseers of the Stetson University College of Law.[2044]

By the terms of the resolution, the Board of Overseers could be composed of not more than twenty regular and two ex-officio members: five selected by the Board of Trustees, five from the membership of the Stetson Lawyers Association, ten selected at large, plus the University president and the College of Law dean as ex-officio members.[2045] Of particular significance to the College of Law was the list of specific managerial powers the University Trustees delegated to the Overseers. Included were the rights to supervise and direct the general operations of the College; to formulate policies, plans, and programs related to financing the College; to provide a sound physical plant and library collection; to oversee the selection and maintenance of an adequate and able faculty and administrative staff, and to provide them with reasonable compensation; to formulate the curriculum as well as the criteria for academic standards; to solicit and accept funds; to negotiate loans and to discharge obligations; and to create and establish loan funds for worthy students.[2046] The members of the Overseers would serve a three-year term.[2047] Initial members were: University Trustees Doyle E. Carlton of Tampa; William J. Clapp of St. Petersburg; Walter H. Mann of New York City; Arthur N. Morris of Jacksonville; and C.H. Bolton of West Palm Beach.[2048] Stetson Lawyers Association members were: Justice E. Harris Drew of Tallahassee; Cecil C. Bailey of Jacksonville; Perry R. Nichols of Miami; Carroll R. Runyon of St. Petersburg; and Francis P. Whitehair of DeLand.[2049] Members at large were to be chosen at a later time.

Sebring was pleased by the creation of the law school's Board of Overseers. One of the dean's continuing concerns had been how the College of Law was

2044. *Id.* at 2.

2045. *Id.* at 2-3.

2046. *Id.* at 4.

2047. *Id.*

2048. *Organization Meeting of the Board of Overseers of Stetson College of Law Minutes* 1 (Feb. 20, 1957) (on file at the Stetson U. College of Law, Gulfport, Fla.) [hereinafter *Feb. 20, 1957 Overseers Minutes*]

2049. *Id.* Whitehair was U.S. Undersecretary of the Navy.

Benefactor Perry R. Nichols

going to pay off the mortgage on its Gulfport campus within the required ten-year period.[2050] Sebring reported to the Overseers that the greatest service the Board could provide was to find a way to relieve the University from the school's mortgage indebtedness.[2051] Reminding the Overseers that the Stetson College of Law was both the state's oldest and newest (at its new Gulfport location) law school, he told the members that they would have to "give unstintingly of their valuable time and talents to solving the financial problems that confront the law school and putting the law school on a solvent basis."[2052] Sebring gave this exhortation to the Overseers at their organization meeting on February 20, 1957.[2053] During the meeting, the Overseers elected Walter H. Mann president, Perry R. Nichols vice-president, Carroll R. Runyon secretary, and William J. Clapp treasurer.[2054] In addition, the Overseers passed several resolutions, including one requesting the University to transfer law school funds held on the DeLand campus to the law school.[2055]

2050. Sebring, *Facts, supra* n. 1685.

2051. *Id.* at 10.

2052. *Id.* at 11.

2053. *Feb. 20, 1957 Overseers Minutes, supra* n. 2048.

2054. *Id.* at 2. Subsequent presidents (later called "chairs") of the Board of Overseers included Perry Nichols, Ralph H. Ferrell, William J. Clapp, William Amory Underhill, William Blews, and Marsha Rydberg, who at the time of this writing is the current chair of the Overseers. Vause, *Centennial History, supra* n. 595, at 139.

2055. *Id.*

Trustee Arthur Morris

Then, in an action welcomed by Sebring, the Overseers resolved to solicit gifts and promised to provide a sum of money "equal to 30 percent of any deficit of the Stetson College of Law for the fiscal year 1956–57, and sums equal to 60 percent of any operating deficits for the fiscal years 1957–58 and 1958–59."[2056] President Edmunds, however, was not pleased with the Overseers' action.[2057] Effectively vetoing the promise of specific financial aid, Edmunds explained that though the University appreciated the Overseers' good intentions, matters pertaining to University budgets, including the law school's, were at the University's sole discretion. Nevertheless, he hoped the Overseers would raise funds for the benefit of the College of Law.[2058]

Sebring and the faculty were also concerned about the University business office continuing to pay bills, receive monies, and handle accounts of the law school.[2059] The system worked poorly, as bills were paid late and, moreover, no accounting was made available to Sebring. University Trustee Arthur Morris, a defender of the law school, took action. According to Bruce Jacob, Morris went in 1956 to the University business office in DeLand and demanded that

2056. *Id.* at 6.

2057. *See Stetson University College of Law Board of Overseers Minutes, Special Meeting* 2 (May 24, 1957) (on file at Stetson U. College of L., Gulfport, Fla.) [hereinafter *May 24, 1957 Special Meeting*]

2058. *Id.*

2059. *Id.*

he be given all financial records of the College of Law.[2060] From that time onward, the law school has managed its financial and business affairs at the Gulfport campus.[2061]

Early on, the College's Board of Overseers realized that the school needed a degree of financial independence from DeLand. As a first step, the Overseers sought permission from the University Trustees to establish a nonprofit corporation that would seek, hold, and disperse funds in order to provide financial stability for the law school. To accomplish this goal, the corporation had to be legally independent of Stetson University.[2062]

10.5 Stetson Law Center Foundation

Water Mann and Arthur Morris spearheaded the drive for an independent foundation for the law school. Their goal was to come up with an arrangement that would free the College of Law from relying on the University for supplemental grants to fund the law school's operations.[2063] After obtaining approval from the University,[2064] the Overseers resolved in April 1957 to establish an independent not-profit-corporation.[2065] The first step was for Overseer Carroll Runyon to secure approval from Pinellas County circuit judges of a not-for-profit corporate charter.[2066] The charter was issued in the name of the "Stetson Law Center." It declared that the corporation's purpose was to "maintain and support Stetson College of Law and its program through gifts and other means."[2067]

Sebring explained:

> This is a corporation that has no legal connection with Stetson University, or its College of Law, but is entirely separate and independent in its

2060. Conversation between Arthur Morris, former member Bd. of Trustees, Stetson U. College of L., and Bruce Jacob, Dean Emeritus, Stetson U. College of L. (Apr. 1995) (on file at Stetson U. College of L., Gulfport, Fla.).

2061. Vause, *Centennial History*, *supra* n. 595, at 139.

2062. *Id.* at 5.

2063. Lycan, *History of Stetson*, *supra* n. 109, at 368.

2064. *Id.*

2065. Harold L. Sebring, *Stetson University College of Law from 1954 to 1968*, at 7 (Feb. 1968) (unpublished report) (on file at Stetson U. College of L., Gulfport, Fla.).

2066. *May 24, 1957 Special Meeting*, *supra* n. 2057.

2067. *Id.* A month later, the Overseers changed the name to "Stetson Law Center Foundation." Then, in 1962, the name was changed again to "Law Center Foundation, Inc." Finally, in 1978, during the administration of Dean Richard Dillon, the corporation became known as the Charles A. Dana Law Center Foundation, Inc.

operations. It was organized under the laws of Florida, its charter being granted on April 18, 1957.[2068]

Over the next decade, this not-for-profit corporation received monies in excess of several hundred thousands dollars, raising funds, then dispersing portions to the law school.[2069] For example, in 1965, the Foundation made a grant to the College, enabling it to acquire twenty-two parcels of land on the south edge of the campus for the price of $60,000.[2070] The Foundation paid $20,000 of the purchase price and arranged for the Union Trust Company to finance the balance.[2071]

The Union Trust Company was crucial in another transaction involving the Stetson law school. On June 11, 1959, the Charles A. Dana Foundation gave $137,500 to the Stetson Law Center Foundation.[2072] This action relieved Sebring of one of his persistent worries, as the dean announced that as a result of the gift, Union Trust's mortgage on the law school property from that point on would be held by the Law Center Foundation.[2073] At that time, the mortgage secured a remaining debt of $137,500 that Stetson University owed on its 1954 purchase of the Gulfport campus.[2074] The donor's intention was that the property be "devoted exclusively to [law] school purposes."[2075] If Stetson University were to sell or use the property in any manner other than for a law school, the gift would have to be returned, meaning Stetson "recaptured" its obligation to pay the outstanding indebtedness secured by the mortgage. Moreover, the Dana Foundation required that if any of the funds be used for other than law school purposes, then "said sums are to be turned over and paid to The Charles A. Dana Foundation, Inc."[2076]

Over the years, many persons served as directors of the Foundation. In 1967, its officers were: E. Harris Drew (Chairman); Gardner W. Beckett, Jr., (President); Amory Underhill (First Vice President); Cecil C. Bailey (Vice Pres-

2068. *Id.*

2069. *Id.*

2070. *Id.*

2071. *Id.*

2072. Ltr. from Harold L. Sebring, Dean, Stetson U. College of L., to the Hon. Doyle E. Carlton, former Gov., St. of Fla. (June 16, 1959) (on file at Stetson U. College of L., Gulfport, Fla.).

2073. *Id.*

2074. *Directors of the Stetson Law Center Foundation Minutes* 1 (Oct. 9, 1959) (on file at Stetson U. College of L., Gulfport, Fla.) [hereinafter *Oct. 9 Foundation Minutes*].

2075. Harold L. Sebring, *Stetson University College of Law: Past, Present, Future, 1954-1959,* at 4 (unpublished paper) (on file at Stetson U. College of L., Gulfport, Fla.) (n.d., circa 1959-60) [hereinafter Sebring, *Past, Present, Future*].

2076. *Oct. 9 Foundation Minutes*, *supra* n. 2074, at 1.

Dana Foundation and Overseer President Gardner W. Beckett, Jr.

ident); Arthur N. Morris (Treasurer); and Carroll R. Runyon (Secretary). Other directors included: Doyle E. Carlton, Walter Mann, Perry Nichols, William J. Clapp, Dr. James Parrish, J. Ollie Edmunds, Wallace Storey, Harold L. Sebring, Cody Fowler, Robert J. Stinnett, and Allan C. Hickok.[2077]

As the list reveals, a majority of the Foundation's directors also served as members of the Board of Overseers, and consequently shared common concerns and ambitions regarding the College of Law. However, the Foundation—being an independent, not-for-profit corporation under Florida law—was not obligated to (and did not) rubber stamp what the University Trustees, the Board of Overseers, or the law school dean wanted done. The Foundation's actions did not always please Sebring, especially when it failed to disperse funds as quickly or for the purpose that Dean Sebring (and later Dean Dillon) desired.

10.6 ABA Once Again Threatens Stetson's Accreditation

a. Walter Mann and Arthur Morris Confront Edmunds

During the first years of Sebring's deanship, obtaining sufficient revenues to finance the law school's operations was his greatest problem. In spite of sev-

2077. *Meeting of the Law Center Foundation Minutes* 1 (June 2, 1967) (on file at Stetson U. College of L., Gulfport, Fla.).

eral large gifts for capital projects,[2078] and in spite of the existence of the Board of Overseers and the Law Center Foundation, the school's annual operational deficits persisted as they had prior to the move to Gulfport.

This situation particularly frustrated Board of Overseers President Walter Mann. In 1959, Mann wrote what can only be described as a blistering memorandum to the members of the Overseers and directors of the Law Center Foundation.[2079] In it, he expressed disappointment in the two bodies, pointedly stating: "The activities and accomplishments of these Boards have not been [what] was envisaged upon their formation."[2080] In a separate letter to Justice E. Harris Drew, Mann wrote: "In the two years since its establishment, the Board of Overseers, as a body, cannot point with pride, and might have to hunt reasons to justify its existence."[2081] And, though in a letter to the dean Mann complimented Sebring for his "inspirational efforts," Mann again scolded the Overseers, exclaiming that the College of Law had become "too important to tolerate a 'Paper Board.'"[2082]

While displeased with the Overseers' performance, Mann was just as critical of the University's Board of Trustees (of which he was a member). In a letter to the ABA Council on Legal Education, Mann declared: "All problems of the University and Law School result from the complete ignorance of four-fifths of the [Board of] Trustees, whose attendance at the meetings could be fairly compared to attendance at Rotary luncheons."[2083]

Mann's voicing of his negative opinions about the University's management vis-a-vis the College of Law began to have an effect. University Trustee Arthur Morris joined Mann in complaining about the University's ignoring the financial crisis Sebring was confronting. Historian Lycan notes that through letters and meetings, Mann built up a "powerful opposition to the president."[2084] These developments, of course, came to the attention of Edmunds, especially

2078. *See infra* n. 2117-2209 and accompanying text.

2079. Memo. from Walter Mann, Pres., Stetson U. College of L. Bd. of Overseers, to the Bd. of Overseers, Stetson U. College of L.; Bd. of Dirs., Stetson L. Ctr. Found. (May 4, 1959) (on file at Stetson U. College of L., Gulfport, Fla.).

2080. *Id.*

2081. *Id.* (quoting from a letter from Walter Mann, Pres., Stetson U. College of L. Bd. of Overseers, to Justice E. Harris Drew, Justice, Fla. Sup. Ct. (May 4, 1959) (on file at Stetson U. College of L., Gulfport, Fla.).

2082. *Id.* at 2.

2083. Lycan, *History of Stetson*, *supra* n. 109, at 368 (citing Ltr. from Walter Mann, Pres., Stetson U. College of L. Bd. of Overseers, to John G. Hervey, Consultant on Leg. Educ., *American Bar Association*) (1960) (on file at Stetson U. College of L., Gulfport, Fla.).

2084. Lycan, *History of Stetson*, *supra* n. 109, at 366.

after Mann complained directly to the president about the University's failure to support the law school.[2085] In a series of acrimonious letters, Mann accused the president of "squandering" the University's monies, of failing to write thank-you letters to donors of the law school; and of refusing to send promised money to Sebring for a law student loan fund.[2086]

Another thing that particularly annoyed Mann was Edmunds' unwillingness to transfer to the law school "The Student Loan Fund," $27,000 of a promised $35,000 transfer authorized by the trustees in 1957.[2087] Mann and the Overseers were also unhappy with the president's non-compliance with the University Trustees' directive of September 26, 1960, to transfer $10,000 to the law school for operations.[2088] In an impulsive five-page letter, Mann presented Edmunds with comparisons between the average money spent per student on the DeLand campus with the lower average amount per student at the College of Law.[2089]

Subsequently, Mann and Morris—without notifying the president—arranged a meeting with members of the University Trustees to plead their case for increased financial assistance to the law school.[2090] This somewhat clandestine meeting particularly angered Edmunds. In a letter to the recalcitrants, the president wrote:

> Holding Trustee Committee meetings without the President is not only bad college administration practice, it is violative of the resolution in creating the Overseers which was: "To supervise and direct the operation of the College of Law in accordance with the recommendations of the President of the University."[2091]

Edmunds added: "[It] is distasteful for me to have to disagree with you and Arthur," noting that Mann's letters, instead of "correcting misunderstandings," have created the "only misunderstandings within the Board of Trustees I have known about."[2092] The president declared: "I object to the kind of letters you

2085. *See* Ltr. from J. Ollie Edmunds, Pres., Stetson U., to Walter Mann, member, Bd. of Trustees, Stetson U. 1 (Oct. 18, 1960) (on file at Stetson U. College of L., Gulfport, Fla.) [hereinafter Edmunds, Oct. 18 Mann Letter].

2086. Lycan, *History of Stetson, supra* n. 109, at 366.

2087. *See* Ltr. from Walter H. Mann, member, Bd. of Trustees, Stetson U. to J. Ollie Edmunds, Pres., Stetson U. (Nov. 4, 1960) (on file at Stetson U. College of L., Gulfport, Fla.).

2088. *Id.*

2089. *Id.*

2090. *See* Lycan, *History of Stetson, supra* n. 109, at 366.

2091. Edmunds, Oct. 18 Mann Letter, *supra* n. 2085, at 2.

2092. *Id.*

write."[2093] As Historian Lycan characterized, with this letter, Edmunds "dug in his heels."[2094] Nonetheless, Mann persisted. In a testy response, Mann wrote that he had "given as much time and money as the total of some fifteen trustees, perhaps more, except Mrs. duPont. Would you like the figures? ... The ridiculous disparity of expenditures for the Undergraduate Schools and the Law College should be conclusive."[2095]

Meanwhile, Arthur Morris expressed his displeasure with the state of affairs. He wrote Comptroller of the University, Graves Edmondson, announcing: "In reply to your recent letter, I have decided to withdraw my pledge to the University until such time as I can be assured of a balanced budget and a lower cost of fund raising."[2096] The arguments and polemics of Mann and Morris notwithstanding, a more compelling incentive would be needed to budge President Edmunds.

b. 1957, 1959, and 1961 ABA Inspections

What moved the president to action—as it had years earlier—was a threat from the American Bar Association's Council on Legal Education to remove the College from the approved list of America's law schools.[2097]

Early in 1957, Dean Russell N. Sullivan of the Illinois University School of Law conducted an ABA-site inspection of Stetson College of Law.[2098] Just as Dean Hervey had found in his 1951 and 1953 ABA inspections,[2099] Dean Sullivan concluded that President Edmunds was continuing "to interfere" with the management of the College of Law. Sullivan criticized Edmunds for the University's lack of sufficient financial support to the school, noting that the school had no budget and was continuing on a "day-to-day" and "month-to-month basis."[2100] Sullivan added:

2093. *Id.* at 1.

2094. Lycan, *History of Stetson*, *supra* n. 109 at 367.

2095. Ltr. from Walter Mann, Member, Bd. of Trustees, Stetson U., to Dr. J. Ollie Edmunds, Pres., Stetson U. (Oct. 27, 1960) (on file at Stetson U. College of Law) [hereinafter Oct. 27 Mann Letter].

2096. Ltr. from Arthur N. Morris, Member, Bd. of Trustees, Stetson U., to H. Graves Edmondson, Comptroller, Stetson U. (Oct. 31, 1960) (on file at Stetson U. College of L., Gulfport, Fla.).

2097. See *supra* nn. 1545-1546, 1552, and accompanying text.

2098. *See* Russell N. Sullivan, *Inspection Report, Stetson University College of Law* (1957) (copy on file at Stetson U. College of L., Gulfport, Fla.) [hereinafter *ABA 1957 Report*].

2099. *See supra* n. 1541-1543 and accompanying text.

2100. *ABA 1957 Report*, *supra* n. 209,8 at 1.

> Stetson ... has had, at least for the past twenty-five years, a very difficult financial problem ... It is imperative that the school have an adequate budget prepared well in advance of each academic year ... [and] that this budget will require an annual supplement to [tuition] income ... The income will need to come from private sources, or from the general University funds.[2101]

Sullivan underscored the negatives of the law school's relocation to Gulfport, noting that because of it being "remote from the campus at DeLand, *the law school is paying heavy administrative costs*" for business operations and personnel "who would not be needed if the law school were in DeLand."[2102] After Sullivan filed his report, the ABA Council of Legal Education again became concerned over the poor financial situation at Stetson's law school, and ordered a reinspection to take place in 1959 (two years hence). Professor Thomas W. Christopher of Emory University School of Law (later of North Carolina University) led the 1959 ABA reinspection. Though he found that the College had made "commendable and substantial progress" over the previous two years, he nonetheless concluded:

> If the University will support the school in meeting its needs outlined [above] (and those needs are great), and if it will help the school supplement its income, and if the school will keep its enrollment down ... Stetson can again provide sound legal training.[2103]

In response to Christopher's assessment, the ABA Council on Legal Education felt that the school's financial problems remained unresolved. It therefore ordered another reinspection in 1961.[2104] In the fall of that year, the ABA learned that the University's trustees had rejected a request from the law school's Board of Overseers that the "law College be allocated its per-student share" of University endowment funds and gifts.[2105] Considering a pro-rata per-student allocation to be a fair solution for providing the law school financial support, the ABA was astonished by the University's refusal to do

2101. *Id.*

2102. *Id.*; *see also* Bd. of Overseers, *Stetson College of Law—American Bar Association Relationships* 6-7 (n.d.) (circa 1963) [hereinafter *Stetson—ABA Relationships*] (emphasis added).

2103. *Id.* at 8 (citing Thomas W. Christopher, *ABA Inspection Report, Stetson University College of Law* (1959)).

2104. *Id.*

2105. *See* President of the Board, *Report to the Board of Overseers of Stetson University College of Law* 1 (Oct. 22, 1960).

so.[2106] Thus, just as had happened in 1953, the ABA Council on Legal Education set a deadline on the University to resolve the law school's funding dilemma or face loss of ABA approval. The ABA 1961 Inspection Report did not use soft praise.

> [T]he Council [on Legal Education] has indulged these [financial] problems at Stetson for many years ... The time is at hand when the Council should [require] that the University allocate to the law school, out of non-student income, a fixed amount per student, the allocation to be on the basis of the total student population of the institution.[2107]

The Council agreed with the ABA site inspector's recommendation. In a letter to Stetson officials, the ABA Council on Legal Education got everybody's attention at the University.

> [T]he parent [Stetson] University has failed to provide the law school with its fair share of the total institutional resources since the school was moved to St. Petersburg.... [T]he authorities of your institution should be advised that unless, by the August 1962 meeting of the Council, they furnish evidence on the [deficiencies listed in the Inspection Report], the Council will recommend to the House of Delegates that the school be dropped from the approved list of ABA schools.[2108]

Deficiencies that immediately needed to be rectified included:

(1) Low faculty salaries;
(2) Too lenient admission and retention standards;
(3) Inadequate funding for the library;
(4) Reversal of economic situation whereby the law school is unsupported by the University general funds; [and]
(5) Provision for funds to be made available to the law school by the University in amounts adequate to accomplish the foregoing objections on a continuing basis.[2109]

In response, Sebring and the Board of Overseers drafted a report for the University Trustees.[2110] The eighteen-page document summarized the school's prior strained relationship with the ABA and warned the trustees: "Without financial support from the University, the Law School can never hope to sat-

---

2106. *Stetson—ABA Relationships*, *supra* n. 2102, at 8.

2107. *Id.*

2108. *Id.*

2109. *Id.* at 10 (emphasis added).

2110. *See Stetson—ABA Relationships*, *supra* n. 2102, at 1, 18.

isfy the qualitative standards mandated by the accrediting agency."[2111] The statement referred to ABA complaints that Stetson admitted students without academic credentials for success in law school, and that some of the marginal students admitted failed the state bar examination after graduating. The Overseers Report acknowledged the truth of these charges:

> It must be stated in all candor that, because of the lack of sufficient funds to keep its operation going, Stetson College of Law has been compelled to accept and retain some students who were below the high standard that should be set for a first rate law school.[2112]

The Overseers report concluded: "These charges and the manner in which they should be dealt are matters which, in our opinion, should engage the serious and immediate attention of every member of the Board of Trustees."[2113]

After six years of attempting to make the president and trustees understand the gravity of the law school funding situation, the point had finally been made. In short order, Edmunds and the University Trustees agreed to annually allocate to the College of Law a share of the University's endowment-generated income and a portion of the unrestricted gifts the University received each year, both amounts to be based on the number of law students as a percentage of the total number of University students.[2114]

These actions represented a significant turning point in the law school's financial situation and its relationship with the University. By 1964, the College of Law reached a position "where its existence or accreditation was no longer threatened because of the scarcity of money."[2115] Historian Lycan declares that the resulting turnaround was a victory for "Walter Mann's crusade," since "he was more active than anyone else in getting the changes."[2116]

Throughout this battle, Sebring worked with, and fully supported, Mann's activism, but usually behind the scene. Sebring understood that good relations with Edmunds and the University Trustees had to be maintained. Nonetheless, no one was more pleased than Sebring when the issue was resolved. The combination of an independent Law Center Foundation, a more powerful Board of Overseers, and new cooperation from Deland provided Dean Harold

---

2111. *Id.* at 18.

2112. *Id.*

2113. *Id.*

2114. Lycan, *History of Stetson*, *supra* n. 109, at 368; *see also* Vause, *Centennial History*, *supra* n. 595, at 138.

2115. Lycan, *History of Stetson*, *supra* n. 109, at 368.

2116. *Id.* (citing interview by Gilbert Lycan, Prof. of History, Stetson U.,with Walter Mann, member, Bd. of Trustees, Stetson U. (Mar. 31, 1980)).

Sebring with an opportunity to rebuild the College of Law's academic quality, an objective he pursued through the remaining years of his deanship. Meanwhile, even more good news was at hand. Major benefactors were beginning to make significant gifts to the College of Law.

10.7 College of Law Benefactors: Charles A. Dana, Roy E. Crummer et al.

a. The Sebring Library

A news release from Stetson University's development office in September 1955 announced that a $250,000 pledge had been given for a "New Law Center," but it did not reveal the donor's identity, only that the gift came from a New York City businessman who preferred to remain anonymous.[2117] The gift was to help pay for a law library and a classroom building (where an auditorium on the second floor could be divided into two classrooms), but only if an equal amount was raised from other sources. The anonymous gift, it was said, would provide one-third of "$750,000 required to develop the [College of Law] into a long-desired law center for all Florida lawyers."[2118]

A campaign to raise the required $250,000 in matching gifts began immediately and was headed by Florida Supreme Court Justice E. Harris Drew as the honorary chairman of the drive.[2119] St. Petersburg businessman Bunie E. Webb (brother of "Doc" Webb of the World's Largest Drug Store fame) led efforts to solicit gifts and pledges from Stetson graduates and Tampa area law firms.[2120] One fund-raising strategy involved the school's pledge that "any graduate of the Stetson College of Law will draw a will without charge if it contains a bequest to Stetson."[2121] The campaign reached its goal within a year.[2122] By then, the anonymous donor was known—the Charles A. Dana Foundation and its president, New York City manufacturer and philanthropist Charles A. Dana,[2123] a business associate and friend of Walter Mann.[2124]

2117. *$250,000 Given University for New Law Center*, 1 Priv. Rpts. from Stetson 1 (Sep. 1955) [hereinafter *New Law Center*].

2118. *Id.*

2119. *Id.*

2120. *Id.*

2121. *Justice Sebring Heads Stetson Law School*, 1 Priv. Rpts. from Stetson 3 (Oct. 1955).

2122. *Law Center Campaign Reaches Its Objective*, 2 Priv. Rpts. 1 (Nov. 1956).

2123. *Law Library Nearing Completion*, 1 Stetson's Law. Rpt. 1 (Oct. 1957).

2124. One story, not verified, is that Charles Dana did not learn about Stetson University College of Law from Mann, but from Stetson President J. Ollie Edmunds. Supposedly,

Benefactor Charles A. Dana

Charles Dana learned about Stetson College of Law through a long-standing business relationship with Walter Mann. The two served on the boards of several New York-based corporations. Mann, originally from Winter Haven, Florida, became a member of Stetson University's Board of Trustees in the 1940s. Overseer Underhill recalled that Mann had an "important connection" with the Dana Foundation and that it was only because of Mann's urging Dana gave the College of Law its first major gift after its move to St. Petersburg.[2125] Overseer Cecil Bailey recollected that Mann always "was very close to the

---

Dana and Edmunds met at a convention on education. Edmunds mentioned to Dana that Stetson University had purchased an old hotel in Gulfport, Florida, as the new home for its law school. Dana asked if it happened to be the Rolyat Hotel. "Yes," Edmunds replied. Surprised, Dana exclaimed that he and his wife spent their honeymoon at the Rolyat, and that the hotel held very special memories for them. Jacob, *Remembering Sebring*, *supra* n. 9, at 143, n. 569 (citing to interview by J. Ollie Edmunds, retired Chancellor, Stetson U., with Bruce R. Jacob, Dean Emeritus, Stetson U. College of L. (early 1980s)). The Dana honeymoon-at-the-Rolyat story came from Edmunds, who on occasion was known to puff up a story. People who know Dana, including Walter Mann, Cecil Bailey, Amory Underhill, and Richard Dillon, never mentioned this connection. Dillon was with the Danas on the occasion of Eleonor Dana's first visit to the Gulfport campus in 1957. Dillon remembers she was impressed by the beauty of the Spanish architecture and never hinted, let alone mentioned, that she had been on the campus before. *May 4 Dillon Interview*, *supra* n. 1885.

2125. *Underhill Interview*, *supra* n. 842, at 12.

Danas," adding that he had persuaded Dana "to take an interest in the law school and he listened to Walter's advice in many instances."[2126]

Charles A. Dana was a good person to have as a friend. He supported higher education through both his words and his pocketbook. A lawyer as well as an industrialist, he graduated from both Columbia University and its School of Law. After law school, he practiced a few years, first with the New York City district attorney's office, then in private practice. Attracted to public service, he entered politics and was elected a New York State legislator and served three terms.[2127] Afterwards, he began building a manufacturing empire. By 1919, he was president of Spicer Manufacturing Company, which in 1946 became the Dana Corporation. It grew to become one of the largest manufacturers of automotive parts in the world.[2128] With wealth, a concern for the body politic, a philanthropist concerned about education—especially, being a lawyer, about legal education—Charles A. Dana through his and Stetson's mutual friend—Walter Mann—caused the campus of the College of Law to dramatically grow.

In the spring of 1957, construction of the Charles A. Dana Library began.[2129] The funds included approximately $75,000 given by Tampa area "friends of the College."[2130] Edmunds thanked the Dana Foundation and the Danas for their generosity, and acknowledged Walter Mann for being the one "chiefly responsible for the Dana interest and Dana Foundation money."[2131]

The Dana library was constructed in thirteen months. As fast as that was, moving the books from the stacks and reading room (today Classroom H) to the much larger and modern facility took less than half an hour because the library collection was "very small."[2132] Richard Dillon, then an assistant professor and law librarian, orchestrated the transfer. He formed a "human chain" of students and staff, men and women standing shoulder-to-shoulder, handing books one at a time down the line directly to be placed on the shelves of the new Dana Law Library.[2133] The books were put in the exact order that they

2126. *Bailey Interview*, *supra* n. 1662, at 15.

2127. *Id. College Receives $200,000 from Dana Foundation; Latest Grant for Library Expansion Swells Total of Dana Gifts to More Than $1,000,000,* 14 Stetson Law. 1 (May 1971) [hereinafter *Dana Foundation Gift*].

2128. *Id.*

2129. Sebring, *Past, Present, Future, supra* n. 2075, at 2.

2130. *Id.*

2131. Harold Sebring, *1958 President's Report* 4 (1958) (on file at Stetson U. College of L., Gulfport, Fla.) [hereinafter Sebring, *1958 President's Report*].

2132. Jacob, *Remembering Sebring*, *supra* n. 9, at 144.

2133. *May 4 Dillon Interview*, *supra* n. 1885.

had been in at the old stacks. The time it took the human chain to move a book from the old shelf to the new one was around thirty seconds.[2134]

In January 1958, students entered the new and spacious library.[2135] Costing $406,718.64,[2136] it provided housing for 70,000 volumes, a study area for 100 students, and a large auditorium for law school and continuing legal education functions.[2137]

On March 8, 1958, the Dana Library was dedicated, with Charles A. Dana present.[2138] Florida Governor LeRoy Collins gave the convocation address.[2139] Collins told those assembled that the strength of the Constitution is not within the instrument itself, nor even in the judiciary, "but in the minds and hearts of the people."[2140] Florida Supreme Court Justice E. Harris Drew presented the new library to Board of Trustees Chairman Charles Bolton.[2141] Then, Stetson's Board of Overseers President Walter Mann unveiled an oil portrait of Charles A. Dana.[2142] Sebring, in accepting the portrait, said it would hang in the Dana Library.[2143]

b. Eleanor Naylor Dana Administration and H. Jackson Crummer Classroom Buildings

In March 1964, a fire caused by defective wiring seriously damaged Stetson's practice courtroom.[2144] After repairs, the room was used as a classroom until 1966 or 1967. Edmunds and Sebring decided it would be best not to restore the facility for use as a courtroom, but rather to replace it with a new facility, though the original courtroom, subsequently moved across campus, is still in use today as Classroom H.[2145] Though all agreed on the desirability of new facilities that would house classrooms, administrative and faculty offices, and a courtroom, the determinative issue was how to finance construction. In addition to anticipated donations, the University Board of Trustees authorized

2134. *Id.*

2135. *New Law Center, supra* n. 2117, at 1.

2136. Sebring, *1958 President's Report, supra* n. 2131, at 4.

2137. Sebring, *Five-Year Report, supra* n. 1896, at 3.

2138. *Governor Speaks at Dedication of Law Library*, 1 Stetson News 1, 5 (Apr. 1958).

2139. *Id.* at 1.

2140. *Id.* at 5.

2141. *Id.* at 1.

2142. *Id.*

2143. *Id.*

2144. H.L. Sebring, *1967 Report on Stetson University College of Law* 5 (Dec. 1967) (on file at Stetson U. College of L., Gulfport, Fla.) [hereinafter Sebring, *1967 Report*].

2145. *Id.*

Edmunds "to apply to the Federal government for a loan and grant under the Federal Higher Educational Facilities Act of 1963."[2146] But the Board's recommendation to seek federal funds was not unanimous and drew sharp criticism from certain members of the Florida Baptist Convention who felt the Baptist-affiliated University should accept no grants or borrow funds from the federal government.[2147]

While Edmunds and the Trustees were contemplating how to finance the new buildings, the law faculty knew very little about the plans. Edmunds on September 8, 1965, attended a special meeting of the law faculty called by Dean Sebring (at Edmund's request). Edmunds informed the faculty of the construction and financing plans for the new buildings on the Gulfport campus and asked them for their input.[2148] The faculty was concerned, not knowing what was coming.

Sebring then appointed professors David Dickson, Paul Barnard, and Calvin Kuenzel to study the University's building and financing plans, and then to report back to the faculty as a whole.[2149] Known as the "Dickson Committee," the group put together a report in twelve days, presenting it to the faculty on September 20, 1965.[2150] Its report concluded that the proposed building program "could be disastrous to the College" because it could jeopardize the school's ability to pay the additional debt service obligation that a proposed $610,653 loan from the government would create. The committee had no problem with grants from the government, but loans for that amount seemed injudicious.[2151] The report was submitted after faculty approval to Sebring along with a letter from Dickson to Perry Nichols.[2152] The concerns were heard. Negotiations between University and government officials resulted in the federal loan being lowered from $610,653 to $361,000, the difference being made up by a $290,000 government grant to the University.[2153]

After University Trustees committed to build new facilities for the law school, Walter Mann encouraged Naylor Eleanor Dana, wife of Charles A.

2146. *Id.*

2147. This was also suggested by Dean Emeritus Richard T. Dillon. *Jan. 29 Dillon Discussion, supra* n. 1969.

2148. *Minutes, Faculty Meeting, College of Law* (Sept. 9, 1965); *May 4 Dillon Interview, supra* n. 1885.

2149. *May 4 Dillon Interview, supra* n. 1885.

2150. *Id.*

2151. David Dickson, *Committee Report to College of Law Faculty* 1–4 (Sept. 20, 1965)

2152. Ltr. from David Dickson, Prof. of L. Stetson U. College of L., to Perry Nichols, Pres., Bd. of Oversees, Stetson U. College of L. 2 (Nov. 3, 1965) (on file at Stetson U. College of L., Gulfport, Fla.).

2153. *May 4 Dillon Interview, supra* n. 1885

Benefactor Eleanor Dana

Dana, to help finance the project.[2154] In response to Mann's entreaty, Eleanor Dana announced in December 1965 that she would contribute $172,000 to help fund the new administrative building.[2155]

Meanwhile, Hewen A. Lasseter—Stetson law graduate (class of 1930), member of the Board of Overseers, and a president of the Stetson Lawyers Association—solicited municipal bond investor Roy E. Crummer of Los Angeles, California, to make a contribution to the Stetson College of Law.[2156] Crummer had purchased Florida municipal bonds in the 1930s after the Legislature (at the depth of the Depression) had forgiven all outstanding property taxes and removed the state's real property from further taxation.[2157] Without *ad valorem* tax revenues, municipal governments defaulted on their bond obligations. Crummer purchased scores of these nearly worthless instruments when most investors considered them far too speculative to touch.[2158] His gamble paid off after the Florida Legislature put the state's privately held real property back on the tax rolls.[2159]

During the 1960s, Board of Overseers member and former President of Stetson Lawyers Association Hewen Lasseter was chief executive of the

2154. Sebring, *1967 Report*, *supra* n. 2144, at 5; *see also* Underhill Interview, *supra* n. 842, at 12–13.

2155. Lycan, *History of Stetson*, *supra* n. 109, at 369.

2156. *Underhill Interview*, *supra* n. 842, at 12–13.

2157. *Id.*

2158. *Id.*

2159. *Id.*

Lawyers' Title Guaranty Fund, headquartered in Orlando. Lasseter helped Crummer evaluate the investment potential of Florida municipal bonds investments.[2160] With encouragement from Overseer Francis Whitehair, Lasseter persuaded Crummer to give the College of Law a "significant gift" to help fund a classroom building.[2161] Crummer pledged $125,000 toward the new structure.[2162] He placed one condition, however, on his gift: the new building had to be named the H. [Henry] Jackson Crummer Classroom building in memory of his deceased son.[2163]

In an article titled "College of Law Launches New Development Program," the *Stetson Lawyer* announced in March 1965 the Dana and Crummer gifts.[2164] Eleanor Dana responded that she was "glad to contribute personally to [the College] becoming one of the most desired law schools in the nation."[2165] Former Governor Doyle Carlton noted that Stetson's plans called for a gradual expansion of student enrollment, while Dean Sebring commented that the campus would serve not only the law students, "but lawyers from across the state as well."[2166]

With the Dana and Crummer gifts in hand—a combined value of $297,000—Stetson University formally applied for federal monies to finance the remaining cost of the two buildings.[2167] In line with prior understandings, the government gave the University a combined grant totaling $290,000 and a loan of $361,000.[2168] Along with contributions from the Law Center Foundation, the College of Law had over one million dollars available for construction. The firm of Parish, Merwin, and Parish of St. Petersburg designed the two buildings to be consistent with the Mediterranean Revival style of the original Rolyat Hotel structures.[2169] The construction contract was awarded to Daniel Construction Company."[2170]

2160. *Lasseter Bows Out as Fund's Chief Executive,* 10 Stetson Law. 5 (May 1967); *see also* Sebring, *1967 Report, supra* n. 2144, at 6; *Underhill Interview, supra* n. 842, at 12–13.

2161. *Underhill Interview, supra* n. 842, at 12–13.

2162. Jacob, *Remembering Sebring, supra* n. 9, at 158.

2163. *Landscaping Is Planned as New Structures Rise,* 11 Stetson Law. 1, 1 (Nov. 1967) [hereinafter *Landscaping*].

2164. *College of Law Launches New Development Program, Gifts Provide for Erection of Two New Buildings to Meet Growing Demand for Legal Education,* 8 Stetson Law.1, 1 (Mar. 1965).

2165. *Id.*

2166. *Id.*

2167. Sebring, *1967 Report, supra* n. 2144, at 6.

2168. *Id.*

2169. *Buildings to Be Dedicated at Stetson Law School,* St. Pete. Times A-2 (Mar. 7, 1969) [hereinafter *Buildings to Be Dedicated*].

2170. *Id.*; *see also Landscaping, supra* n. 2163, at 1.

Dean Sebring and Law Faculty

On June 3, 1966, the groundbreaking took place. Among the scoopers were Edmunds, benefactor Eleanor Dana, Overseer Hewen Lasseter (representing Roy Crummer), University Trustee and Overseer Walter Mann, Florida Bar President Fletcher G. Rush, Student Bar Association President James Ron Smith (later an official of Florida), and Stetson Lawyers Association President Robert Stinnett.[2171] Sebring described the Eleanor Dana and Roy Crummer halls as two modern, air-conditioned, two-story buildings with a connected covered arcade, all of Spanish design. He noted that the Eleanor N. Dana Hall would provide offices for administrators and seventeen faculty offices, a faculty research library, a conference room, and a faculty lounge. The H. Jackson Crummer Hall would contain seven classrooms with seating capacity for 500 students.[2172]

Sebring predicted that the final cost of the buildings and furnishings would be close to $900,000, and that $583,000 of that amount would be paid off, leaving a debt of $361,000 owed to the federal government. Sebring concluded his address with the following remarks:

> When these buildings are completed, Stetson University College of Law will have one of the finest small law school plants in the country—one that, for the first time in the 67-year history of the College, will meet

2171. *Id.*
2172. *Id.*

> reasonable requirements or standards laid down by the American Bar Association.[2173]

Though Harold Sebring lived to see the halls completed in April 1968, by then he was suffering from his recurring heart ailment. On July 26, five weeks short of his scheduled retirement and several months prior to the dedication of Dana and Crummer halls, Harold L. "Tom" Sebring died.[2174] On March 8, 1969, the Eleanor Dana and Roy Crummer buildings were dedicated without the man who had made them a reality.[2175]

The dedication ceremony was impressive. Stetson's new College of Law Dean, Richard T. Dillon, had invited Florida's ranking member of Congress, Robert L.F. Sikes, to give the keynote address.[2176] Beginning in 1940, Sikes served fourteen consecutive terms in the U.S. House of Representatives.[2177] Others attending the ceremony included Pinellas Circuit Judge William Patterson (1960) who served as chair of the reception committee, and Robert Coker, President of Stetson's Student Bar Association.[2178] Alumnus Perry Nichols (1937) moderated a trial advocacy workshop arranged by Stetson law professor McKinley Smiley.[2179] Meanwhile, the College invited all women attendees to a tea in honor of Mrs. Roy Crummer. Mrs. Richard T. Dillon served as hostess.[2180] Among those attending were Mrs. Doyle E. Carlton and Mrs. Eleanor Dana.[2181] Chester Bedell of Jacksonville, a fellow of the American College of Trial Lawyers and member of the Board of Governors of the Florida Bar, addressed the Inns of Court gathering, emphasizing the ethical obligations of attorneys.[2182] Also present were Judge Robert E. Beach, former law dean Paul Raymond, attorney Marshal Criser (later, President, University of Florida), Judge Robert Williams, Justice E. Harris Drew, Walter Mann, Professor Everett Cushman, Hewen Lasseter, recently hired University President Paul F. Geren, and now-University Chancellor J. Ollie Edmunds.[2183]

2173. *Id.*

2174. *See infra* nn. 2576–2579 and accompanying text.

2175. *Buildings to Be Dedicated, supra* n. 2169, at 2.

2176. *Crummer, Dana Halls to Be Dedicated; Formal Ceremonies Will Be Part of Two-Day Program of Events Honoring Stetson Donors*, 12 Stetson Law. 1, 1 (Feb. 1969).

2177. *Id.*

2178. *Id.*

2179. *Some Highlights of Dedication Festivities of Eleanor Dana Hall and H. Jackson Crummer Hall*, 12 Stetson Law. 4–5 (May 1969).

2180. *Id.*

2181. *Id.*

2182. *Id.* at 6.

2183. *Id.* at 5.

c. Other Significant Benefactors During the Sebring Era

Between 1900 and 1970, major benefactors—including Henry Flagler, Harvey S. Firestone, Jr. (and his brothers), the Dana Foundation, Charles A. Dana, Eleanor Naylor Dana, and Roy E. Crummer—enabled the College of Law to construct and renovate the physical facilities it needed. Of course, additional donors also contributed to the law school during this seventy-year period, especially during Sebring's deanship.

Among these benefactors was Mrs. Alfred I. duPont, a member of another well-known philanthropic family. President Edmunds, when he was a county judge in Jacksonville, became a friend of the duPonts and presided over the duPont estate.[2184] Mrs. DuPont was the wife of industrialist Alfred I. duPont and served on the Stetson University Board of Trustees. Over the years, she gave several financial gifts to the University, including a 1958 pledge of $21,000 to the College of Law, an amount the Dana Foundation matched.[2185]

Meanwhile, in 1957, St. Petersburg resident Mrs. Ambrose L. Cram of St. Petersburg gave the law school one of its more interesting gifts, "a beautiful set of carillon bells" that were installed in the central tower.[2186] Cram presented the bells as a memorial to her late husband and to her deceased brother.[2187] According to Stetson University historian Olga Bowen, Cram donated the bells to Stetson in part because her brother had served as superintendent of a Baptist school in Philadelphia, a school established by the same John B. Stetson for whom Stetson University was named.[2188] Cram's gift was in recognition of John Stetson's "influence" on her late brother.[2189]

The "bells of Stetson" apparently did not ring long. Some of the College's neighbors complained of the disturbingly loud "noise" levels the bells produced.[2190] They were able to persuade school officials to stop the clanging, resulting in an acoustic quiescence that continues to this date.

2184. *See supra* n. 1501–1502 and accompanying text.

2185. Sebring, *Five-Year Report*, *supra* n. 1896, at 3; *see also Special Meeting of the Board of Trustees of John B. Stetson University, St. Petersburg, Florida Minutes*, 1 (Sept. 25, 1958) (on file at Stetson U. College of L., Gulfport, Fla.).

2186. *See Special Meeting of the Board of Overseers of Stetson University College of Law Minutes* 2 (Oct. 30, 1957) (on file at Stetson U. College of Law, Gulfport, Fla.).

2187. *Id.*

2188. Bowen, *supra* n. 455, at 14.

2189. *Id.*

2190. This story has been told by local Gulfport town's people but no written reference to the Stetson bells has been located.

During the Sebring era, several members of the Board of Overseers made significant financial contributions to the law school,[2191] donations used primarily to renovate campus facilities.[2192] Sebring reported that the law school by 1960 had spent $784,000 for "improvements, renovations, additions, and repairs."[2193] Sebring was pleased that most of this money had come to the College "either directly, or as the result of gifts from the members of the Board of Overseers, or indirectly as the result of solicitations made by them."[2194]

Though Walter Mann had been disappointed over the Overseers' lack of support a few years earlier,[2195] he was pleased with their newfound gifts and fund-raising success. The Overseers' increased giving resulted not only from the prodding of Mann and Morris, but also from the example set by Charles A. Dana, especially following his foundation's contribution of a quarter of a million dollars to the new library.[2196]

Though the new Dana library began with 20,000 volumes in 1957, the collection tripled during Sebring's deanship, largely due to an annual stream of book donations. For example: in 1957, Mrs. P.H. Odom, widow of a prominent Jacksonville lawyer, donated 2,257 volumes; Manley Caldwell of West Palm Beach, 140 volumes; the Jacksonville law firm of Marks, Gray, Yates, and Conroy, twenty-four boxes of books; Seth G. Widener of St. Petersburg, 180 volumes; and Louis Wallace of Madeira Beach, eighty-nine volumes.[2197] Then, in 1964, University Trustee (and later chair of the Dana Law Center Foundation) Ralph H. Ferrell of Miami gave a complete set of the National Reporter System to the Dana Law Library, comprising over 3,000 volumes.[2198] That same

2191. Board of Overseers, Stetson College of Law 1–3 (n.d.) (six-page internal memo, on file at Stetson U. College of L., Gulfport, Fla.); *see also* Sebring, *Five-Year Report, supra* n. 1896, at 4. The benefactors included Walter H. Mann, Arthur N. Morris, William J. Clapp, Francis P. Whitehair, Perry Nichols, Ralph H. Ferrell, Hewen A. Lasseter, J. Ben Watkins, Cecil C. Bailey, Cody Fowler, Hal P. Dekle, Gardner Beckett, Mrs. Charles A. Dana, Robert Stinnett, William Gay, Judge J. Thomas Gurney, Charles Campbell, Wallace Storey, Amory Underhill, B.E. "Beunie" Webb, Earl B. Edington, Richard D. Pope, Sr., Arthur Morris, L. Leroy Highbaugh, Sr., and Carroll R. Runyon.

2192. Harold Sebring, *A Few Facts about the Stetson College of Law* 3 (1967) (a report to the Board of Overseers) [hereinafter Sebring, *A Few Facts*].

2193. Sebring, *Five-Year Report, supra* n. 1896, at 4.

2194. *Id.*

2195. *See supra* n. 2081–2082 and accompanying text.

2196. *See supra* n. 2217–2218 and accompanying text.

2197. *Library Donations*, 1 Stetson L. News 3, 3 (Jan. 1958).

2198. *Trustee's Gift Tops New Book Donations*, 7 Stetson Law. 3, 3 (July 1964).

year, Judge A.O. Kanner, a graduate of the Stetson law class of 1915, donated sets of Florida Statutes, Annotations to Florida Statutes, Florida Digests, and Florida Jurisprudence to the College.[2199]

The largest gift the law library received, however, was a $250,000 bequest from the estate of Sarah E. Armstrong of St. Petersburg.[2200] Ms. Armstrong, who died on February 27, 1962, had established two trusts in her will, each naming the College of Law the residual beneficiary. She wanted her bequest to be used for the sole purpose of expanding the library collection.[2201] Ms. Armstrong, president of the St. Petersburg Woman's Club for several years, made her bequest to Stetson in memory of her husband, William W. Armstrong, who had been a prominent New York attorney.[2202]

Shortly after the College of Law opened in Gulfport, Mr. and Mrs. L. LeRoy Highbaugh, Sr., Baptists from Louisville, Kentucky, began making contributions to the school.[2203] According to Sebring, the Highbaughs made their "generous gifts to train Christian Lawyers."[2204] Some of the funds were used to renovate student dormitory rooms.[2205] The largest portion of their gifts were used to establish the "Highbaugh Scholarships Fund."[2206] The fund afforded up to twelve students a year full-tuition grants. Recipients were designated as "Highbaugh Scholars."[2207] One of them was Bruce Jacob.[2208]

d. The Highbaugh Gift of a Charles Wilson Peale Painting Masterpiece

The donation of cash and books to a law school is expected. But the Stetson College of Law received an oil portrait painting that was not only unanticipated, but also turned out to have remarkable historical and artistic value. The painting first came to the law school in the late 1950s. No one knew either the artist's identity or that of the man depicted in the large seventy-nine

2199. *Id.*

2200. *St. Petersburg Woman Wills College of Law $250,000 for Purchase of Library Books*, 5 Stetson Law. 1 (Apr. 1962)

2201. *Id.*

2202. *Id.*

2203. Bowen, *Law School History*, *supra* n. 455, at 13

2204. Harold L. Sebring, *Annual Report to Board of Overseers* 5 (1955) (on file at Stetson U. College of L., Gulfport, Fla.).

2205. *See* Sebring, *A Few Facts*, *supra* n. 2192, at 3.

2206. *Id.* at app. 6, pg. 1.

2207. Jacob, *Recollections*, *supra* n. 1678, at 18

2208. *Id*; *see also* Jacob, *Remembering Sebring*, *supra* n. 9, at 150.

inch by fifty-eight inch portrait.[2209] Several years would pass before the College learned that the portrait was painted in Maryland in 1770 by Charles Wilson Peale, an American artist born in 1741 in Kent County, Maryland.[2210] The painting portrayed a distinguished aristocrat attired in white leggings, formal waistcoat, and shirt with frill cuffs. The subject of Peale's painting turned out to be a Maryland planter and judge named John Beale Bordley.[2211] Bordley's mother and her husband Edmund Jennings in the 1870s lived in London and, according to an account from the National Gallery of Art, may have commissioned their son's portrait.[2212] Another explanation, however, may be that Peale painted the portrait because Bordley agreed to pay Peale's trip to London to study under the renown artist Benjamin West.[2213]

The National Gallery of Art's interpretive description of Peale's rendition of Bordley in part follows:

> The theme of tyranny dominates.... Trained as a lawyer, Bordley raises his hand in a gesture of debate. He points to a statute of British liberty, holding a scales of justice, reminding [the British] that the American colonists lived under British law and thus were entitled to the rights it guaranteed. Britain's violation of these rights is signified by the legal document, torn and discarded at Bordley's feet.[2214]

2209. Memo. from Ollie Edmunds, Pres., Stetson U., to Bd. of Trustees, *Memorandum to Board of Trustees* (Oct. 29, 1969) (on file at Stetson U. College of L., Gulfport, Fla.) [hereinafter Edmunds, *1969 Memorandum*].

2210. The leading authority on the life and paintings of Charles Wilson Peale is art historian Charles Coleman Sellers. *See e.g.* Charles Coleman Sellers, *Charles Wilson Peale with Patron and Populace: A Supplement to Portraits and Miniatures by Charles Wilson Peale* (Am. Phil. Socy. 1969); Charles Coleman Sellers, *Portraits and Miniatures of Charles Wilson Peale* (Am. Phil. Socy. 1952) [hereinafter Sellers, *Portraits and Miniatures*]; *see also New Perspectives on Charles Wilson Peale* (Lilian B. Miller & David C. Ward eds., U. of Pittsburgh Press 1991).

2211. Charles Coleman Sellers, *Charles Wilson Peale and John Beale Bordley,* 12 Pharos 20 (Summer–Fall 1969) [hereinafter Sellers, *Peale*].

2212. *Id.*

2213. In London, Peale honed his skills under the legendary artist Benjamin West. West was "one of the most prominent artists in late eighteenth-century London" and was president of the prestigious British Royal Academy. He painted sixty works, including several considered masterpieces, at the request of King George III, whom West served as a royal patron of the arts. West, at the King's request, also designed the stain glass windows in two chapels at Windsor Castle. He was the tutor of Peale and surely influenced his painting of the Bordley portrait.

2214. *Id.*

Peale and Bordley shared similar political views over England's trampling on the rights of the colonists. Peale used his painting as a vehicle to make a political statement. In the "stormy years" prior to America's War for Independence, the painting was intended as a warning to the British not to limit the civil liberties of colonialists in America.[2215]

In March 1771, according to art historian Charles Coleman Sellers, the great painting was packed (or so Peale thought), ready for shipment to London.[2216] But then the painting disappeared for roughly 180 years. As historian Sellers observes in his 1952 book *Portraits and Miniatures by Charles Wilson Peale,* the portrait remained "unlocated."[2217]

Then, near the end of the 1950s, Peale's portrait of Bordley serendipitously turned up in the attic of a Louisville, Kentucky, house owned by L. LeRoy Highbaugh, Sr., and his wife. Their son, LeRoy Highbaugh, Jr., apparently with Stetson University Chancellor J. Ollie Edmunds, rummaged through the attic of the home, where they found the large portrait which, unbeknownst to them, was Peale's portrait of Bordley.[2218] The painting was covered with grime, and the artist's identity was not discernible.

Highbaugh, Sr., told Edmunds that he did not wish to go to the bother and expense of cleaning the portrait, that it was of no use to him in its present condition. Edmunds responded by noting that a large painting was needed for the College of Law lounge.[2219] A previous benefactor of the law school, Highbaugh, Sr., agreed to ship the portraiture to Gulfport. Upon its arrival, the anonymous painting was hung in the Stetson Inn large public room (later named the Mann Lounge), where it remained several years.

Then, a fortuitous event took place—the visit of President Hugh McKean of Rollins College to give the 1960 commencement address to graduating law students.[2220] McKean, a lover of art, observed the portrait and "became quite excited," believing that it might be a masterpiece, adding that the painting should be cleaned and restored.[2221]

During his visit, McKean photographed the painting and took the photograph to Creighton Gilbert, Curator of the John and Mable Ringling Mu-

2215. Sellers, *Peale, supra* n. 2211, at 20–21.

2216. *Id.* at 25.

2217. Sellers, *Portraits and Miniatures, supra* n. 2210.

2218. Bowen, *supra* n. 455, at 13; *see also* Edmunds, *1969 Memorandum, supra* n. 2209.

2219. Edmunds, *1969 Memorandum, supra* n. 2209.

2220. *Id.*

2221. *Id.*

seum of Art in Sarasota.[2222] Subsequently, Gilbert wrote Stetson officials that "as far as we can observe from [the photograph], the painting is of a certain quality and it would be worthwhile to study it."[2223] Assistant Dean Richard Dillon responded to Gilbert's letter and, after further discussions with Ringling officials, Sebring and Dillon decided to transport the work to the Ringling Museum so that a specialist could evaluate and hopefully identify both the painter and the person portrayed.[2224] After a professional cleaning and restoration, specialists at Ringling determined that Charles Wilson Peale was the artist and that Judge John Beale Bordley was the subject.[2225] Peale painted Bordley in 1770, a few years prior to America's War for Independence.[2226]

After the Ringling Museum returned the portraiture to the College of Law, Edmunds and Sebring "agreed to let the Museum of Fine Arts," just then being organized in St. Petersburg, "display this painting on a loan basis."[2227] Edmunds later reported that after the identity of Peale and Bordley became known, "the University in recent months has had several tempting offers from persons wanting to buy it, but we have declined all offers."[2228]

In fact, it was not clear in 1969 that the University even owned the painting. Highbaugh, Sr., over a decade earlier, had told Edmunds it could be hung in the law school lounge in St. Petersburg.[2229] Highbaugh's son, L. LeRoy Highbaugh, Jr., then a member of the Stetson University Board of Trustees, along with his wife, Dorothy L. Highbaugh, on April 3, 1973, executed a document transferring the title of the painting to the University.[2230] The transfer document declares in part:

2222. Ltr. from Creighton Gilbert, Curator, John and Mable Ringling Museum of Art, to Dean of the Stetson U. College of L. (Apr. 6, 1960).

2223. *Id.*

2224. *See* Ltr. from Creighton Gilbert, Curator, John and Mable Ringling Museum of Art of Sarasota, to Richard T. Dillon, Dean, Stetson U. College of L. (Apr. 23, 1960) (on file at Stetson U. College of L., Gulfport, Fla.) (in turn referring to a letter from Richard T. Dillon to Creighton Gilbert (Apr. 15, 1960) (on file at Stetson U. College of L., Gulfport, Fla.)).

2225. Edmunds, *1969 Memorandum*, *supra* n. 2209, at 1.

2226. *Id.*

2227. *Id.*

2228. *Id.*

2229. *Jan. 29 Dillon Discussion*, *supra* n. 1969.

2230. Gift from L. LeRoy Highbaugh, Jr., and Dorothy L. Highbaugh, to John B. Stetson University (Apr. 3, 1973) (a one-page typed document signed by Mr. and Mrs. Highbaugh, and by Stetson University Business Manager, H. Graves Edmundson, on file at Stetson U. College of L., Gulfport, Fla.).

> WHEREAS, L. Leroy Highbaugh, Jr., and Dorothy L. Highbaugh are the absolute owners of a certain portrait of Judge John Beale Bordley, painted by Charles Wilson Peale (the "Portrait);
> NOW THEREFORE, L. LeRoy Highbaugh, Jr., and Dorothy L. Highbaugh hereby give and deliver the Portrait to John B. Stetson University [and that] John B. Stetson University shall have full and absolute fee simple legal title to the Portrait without reservations of any kind. . . .[2231]

In 1973, only months after the Highbaughs' executed the document, Stetson University sold the Peale painting to the Kennedy Galleries of New York City, which paid Stetson $250,000.[2232] One year later, the Kennedy Galleries sold the portrait of John Beale Bordley to the Barra Foundation, Inc. (near Philadelphia) for an undisclosed price. Then, in 1984, the Barra Foundation gifted the portrait to the National Gallery of Art in Washington, D.C.[2233]

The $250,000 Stetson University received in 1973 remained in University coffers in DeLand for a number of years, though law school Dean Richard Dillon argued that the money belonged to the College of Law that had been the recipient of Highbaugh family gifts as far back as 1955.[2234] Moreover, the painting had originally been delivered to the law school by Highbaugh, Sr., and had remained under the school's control until it was sold. Dillon's arguments prevailed, and in 1979, University President Pope Duncan authorized the proceeds of the sale of the Peale painting be given to the College of Law.[2235]

The College used the funds to establish the second academic chair in the College of Law's history, the first being the Charles A. Dana Professor of Law. At a meeting of the law faculty in 1981 and at graduation ceremonies the following evening, Dean Dillon announced that the University Board of Trustees had ratified his recommendation that the University appoint Professor Calvin A. Kuenzel the first L. LeRoy Highbaugh, Sr., Professor of Law at the College of Law.

2231. *Id.*

2232. The purchase is documented in a letter located in the curatorial file of the National Gallery of Art from Russell E. Burke III, Senior Vice President of Kennedy Galleries, Inc. This transfer is documented in a letter in the curatorial file of the National Gallery of Art from Gail H. Fahmer, program officer of the Barra Foundation.

2233. *Id.*

2234. *Jan. 29 Dillon Discussion*, *supra* n. 1969.

2235. *Id.*

Calvin A. Kuenzel

10.8 Faculty: The Greening of the Faculty: Kuenzel, et al.

a. Sebring's Plan: "A Well-Rounded Faculty"

Dean Sebring believed the school needed a different law faculty composition than the one he inherited when becoming dean in 1955. Within four years of Sebring's arrival, none of the 1954–55 full-time faculty—Roy Howes, Charles Hilkey, Louis James, Harvey Jernigan, and C.W. Leaphart—remained, both Jerningan and Leaphart having left even before Sebring became dean. Some retired, while others went elsewhere. Also gone were the new faculty members Hilkey had hired—Burton Stevenson and William O. Morris.[2236]

In contrast to the lack of varied experience and age diversity characteristic of the Haslup and Hilkey faculties, Sebring believed that a "well-rounded faculty" must include distinguished judges, experienced law teachers and administrators, leading practitioners with legal expertise in specific areas of law, and top-of-the-class recent law school graduates with potential to become demanding teachers.[2237] This mix, he believed, afforded law students the best op-

2236. Sebring did retain, however, a few part-time faculty members from the 1954–56 faculty, including Victor O. Wehle and Reese Smith.

2237. *See Stetson College of Law Begins Its 61st Year with Largest Faculty in Its History* 1 (six-page, legal size typed paper, author unknown (though probably Sebring) (1961) (on file at Stetson U. College of L., Gulfport, Fla.) [hereinafter *Largest Faculty*].

portunities for theoretical, doctrinal, and practical training. Older faculty members draw upon their varied experiences, he believed, while the younger ones have ambition, bright intellect, and energy. In addition, the younger faculty members can develop not only teaching and scholarly skills, but also can provide a needed long-term stability for the College of Law—one of the school's deficiencies that the ABA had identified.

In a 1959 report to the Trustees and Board of Overseers, Sebring summarized the new faculty's composition:

> On the faculty are four former judges (two of whom were Chief Justices of State Supreme Courts and judges at the Nuremberg Trials) ... two former distinguished deans of other law schools, two former presidents of their state bar associations, and several highly successful practitioners. These elder scholars supplement a "permanent" faculty of younger men who, while they have had only limited teaching experience, show great promise as future law teachers and law school administrators.[2238]

Those who fulfilled Sebring's "young, bright, and demanding" criteria were Richard T. Dillon,[2239] Calvin A. Kuenzel,[2240] Paul Barnard,[2241] Frank E. Booker,[2242] Wallace Storey,[2243] Everett Cushman,[2244] Charles M. Waygood,[2245] and Kenneth Evans.[2246] As for experienced jurists, Sebring hired James T. Brand, retired Chief Justice of the Oregon Supreme Court and a principal judge at the Nuremberg trials (as was Sebring);[2247] Judge Stanley Milledge of the Eleventh Judicial Circuit (Miami);[2248] Judge Peabody Howard of the Tennessee Court of Appeals;[2249] and Judge Victor O. Wehle of the Sixth Judicial Circuit (St. Petersburg).[2250] Sebring's third group of seasoned law teachers and former law deans consisted of Joseph A. McClain, Jr., who had been dean at four law schools;[2251] Edward L. Platt, both a law teacher and a former acting

2238. Sebring, *Five-Year Report*, *supra* n. 1896, at 8.
2239. *See infra* nn. 2270–2280 and accompanying text.
2240. *See infra* nn. 2281–2319 and accompanying text.
2241. *See infra* nn. 2342–2350 and accompanying text.
2242. *See infra* nn. 2369–2372 and accompanying text.
2243. *See infra* n. 2258 and accompanying text.
2244. *See infra* nn. 2373–2382 and accompanying text.
2245. *See infra* nn. 2396–2400 and accompanying text.
2246. *See infra* n. 2473 and accompanying text.
2247. *See infra* nn. 2320–2333 and accompanying text.
2248. *See infra* nn. 2334–2341 and accompanying text.
2249. *See infra* n. 2423 and accompanying text.
2250. *See infra* nn. 2392–2395 and accompanying text.
2251. *See infra* nn. 2259–2269 and accompanying text.

Nuremberg Justice and Stetson Professor James T. Brand
with Students below Portrait of Charles Dana

dean;[2252] and experienced law professors David L. Dickson (also a former assistant general counsel of Montgomery Ward),[2253] Harold I. Lindsey,[2254] and Harry H. Haden.[2255] Finally, newly hired adjunct professors included distinguished practitioners John J. Trenam, Sherwin P. Simmons, and Granville Mason Alley, Jr., all members of the Tampa law firm (then-called) Fowler, White, Collins, Gillen, Humkey and Trenam; Wm. Reece Smith[2256] (initially hired by Dean Hilkey), future president of the American Bar Association and head of the Tampa-based law firm of Carlton Fields; Paul Roney, a prominent St. Petersburg attorney who later became a judge on the United States Court of Appeals for the Eleventh Circuit,;[2257] William J. McLeod, tax specialist from St. Petersburg; Tampa attorney James Davis, and former F.B.I. agent Col. Henry A. Fisher, Jr. In addition, Sebring hired Wallace Storey in 1959, who later became secretary and treasurer of the Board of Overseers and of the Law Center Foundation.[2258]

2252. *See infra* nn. 2351–2367 and accompanying text.

2253. *See infra* nn. 2384–23 91 and accompanying text.

2254. *See infra* nn. 2401–2410 and accompanying text.

2255. *See infra* nn. 2411–2417 and accompanying text.

2256. *See infra* nn. 3836–3852 and accompanying text.

2257. Judge Roney's chambers were in St. Petersburg, though the Eleventh Circuit usually sits in Atlanta.

2258. *See infra* nn. 2418–2422 and accompanying text.

b. The Mix: The Young, the Experienced, and the Demanding

(1) Joseph A. McClain, Jr.

Dean Sebring's first faculty hire, Joseph A. McClain, Jr., was noted in the *New York Times:*

> Dr. Joseph A. McClain, Jr., Dean of Duke University School of Law for the last six years, will join the faculty of Stetson University's College of Law in September. Dr. McClain, who has thirty years in law, will be a visiting professor and will open a private practice in this area.[2259]

His appointment also engendered a laudatory editorial in the *St. Petersburg Times,*[2260] which reads in part:

> Stetson University College of Law, a prize academic facility of St. Petersburg ... is beginning to demonstrate a magnetic attraction for top thinkers.... Dr. Joseph A. McClain Jr., dean and professor of law of Duke University School of Law for the past six years will join the Stetson Law Faculty this September as a visiting professor of law.
> As a result, the school's prestige takes a distinct jump upward. [McClain is] one of the country's distinguished teachers and practitioners in the field of law.... Stetson's impressive growth is becoming a model for the Suncoast ... as the nation's intellectual climate moves South.[2261]

A Georgia native, McClain earned his B.A. and LL.B. degrees from Mercer University, and J.S.D. from Yale Law School.[2262] Later, he received two honorary degrees—one from Mercer, the other from Tulane University.[2263] After serving on two law faculties, McClain became dean at four law schools: Mercer University (1932–34); University of Louisville (1934–36); Washington University of St. Louis (1936–42); and Duke University (1950–56).[2264] Previously, he was a general counsel of the Terminal Railroad Association, and later, general counsel of the Wabash Railroad.[2265] Active in the American Bar Association, McClain served as chair of the Council on Legal Education

2259. *Duke Law Dean Joins Stetson,* N.Y. Times 25 (Mar. 4, 1956) (reprinted in St. Pete. Times; page and date not shown on clipping) [hereinafter *Duke Law Dean*].

2260. Editorial, *Intellectual Climate Moving South,* St. Pete. Times 8 (Mar. 5, 1956).

2261. *Id.*

2262. *Duke Law Dean, supra* n. 2259.

2263. *Id.*

2264. *Id.*

2265. *Id.*

and as a member of the House of Delegates.[2266] In accepting Sebring's offer to join the Stetson faculty as an adjunct, McClain said: "My decision is not a sudden one. I have considered for some time the desirability of living in the St. Petersburg area, particularly since Judge Sebring became the dean of Stetson."[2267] Bruce Jacob took both criminal law and trusts from McClain and remembers him as "an unbelievably good teacher."[2268] While teaching at Stetson, McClain practiced law full-time, first in Sarasota and then in Tampa.[2269]

(2) Richard T. Dillon

In the spring of 1953, Richard T. Dillon graduated valedictorian of his class at the University of Tampa.[2270] The Tampa native and Navy veteran of World War II entered Stetson University's College of Law in the fall of 1954, a member of the first class initially admitted on the school's Gulfport campus.[2271] In 1957, Dillon received his LL.B. degree from Stetson, graduating near the top of his 1954 charter class.[2272] As a Ford Foundation Fellow, he later earned the LL.M. degree from New York University, a program for law deans and professors. NYU law school Dean Robert McKay said, "Dillon's work for the LL.M. was completed with one of the highest averages ever to be achieved in that particular program ... we are most enthusiastic about him."[2273] Dillon was a tireless worker. During his years as a Stetson student, he supported his family by teaching at Florida Central College and the University of Tampa.[2274] Prior to entering law school, Dillon had owned and operated several business, including a successful real estate brokerage and licensing school.

In law school, Dillon was Chief Justice of the Stetson Honor Court, head of his legal fraternity, *Phi Alpha Delta*, and an Overseer's scholar. Like Dean McKay, Dean Sebring was "most enthusiastic" over Dillon's performance as a student, so much so that following his graduation, the dean invited Dillon to

2266. *Id.*

2267. *Id.*

2268. Memo. from Bruce R. Jacob, Dean Emeritus, Stetson U. College of L., to W. Gary Vause, Dean, Stetson U. College of L. 13 (Sept. 17, 2001).

2269. *Largest Faculty*, *supra* n. 2237, at 3; *see also Duke Law Dean*, *supra* n. 2259.

2270. Dick Bothwell, *Stetson at 20*, St. Pete. Times 8, 10 (Sept. 29, 1974).

2271. *See supra* n. 1891 and accompanying text.

2272. *Dillon Succeeds Sebring as Dean, September 1*, 11 Stetson Law. 1, 1 (Mar. 1980) [hereinafter *Dillon Succeeds Sebring*].

2273. *Id.*

2274. *Id.*

join the Stetson law faculty.[2275] He accepted and, in the fall of 1957, began a thirty-four year career with Stetson College of Law, including nine as assistant dean, and thirteen as dean of the law school.[2276] Throughout his years of decanal service, Dillon continued to teach property in addition to other courses.

Sebring initially hired Dillon as an assistant professor of law and as the librarian of the law school. He was relieved of his librarian duties in 1958.[2277] The young teacher soon proved his worth as students considered Dillon an "excellent," though "tough," teacher. One of his students, Ruth Thurman (who later joined the Stetson faculty),[2278] took four courses from him and describes him as "a wonderful teacher" because he was able to communicate the legal intricacies of "future interest."[2279] Another Dillon student, Bruce Jacob, echoes Thurman's sentiment: "Dillon was a very good teacher, very well organized. He did his research on Florida law, gave us Florida citations, and I always liked him as a teacher."[2280]

(3) Calvin Arnold Kuenzel

He was young and debonair with eyes that could penetrate. His appellation was Calvin Arnold Kuenzel, a name variously pronounced as either K U N zel, or K I N zel—he didn't care. He came from America's heartland, Iowa, the Hawkeye state. The twenty-nine year old northerner, never in Florida before, arrived in the summer of 1958 to a hot and steamy St. Petersburg.[2281] He was starting his career—teaching law. From that moment on he never looked back, never longed to do anything or be anywhere else. He would say: "You've got to be somewhere," and he knew the environs of the old Rolyat Hotel was the place to be. On those grounds, Professor Kuenzel taught over the course of four decades approximately 4,000 law students and, in doing so, established a reputation unlike any other professor before or since.

2275. Vause, *Milestones*, *supra* n. 1370, at 24.

2276. *See infra* n. 3210 and accompanying text.

2277. *Dillon Succeeds Sebring*, *supra* n. 2272, at 1.

2278. *See* Interview by Michael I. Swygert, Prof. Emeritus, Stetson U. College of L., with Ruth Thurman, Professor of Law, Stetson U. College of L., *Stetson University College of Law Oral History Project* (May 18, 2004) [hereinafter *Thurman Interview*].

2279. *Id.* at 28.

2280. Interview by Michael I. Swygert, Prof. Emeritus, Stetson U. College of L., with Bruce R. Jacob, Dean Emeritus, Stetson U. College of Law, *Stetson University College of Law Oral History Project*, 24 (Apr.14, 2004) (on file at Stetson U. College of L., Gulfport, Fla.) [hereinafter *Jacob Interview*].

2281. *Calvin A. Kuenzel*, 2 Stetson L. News 4 (Nov. 1958).

Calvin Kuenzel's credentials were good, very good, but not extraordinary for one seeking to join a law faculty. He earned the A.B. and J.D. degrees from Iowa University, and later the LL.M. and S.J.D. degrees from the University of Illinois.[2282] After coming to Stetson, Kuenzel continued to hone his expertise. In the summer of 1962, he attended a conclave for contracts teachers at New York University.[2283] There, he studied with leading experts in the fields of contracts and commercial law. Subsequently, two of these scholars, Professors Donald King and Bradford Stone, joined Kuenzel in writing an authoritative and popular casebook on commercial law.[2284]

But his expertise was in an early stage in the summer of 1958 when Kuenzel "showed up" (one of his favorite expressions) at Stetson. Dorothy Bishop was at that time an assistant to law school admissions director, Mrs. Kay Eddy.[2285] Bishop recalls vividly her first impressions of "Cal."

> I saw this young man walking toward me. I knew right away that it was Cal Kuenzel. I thought he was so handsome, such a nice young attractive man. I spoke to him and he was on his way to the dean's office. This was my first meeting with him. I can see it today.[2286]

Dorothy Bishop later became administrative assistant to Dean Richard Dillon (and subsequently to four of his successors).[2287] She recalls that Calvin Kuenzel—whom Dillon made assistant dean—possessed a style of interacting with people that contrasted yet complemented the style of Dean Dillon. Whereas Dillon "was so serious," Bishop points out "Professor Kuenzel was just the opposite. He just didn't take things seriously."[2288] The distinction was apparent in the way they spoke. Dillon was direct and to the point—no obfuscation. However, Kuenzel typically spoke in an enigmatic and tongue-in-cheek manner. "You weren't sure if he was being serious or not,"[2289] Bishop says. A case in point follows.

2282. *Id.*

2283. *Faculty Vacations*, 6 Stetson Law. 2 (Nov. 1962).

2284. *See* Donald B. King, Calvin A. Kuenzel & Bradford Stone, *Commercial Transactions under the Uniform Commercial Code* (5th ed., Matthew Bender 1997).

2285. Bishop Interview, *supra* n. 1953, at 3.

2286. *Id.* at 9.

2287. *See infra* nn. 3188–3192 and accompanying text.

2288. *Bishop Interview*, *supra* n. 1953, at 10.

2289. *Id.* at 11. The candidate was the co-author of this volume, Michael I. Swygert. The dinner occurred at the Sunbird Restaurant (no longer in existence) in St. Petersburg in mid-January 1979. At that time, Swygert was a tenured faculty member of DePaul University College of Law in Chicago. The northern school referred to in the text, however, was

In 1979, Kuenzel met with a Stetson faculty candidate who had taught at Valparaiso law school in Northern Indiana.[2290] The applicant talked about student protests during the 1960s and '70s against the Vietnam War, recalling events in May of 1970, when members of the Ohio National Guard killed three Kent State University students who were protesting the war and throwing stones at the guardsmen. In response to the killings, the applicant told how undergraduate students at his university burned down the school's administration building. A few days later, senior law students petitioned the faculty to cancel their pending final examinations. The faculty did, and a controversy ensued between the law school and the state's (Indiana) supreme court over whether the examless students could sit for the bar examination[2291] (eventually, they were allowed to do so).[2292]

The applicant then asked Kuenzel: "What did Stetson's students do after the Kent State killings?"[2293] Eyes narrowing, chin lowering, and lips dropping, Kuenzel uttered: "The day after Kent State, our boys enlisted in the National Guard."

Stunned, the faculty applicant sat in silence. Then, Kuenzel's chin began to rise, the ends of his lips turning upward, and his facial muscles softening—subtle modifications which transformed his melancholic appearance into Kuenzel's trademark Mona Lisa, "Am-I-serious-or-not?" look. The applicant was bewildered. Kuenzel smiled and with eyes sparkling, looked at the befuddled stranger, silently shouting: "I got yah."

Though loving to put one over on students and colleagues whenever the chance arose, Kuenzel's sly humor was only a small part of his probing, demanding, and distinctive manner of teaching.[2294] In the classroom, a certain gruffness and even a dash of cynicism cropped up. With students, he could be both gentle (soft spoken) and hard (relentless) at the same time.

---

the Valparaiso University School of Law in northern Indiana, where Swygert taught from 1969 through 1972.

2290. The faculty candidate was Michael I. Swygert, Professor Emeritus, Stetson U. College of L.

2291. Swygert, *supra* n. 80, at 245–254.

2292. The background and decision of the Indiana Supreme Court are discussed in a newspaper article published in the *Indianapolis Times.* Jack Averitt, *Skipping Law Exams Ends in Court Hassle*, Indianapolis Times 1–2 (June 11, 1970); *see also* Jack Averitt, *In, Around Statehouse*, Indianapolis Times 1, 4 (June 14, 1970).

2293. Swygert's question was serious and he expected a straightforward answer. Of course, he had not met Professor Kuenzel prior to that day and did not realize that by asking the question, Swygert was venturing into a Kuenzel engineered conundrum.

2294. *See* Michael I. Swygert, *Calvin Arnold Kuenzel, Master Teacher*, 28 Stetson L. Rev. 1001 (Feb. 2000) [hereinafter Swygert, *Tribute to Kuenzel*].

Kuenzel's military background added still another dimension to the classroom kinetics. Though his students adopted various names for their demanding professor—"Cool Cal" was their favorite—friends and colleagues simply called him "Cal." But when he served in the U.S. Army, he was referred to as "Captain Calvin A. Kuenzel." His military service included tours of duty with both the U.S. Navy and the U.S. Army.[2295] He ended up a Colonel in the Army Reserve. While teaching at Stetson, Kuenzel participated in the Army reserves for several years, attending training programs during the summers.[2296] When he addressed military subordinates, they stood and responded to his questions. Similarly, when he taught and asked a law student a question, the student was expected (as in all law school classes) to stand and respond. The difference in Cal's classes was that each rose with nervous disquietude.[2297]

Kuenzel initially taught personal property and domestic relations, courses far removed from what became his principal areas of expertise: contracts and commercial law.[2298] But whatever he taught, students' reactions were the same.

One of his students from the 1970s, Susan Schaeffer, recalls that in class "you could not figure out what he was saying at the moment. You just didn't know."[2299] Though many students never did understand Kuenzel's use of the Socratic pedagogy (in the manner Socrates had intended), Susan Schaeffer did. She explains:

> [Students] would ask me. "What is he saying?" I'd say "I have no idea." So I just started writing everything he said, every question he asked ... I could tell that he was trying to dig something out ... Then, as part of my study, I'd go back and [review his questions]. The case didn't seem to be so terribly important, but I'd have all that stuff he asked ... Sooner or later, I could figure out what he was getting at. Once I figured that out, I knew what was important.[2300]

Not surprisingly Schaeffer graduated number one in her class. She became one of the law school's highest achieving graduates as a leading jurist and public

2295. *See* Thomas Marks, *From "Professor Kuenzel" to "Cal"*, 28 Stetson L. Rev. 991, 991–992 (Feb. 2000).

2296. *Faculty Doings*, 5 Stetson Law. 7 (Oct. 1961).

2297. Other professors besides Kuenzel expected students to stand up when they recited in class.

2298. *Faculty Doings*, *supra* n. 2296, at 7.

2299. Interview by Michael I. Swygert, Prof. Emeritus, Stetson U. College of L., with Judge Susan Schaeffer, Circuit Judge of the Sixth Judicial Circuit, 79–80 (Jan. 20, 2005) [hereinafter *Judge Schaeffer Interview*].

2300. *Id.* at 81.

servant in Florida.[2301] In February 2005, she was installed into the Stetson University College of Law Hall of Fame.[2302]

Another achieving survivor-of-contracts-with-Cal student was Ruth Fleet Thurman of the law class of 1963.[2303] Thurman, like Schaeffer, notes that Kuenzel "invoked such positive and negative feelings in students that they thought either he was the best teacher they ever had, or they were incensed by him."[2304] Kuenzel once told Thurman that if a student left his class without more questions that he or she came in with, Cal "felt he hadn't had a good class."[2305] Thurman notes that students never figured out what Kuenzel was driving at. But, she adds, if they were willing to "dig into the books, pretty soon the light would dawn on them."[2306] Ruth Thurman shares her insights about Kuenzel's teaching philosophy. She explains:

> He didn't give [students] the answers, but steered them in the right direction. He felt that ... you had to "be in the question," because once you think you have the answer, learning stops. He wanted students to take responsibility for their own education. He understood that our job was not to teach law to the students, but to teach the students to teach themselves law.[2307]

At times, the keep-the-ball-hidden professor became frustrating. During his early teaching years, Kuenzel "would fling an eraser or a piece of chalk" in the direction of an unprepared, or unthinking, student. Ruth Thurman recollects: "If you gave a stupid answer, you could expect to have something sailing past you."[2308]

An older student, while sitting in class, was struck by a small piece of chalk put into motion by Professor Kuenzel. The student was incensed. He stood and told Kuenzel to never ever throw chalk at him again. The student then picked up his books and left the room while the class was still in session.[2309]

2301. *See infra* nn. 2957–2977 and accompanying text.

2302. The College of Law's establishment of a Hall of Fame and the other members are discussed *infra* nn. 4506–4523 and accompanying text.

2303. *Thurman Interview*, *supra* n. 2278.

2304. *Id.* at 83.

2305. *Id.* at 93–94.

2306. *Id.*

2307. *Id.* at 84–85.

2308. *Id.* at 35.

2309. The story related above concerning the incident involving Kuenzel and the incensed student over the latter's being struck by chalk has been mentioned by numerous graduates who witnessed some or many of the events. In addition, Professor Kuenzel reportedly told the story at an alumni function years after it took place. Dean Emeritus

The student went directly to Dean Sebring's office to report the incident. As he entered the Dean's outer office, he was cordially met with a "how are you" greeting by the College's beloved Director of Admissions, Mrs. Kay Eddy, who also functioned as gate-keeper for the Dean.[2310] The obviously angry student informed Eddy about his grievance and asked to see Sebring. Because of her work in Admissions, Eddy remembered that the student had a military background and that he was a highly decorated combat veteran. Eddy was guided by her protective instincts and referred the student to Assistant Dean Richard Dillon.[2311]

The student's cooling down mechanism had not yet kicked in by the time he reached Dillon's office. He made it abundantly clear that if Kuenzel ever threw chalk at him again, Kuenzel could expect swift retaliation in the form of physical harm.

Dillon went to Kuenzel's office and repeated the student's warning. Dillon then volunteered to his old friend his assessment of the probability of the student resorting to violence if the incident occurred again as a nine on a scale of one to ten. For the next thirty seconds, the sound of muffled voices emanated from the room, much to the delight of several students and faculty who were standing silently outside the office. Suddenly the door opened and as Dillon emerged he was overheard to say: "Don't expect me to attend your funeral, I'll be too busy assisting with the defense." He closed the door, reopened it, leaned back in and said: "stay well."[2312]

Another Stetson law professor tells the story of how Kuenzel once called on a student throughout two class periods. Nobody knew why.[2313] The student became frustrated by the non-stop questions of the grand inquisitor. At some point, a nearby student whispered: "Remove your baseball cap." The student did and Kuenzel immediately turned to another student and fired away.

Professor Thurman believes that Kuenzel was the most "admired" and most "feared" of all Stetson law professors.[2314] As such, he is indisputably the most memorable teacher in the minds of the largest number of students in Stetson's

---

Richard Dillon also vividly recalls the incident and has supplied some of the details. May 4 Dillon Interview, *supra* n. 1885.

2310. *Id.*

2311. *Id.*

2312. *Id.*

2313. The story was told to Professor Michael Swygert by several College of Law students who were in Professor Kuenzel's class when the alleged incident took place.

2314. *Thurman Interview*, *supra* n. 2278, at 28; *see also* Swygert, *Tribute to Kuenzel, supra* n. 2294.

history. Of those who condemned him when in school, many later changed their minds, realizing that he was the professor who had best taught them how to think, how to go beyond the obvious, and how "to dig."[2315] Professor Swygert has written:

> Cal combined his vast pedagogical talents with a caring heart. Cal viewed each student [as having] within themselves infinite possibilities ... He was a successful and ultimately a most influential teacher.[2316]

On July 20, 1998, Calvin A. Kuenzel died at the age of seventy.[2317] At the time of his death, the dynamic professor was teaching at the Stetson law school as he had done for four decades. Following his passing, students of the Stetson University College of Law named their organization in his honor—the Calvin A. Kuenzel Student Bar Association.[2318] It was the right thing to do. The story of Professor Calvin Kuenzel's exceptional contributions to the Stetson University College of Law continues in later chapters.[2319]

(4) Justice James Tenney Brand: "Judgment at Nuremberg"

The same year Sebring hired Kuenzel, the dean appointed former chief justice of the Oregon Supreme Court—and fellow Nuremberg judge—James Tenney Brand to the faculty.[2320] Justice Brand earned his undergraduate degree from Oberlin College in Ohio and his law degree from Harvard.[2321] In 1947, President Harry Truman named Brand to be one of the principal judges at the Nuremberg Nazi War Crime Trials. Brand served on the "Justice Trial" tribunal. In that case, the United States prosecuted judges and other officials for giving legal sanction to, and validation of, Nazi atrocities, including the is-

---

2315. On various occasions when alumni of the Stetson College of Law returned to the campus, such as the fiftieth anniversary of the College being on the Gulfport campus in September 2004, many would reminisce about their feelings (often quite negative) about Professor Kuenzel when they were students at the College, then express their appreciation today for how Kuenzel had made them better lawyers.

2316. Swygert, *Tribute to Kuenzel*, *supra* n. 2294, at 1004.

2317. *See Professor Calvin A. Kuenzel, 1928–1998,* 39 Stetson Law. 1, 8–9 (Fall 1998/Winter 1999).

2318. *Stetson Announces Student Bar Association Officers*, 40 Stetson Law. 1, 37 (Fall 2000).

2319. *See supra* nn. 2274–2275; 2278–2279 and accompanying text; *infra* nn. 2815–16 and accompanying text.

2320. *Distinguished Jurists Among New Faculty Members*, 2 Stetson L. News 2 (Nov. 1958).

2321. *Id.*

suing of orders removing Jewish men, women, and children to concentration camps.[2322]

The Justice Trial became the basis of a television play (and later Hollywood movie) titled "*Justice at Nuremberg*."[2323] In the television version (aired in 1959 on *Playhouse 90*) actor Claude Rains played Brand's role as the presiding judge.[2324] In the movie version, Spencer Tracy portrayed Justice Brand.[2325] In preparing for his role as the presiding judge, Claude Rains came to Stetson law school to familiarize himself with the personality, character, and mannerisms of Professor Brand, and to learn firsthand what happened.[2326] Students saw Rains and Brand working together at the law school.[2327]

Brand and Sebring had become friends while they both served as judges at Nuremberg. After Brand retired at the age of seventy-three from the Oregon Supreme Court in 1958, Sebring persuaded him to join the Stetson law faculty. At Stetson, Brand taught torts, constitutional law, and municipal corporations.[2328] Bruce Jacob notes that, as a student, he and Professor James Brand became friends and "were together constantly."[2329] Students called them the "Gold Trust Twins" because Brand had sprouted white hair and Jacob light blond hair.[2330] Jacob remembers Brand as a "magnificent teacher and a magnificent man." The justice taught three years at Stetson, then retired in 1960.[2331] On February 29, 1964, James Tenney Brand died. He was in his late seventies.[2332] The *Stetson Lawyer* observed: "His students loved him, as he loved them and Stetson."[2333]

(5) Judge Stanley Milledge

Sebring appointed four new faculty members for the 1958–59 academic year. Besides Brand and Kuenzel, he hired Judge Stanley Milledge and Paul Barnard. Milledge had been judge of the Eleventh Judicial Circuit of Florida

2322. *Id.; see also Jacob Interview, supra* n. 2280, at 13.
2323. Jacob, *Remembering Sebring, supra* n. 9, at 110.
2324. Sebring, *Largest Faculty, supra* n. 2237, at 2.
2325. Jacob, *Remembering Sebring, supra* n. 9, at 110 n. 295.
2326. *Id.*
2327. *Id.*
2328. Vause, *Centennial History, supra* n. 595, at 155.
2329. *Jacob Interview, supra* n. 2280, at 13.
2330. *Id.*
2331. *Id.* at 12.
2332. *James T. Brand*, 7 Stetson Law. 1,1 (Mar. 1964).
2333. *Id.*

from 1945 to 1958.[2334] He earned his law degree at the University of Georgia and also had taken courses at Florida, Tennessee, and Michigan universities.[2335] Prior to going on to the bench, Milledge served as mayor of Miami Shores and was state's attorney for the Eleventh Judicial Circuit.[2336]

At Stetson, Milledge was considered an intellectually engaging professor who enjoyed digressing into "philosophical colloquies on almost every facet of the law."[2337] Many considered him "an excellent professor."[2338] His specialty was legal ethics.[2339] Described as an affable and soft-spoken professor, he once was an "implacable foe of racketeers" when serving as a state's attorney.[2340] Judge Milledge died unexpectedly at the age of sixty-nine, during his eighth year on the Stetson faculty. A story in the *Stetson Lawyer* lamented that "a faculty chair was vacant, a familiar face was missing from the cafeteria, the campus flag was at half mast, and strained faces of faculty and students reflected a great loss; [Milledge] was a beloved professor and a distinguished judge."[2341] Throughout his years at Stetson, Judge Milledge ate with students in the cafeteria.

(6) Paul Barnard

Paul Barnard, like professors Dillon and Kuenzel, was a recent graduate of the law school when Sebring invited him to join the faculty. Barnard was an FBI agent for several years before studying law.[2342] At Stetson, he served as chief justice of the school's Honor Court and won first place in the moot court competition.[2343] Prior to earning his Stetson law degree, Barnard earned a bachelor's degree from Wheaton College, and then a master of arts degree from Florida State University.[2344] Sebring hired Barnard in 1958 as assistant professor and law school librarian.[2345] Paul Barnard spent eighteen years on the Stetson law faculty before resigning in 1976. He taught a variety of courses, in-

2334. *Stanley Millege*, 2 Stetson L. News 4, 4 (Nov. 1958).

2335. *Id.*

2336. *Id.*

2337. *Beloved Professor, Distinguished Milledge, 69, Dies Suddenly*, 9 Stetson Law. 5, 5 (Nov. 1965).

2338. *Id.*

2339. Vause, *Centennial History*, *supra* n. 595, at 184.

2340. *Id.*

2341. *Id.*

2342. *Id.* at 160.

2343. *Paul Barnard*, 2 Stetson L. News 4, 4 (Nov. 1958).

2344. *Id.*

2345. *Id.*

cluding criminal law and creditor rights.[2346] Though bright and respected by his colleagues, student reactions about Professor Barnard's teaching were mixed.[2347] However, Barnard contributed to the development and quality of the College of Law. As discussed below, he and alumnus Robert Jagger set up Stetson's Public Defender Clinic.[2348] Moreover, Barnard convinced the Florida Supreme Court to allow third-year law students to practice in court under members of the bar.[2349] Dean Emeritus Richard Dillon remembers that Professor Barnard had personally raised much of the funding for Stetson's Public Defender Clinic, not only during Dean Sebring's administration, but also during Dillon's administration. Dillon declares: "Paul Barnard was an advocate for practical legal education when theoretical legal education was king. As a pioneer in clinical training, he set the markers for others to follow."[2350]

(7) Edward L. Platt

In 1956, Sebring appointed Edward L. Platt "visiting senior professor of law,"[2351] describing Platt as an experienced legal educator who had taught "practically every subject offered in law colleges."[2352] It proved true. At Stetson, Platt taught civil procedure, creditor rights, corporations, "and anything else that needed teaching."[2353] Prior to joining the Stetson faculty, Platt served as acting dean at "South Jersey Law School" (renamed Rutgers University College of Law, Camden).[2354]

The year following Platt's arrival at Stetson, the ABA inspected the school. In the ensuing ABA report, Professor Russell Sullivan described Professor Platt as "a man of only limited legal ability."[2355] Though perhaps a harsh and unfair criticism, many Stetson law students of the 1950s and '60s would agree. One recalls:

2346. Vause, *Centennial History*, *supra* n. 595, at 155.

2347. *See e.g. Jacob Interview*, *supra* n. 2280, at 12–13.

2348. *See infra* nn. 2438–2460 and accompanying text.

2349. *Id.*

2350. Discussion between Silvia Manzanero, Paralegal, Stetson U. College of L., and Richard T. Dillon, Dean Emeritus, Stetson U. College of L. (Aug. 3, 2005) [hereinafter *Dillon-Manzanero Aug. 3 Discussion*].

2351. Dorothy Bishop, *List of Law Faculty and Dates of Appointment from 1954 through 2004*, at 1 (on file at Stetson U. College of L., Gulfport, Fla.) [hereinafter Bishop, *List*].

2352. *Learning, Versatility*, *supra* n. 1974, at 5. Today, legal educators would consider "teaching the curriculum" not to be an asset, since doing so would mean that the person would teach any given course superficially at best.

2353. Vause, *Centennial History*, *supra* n. 595, at 155.

2354. *Id.*

2355. Vause, *Centennial History*, *supra* n. 595, at 141, 144.

> [Platt's] classes were really not very good and you never learned anything from him. He really didn't teach; he would cover four cases per day. Students would recite. He would say a few words, but the coverage was so superficial it was laughable.[2356]

Less laughable were Platt's grading practices. Bruce Jacob remembers that Platt "was a one-man crusade to save as many students as he possibly could from flunking out."[2357] Platt would ask how many quality points a student needed to stay in school, then would provide that student with the necessary grade.[2358] Back then, the law school did not have an anonymous grading system. Years later, Professor Kuenzel explained that the faculty adopted anonymous grading as a direct response to Platt's grading practices.[2359] Confirming the practice, a student of the era remembers that Platt had "sympathy on students who needed good grades."[2360]

Platt also treated women students differently than men. Ruth Thurman recalls: "He paid a lot of attention to women students and to students' wives. He was always glad to give us a hug."[2361] The Student Bar Association on one occasion invited women from area colleges to a reception at the law school.[2362] Upon entering the lounge each woman was told to write her name and phone number on a tablet. Though faculty members had not been invited, Professor Platt was there, hugging and kissing each woman as she entered the lounge.[2363]

Platt remained on the law faculty through the 1965–66 academic year. In fairness to Platt, his teaching difficulties probably resulted in large measure because of a severe hearing problem. One student recalls that "he was nearly deaf" and could rarely hear what students said in class, adding that students were often "horsing around and talking" while Platt was unaware of their actions.[2364] In one area, Platt served the law school well. For several years, he was the librarian.[2365] In that capacity, he oversaw the collection increase to 51,000

2356. *Jacob Interview*, *supra* n. 2280, at 17–18.
2357. Jacob, *Recollections*, *supra* n. 1678, at 3.
2358. *Id.*
2359. *Id.*
2360. *Thurman Interview*, *supra* n. 2278, at 30.
2361. *Id.*
2362. *See* Vause, *Centennial History*, *supra* n. 595, at 158.
2363. *Id.*
2364. *Jacob Interview*, *supra* n. 2280, at 17.
2365. *Retiring Librarian Describes Four-Year Term as One of "Substantial Progress"*, 8 Stetson Law. 3 (June 1965).

volumes, compared with less than 20,000 when the school moved to Gulfport.[2366] Platt retired in 1966 when he was seventy-six.[2367]

(8) Frank E. Booker

A Duke law school graduate, class of 1954, Frank E. Booker practiced law for six years in St. Louis prior to joining the Stetson law faculty in 1960.[2368] At Duke, he was a member of the law review and graduated with honors.[2369]

While a member of the Stetson law faculty, Booker taught torts, civil procedure, and evidence. Many students considered him an extraordinary teacher, one of them declaring that Booker "was very powerful, an excellent teacher."[2370] In addition to teaching, Booker researched and wrote scholarly articles published in law reviews. One had "double" significance for Stetson, because it involved a Stetson professor and a Stetson alumnus. Professor Booker co-authored an article with Richard Morton, "a former Stetson law student," in the *University of Denver Law Journal*, titled "The Paradoxical Nature of Federal Securities Regulation."[2371] After serving eight years on the Stetson law faculty, Booker left to join the faculty at the University of Notre Dame Law School.[2372]

(9) Everett E. Cushman

Everett E. Cushman came to Stetson in the fall of 1960, the same year as Frank Booker.[2373] Like Dillon and Barnard before him, Cushman, though older than the others, had just graduated from law school when Sebring hired him.[2374] In law school, Cushman also was editor of the Student Bar Association publication *The Brief*.[2375] He held an A.B. degree from Bates College, an M.A. from the University of Miami, and an LL.B. from Stetson (1959).[2376] Before en-

2366. *Id.*

2367. Bishop, *List*, *supra* n. 2351.

2368. *Assistant Professors*, 4 Stetson Law. 5, 5 (Oct. 1960).

2369. Harold Sebring, *New Members of Stetson College of Law Faculty, Fall Semester 1960–1961* (1960) (on file at Stetson U. College of L., Gulfport, Fla.) [hereinafter Sebring, *New Members*]

2370. Thurman Interview, *supra* n. 2278, at 29.

2371. *See Recent Articles by Stetson Professors*, 11 Stetson Law. 3, 3 (Nov. 1967).

2372. *Booker Will Join Notre Dame Faculty This Fall*, 11 Stetson Law. 4, 4 (May, 1968).

2373. Bishop, *List*, *supra* n. 2351.

2374. Sebring, *New Members*, *supra* n. 2369, at 5.

2375. *Id.* at 1, 2.

2376. *Id.*

tering law school, he spent fifteen years teaching English and social sciences in secondary schools in Maine.[2377] In addition, he was a Navy Veteran of WWII.

After joining the Stetson law faculty, Cushman taught real property, legal research and writing, and constitutional law.[2378] In addition to teaching, Cushman served as editor of the *Stetson Lawyer* (a job he had begun earlier in 1959 when still a student).[2379] On the faculty, he continued editing the twice yearly publication through the spring of 1976, when Professor Ruth Thurman took over.[2380] After he left, Thurman took over various administrative tasks that he had performed for Dillon.[2381] Cushman returned in 1977 to teach for one final year.[2382] Afterwards, he resumed his editorship of the *Stetson Lawyer* for several years.

Everett Cushman contributed to Stetson College of Law in many capacities. Dean Emeritus Dillon recalls that Cushman was dedicated to the school and was one of the more significant figures in bringing about its improvement.[2383] Cushman did so in several ways. He was a good teacher who liked to get to the "heart of the matter" in any discussion. An excellent writer, he kept good records, which he used to write the developments of the law school for twenty years. Moreover, because he was the tutor and good friend of Harvey Firestone, III, he was instrumental in persuading Harvey Firestone, Jr. to make significant gifts to the College.

(10) David L. Dickson

David L. Dickson came to Stetson with impressive credentials, having obtained an LL.B. degree from Harvard Law School (1930) and an A.B. degree from Harvard College (1927), where he graduated *cum laude* and was a member of the *Phi Beta Kappa* academic honor society.[2384] He practiced law in Chicago, then served several years as assistant general counsel to the retail giant Montgomery Ward & Company.[2385] Before coming to Stetson, Dickson taught five years on the Loyola (Chicago) law faculty and was an active member of the ABA.[2386] His scholarly proclivity appeared early in his career, and he pub-

2377. *Id.*

2378. *Id.*

2379. *See* 2 Stetson Law. 8 (Apr. 1959).

2380. *Thurman Interview, supra* n. 2278, at 31; *see also* 19 Stetson Law. 1, 8 (Aug. 1976).

2381. *Thurman Interview, supra* n. 2278, at 31.

2382. Bishop, *List, supra* n. 2351, at 2.

2383. *May 4 Dillon Interview, supra* n. 1885.

2384. *Professor Dickson*, 5 Stetson Law. 4 (Oct. 1961).

2385. *Id.*

2386. *Id.*

lished several articles in the *Chicago Bar Record*.[2387] He further developed his research and scholarly skills at Stetson. Dickson authored several articles, including one titled "Declaratory Remedies and Constitutional Change," published in the *Vanderbilt Law Review*,[2388] and another on Florida law published in the *University of Miami Law Review*.[2389]

Dickson retired from the College when he was seventy. Students asked Dean Dillon to allow Dickson to make the commencement address. The address was described as "inspiring."[2390] At the commencement, the College of Law gave David Dickson the Distinguished Service Award for his contributions to the school.[2391]

(11) Judge Victor O. Wehle

Victor O. Wehle was a Circuit Judge in Pinellas County when Sebring appointed him to the part-time faculty in 1958 to teach trial practice. Wehle earned his LL.B. degree from Cornell Law School.[2392] He became a full-time faculty member in 1961, and remained on the faculty for ten years until he retired in 1971 as professor emeritus of law.[2393] Before coming to Stetson, Wehle was a city judge for St. Petersburg, and later was appointed to Florida's Sixth Judicial Circuit.[2394] Judge Wehle was well-known throughout Florida. He served as president of both the Circuit Judges Association of Florida, and the St. Petersburg Bar Association.[2395]

(12) Charles M. Waygood

In 1960, Sebring hired another recent honors graduate of the Stetson College of Law—Charles M. Waygood. A 1957 graduate of Stetson University and a 1960 graduate of the College of Law, Waygood began teaching and serving as law school librarian four months after earning his LL.B. degree.[2396] While a

---

2387. *Id.*

2388. David L. Dickson, *Declaratory Remedies and Constitutional Change*, 24 Van. L. Rev. 47 (1972).

2389. David L. Dixon, *Declaratory Judgments in Florida: Jurisdiction and Judicial Discretion*, 27 U. Miami L. Rev. 47 (Fall–Winter 1972).

2390. *Dillon-Manzanero Aug. 3 Discussion*, *supra* n. 2350.

2391. *Id.*

2392. *Professor Wehle*, 5 Stetson Law. 4 (Oct. 1961).

2393. *Id.*

2394. *Id.*

2395. *Id.*

2396. Sebring, *New Members*, *supra* n. 2369, at 3.

law student, Charles Waygood three times received a full-tuition scholarship awarded annually by the College of Law Overseers to the student with the highest academic average in his class.[2397] Waygood excelled not only academically, but also as a student leader, serving as a justice on the Honor Court and as president of the SBA.[2398] He stayed on the faculty one year. Waygood subsequently practiced law in New York City with Olwine, Connelly, Chase, O'-Donnell and Wether.[2399] Specializing in antitrust practice, he represented the International Business Machines Corporation. Retiring from his firm in 1992, Waygood returned to the Stetson law faculty, where he taught classes in alternative dispute resolution and trade regulation and also served as assistant dean to Dean Bruce Jacob.[2400]

(13) Harold I. Lindsey

A native of Spartanburg, South Carolina, Harold I. Lindsey joined the Stetson law faculty after teaching law at Mercer, Cumberland, and South Carolina universities.[2401] He earned both A.B. and LL.B. degrees from the University of South Carolina, and was admitted to the honorary society the Order of the Wig and Robe.[2402] He also earned an LL.M. degree from Duke University.[2403] For many years, Lindsey practiced law in Charleston, South Carolina. During WWII, he served as a trial counsel in the Judge Advocate General's Corps.[2404] He was admitted to practice before the United States Court of Military Appeals and before various federal and state courts in South Carolina.

Lindsey was a full-time faculty member of the College of Law for twenty-six years, retiring in 1990. It is unlikely that any student who had him as an instructor would forget him. Though dour much of the time, Lindsey had a winning smile, and his demeanor often typified the quintessential laid back professor. He strolled into the classroom, usually several minutes late, then took several minutes to take the roll, calling out each student's name and checking his or her attendance on a sheet of paper.[2405] About ten minutes into a fifty-minute class, Lindsey would turn to the subject at hand.

2397. *Id.*
2398. *Id.*
2399. *News from Alumni Files*, 5 Stetson Law. 8 (Nov. 1962).
2400. Bishop, *List*, *supra* n. 2351, at 2.
2401. *Former Mercer Instructor Joins Faculty*, 8 Stetson Law. 2 (Nov. 1961).
2402. *Id.*
2403. *Id.*
2404. *Id.*
2405. *Id.*

When it came to teaching, Harold Lindsey was never accused of using the Socratic method, at least not during his last decade on the faculty. In fact, he may qualify as the all-time *reading lecturer* in the school's history. Alumnus and now Judge of the Second District Court of Appeals Thomas Stringer, '74, comments:

> [Lindsey] was a character ... the butt of jokes. He would tell you stories ... [In class] you were relaxed because he wasn't going to call on you.[2406]

Lindsey, rather than asking questions, was a professor who "laid out the law." Moreover, in the last few years of teaching, he did so by reading to his class from a typed manuscript, one he used year after year.[2407] It is claimed that students paid little attention in his classes, many occupying their time by reading extraneous materials, preparing for other classes, or dozing off as Lindsey kept on reading. One deceitful (though enterprising) student clandestinely recorded his lectures.[2408] Later, the tapes were transcribed and copies were made available to students the following year. The incoming students were not surprised that their professor was reading a script, as some read along with him, word for word, from their own hard copy.

His method of teaching notwithstanding, Lindsey was well versed in the law and knew the subjects which he taught, primarily torts and equity. Outside of class, it was difficult not to like Lindsey. He was kind, humble, gracious, often shy, and radiated genuine warmth when in social settings. He especially enjoyed clogging, a distinct kind of dance, and regularly participated in both clogger and a square dance clubs.[2409]

Lindsey did have a few idiosyncracies. Each day he would bring to school an extra set of clothes. At some point, he changed into the second outfit. Though there are countless stories about Harold Lindsay, he will be remembered above all for one incident. At the end of class, in a classroom on the second floor of Crummer Hall, Lindsey, as he was departing, opened the wrong door and, by accident, walked straight into a broom closet.[2410] What the stu-

---

2406. Interview by Michael I. Swygert, Prof. Emeritus, Stetson U. College of L., with Hon. Judge Stringer, Judge of the Second Dist. Ct. of Appeal, 12 (Apr. 7, 2005) [hereinafter *Judge Stringer Interview*].

2407. Conversation between Bruce Jacob, Dean Emeritus, Stetson U. College of L., and Michael Swygert, Prof. Emeritus, Stetson U. College of L. (Apr. 2005).

2408. *Id.*

2409. Faculty members attended a party during the 1980s where Professor Lindsay demonstrated his clogging skills.

2410. One of the students who was present and who witnessed this incident was Peter Munson, class of 1972, now a prominent attorney in Lakeland, Florida. Discussion between

dents in attendance still roar about today is that Lindsey, overcome with embarrassment, simply shut the door behind him and remained in the cramped and darkened space several minutes. He came out, presumably, only when he assumed all students had vacated the room. Of course, they had not, and were waiting for his re-appearance. Everyone had a good laugh when he emerged, strolling out as if it was perfectly normal to spend some quiet time inside a dark janitor's supplies closet.

(14) Henry H. "Harry" Haden

Henry H. Haden, described as "a little man who thinks big," joined the faculty in 1967.[2411] Though short in height, he was tall in credentials. He earned LL.B. and LL.M. degrees from the University of Virginia law school.[2412] Following a brief period in practice, Haden served on the University of Alabama law faculty for twenty-one years. He came to Stetson after reaching the mandatory retirement age at Alabama.[2413] Haden was the most prolific scholarly author that Stetson law school had hired, having published eight law review articles and two books, one titled "Fundamentals of Federal Taxation," and the other, a co-authored casebook on tax law.[2414] Every morning, Haden jumped rope for one hour in his office.[2415] Haden remained on the Stetson faculty through 1972, then returned for the 1974–75 academic year.[2416] In 1972, Harry Haden was graduation speaker and received the Stetson University Distinguished Service Award.[2417]

(15) Henry A. Fisher, Jr.

Lieutenant Colonel Henry A. Fisher, Jr., came to Stetson after teaching law at the United States Military Academy at West Point.[2418] He obtained both his undergraduate and law degrees from the University of West Virginia. After working for the Federal Bureau of Investigation, he entered the U.S. Army in

---

Michael I. Swygert, Prof. Emeritus, Stetson U. College of L., and Peter Munson, alumnus, Stetson U. College of L. (May 4, 2005).

2411. *New Faculty Member a Teacher for 21 Years*, 11 Stetson Law. 6, 6 (Nov. 1967).

2412. *Id.*

2413. *Id.*

2414. *Id.*

2415. *May 4 Dillon Interview*, *supra* n. 1885.

2416. Bishop, *List*, *supra* n. 2351, at 3.

2417. *Id.*

2418. *West Point Professor Joins Teaching Staff*, 10 Stetson Law. 3, 3 (Nov. 1966).

1942 and served in India, China, and Japan, before mustering out in 1946.[2419] In 1951, Colonel Fisher began a long career in international law on behalf of the U.S. Army, and later, for the U.S. government. Fluent in several languages, he served on several U.S. missions dealing with international legal transactions between the U.S. and foreign nations, including Japan, Korea, and Germany.[2420] For his public service, Fisher was awarded a Presidential Citation, a Commendation Medal, the Oak Leaf Cluster, and a Bronze Star.[2421] Colonel Fisher taught three years at Stetson, dying in 1969, eight months after resigning from the faculty.[2422]

(16) Other Faculty Appointments

In addition to the fifteen Sebring faculty appointments discussed above, the dean hired four other full-time faculty members: Wallace L. Storey (1959–60), a 1959 graduate of the College of Law who later became a member of the Board of Overseers and also secretary to the Stetson Law Foundation; Judge Peabody Howard (1962–64); Connie E. Bolden (1965–66); and Kenneth Evans (1966–71) (later dean at New England School of Law), who worked in the library when a Stetson law student, and was hired by Sebring as an assistant professor and head librarian after his graduation.[2423] Part-time instructors, in addition to those mentioned earlier, included Granville M. Alley, Jr.; Baya M. Harrison, Jr. (president of The Florida Bar); Judge John U. Bird; Dr. Earl S. Leinbach (physician); Judge William J. McLeod; William Carey; James A. Stewart (the University Chaplain and a Stetson undergraduate faculty member who taught philosophy and law); and Circuit Judge Ben F. Overton (later justice, then chief justice of the Florida Supreme Court).

(17) Ten Librarians in Thirteen Years

From the time the law school moved to Gulfport in 1954 through the end of Sebring's deanship in 1968, ten law librarians were appointed, eight of which served for only one year. They were: Francis Nicholson (1954–55); Gladys Henderson (1955–56); Jack Rappaport (1956–57); Richard Dillon (1957–58); Paul Barnard (1958–59); Wallace Storey (1959–60); Charles Way-

2419. *Id.*

2420. *Id.*

2421. *Id.*

2422. Bishop, *List, supra* n. 2351, at 2.

2423. *Graduate Evans Named Librarian, Professor*, 11 Stetson Law. 6, 6 (Nov. 1967); *see also* Bishop, *List, supra* n. 2351, at 2, 3.

good (1960–61); Edward Platt (1961–65); Connie Bolden (1965–66); and Ken Evans (1967–69).[2424]

(18) Faculty Meetings

Under Sebring, faculty meetings were intermittent, though he did hold an organizational meeting at the beginning of each academic year.[2425] Consequently, relatively few sets of minutes of Sebring-led faculty meetings are available. The earliest set covers a particularly significant meeting held on September 17, 1956. Nine faculty members—both full and part-time—were present. The business at hand consisted of approving a dean's proposal to change the time of classes and a discussion to consider the re-admission of several students who had been academically excluded.[2426] The minutes list eight students who were permitted to reenter on probation.[2427]

(19) Faculty Tensions between DeLand and Gulfport

From 1954 onward, the 150-mile physical separation between the DeLand and Gulfport campuses of Stetson University also led to a cultural separation between the two faculties. In his 1961 annual report to University Trustees, President Edmunds commented that from the time the law school had relocated to Gulfport, "we have experienced the problems attendant upon any university that has two campuses," adding that the distance between the campuses [had] resulted in a division "that is psychological as well as geographical."[2428]

Edmunds pointed out that the faculty in DeLand feels "that the College of Law has not properly recognized the growing respect" that outside educators were giving the DeLand faculty.[2429] At the same time, Edmunds wrote, the law faculty feels that "it has been left to its own devices and assisted only grudg-

---

2424. The above list was provided by Dean Emeritus Richard Dillon to Professor Michael Swygert on May 10, 2005. Swygert verified the names and years of service of the ten law librarians.

2425. Conversation between Richard T. Dillon, Dean Emeritus, Stetson U. College of L., and Michael I. Swygert, Prof. Emeritus, Stetson U. College of L. (May 9, 2005).

2426. *Minutes of Faculty Meeting* 1 (Sept. 17, 1956) (on file at Stetson U. College of L., Gulfport, Fla.).

2427. *Id.*

2428. J. Ollie Edmunds, *Stetson University President's Annual Report to the Board of Trustees*, 5 (Feb. 1961) (on file at Stetson U. Archives, DeLand, Fla.).

2429. *Id.* at 6.

ingly—and then not sufficiently."[2430] Edmunds surely was referring to the demands for increased financial assistance to the law school.[2431]

Edmunds believed he had a solution. He proposed the exchange of professors from the two campuses, "for lectures, special academic functions, and social occasions."[2432] Edmunds said that there must be "unity in the University," adding "I have no doubt that as the two faculties get to know each other and understand each other's problems, most of the friction will disappear."[2433]

Over the next several years, the records indicate that only two professors from the DeLand campus came to teach at the law school in Gulfport. One was University Chaplain James Stewart, who taught a course on philosophy and law.[2434] The other was Gilbert L. Lycan, a history professor who in 1961 conducted a class on international law.[2435] In the same year, Calvin Kuenzel taught undergraduates at DeLand a course on nature and function of law.[2436] Nevertheless, through the present day, interaction between the two faculties as a whole is very sparse. True, individual faculty members both at the law school and at DeLand contact each other and, on occasion, jointly engage in short-term teaching or scholarly activities.[2437]

10.9 Barnard and Jagger Establish Legal Clinic

As discussed earlier, the first student legal clinic at the College of Law was established in 1939 during Dean Paul Raymond's administration.[2438] Designed specifically to aid indigents in Volusia County, the clinic was in operation for only two years, partly because few clients qualified as indigents and partly due to the advent of WWII.

Two decades later, in 1961, St. Petersburg lawyers established a Legal Aid office to serve residents unable to pay for legal services.[2439] The attorney most

2430. *Id.*

2431. President Edmunds recognized that the DeLand law faculty felt it was not getting its fair share of University resources.

2432. *Id.* at 2.

2433. *Id.*

2434. *Id.*

2435. *Exchange Program*, 5 Stetson Law. 4, 4 (Oct. 1961).

2436. *Id.*

2437. Conversation between Michael I. Swygert, Prof. Emeritus, Stetson U. College of L., and Darby Dickerson, V.P. and Dean, Stetson U. College of L. (Apr. 2005).

2438. *See infra* nn. 1216–1219 and accompanying text.

2439. Vause, *Foundations for Excellence*, *supra* n. 308, at 336.

Public Defender Robert E. Jagger

responsible for its creation was Stetson law alumnus Robert E. Jagger, class of 1958.[2440] Three years after graduating from the law school, in 1961 Jagger was appointed Public Defender for Pinellas County by the County Commissioners pursuant to a special act of the Florida Legislature.[2441] He was the County's first public defender.[2442] Later, he became member of the Board of Overseers during the Dillon administration.

Jagger came to Stetson in the fall of 1962 to talk with Dean Sebring, Assistant Dean Dillon, and Professors Kuenzel and Barnard about starting up a public defender clinic.[2443] They all supported the plan, especially Paul Barnard. Jagger and Barnard knew the value to students being involved in actual clinical situations where their work would be guided by supervisory attorneys. Initially, students would do research and would assist in interviewing clients and witnesses. But Jagger and Barnard envisioned that at some point students would also be allowed to assist defense counsel in the courtroom to defend their clients and, in time, be permitted to represent clients in court on their own.[2444]

2440. *Notes from Alumni Files*, 5 Stetson Law. 8, 8 (Oct. 1961).

2441. Fla. Stat. §832.07(i)(a) (1964) (as revised).

2442. Jerome C. Latimer, *Stetson Univesity: Clinical Programs—Pioneering, Innovative, and Effective*, Fla. B.J. 43 (July/August 1991) [hereinafter Latimer, *Clinical Programs*].

2443. Robert E. Jagger, *Stetson: The First Public Defender Clinic*, 30 Stetson L. Rev. 189, 191 (2000) [hereinafter Jagger, *Clinic*].

2444. *Public Defender Clinic Conceived as a Learning through Service Program*, 6 Stetson Lawyer 3 (May 1963) [hereinafter *Public Defender Clinic*].

How far the program would be developed was unclear in the beginning, but with the support of the faculty and Dean Sebring, the Stetson College of Law announced in 1963 the formation of a public defender clinic "course." The announcement reads in part:

> "The Public Defender Clinic" is a new course that marks another step ... by the College of Law ... designed with a two-fold objective—to produce more mature and competent lawyers, while at the same time meeting the obligation of service to the community.[2445]

Besides Jagger and Barnard, Judge John U. Bird of Florida's Sixth Judicial Circuit supported the endeavor.[2446] About this time, the United States Supreme Court decided the landmark case of *Gideon v. Wainwright.*[2447] The Court held that an indigent defendant in a criminal prosecution has a legal right to be represented by counsel.[2448] Following the *Gideon* decision, state bar associations began to look to law schools for helping furnishing legal assistance to attorneys in representing indigent defendants in criminal cases.[2449] Consequently, the rise of legal defender clinics involving law students in the United States was, to a large extent, directly related to the Court's decision in *Gideon.* The case also prompted the AALS to put pressure on law schools to provide students with more opportunities for clinical education.[2450]

Incidentally, the *Gideon* case has special historical significance for Stetson College of Law. Stetson law graduate and now Dean Emeritus, Bruce Jacob, argued the case before the United States Supreme Court on behalf of the respondent, the State of Florida. Opposing Jacob was the legendary lawyer (and later United States Supreme Court Justice) Abe Fortas.[2451] (The *Gideon* case is discussed below.)[2452]

The law school in Gulfport was the first in Florida to establish a public defender clinic.[2453] The clinic gave one hour of academic credit to students who

2445. *Id.*

2446. *Id.*

2447. 327 U.S. 335 (1963).

2448. Stetson College of Law Dean Emeritus Bruce Jacob represented the respondent in the *Gideon* case, the state of Florida.

2449. Vause, *Foundations for Excellence, supra* n. 308, at 336.

2450. *See* Assn. of Am. L. Schs., *Annual Meeting, Program and Reports of the Committees* 188 (1963).

2451. Anthony Lewis, *Gideon's Trumpet* (Random House 1964).

2452. *See infra* nn. 2479–2488 and accompanying text.

2453. Vause, *Foundations in Excellence, supra* n. 308, at 336.

chose to participate.[2454] As initially structured, students were assigned to pending cases in the Office of the Public Defender. The defendants were indigents unable to afford private counsel.[2455]

Professor Barnard, however, became frustrated with the program, since students were limited to only interviewing and conducting legal research.[2456] He investigated how other states handled students working with indigents and discovered that three states (Michigan, Massachusetts, and Colorado) had opened up their courtroom doors to "certified" law students, permitting them to practice law on behalf of indigent clients, though in a supervised manner.[2457]

With his research in hand, Barnard filed a petition with the Florida Supreme Court, asking it to permit senior law students to work with public defenders and other appointed counsel in conjunction with Stetson's public defender clinic.[2458] The reaction of the organized bar was hostile to the idea, and The Florida Bar filed a brief opposing Professor Barnard's petition, the Florida Supreme Court promulgated "Criminal Procedure Rule 2," which permitted senior law students in faculty-supervised legal aid programs to appear in both trial and municipal courts, provided a public defender supervised the student.[2459] The court's new rule was a great victory for Professor Barnard personally. It also was good for the Stetson law school, all other Florida law schools, and for indigent defendants.

Public Defender Robert Jagger remained in office through 1996, when he retired. One of the nation's longest employed and most respected public defenders, he received numerous national and state awards, including the Reginald Heber Smith Award from the National Legal Aid and Defender Association, the Selig I. Goldin Memorial Award by the Criminal Law Section of The Florida Bar; the Ben C. Willard Memorial Award from the Stetson Lawyers Association; the Distinguished Alumni Award from the Stetson University Alumni Association; and the L. Clayton Award from the Florida Public Defender Association.[2460]

10.10 The Best and the Worst

During Sebring's administration, two notable events regarding alumni of the College occurred. The first involves one of Stetson's most-acclaimed law

2454. Latimer, *Clinical Programs*, *supra* n. 2442, at 43.
2455. *Public Defender Clinic*, *supra* n. 2444, at 3.
2456. Latimer, *Clinical Programs*, *supra* n. 2442, at 43.
2457. *Public Defender Clinic*, *supra* n. 2444, at 3.
2458. *The Adoption of Student Practice Rules*, Fla. B.J. 35 (July/Aug. 1991).
2459. *In re Criminal Procedure Rule No. 2,* 167 So. 2d 574 (Fla. 1964).
2460. *See also* Jagger, *Clinic*, *supra* n. 2443, at 189.

General Roy S. Geiger

graduates, General Roy Stanley Geiger. The second concerns Joseph Alexander Peel, Jr., a public official who paid for the assassination of respected Florida Circuit Judge Curtis E. Chillingworth of Palm Beach.

(1) General Roy Stanley Geiger, USMC

In 1907, Roy Geiger, a native Floridian, earned an LL.B. degree from Stetson College of Law.[2461] He never practiced law, but nonetheless made the law school proud. For reasons that remain unclear, during his last year of law school, Geiger decided to join the United States Marine Corps.[2462] On November 2, 1907, a few months after graduating, Geiger enlisted in the Corps. He rose through the ranks from private to three-star general. He was awarded a fourth star posthumously by the Eightieth Congress of the United States.[2463]

Throughout his military career, Geiger took every opportunity for advanced training, learning to be a pilot in Pensacola and later attending the Naval War College. When America entered World War I, he was combat ready. The Marine aviator participated with the Royal Air Force in the bombardment of Dunkirk.[2464] For the next two decades, Geiger continued to advance in rank,

2461. *Classmates Unveil Portrait of Marine Hero*, 5 Stetson-Ltr. 6 (DeLand, Fla. June 1957) [hereinafter *Marine Hero*].

2462. *Id.*

2463. *Id.*

2464. *Id.*

until during World War II he became Commanding General, First Marine Aircraft Wing, Fleet Marine Force. His most famous victory was the success of his Marine Aircraft Wing at Guadalcanal. A report of the battle notes:

> [General Geiger] served gallantly at Guadalcanal, where his unit in 1942 shot down 268 Japanese aircraft and damaged a number equally as great, sank six enemy vessels, possibly sank four others, and damaged eighteen. [Then in 1944] he assumed command of the Marine Third Amphibian Corps and captured Guam, Palau, and Okinawa.[2465]

As a consequence of his war-time triumphs, General Geiger was awarded in excess of twenty-five decorations, including a Presidential Citation for the battle of Guadalcanal, a Distinguished Service Metal, and a World War II Victory Metal.[2466] General Geiger died in 1947, forty years after receiving his law degree from Stetson and after having enlisted in the Marine Corps. Today, the Marine Corps's Camp Geiger, a part of the larger Camp Lejeune in North Carolina, is named after the war hero.[2467]

Ten years after his death, Geiger, described as "one of the most distinguished leaders in the history of the United States Corps," was honored by Stetson College of Law as part of the school's 1957 commencement.[2468] With Dean Sebring looking on, two of Geiger's classmates from 1907—Russell W. Farnell of Lake City, Florida, and George Leitner of Arcadia, Florida—unveiled an oil portrait of General Roy Stanley Geiger on the occasion of the fiftieth anniversary of his and their graduation from the College of Law.[2469] The portrait was given to the College of Law by Mrs. Robert J. Johnson, daughter of General Geiger.[2470] The portrait hangs today in the Law Library of the College.

In recent decades, few who passed the painting knew who the handsome man, attired in a Marine Corps Uniform, was, or that he was a Stetson graduate. Stetson professor Tom Marks tells that when he was reading a book about the battle of Guadalcanal several years ago, he came across the name of General Geiger. The book noted that Geiger was a graduate of Stetson College of Law. Marks, not sure if anyone at that time knew that Geiger was a graduate

2465. *Id.*

2466. *Id.*

2467. E-mail from William R. Eleazer, Distinguished Professor Emeritus, Stetson U. College of L., to Michael I. Swygert, Professor Emeritus, Stetson U. College of L. (Mar. 21, 2005). Prof. Eleazer wrote that he knew of General Geiger, "but had no idea he was a Stetson grad." *Id.*

2468. *Marine Hero*, *supra* n. 2461, at 6.

2469. *Id.*

2470. *Id.*

of the law school, wrote a letter to then University President Pope Duncan, exclaiming, "Look what I found out about Roy Geiger. See what one person can do with a law degree."[2471]

(2) Joseph Alexander Peel, Jr. (Raiford State Penitentiary, Florida)

The headline read: "Judge's Lust for Power Leads to Deaths at Sea."[2472] The report began: "When West Palm Beach Circuit Judge Curtis E. Chillingworth, 58, a punctual man, did not appear for court the morning of June 15, 1955, colleagues knew something had happened." They were right.[2473] Judge Chillingworth and his wife Marjorie had disappeared from their oceanfront home the previous day, in the early hours of June 14th.[2474] Though footprints were found on the beach along with patches of blood, their bodies were never found. Their mysterious disappearance remained unsolved for six years. Then the facts became known and they turned out to be far beyond even the imagination of the police who investigated.

Early on June 13, 1955, Judge and Marjorie Chillingworth were awakened in their home by two men who overpowered, gagged, and tied them up, then dragged the two to a boat. The bound couple was taken several miles off shore into the Atlantic. There, the two thugs weighted down the Chillingworths. Marjorie Chillingworth was thrown over the side. Her husband jumped in to save her but was hit over the head and both drowned.[2475] The two men carrying out this deadly scheme—Floyd "Lucky" Holzapfel and George "Bobby" Lincoln, both thirty-one, turned out to be "contract killers." Holzapfel, after being arrested for another murder, confessed to the murder-for-hire arrangement of Judge Chillingworth.[2476]

The person who hired the two thugs to murder Judge Chillingworth was, shockingly, another judge from Palm Beach County, Joseph Alexander Peel, Jr.

2471. Interview by Michael I. Swygert, Prof. Emeritus, Stetson U. College of L, with Thomas C. Marks, Jr., Prof. of L., Stetson U. College of L, 27 (Apr. 8, 2004) [hereinafter *Marks Interview*].

2472. Edna Buchanan, *Fatal Politics*, Miami Herald, http://history.jupiter.fl.us/kids/PI%20Menuu/miami_article.htm, (accessed on May 10, 2005) [hereinafter Buchanan, *Fatal Politics*].

2473. *Id.*

2474. Bruce R. Jacob, *Memories and Reflections about* Gideon v. Wainwright, 33 Stetson L. Rev. 181, 215 (Fall 2003) [hereinafter Jacob, *Gideon*] (citing *National Affairs*, *Newsweek* 26, 27 (Mar. 20, 1961)).

2475. Buchanan, *Fatal Politics*, *supra* n. 2472, at 1.

2476. Jacob, *Gideon*, *supra* n. 2474, at 215.

He was municipal judge for the city of West Palm Beach. It turned out that Judge Peel was corrupt. He not only took bribes, but was also connected with illegal gambling and liquor activities.[2477] Among other things, investigators discovered that Peel and Holzapfel had split about $3,000 a week for tip-offs they passed to mobsters when police were going to raid moonshine stills and gambling dens, all the raids to take place pursuant to search warrants issued by Judge Peel.[2478] *Newsweek* reported that Chillingworth learned of these corrupt actions and was "about to blow the whistle" when Peel contracted for Chillingworth's murder. The evidence against Peel was overwhelming. Convicted of murder, he was sentenced to life in the Florida State Penitentiary at Starke.

Interestingly, while in prison, Peel's legal training and law degree from Stetson College of Law[2479] allowed him to play a key role in the landmark case of *Gideon v. Wainwright.*[2480] Clarence Earl Gideon on June 3, 1961, allegedly broke into a pool hall and stole cigarettes from a vending machine. The alleged crime took place in the Bar Harbor neighborhood of Panama City, Florida. At the beginning of his trial, Gideon, who had no funds to hire his own lawyer, asked for but was not given a court-appointed attorney. At the close of trial, he was convicted for the felonious breaking and entering of an establishment to commit petit larceny,[2481] and, on the basis of prior convictions, was given a five-year sentence to be served in the Florida's penitentiary at Starke, Florida.[2482]

It was from his prison cell that Clarence Gideon in January 1962 filed a petition for certiorari in the United States Supreme Court, claiming that Florida had denied him his constitutional right to have counsel at trial, a right he argued was available not only for those who can hire lawyers, but for those who do not have the financial means to do so.[2483] In researching the law and preparing his legal petitions in jail, Gideon, it is said, was assisted by Joseph Alexander Peel, Jr., the Stetson law graduate and convicted murderer of the Chillingworths.[2484]

2477. *Id.*

2478. *Id.*

2479. *Id.* at 214.

2480. As noted earlier, Stetson College of Law Dean Emeritus Bruce Jacob was Assistant Attorney for the State of Florida in the famous case of *Gideon v. Wainwright,* in which Jacob represented Florida before the United States Supreme Court in a matter where Gideon, a convicted criminal defendant, claimed that Florida had denied him his rights to counsel by not appointing a lawyer for him in a criminal prosecution.

2481. *Id.* at 200.

2482. *Id.* at 212.

2483. *Id.* at 212–214.

2484. *Id.* at 214–215.

On March 18, 1963, a unanimous United States Supreme Court handed down its decision in the *Gideon* case, declaring that the Sixth Amendment's right to counsel provision applied to state courts in addition to the federal courts.[2485] The Court then remanded the case to Panama City for retrial.[2486] The court appointed a Panama City lawyer named W. Fred Turner, Sr., (later a Circuit Court Judge) to represent Gideon. At the retrial, Clarence Gideon was acquitted of all charges originally brought against him.[2487] During the retrial, Gideon informed his attorney, Fred Turner, that while in jail at the penitentiary in Starke, he was aided in putting together his legal arguments by none other than Stetson graduate and now convict, Joseph Alexander Peel. Peel, Turner asserted, "stood over Gideon's shoulder and told him what to say."[2488]

10.11 Integration Postponed

Discrimination by law schools on the basis of race at one time was nearly universal in the South,[2489] at least until the U.S. Supreme Court's historic 1954 decision of *Brown v. Board of Education.*[2490] Four years prior to that decision, an effort had been initiated to prohibit law schools from denying admission to any applicant on the basis of race. In 1950, the faculty of the Yale Law School proposed that the standards of the Association of American Law Schools (AALS) be amended to add the following requirement: "No school which follows a policy of excluding or segregating qualified applicants or students on the basis of race or color shall be qualified to be admitted to or to remain a member of the Association."[2491] The proposal was distributed to all schools that were members of the AALS, including the Stetson College of Law.[2492]

2485. *Id.* at 251.

2486. *Id.* at 257.

2487. *Id.*

2488. *Id.* at 214–15. Turner repeated this assertion while serving on a panel about the Gideon case with Bruce Jacob at the University of Tampa on April 19, 2001. *Id.* at 214 n. 179.

2489. *See e.g.* Nancy E. Dowd, Kenneth B. Nunn & James E. Pendergast, *Diversity Matters: Race, Gender, and Ethnicity in Legal Education*, 15 U. Fla. J.L. & Pub. Policy 11 (2003).

2490. *See Brown v. Bd. of Educ.*, 349 U.S. 294 (1955).

2491. Memo. from F.D.G. Ribble, Sec.-Treasury, Assn. of Am. L. Schs., to the Member Schools of the Assn. of Am. L. Schs. (Oct. 24, 1950) (copy on file at Stetson U. College of L., Gulfport, Fla.).

2492. *Id.*

In response to the AALS proposed requirement prohibiting member schools to use race or color as a basis for refusing admittance of applicants of color, Stetson President J. Ollie Edmunds wrote the presidents or law school deans at eleven Southern universities: Baylor (William R. White); Wake Forest (Carroll W. Weathers); Tulane (Paul Brosman); Mercer (Spright Dowell); Richmond (George M. Modlin); Southern Methodist (R.G. Storey); Duke (A. Hollis Edens); Vanderbilt (Harvie Branscomb); Emory (Goodrich C. White); Washington and Lee (Frances P. Sarnes); and Miami (B.F. Ashe).[2493] In each letter, Edmunds wrote: "Those of us in states where segregation is enforced by law would find ourselves in a very embarrassing position."[2494] Most of the recipients of Edmunds' letters responded, indicating they did not want Yale's proposal to become an AALS requirement, with one exception, President of Duke University A. Hollis Edens, who said only that he had discussed the proposal with his law school dean.[2495]

At the AALS 1950 annual meeting, the body tabled the Yale proposal, sending it to a committee to consider how the AALS should respond, directing the committee to report back in one year.[2496] The committee did so, and as a result, in December 1952 the AALS formally adopted a resolution requiring member schools not to engage in racial discrimination as a basis for denying admission of people of color, a resolution that had its genesis in the1949 Yale original proposal.[2497] Dean F.D.G. Ribble of the University of Virginia School of Law and President of the AALS, wrote Edmunds, stating that the report of the committee upon which the resolution passage came about "was a very wise one."[2498] It is not clear whether all the presidents of southern universities having law schools shared Ribble's sentiment.

Though nothing in the official announcements, records, or faculty minutes of Stetson of College of Law has been found expressly stating or implicitly sug-

2493. Ltrs. from I. Ollie Edmunds, President, Stetson U., to presidents or deans of eleven southern universities (Nov. 29, 1950) (listed in the text, with the names to whom they were sent (originals on file at Stetson U. College of L., Gulfport, Fla.)).

2494. *Id.*

2495. *See* Ltr. from A. Hollis Edens, Pres., Duke U., to J. Ollie Edmunds, Pres., Stetson U. (Dec. 13, 1950) (a copy on file at Stetson U. College of L., Gulfport, Fla.).

2496. Ltr. from David F. Cavers, et al., Prof. Harvard U. L. Sch. (and member of an AALS special committee to Committee to study Yale Law School proposed amendment to AALS articles for membership), to the Deans and Faculty Members of Association Schools 1 (Mar. 26, 1951).

2497. Association of American Law Schools Resolution (adopted at the Annual Meeting Dec. 28–30, 1951).

2498. Ltr. from F.D.G. Ribble, President, Assn. of Am. L. Schs., to J. Ollie Edmunds, Pres., Stetson U. (Jan. 14, 1952) (copy on file at Stetson U. Archives, DeLand, Fla.).

gesting that African-Americans would not be welcomed at the law school, the fact is that not a single African-American was admitted throughout the thirteen years of Sebring's deanship, beginning in 1955 (the year after the Supreme Court's decision in *Brown*), and continuing through 1968.

10.12 Student Activities

During the Sebring era, America experienced sweeping changes: from the comparatively placid 1950s, when Sebring became dean, to the turmoil of the late 1960s during the Vietnam War. But there was more to it than the shift from a sense of national contentment to one of tumultuousness. America's attitudes were rapidly changing, as demonstrated by the civil rights movement for racial equality and the increasing demands of women for access to educational and employment opportunities. Stetson law school was not exempt from the attitudinal shift regarding these important social matters. The impact of these changes on the Stetson community are apparent when comparing two organizations: one active in the mid-1950s, and the other during the late 1960s.

After the College moved to Gulfport, students engaged in their traditional activities and were members of long-standing organizations, including moot court competitions, student bar activities, various clubs, Inns of Court functions, and three law fraternities. Male students predominantly participated in these organizations and activities.

But one organization at the school did not fit this model: it had no males, and, in fact, had no student members. Called the *Lawyerettes*, the group was composed of law students' wives.[2499] It is unclear exactly when the women's group was formed, but a published reference indicates it was active by 1957.[2500] At the dedication of the Charles A. Dana Law Library, Stetson's *Lawyerettes* hosted a tea.[2501] The engraved invitation reads in part:

> The Lawyerettes of Stetson University College of Law
> request the pleasure of your company at a tea in honour
> of Mrs. Leroy Collins [and] Mrs. Charles A. Dana on
> Friday afternoon, the seventh of March, at four o'clock
> in the lounge of the Stetson Inn.[2502]

2499. *Lawyerettes Aid Children's Hospital*, 2 Stetson L. News 6 (Nov. 1958) [hereinafter *Lawyerettes Aid*].

2500. *Id.*

2501. *Id.*

2502. *The Lawyerettes Invitation* (engraved card 1957).

The *Lawyerettes* often held tea parties. Another example was a benefit they sponsored in 1959 to raise donations for the American Legion Crippled Children's Hospital in St. Petersburg.[2503] "Mrs. Don McGregor," president of *Lawyerettes*, assigned each member to specific tasks. She appointed as the "Chairman," Mrs. William Hereford.[2504] In just one academic year, the *Lawyerettes* gave a swimming party for new students; hosted a faculty reception; held a "Get-Acquainted Dance" at the Army-Navy Club; sponsored a "charity Christmas Party;" put on a Christmas party where children could meet Santa; delivered food and clothing to three needy families in the community; put together a fund-raising event; and hosted a reception honoring mid-semester graduates of the school.[2505]

Stetson's *Lawyerettes* upheld the stereotype of women in the '50s and '60s as being perky housewives who supported their husbands' careers and who spent their time at home, though perhaps involved in outside social and charitable activities. It should not be overlooked, however, that in those days, many wives worked outside the home to pay for their husbands' legal education.

Today, law students at Stetson (and elsewhere) would probably consider an organization of law students' wives ridiculous and sexist. On the other hand, support groups for spouses of law students (including significant others) are found on many law school campuses today, in contrast to the 1950s and 1960s, when numerous schools had organizations of law wives.[2506]

A generation later, it was clear that both male attitudes and women's choices were changing. Consider the following story published in the March 1968 edition of the *Stetson Lawyer*: "It was bound to happen; it has happened. A woman has become the leader of a law fraternity on the College of Law campus. Furthermore, it is all strictly legal."[2507]

Indeed! Helen Hansel, a third-year student (later to become a judge on Florida's Sixth Judicial Circuit), was installed as "Chancellor" of a new legal fraternity at Stetson, the Harold L. Sebring chapter of *Nu Beta Epsilon*.[2508] Writing with tongue in cheek, the author of the account purported to reflect the attitudes of Stetson's law alumni when he wrote:

> To forestall a deluge of inquiries, the writer hastens to assure all alumni who are members of *Phi Alpha Delta, Phi Delta Phi,* or *Delta Theta Phi*

2503. *Lawyerettes Aid, supra* n. 2499, at 6.

2504. *Id.*

2505. *Id.*

2506. One group was called *Amicae Curiae* (which translates into "friends of the court"). Swygert, *supra* n. 80, at 232.

2507. *Woman Chancellor of New Legal Fraternity*, 11 Stetson Law. 6, 6 (Mar. 1968).

2508. *Id.*

> that to these organizations [fraternities], is still translated "brotherhood," and that the pristine purity of their membership remains unsullied.[2509]

But the author of the report revealed his own sentiments when he wrote:

> In 1964, the United States Supreme Court sagely deduced that voters are people, not trees or pastures. Following the same logic, devastating to some, *Nu Beta Epsilon* has concluded that lawyers on a professional level are not "guys and dolls," or distinguishable on the basis of race, color, creed, or sex. It accepts members whether they be Negroes, Jews, Catholics, Protestants, or what is more directly in point, "shes."[2510]

The student author concluded the homily by acknowledging that not all Stetson law students accepted gender equality. For example, a member of a male fraternity quoted humorist Irvin S. Cobb: "Now that woman has been made our equal, we hope she will be on the level with us."[2511] The time of sexist humor was then in full swing.

In 1968, when Hansel became chancellor of her Stetson fraternity, it consisted of eight women (including two graduate attorneys) and four men.[2512] That same year, only six women were enrolled at Stetson law school, or three percent out of 214 total registrants.[2513] Stetson's numbers compared with a national total of 3,704 women, or five percent, out of 62,000 law students in ABA-approved law schools.[2514] Ten years later, the number of women law students in America had risen to 37,534 out of 117,229 law students.[2515] At Stetson, the numbers reflected this national trend. In the fall of 1977, 140 of the 470 students in the school were women, or roughly thirty percent.[2516] These figures are in sharp contrast with the numbers a decade earlier. In the fall of 1960, fourteen women registered at Stetson's law school out of 226 students.[2517] In 1966, the number was sixteen.[2518] Moreover, the proportion of women fell

---

2509. *Id.* (emphasis in original).

2510. *Id.* (emphasis in original).

2511. *Id.*

2512. *Id.*

2513. *Id.*

2514. Stevens, *Law Education*, *supra* n. 196, at 246.

2515. *Id.*

2516. *Freshman Statistics*, 20 Stetson Law. 2, 2 (Aug. 1977).

2517. *Enrollment Statistics*, 4 Stetson Law. 7, 7 (Oct. 1960).

2518. *Women Vie with Men for Grades, Scholarships*, 10 Stetson Law. 1, 1 (Nov. 1966); *see also* Harold L. Sebring, *Final Report* 8 (Feb. 1968) (submitted to the Board of Overseers and to the president and trustees of Stetson University) [hereinafter Sebring, *Final Report*].

the remainder of the decade. In the fall of 1969, only sixteen women once again attended the Stetson law school, but that year the total enrollment was 327 students, meaning that women were less than five percent of the student body.[2519] However, with the coming of a new decade, women began to enter law school in greater numbers. In time, male law students began to overcome gender prejudices about women classmates.

Around this same time—by the end of the 1960s—a national political issue took center stage, one that embroiled the country in turmoil to a level not seen since the Civil War. The controversy centered on America's involvement in what was essentially a civil war between Communists and non-Communists in Vietnam. While the war was raging in the South Pacific, and U.S. troops were dying, Americans at home were sharply divided over the rightness or wrongness of the war. Anti-war groups were concentrated on college campuses, where they engaged in emotive protests.

In many instances, student anti-war demonstrations turned violent, but not so at Stetson University.[2520] Both University and College publications during the 1966–1972 period indicate that little, if any, anti-war activities took place at the College of Law.[2521] Nonetheless, student resentment about the war did exist.[2522] The same can almost be said about the University. According to historian Gilbert Lycan, only one organized anti-war rally occurred in DeLand, a 1972 protest called a "Peace Rally."[2523] Revealing a southern conservatism to unpleasantness, Stetson University officials demanded—and the students acceded—that they not call their demonstration an "anti-war rally," which had been their preference, but a "peace rally."[2524]

Student activities, like in the past, included traditional weekend parties. Alumni of that era remember spending evenings drinking beer at the "Blinker" and at "Chill's Bar."[2525] Student consumption of alcoholic beverage was commonplace. At one fraternity rush party, the "chairman" purchased "large pret-

---

2519. *Record Enrollment as College Enters 70th Year*, 13 Stetson Law. 1, 1 (Dec. 1969).

2520. *See e.g.* Swygert, *supra* n. 80, at 247–254.

2521. The only story about the Vietnam War appearing in the *Stetson Lawyer* during the period concerned the impact of the removal of the deferment for law students from the draft on law school enrollment. *See New Students May Receive Summer Grants, Part of Stepped-Up Recruiting Program to Offset Anticipated Inroads on Enrollment by Draft Boards*, 11 Stetson Law. 1, 1 (May 1968).

2522. Vause, *Centennial History*, *supra* n. 595, at 181.

2523. Lycan, *History of Stetson*, *supra* n. 109, at 469.

2524. *Id.*

2525. Jacob, *Recollections*, *supra* n. 1678, at 13.

zels and two kegs of beer."[2526] When Bruce Jacob was nearing graduation, he and his classmates attended a farewell party at the Beachcomber Hotel on St. Petersburg Beach. The merry makers danced and drank. The next day, photographs of the event appeared in the *St. Petersburg Times*, showing several students holding drinks.[2527] The law school business manager, Harold F. Archibald, told SBA President Jacob that the school did not object to law students drinking off campus, but in the future to "keep this out of the press."[2528]

During Sebring's deanship, students began a short-lived publication called *The Brief*,[2529] described as a "new student newspaper." The editors were Everett Cushman (later a member of the faculty)[2530] and William H. Unger, a recent graduate who in 1964 became the College's business manager, succeeding Harold F. Archibald.[2531] *The Brief* re-emerged as a student newsletter in December 2004.

In 1955, Stetson students went to Sebring and asked if they could start a law review.[2532] The students wanted to publish a *Stetson Law Quarterly*, with the first issue being a symposium on Florida mechanic liens. According to Sebring, the students grew tired of the project and gave up.[2533] Three years later, students James Druck and Bruce Jacob approached Sebring and asked if they could start a law review.[2534] Sebring said yes, but only if they could convince ten second-year students who were in the top twenty percent of their class to commit one year to the project prior to issuance of a first issue.[2535] However, Druck and Jacob were unable to enlist the needed number. Eleven years later, in 1969, Stetson law students proposed a student-edited law review for the third time, this time to Dean Richard Dillon. By then, the numbers of highly qualified students had risen and Dillon agreed. The story of the beginning of Stetson's law review appears in the next chapter.[2536]

Though not having a law review, students enjoyed an interesting distraction on the Gulfport campus in 1956. Hollywood came to the law school. A

2526. *Id.* at 16.
2527. *Id.*
2528. *Id.*
2529. *Student Paper Available*, 1 Stetson L. News 4, 4 (Jan. 1958).
2530. *See supra* nn. 2374–2377 and accompanying text.
2531. *Stetson Grad Named Business Manager*, 8 Stetson Law. 2, 2 (Nov. 1964).
2532. Jacob, *Recollections*, *supra* n. 1678, at 15.
2533. Jacob, *Remembering Sebring*, *supra* n. 9, at 166.
2534. *Id.*
2535. Jacob, *Recollections*, *supra* n. 1678, at 15.
2536. *See infra* nn. 2806–2871 and accompanying text.

movie, titled "*The Strange One*," was filmed on the College of Law campus. The plot concerned a student officer in a boys' military academy who tormented and hazed a younger cadet. In line of the requirement of "good endings" of 1950 movies, by the end of the film justice prevailed, as the "hazor" was booted out and the "hazee" had become the hero.[2537] Stetson was chosen as the site for the film since only seven years earlier, the campus housed a boys military academy.[2538]

The film's director was Jack Garfein, a survivor of the Nazi Auschwitz concentration camp.[2539] Two well-known actors starred in the film—George Peppard and Ben Gazarra.[2540] Among the extras was Gardner Beckett, a third-year law student who had transferred to Stetson from Harvard University in 1955. Years later, Beckett served as President of the Stetson Law Center Foundation.

10.13 Academic Standards

During Sebring's deanship, the academic quality and performance of the Stetson law students rose, due largely to the raising of standards for admission. The higher quality and performance of the students is confirmed by reviewing graduation data from 1955–58.[2541]

2537. Bruce R. Jacob, Speech, *Orientation Remarks Regarding the History of Our Law School* 3 (Gulfport, Fla., n.d.) [hereinafter, Jacob, *Orientation*] (copy on file at Stetson U. College of L., Gulfport, Fla.).

2538. *See supra* nn. 1839–1873 and accompanying text.

2539. IMDB, Earth's Biggest Movie Database, *The Strange One* (1957), www.imdb.com/title/tt0051019/ (accessed May 10, 2005).

2540. Jacob, *Orientation*, *supra* n. 2537, at 3.

2541. Beginning on January 28, 2005, through June 22, 2005, Richard T. Dillon, Dean Emeritus, Stetson University College of Law and Michael I. Swygert, Stetson University College of Law, reviewed early student graduation data and did a statistical analysis.

From February 1955 until February 1958, Stetson University College of Law had nine graduating classes and graduated a total of 104 graduates during this period. Forty-four of the 104 graduates had not initially enrolled in Stetson but had transferred to Stetson from another law school. The number of graduates who were transfer students was 42% of the 104 graduates during this period examined. Of course, sixty grads, or 58% of the total number for the same period, were students who were not transfer students, but had been admitted to Stetson ab initio. Forty-one of the forty-four grads who transferred to Stetson took the Florida Bar Exam, and thirty-two of them passed the exam on the first try for a passing rate of 78%. Most of the transferees who failed the bar exam passed on their second attempt.

Fifty-six of the grads who were initially admitted to Stetson (non-transferees) took the Florida Bar Exam, and thirty-seven of them passed on their first attempt, for a passing rate

Before admission standards rose, however, the number of students on academic probation or excluded on the basis of grades was unacceptably high.[2542] A review of faculty minutes of a 1956 meeting reveals that eight students "had been dropped for low grades."[2543] Nonetheless, seven first-year students were readmitted on probation, but only for one time.[2544] Yet, according to the ABA 1957 Inspection Report of Stetson College of Law, of seventy-five students admitted in the fall of 1955, only thirty-nine remained in school at the end of their second year.[2545]

Though student attrition remained high throughout Sebring's era, the preparedness for entry into the legal profession increased. One indication was the rising rate of success Stetson law graduates achieved on bar examinations. By the 1960s, the school regularly, though not in every instance, achieved the

---

of 66%. Three of the (non-transferees) grads received the diploma privilege and were not counted as having taken the exam. Some of the non-transferee grads who failed the bar exam on their first attempt passed on their second try, while others gave up, and some continued to take the bar multiple times with varying degrees of success. Each time a graduate repeated the exam and failed, that failure was counted negatively in Stetson's overall bar results.

Another fact learned from our study was that twenty-two graduates, or 21% of the 104 grads in the study, had LSAT scores of less than 400. Thirteen of the twenty-two grads in this category took the Florida Bar Exam and failed on the first try for a passing rate of 41%. Less than half of those who failed on the first try passed on the second attempt.

Another fact learned from this study: thirty out of 104 of the graduates studied during this period had been admitted to Stetson College of Law on a three-three program.

The College of Law Official Bulletin (1965) on page 28 announced two changes in admission requirements. First, the three-three program would be abolished at the College beginning with the fall semester of 1966 by requiring all applicants for admission to hold an A.B. degree or its equivalent. Had this policy or requirement been in effect for the graduates in our study at the time of their admission to law school, 28.84% (thirty out of 104) of the graduates in the first nine graduating classes in Gulfport would not have been eligible to be considered for admission until they had completed one more year of undergraduate study. Another announcement in 1965 was that "an application showing less than a 1.25 undergraduate average (based on a 3.0 grading system) and a Law School Admission Test score of less than 400 will not be considered for admission."

Information about GPAs of early graduates is incomplete, but this minimum requirement of a 400 LSAT, put into effect in 1965, would have denied admission to 21% of the graduates in our study, had that standard been in effect and applied at the time of their admission to law school.

2542. Vause, *Centennial History*, *supra* n. 595, at 143–44.

2543. *Minutes, Faculty Meeting* 1 (Sept. 1945).

2544. *Id.*

2545. Vause, *Centennial History*, *supra* n. 595, at 144 (citing *ABA 1957 Report*, *supra* n. 2098, at 3.

highest passage rate of any law school in Florida.[2546] In 1965, 100% of Stetson's graduates (twenty out of twenty) passed the bar;[2547] Stetson again hit 100% in 1966 (twenty-six out of twenty-six);[2548] but dropped to 98% in 1967 (forty-five out of forty-six).[2549] Under Dean Dillon's administration, 1968–81, Stetson graduates continued to do exceptionally well on the Florida Bar Examination, attaining a 100% passage rate on a number of occasions, and leading the state with unprecedented frequency.[2550]

10.14 National Trial Seminars and Continuing Legal Education

Though the College of Law on occasion had sponsored continuing legal education (CLE) programs in DeLand, not until the school moved to the Tampa Bay area did CLE become a significant component of Dean Sebring's concept of a law center. And, in line with Stetson's historical focus, the emphasis was on trial practice.

(1) Stetson National Trial Seminars

The first Stetson "Trial Lawyer Seminar" took place in March 1958, a three-day, on-campus event where "the top legal talent of the nation was represented."[2551] Stetson law graduate Perry Nichols of Miami organized the CLE program and put together a national faculty.[2552] Participants included: Truman B. Rucker, New York City, president of the International Academy of Trial Lawyers; James A. Dooley, Chicago, president of the American Trial Lawyers Association; Harry A. Gair and Emile Zola Berman, New York City trial attorneys; William Frates, Miami, president of the Law Science Foundation of America; former Stetson dean Thomas Lambert of Boston; Tampa trial lawyer T. Paine Kelley, Jr.; Florida Supreme Court Justice and Stetson graduate E. Harris Drew; as well as Florida district court of appeals judges W.E. Sturgis, A.O.

2546. Sebring, *Final Report*, *supra* n. 2518, at 9.

2547. *Score: Stetson 100% on Bar Exam*, 8 Stetson Law. 4, 4 (June 1965).

2548. *See e.g. 100%—Twenty Six of Twenty Six Pass Bar*, 9 Stetson Law. 4, 4 (June 1966);

2549. *Stetson Grads Again Lead Bar Examinees*, 11 Stetson Law. 7, 7 (Nov. 1967)

2550. *See e.g. 100%, 43 Try, 43 Pass*, 13 Stetson Law. 4, 4 (Dec. 1969).

2551. *Top Legal Talent of Nation at Mid-Winter Trial Seminar*, 1 Stetson L. News 2, 2 (Apr. 1958).

2552. *Id.*

Kanner, and Charles A. Carroll.[2553] In a report to University Trustees, Sebring described the event as "outstanding."[2554]

Seven years later, Nichols and Sebring put on an even more ambitious three-day "Mid-Winter Trial Seminar" at the American Hotel in Miami Beach.[2555] They invited twenty of the nation's premier trial attorneys from New York City, Philadelphia, Chicago, Cleveland, Birmingham, Tulsa, Boston, Urbana, Tallahassee, Tampa, and Miami.[2556] Though no record has been found as to the number of lawyers who attended or where they came from, the planners goal was to draw trial lawyers far beyond Florida. To promote this objective, the seminar was held in mid-March at the height of the winter tourist season. An advertising brochure proclaimed that "sightseeing tours and cruises" would be available, a fashion show "for the ladies by Burdine's Sunshine Fashions" would be held, and that "Florida Orange Juice (The world's best beverage) would be given away throughout the seminar."[2557]

One year later, Stetson law school put on a third trial seminar in the spring, again at Miami Beach.[2558] Among the new speakers and moderators was Houston, Texas, trial lawyer Percy Foreman, who spoke on practicing in the area of criminal defense.[2559] Stetson law graduate Murray Sams, Jr., of Miami, headed a panel on cross examination.

The fourth (and last) of Stetson's mid-winter trial seminars occurred in Miami Beach in March 1967, and was expanded to four days.[2560] Two Stetson law graduates spoke: Florida Supreme Court Justice E. Harris Drew, class of 1923, and the person who became Drew's successor on the Supreme Court, Circuit Judge Hal P. Dekle, class of 1940.[2561] Moderators included U.S. Fifth Circuit Court of Appeals Judge John R. Brown, and attorneys Chester Bedell, Jacksonville, and J.B. Spence, Miami.[2562] Stetson's annual national trial seminars off campus came to an end in part due to Dean Sebring's health problems, but

---

2553. *Id.*

2554. Sebring, *1959 Overseers Report*, *supra* n. 1883, at 6.

2555. *Stetson Mid-Winter Trial Seminar*, 8 Stetson Law. 2, 2–3 (Mar. 1965).

2556. *Id.*

2557. *Id.*

2558. *1966 Annual Mid-Winter Trial Seminar*, 9 Stetson Law. 1, 1–6 (Feb. 1966).

2559. *Id.* at 5.

2560. *1967 Annual Stetson Mid-Winter Trial Seminar*, 10 Stetson Law. 2, 2–6 (Feb. 1967) [hereinafter *1967 Annual Seminar*].

2561. Judge Dekle, *'40, Seeks to Succeed Justice Drew, '12*, 13 Stetson Law. 3, 3 (Dec. 1969).

2562. *1967 Annual Seminar*, *supra* n. 2560, at 3, 5.

even more so because of the monetary cost.[2563] The dean acknowledged that the annual seminars held in Miami Beach had cost the school dearly.[2564]

(2) Stetson Space Law Seminar

Though putting on CLE conferences in Miami Beach was not profitable, Dean Sebring made sure that the College provided lawyers with varied CLE programs on the school's Gulfport campus. One topic was out of this world—"A Space Law Seminar."[2565] Described as "a unique, all-day program devoted to an examination of the research frontier between law and space," the speakers included Garrett D. Quick, Stetson law '54 graduate.[2566] Quick was legal counsel for contractors involved with "Cape Canaveral projects."[2567] Other speakers were Andrew G. Halley, general counsel of International Astronautical Federation and the American Rocket Society; Walter D. Smith, chief engineer, Martin Company, Cape Canaveral; B.G. MacNabb, operations manager for General Dynamics, Astronautics, Air Force Missile Test Center; and Stetson law professor Frank E. Booker and former dean Paul E. Raymond.[2568]

The *Stetson Lawyer* described the program as follows:

> The panel [is] comprised of attorneys, scientists, and executives who specialize in the fields of space, electronics and nuclear energy. It is reasonably certain that the lawyers of no other state have even been offered in a single program an opportunity to learn from so competent a group of men the legal problems presented by the space age.[2569]

(3) Labor Forums and other CLE Programs

In 1958, the College of Law held a two-day "Medical-Legal Institute" co-sponsored by The Florida Bar and the Florida Medical Association. A reported 300 to 350 lawyers and doctors attended."[2570] Other CLE programs during Sebring's deanship included an institute on "The Child and the Law";[2571] annual "Labor

---

2563. Vause, *Milestones*, *supra* n. 1370, at 25.
2564. Sebring, *Final Report*, *supra* n. 2518, at 6.
2565. *Space Seminar Highlights Law Day, 1961*, 5 Stetson Law. 1, 1 (Oct. 1961).
2566. *Id.* at 2.
2567. *Id.*
2568. *Id.*
2569. *Id.*
2570. Sebring, *1959 Overseers Report*, *supra* n. 1883, at 6.
2571. *Id.*

Relations Forums" (which first began in 1947 under Dean Haslup);[2572] a Prosecuting Attorney Seminar;[2573] and a "Real Property Practice Institute" put on in conjunction with the Real Property Section of The Florida Bar.[2574] In addition, at the school's annual law day celebration each spring, CLE programs were included for the benefit of Florida attorneys. Associate Justice Tom C. Clark of the United States Supreme Court spoke at one law day as the guest of Dean Sebring.[2575]

10.15 The Goal of Dean Sebring Is Realized

Stepping foot on the Gulfport campus in 1955, Sebring found it "in shambles," with buildings in need of rehabilitation. He inherited a faculty that was largely unenergetic and unproductive. He had little financial support from the University, and was threatened with loss of accreditation by the ABA. The school had a number of marginal students that resulted in high academic attrition and a mediocre success rate on the Florida bar examination. Perhaps most challenging of all, Sebring faced a University president who at that point appeared to be unsympathetic to the needs of the law school, and who seemed to oppose the school having a high level of autonomy to perform its functions.

Then the former Chief Justice of the Florida Supreme Court, Justice at Nuremberg, and University of Florida head football coach was ready to push ahead. But only nine months after his arrival, Sebring suffered a heart attack requiring a long recuperation in his home. After regaining his health, he went to work, notably by hiring a bright, dedicated, productive faculty. Calvin Kuenzel, Justice James Brand, Paul Barnard, Richard Dillon, David Dickson, and others raised students' performance to a level that, by the end of Sebring's deanship, was reflected by Stetson's graduates passing the bar year after year at virtually a one hundred percent rate. Sebring and the faculty had begun the long process of building the academic integrity and standards of the College of Law.

Sebring turned to those who supported the school, and with the leadership of Walter Mann convinced Edmunds and the Board of Trustees to establish a Board of Overseers as well as a separate, legally independent Stetson Law Foundation. Key supporters, in addition to Walter Mann, included Arthur

---

2572. *Labor Forums*, 5 Stetson Law. 5, 5 (Oct. 1961).

2573. *Prosecuting Attorney Seminar*, 7 Stetson Law. 5, 5 (Mar. 1964).

2574. *Florida Bar Property Institute at Stetson*, 9 Stetson Law. 7, 7 (Nov. 1965).

2575. *Sebring Administration at College of Law an Era of Development and Progress*, 11 Stetson Law. 2 (Nov. 1967).

Morris, Doyle Carlton, Bill Clapp, Cecil Bailey, Perry Nichols, Francis Whitehair, Ralph Ferrell, Carroll Runyon, Harris Drew, Earl Echdington, Amory Underhill, Ben Watkins, and Wallace Storey. These men assisted Sebring in building financial security and a degree of administrative autonomy from DeLand.

Subsequently, through Sebring's efforts and those of the Overseers and Law Center Foundation directors, the College received several substantial gifts that were instrumental in financing the construction of the administration and classroom buildings. The donors included nationally known philanthropists: duPonts, Danas, and Firestones.

Even more important to Sebring's ultimate goal of enhancing the College of Law's reputation was his raising academic standards, increasing the books in the library count from 20,000 to 60,000 volumes, sponsoring national programs on trial practice, and promoting on-campus CLE programs in addition to an off-campus Public Defender Clinic. All of these achievements led the ABA and AALS to declare that Stetson law school was in full compliance with standards for accreditation. The school's reputation had been restored. By the time he had planned to resign at the end of August 1968, Harold L. "Tom" Sebring had overseen the rebuilding of the Stetson College of Law physically, financially, and qualitatively.

Only five weeks prior to his retirement, Judge Harold Leon "Tom" Sebring died, July 26, 1968, in his St. Petersburg home at the age of seventy.[2576] Both at Stetson University in DeLand, and at the College of Law in Gulfport, the American flags were lowered to half staff.[2577] Later, the Florida Senate passed a resolution (drafted by Joseph McClain, then a member of the Senate) in honor of Justice and Dean Harold (Tom) Sebring.[2578] It reads in part:

> [T]ruly a man whose distinction circled the globe, he performed nobly as athlete, soldier, attorney, jurist, and educator, but probably the greatest tribute to his memory remains enshrined in the hearts of his students who shared his hopes and ideals and who will strive to build upon them.[2579]

The building of Stetson law school's standards, reputation, and physical plant did continue. The story of the Dillon administration follows.

2576. *Deaths, Stetson Law Dean, Judge Harold Sebring*, St. Pete. Indep. C6 (July 26, 1968).

2577. *Dean Sebring, Noted Jurist, Law Dean Dies*, St. Pete. Times B13 (July 27, 1968).

2578. Fla. Sen. Res. 1704, 1st Leg., at 2.

2579. *Id.*; *see also* Jacob, *Remembering Sebring*, *supra* n. 9, at 172–173.

CHAPTER ELEVEN

Raising Academic Standards, Money—Dean Dillon

11.1 The New Dean

a. Young and Qualified

Dean Harold "Tom" Sebring intended to relinquish the deanship of the College of Law on August 31, 1968,[2580] and to remain on the faculty.[2581] However, only five weeks short of retiring, he died. At that point, Richard T. Dillon assumed all decanal responsibilities.[2582] Nine years earlier, in 1957, Sebring had invited Dillon—who recently had received his Stetson LL.B. degree—to join the College of Law faculty. Within two years, Sebring named Dillon assistant dean, the first sub-dean in the College's history.[2583] Subsequently, he served both as assistant dean and a full-time teaching member of the faculty for eleven years until he was elevated to the deanship in 1968.

On the recommendation of University President Paul Geren, the Board of Trustees elected Dillon to be Sebring's successor.[2584] An article in the *Stetson Lawyer* indicates Dillon's choice had been widely recommended:

> President Geren's selection [of Dillon] is heartily endorsed by all members of the Stetson family. Immediately following Dean Sebring's announcement this fall that he intended to retire September 1, 1968, the

2580. *Harold "Tom" Sebring, 1898–1968: Scholar, Athlete, Lawyer, Jurist, Legal Educator and Former Dean*, 12 Stetson Law. 1, 6 (Feb. 1969).

2581. W. Gary Vause, *The Dillon Years*, 30 Stetson Law. 1, 22, 24 (Fall 1990) [hereinafter Vause, *Dillon Years*].

2582. *Bishop Interview*, *supra* n. 1953, at 12.

2583. *Many "Firsts" on Dean-To-Be's Record*, 11 Stetson Law. 2, 4 (Mar. 1980) [hereinafter *Dillon Firsts*]; *see also Dillon Succeeds Sebring*, *supra* n. 2272, at 2.

2584. *Dillon Succeeds Sebring*, *supra* n. 2272, at 1.

> [law] faculty unanimously recommended to the President that Professor Dillon be appointed to fill the vacancy.[2585]

In addition to the unanimous recommendation of the faculty, Dillon received support from "scores of alumni from all over the country and several leading educators and friends."[2586] After his appointment was announced, he had Dean Sebring's full approval to make plans and decisions that would affect his future administration of the College. In conjunction with the faculty, he made plans to continue the Public Defender Clinic, to admit first-year students to the 1968 summer season, and to revamp faculty support services.[2587]

Sebring was relieved and pleased by Geren's appointment of Dillon, as it clearly took the administrative responsibility of running the school off his back. Sebring wrote:

> In my opinion, Dr. Geren, President of Stetson University, made an excellent choice when he selected Dr. Dillon to become Dean of Stetson College of Law ... He is in complete sympathy with the program of legal education under which we have had such singular success in training students to become lawyers and ... [he] intends to expand this program.[2588]

Sebring noted that Dillon had become "familiar with every aspect of the law school's operation." In turn, Geren pledged that he would "give his unqualified support to Dean Dillon and his administration."[2589] Sebring's strong recommendation was but one, albeit an important, factor in President Geren's decision to appoint Dillon dean. Another was Dillon's list of accomplishments. A story in the *Stetson Lawyer* reported that he had a "number of firsts"[2590] that related to his association with the law school as student, professor, and assistant dean. He was a member of the first law class initially admitted in 1954 on the Gulfport Campus, and was the first Stetson law graduate from the Gulfport campus to speak before the Florida Supreme Court on behalf of all the new lawyers being admitted to The Florida Bar at its "Induction Ceremony."[2591] As a teaching member of the law faculty, Dillon served as the first librarian of

---

2585. *Id.*

2586. *Id.*

2587. *July 25 Dillon Conversation*, *supra* n. 1986.

2588. *Sebring Successor: "An Excellent Choice,"* 11 Stetson Law. 2, 4 (Mar. 1968).

2589. *Id.*

2590. *Dillon Firsts*, *supra* n. 2583, at 4.

2591. *See Response on Behalf of Newly Admitted Members*, Fla. B.J. 528 (Nov. 1957). Dillon quoted Justice Sharswood to his fellow inductees: "Let it be remembered in the heart of every student that no man can ever be a truly great lawyer" who is not in every sense "a good man." *Id.*

Dean Richard T. Dillon

the Charles A. Dana Law Library. In addition, he was the first professor on the Gulfport campus awarded tenure, and was the first administrator in the College's history to be appointed assistant dean.[2592] In one matter, however, Dillon was last, according to his wife, Betty Vallejo Dillon. She predicted that her husband, "would be the *last* to leave his office every night."[2593] In time, Dillon would receive honorary degrees from his alma maters, the University of Tampa and Stetson University.

Dillon brought to the deanship several other awards and recognitions. He was valedictorian of his college class, an Overseers' Scholar, a recipient of the Perry Nichols Award for outstanding performance in trial practice class, and a holder of a Ford Foundation Fellowship for graduate work in law at New York University, where he earned an LL.M. degree.[2594]

b. New Dean Faces Challenges

Upon taking office, the highly qualified dean confronted serious problems. First, Dean Sebring's emphasis on capital improvements meant that funds for operating expenses of the law school were limited. In his final year as dean, Sebring finalized the budget for the 1968–69 academic year, the year Richard

2592. *Dillon Firsts*, *supra* n. 2583, at 4.
2593. *Id.* (emphasis in original).
2594. *Id.*

Dillon would take over. The budget provided for $50,000 additional annual support from the University.[2595] Looking back, Dillon describes the problem:

> We faced the 1968–69 year with an operating budget that had already been approved by the Board [of Overseers] in February of the preceding academic year, a budget that contained no provision for continuation for the Public Defender Clinic ... Of greater immediate concern to me at the time was the fact the Board of Trustees amended the [law school] budget that had been approved by the Board of Overseers and the final document had expenses exceeding income by $50,000.[2596]

Besides budgetary concerns, Dillon was aware of the school's ongoing financial obligations, which included amortizing the federal loans used to help finance construction of the Dana and Crummer buildings.[2597] Business Manager William Unger, within days after Dillon's appointment, notified him that the school would have to borrow $100,000 to open in the fall of 1968.[2598] Dillon replied that closure was impossible, saying that additional revenues had to be found.[2599] By cutting back on budgeted expenditures, and by successfully soliciting gifts from Overseers, alumni, and friends of the College, Dillon kept the school operating and avoided additional financial encumbrances.

But Dillon also recognized that major capital building improvements needed to be made. Though several campus buildings were air conditioned, the majority of the students' dormitory rooms were not.[2600] Dillon promised to do something about it.[2601] He did, and by 1970, all on-campus student living quarters had air conditioning, to the relief of suffering residents. One stu-

---

2595. Vause, *Dillon Years*, *supra* n. 2581, at 24.

2596. Richard T. Dillon, *Address to Stetson Lawyers Association*, 1 (Washington, D.C., Spring 1973) (on file at Stetson U. College of L., Gulfport, Fla.) [hereinafter Dillon, *Address*].

2597. *Id.*

2598. Vause, *Dillon Years*, *supra* n. 2581, at 24.

2599. *Id.* Unger died soon after Dillon's appointment. Dillon then took on the additional responsibilities of the College's business manager until 1971, when Dillon appointed Al Lane business manager, because there was no money in the budget to pay for a business manager during that period. *Id.* at 25.

2600. *Dormitory Area Is Now Fully Air-Conditioned*, 13 Stetson Lawyer 2 (July 1970) [hereinafter *Dormitory Area*]; *see also A Glance Backward—Past Five Years Have Been Years of Steady Progress at College of Law*, 16 Stetson Lawyer 3 (Aug. 1973) [hereinafter *Glance Backward*].

2601. *Dormitory Area*, *supra* n. 2600, at 2; *see also* Vause, *Foundations for Excellence*, *supra* n. 308, at 334, n. 132.

dent commented that before air conditioning, "a Turkish bath would have had the chilling effect of a cold shower."[2602] Cool air in Florida's climate, however, did not come cheaply. Not only were air conditioning units expensive; so, too, was electricity. In the mid-1950s, the College's average annual electric bill approximated $8,000, compared with $38,000 in 1969, and $80,000 by 1974.[2603]

Though Dillon was challenged by financial conditions at the school, he soon faced another problem—a predicted major decline in student enrollment. His deanship began in 1968 at the height of the Vietnam War. A few months earlier, the federal government had abolished draft deferments for law students.[2604] Thus, many believed that the loss of deferments would impact law school enrollment hard, at least during the 1968–1970 period.[2605] This, in turn, would cause the school's budgetary assumptions to be far off the mark.[2606]

In light of an estimated 30% to 50% decline in law school enrollment, University officials worried that the College was entering a precarious period.[2607] To minimize the projected enrollment declines, Dillon and the faculty decided to admit new students three times a year by adding a summer entering class (in addition to those in the fall and spring), a policy taking effect in the summer of 1968.[2608] It was a wise move, as the school's enrollment levels held steady. In June 1968, thirty-six students matriculated, followed by ninety-two in the fall, then thirty-one in the spring of 1969.[2609] Though thirty-three students graduated in January,[2610] the school's total enrollment of 269 students was only one percent below the 1967–68 number.[2611] Nonetheless, due to the potential impact of the draft, Dillon and the faculty remained concerned about potential declines in enrollment for the 1969–72 years. Their fears, however, did not materialize.

Rather than declining, the law school's total enrollment by September 1970 had risen to 327 students, an all-time high according to the school's registrar,

2602. *Dormitory Area*, *supra* n. 2600.

2603. Dillon, *Address*, *supra* n. 2596, at 3; *see also College of Law Will Enter Seventy-Fifth Year*, 17 Stetson Law. 1, 1 (Aug. 1974).

2604. *Anticipated Inroads on Enrollment by Draft Boards*, 11 Stetson Lawyer 3, 1 (May 1968) [hereinafter *Anticipated Inroads*].

2605. Dillon, Address, *supra* n. 2596, at 1.

2606. Vause, *Dillon Years*, *supra* n. 2581, at 24.

2607. *Anticipated Inroads*, *supra* n. 2604, at 1.

2608. *Glance Backward*, *supra* n. 2600, at 3.

2609. *College of Law Looks to Future; 1968–1969 Academic Year Heralds Many Changes*, 12 Stetson Law. 1, 2 (Feb. 1969).

2610. *Id.*

2611. *Glance Backward*, *supra* n. 2600, at 3.

Kay Eddy.[2612] The entering first-year class numbered 180 students.[2613] The entire student body included ninety-six returning Vietnam War veterans and twelve women.[2614] The students came from 123 colleges and thirty-one states.[2615] Moreover, close to half of the students were married.[2616]

Three factors triggered larger enrollments than earlier predicted. First, an unexpected number of returning war veterans offset prospective students who were drafted. Second, both the percentage and number of women law students in proportion to men increased, a trend that accelerated during the remainder of the 1970s. Third, older students, many of whom were married, represented a statistically higher percentage of the student body. As the *Stetson Lawyer* reported:

> Surprisingly, in view of the abolishment of the draft deferments for most graduate students, applications for admission [to the law school] for the 1969–1970 academic year greatly exceeded expectations, enabling the College to select its largest entering class ever.[2617]

The larger enrollments at the beginning of the 1970s gladdened Dean Dillon and the faculty. They were further pleased when gifts to the College ensued.

11.2 Dillon Brings in Major Capital Funds

a. Dana Gifts Top One-and-One-Half Million Dollars

When Dillon served as assistant dean, he became well acquainted with Charles and Eleanor Dana, and with the Danas' friend, Walter Mann, who, as noted earlier, was a University trustee and member of the law school's Board of Overseers. Near the end of 1969, Mann informed Dillon that the Charles A. Dana Foundation was making a $100,000 gift to the College of Law.[2618] In addition, Eleanor Dana and Ralph Ferrell, a member of the Board of Overseers, gave gifts to the College. Dillon used the Eleanor Dana and Ferrell donations to renovate and refurbish guest suites in the Stetson Inn, which today are named after the donors.[2619]

2612. *Record Enrollment as College Enters 70*th *Year*, 13 Stetson Lawyer, 1, 1 (Dec. 1969).
2613. *Id.*
2614. *Id.*
2615. *Id.*
2616. *Id.*
2617. *Id.*
2618. *$100,000 Gift*, 13 Stetson Law. 1 (Dec. 1969).
2619. Vause, *Foundations for Excellence*, *supra* n. 308, at 334 n. 132.

In 1970, Dillon submitted a proposal to the Dana Foundation for funds to build an addition to the Dana Law library.[2620] An expanded library was needed because of acute space problems caused by the doubling of students—from about 200 in 1958 (when the library was dedicated) to near 400 in 1972—and due to the growth in the library collection. The Dana Foundation favorably responded to Dillon's request with a pledge of $200,000.[2621] At that point, the total of Dana gifts to the school exceeded one million dollars, consisting of approximately $200,000 from Charles A. Dana personally, $200,000 from his wife Eleanor Naylor Dana, and $600,000 from the Dana Foundation.[2622]

The object of the 1971 Dana gift was to double the size of the library, the facility the Foundation had earlier financed.[2623] The $200,000 donation was contingent upon the College contributing an equal amount from outside sources, a condition in line with the Foundation's policy—financial "help should be given to those willing to help themselves." In time, Dillon raised the required matching funds from "alumni, members of the bar, and other friends of Stetson."[2624] In 1973, the addition to the library was completed and dedicated.[2625] After its expansion, the library accommodated 275 students—compared with 140 previously—and had space to shelve 160,000 volumes—compared with 70,000.[2626] In addition, the larger library included private study rooms, typing centers, and conference areas to accommodate seminars and student-group studying.[2627]

In 1958, the library's book count totaled 60,000 volumes, but during the Dillon era the number rose appreciably. One reason was a challenge gift of $25,000 per year for three years from the Edyth Bush Charitable Foundation of Orlando.[2628] The Bush Foundation gift, like the Dana library-expansion donation, was contingent on the school providing matching funds, which it did.[2629] Among scores of other gifts to the library, The Florida Bar also contributed $1,000 for books on professional responsibility.[2630] Moreover, the

2620. Vause, *Dillon Years*, *supra* n. 2581, at 25.

2621. *Dana Foundation Gift*, *supra* n. 2127, at 2.

2622. *Id.*

2623. *See supra* n. 2117–2126 and accompanying notes.

2624. *Dana Library Symbolizes College of Law's Growth*, 18 Stetson Law., 1, 1 (Aug. 1975) [hereinafter *Dana Library Growth*].

2625. *Id.* at 1; *see also Glance Backwards*, *supra* n. 2600, at 6.

2626. Dillon, *Address*, *supra* n. 2596, at 4, 5.

2627. Vause, *Dillon Years*, *supra* n. 2581, at 25.

2628. *See Library Gift*, 23 Stetson Law. 1, 2 (Feb. 1979).

2629. *Dana Library Growth*, *supra* n. 2624, at 7.

2630. *Id.*

Charles A. Dana Library collection was further augmented by being designated the first law library in Florida to be a depositary for Federal Government documents.[2631] Expansion of the library's collection happened because the Dana Foundation helped finance the library's addition.[2632] Fortunately for the College of Law, additional Dana contributions would be forthcoming.

Before the end of the Dillon administration, and after the death of Charles A. Dana in 1975, the Dana Foundation in 1979 announced that it was granting $500,000 to the Stetson Law Center Foundation[2633] (the independent, non-profit corporation established to benefit the Stetson law school).[2634] The gift raised the total of Dana contributions to more than one-and-one-half million dollars.[2635] The donation was the largest received by the Stetson Law Center up to that point. Prior to Stetson's receipt of the half-million dollar gift, two members of the Dana Foundation approached Dean Dillon and suggested that the Foundation might consider a one million dollar grant to the school in memory of Charles A. Dana. With the knowledge of Eleanor Dana, representatives suggested that in return, the Foundation might condition the gift on Stetson University renaming the law school the "Charles A. Dana College of Law of Stetson University."[2636] Dillon responded that he would present the idea to Stetson University President John Edwin Johns. Upon hearing about the possibility of a gift that would require the University renaming the College of Law, President Johns told Dillon the University could not approve.[2637] Dillon concurred. Dillon says that there were never any negotiations about the matter and that he opposed the million dollar Dana gift from the outset.[2638]

At some point following President Johns' negative reaction, Dillon became aware that certain members of the Foundation's trustees were unhappy with Stetson. Dillon wrote the director of the Foundation at its Greenwich, Connecticut, headquarters, and expressed the University and law school's appreciation for Dana Foundations's generosity in the past, noting how significant

---

2631. *Id.*

2632. *See supra* n. 2628 and accompanying text.

2633. *Dana Foundation Grant Benefits Law School*, 22 Stetson Law. 1, 1 (Feb. 1979) [hereinafter *Foundation Grant*].

2634. *See supra* nn. 2063–2077 and accompanying text.

2635. *See Dana Foundation Gift, supra* n. 2127, at 2.

2636. Conversation with Richard T. Dillon, Dean Emeritus, Stetson U. College of L., and Michael Swygert, Prof. Emeritus, Stetson U. College of L. (May 7, 2005) [hereinafter *May 7 Dillon Conversation*].

2637. *Id.*

2638. *Id.*

its gifts had been for the College.[2639] Dillon also reminded Dana Foundation leaders of the strong personal ties that had developed between himself and the Dana family, in particular, with Eleanor, or "Nel," as he called her. Dillon and Mrs. Dana were close friends for twenty years. She had spent several winters residing on the Stetson campus, an inviting environment she described as "my second home."[2640] One winter, after her husband died, Eleanor Dana became seriously ill, she told Dillon that she wished to remain in her Stetson apartment while recuperating.[2641] Dillon made sure she received the best possible medical care, a courtesy Eleanor Dana greatly appreciated and which, among other reasons, caused her to hold Dillon in high esteem throughout the remainder of his deanship.

Given Dillon's strong ties with Charles and Eleanor Dana, he was determined to demonstrate to Foundation trustees how highly the school valued its relationship with the charitable institution. He found a way to do so. Dillon called upon alumnus Cecil Bailey, president of the St. Petersburg Law Center Foundation,[2642] and suggested that the Center consider renaming itself the Charles A. Dana Law Center Foundation.[2643] Bailey agreed and the Center's directors unanimously agreed to change the name,[2644] which became official when the Foundation's charter was amended on March 13, 1978.[2645] Less than one year later, the Dana Foundation in Connecticut announced a grant of $500,000 to the renamed Charles A. Dana Law Center Foundation in St. Petersburg.[2646]

In disclosing that the Dana Law Center Foundation had received the half-million dollar gift, its president, Cecil Bailey, stated that income from the grant would be used in three ways: first, to purchase additional books for the Dana Law Library; second, to establish Dana Scholarships; and third, to supplement the salary of a distinguished professor to be designated the Charles A. Dana Professor of Law.[2647] In keeping with the philosophy of Charles A. Dana, the Foundation expected the College to provide an equal amount in matching

---

2639. *Id.*

2640. *College of Law First on Mrs. Dana Personal List*, 22 Stetson Law. 1, 2, 11 (Feb. 1979). "A familiar sight in the 1960s was Mrs. Dana, seated comfortably in a lounge chair near one of the inner court fountains." *Id.*

2641. *See Dana Foundation Grant*, *supra* n. 2633, at 1.

2642. *See supra* n. 2077 and accompanying text.

2643. *May 7 Dillon Conversation*, *supra* n. 2636.

2644. *Foundation Changes Name to Honor Dana*, 22 Stetson Law. 1, 1 (Feb. 1979).

2645. *Id.*

2646. *Dana Foundation Grant*, *supra* n. 2633, at 1.

2647. Dean Emeritus Richard T. Dillon was the first person to hold the Charles A. Dana chair. *See infra* nn. 3199–3200 and accompanying text.

funds. Dillon was able to do so by soliciting gifts and by allocating a portion of law school revenues to meet the requirement.[2648]

b. Harvey S. Firestone, Jr.

During the Dillon years, another major benefactor was a well-known industrialist from Akron, Ohio, Harvey S. Firestone, Jr. (whom Sebring had first contacted). Beginning in 1956, and continuing every year until his death in 1973, Firestone made financial contributions to Stetson College of Law.[2649] His son, Harvey Firestone, III, who was physically disabled, having other options, chose Stetson for law study. Matriculating in the fall of 1955, he graduated in 1959, ranking third in his class.[2650]

During the time Firestone, III was a law student, his father donated money for a campus swimming pool and for the renovation and refurbishment of a suite of rooms in the Stetson Inn.[2651] Prior to his graduation, Firestone, III resided two years in what today is known as the Firestone Apartment. His father, Harvey Firestone, Jr., also financed construction of new faculty offices, then called "the faculty row."[2652] A short time after Harvey Firestone, III graduated from law school, the thirty-year old heir to the Firestone fortune suffered a tragic death while vacationing in Havana, Cuba.[2653]

Thirteen years after his son's death, the senior Firestone gave $150,000 to the College of Law in 1973 to rebuild and expand the school's "Recreation Center" in memory of his son. The funds were used to refurbish the swimming pool, and to build new tennis courts, a basketball court, and a work-out area.[2654] In addition, Harvey Firestone, Jr., arranged for the Firestone Foundation to make gifts for perpetual maintenance of the Recreational Center, to pave and light the parking lot, and supplement faculty salaries.[2655] Unfortunately, only one year after his donation to the College of Law, Harvey Firestone, Jr., died, just prior to the dedication of the Recreation Center bearing the name of his son.[2656]

2648. *May 7 Dillon Conversation, supra* n. 2636.

2649. *Harvey S. Firestone, Jr., Dead at Age 75, Was One of the College of Law's Major Benefactors,* 16 Stetson Law. 1, 2 (Aug. 1973) [hereinafter *Firestone*].

2650. *Id.*

2651. Vause, *Dillon Years, supra* n. 2581, at 25.

2652. *Firestone, supra* n. 2649, at 2.

2653. *May 4 Dillon Interview, supra* n. 1885.

2654. Vause, *Foundations of Excellence, supra* n. 308, at 334 n. 132.

2655. *Firestone, supra* n. 2649, at 2.

2656. *Dedication of Harvey Firestone III Memorial Recreation Center,* 17 Stetson Law. 1, 4–5 (Aug. 1974).

The dedication of the Firestone Center was held in the summer of 1974 under the shade of a banyan tree.[2657] Those present included College of Law Dean Richard Dillon; Stetson University President John E. Johns; University Chancellor J. Ollie Edmunds; University Trustee Earl B. Edington; the sister of Harvey Firestone, III, Martha Firestone Ford; the fourteen-year-old daughter of Harvey Firestone, III, Diane Firestone; and Stetson faculty and students. Student Bar Association President Benton E. Kay, among many others, paid homage both to the father (the benefactor), and to the son (the late Stetson law graduate and member of The Florida Bar).[2658] Today, on a large granite stone in front of the original center, the following engraved inscription appears:

Stetson University College of Law
RECREATION CENTER
IN MEMORY OF
HARVEY S. FIRESTONE, III
1930–1960
Graduated LL.B., Class of 1959
Admitted to The Florida Bar, 1960

c. The Estate of John T. Rosa: A Multi-Million Dollar Bequest

Clifford B. Rosa was one of Stetson University's earliest administrators, having been appointed bursar in 1897 by the University's first president, John B. Forbes.[2659] Three years earlier, Forbes had hired Clifford Rosa to teach "commercial branches," and "military tactics and drill" (Rosa had graduated from a military academy).[2660] Students referred to Clifford Rosa as the "Professor of Accounts," because he taught accounting.[2661] Initially, Forbes appointed Rosa chairperson of the "Commercial Department" of Stetson University, but the president soon recognized that Rosa's keen knowledge of business and accounting could be of great aid to the University.[2662] Thus, in 1897, Forbes el-

2657. *Id.*

2658. *Id.* at 4.

2659. Lycan, *History of Stetson*, *supra* n. 109, at 22.

2660. *Id.* That same year, the University's first ever intra-mural football game took place on campus. One team was called the "Forbes Team" and was coached by Professor Rosa. The other was called the "Stetson Team" and was coached by English Professor Harvey M. MacQuiston. *Id.* at 210. The Rosa team won. *Id.* An account of the game, written by Clifford Rosa long after he retired, appears in a 1948 edition of Stetson University publication *Alumnus*. *Id.* at 227; Henry B. Plant Museum, *supra* n. 4.

2661. Lycan, *History of Stetson*, *supra* n. 109, at 22.

2662. *Id.* at 84.

Benefactor John T. Rosa

evated Clifford Rosa to be the University Comptroller, a post he held for over forty years.[2663]

Clifford B. Rosa and his wife, Olive Tawney Rosa, had a son named John T. Rosa. In 1929, John T. Rosa graduated from Stetson College of Law in DeLand with an LL.B. degree.[2664] A few years after his graduation, he moved to Red Bank, New Jersey, and became a businessman and a real estate investor.

Interestingly, the authors have found no evidence that Rosa contacted anyone at the law school from the time he graduated in 1926 until the mid-1970s, a period of almost fifty years (though he surely kept in touch with his parents in DeLand). Then, in the mid-1970s, Dean Richard Dillon received a phone

---

2663. *Id.* at 265, 375. After Stetson's second president, Lincoln Hulley, died in 1934, the Trustees appointed seventy-seven-year-old Stetson University Professor Charles Sherwood Farris, who, according to historian Gordon Lycan, "notably lacked in administrative abilities," as interim president. *Id.*

At that time, John B. Stetson, Jr., (son of John B. Stetson for whom the University is named), was chairperson of the Board of Trustees. John B. Stetson admired Rosa and, following the end of the Hulley presidency, considered Rosa "the key man at the University." Stetson often wrote confidential letters to Rosa, giving him instructions on managing the University until a permanent president could be appointed, even though Professor Farris was nominally in charge. *Id.* at 264, 265.

2664. Bruce R. Jacob, *1986 Annual Report on College of Law* 1 (July 17, 1986) (submitted to University President, Dr. Pope Duncan); *see* Ltr. from Bruce R. Jacob, Dean, Stetson U. College of L., to Dr. Pope Duncan, Pres., Stetson U. (July 17, 1986) (on file at Stetson U. College of L., Gulfport, Fla.)).

call from John T. Rosa (who then lived in Long Branch, Monmouth County, New Jersey).[2665] After introducing himself, Rosa told Dillon that he was considering making a gift to his alma mater, Stetson College of Law. Dillon, of course, was pleased and invited Rosa and his wife (Mildred) to come to Gulfport to see the law school's campus (which they had never seen), and to discuss the opportunities for assisting the College's needs.

Rosa accepted Dillon's invitation, and he and his wife traveled to St. Petersburg. Over dinner, Dillon and Rosa talked about the possibility of Rosa becoming a benefactor of the school. They continued their discussion the following morning at breakfast.[2666] Later, in Dillon's office, Rosa expressed his wish to give the College money for a building that would bear his name.[2667] Dillon describes what happened next:

> [Rosa] asked me what kind of building the school needed. I told him that many of our students were married and in need of reasonably priced housing, and that a building ... containing rental apartments for married couples was needed. He indicated an interest in pursuing my suggestion further, and we took a tour of the campus and adjoining neighborhood looking at possible building sites. Later that day he told me that he planned to include a bequest in his will for such a building.[2668]

Dillon thanked Rosa for his magnanimous generosity and told him that the building, "would be a great benefit to our married students and to our school."[2669] Dillon then asked if Rosa would consider including in his bequest, funds not just for the building, but also for its maintenance, to which Rosa responded that he would provided his estate was not exhausted after funding the building and providing for other gifts he intended to make.[2670]

During the same time Rosa was talking with Dillon about making a substantial gift to the law school, he was also discussing with University officials

---

2665. This information regarding Rosa was furnished by Dean Emeritus Richard T. Dillon to Stetson law professors Kristen Adams, Tom Marks, and Michael Swygert in January 2005 [hereinafter Dillon, *Discussion of Rosa Gift*].

2666. *Id.*

2667. Aff. Richard T. Dillon 1 (July 19, 1985) [hereinafter Dillon, *Rosa Estate Affidavit*].

2668. *Id.* Dillon explained to Rosa that due to the Vietnam War and the loss of law-student deferments, the law school had actively recruited women and married students in the late 1960s, two groups which were not subject to the draft. Dillon explained that that could happen again. Dillon, Discussion of Rosa Gift, *supra* n. 2665.

2669. Dillon, *Rosa Estate Affidavit*, *supra* n. 2667.

2670. *Id.*

his possible funding of an administration building in DeLand, one to be named after his deceased father and mother—Clifford B. and Olive Tawney Rosa.[2671] At one point, Stetson University Vice President for Finances H. Graves Edmondson called Dillon to advise him that John Rosa was coming to DeLand to discuss the proposed administration building. Edmondson invited Dillon to confer with Rosa regarding his promised funding of a new building for married students. In Dillon's subsequent meeting in DeLand with Rosa, he inquired what the amount, in general terms, Rosa's bequest might come to, since Rosa had previously given no hint. As he had done in the past, however, Rosa did not specify what the amount of his gift might be.[2672]

Then, years later, in February1981, Dillon received a letter from attorney John Warren, Jr., of the Red Bank, New Jersey, law firm of Parsons, Canzona, Blair & Warren.[2673] Warren wrote that John T. Rosa had died on January 11, 1981, and that the directives in Rosa's Last Will and Testament and in a subsequent Codicil included "a provision concerning [the College of Law]."[2674] It turned out that Rosa's will, executed in February 20, 1976, bequeathed through a charitable remainder trust, his entire residual estate to Stetson University and to the College of Law, subject to a trust for the life of his wife, Mildred.[2675] The will bestowed 60 % of the residual estate to John B. Stetson University specifically to be used for:

> [T]he construction of a new administration building on Stetson University property located at the northeast corner of North Boulevard and East Michigan Avenue in DeLand, Florida. I direct that such building be named "The Rosa Administration Building" in memory of my father and mother, Clifford B. And Olive Tawney Rosa.[2676]

The will directed the administrator to direct the remaining 40 % of the residual estate to:

> [The] John B. Stetson Law College, St. Petersburg, Florida. I direct that those funds shall be devoted to construction of a building as a self-contained unit

2671. Dillon, *Discussion Rosa Gift*, *supra* n. 2665.

2672. *Id.*

2673. Ltr. from John Warren, Jr., to John B. Stetson L. College (Feb. 4, 1981) (on file at Stetson U. College of L., Gulfport, Fla.).

2674. *Id.*

2675. *See* John T. Rosa, *The Last Will and Testament of John T. Rosa* (Feb. 20, 1976) (on file at Stetson U. College of L., Gulfport, Fla.).

2676. *Id.* at 5, ¶ 6, B(1).

> and not connected with any other branch or division of the University and that such building shall be known as "The John T. Rosa Building."[2677]

At the time Rosa executed his will in 1976, Mildred was alive. Therefore, he established a trust on her behalf directing that after his death all his estate's assets be used for her support for life. After executing his will, Rosa learned that Stetson University officials, in need of new administrative quarters, proceeded to restore and refurbish DeLand Hall to serve as the new headquarters for the central administration.[2678] Aware of these developments, in 1979 Rosa added a codicil to his 1976 will, changing the allocation percentages of his residual estate going to the University and to the College of Law.[2679]

Rosa, however, had not signed the codicil, which meant that after his death, the document failed to meet New Jersey's requirements for legal authenticity. Nevertheless, the executors of the Rosa estate, including Mildred Rosa—John Rosa's widow—petitioned a New Jersey Probate Court to declare the codicil legally valid.[2680] Mildred Rosa and the testator's attorney, John Warren, along with the trustees and other Rosa executors, all gave evidence that the 1979 unexecuted codicil accurately reflected Rosa's last expressed wishes as to how he wanted his residual estate disposed.[2681] Persuaded, the New Jersey court allowed Rosa's 1979 codicil to his last will and testament to be probated.

The codicil reversed the percentages of the estate to go to the University (originally 60%), and to the College of Law (originally 40%). Under the codicil, the University was to be allocated 40%, while the law school would receive 60% of the estate.[2682] Then University Vice-President Edmondson later explained why Rosa made the change.

> The proposed administration building for the DeLand campus no longer represented a need with the [University's] decision to restore DeLand Hall for such purposes. The apartment complex had been suggested [by

2677. *Id.* at 5, ¶ 6, B(2).

2678. Ltr. from H. Graves Edmondson, V.P. and Bus. Mgr., Stetson U., to Bruce R. Jacob, Dean, Stetson U. College of L. 1 (Jan. 26, 1982) (on file at Stetson U. College of L., Gulfport, Fla.) [hereinafter *Edmondson Letter*].

2679. *See* John T. Rosa, *Codicil to Last Will and Testament of John T. Rosa* (unexecuted and undated except for 1979) [hereinafter Rosa, *1979 Codicil*).

2680. *Edmondson Letter*, *supra* n. 2678 at 1.

2681. *Id.*

2682. Rosa, *1979 Codicil*, *supra* n. 2679, at 3.

> Dillon] for the College of Law ... The shift of percentages was a recognition of the reality of building costs, and that the apartment construction might [be expensive].[2683]

Though Rosa's 1979 codicil changed the percentages between the University and the College of Law, it did not change how the College of Law was to use the monies. The language in the 1976 will specified that the law school's portion could only be used for construction of a self-contained building to be named the John T. Rosa Building. That portion of the will's language was not altered by the 1979 Codicil.[2684] Conversely, Rosa's testamentary bequest to the University in DeLand, under provisions of the 1979 codicil, Rosa directed that the monies be used for scholarships in his parents' names.[2685]

Thus, by the early 1980s, both University and law school officials knew what percentage of Rosa's residual estate would to go to each entity. The law school was also aware that certain limitations on the use of its portion of the Rosa monies had not changed. But neither the University or College of Law knew (or could have known) the ultimate worth of the respective bequests. They would learn that only after Mildred Rosa's death, and that occurred in 1984. Shortly thereafter, the Rosa estate executors reported that the value of the combined bequests to the University and to the law school totaled approximately \$6.1 million.[2686] Of that amount, the College of Law was entitled to \$3.7 million.[2687] In 1985, Bruce Jacob, who by then had succeeded Richard Dillon as dean, requested in writing that the executors of the Rosa estate permit the College of Law to use the monies in the following manner:

1. Purchase or construction of the "John T. Rosa Apartment Building" or "John T. Rosa Apartment Complex."	$1,400,000
Contingency	$150,000

2683. *Edmondson Letter*, *supra* n. 2678, at 1.

2684. Rosa, *1979 Codicil*, *supra* n. 2679, at 3.

2685. *Id.* Rosa's intention that his bequest to the University fund scholarships in his parents' names is confirmed by Richard Dillon in a letter to attorney John Warren, Jr., dated March 29, 1982. Dillon wrote Warren that Rosa, "did reveal to me his desire to establish scholarships at the University in memory of his mother and father." *See* Ltr. from Richard T. Dillon to John Warren, Jr. (Mar. 29, 1982) (on file at Stetson U. College of L., Gulfport, Fla.).

2686. Bruce R. Jacob, *The John T. Rosa Bequest to the Stetson College of Law* 1 (1985) (submitted to the executors of the John T. Rosa Estate).

2687. *Id.*

2. Renovation of existing Stetson Inn, to be named	
"John T. Rosa Inn" or "John T. Rosa Hall."	$1,000,000
Contingency	$110,000
3. Endowment for operation and maintenance of the	
"John T. Rosa Apartment Building" or "Complex."	$1,000,000
TOTAL	$3,660,000

Jacob added: "We respectfully request that the recommendation contained herein be judged to be in accordance with the wishes of John T. Rosa as set forth in his Last Will and Testament [including the 1979 Codicil]."[2688] The law school's petition to the New Jersey court overseeing the administration of the Rosa estate sought permission, first, to acquire a property for married student housing as an alternative to building one as Rosa's will and codicil directed; and second, to use the monies to renovate existing rooms in the Stetson Inn. Neither of these uses of the Rosa monies were permitted by the express language in either Rosa's will or codicil.

With approval of the New Jersey court overseeing the administration of the Rosa estate, the college of law used a portion of the Rosa money to purchase the Tarreyton Apartments, three blocks east of the school, for $950,000, for married student housing.[2689] The college also petitioned the court for permission to spend the balance of the bequest to renovate the dormitory rooms of the Stetson Inn (old Rolyat Hotel).[2690] The court granted Stetson's petition and the rebuilding of the old hotel rooms followed.[2691] The Stetson Inn, however, was not renamed the John T. Rosa Inn, or John T. Rosa Hall, as had been earlier suggested, but simply the Rosa Inn.[2692]

In time, the College renamed the former Tarreyton Apartments the "John T. Rosa Apartment Complex," though no formal dedication ceremony took place. Regardless, the $6.1 million bequest from the John T. Rosa estate to Stetson University, with $3.7 million going to the College of Law, exceeded in amount gifts from any of the College's earlier major donors.[2693] It was the largest charitable contribution given to the College of Law up to that time. Dillon had successfully courted the donor and Jacob had used the resulting proceeds of Rosa's gift to good advantage for the College of Law.

2688. *Id.* at 3–4.

2689. *Estate Gift Provides Needed Expansion,* 27 Stetson Law. 8 (Fall 1987).

2690. *Id.*

2691. *See infra* n. 3356 and accompanying text.

2692. *See supra* n. 2682 and accompanying text.

2693. *See supra* nn. 2117–2122; 2155–2167; 2184–2185 and accompanying text.

d. Mann Lounge; Sebring Courtroom

In 1974, Walter H. Mann (at the suggestion of Dean Dillon) contributed money to the law school to restore the lounge of the Rolyat Hotel to its original condition.[2694] In gratitude, the law school named the room the Walter H. Mann lounge in his honor.[2695] The College hired Fanitsa Meehan, the wife of Stetson graduate Geroge Meehan, to oversee the project.[2696] An interior decorator, Meehan was assisted by Karen Mullendore, and together they brought in a skilled craftsman from Clearwater to recreate the intricate and brightly colored painting designs on the massive wooden beams supporting the lounge's ceiling.[2697] His name was Dino DiLiberti.[2698] Other artisans marbleized the oyster-white supporting columns, while still others covered the floor with imported glazed Italian tiles.[2699] Meehan kept existing antique pieces while purchasing complimentary new furnishings, including several customized wool area rugs from New York City. The project took two years to complete.

Dillon was pleased with the results that Meehan and Mullendore had achieved. The decorators responded, "Dean Dillon was so appreciative, and understanding of what we were striving for, it made our work much easier."[2700] The *St. Petersburg Times* lauded the results, describing the restorative work as updating "elegance."[2701] Three years after the restoration, Walter Mann stood in the elegant lounge bearing his name. He was present to receive the Champion of Higher Independent Education in Florida award (CHIEF) from the Association of Independent Colleges and Universities of Florida.[2702] Mann, who had made restoration of the Rolyat's lounge possible, had by then served on the University Board of Trustees thirty years.[2703]

Only a year after Mann pledged money to restore the Rolyat's lounge, law school alumni E. Harris Drew and Perry Nichols approached Dillon and said that they would like to pay for the renovation of an existing courtroom in memory of their friend and former Stetson dean, Judge Harold Sebring.[2704]

2694. *Student Lounge Becomes Walter Mann Lounge,* 18 Stetson Law. 6 (Aug. 1975).

2695. *Id.*

2696. Jean Miller, *Updated Elegance: Designer Takes Pride in Restoring a Part of Stetson's Past*, St. Pete. Times F1 (Oct. 5, 1975).

2697. *Id.*

2698. *Id.*

2699. *Id.*

2700. *Id.*

2701. *Id; see also* Vause, *Dillon Years, supra* n. 2581, at 25.

2702. *Newly Named Chief*, 7 Cupola (Stetson U.) 1 (Jan. 1979).

2703. *Id.* Mann also continued to serve as a director of the Dana Law Foundation.

2704. *New Courtroom Planned in Memory of Late Dean*, 18 Stetson Law. 7, 7 (Aug. 1975).

Drew and Nichols contacted members of the Stetson Lawyers Association to enlist their support. The memorial to Dean Sebring was welcomed by Dillon and the faculty. The fund drive raised sufficient money to pay for other campus renovations as well.

On February 23, 1976, the College let contracts for complete renovation of the courtroom and for partial renovation of the Eleanor Dana Hall to make room for additional faculty offices.[2705] The courtroom was gutted and rebuilt, while in Dana Hall, three faculty offices were added along with a new faculty library.[2706] The Harold L. Sebring Courtroom was dedicated on November 11 and 12, 1976, with Dillon leading the ceremonies honoring former Justice Sebring.[2707] The Florida Supreme Court sat en banc throughout the event. Following the formal dedication, the attendees moved to the Mann Lounge, where the widow of Dean Sebring unveiled a portrait of Walter Mann.[2708]

11.3 Faculty

a. Faculty Governance

After Dillon became dean, he gave the faculty greater power in governing the affairs of the law school than had Sebring.[2709] Moreover, in contrast to Sebring, who rarely held faculty conclaves, Dillon scheduled faculty meetings twice a month.[2710] While governance was never part of Sebring's vision for the College of Law,[2711] Dillon saw things differently, and vested in the faculty a wide-range of responsibilities addressing critical issues affecting the law school. This point is underscored by Professor Thomas "Tom" Marks, Jr. (who began his long association on the faculty during Dillon's era). "Dick Dillon," says Marks, "involved the faculty heavily in governance."[2712] This was a significant change, since it was the first time in the school's history that a law dean delegated to the faculty authority over the critical personnel issues of hiring, re-

2705. *The Sebring Courtroom* (Stetson U. n.d.) (brochure on file at Stetson U. College of L., Gulfport, Fla.).

2706. *Id.*

2707. *Id.*

2708. *Id.*

2709. Vause, *Dillon Years*, *supra* n. 2581, at 27.

2710. *Id.*

2711. *Id.* In response to a question by University Dean William McEniry whether the law school had faculty meetings, Sebring responded: "Most of our plans and problems are dealt with informally over the luncheon table." *Id.*

2712. *Marks Interview*, *supra* n. 2471, at 38.

tention, promotion, and tenure of faculty members.[2713] Dillon's actions were in accordance with ABA standards requiring a level of "shared governance" between the dean and faculty of an ABA-approved law school.[2714] Consequently, the dean no longer made decisions unilaterally in reference to faculty retention, dismissal, promotion, and tenure. From Dillon's era onward, Stetson faculty members were selected and retained according to the collective views of the dean and the faculty.[2715] Moreover, to assure the process was both workable and fair, Dillon delegated to the faculty the task of formalizing standards for promotion and tenure, criteria that emphasized teaching competence, research, writing, and participation in national conferences or those sponsored by The Florida Bar.[2716]

In addition, Dillon delegated to the faculty the task of formulating policies as to student admissions, retention, and readmissions, as well as academic standards concerning grades, grade appeals, minimum grade-point averages, and academic requirements for graduation.[2717] Finally, in reference to the law school's finances, Dillon asked faculty members to provide input regarding the school's financial priorities.[2718]

Though Dillon worked with the faculty, he strongly influenced its activities, first, by expressing his own opinions and, second, by exercising control over the agenda.[2719] Nonetheless, according to Dillon, every faculty member had the right to raise any matter of concern by asking the dean's secretary to put it in the agenda for the next faculty meeting.[2720] Students and student or-

---

2713. Vause, *Foundations for Excellence*, *supra* n. 308, at 337.

2714. The official standards of approval promulgated by the American Bar Association are located in the Stetson College of Law Library, Gulfport, Florida.

2715. Vause, *Foundations for Excellence*, *supra* n. 308, at 337. Not all faculty members were permitted to vote on these matters during the Dillon era, only those who were tenured. Under the Bruce Jacob deanship, the appointment, retention, promotion and tenure decisions began to be made by the entire full-time faculty, both tenured and un-tenured members. *See* Interview by Michael I. Swygert, Prof. Emeritus, Stetson U. College of L., with Robert Batey, Prof. of L., Stetson U. College of L., (Apr. 8, 2004 35) (on file at Stetson U. College of L., Gulfport, Fla.) [hereinafter *Batey Interview*].

2716. *See generally* Vause, *Dillon Years*, *supra* n. 2581, at 27; Minutes of the Stetson College of Law Faculty for the years 1975 through 1980 (on file at Stetson U. College of L., Gulfport, Fla.).

2717. Vause, *Dillon Years*, *supra* n. 2581.

2718. *Id.*

2719. *Judge Schaeffer Interview*, *supra* n. 2299, at 34.

2720. Silvia Manzanero, Paralegal, Stetson U. College of L., Discussion with Richard T. Dillon, Dean Emeritus, Stetson U. College of L. (Aug. 20, 2005) [*Aug. 20 Dillon-Manzanero Discussion*].

ganizations also were given the privilege of appearing before the faculty at its scheduled meetings.

When Dillon became dean in 1968, he had no funds to pay for an assistant dean. He knew that Cal Kuenzel was knowledgeable about admissions and was familiar with every aspect of the operation of the registrar's office; that scheduling classes and teaching assignments were Cal's forte; and that he wouldn't provide the students a shoulder to cry on, but he could give them meaningful counseling and advice about most problems they would confront as law students.[2721] Moreover, Dillon was impressed by Kuenzel's having recently earned a doctor of jurisprudence degree from the University of Illinois, and by the publication of his authoritative work, *The Florida Uniform Commercial Code.*[2722] Last, but not least, Kuenzel had by then become a close friend of Dillon.[2723] Thus, no other choice for assistant dean was conceivable and, consequently, Dillon appointed Kuenzel to that post, effective November 1, 1969, fifteen months after Dillon himself had become dean.[2724]

Over the next twelve years, Dillon and Kuenzel, together with the faculty, charted the future course of Stetson College of Law. In the process, the school became financially more secure and academically more respectable. Naturally, along the way disagreements over policy arose. Alumna Susan Schaeffer, a member of the law faculty for a short time during this era, says that if she, Cal Kuenzel, and Paul Barnard were opposed to a particular proposal Dillon wanted to bring to the faculty, the three of them controlled enough votes to defeat it.[2725] Dillon, however, was aware of this potential "political block," Schaeffer says, and he would "take the matter off the agenda, and wait until he had the votes."[2726] In any event, whatever the internal politics were, a more significant point for the school's history was Dillon's establishing a shared faculty governance aptly described as "one of the hallmarks of his administration."[2727]

b. Emphasis on Scholarship

Throughout the Sebring years, the faculty engaged in minimal research and produced only meager scholarship. This was not due to any collective lack of

2721. *Id.*

2722. *Id.*

2723. *Judge Schaeffer Interview*, *supra* n. 2299, at 34.

2724. *Kuenzel New Assistant Dean Will Teach,* 13 Stetson Law. 1, 4 (Dec. 1969).

2725. *Judge Schaeffer Interview*, *supra* n. 2299, at 34.

2726. *Id.*

2727. Vause, *Dillon Years, supra* n. 2581, at 27.

ambition; rather it was because the small number of full-time faculty members had to instruct multiple courses to cover the required curriculum. As regards scholarship, Dean Gary Vause made the following assessment:

> The truth of the matter was that no one had enough time for serious research and writing projects. While there were a few notable exceptions, most faculty members were preoccupied with an enormous teaching load in a wide variety of unrelated subjects. The dual tasks of keeping current in the law and preparing for class constituted a full-time job.[2728]

(1) Library Books Increase Ninefold

Another hindrance to scholarly production was the library's meager holdings, consisting of fewer than 18,000 books in 1954 when the school relocated to Gulfport. One consequence was that neither students nor faculty could conduct in-depth comparative or theoretical research. When Harold Sebring and Walter Mann convinced Charles A. Dana to provide funds for the new Dana Library,[2729] Sebring foresaw a day when the Stetson law library would be filled with the needed materials to properly serve faculty and students as a comprehensive legal research center.[2730] In contrast to the situation in 1954, by 1969, the year after Dillon became dean, the Dana library held 59,400 volumes.[2731] When Dillon left the dean's office to return to full-time teaching, the number of volumes had grown to 165,182.[2732] Only one year earlier, the number had been 150,000 volumes, meaning that the collection had grown ten percent in one year.[2733]

Thus, over the twenty-six years of the combined Sebring and Dillon deanships, the library volume count had risen ninefold from what it had been in 1955. In his early years as dean, Sebring had no library staff except for a faculty member who served as part-time librarian. In contrast, by the end of the Dillon era, the library staff consisted of three professional librarians, four clerical assistants, and ten student assistants.[2734] Dillon made sure that Sebring's

---

2728. Vause, *Foundations of Excellence*, *supra* n. 308, at 337, 338.

2729. *See supra* nn. 2117–2125 and accompanying text.

2730. *Jan. 29 Dillon Discussion*, *supra* n. 1969.

2731. *Plans Being Prepared for Library Expansion*, 12 Stetson Law. 2, 2 (May 1969).

2732. J. Lamar Woodard, *Report on Charles A. Dana Law Library* (Mar. 31, 1981) (on file with Richard T. Dillon, Dean Emeritus, Stetson U. College of L., Gulfport, Fla.).

2733. *150,000th Library Book Accessioned in March; Volume Count Has Doubled in Last Seven Years*, 24 Stetson Law. 1, 3 (May 1980).

2734. *Id.*

vision of a library research center was fulfilled. Dillon and Law Librarian and Professor Emeritus of Law J. Lamar Woodard continued assembling essential resources needed to facilitate faculty and student scholarly research and writing. Dillon also bettered the institution's scholarly environment by lightening faculty teaching loads during the latter years of his deanship. Moreover, he went one step further—he initiated faculty sabbaticals.

(2) Sabbaticals; Faculty Support; Scholarship

Today, faculty sabbaticals are commonplace throughout American legal education, but that was not always the case. Not until the 1970s did Stetson College of Law adopt a formalized sabbatical policy permitting a faculty member, after a specified period of employment, to apply for a paid leave of absence, a policy that has continued through the present.[2735] In recent years, however, the requirements for a faculty member applying for a paid sabbatical have become more rigorous than they had been earlier. Today, administrators and faculty understand that sabbaticals have to be earned and are expected to involve a significant academic and scholarly activity. At one point in the school's history, various faculty members believed that a sabbatical was a right that they had earned for time spent in teaching—in essence, deferred compensation for "being around" for the required period of time (usually seven years). This is not the case at Stetson today.

In addition to research sabbaticals, Dillon assisted faculty scholarship by adding Faculty Support Services. During Sebring's deanship, the faculty had little, if any, secretarial support. The school could not afford it. Dean Sebring had one full-time secretary, while the assistant dean and faculty had none until 1963. From 1963 until 1968, Dorothy Bishop was the sole secretary for the assistant dean and for "the entire faculty."[2736] Of course, there were neither computers nor word processors, let alone electronic databases for locating legal materials. Gary Vause has noted: "No one could fault Stetson law faculty members prior to the late 1970s for lack of scholarship."[2737] The faculty worked at a distinct disadvantage when it came to scholarly writings. They had no research assistants or, for that matter, even telephones in their offices. During Dillon's deanship, he established a secretarial pool for the faculty, installed

2735. Vause, *Dillon Years, supra* n. 2581, at 27. Prior to sabbaticals, the only way a Stetson professor could leave for graduate study or to research was to ask the dean for an unpaid leave of absence.

2736. *Aug. 20 Dillon-Manzanero Discussion, supra* n. 2720.

2737. *Id.*

phones in each office, and began a student research assistance program, all intended to promote the faculty's scholarship.[2738]

Did these changes demonstrably affect the faculty's scholarly productivity? Without question. Reference Librarian and Adjunct Professor Sally Waters conducted a study of Stetson law faculty scholarly publications over three time spans: 1970–75, 1975–80, and 1980–85. She compared the last two five-year periods with the 1970–75 period as the base.[2739] Waters found that the average number of faculty publications tripled during the 1975–80 time span, then quadrupled between 1980–85, over the base period of 1970–75.[2740]

During the thirteen-year Sebring deanship, the faculty produced little in the way of scholarship, though professors Barnard, Booker, Cushman, Dixon, Kuenzel, and Milledge each published at least one piece. During Dillon's subsequent thirteen-year deanship, the number of faculty engaged in scholarly work increased dramatically, as did the overall number of works published. Professor Tom Marks was the most prodigious author during the 1970s and 1980s.[2741] While only five Stetson professors published articles during the 1955–65 decades, thirty-five did so during the 1975–85 time frame.[2742]

c. *Relations with Students*

(1) "Life Grants Nothing Without Hard Work"

Over two thousand years ago, the Roman poet Horace (Quintus Horatius Flaccus) wrote: "Life grants nothing to us mortals without hard work."[2743] No one in legal education doubts that law school is serious business and that it places a premium on hard work. For a long time at Stetson College of Law, students understood that they had to make great efforts just to stay in school,

---

2738. *Id.*

2739. Vause, *Foundations of Excellence, supra* n. 308, at 338 n. 141.

2740. *Id.*

2741. *See e.g. Recent Writing Activity by Faculty*, 17 Stetson Law. 1, 2 (Aug. 1974).

2742. Vause, *Foundations of Excellence, supra* n. 308, at 338. During the period of 1975–85, faculty members who published law review articles, books, or other legal materials included deans Richard Dillon and Bruce Jacob, and professors Howard Oleck, Calvin Kuenzel, Thomas Marks, Gary Vause, Jerome Latimer, Ruth Thurman, Robert Batey, Jon Bruce, Millard Clark, Everett Cushman, James Byrne, Kenneth Deacon, Edward Craig, Terry Deutsch, Mary Greenwood, McKinley Smiley, Harry Fogle, James Falco, Robert Bickel, McGruder Farris, Randolph Monsur, Elvin Lashbrooke, Michael Swygert, Jonathan Alpert, Charles McCarter, Beverly Greenley, James J. Brown, Michael Finch, Mark Brown, Suzanne Armstrong, Diane Clark, and William Eleazer.

2743. John Bartlett, *Familiar Quotations* 106–117 (15th edit., Emily Morison Beck ed., 15th ed. Little, Brown & Co. 1980).

let alone excel, as large numbers each year were excluded for academic deficiency.[2744] Alumna Judge Susan Schaeffer, '71, describes her experience when she began law school at Stetson:

> When they said, "Look to your right; look to your left. One of you students won't be here [at graduation]," that was the absolute truth and that's what the students expected ... I worked really hard as a student because I didn't know [if I would be one of those] "gone."
> [F]or the first semester, I just worked as hard as I could work. I thought I'd see just what happens and then I'd see if I was going to make it. When the grades came out, I was number two in the class. So then I knew I was going to make it. I just had to work hard. [Later] I was fortunate enough to graduate cum laude and first in my class.[2745]

Not only did the students work hard in the 1970s, so did Dean Richard T. Dillon. Professor Robert Bickel (an assistant dean during Dillon's era) comments that when "Richard was working in his office, he was the epitome of productivity,"[2746] adding that Dillon seemed to embody the adage: "If you're not eating or sleeping, you should be working."[2747] But that was not the entire case, as there is a page two in describing Dillon's life at Stetson.

True, Dillon worked hard, but he also spent considerable non-working time with students, much of it on Stetson's tennis courts. Typically, he and students arrived on campus around 7 a.m., to play tennis until 8:15 to 8:30.[2748] Dillon then went to his office to begin the day's work.[2749] Among students Dillon recalls playing with were Christian Searcy, Sr., Richard Rahdert, Dan Burton, Charles Morachnick, and Joe Chambers.[2750] Chris Searcy and Dillon regularly scheduled matches throughout the time Chris was a student.

In addition to playing tennis with students most mornings, for over ten years Dillon took part in student-sponsored tennis tournaments.[2751] In 1972,

2744. *See Judge Schaeffer Interview*, *supra* n. 2299.

2745. *Id.*

2746. Interview by Michael I. Swygert, Prof. Emeritus, Stetson U. College of L., with Robert Bickel, Prof. of L., Stetson U. College of L (Apr. 14, 2004). [hereinafter *Bickel Interview*].

2747. *Id.*

2748. *Jan. 29 Dillon Discussion*, *supra* n. 1969.

2749. *Id.*

2750. *Id.*

2751. Michael I. Swygert, Prof. Emeritus, Stetson U. College of L., Conversation with Richard T. Dillon, Dean Emeritus, Stetson U. College of L. (July 24, 2005) [hereinafter *July 24 Dillon Conversation*].

he and his partner, Gill Olson, won the doubles championship, after having played seven matches against seven different teams.[2752] Dillon still cherishes the trophy, saying, "it is one of my favorite awards."[2753]

Still, working hard to push the school forward was Dillon's principal preoccupation. Stetson law professor Jerome Latimer (who joined the faculty in the 1970s) remembers that though Dillon was "relatively autocratic and fairly controlling, ... [he] got things done."[2754] Indeed he did. Professor Bickel declares: "Dillon was the right man at that time."[2755]

(2) Student-Faculty Relations

As an educator, Dillon during his deanship believed that faculty members need to maintain a professional relationship with their students, and, correspondingly, that students need to respect their professors.[2756] Dillon perceived how students' respect for their instructors could be diminished by faculty members "hanging out with students and drinking alcoholic beverages with them."[2757]

Dillon's core belief should not be interpreted as meaning a faculty member should not fraternize with students; it does mean, however, that those student-faculty activities that might affect, or even have the appearance of affecting, a teacher's professional responsibility to evaluate student performance in accordance with all other students, should be off limits.[2758] For the record, Stetson College of Law has a professional standard applicable to faculty that prohibits any dating or sexual relationship between a professor and a student enrolled in the College.[2759]

In the 1970s, many students felt that the faculty was standoffish.[2760] At Stetson law school during the 1950s, 1960s, and 1970s, academic attrition was

2752. *Id.*

2753. *Id.*

2754. Interview by Michael I. Swygert, Prof. Emeritus, Stetson U. College of L., with Jerome C. Latimer, Prof. of L., Stetson U. College of L. 12 (Apr. 2, 2004) [hereinafter Latimer Interview].

2755. *Bickel Interview*, *supra* n. 2746, at 31.

2756. *July 24 Dillon Conversation*, *supra* n. 2751.

2757. *Id.*

2758. *Id.*

2759. Full-Time Faculty Policies, *Consensual Relations Policy*, (Stetson U. College of L., 2005). "[T]he University has adopted a policy to prohibit consensual relations and to place all employees 'on notice' that the University views consensual relationships as unwise and of a high risk, especially when students are involved." *Id.*

2760. Professor Robert Batey said in an interview that he did not favor faculty keeping "a distance from students," saying that in his opinion to do so is "to imply that we're some-

quite high. Alumna Susan Schaeffer notes that one-third of her entering class failed to graduate.[2761] This weeding-out process affected student attitudes. Schaeffer explains:

> We lost a lot of students, and the attitude at that time in the student body was not good. You lost a lot of your friends, and the sense at Stetson at that time, by a lot of alumni, was that they weeded out too many people."[2762]

Along the same line, Professor Tom Marks comments:

> For a very long time, there was [at Stetson] what might be called an era of bad feelings because of academic attrition and the real pressures put on the students. I mean it was tough here. It really was, because the teachers were hard and to some extent may have appeared to be unfeeling.[2763]

Dillon agrees with statements describing the faculty in the 1960s and 1970s as demanding, pointing out that it was the faculty's responsibility to prepare students to enter a regulated profession, one that serves members of the public who became either "beneficiaries or victims" of their lawyers.[2764] Despite this reasoned justification for Stetson law professors demanding students work hard and be graded rigorously, many students left the law school with strong negative feelings. Professor Marks remembers going to alumni meetings where several graduates at that point said they "wanted nothing to do with Stetson."[2765]

One who never turned her back on Stetson is Judge Schaeffer, who found law school to be "very difficult, [because] the professors were tough and had very high expectations for us.[2766] Years later, and at the pinnacle of her career as a lawyer and judge,[2767] Schaeffer concluded that the demands of law school "made me more appreciative of what I gave up to get there," adding, "we were conditioned to excel; to always be better prepared than anyone else."[2768]

---

how different from the students. I was just unable to do that." *Batey Interview*, *supra* n. 2715, at 21.

2761. *Judge Schaeffer Interview*, *supra* n. 2299, at 19.

2762. *Id.*

2763. *Marks Interview*, *supra* n. 2471, at 35.

2764. *July 25 Dillon Conversation*, *supra* n. 1986.

2765. *Marks Interview*, *supra* n. 2471, at 35. Some students began a "I'll never give a dime" club, according to Bruce Jacob and Tom Marks.

2766. Susan Shulins, *Women of Stetson, Creating a Foundation for Change* 7 (ten-page brochure 2003).

2767. *See infra* nn. 2967–2969 and accompanying text.

2768. Shulins, *supra* n. 2766, at 7.

11.4 Raising Academic Standards

a. Tightening Admissions

During the deanship of Harold Sebring, the school's need for tuition revenues kept admissions standards lower than the dean and faculty would have preferred.[2769] To say that many students did not graduate is to understate the realities. On some occasions, the attrition exceeded fifty percent.[2770] For example, in 1954, of fifty-five newly enrolled first-year students, only twenty-six graduated three years later.[2771]

In contrast to the Sebring deanship of the 1950s and 1960s, during the 1970s, Dillon was able to institute a "more rigorous screening of applicants."[2772] He and Kuenzel understood that what the College of Law needed above all was a higher-quality student body, not just to lower the rate of academic failure, but also to enhance the interactive learning environment for all students in the classroom. They understood that the better academic students pull up the level of understanding and performance of those below.

Wallace L. Storey, a 1959 graduate of Stetson law school, witnessed the transition to higher standards. After graduating, Storey taught one year on Sebring's faculty, then served nearly two decades on both the College of Law Board of Overseers and the Dana Law Foundation, a period encompassing the entire Dillon administration.[2773] In an interview with co-author Gary Vause, Storey recalled:

> As dean, [Dillon] stood his ground against those who wanted to relax enrollment requirements for economic reasons. He maintained that excellence and only excellence would sustain Stetson University College of Law over the long term. His leadership and unrelenting insistence on quality over quantity proved to be the making of a first-rate school.[2774]

The evidence bears out Storey's recollections. From a rate of attrition that exceeded fifty percent in 1967, the numbers fell to approximately thirty-three

2769. Vause, *Dillon Years, supra* n. 2581, at 27.

2770. *Id.*

2771. *May 4 Dillon Interview, supra* n. 1885; *see also* Vause, *Foundations for Excellence, supra* n. 308 at 332.

2772. Vause, *Foundations for Excellence, supra* n. 308; *see also Dillon Jan. 29 Discussion, supra* n. 1969.

2773. *Raleigh Greene New President of Law Center Foundation,* 25 Stetson Law. 2 (May 1981).

2774. *See* Vause, *Dillon Years, supra* n. 2581, at 27.

percent by 1971.[2775] A decade later, near the end of Dillon's deanship, the attrition rate had fallen to around fifteen percent.[2776]

In January 2005, Dean Emeritus Richard T. Dillon reflected on his deanship in a conversation with co-author Michael Swygert, and remarked, "I can say without a moment's hesitancy that raising standards for admission was the greatest challenge of my administration."[2777] A statistical analysis of entering class credentials and the rate of academic attrition proves he succeeded. In meeting this challenge, Dillon singles out his colleague, Calvin Kuenzel, whom Dillon describes as having made an "enormous contribution to increasing the school's academic standards."[2778]

Dillon's and Kuenzel's persistent pursuit of higher admissions criteria was significantly assisted by a sharp increase in student applications during the 1970s, especially in reference to the number of women applying to law schools. In a 1981commencement address, Dillon enthusiastically noted that women represented more than fifty percent of the spring entering class.[2779] Indeed, a higher number of female students, and an increase in applications, higher admission standards, rigorous grading, and Dillon's steadfastness in not falling to the temptation of lowering standards to bring in more students, all contributed to the rise in the academic quality of the Stetson College of Law. It was a crucial step forward.

b. Results

Measuring the quality of the education that students receive in law school is, of course, best reflected years later in their career achievements. Using that as the measure, Stetson law graduates have received a legal education that prepared them well for their profession.[2780] A more immediate indicator of the

2775. *Judge Schaeffer Interview*, *supra* n. 2299, at 38.

2776. These figures are based on a comparison of the enrollment of students in the spring semester of their first year with the number of that class who graduated. *See also* Vause, *Foundations for Excellence*, *supra* n. 308 at 335.

2777. *Jan. 29 Dillon Interview*, *supra* n. 1969.

2778. *Id.*

2779. Richard Dillon, *Commencement Address* 3 (Stetson U. College of L., May 9, 1981) (on file at Stetson U. College of L., Gulfport, Fla.).

2780. Indicative of this success are the large number of Stetson College of Law graduates who are or have been judges, prosecutors, public defenders, legislators, successful private practitioners, partners in well-known law firms, business entrepreneurs, and the counsel to major corporations and other businesses. These successes are found in the records of the alumni of the Stetson College of Law in Gulfport. In one area of practice, Stetson law graduates have had a particularly remarkable success throughout the school's 100 plus

quality of law school training—certainly not as important as the real-world achievements of its school's graduates—is the school's student bar passage rate on bar examinations. Applying that measure of a law school's competency in preparing students for the bar examination, data provide strong evidence that during the Dillon era, Stetson College of Law performed well. In contrast to the early years of Sebring's administration, when Stetson's success on the Florida bar examination was mediocre,[2781] from the late 1950s onward, Stetson law graduates' first-time rate of passage of the Florida bar examinations increased dramatically, leading all other Florida law schools in most of the years between 1963 and 1968,[2782] and continues on into the Dillon and Jacob administrations.[2783]

In assessing the numerical medians of entering students in the 1970s, one sees that the overall quality of Stetson law students improved throughout the decade.[2784] In 1972, the 108 first-year students enrolled the College of Law had a class median grade-point average (GPA) of 1.9 on a 3.0 scale, and a median LSAT score of "less than 600."[2785] In comparison, by 1979 the statistical indicia of the overall quality of the student body reflected significant increases. As

---

years—the large number of successful and recognized civil and criminal trial attorneys. William Eleazer, *Trial Advocacy at Stetson: The First Hundred Years*, 30 Stetson L. Rev. 243, 243 (2000) [hereinafter Eleazer, *Trial Advocacy*].

2781. *See supra* n. 2541–2545 and accompanying text.

2782. *See e.g. Stetson's Bar Passage Rate Was 83% on the August 1958 Examination—36 Stetson Grads Pass Bar*, 2 Stetson L. News 3 (Nov. 1958); *92% on the 1963 March Exam; 100% on August 1963 Exam; 97% on March 1964 Exam—Bar Exams No Bar to College of Law Grads*, 7 Stetson Law. 3 (July 1964); *100% on March 1965 Exam—Score: Stetson 100% on March Bar Exam*, 8 Stetson Law. 4 (June 1965); *97% on August 1966 Exam—Exam Results Reveal Stetson Grads Excel*, 10 Stetson Law. 7 (Nov. 1966); *100% on March 1966 Exam, 100% on March 1967 Exam—Stetson Again Hits Jackpot: Grads Excel on Bar Exam, 100 Percent Passing*, 10 Stetson Law. 7 (May 1967); *98% on the August 1967 Exam—Stetson Grads Again Lead Bar Examinees*, 11 Stetson Law. 7 (Nov. 1967).

2783. *See e.g. Stetson's Success was 100% on the August 1969 Bar Examination—100%, 43 Try, 43 Pass Latest Bar Examination*, 13 Stetson Law. 4 (Dec. 1969); *100% on March 1970 Exam—Successful Candidates, Spring Candidates Pass Spring Bar Examination*, 13 Stetson Law. 3 (July 1970); *100%, Feb. 1971 Exam—Enrollment Records Shattered Through 1970–1971*, 14 Stetson Law. 3 (May 1971).

2784. These numbers in themselves, of course, do not assure that the students with high numbers will succeed in law school while those with lower numbers will fail or end up near the bottom of the class. In every year, students with high paper credentials do poorly and those whose numbers may be described as marginal exceed spectacularly. Still, in a large sample, those having higher GPA and LSAT scores do generally do better than those whose scores and grades are lower.

2785. *Glance Backward, supra* n. 2600, at 7.

reported in the *Stetson Lawyer,* the median undergraduate grade-point average of the entire student body, comprising 486 students, incremented to 3.15 on a 4.0 scale (tantamount to a B+), while the median LSAT was then over 600, significantly above the fiftieth percentile score of 500 on the LSAT range of 200 to 800.[2786] The College of Law always attracted highly qualified students, but beginning in the Sebring era and accelerating during the Dillon administration, the proportion of better qualified students to the entire student body increased. When Dillon became dean, the College's Bulletin indicated that a 1.25 GPA on a 3.0 scale and an LSAT score of at least 400 were minimum requirements for admission.[2787] The minimum numbers rose by the end of his deanship.

Among the factors causing the median academic credentials of entering Stetson students to go up was the school's decision, beginning in 1970, to award half-tuition scholarships to applicants considered to have above average prospects for success.[2788] In 1972, these academic scholarships were extended to student assistants in research and writing and to members of the law review.[2789]

Another factor that contributed to the rise in student quality was Dillon's placing a cap of 500 students on the school's total enrollment. He knew that by keeping the total number of students at a stable level during a period of rising law school applications, the academic quality of the student body should increase, thereby helping to achieve one of his priorities.[2790] Of course, capping enrollment also meant losing potential income from additional students that would have been admitted otherwise. For this and other reasons, Dillon continued to struggle with a budget that was far less than he would have preferred. Professor Tom Marks comments that Dillon's "great accomplishment was to get the law school through some very bad financial times" when the College of Law was operating under a cap in enrollment and in an era of barely rising student tuition.[2791] Nonetheless, the goal of raising academic standards trumped most other considerations. Indeed, throughout the unfolding history of Stetson College of Law, upgrading the academic quality of both students

2786. *Survey of Past Quarter of a Century Shows Abundant Evidence of Qualitative Growth,* 22 Stetson Law. 1, 4 (Feb. 1979).

2787. *Dean Dillon's Administration Characterized by Physical Improvements and Academic Growth,* 25 Stetson Law. 4 (May 1981) [hereinafter *Dillon's Administration*].

2788. *Glance Backward, supra* n. 2600, at 7.

2789. *Id.*

2790. *Jan. 29 Dillon Discussion, supra* n. 1969.

2791. *Marks Interview, supra* n. 2471, at 40, 41.

and faculty turned out—not surprisingly—to be the most crucial undertaking that bore on the school's reputation.[2792]

c. Adjusting the Curriculum: Remedial Writing and New Clinics

A legal education bromide has it that remedial writing is for students who can't write, while law review is for those who can. Though the comparison exaggerates the realities, for a short time it described the situation at the law school. During the Dillon years, both a remedial writing course and a student-edited law review came into existence. Though all Stetson students were required to take a two-hour research and writing course, in the fall of 1968 Dillon and the faculty added a remedial writing course for students who "were deficient in their writing skills."[2793] An article in the *Stetson Lawyer* describes the course:

> Under the direction of Dean Dillon, Stetson may well have taken the lead in the long quest by the country's law schools to find the most effective teaching technique for helping students who ... reveal deficiencies in organizing and writing solutions to legal problems....
>
> Professor Kenneth Evans, in cooperation with Dr. Arthur Pollock, Chairman of Directed Studies at St. Petersburg Junior College, [have] developed a first semester, two-hour course [in] the essentials of proper expression involving legal problems and geared to the legal thought process.[2794]

Legal writing is based in part on effective and efficient legal research. To these ends, in 1980, Stetson College of Law installed its first computer-assisted information-retrieval system—a LEXIS data retrieval terminal located in the Dana Law Library.[2795] This event represents the first step in the College's continuing incorporation of computer technology into every aspect of the institution, a process and emphasis championed and implemented by Woodard.[2796]

Continuing through today, Stetson law school emphasizes computer-assisted research and requires students to become proficient in using personal

---

2792. What Sebring, Dillon, and later Jacob each were able to accomplish during their respective thirteen-year deanships was to lay the foundations for today's Stetson University College of Law. As co-author Gary Vause has put it, they built "the foundations of excellence." *See* Vause, *Foundations for Excellence*, *supra* n. 308.

2793. *New Course Bolsters Basic Writing Skills*, 12 Stetson Law. 2, 2 (Feb. 1969).

2794. *Id.*

2795. Stetson College of Law Purchase Order to Mead Data Control, Inc. (May 8, 1980) (on file at Stetson U. College of L., Gulfport, Fla.).

2796. *See infra* nn. 3093–3104 and accompanying text.

Prosecutor James T. Russell

computers in this process. At the same time, the school continues to emphasize the teaching of legal writing skills. In 2005, Stetson's legal writing program achieved national recognition when *U.S. News & World Report* ranked the College's program among the top four in the nation.[2797] The climb up this mountain began, it seems fair to say, when Dillon and the faculty required a legal writing course back in 1968. During the 1960s and '70s, Stetson's first-year core curriculum, like most other law schools, was similar to what it had been decades earlier.[2798] On the other hand, the number of elective courses in the 1970s expanded dramatically, a reflection of emerging specialties in the law practice.[2799]

During the same late 1960s and throughout the 1970s, however, America's judges and lawyers nudged law schools to place greater emphasis on skills training and clinical education.[2800] Stetson College of Law had initiated clinical instruction in the 1960s.[2801] Then, in the 1970s, the school created a new Prosecution Clinic with encouragement and strong support from the State's Attorney for the Sixth Judicial Circuit, James Russell, a Stetson law graduate

2797. *Stetson Ties as America's Top School for Advocacy; Legal Research and Writing Ties as Nation's Third Best,* 45 Stetson Law. 3, 3 (Spring 2005) [hereinafter *Stetson Ties as America's Top School*].

2798. *See supra* nn. 362–366 and accompanying text.

2799. *See* Vause, *Foundations for Excellence*, *supra* n. 308, at 337.

2800. Stevens, *Law School*, *supra* n. 196, at 216, 240–241.

2801. *See supra* nn. 2443–2445 and accompanying text.

who died in 2005.[2802] With the faculty's approval, Dillon adjusted the school's curriculum to accommodate both clinical (or "practical") instruction with academic (or "doctrinal") classes to better prepare students for the profession of law.[2803]

After the Stetson Public Defender and Prosecutor Clinics were established, Stetson reaped benefits beyond the primary and educational value for students. Not only were Public Defender Robert Jagger and State's Attorney James Russell pleased, so too were members of the region's bench and bar. Judges, lawyers, and public officials sent numerous congratulatory letters and messages to the school.[2804] The favorable reaction removed any doubts in reference to expanding the clinical program of the school. Civil legal aid clinics were added in Clearwater and St. Petersburg in the early 1970s.[2805]

11.5 The Stetson Law Review *Begins*

In the late 1950s, a few determined Stetson law students had failed to persuade Dean Sebring to start a law review, in part, because they did not assemble a sufficient number of interested and qualified classmates.[2806] That was not, however, the case a decade later. As noted earlier, the number of students both quantitatively and qualitatively rose throughout Dillon's administration.[2807] The faculty knew that to become a prestigious law school, Stetson College of Law needed a student-edited law review.[2808] Emeritus Law Librarian Lamar Woodard explains:

> Dillon understood that for a law school to have any prestige at all, it needed a publication.... Apparently Dean Sebring didn't think that much of a law review, but Dean Dillon did and realized that we needed to ... have a publication. [He] proceeded to set aside the money and get someone in here to supervise it.[2809]

2802. *See Public Defender Clinic,* 1 Prelude 1 (Oct. 29, 1971).

2803. Vause, *Dillon Years, supra* n. 2581, at 27.

2804. *Jan. 29 Dillon Discussion, supra* n. 1969.

2805. Vause, *Dillon Years, supra* n. 2581, at 26.

2806. *See supra* nn. 2532–2536 and accompanying text.

2807. *See infra* n. 3205 and accompanying text.

2808. *Jan. 29 Dillon Discussion, supra* n. 1969.

2809. Robert Batey & Scott William Fitzpatrick, *The Early Years of the Stetson Law Review,* 30 Stetson L. Rev. 213, 215 (2000).

Woodard's statement, though 99% accurate, is not completely so, as Dillon's budget did not have sufficient money to fund the venture. Rather, Dillon relied on the donations from Board of Overseers members William Amory Underhill of Washington, D.C., and J. Ben Watkins of Miami.[2810]

Once the faculty decided to institute a student-edited law review, the overriding issue became how could it develop into a distinctive journal, especially given Stetson's publication would be a late entrant among American law schools in publishing a scholarly journal.[2811] Kuenzel and others understood that Stetson College of Law's reputation would be directly impacted by the journal's quality or lack thereof. Years later, one student noted that Kuenzel "was sensitive" to the pitfalls of a fast start and persuaded his colleagues that the publishing venture should start slowly.[2812]

According to Robert Batey and Scott Fitzpatrick, authors of a history of the *Stetson Law Review,* the faculty decided that to aim for excellence, the review should begin as an "intramural" publication.[2813] No lead articles by legal academicians or practitioners would be included, only the work of students who would research and write casenotes and comments. When completed, the issues would circulate within "the Stetson community until the product was worthy of wider distribution."[2814]

A member of the initial board of editors said, "If we were going to have a law review ... it was to be of a quality that would satisfy Kuenzel's muster." Though Kuenzel was the most ardent supporter of the school publishing a law review, he also was (as the editor's comments make clear) the most demanding critic. An early editor recalls that Kuenzel "was very, very adamant that quality come before any publication."[2815]

Once the faculty made the commitment to start an intramural law review, the first step was to assemble a group of qualified students. During the summer of 1969, Kuenzel and Dillon sought out high-ranking students who had completed their second year of law school, inviting each to help start up a student-edited law review.[2816] To be invited, a student needed to have a grade-point average of 1.75 (a B-minus) or better on a 3.0 scale.[2817] Though only high-ranking

2810. *Id.* at 215 n. 16.

2811. *Id.* at 216.

2812. *Id.*

2813. *Id.*

2814. *Id.* at 217.

2815. *Id.* at 219.

2816. *Id.* at 218.

2817. *Stetson Law Review May Soon Be a Reality*, 13 Stetson Law. 5, 5 (Dec. 1969).

students were eligible for appointment to the board, the faculty decided that any student could submit an article to the editors to be considered for publication.[2818]

Dillon and Kuenzel chose the initial editorial board's members, consisting of Thomas E. Kingcade, editor-in-chief from St. Petersburg; Stephen C. Watson, managing editor from Lakeland; Barry F. Spivey, notes and comments editor from DeLand; and Thomas W. Ulrich, lead articles editor (and a future business manager of the College of Law) from Falls Church, Virginia.[2819] Additionally, four other students were later selected as members of the first editorial board: J. Dana Fogle, Thomas C. Garwood, Jr., Joan LoBianco Walker, and C. Allen Watts.[2820]

The next question: Who would supervise the students? Dean Dillon invited a former law review advisor, Joseph Long, to teach on the Stetson law faculty in the fall of 1969.[2821] The faculty approved his hiring not only to teach corporations, but also to be the faculty advisor to the embryonic *Stetson Intramural Law Review*.[2822] Long was short at Stetson, however, leaving in less than a year to join the faculty at the University of Oklahoma.[2823] His influence on the law review, unlike Kuenzel's, appears to have been minimal.

2818. *Id.*

2819. *Id.* Editor in Chief Thomas Kingcade is a well-known, Board-certified lawyer in the West Palm Beach firm of Kingcade & Campbell. *See* Ltr. from Thomas E. Kingcade, Atty. at L., to W. Gary Vause, Prof., Stetson U. College of L. (Sept. 15, 1987) (on file at Stetson U. College of L., Gulfport, Fla.).

2820. Batey & Fitzpatrick, *supra* n. 2809, at 220. Other members of the board of editors of the *Stetson Intramural Law Review* who published student casenotes or comments included: Wayne L. Hogeboom, W. Scott Lovejoy, III, Bernard J. McCabe, Jr., Donald E. Pellecchia, Wendell L. Schollander, Jr., Edward F. Simpson, Jr., James D. Henry, Jr., Peter Brick, Robert R. Carbonell, Edward D. Foreman, John N. Jenkins, Ronald G. Meyer, A.J. Musial, Jr., David C. Park, Peter W. Rotella, O. Stephen Thacker, II, John P. Warren, Howard M. Zaritsky, Worth T. Blackwell, Keith M. Casto, C. Thomas Ferrara, John A. Friedman, Lawrence E. Fuentes, George D. Lynn, Jr., Robert A. Meade, Jr., Ronald G. Meyer, Philip Padovano Jr., Carlisle Rogers, Jr., Maryin E. Rooks, Cary R. Singletary, Charles R. Stepter, Jr., William H. Walker, John Asbell, W.M. Chanfrau, Timothy G. Hains, William L. Livingston, Jr., James N. Powell, Joseph C. Rubel, Marguerite Smith Stephens, G. Alex Weller, W. Walker, John E. Woodbury, Ron Goldstein, Gary Simon, Gary Trombley, Michael Lenehan, A., Thomas Mihok, Gerald M. Taylor, Harry O. Thomas, Larry Bergman, Jeff Brown, William A. Grimm, Gary A. Carnal, William R. Dickey, William H. Green, Leslie Reicin Stein, William C. Davell, Marsha Griffin Rydberg, J. Brent Walker, James H. Siesky, Alice K. Nelson, Judy A. Schropp Burnett, Jerry E. Aron, Dennis E. Dabroski, Joseph G. Burns, Nelson A. Faerber, Jr., Richard A. Kupfer, Kenneth A. Marra, Stephen C. Page, Paul T. Scheverman, and Archie J. Thomas, III. *Id.*, at 221, 223–224, 226–229, 231.

2821. *Faculty, Staff Enriched by Three New Members*, 13 Stetson Law. 6, 6 (Dec. 1969).

2822. *Id.*

2823. Batey & Fitzpatrick, *supra* n. 2809, at 219.

That was not the case for the new publication itself. In 1970, when the first issue of the *Stetson Intramural Law Review* was published, it had a significant influence on Stetson's students, faculty, and administrators. Batey and Fitzpatrick comment that "the school was apparently not embarrassed, [because] the administration distributed copies of Volume I, Number 1 to the entire graduating class at the awards dinner preceding the spring 1970 [graduation] ceremony."[2824]

The fact that Stetson law students began to write and edit a school law review soon became known among alumni and friends of the College.[2825] An article in the *Stetson Lawyer* described the venture as "the most exciting new undertaking in the College of Law this year."[2826] Upon seeing the first issue in print, the *Stetson Lawyer* called it one of the "most unprecedented accomplishments of the year."[2827] Consisting of ninety-four pages, the issue contained all student-authored work—three comments and seven casenotes.[2828] The ten pieces were divided between articles pertaining to substantive law questions and those addressing litigation problems. Articles dealing with trial issues included questions involving the use of unsworn attorney statements regarding unavailability of witnesses to appear for trial; dismissal of civil suits upon assertion of privilege; the problem of voluntary self-incrimination through interrogation and waiver; and the admissibility of parol evidence to rebut a presumption of law.[2829] Substantive law topics included product liability under the Florida Uniform Commercial Code; government in the sunshine and the public's right to know; negligent misrepresentations giving rise to products liability; whether lecturers have a copyright to their material; community standards for determining obscenity; and what constitutes the criminal possession of marijuana.[2830]

Any new venture typically has a few things go wrong, and that was true of the *Stetson Intramural Law Review*. One of the editors discovered that a student author had submitted a work that was "a pretty gross example of plagiarism."[2831] The student editor explained that the writer had "copied the whole hog article."[2832] Fortunately, the purloined piece never appeared in print.

2824. *Id.* at 221.
2825. *Past Year One of Achievements*, 13 Stetson Law. 1, 1 July 1970.
2826. *Id.*
2827. *Id.*
2828. 1 *Stetson Intramural L. Rev.* 1 (1970).
2829. *Id.*
2830. *Id.*
2831. Batey & Fitzpatrick, *supra* n. 2809, at 225.
2832. *Id.*

Another snafu occurred regarding a student's casenote praising the Florida Supreme Court's reversal of a trial court's conviction of a defendant. The trial judge—whose decision the Supreme Court had overturned—became incensed upon learning of the student's published analysis.[2833] The judge reportedly called the student author at his home and "raised holy hell," after which the judge called the dean and complained (likely with more holiness and less hell). To the credit of Dillon and the faculty, they supported both the actions and the integrity of the law review editors generally and the student author in particular. Nothing in the article could be construed as derogatory about the judge personally, it was decided. The student merely had criticized how the judge seemed to have misapplied the law in a given case. Afterwards, the student author commented that the response of the dean and faculty to the sensitive judge "made us all feel good."[2834]

Then there is the story about the *Review* publishing an article co-authored by a well-know Miami lawyer, J.B. Spence, and by a student from the University of Miami Law School, Jeffrey Roth.[2835] The student author's first name—Jeffrey—was incorrectly spelled in the published article as "Jeffery." Attorney and lead-author J.B. Spence was more than displeased over the misspelling and with other errors, as well, demanding that a corrected version of the entire article be published, along with an apology in a later issue of the *Review*.[2836] The *Review* did so.[2837]

The misspelling of an author's first name likely would have been a rare occurrence during the six years that Professor Elizabeth M. Leeman served as advisor to the intramural periodical. Batey and Fitzpatrick note that throughout this period, Leeman "upgraded the editorial standards" of the *Review*.[2838] About the same time that Volume I, Number 1 came out (1970), Dillon appointed her to the faculty in the dual positions of assistant librarian and assistant professor of law.[2839] Dillon also asked her to serve as the advisor to the *Intramural Law Review*, since the *Review*'s initial advisor, Joseph Long, had resigned from Stetson three months earlier. Thus, Leeman became the first woman advisor of the *Stetson Law Review*. Of greater significance, however, was that she was

---

2833. *Id.*

2834. *Id.*

2835. J.B. Spence & Jeffery [sic] Roth, *Closing the Courthouse Door: Florida's Spurious Claims Statute*, 10 Stetson L. Rev. 398 (1981); *see also* Mary Ann S. Kokoszyna, *June Issue of Law Review Readied for Publication*, 25 Stetson Law. 2, 2 (May 1981).

2836. Batey & Fitzpatrick, *supra* n. 2809, at 236, 237.

2837. *See* J.B. Spence & Jeffrey Roth, *Closing the Courthouse Door: Florida's Spurious Claims Statute,* 11 Stetson L. Rev. 283, 283 n. * (1982).

2838. Batey & Fitzpatrick, *supra* n. 2809, at 236.

2839. *See infra* nn. 2950–2956 and accompanying text.

Elizabeth M. Leeman

the first woman lawyer appointed to the Stetson College of Law faculty, a historical event discussed below.[2840]

As faculty advisor to the *Review,* Leeman meticulously focused on the editorial production of each issue, reading and rereading all manuscripts, and checking organization, punctuation, syntax, spelling, and citation in every submitted writing.[2841] A student editor said that Leeman's critiquing skills were "so outstanding" that she eventually took over most of the editorial functions.[2842] However, that did not sit well with many of the student editors, as they believed Leeman was usurping their editorial prerogatives.[2843] Moreover, the *Review* often came out months late because, some believed, Leeman "did not care how long it took to produce work that met her standards."[2844]

Of less consequence (except for one's health), staff members also complained about "Leeman's incessant smoking," one former editor commenting that "she liked her cigarettes. I'd meet with her; I'd have to brush away the smoke."[2845] Still, not all the *Review*'s staff held negative opinions about their advisor. Several continued to recognize that she contributed, perhaps more

2840. *See infra* n. 2951 and accompanying text.
2841. Batey & Fitzpatrick, *supra* n. 2809, at 226.
2842. *Id.* at 227.
2843. *Id.* at 229.
2844. *Id.* at 230.
2845. *Id.* at 229 n. 28.

than anybody, to raising and maintaining high editorial standards.[2846] Leeman retired from teaching in 1976.[2847] Her expertise was missed.

That fall, Dillon and the faculty hired a new assistant professor, Norman Terry Deutsch, who took Leeman's place as advisor to the *Law Review*.[2848] When he was a law student at the University of Maryland, Deutsch served on the *Maryland Law Review*.[2849] After joining the Stetson faculty, he discovered that the *Stetson Law Review* was not following traditional ways of doing things in effect at more established law reviews. Deutsch assigned the editors to draft a manual of internal procedures and responsibilities, then he oversaw the project.[2850] Deutsch recommended specific provisions be included that were found in law review manuals of other schools. The resulting Stetson manual, Batey and Fitzpatrick observe, required first, that the "Blue Book" citation guide be followed, and second, that the editor-in-chief delegate specific tasks to each member of the staff. The goal of these prescriptions was to establish a standardized citation format and to instill clarity of tasks and work habits that made the law review more professional.[2851] Upon Deutsch's suggestion, the editors also drafted a constitution that the faculty approved.[2852]

In mid-1978, the first issue of the *Stetson Intramural Law Review* produced in accordance with the manual of internal procedures (Volume VII, Number 2) was published.[2853] It turned out to be the final issue in the seven-year history of the intramural edition, and was described as the "breakthrough" issue.[2854] The volume was the largest issue yet published (190 pages). Moreover, it was the first produced entirely by students, with minimal guidance from a faculty advisor.[2855]

2846. *Id.* at 229.

2847. *See infra* n. 3187.

2848. *Id.*

2849. Batey & Fitzpatrick, *supra* n. 2809, at 231.

2850. *Id.*

2851. *Id.*

2852. *Id.* at 85.

2853. *See also Editor's Page*, 7 Stetson Intra. L. Rev. i (1977).

2854. Batey & Fitzpatrick, *Law Review*, *supra* n. 2809, at 234.

2855. The editorial staff and student authors of Volume VII of the *Stetson Intramural Law Review* consisted of: Steven R. Anderson, Ann S. Azdell, William David Dugan, Gary M. Fader, Fred F. Harris, Lucy Harrison Harris, Michael P. Jones, Michael J. Keane, Robin Richards Lane, Carol C. Murphy, Eileen Murphy, Michael L. Reda, Robert S. Schumaker, John Cameron Story, William G. Berzak, Joel T. Daves, IV, Cheryl Flax-Davidson, James C. Hauser, Kevin B. Krauss, Harley K. Look, Jr., John Harrison Rains, III, Julia C. Roberts, and Diane M. Van Keane.

That same year—1978—and at the suggestion of Editor-in-Chief Michael J. Keane and his staff, the *Stetson Law Review* established an award for the best student work published in each issue of the *Review*.[2856] They decided that the prize should be named after the first significant *Review* faculty advisor, Elizabeth M. Leeman, "in recognition of her efforts as the guiding force during her term as faculty advisor."[2857] With annual awards for the best student work in place, and with the successful publication of Volume VII, Number 2, the Stetson law school community recognized that one era of the student publication was ending and that a new one was beginning. On the "Editor's Page" of the last issue of the Intramural publication, the editors proclaimed:

> Established in 1970, the *Stetson Intramural Law Review* has sought to provide the practicing attorney in Florida with current, informative, and noteworthy articles. The Editorial Board is happy to announce that the Review will continue to strive to meet these objectives under a new format. Rather than continue as a strictly in-house publication with limited distribution, the *Review* will begin publishing articles submitted by outstanding members of the legal profession, and distributing on a subscription basis.[2858]

As the planned fall 1978 publication of the renamed *Stetson Law Review* approached, the editors were excited and proud over what some called the "legitimate" journal's birth. A three-column headline on the front page of the law student newspaper, the *Prelude*, proclaimed: "Law Review Plans National Publication."[2859] The story set out an aspirational goal for the editors:

> Both the faculty advisor Professor R. Batey and the Chief Editor Mike Keane feel that the challenge presented by the production of a truly national law review will stimulate a continued improvement in the quality of the articles. The inception and growth of a true law review will require the sincere efforts of all the students who edit and write.[2860]

The initial issue of the new "national" version of the *Stetson Law Review* came out on schedule. For the first time, it contained lead articles not written

---

2856. *Id.*
2857. *Id.*
2858. *Editor's Page*, 7 Stetson L. Rev. i (1978).
2859. Jim Hardman, *Law Review Plans National Publication,* Prelude 1 (Feb. 2, 1978).
2860. *Id.*

by students (though student-authored casenotes and comments continued).[2861] Rather, Stetson law professors Calvin A. Kuenzel and W. Gary Vause authored the two lead articles.[2862]

Within several years, the *Review* published as many as four issues a year. A volume (later called "book" by the staff) often was more than 1,000 pages in length, (one issue exceeded 1,500 pages),[2863] in sharp contrast to the first issue's ninety-four page total.[2864] In time, the *Stetson Law Review* began (and continues) to publish lead articles and comments authored by nationally known jurists,[2865] such as associate justice of the U.S. Supreme Court of the United States, Ruth Bader Ginsberg;[2866] public officials;[2867] and law deans and professors;[2868] as well as internationally renowned figures, including Russian poet Yevgeny Yevtushenko.[2869]

2861. *See* Table of Contents, 8 Stetson L. Rev. (1978).

2862. *See* Calvin A. Kuenzel, *The Bulk-Sales Risk—Who Needs UCC Article 6?*, 8 Stetson L. Rev. 1 (1978); and W. Gary Vause, *Occupational Safety and Health Law for Agricultural Employment*, 8 Stetson L. Rev. 13 (1978).

2863. *See* 30 Stetson L. Rev. (2000).

2864. *See supra* nn. 2824–2828 and accompanying text.

2865. From 1994 through 2004, jurists who published in the *Stetson Law Review* have included Ben F. Overman, Florida Supreme Court; Marvin Aspen, Chief Judge, U.S. District Court, N. Ill.; Thomas M. Reavley, U.S. Court of Appeals, 5th Cir.; Gregory W. Carman, U.S. Court of International Trade; Abner J. Mikva, U.S. Court of Appeal, District of Columbia; Joseph W. Hatchett, U.S. Court of Appeal, 11th Cir.; Charles R. Wilson, U.S. Court of Appeal, 11th Cir.; Philip J. Padovano, Fla. 1st DCA; John M. Scheb, 2nd Fla. DCA; Thomas F. Stringer, Jr., Florida 2nd DCA; and Chris W. Altenbernd, Florida 2nd DCA.

2866. Ruth Bader Ginsburg, *Remarks in Celebration of Stetson's Law Library and Information Center*, 28 Stetson L. Rev. 2, 231–39, (1998).

2867. Robert A. Butterworth, Florida Attorney General.; Lucia A. Dougherty, Miami City Attorney.; James E. Goodby, U.S. Ambassador; Emeline C. Acton, Hillsborough Cty. Attorney.; Herbert W.A. Thiel, Leon City Attorney; Chon-ho Park, Member, International Tribunal, Law of the Sea.

2868. Melvin Eisenberg (Cal. Berkeley), Steven Lubet (Northwestern), John Stephan (Virginia), Jon Bruce (Vanderbilt), Susan Koniak (Boston College), Francis Cullen (Cincinnati), Kenney Hegland (U. Arizona), Edward Spurgeon (Georgia), Frank Macchiarola (Cardozo), Naomi Cahn (George Washington), Lawrence Frolik (Pittsburgh), Laura Rothstein (Houston), Gary Pavela (Maryland), Michael Gordon (Florida), John Spanogle (George Washington), Ellen Wertheimer (Villanova), Edward Ohlbaum (Temple), Edward Imwinkelreid (Cal. Davis), Peter Salsich (St. Louis), Patrick Longan (Mercer), Larry Teply (Creighton), Gary Gildin (Dickinson/Penn State), Jack Hiller (Valparaiso), Katherine Butler (S. Carolina), Mary Radford (Georgia St.), Roberta S. Karmel (Brooklyn), Seymour Moskowitz (Valparaiso), Franklin Gevurtz (McGeorge/Un. of Pacific), John Martinez (Utah), and David Callies (Hawaii).

2869. Yevgeny Yevtushenko, *Russia's Amateur Justice*, 25 Stetson L. Rev., 1121–29 (1996).

During the past dozen years, the *Stetson Law Review* has published on average two symposia a year, including one pertaining to state and local government law in Florida.[2870] Other symposia have focused on elder law; limited liability companies; voting rights; higher education law; economic sanctions, trade controls and foreign policy; corporate philanthropy; state constitutional law; guardianship law; international environmental law; labor law; litigation ethics and professionalism; economic relations with Latin America; criminal prosecutions; and comparative corporate governance.[2871]

Over the past thirty-five years, the *Stetson Law Review* has grown into a highly professional and respected journal, one that has contributed to legal academia and to the legal profession.

11.6 Student Activities and Concerns

a. The Prelude

During Dillon's era, when the *Stetson Law Review* began, the majority of the Stetson students took part in traditional school activities, including: legal fraternities;[2872] Inns of Court banquets;[2873] client counseling competitions;[2874] moot court competitions;[2875] Honor Court;[2876] and the "Lawyerettes" group,[2877] in 1973 renamed "Law Wives"[2878] (which should not be confused

---

2870. The *Review's* symposium editor and Professor James J. Brown, along with the Local Government Section of The Florida Bar, together put this special issue together.

2871. The above list was provided by Legal Assistant/Paralegal Michael Sepe of the *Stetson Law Review* staff.

2872. *See e.g.* Peter Keating, *Phi Alpha Delta Law Fraternity*, 4 Prelude 9 (Apr. 30, 1973). The same issue also refers to Delta Theta Phi and Phi Delta Phi fraternities.

2873. *See e.g. Varied Programs Presented at Inns of Court Dinners; Speakers Include the Attorney General, a County Solicitor, a Conservationist, Practicing Lawyers*, 14 Stetson Law. (May 1971); Tom Drage, *Inns of Court, 1 Stetson College of Law*, Prelude 3 (Oct. 15, 1971).

2874. *See e.g. Client Counseling Competition Nears*, Prelude (Nov. 8, 1978); *Client Counseling Competition*, 20 Stetson Law. 7 (Aug. 1977).

2875. Stetson students Mike Keane and Steve Whitaker won the regional competition two years in a row. *See* Mike Keane, *Whitaker Moot Court Winners*, Prelude 1 (Sep. 30, 1977); *see also Stetson Moot Court Teams Seek to Repeat 1970 Triumph*, 14 Stetson Law. 2 (May 1971). "Law students David A. Demers, C. Allen Watts, Thomas C. Garwood, Jr., and George Meehan" represented Stetson. *Stetson Moot Court Teams*, *supra* n. 2875, at 2.

2876. *See e.g. Honor Court*, 3 Prelude 7 (Oct. 1972).

2877. *See e.g.* Vicki Rubel, *Wives*, 3 Prelude 1, 6 (Oct. 1972).

2878. Laura Alcott, Stetson *Women's Association Welcomes New Wives*, 4 Prelude (July 4, 1973).

with "Women in Law," an organization comprised of Stetson women law students).[2879] Of course, since law students have a propensity for partying, this modus vivendi continued throughout the 1970s. The merry-making took place at several nearby "watering holes," which included the "Blinker," "Shadracks," "Beach Pub," "Nick's," "Ringside Café," and "Gulfport on the Rocks."[2880] In addition to traditional activities, students found new enterprises to pursue.

In October 1971, Stetson students began a campus newspaper called the *Prelude*.[2881] In the publication's initial issue, Editor-in-Chief Robert Kunkel explained why it was named the *Prelude*. "It has a musical ring to it; it's classy; it would mean we are starting off on the right note."[2882] Exhausting his supply of puns, Kunkel noted that going to law school represents the beginning of a lifetime of study and, therefore, the commencement of a law student's professional career. As to the *Prelude*'s function, Kunkel wrote:

> There are [students] who feel that the administration is a Group [sic] of individuals who sit in the bell tower looking down and thinking of ways to zap members of the student body.... The *Prelude*, this beginning, has a very real importance at Stetson. We have the opportunity to have a two way street of thought.[2883]

The initial issue fulfilled that goal. Informative articles by Dean Dillon on the status of the law school, and by Student Bar Association President Dave Demers (later Chief Judge of the Florida Sixth Judicial Circuit) on the SBA's plans for the upcoming school year, appeared.[2884]

Stetson law students wrote and disseminated the *Prelude* throughout the Dillon administration and into the late 1980s. No serious problems with the student paper arose during Dillon's deanship. But a serious problem did develop near the end of Jacob's deanship when the paper's professional standards and decency fell. The following excerpt is typical:

2879. *See e.g.* Cheryl Flax-Davidson, *Women in Law Hosts Interesting Speakers*, *Prelude* 6 (Nov. 8, 1977).

2880. *See e.g. Judge Schaeffer Interview*, *supra* n. 2299, at 37. "[When a Stetson law student] I was a fun loving girl. I'd like to go out and have my drinks. We'd go over to Gulfport on the Rocks and we'd party." *Id*; *see also Entertainment:* Prelude *Guide to Extracurricular Fun*, Prelude 3 (Nov. 8, 1977). The article said that the "Blinker has served Stetson students since 1954." *Id*.

2881. *See* Bob Kunkel, *Editors' Notes*, 1 Prelude 1 (Oct. 1. 1971).

2882. *Id*.

2883. *Id*.

2884. *Id*. at 2.

> In order to prove that the editors give every point of view an opportunity to speak, we now publish the following garbage. [There follows a short letter with sections marked out with a black marker, after which the editors continue] The editorial staff refuses to print portions of this letter. We reserve the right to edit whatever the hell we feel deserves editing. The Prelude dictatorship lives![2885]

The same issue has a series of fictional "Valentine Personals." Each of the eight "personals" refers to sexual acts. On the same page, a personal advice column titled "Ask the Expert," authored by Ima [followed by an obscenity]. To describe the column as unprofessional and in poor taste may understate the matter. In the late 1980s, the *Prelude* ceased publication. There has been no student-edited law school newspaper at Stetson since.

b. Student Skit Nights

Another new student enterprise—though short lived—began during Dillon's administration, an annual social and drinking fraternity event called "skit night."[2886] Held off campus (where alcohol could be served), the annual combination of drama, music, comedy, and perhaps most of all, sarcasm, revealed that many law students had "show business talent."[2887] But the skits also suggested that certain students had gripes about their law school experience. One professor commented that the student skit nights in the late 1970s and early 1980s were "an outlet for student dissatisfaction."[2888]

One skit that Professor Batey remembers well was a takeoff of *The Wizard of Oz.* The movie's characters were renamed to resemble those of faculty members. For example, the dog "Toto" became "Bic-Key," suggestive of the name of Professor Dickel.[2889] Then the students changed the character called the "Wizard" to the "Dean," a veiled reference to Dean Dillon.[2890] So far, so good, but when the lyrics of the story's principal song—"We're off to see the wizard because, because, because, because of the wonderful things he does"—were changed to, "He is the dean because, because," (pause) "because of the very few things he does, he does, the very few things he does," not all found it amusing.[2891] Besides Dillon, many Stetson faculty members were

2885. Prelude 6 (Feb. 24, 1988).
2886. The precise year when student skit nights began is unclear.
2887. *Batey Interview*, *supra* n. 2715, at 22.
2888. *Id.*
2889. *Id.* at 23.
2890. *Id.*
2891. *Id.*

spoofed at the student skit night, including professors Kuenzel, Thurman, and Oleck.

c. Student Evaluations of Faculty

Even though today student evaluations of faculty teaching is the universal norm throughout higher education, it was not always so. At Stetson College of Law, students had no school-sponsored system for evaluation of their professors from its opening in 1900 until 1982, when an institutionalized practice began. At that point, shortly after Bruce Jacob became dean, the school implemented an anonymous system of student evaluations.[2892] Throughout Dillon's administration, however, there existed little, if any, interest by the faculty to obtain students' evaluations of their performance.

But then, in the fall of 1979, the American Bar Association and Association of American Law Schools conducted one of its periodic site inspections of the College of Law, a process that occurs at all ABA-approved law schools at least once every seven years.[2893] According to an article appearing in the student newspaper, the *Prelude*:

> Some consternation about the lack of teacher evaluations was reportedly expressed by a member of the accreditation team which recently visited Stetson. Discussions with the [ABA and AALS] accreditation board revealed that faculty evaluations are often mandatory at other law schools and that the board was surprised to find no such program at Stetson.[2894]

It should be noted, however, that the ABA had no rule or standard that law schools had to conduct student evaluations. Even before the ABA and AALS inspection team visited Stetson, certain newer members of the law faculty were urging their colleagues to institute student evaluations of faculty teaching. Three professors—Bob Batey, Jon Bruce, and Mike Swygert—before coming to Stetson were members of other law school faculties[2895] where students routinely evaluated faculty.[2896] Nonetheless, no formal proposal for student eval-

2892. *See infra* nn. 3252–3263 and accompanying text.

2893. *Students Meet With Accreditation Committee*, Prelude 1 (Apr. 1980).

2894. *Future of Teacher Evaluations Is in Doubt*, Prelude 2 (Feb. 1980) [hereinafter *Teacher Evaluations*].

2895. Before joining the Stetson law faculty, Robert Batey was a professor at West Virginia University College of Law; Jon Bruce was a professor at Oklahoma City University School of Law; and Michael Swygert was a professor at DePaul University College of Law.

2896. Professor Swygert was one of the "newer" professors in favor of student evaluations. Having been a tenured faculty member at DePaul College of Law for seven years, where the dean and faculty had always supported student evaluations, Swygert tried to per-

uations was taken to the Stetson faculty for a vote. Realizing that the majority of the faculty did not favor implementing student evaluations, the proponents retreated, and suggested that students be permitted to evaluate only those professors who volunteered, but that proposition was not accepted either.[2897]

In February 1980, an article in the *Prelude* reported that the Academic Affairs Committee of the faculty met and debated whether voluntary teacher evaluations should be established.[2898] Though several faculty members supported the idea, the majority did not.[2899] A major roadblock concerned what questions should be given to the students to respond to.

At the end of the fall 1979 semester, the Stetson Student Bar Association decided to conduct its own student teaching evaluations of Stetson faculty, which, of course, it had the right to do and had, in fact, done in the past.[2900] Students were asked four questions in reference to each of their instructors who taught in seven designated subject areas. In three of the subjects, two professors each taught a section. Thus, ten instructors were subject to the evaluations.[2901] The courses were criminal law, pleading & procedure, contracts, real property (two sections), federal tax (two sections), U.S. constitutional law (two sections), and torts. The results of the evaluations were published in the *Prelude.*[2902]

The results revealed that students rated their professors on a scale of one (lowest) to four (highest) in response to five specified student concerns: (1) Instructor's awareness of student difficulties; (2) Instructor's efforts to alleviate student difficulties; (3) Instructor's encouragement of free expression of ideas; (4) Necessity of assigned material for understanding the subject; and (5) Reasonableness of credit hours compared to amount of work required.[2903]

The printed results, though showing how those students who participated ranked their professors in reference to the five concerns, did not reveal either the number or percentage of students who took part. In theory, percentage could be anywhere from zero to 100 percent. Moreover, the "concerns" were not

---

suade colleagues who did not favor student evaluations that they enabled professors to learn more about their teaching manner, style, and effectiveness, and that as a result they would be able to make adjustments that would improve their teaching skills in the classroom.

2897. *Teacher Evaluations*, *supra* n. 2894.

2898. *Id.*

2899. *Id.*

2900. *Prelude* 3 (Apr. 1980) (one entire page consisting of fifty bar graphs, five columns wide, and ten up and down, with five lines in each column).

2901. *Id.*

2902. *Id.*

2903. *Id.*

particularly representative of what is considered to constitute effective teaching. Thus, the published "evaluations" were incomplete, misleading, and were more in the nature of a popularity ranking rather than a serious teaching assessment. In a few years, Stetson College of Law did institute faculty reviews by students.

d. Stetson Law School's Standard of Appearance and Attire ("Dress Code")

During the administration of Richard Dillon, the College faculty promulgated the "Standard of Appearance and Attire," often erroneously referred to as "the student dress code," since it applied not only to students, but also to faculty.[2904] Its rationale was said to be based on a statement by Warren E. Burger, Chief Justice of the United States, who at a prayer breakfast at an annual meeting of the ABA in Dallas, Texas, said: "The law school is uniquely situated to shape and form the habits of the students in the period when his professional ideas and standards of ethics, decorum, and conduct are being formed."[2905] The Stetson faculty and Dillon believed that if "respect for the law is to be preserved," the law school must create in the student "an awareness of the image a lawyer must present to the public."[2906]

The Standard of Appearance and Attire was adopted by faculty on November 13, 1969, but did not go into effect until June 1, 1970 (coincidentally at the height of student concerns over the Vietnam War).[2907] Drafted by Professor David Dickson, the Standard's language is challenging. It reads:

> The Faculty of Stetson University College of Law adopts as a standard of appearance and attire the standard that may from time to time exist for attorneys appearing before the Circuit Court in the Sixth Judicial Circuit of the State of Florida. Such standards shall be applicable to all persons in the following designated locations:
>
> In the *Courtroom* when official functions of the College are being held therein or when it is being used as a courtroom.
>
> In the Great Hall when official functions of the College are being held therein.

2904. *Faculty Sets Standard of Attire, Appearance*, 13 Stetson Law. 5 (Dec. 1969) [hereinafter *Faculty Sets Appearance Standard*].

2905. *Id.* (quoting Chief Justice Burger, but with no specific attribution).

2906. *Faculty Sets Appearance Standard, supra* n. 2904.

2907. *Standard of Appearance and Attire*, Stetson U. College of L. (Nov. 12, 1969) (a three-inch by seven-inch single page (green) (on file at the Stetson U. College of L., Gulfport, Fla.). To see the text of the *Standard of Appearance and Attire* in print, see *Faculty Sets Appearance Standard, supra* n. 2904.

> In the *Crummer Auditorium* when official functions of the College are being held therein.
>
> Appearance and attire in the classroom shall be the standard adopted for the above locations except that a jacket need not be worn if a jacket is required under the adopted standard.
>
> Appearance and attire in the library shall be the standard adopted for the above locations except that in the library until 5:00 p.m., Monday through Friday, a jacket need not be worn if a jacket is required under the adopted standard, and after 5:00 p.m. and over weekends, neither jacket nor tie shall be required if a jacket and tie are required under the adopted standard.[2908]

Dillon opines that the "Standard of Appearance and Attire" is perhaps the most discussed and least understood policy the faculty adopted during his administration.[2909] First, as noted above, it has been called the "student" dress code, but it applied to faculty as well. Second, it was not a Stetson delineated dress code, but rather was tailored to conform to whatever the Sixth Judicial Circuit adopted as its standard of appearance for attorneys appearing in its courts. Moreover, it was conceived to be a changeable standard based on prevailing judicial norms. And third, as Dillon points out, the Stetson law faculty "unanimously" adopted the appearance standard only after holding meetings with area judges and attorneys.[2910]

Not long after the Stetson Attire Standard went into effect in the fall of 1970, women in increasing numbers entered the College of Law (as they did in law schools throughout the country).[2911] This created a problem, since Stetson's Standard of Appearance and Attire was based on what the Sixth Circuit required male attorneys to wear in court. But the courts had no similar standard in place for women lawyers. Consequently, the Stetson faculty in the mid-1970s voted to abolish the Standard of Appearance and Attire.[2912]

2908. *Id.* (emphasis in the original).

2909. Handwritten notes from Richard T. Dillon, Dean Emeritus, Stetson U. College of L., to Michael I. Swygert, Prof. Emeritus, Stetson U. College of L. 14 (Jan. 2005) (on file with co-author Michael I. Swygert).

2910. *Id.*

2911. *Id.*

2912. *Id.*

Judge Thomas E. Stringer, Sr.

11.7 African-Americans Come to the College of Law

It was during Dean Dillon's administration when the first African-Americans enrolled in the Stetson College of Law.[2913] From the school's opening in 1900 through Sebring's administration, the *de facto* policy of Stetson law school was not to seek applicants of color.[2914] There is no evidence, however, that the school ever denied admission to a black applicant. The fact is none applied during the school's first seventy years.

In the school's seventy-first year, African-American Thomas E. Stringer, Sr., in 1971 applied and was admitted to the Stetson University College of Law.[2915] In the spring of 1974, Stringer graduated, thereby becoming the first African-American to receive a law degree from Stetson College of Law.[2916]

Thomas Stringer was born in 1944 in Peekskill, New York, close to the small village of Montrose, where his father worked as a mechanic and his mother as a domestic.[2917] After graduating with high grades from Henry Hudson High

---

2913. *See* Mark R. Brown, *Affirmative Inaction: Stories from a Small Southern School*, 75 Temp. L. Rev. 201 (2002) [hereinafter Brown, *Affirmative Inaction*].

2914. *See supra* n. 2489–2495 and accompanying text.

2915. *Judge Stringer Interview*, *supra* n. 2406, at 1.

2916. *See* Board of Overseers, Stetson University College of Law, *A Resolution in Honor of Thomas E. Stringer, Sr.* (Dec. 3, 2003) [hereinafter *Judge Stringer Resolution*].

2917. *Judge Stringer Interview*, *supra* n. 2406, at 7.

School, Stringer received a full scholarship to attend New York University, where he enrolled in 1962 and from which he graduated in 1967 with a B.A. in mathematics.[2918] He then entered the United States Air Force, took pilot training, and attained the rank of Captain. He mustered out in 1971, having the benefits of the G.I. Bill to pay for graduate education.[2919]

Captain Stringer, USAF (retired), applied and was accepted at both Florida and Stetson law schools. Florida would not consider him a resident, even though he had spent three years at Elgin Air Force Base in Pensacola. As he puts it, "Well, for that money, I'll go to Stetson," and he did.[2920] Stringer quickly became aware that there were no other African-Americans in the Stetson student body. He explains what took place one morning:

> I was walking across campus and there was an African-American groundskeeper, a guy named Norman, and he stopped raking and looked at me very curiously … I thought, "that's strange." [Later] I was coming back and he looked at me again and said: "Excuse me, can I ask you a question?" I said, "Sure." "Are you planning to go here?" The way he said it made me, you know, a little [suspicious].
>
> I said, "Sure, and why do you ask?" He said, "Well, you know a lot of black kids [potential applicants] come here and look around and they never come back." That was the first time I had an inkling that there were no other African-American students."[2921]

Stringer recalls that while he was a student at Stetson law school, he witnessed no overt racism, nor did he feel that he was discriminated against due to the color of his skin.[2922] On the other hand, a law school friend (and later Stringer's law partner), John Scott, told Stringer that there were times when he and Stringer would go to the library and sit down, followed by a few students immediately getting up and leaving.[2923]

After graduating from the law school, Stringer worked in the Hillsborough State Attorney's Office under E.J. Salcines (later a colleague of Judge Stringer on the Florida Second District Court of Appeal). From 1976 through 1984, Stringer was in private practice.[2924] Hearing about a judicial vacancy, he ap-

2918. *Judge Stringer Resolution*, *supra* n. 2916.

2919. *Judge Stringer Interview*, *supra* n. 2406, at 3, 4.

2920. *Id.* at 4.

2921. *Id.* at 5.

2922. *Id.* at 6.

2923. *Id.*

2924. *Judge Stringer Resolution*, *supra* n. 2916.

plied for and was appointed in 1984 Hillsborough County Judge, and subsequently elected to the post a few years later.[2925] Then, in 1988, Florida Governor Robert Martinez appointed Judge Stringer circuit judge on the Thirteenth Judicial Circuit, the first African-American to hold that position.[2926] Stringer's climb up the judicial ladder continued when, in 1997, Florida Governor Jeb Bush elevated him to Florida's Second District Court of Appeals, a post he currently occupies.[2927]

The first African-American graduate of the College of Law is one of the school's strongest supporters. Judge Stringer has worked—and continues to work—on behalf of the school's Black Student Lawyers Association (BALSA) now named for him. In addition, he has served on both the Board of Trustees of Stetson University and on the Board of Overseers of the College of Law.[2928] He was chair of the Overseers from 1999 through 2003.[2929]

In recognition of his contributions to the African-American community, BALSA honored Judge Stringer by instituting an annual celebration called the Judge Thomas Stringer Youth Day.[2930] At the December 2003 graduation at the College of Law, the Board of Overseers presented Judge Stringer with a Resolution that reads in part: "This Resolution is adopted to honor Thomas E. Stringer, Sr., for his selfless devotion, and the advancement of legal education.[2931]

The second African-American to graduate from Stetson College of Law was David A. Lister, in May 1977.[2932] Unlike Thomas Stringer, David Lister neither stayed in Florida nor practiced law. Rather, he became a highly successful corporate manager, working for several companies headquartered in the New York and New Jersey region. Prior to studying law at Stetson, Lister earned his undergraduate degree from Central State University in Wilberforce, Ohio.[2933]

2925. *Judge Stringer Interview*, *supra* n. 2406, at 15.

2926. *Id.*

2927. *Id.* at 15, 16.

2928. *Judge Stringer Resolution*, *supra* n. 2916

2929. *Id.*

2930. *Id.*

2931. *Id.*

2932. The information about David A. Lister's graduation from Stetson College of Law was given to Michael I. Swygert, Prof. Emeritus, Stetson U. College of L., by officials of Stetson College of Law Office of the Registrar on July 25, 2005.

2933. The information about David Lister comes from Judge Stringer, the University of Medicine and Dentistry of New Jersey, and from a telephone conversation Professor Michael Swygert had with Mr. Lister in June 2004.

After law school, Lister moved to the northeast. There, he held high managerial positions in personnel and affirmative action administration for a quarter of a century. Lister served as an affirmative action and personnel administrator at Beech-Nut, Inc., the Yale-New Haven Medical Center, The John Hopkins Medical Institutions, the University of Massachusetts Medical Center, and the Institute of International Education in New York City.[2934]

In addition, Lister served as Assistant Vice President for Administration at Fairleigh Dickinson University in Teaneck, New Jersey.[2935] His last position prior to his 1993 retirement and return to the Tampa area was the most prestigious one of all—Vice President for Human Resources of the University of Medicine and Dentistry in New Jersey (UMDNJ), a position he was appointed to by the University Board of Trustees after it conducted a nationwide search.[2936] UMDNJ at the time employed 9,000 people on campuses in Newark, New Brunswick, and Camden/Stratford, New Jersey.[2937]

Though Stringer and Lister were the first two African-Americans graduates of the Stetson school, beginning in the mid-1970s and continuing ever since, the numbers have grown, though not as fast as they could have under a more aggressive affirmative action program.[2938] One former Stetson faculty member—Professor Mark Brown—in particular was vociferous in his belief that the College of Law has lagged when it comes to admitting African-Americans. Brown set out his arguments in an article published in the *Temple Law Review*.[2939] Most faculty members and the dean felt that many of his assertions were wrong. At the same time, Stetson law students sent letters, including e-mails, to him disputing his claims about race relations at the school.

11.8 Dillon Builds the Faculty

(i) W. McKinley Smiley, Jr., was initially hired as an adjunct instructor during Dean Sebring's administration. He was later appointed a full-time faculty member, along with Marion Fallwell and Joseph Long, by Dillon in the fall of

2934. U. of Med. & Dentistry of N.J., *News Release* 1, 2 (2001) (on file at Stetson U. College of L., Gulfport, Fla.).

2935. *Id.* at 1.

2936. *Id.*

2937. *Id.*

2938. Brown, *Affirmative Action, supra* n. 2913, at 201.

2939. *Id.* at 227, 228.

W. McKinley Smiley, Jr.

1969.[2940] Of the three, only Smiley remained after one year. A Bradenton, Florida, native, Smiley began law school at Stetson, but transferred to Emory University. A Duke University undergraduate, Smiley later earned an LL.M. from Miami. He also spent several months at Yale Law School as a visiting scholar.[2941]

"Mickey," as Smiley was called by colleagues, was a member of the Stetson law faculty from 1969 through 2004. His involvement with the school took many paths. Along with Professors Latimer, Marks, and William Eleazer, Smiley was an early strong proponent for the school's trial advocacy program.[2942] He founded both the Trial Advocacy Society and the International Law Society at Stetson.[2943] In 1993, he coached a group of Stetson students who came in first place in the American Trial Lawyers' Association Student Trial Advocacy Competition.[2944]

Smiley's commitment to promoting and teaching trial practice became widely known. In 1991, he received the Award of Merit of the Academy of Florida Trial Lawyers, and in 2002, the Perry Nichols Trial Award from the Academy of Florida

2940. *Faculty Staff Enriched by Three New Members*, 13 Stetson Law. 6, 6 (Dec. 1969).

2941. *Id.*

2942. Eleazer, *Trial Advocacy, supra* n. 2780, at 259–260.

2943. *International Law Society Returns to the Stetson Campus*, 31 Stetson Law. 11 (Spring 1991).

2944. *Id.*, at 260; *see also Stetson ATLA Trial Team Places First and Second in State Competition*, 27 Stetson Law. 5, 5 (Fall 1987).

Trial Lawyers.[2945] Smiley served as officer of both state and national trial lawyers' associations;[2946] a member of the Task Force Advisory Commission of the American Trial Lawyers' Association (ATLA); and was Florida's representative on the American Trial Lawyers Association Committee on Professional Ethics.[2947]

At Stetson, Smiley taught torts, product liability, and medical jurisprudence. He often invited recognized experts to his classes who lectured, led discussions, and shared with students their experiences in practice.

Smiley loves music. Frequently, he played both the guitar and the banjo, and sang ballads and country and western songs at various functions, including law school parties.[2948] In 2004, Mickey Smiley retired. Students who took Smiley's courses generally found his classes invigorating. Many liked his digressions into real-life stories about the "hard-ball" practice of law.[2949] During his thirty-five years on the faculty, Smiley served under six deans—Sebring, Dillon, Jacob, Moody, Vause, and Dickerson. He contributed much to the school.

(ii) Elizabeth M. Leeman was appointed in the fall of 1970 to the faculty as assistant professor of law and assistant librarian.[2950] Leeman was the first woman with a law degree to join the Stetson law faculty.[2951] She had been librarian at Florida State University Law School, and also at Texas Tech University.[2952] Leeman had a B.A. degree from Winthrop College, an M.A. from University of Texas, an LL.B. degree from St. Mary's law school (Texas), and an M.A. degree in law librarianship from University of Washington.[2953] After law school, she was project manager compiling current state legislation for the American Bar Foundation.[2954] When she came to Stetson, Leeman taught

2945. *Professor Mickey Smiley Honored by Academy of Florida Lawyers*, 35 Stetson Law. 11, 11 (Spring 2003).

2946. W. McKinley Smiley, Jr., *The Faculty of the College of Law*, Stetson College of L. Bull. 1991–1992, at 17 (1991).

2947. *Stetson Professor on ATLA Ethics Committee*, 13 Stetson Law. 2, 2 (Dec. 1969).

2948. *See e.g. Maestros*, 17 Stetson Law. 5 (Aug. 1974); *see also Homecoming 1975 Style, Varied Programs Attract over 300 Alumni, Guests*, 18 Stetson Law. 4 (Aug. 1975).

2949. These observations are based on discussions co-author Swygert has had with Smiley's students over the years and on Smiley's repeated assertion that "litigation is hard ball."

2950. *Enrollment Records Shattered through 1970–1971*, 14 Stetson Law. 3, 3 (May 1971).

2951. Vause, *Foundations for Excellence*, *supra* n. 308, at 323. When the College of Law opened in 1900, University President Forbes appointed a woman to teach on a part-time basis at the school, but she did not have a law degree. *See supra* nn. 403–405 and accompanying text. From 1902 through 1970, no woman was appointed to a professorial position at the law school.

2952. Vause, *Foundations for Excellence*, *supra* n. 308, at 323.

2953. *Id.*

2954. *Id.*

Judge Susan F. Schaeffer

classes in legal research and writing, served as assistant librarian, and was advisor to the *Stetson Intramural Law Review*.[2955] She retired with the rank of associate professor in July 1976.[2956]

(iii) Susan F. Schaeffer was the second woman Dillon appointed to the Stetson law faculty. Schaeffer remained on the faculty for approximately three semesters. She was born in 1942 in Pennsylvania, but when six, she and her mother moved to St. Petersburg.[2957] She studied music in St. Petersburg Junior College, and then enrolled in the School of Music at Florida State University.[2958] Schaeffer at that point had no thoughts about law school. Attorney Susan Shulins describes:

> [Her] original aspirations were far from the courtroom. Her hopes were set on becoming a musician and composer and someday making her way to Broadway. Today, as the Chief Judge of ... Florida's largest trial court, Schaeffer can't imagine being in any other profession.[2959]

2955. *See supra* nn. 2838–2840 and accompanying text.; *see also* Batey & Fitgerald, *supra* n. 2809, at 222.

2956. Bishop, *List*, *supra* n. 2351, at 3.

2957. *Judge Schaeffer Interview*, *supra* n. 2299, at 2, 3.

2958. *Id.* at 4–6.

2959. Shulins, *supra* n. 2766, at 4,6.

Before entering a courtroom, however, Schaeffer went down another road. She explains:

> I got up there at the big school [FSU] and I saw skilled musicians [who] were far better than I ... Though I had hoped that maybe I could go into composition and write Broadway musicals ... I realized that was probably pie in the sky ... So I went from the School of Music to business and majored in accounting.[2960]

After graduating from FSU in 1964, Schaeffer confronted gender bias when she sought a job at the Internal Revenue Service. The hiring agent told her she had the credentials, but then said, "except you're a woman."[2961] Schaeffer replied: "I can get along with men. If you hire me, you will see."[2962] He made her an offer, she accepted, and he learned she was right.

As an IRS auditor, Schaeffer found she liked researching tax law and began to consider the possibly of law school.[2963] Schaeffer says: "So, I thought, okay. I took the LSAT."[2964] Accepted at Stetson University and UF law schools, she chose Stetson.[2965] She entered in the fall of 1968, and found many of her classmates were returning Vietnam veterans, which pleased her since, like her, they were older than law students coming directly from college.[2966]

Schaeffer graduated number one in her class, was president of the Student Bar Association,[2967] and was on the Stetson winning team at the Florida Moot Court Competition.[2968] The justices voted Schaeffer "the outstanding speaker of the state competition."[2969] As a law student, Schaeffer worked part-time, clerking for Sherwin Simmons of the Tampa firm of Simmons, Kempler,

2960. *Judge Schaeffer Interview*, *supra* n. 2299, at 5.

2961. *Id.* at 9.

2962. *Id.*

2963. *Id.* at 10–14.

2964. *Id.* at 14.

2965. *Id.* at 15.

2966. *Id.* at 20.

2967. Shulins, *supra* n. 2766, at 7.

2968. She and classmate Wendell Tucker argued the final round of the competition before seven members of the Florida Supreme Court. To get there, Schaeffer and Tucker had beaten teams from Florida, Miami, and Florida State. As it turned out, the final round was between two Stetson teams—Schaeffer and Tucker arguing (and winning) against classmates Dana Fogle and Allen Watts. *Past Year One of Growth, Achievement and Firsts*, 13 Stetson Law. 1, 1 (July 1970).

2969. Susan Schaeffer, *New Faces, Retirements Characterize 1971–1972*, 15 Stetson Lawyer 1, 2–3 (Aug. 1972) [hereinafter Schaeffer, *New Faces*].

Sharpe, and Butler.[2970] Simmons invited her to join the firm, even though he earlier had told her that his firm did not hire women.[2971] To Simmons' surprise, she turned down the offer to accept the position of assistant professor of law at Stetson College of Law.[2972]

Dean Dillon was impressed with Schaeffer's performance as a law student, and asked if she would join the faculty.[2973] She accepted and became assistant professor of law.[2974] After teaching agency and partnership for two semesters and a summer session, Schaeffer left the law school to enter practice.[2975] Pinellas County Public Defender Robert Jagger hired her and soon promoted her to be assistant.[2976] In 1982, Florida Governor Robert Graham appointed Schaeffer to be Circuit Court Judge for the Sixth Judicial Circuit.[2977] In 1995, she was elected the Circuit's chief judge.[2978] Judge Schaeffer retired from the bench on December 31, 2004, because of throat cancer, a disease she is battling as of the time of this writing.[2979]

Sixth Circuit Stetson alumnus Chief Judge David Demers, himself a Stetson alumnus, describes Judge Schaeffer's twenty-two years of service to the Sixth Judicial Circuit of Florida and to the people of Florida as being "absolutely immeasurable."[2980] In February 2005, Susan F. Schaeffer, class of 1971, was inducted into the Stetson University College of Law Hall of Fame.[2981]

2970. *Judge Schaeffer Interview*, *supra* n. 2299, at 26.

2971. *Id.* at 26, 27.

2972. *Id.* at 28.

2973. *Jan. 29 Dillon Discussion*, *supra* n. 1969. Initially, Schaeffer was also offered the position of acting registrar to replace the long-time registrar Kay Eddy, who had retired. Ms. Eddy was registrar at the law school from 1955–71. She was loved by the students, whom she called "my boys." Richard Dillon and Bruce Jacob, both students when Eddy was Registrar, speak glowingly about her role at Stetson. *See Mrs. Eddy Retires*, Prelude 2 (Oct. 15, 1971).

2974. *Id.*

2975. *Judge Schaeffer Interview*, *supra* n. 2299, at 30.

2976. *Id.*; *see also* Shulins, *supra* n. 2766, at 7.

2977. Scott E. Schiltz, *Judicial Profile: Honorable Susan F. Schaeffer*, Newsltr. (Clearwater B. Assn.) 1 (Dec–Jan. 2002).

2978. *Id.*

2979. William R. Levesque, *Ailing Circuit Judge Susan Schaeffer to Retire, after a Distinguished 22 years on the Bench, the Judge Will Leave at the End of the Year*, St. Petersburg Times Online www.sptimes.com/11/03/news_pf/Tampabay/Ailing_Circuit_Judge_.shtml (accessed on Jan. 19, 2005).

2980. *Id.*

2981. *Stetson University College of Law Hall of Fame*, www.law.stetson.edu/HallofFame/2005_inductees.asp (Mar. 2005).

Thomas Clark Marks, Jr.

(iv) Retired Sixth Circuit Judge Orvil L. Dayton, Jr., in 1972 accepted Dillon's offer to join the law faculty.[2982] Dillon wanted to "restore the judicial balance" the faculty lost when Judge Victor Wehle retired in the spring of 1972.[2983] A visiting professor, Dayton expected to stay two years, but quickly found that he loved teaching law. Consequently, he became a regular member of the faculty, where he remained until retiring.[2984]

Dayton's Stetson colleagues recall that during the 1980s, he returned to the school with regularity to lunch with the faculty. He told stories about his years as an active judge, especially recounting humorous encounters with lawyers. Dayton would also tell jokes, a few mildly off color, but which, according to Professor Tom Marks, were "belly shakers."[2985]

(v) Thomas Clark Marks, Jr., has the felicity for surprise. A student sat encamped outside Professor Marks' office one morning, waiting to see him. Walking down the hallway en route to class, Professor Bruce Jacob spotted the young woman sitting in a hallway chair. He asked her who she was waiting to

2982. *Judge Dayton Called, New Faces, Retirements 1971–1972*, 15 Stetson Law. 3, 3 (Aug. 1972).

2983. *Id.*

2984. Bishop, *List*, *supra* n. 2351, at 3.

2985. Professor Michael Swygert often attended these lunches and, like Professor Marks, recalls the robust times when Judge Dayton was present.

see. She replied, "Professor Marks, but he has someone in his office."[2986] Jacob went to teach his class and an hour later returned, only to see the student still sitting in front of Marks' office. "Haven't you seen Professor Marks yet?" Jacob asked. "No, there's still someone with him," she replied. Jacob looked through the small glass window and laughed. "There's no one but Marks in his office," Jacob chuckled. "That can't be," said the student, "I saw someone in there." She looked through the window again and exclaimed, "He's still there, standing next to Dr. Marks." Jacob advised the befuddled student: "The person you see next to Professor Marks is a six-foot cut-out of John Wayne."[2987]

Marks typically arrived at Stetson school early in the morning.[2988] The friendly professor frequently took the entire faculty-support staff out to lunch, an event the staff looked forward to and appreciated, said Connie Evans, Director of Faculty Support Services.[2989]

Whether called "Professor," "Tom," "Doctor," or "Major, "Marks has contributed something often needed at the school—a calming influence. With an optimistic and unflappable persona, his mere presence can defuse situations, such as faculty meetings, where rational lawyers have a proclivity to speak and act irrationally on occasion.

Marks was born in 1938 in Tampa, Florida. He graduated from Florida State University in 1960 with a B.S. degree, and from Stetson College of Law in 1963 with an LL.B. degree.[2990] Following his military duty in Vietnam,[2991] he joined

---

2986. Somewhat embarrassed but relieved, the student softly knocked on Marks' door and, after a "come in," took herself into an eclectic sanctuary with strewn papers, handwritten notes and law books, a life-size reproduction of President George Bush, two H.O. scale steam locomotives, (one lettered for the Atlantic Coast Line and the other for RFTC), various mementoes from the United States Army, and, yes, a life-size reproduction of John Wayne. The story about this incident has been told countless times over the past decade by Dean Emeritus Bruce Jacob.

2987. *Id.*

2988. Marks prefers to teach early in the morning, and for years asked for 8 a.m. classes. However, the majority of his students do not share his adherence to the famous adage of Benjamin Franklin, "Early to bed, early to rise, makes a man healthy, wealthy, and wise." The person who arrives the earliest on most days (in addition to Dean Darby Dickerson) is the Director of Faculty Support Services, Connie Evans, who typically arrives between 6:30 and 7:00 a.m.

2989. Statement of Connie Evans, Dir. of Faculty Support Staff, Stetson U. College of L., to Michael Swygert, Prof. Emeritus, Stetson U. College of L. (June 12, 2005).

2990. Schaeffer, *New Faces*, *supra* n. 2969.

2991. Before coming to Stetson, Marks had compiled a distinguished record of military service. In 1960, he was commissioned an Army Second Lieutenant. Subsequently, he served with a reserve artillery unit until, in 1963, he transferred to the Army Judge Advo-

the Tampa law firm of Gibbons, Tucker, McEwen, Smith and Cofer, where he practiced for two years.[2992] However, Marks desired to return to school for a doctorate degree. He chose UF, and in 1971 earned his Ph.D. in political science.[2993] He then took a job teaching criminal justice and political science at the University of South Alabama in Mobile. In 1973, he received an offer from Dean Dillon to join Stetson's law faculty.[2994] Marks began his thirty-third year on Stetson's law faculty in the fall of 2005, where he has taught United States and Florida constitutional law, basic and advanced courses, and criminal procedure. In his Florida constitutional law class, he uses a published casebook that he and his colleague, John F. Cooper, co-authored.[2995] Moreover, while teaching a full schedule, Marks served as the initial director of the school's Public Defender Clinic, and later, as director of the Prosecution Clinic.[2996]

As to scholarly activity, Marks has had more works published than any other professor at the law school to date, a number approaching sixty.[2997] Five

---

cate General's Corps, and was promoted to First Lieutenant, and one year later to Captain and assigned a staff and faculty position in the non-resident training department at the Army Advocate General's School in Charlottesville, Virginia. From 1965–66, he was assistant staff judge advocate and acting staff-judge advocate in the Fourth Transportation Command in the Republic of Vietnam. He returned from Vietnam in 1967 to Charlottesville. Captain Marks remained nine years in the Army's Ready Reserve as a "Mobilization Designee" for the Judge Advocate General's School at Charlottesville. He was promoted in 1976 to Major. He became an inactive reservist and was honorably discharged from the Army in 1982. For his service to his country, Major Thomas Marks received the National Defense Service Medal, Vietnam Campaign Medal, Army Commendation Medal with First Oakleaf Cluster, and Republic of Vietnam Service Medal.

2992. *Id.*

2993. *Id.* It must be pointed out for historical accuracy that Marks, though having earned a higher degree from the University of Florida, continues to put the institution that awarded him a lower degree, Florida State University, at the top of his loyalty list. There is never any doubt around the law school about this matter when the annual Seminole-Gator football game approaches, the outcome of which, should the Seminoles lose, causes Marks to momentarily stop smiling.

2994. *Id.*

2995. Thomas C. Marks, Jr. & John F. Cooper, *Florida Constitutional Law* (3d ed., Carolina Academic Press 2003).

2996. Schaeffer, *New Faces, supra* n. 2969, at 1.

2997. The number of publications does not include subsequent editions or revisions of works previously written. Other Stetson law professors who have over forty works published include professors W. Gary Vause, Robert Batey, and Michael Swygert. When it comes to books, however, Stetson Professors Bradford Stone and the late Howard Oleck have the highest totals.

of these are books.[2998] His articles have appeared in numerous law reviews and other periodicals.[2999] In recognition of his scholarship, Marks twice has received the Homer and Dolly Hand Award for Excellence in Scholarship.[3000] As active in the classroom as in the library,[3001] Marks engages his students in the great themes and nuances of Constitutional law. His classes often focus on controversial social and political issues.

(vi) Ruth Fleet Thurman once participated in a student-sponsored "sack-in" in Cal Kuenzel's contracts class. Placing a brown paper bag over her head (with cut outs for eyes and nose), she and the students marched into the classroom.[3002] Thurman recalls the happening: "Cal just taught the class in the normal way. [He] called on students as he always did. Students, Thurman explains, would "take their paper bag off and stand up to recite. [Cal] never let on that he even noticed those paper bags."[3003] This story reveals not only Professor Kuenzel's "coolness," it also demonstrates Professor Thurman's adventurousness.

Ruth Thurman received an A.B. degree from Smith College.[3004] She later enrolled in Stetson College of Law, earning her law degree in 1963. Later, she earned an LL.M. from Columbia University while on sabbatical. When Thurman was admitted to practice in Florida in 1963, only 2.7 percent of the nation's lawyers were women.[3005] Her 1960 entering law class, however, included

---

2998. *See* Thomas C. Marks, Jr. & John F. Cooper, *Florida Constitutional Law—Cases and Comments* (1st, 2d, & 3d eds., Carolina Academic Press 1992, 1996, 2003); Thomas C. Marks, Jr., & John F. Cooper, *State Constitutional Law in a Nutshell* (1st, 2d eds., West 1988, 2003); Thomas C. Marks, Jr. Jerome C. Latimer & Robert Batey, *Arrest: The Law in Florida* (1981 & 1982 Supp.); Thomas C. Marks, Jr., & Tim Reilly, *Constitutional Criminal Procedure* (Duxbury Press 1979); Thomas C. Marks, Jr., Richter H. Moore & Robert V. Barrow, *Readings in Criminal Justice* (Bobbs-Merrill 1976).

2999. The periodicals include those published by Albany, Brigham Young, Temple, Nova, Missouri, Campbell, Oklahoma City, Ohio Northern, Detroit, Mercer, and Stetson universities.

3000. Records, Office of the Dean, Stetson College of Law.

3001. For many years, the College of Law maintained a small law library of essential materials for the faculty, located on the second floor of the Dana administration building. In addition to books, there were two large tables with chairs. One of the tables was continually occupied by Professor Marks, with what seemed to be half of the library's books opened up scattered all around intermingled with yellow pads full of notes. No one complained. After all, no one worked as diligently (or at least not as demonstratively) on scholarship as did Marks.

3002. *Thurman Interview*, *supra* n. 2278.

3003. *Id.* at 86, 87.

3004. *Stetson Announces Expanded Faculty,* 18 Stetson Law. 2, 2 (Aug. 1975) [hereinafter *Expanded Faculty*].

3005. ABA, *The American Lawyer: Statistical Report* 15 (Am. B. Found. 1968).

Ruth Fleet Thurman

seven women, but only two of whom graduated;[3006] Thurman and Jan King from Lakeland, Florida.[3007] King later became a judge in Lakeland and was a member of Stetson's Board of Overseers.[3008]

When Thurman began law classes, she already knew about Professor Kuenzel's reputation.[3009] How should she survive his class? Fortunately, she got some words of wisdom. She recalls:

> One of the best pieces of advice that I received as a first-semester student was from Bob Ulrich, who was a senior when I was a freshman. [Ulrich was later Mayor of St. Petersburg.] His advice was, "Don't ever raise your hand in Cal Kuenzel's class." I saw people do that and I saw them get decimated.[3010]

Thurman not only "survived Cal," it turned out that she had performed quite well.

After law school, Thurman practiced law in St. Petersburg. For a time, she and her sister, Lucille Ford, Stetson '65, had their own firm.[3011] Thurman returned to Stetson in 1975 as a member of the faculty. She had received a

3006. *Thurman Interview*, *supra* n. 2278, at 16.
3007. *Id.* King graduated midyear and Thurman graduated in June. *Id.*
3008. *Id.* at 78.
3009. *Id.* at 36.
3010. *Id.*
3011. *Id.* at 43.

phone call from Dillon inquiring if she would be interested in joining the faculty.[3012] She was, and accepted a position on a tenure-track.[3013] Though the College had earlier hired Elizabeth Leeman and Susan Schaeffer on the faculty, Thurman was the first woman to become tenured at Stetson College of Law.[3014]

At the law school, Thurman has taught a required Research and Writing course to the first-year class, a course she describes as "one of the most important in law school."[3015] The course began with a seven-week segment on legal bibliography.[3016] In time, Law Librarian Lamar Woodard taught that portion, but that did little to relieve the burden Thurman faced: assigning, then grading, a series of student writings—opinion letters, memoranda of law, and moot court legal briefs.[3017] Dillon assigned her responsibility for placement, continuing legal education, and both alumni and public relations.[3018] Many of these administrative duties had previously been discharged by Professor Everett Cushman, who had retired.[3019] Overseeing public and alumni matters, Thurman wrote and edited the *Stetson Lawyer*, a publication that Cushman had edited for seventeen years.[3020]

In the area of CLE, Thurman helped to establish what became a prominent national seminar on bankruptcy law. Dillon suggested that she call U.S. Bankruptcy Judge Alexander L. Paskay to talk about the possibility of starting a Stetson conference on bankruptcy law.[3021] Thurman recalls:

> We went to the Southeast Regional Bankruptcy Seminar in Atlanta that had been very successful and scoped it out, and came home and put together our own Bankruptcy Seminar. Judge Paskay contacted and organized all the speakers and the program, and I did [the administrative details]. We held it at the Host Marriott Hotel at the Tampa International Airport.[3022]

3012. *Id.*

3013. *Stetson Appoints Six Full-Time Professors*, St. Pete. Indep. A-7 (Sept. 10, 1975) [hereinafter *Full-Time Professors*].

3014. *Thurman Interview*, *supra* n. 2278, at 48. Thurman was granted tenure in 1979. *Id.*

3015. *Id.*

3016. *Id.* at 50.

3017. Thurman recalls that at the time she began teaching at the law school, "We probably had 480 students, something like that." *Id.* at 53.

3018. *Id.*

3019. *Id.*

3020. *Id.* at 55.

3021. *Id.* at 58.

3022. *Id.*

Judge Paskay induced several of the nation's leading experts on bankruptcy law to come to Tampa in November 1976 to serve on the initial seminar's faculty.[3023] The seminar has since taken place each year since; in 2005, Judge Paskay and the College of Law sponsored the school's 30th "Paskay Bankruptcy Law Seminar."[3024]

In the fall of 2005, Thurman began her thirty-first year on Stetson's law faculty. Her contributions to the school include her activities with the American Bar Association, The Florida Bar, and the Association of American Law Schools. For years, she was Stetson's delegate to the AALS House of Representatives.[3025]

At the law school, Thurman served as CLE director and worked with the state bar in putting on CLE programs.[3026] In 1975–76, she helped put together six Bar CLE courses on campus.[3027] The following year, with Thurman's assistance, The Florida Bar scheduled eight seminars at Stetson College of Law.[3028] Of her various services to the Bar, the most rewarding, she says, was working as a member of the state's Board of Bar Examiners,[3029] a position Thurman describes as a "fantastic experience."[3030]

3023. *Bankruptcy Seminar Scheduled for Nov. 12–13*, 19 Stetson Law. 2, 2 (Aug. 1976).

3024. *See infra* nn. 3895–3915 and accompanying text.

3025. *Thurman Interview*, *supra* n. 2278, at 70–74.

3026. *Id.* at 61.

3027. *Stetson Hosts Florida Bar CLE Courses*, 19 Stetson Law. 3, 3 (Aug. 1976).

3028. *Id.* From the 1980s through today, Professor Thurman has served as secretary and on the executive board of the St. Petersburg Bar Association, board member of the St. Petersburg Legal Aid Society, the St. Petersburg Lawyer Referral Service, and member of the Editorial Board of *The Florida Bar Journal* and *Florida Bar News*. She was President and member of Board of Directors of the Florida Association of Women Lawyers, a member of The Florida Bar Special Study Committee of its Model Rules of Professional Conduct, and a member of the Committee on Professionalism and Committee on Professional Ethics.

3029. Ruth Thurman remembers through this day most of her classmates. Recently, she spoke of Stetson law students she was in school with who became judges. She recalls they included Judge Elizabeth Kovachevich, Chief Judge of the United States District Court for the Middle District of Florida; Florida Circuit Court judges David Seth Walker; David Patterson (later judge on Florida's Second District Court of Appeal); Jan King, Lakeland municipal judge; Florida circuit judges Robert Mitcham; Elvin Martinez; Rom Powell; Charles Prather; Charles McClure; Ray Steinhardt; Dan Futch; Fred Bryson; Joe Donahey; Charles Carrera; Robert Michael; Ray "Gene" Ulmer; Charles Carlton; Harry Lee Coe; E. J. Salcinas (Florida's Second District Court of Appeal); John Blue (Florida's Second District Court of Appeal); and Jay Dauksch (Florida's Fifth District Court of Appeal). Thurman also mentions classmates Joe D'Alessandro, State Attorney for the Second Judicial Circuit, and Richard McFarlain, Counsel to The Florida Bar, whom she describes as its "very successful lobbyist." And she points out that her classmate Carl Kuttler, president of the Stetson Student Bar Association, today is the highly acclaimed President of St. Petersburg College. *Id.* at 65, 66.

3030. *Id.* at 65.

Since coming to Stetson, Thurman has worked for the betterment of the school and the legal profession. Her expertise is in the critical area of professional responsibility. The first woman to attain tenure at Stetson College of Law, Professor Ruth Thurman looks around the campus in 2005 and sees that women are in the majority. She never imagined that would be the case in 1960 when she started law school. In 2005, Professor Thurman was inducted in to the Stetson College of Law Hall of Fame.

(vii) William H. Namack III, joined the College of Law faculty in 1973.[3031] A graduate of Syracuse University, he later received an LL.B. from Albany University, followed by an LL.M. from New York University. A story about Namack noted that, "After building a lucrative law practice in the Bradenton-Sarasota area, he succumbed to the urge to teach."[3032] During twelve years in practice, he specialized in wills, trusts, and estate planning, and for a time, worked for United States Trust Company in New York. After setting up practice in Bradenton, he continued to represent U.S. Trust in Florida.[3033] An author of articles on trust law in the *Florida Bar Journal*,[3034] at Stetson, Namack taught decedents' estates, estate planning, real property, and condominium law, while serving as a lecturer for the Florida Bankers Association Trust School.[3035] Namack was a full-time faculty member from 1973–75, then taught part time for several more years.[3036]

(viii) Jerome C. Latimer leaves an impression. "Who can forget evidence class with Latimer," a 2005 graduate of the College of Law told her contracts professor. "It was the most challenging and demanding course I took at Stetson. I'm happy I survived."[3037] Very few law schools require students to take evidence, but Stetson does, and the subject is not easy. Latimer has been a master of the complex subject by teaching the critical relationship between theory and practice by demonstrating how doctrine interacts with the realities of trying a case in court.[3038]

When asked about his background, Latimer comments that he "was raised about a nine-iron shot from the Stetson law school campus" in the nearby

3031. William J. Namack III, *College of Law Ready for New Academic Year* 16 Stetson Law. 1, 7 (Aug. 1973).

3032. *Id.*

3033. *Id.*

3034. *Expanded Faculty, supra* n. 3004, at 2.

3035. Am. Assn. of L. Schs., *Association of American Law Schools Directory of Law Teachers, 1977*, at 593 (Am. L. Found. 1977) [hereinafter *AALS 1977 Directory*].

3036. *See* Bishop *List, supra* n. 2351, at 6.

3037. The student made these remarks to Stetson Professor Michael I. Swygert at her graduation celebration dinner with her family.

3038. *Full-Time Professors, supra* n. 3013.

Jerome C. Latimer

Pasadena Community Golfclub Estates."[3039] He soon moved to Washington, D.C., where his father was an executive with the Veterans Administration.[3040] After returning to Pinellas County, Latimer attended St. Petersburg's Boca Ciega High School.[3041] In 1967, he earned his B.A. from Florida State University, majoring in history and minoring in economics.[3042]

Not sure that he wanted to become a lawyer, Latimer nonetheless was admitted to the University of Florida Law School.[3043] At orientation, he listened to justices of the Florida Supreme Court speak on the law's noble ends, and the role of lawyers in their pursuit. Any doubts he had about law as a career evaporated. As he puts it, "I was hooked."[3044]

Latimer graduated from UF law school with honors in 1970,[3045] where he became a member in the Order of the Coif, the national law-school honor society.[3046] After admission to The Florida Bar, he volunteered to assist Robert Jagger, Sixth Judicial Circuit Pinellas County Public Defender. Jagger accepted

3039. *Latimer Interview*, *supra* n. 2754, at 1.

3040. *Id.* at 2.

3041. *Id.*

3042. *Id.*

3043. *Id.* at 4.

3044. *Id.*

3045. Am. Assn. of L. Schs. *The AALS Directory of Law Teachers 2004–2005*, 673 (West Pub. Co., 2004) [hereinafter *AALS 2004–2005 Directory*].

3046. *Latimer Interview*, *supra* n. 2754, at 5.

Latimer's offer, and when funds became available, hired him as an Assistant Public Defender for Pinellas County.[3047] Working with Jagger, Latimer became acquainted with Stetson law Professor Paul Barnard, who with Jagger, earlier had started Stetson's Public Defender Clinic.[3048]

In 1974, Barnard was considering leaving the Stetson Public Defender Clinic to pursue other interests.[3049] He went to Latimer and suggested that the latter come to Stetson and become the Clinic's new director.[3050] Though Latimer "liked" working as a trial lawyer and had little desire to leave his public defender position, Barnard persuaded him to do so. Latimer explains: "I was flattered enough, and Barnard encouraged me to take the position and I did. But I got a guarantee from Bob Jagger if I didn't like [working at Stetson], he would hire me back."[3051] Latimer never exercised his right of first return, for he loved teaching law and working with Stetson students. At Stetson, he has taught, in addition to evidence, criminal law, criminal procedure, and trial advocacy.

Over many years, Latimer has been the faculty's leading voice for placing greater emphasis on skills training. Recognizing his dedication to strengthening skills programs at the school, each of the last three deans has asked him to chair the school's committee overseeing the skills component of the curriculum.

Outside the College, Latimer, like Thurman, has actively participated in The Florida Bar. For three decades, he has been on the executive counsel of its Criminal Law Section.[3052] In addition, he has been a member of the Criminal Procedure Rules Committee, a body established by the Florida Supreme Court to suggest modifications of Florida's Rules of Criminal Procedure.[3053]

Beyond teaching and work for the Bar, Latimer researches and publishes. He is the co-author with Tom Marks of a book on the law of arrest.[3054] More recently, Latimer wrote a definitive article pertaining to the United States Supreme Court decision in *Crawford v. Washington*.[3055] At the time of this writing, his article has been scheduled to be published in the *Seton Hall Law Review*.[3056]

3047. *Id.* at 6.

3048. *See supra* nn. 2443–2455 and accompanying text.

3049. *Latimer Interview*, *supra* n. 2754, at 7, 8.

3050. *Id.* at 9.

3051. *Id.*

3052. *Latimer Interview*, *supra* n. 2754, at 26.

3053. *Id.* at 26, 27.

3054. Thomas C. Marks, Jr., Jerome C. Latimer & Robert Batey, *Arrest: The Law in Florida* (Harrison 1981).

3055. *Crawford v. Washington*, 541 U.S. 36 (2004).

3056. Jerome C. Latimer, *Confrontation after* Crawford: *The Decision's Impact on How Hearsey Is Analyzed Under the Confrontation Clause*, 36 Seton Hall L. Rev. 328 (2006).

Robert D. Batey

(ix) Robert D. Batey joined the Stetson law faculty in 1977, after teaching law two years at the West Virginia University.[3057] In the fall of 2005, Batey will begin his twenty-eighth year as a member of the Stetson law faculty. Born in Corpus Christi, Texas, Robert Batey received his undergraduate degree in 1970 from Yale University, majoring in history, and earned his law degree in 1974 from the University of Virginia School of Law.[3058] He then went to the University of Illinois School of Law, where he received an LL.M. degree in 1975 while serving on the faculty as a teaching assistant in legal research and writing.[3059] After his year at Illinois, Batey joined the West Virginia law faculty. From there, he came to Stetson. Soon after his arrival at the school, Batey told an editor of the *Prelude* that he never wanted to practice law; rather, that he went to law school because he wanted to teach law.[3060]

At Stetson, he found the students were "overwhelmingly Caucasian, with a smattering of Hispanics and African-Americans."[3061] Asked how Stetson's students at that time compared academically with those he had been in school with

3057. *School Starts with Early Calendar and New Faculty*, 20 Stetson Law. 1 (Aug. 1977) [hereinafter *School Starts*].

3058. *Batey Interview*, *supra* n. 2715, at 2.

3059. *Id.*

3060. Marc Gilner, *Former Prof. Cushman, Newcomer Batey Join Faculty*, Prelude 3, 8 (Sept. 30, 1977).

3061. *Batey Interview*, *supra* n. 2715, 8, at 11.

at Yale and Virginia, he replied that he "saw no problem with [Stetson's students] intellectual stature."[3062] Nor, for that matter, has he seen any unfriendliness. Batey does and has always maintained excellent relations with students. He remembers the names of nearly all his students long after they graduate. He considers learning each of his students' names as soon as possible a top priority.[3063]

Though Batey's involvement as faculty advisor to the *Stetson Law Review* was noted earlier,[3064] here we note that his working relationship with the *Review*'s editors resulted in long-term friendships with many of the editors, friendships that continue through the present.[3065] Batey is among the school's professors who has an open-door policy for students who wish to see him.[3066] Moreover, he schedules course reviews and tutoring with each of his students on a regular basis.

Batey has taught criminal law ever since he came to Stetson. His expertise in the subject has become widely recognized. Television and radio stations of the Tampa Bay area routinely contact him for his professional opinion on national and local matters involving criminal justice. It is commonplace to watch the evening news and see Batey being interviewed, or read an op-ed piece he authored in the state's newspapers.

Batey is not just an excellent teacher and commentator on criminal law, he is also a scholar. One of the more prolific writers on the Stetson law faculty, his scholarship is both in depth, yet covers a wide range of subjects.[3067] The rich curriculum of Batey's seminar in law and literature reveals his intellectual

---

3062. *Id.*

3063. In contrast to Professor Batey's patter of face-name identification of his students, a few Stetson professors have difficulty in learning, let alone remembering the names (and sometimes even the faces) of their students. For example, in one instance a professor who was attending a social occasion at his neighbor's home was approached by a young woman, who said, "Professor, it is good to see you." The professor replied, "It's wonderful to see you, too. Help me a little, when did you graduate?" "Graduate?" she replied, "I am in your contracts class!"

3064. *See supra* nn. 2801–2871 and accompanying notes.

3065. *Batey Interview*, *supra* n. 2715, at 11.

3066. *Id.*

3067. *See e.g.* Robert D. Batey, *Hawthorne's "'The Custom House, Introductory to the Scarlet Letter," and the Conflict between Individual Liberty and Social Control,* 53 Syracuse L. Rev. 1279 (2003); *Judicial Exploitation of Mens Rea Confusion at Common Law and under the Model Penal Code,* 18 Georgia State U. L. Rev. 341 (2001); *Falconer: John Cheever's Prison Novel,* 25 Leg. Stud. Forum 377 (2001); Parker v. Levy: *A Premier in Judicial Persuasion*, 49 J. Leg. Educ. 97 (1999); *Literature in a Criminal Law Course: Aeschylus, Burgess, Oates, Camus, Poe, and Melville,* 22 Leg. Stud. Forum 45 (1998); *Vagueness and the Construction of Criminal Statutes—Balancing Acts,* 5 Va. J. Soc. Policy & L. 1 (1997).

breadth.[3068] In addition to his thought-provoking teaching and scholarship, Batey was an associate dean for a period during Jacob's administration. The chair of numerous committees, he drafted the College's long-range plan in the mid-1980s, and helped put together several law school self-studies required by the ABA and the AALS.

Contributing to the pleasure of students and colleagues, Batey has adorned his office door with more political statements than any other professor in the history of the school. Moreover, as a devoted reader of the *Chronicle of Higher Education,* the *Washington Post,* and other publications, he circulates to the faculty stories of special interest regarding legal education, public policies, criminal justice issues, and the Unites States political process.

Professor Batey has received recognition for his "outstanding leadership and commitment to the legal community."[3069] In 1997, the *Stetson Law Review* named him recipient of the J. Ben Watkins Award for Professional Excellence.[3070] The *Stetson Law Review* began the Watkins Award in 1993. It is given annually to a person "who has demonstrated outstanding service to the legal community.[3071] The first recipient was Rose Mary Barkett, Chief Justice, Florida Supreme Court.[3072]

Batey's services have extended not only to the law review and the College of Law, but also to the greater Tampa Bay area. He volunteers at the St. Petersburg Center Against Spouse Abuse and for Families Against Mandatory Minimum Sentences, both organizations and programs he strongly supports.[3073]

Personable, knowledgeable, intellectual, hard working, a vociferous advocate in speech and action for racial, gender, ethnic, and sexual orientation diversity, Professor Robert "Bob" Batey has been, and remains, an influential and significant member of the faculty in the ongoing history and evolution of Stet son College of Law. Since his arrival in 1977, Batey's concern about legal education has served as a catalyst for the school's periodic introspections. He al-

3068. Professor Batey's law and literature seminar has explored scores of books over the years. A few of the assigned works included: William Shakespeare, *Measure for Measure;* Fydor Dostoyevsky, *Crime and Punishment*; Franz Kafka, *The Trial;* Truman Capote, *In Cold Blood*; Nathaniel Hawthorne, *The House of Seven Gables*; Toni Morrison, *Tar Baby*; Jane Carol Oates, *Foxfire: Confessions of a Girl Gang*; Vladimir Nabokov, *Invitation to a Beheading*; William Styron, *The Confessions of Nat Turner*; and Elie Wiesel, *The Night Triology.*

3069. *Professor Batey Wins Watkins Award,* 38 Stetson Law. 6 (Fall 1997).

3070. *Id.*

3071. *Law Review Establishes J. Ben Watkins Award,* 34 Stetson Law. 24, 24 (Winter 1993).

3072. *Id.*

3073. *Id.*

Robert Dale Bickel

ways asks why things are done in a particular way, what are the results, and what are the alternatives.

(x) Robert Dale Bickel, though he came from humble beginnings, has risen to be one of the country's leading authorities in law and higher education.[3074] Born in the rural community of Easton, Pennsylvania, Bickel grew up on a family farm.[3075] He attended Pennsylvania public schools until his family moved to Florida.[3076]

In 1956, the University of South Florida (USF) began to construct a campus in Tampa, and in the fall of 1960, took in its first class. Bickel was one of the students. By the time he graduated from USF in 1964, Bickel knew he wanted to be a lawyer.[3077] He applied to Florida State University (which was opening up a new law school) and was accepted.[3078] In 1969, he graduated first in his class, and was admitted to The Florida Bar.[3079] He accepted an

---

3074. In 1997, the American Bar Association bestowed on Professor Robert Bickel its prestigious Tweed Award for his innovating interdisciplinary continuing legal education, specifically in the field of law and higher education.

3075. Adrian G. Soud, *Professor Robert Bickel Wins National Award*, 38 Stetson Lawyer 34 (Fall 1997) [hereinafter Soud, *National Award*].

3076. *Bickel Interview*, *supra* n. 2746, at 1–36.

3077. *Id.* at 3.

3078. *Id.* at 8. Bickel was awarded a full scholarship to law school based on his undergraduate performance at the University of South Florida. *Id.*

3079. *Id.* at 10, 17.

offer to join the Tampa law firm then named Fowler, White, Collins, Gillen, Homkey and Trenam, where one of the partners, Leroy Collins, was a former Florida governor.[3080] Shortly after Bickel joined the firm, however, its partners split up.[3081] He then went into the Honors Program of the United States Department of Justice, where he represented the Commissioner of the Internal Revenue Service in various United States Circuit Courts of Appeals.[3082]

In 1970, FSU Executive Vice-President Cecil Mackey called Bickel and said Florida's public universities were establishing internal offices of legal counsel, and that FSU President Stan Marshall was doing so at FSU. Mackey asked Bickel, "Would you be interested?"[3083] President Marshall then met Bickel in Washington, urging him to be a candidate for FSU's general counsel post.[3084] Though only twenty-eight years old, Bickel applied and was pleased and somewhat surprised when he was offered the post.

As FSU general counsel, Bickel oversaw its office growth and development for seven years.[3085] During that period, he also represented the Florida Board of Regents, the body that had authority over Florida's public universities.[3086] By the mid-1970s, as FSU General Counsel, Bickel was traveling around the country, lecturing on the legal problems confronting colleges and universities. His first contact with Stetson occurred at one of these lectures in Chicago, where he spoke at a conference of the National Organization on Legal Problems of Education.[3087] Following his return to Tallahassee, Bickel received a phone call from Dean Dillon, who invited him to Stetson to talk about the possibility of his joining the faculty.[3088] He learned that Dillon's interest extended beyond his teaching to include Bickel's serving as assistant dean.[3089] Offered the dual positions, he accepted. Like Kuenzel, Smiley, Marks, Latimer, and Thurman before him, once at Stetson, Bickel never left the Col-

3080. *Id.* at 10.

3081. *Id.* at 13.

3082. *Id.* at 13, 14.

3083. *Id.* at 15.

3084. *Id.* at 16.

3085. *AALS 2004–2005 Directory*, *supra* n. 3045.

3086. Bickel Interview, *supra* n. 2746, at 19. While working at FSU, Bickel and the General Counsel of the University of Florida, Judith Breckner, co-authored a book titled *The College Administrator and the Courts.*

3087. *Id.* at 23.

3088. *Id.*

3089. *Id.* at 24. The school's then assistant dean, W. Gary Vause, was going to the University of Virginia pursuing a S.J.D. degree., and a replacement was needed. Dillon pro-

lege of Law. To this point, he has served on Stetson's law faculty for almost thirty years.

At Stetson, Bickel's expertise extends beyond higher education law to include civil procedure and torts, subjects he teaches today. His most significant contribution to Stetson College of Law, and to higher education throughout the United States, is his establishing in 1980 what became—and remains—a premier national conference on law and higher education. This annual gathering of the nation's college administrators and attorneys has been ongoing for twenty-seven consecutive years.[3090] Due to the success of these interdisciplinary seminars, Professor Bickel was awarded in 1997 the Harrison Tweed Award, given annually by the American Law Institute—American Bar Association (ALI-ABA) Committee on Continuing Professional Education, for "outstanding contributions to continuing legal education."[3091] A talented but modest person, Bickel "deflected" credit for his award to former ABA President, and current Stetson Distinguished Professorial Lecturer, Wm. Reece Smith, Jr.; Stetson's Dean Emeritus Bruce Jacob; Tampa attorney Sherwin Simmons; Stetson Dean Emeritus Lizabeth Moody; and to "many distinguished lawyers in higher education."[3092] He presently heads Stetson's Center for Excellence in Higher Education Law.

(xi) J. Lamar Woodard at first wanted to be a civil engineer. He went to the University of Florida's Engineering School, but soon transferred to the college of Liberal Arts.[3093] There, he majored in political science, earning a B.A. degree in 1959.[3094] He then entered UF's law school, receiving an LL.B degree in 1962.[3095] Because Woodard's family could not pay for his education, he worked his way through both college and law school. Upon enrolling at UF in 1956, Woodard took a job at the University's library, where he remained six years until he graduated from law school in 1962.[3096]

posed that during the time Vause was away, Bickel serve as interim assistant dean, in addition to teaching civil procedure.

3090. The national conferences are discussed further in Chapter Twelve.

3091. Soud, *National Award*, *supra* n. 3075, at 34.

3092. *Id.*

3093. Interview by Michael I. Swygert, Prof. Emeritus, Stetson U. College of L., with J. Lamar Woodard, Prof. Emeritus and Libr. Emeritus, Stetson U. College of L. 2 (Apr. 21, 2004) [hereinafter *Woodard Interview*].

3094. *Id.* at 2, 3.

3095. *Id.* at 3

3096. *Id.* Prior to going to college, Woodard spent six months in the U.S. Army, and afterwards joined the Army Reserves in order to earn additional money to help pay his college and law school tuition.

Librarian and Professor J. Lamar Woodard

After law school, and with law library experience, Woodard decided to obtain a masters of library science degree, and did so at Columbia University.[3097] At Columbia, he again worked full-time as assistant reference librarian in the University library.[3098] With degrees in law and library science, Woodard was hired as assistant law librarian in the then eight-member New York City firm of Cahill, Gordon, Reindel & Ohl.[3099]

In 1965, Woodard left New York to accept an offer from Dean Cecil Morgan of Tulane University law school to be its head law librarian.[3100] At Tulane, he learned to manage all the operations of a law school library, thereby gaining knowledge and skills that would benefit Stetson law school in the future. He stayed at Tulane through 1969, and then chose to enter private practice in St. Petersburg.[3101] While practicing law, Woodard was offered a part-time, four evenings a week job as reference assistant in Stetson's law library. At that time, Stetson's law librarian was Kenneth Evans, but he did not have a professional library degree, and "Dillon was insisting that [Evans] go to library school and

3097. *AALS 2004–2005 Directory*, *supra* n. 3045, at 1094.

3098. *Id.*

3099. *Woodard Interview*, *supra* n. 3093, at 4, 5. Cahill, Gordon was and remains one of the country's foremost law firms, today having several hundred members. Even when Woodard worked there, the firm was the tenth largest in New York City.

3100. *Id.* at 6, 7.

3101. *Id.* at 8.

William R. Eleazer

get one."[3102] Evans had little choice. Prior to his leaving to study library science, Evans talked with Woodard about his taking a full-time position at Stetson's law library.[3103] But when Evans did not return to Stetson, he created an opening for a head librarian. Dillon turned to Woodard and asked him to take the job. He agreed, and was appointed Director of Stetson Law Library and Information Services, effective February 1, 1971, a position he held until retiring from the law school in 2001, having directed the library for thirty years.[3104]

Within that time span, Professor Emeritus of Law and Librarian Emeritus J. Lamar Woodard transformed the Stetson University College of Law Library qualitatively, quantitatively, and physically. Today, the grand Stetson Law Library and Information Center, with its state-of-the-art technology and highly trained professional staff, stands as a testament to the vision and service he gave to the College of Law.

(xii) William R. Eleazer, during his twenty-five years on the faculty, did more to further the reputation of Stetson College of Law than any other single person. He put together what became repeatedly ranked as the premier trial advocacy program in the nation.[3105] Eleazer, like Julius Cesar, *came* to the College of Law; *saw* that it needed to improve its trial advocacy program; and

3102. *Id.* at 10.

3103. *Id.* at 14.

3104. *Id.* at 15.; *see also AALS 2004–2005 Directory*, *supra* n. 3045, at 1094.

3105. *See infra* Ch. 13.

then, with his troops (students and area judges and lawyers) *conquered* other law school programs in the land. Because of the College's national reputation for advocacy, the topic is discussed subsequently in a special chapter. Here, we discuss Professor Eleazer's background and achievements.

William Eleazer, a native South Carolinian, did his undergraduate education at Vanderbilt University, earning a B.A. degree in 1953.[3106] After college, Eleazer entered the United States Marine Corps as an officer and remained in the Corps for twenty-five years until 1978, when he retired from active duty with the rank of Colonel.[3107] While in the Corps, he attended both the Naval Justice School at Newport, Rhode Island, and the Army Judge Advocate General School at Charlottesville, Virginia. The Corps sent Eleazer to law school at George Washington University, where he earned his juris doctor degree in 1967.[3108]

During Colonel Eleazer's military career, the Corps assigned him to tours of duty in Korea, Vietnam, and other countries.[3109] In the states, Eleazer served as Circuit Military Judge for California and Arizona, and as Prosecutor, Trial Defense Council, Appellate Defense Counsel, and Staff Judge Advocate for the First Marine Division.[3110]

Upon his retirement in 1978 from active duty, Eleazer moved to Florida and became assistant state attorney and felony prosecutor for the Fifth Judicial Circuit.[3111] In that capacity, he prosecuted homicide and other serious criminal cases.

Learning in 1979 that Stetson College of Law was seeking a trial advocacy teacher, Eleazer came to Stetson to interview with Dillon and the faculty. He was soon invited to join the faculty, beginning his service in the fall of 1979. He became a full professor with tenure in 1984.[3112]

During twenty years on the Stetson law faculty, Eleazer taught trial practice, advanced trial practice, and evidence, and in addition served as director of the College's Prosecution Clinic, working with Sixth Judicial Circuit State Attorneys James T. Russell and, later, Bernie McCabe.[3113] In 1990, Eleazer received Stetson University's Outstanding Teacher Award.[3114] During his entire time on the faculty, he worked countless "overtime" hours during

---

3106. *AALS 2004–2005 Directory, supra* n. 3045, at 437.

3107. *William R. Eleazer Information Record* 1 (on file at Stetson U. College of L., Gulfport, Fla.) (1999) [hereinafter *Eleazer Record*].

3108. *Id.*

3109. *Id.*

3110. *Id.*

3111. *Id.*

3112. *AALS 2004–2005 Directory, supra* n. 3045.

3113. *Eleazer Record, supra* n. 3107, at 1.

3114. *Id.*

evenings, Saturdays, and every other opportunity he could find coaching, guiding, and assisting students in preparing for state, regional, and national trial competitions.[3115]

To further his commitment to be the best he could be in teaching trial advocacy, he attended Emory University School of Law during the 1986–87 academic year, where he earned a Masters of Law Degree in Litigation.[3116] Emory's faculty was so impressed with Eleazer that they invited him to come back four summers to teach in the school's Trial Techniques Program.[3117] In 1983 and 1984, Eleazer was the organizer and director of two eight-day-long Prosecutor-Public Defender Trial Training Programs sponsored by The Florida Bar's Section on Criminal Law.[3118] In addition, he served both as instructor and team leader at the University of Florida Prosecutor-Public Defender Trial Training Programs.[3119] During his years at Stetson, Eleazer frequently lectured and served on panels at continuing legal education programs.

Like professors Thurman and Latimer, Eleazer has been actively involved with both The Florida Bar and the American Bar Association. He has served as Vice Chairman of the ABA Military Law Section;[3120] was elected to the The Florida Bar's Executive Council of the Criminal Law Section; and served on The Florida Bar's Code and Rules of Evidence Committee.[3121] Regarding writing, Eleazer has authored or co-authored several books, including *Florida Evidence Courtroom Manual*,[3122] *Florida Objections at Trial*,[3123] and *Florida Criminal Trial Practice*.[3124] In addition to books, he has written several articles and has contributed chapters to Florida practice manuals.[3125] Even in retirement, he continues to write trial practice books for lawyers.

3115. Professor Eleazer's record of success with his trial advocacy teams is documented in Chapter Thirteen.

3116. *Id.* at 1. Emory was the only school in the country at that time that offered a graduate trial program leading to a degree.

3117. *Id.*

3118. *Id.*

3119. *Id.* The years were 1987, 1990, 1991, and 1993. *Id.*

3120. *Id.* at 2.

3121. *Id.*

3122. William R. Eleazer & Glenn Weissenberger, *Florida Evidence Courtroom Manual* (Anderson Publg. Co. 1992) (updated anually).

3123. William R. Eleazer, Myron H. Bright & Ronald L. Carlson, *Florida Objections at Trial* (Butterworth Leg. Publishers, 1992).

3124. William R. Eleazer, Stephen M. Masterson & Martin E. Rice, *Florida Criminal Trial Practice* (Harrison & Co. 1982).

3125. *See e.g.* William R. Eleazer, *Demonstrative Evidence*, in *Evidence in Florida* (Fla. B. 1989, rev. 1993); William R. Eleazer, *Survey of Florida Criminal Law*, 10 Nova L. Rev. 973

Though Eleazer always worked hard, he also enjoyed beating opponents in racketball, playing poker on occasion, helping design and build homes, and celebrating birthdays, especially on November 10—the birthday of the United States Marine Corps. Each year on that date, Colonel Eleazer marched into his class at Stetson with the Stars and Stripes and the Marine Corps banner. He then led the class in singing the Marine Corps hymn. On one occasion, Eleazer invited Connie Evans, Director of Faculty Support Services, and her staff to march into class with him to help celebrate the Marine Corps birthday. He asked Evans if she would carry a large birthday cake into the room. She agreed, but did more. Evans explains:

> Well, we really surprised him [Eleazer] because we went up and down the hallway and we found every active faculty member that we could find ... When we opened the door and walked in with the cake, there was a stream of people who walked in with us. We all pretended that we were playing instruments as we sang the Marine Corps hymn. Professor Eleazer was dumbfounded and excited. Well, today at Stetson we have a professor who was a student in that class, Stephanie Vaughan, who says that that was one of her fondest classroom memories.[3126]

The retired Marine Colonel and Distinguished Professor of Law Emeritus of Stetson University College of Law never forgets the anniversary of his marriage to his wife, Jan. Eleazer made sure they got married on November 10, the birthday of the United States Marine Corps.[3127] His wife worked with him in getting the administrative chores done the year he took trial teams around the country. She accompanied the teams and says she was "their number-one fan."

In 2005, Stetson College of Law named a new courtroom in Eleazer's honor, and in the same year made him a member of the Stetson Hall of Fame.[3128]

(1986); William R. Eleazer, *Trial Advocacy and Client Counseling Competition*, 12 Stetson L. Rev. 747 (1983).

3126. Interview by Michael I. Swygert, Prof. Emeritus, Stetson U. College of L., with Connie Evans, Dir., Faculty Support Serv., Stetson U. College of L. 40 (May 13, 2005) [hereinafter *Evans Interview*].

3127. Professor Eleazer's wife, Jan Eleazer, loves to tell this story and admits that she was honored "to marry Bill" on November 10, the birthday of the United States Marine Corps. In response, Professor Eleazer assures her that she has been and remains the love of his life, followed, naturally, by the Corps.

3128. *See infra* n. 4075 and accompanying text.

(xiii) Jon W. Bruce joined the faculty in 1976, and became an excellent teacher and top scholar. Though teaching at Stetson only a few years, during that period Bruce exerted a positive influence on faculty scholarship. At Stetson, he authored *Real Estate Finance in a Nutshell* (today in its fifth edition),[3129] along with a scholarly article on real estate financing, a work published in the *Georgetown Law Review.*[3130]

During Bruce's fourth year on the Stetson faculty, Vanderbilt University Law School invited him to come to Vanderbilt as a visitor. With Dean Richard Dillon's consent, Bruce went to Nashville. Pleased by the quality of his teaching and scholarship, Vanderbilt invited Bruce to join its law faculty on a permanent basis. The offer was, to borrow the cliché, one he could not refuse.[3131]

Before leaving Stetson, Professor Bruce had an impact on the importance of scholarship. Besides his own output, he and Professor Swygert believed that tenure and promotion standards of the College be strengthened to require "substantial" and "quality" scholarship for advancement.[3132] Though their ideas were not adopted at that time, a few years later the Stetson faculty put in place more demanding promotion and tenure requirements regarding scholarship. After leaving Stetson, Bruce accelerated his scholarly output, including co-authoring a long-standing property law casebook.[3133]

3129. *See* Jon W. Bruce, *Real Estate Finance in a Nutshell* (5th ed., Thomson-West, 2004).

3130. Jon W. Bruce, *Mortgage Law Reform under the Uniform Land Transaction Act*, 64 Geo. L.J.1245 (1976).

3131. The source of the information about Professor Bruce leaving Stetson and joining the Vanderbilt Law School faculty is based on the personal knowledge of Michael Swygert, Professor Emeritus, Stetson University College of Law. Swygert was a colleague of Jon Bruce at Stetson and has remained a close friend since. The two have co-authored two articles, including one on the history of American law reviews published in the *Hastings Law Journal. See* Michael I. Swygert & Jon W. Bruce, *The Historical Origins, Founding, and Early Development of Student-Edited Law Reviews*, 36 Hastings L. J. 739 (1985).

3132. *See* Memo. from Michael Swygert, Prof., Stetson U. College of Law, to Faculty, Stetson U. College of L. (1980). On another matter, Bruce and Swygert felt that the College was not taking advantage of the AALS annual faculty-hiring meetings. Their belief prompted them to write an article detailing the hiring process used by most law schools. The piece was published in the *Houston Law Review.* Not long thereafter, during Jacob's administration, Stetson began to go each year to the AALS hiring meetings. *See* Jon W. Bruce & Michael I. Swygert, *The Law Faculty Hiring Process*, 18 Houston L. Rev. 215 (1981).

3133. *See* Jon W. Bruce, C. Dent Bostick & James W. Ely, Jr., *Cases and Materials on Modern Property Law* (5th ed., Thomson-West 2003); Jon W. Bruce & James W. Ely, Jr., *The Law of Easements and Licenses in Land* (West Group 2001 ed. & semi-annual supps., Thomson-West).

(xiv) Michael I. Swygert came to Stetson in 1979, after having served on the faculty of DePaul University College of Law in Chicago (seven years),[3134] and as assistant dean and assistant professor of law at Valparaiso University School of Law (three years).[3135] During his legal education career, Swygert was a law faculty member or a law student at nine universities: Valparaiso, Yale, Indiana, Stetson, Emory, Cambridge, DePaul, Wake Forest, and Notre Dame.[3136] During the 1986–87 academic year, he visited on the law faculty at Cambridge in England.[3137] Though he neither tutored students nor taught classes, he attended lectures and sat in on tutoring sessions. His main activity was researching and comparing the American and Scandinavian theories of legal realism.[3138] Swygert found his year at Cambridge satisfying. Subsequently, two Stetson colleagues—professors Robert Batey and Ruth Thurman—also were appointed visiting members of the Cambridge law faculty. Swygert was born in Hammond, Indiana, and though his father was a judge, he had no interest in becoming a lawyer.[3139] He began his undergraduate education at Carleton College, but left after two years and became a newspaper reporter in Fort Wayne, Indiana.[3140] In 1962, Swygert enrolled at Valparaiso University, majoring in political science, where the chair of the

---

3134. Swygert was on the DePaul College of Law faculty from 1972 through 1980, but was on leave at Stetson during the 1979–1980 academic year.

3135. Swygert taught at the Valparaiso School of Law from 1969 through 1972.

3136. Swygert has visited at Indiana, Emory, Cambridge, DePaul, Wake Forest, and Notre Dame universities. At Emory, he was given the "best teaching award" from the first-year students.

3137. Swygert's invitation to be a visiting scholar at Cambridge University was due to Stetson College of Law graduate Matthew ("Matt") Towery. Towery had attended Cambridge University, where he earned a Master of Philosophy degree. At Cambridge, Towery became a close friend of Cambridge Professor Christopher Greenwood who, in 1986, was Dean of the Cambridge University Faculty of Law. Towery told Professor Greenwood that Professor Swygert would "fit in well" at Cambridge. As a result, Greenwood invited Swygert to be a visiting member of the faculty.

3138. After his return from Cambridge, Swygert began to teach jurisprudence courses at Stetson, including a course he team taught with Professor Rebecca Morgan on feminist legal theory, as well as jurisprudence seminars with emphases on post-modern jurisprudence, law and economics, creativity and the law, and law and morality.

3139. When Michael Swygert was two years old, his father, Luther M. Swygert, was appointed by President Franklin D. Roosevelt judge on the United States District Court for the Northern District of Indiana. In 1961, President John F. Kennedy elevated Swygert to the United States Court of Appeals for the Seventh Circuit, where he later served as chief judge. Yet, despite his father's forty-six year judicial career, the last thing Mike Swygert wanted to be was a lawyer.

3140. The newspaper was the *Fort Wayne Journal-Gazette.*

Michael I. Swygert

department, a lawyer, convinced him to attend law school.[3141] It was the right thing to do.[3142]

After earning an A.B. degree cum laude, Swygert entered Valparaiso University school of law, where he found law study the intellectual adventure he had been seeking. Legal issues were grounded in the richness of the social sciences—history, sociology, economics, psychology, semantics, linguistics, empiricism, natural law, epistemology, and political science. Swygert did well in law school. He was appointed editor-in-chief of Volume One of the *Valparaiso University Law Review*;[3143] was a member of the school's national moot court team that advanced to the Midwest regional finals in Chicago;[3144] and graduated number one in his class, earning in 1967 a J.D. degree *summa cum laude*. Subsequently, he was accepted into the Yale Law School graduate program.[3145]

3141. The department chairman was Dr. Albert Wehling, who had a J.D. degree from University of Illinois College of Law.

3142. From the time he was in high school through his final year of undergraduate school, Swygert had no idea what he wanted to do with his life. He loved philosophy, but realized it had few career possibilities that provided a decent standard of living.

3143. *See* 1 Valparaiso U. L. Rev. 1–200 (1966); 1 Valparaiso U. L. Rev. 201–442 (1967).

3144. Besides Swygert, the other member of the team was his classmate Bruce Berner, who, like Swygert, went on to Yale and became a law professor. Today, Berner is associate dean and professor of law at Valparaiso, and holds the Seegers chair at the University.

3145. There were only twelve Americans in the Yale graduate law program. Two of the others were or became professors at the University of Florida College of Law—Robert Mann and Fletcher Baldwin.

There, he concentrated in antitrust and law and economics, and in 1968 earned an LL.M. degree.[3146] Following Yale, he joined a Chicago law firm, where he worked on a single antitrust case—*International Telephone and Telegraph Company v. American Telephone and Telegraph Company.*[3147] The narrowness was a disappointment for Swygert.

In 1969, Alfred W. Meyer, Dean of the Valparaiso law school, invited Swygert to join the faculty.[3148] There, he taught commercial paper, sales, and secured transactions—European-style black-letter law code courses, not particularly amenable to teach in a social science, integrative manner. After coming to Stetson, however, he began to teach contracts and jurisprudence, courses that accommodated his desire to bring law and economics, semantics, theories of morality, and philosophy into the classroom.

In the mid-1980s, Professor E. Allan Farnsworth, Alfred McCormack Professor of Law at Columbia University, nominated Swygert for membership into the American Law Institute (ALI). Judge Richard Cudahy of the United States Court of Appeals for the Seventh Circuit, and Nathaniel E. Gozansky, Associate Dean and Professor of Law at Emory University, seconded the nomination. Swygert became the first person on Stetson's faculty to be elected into the ALI, where he served on two ALI consultative committees, one revising Article Nine of the Uniform Commercial Code, and the other, drafting a new Restatement of the Law of Suretyship.[3149]

At Stetson, Swygert twice received Stetson University's Outstanding Teacher Award, and twice the Homer and Dolly Hand Award for Excellence in Faculty Scholarship. He has authored or co-authored several books and over forty other pieces consisting of articles, comments, notes, and book reviews.[3150]

3146. Swygert's antitrust instructors at Yale included professors Robert Bork, Richard Spivack, Ward Bowman (an economist), and Friedrich Kessler.

3147. ITT sued GT&E in the U.S. District Court for the District of Hawaii, seeking divestiture of the vertically integrated company, specifically, the telephone operating companies from the manufactures of telephone equipment. It was the first time in the history of U.S. antitrust law that a private litigant sought divestiture as a remedy. The litigation lasted years, resulting in a settlement that was costly to GT&E. Swygert worked on the case two years.

3148. Dean Meyer told Swygert that in addition to his duties as assistant dean, he would have to teach nineteen to twenty-one class hours per academic year. Swygert did so for three years.

3149. Stetson Professors Robert Bickel, Marlen O'Connor-Feldman, and Kristen Adams have since became elected members of the American Law Institute. Deans of law schools are non-elected ALI members during their deanships.

3150. *See* Stetson U. College of L., *Faculty Home Page, Michael I. Swygert*, www.law.stetson.edu./faculty/swygert.htm.

One study he co-wrote caught the eye of both legal educators and the nation's press. With Emory professor Nathaniel Gozansky, in 1983 Swygert conducted an empirical study of the publishing histories of all tenured law faculty at each of the country's then-172 ABA-accredited law schools. The study—published in the referred *Journal of Legal Education*[3151]—found that nearly fifty percent of "senior" law faculty had not authored articles or books related to law during a five-year period.[3152] The high percentage implied that though most professors need to publish to gain tenure, after attaining that status a large number choose to "retire" into a less stressful and demanding professional life. Following publication of the Swygert-Gozansky study, its findings and methodology were discussed at national conferences of law school deans, and were reported and commented on in legal journals and newspapers around the country, including *The New York Times*, *Los Angeles Times*, *Washington Post*, *Chicago Tribune*, and the *International Herald Tribune*.[3153]

In 2004, Swygert authored a 125-year history of his alma mater, the Valparaiso University School of Law.[3154] This volume—the history of the Stetson University College of Law—is his second law-school documented chronology of an American law school. Swygert retired from Stetson in May 2005.[3155] Af-

3151. Michael I. Swygert & Nathaniel E. Gozansky, *Senior Law Faculty Publication Study: Comparisons of Law School Productivity*, 35 J. of Leg. Educ. 373 (Sept. 1985).

3152. *Id.* at 393.

3153. *See e.g.* David Margolick, *Lack of Scholarly Writing by Law Professors Cited*, N.Y. Times, Educ. Sec. 2, col. 2 (Dec. 22, 1985); *Short Takes*, Intl. Herald Trib., 3, col. 5 (Dec. 29, 1985); Warren, Possley, & Tabor, *Not to Publish Is Not to Perish*, Chicago Trib., Bus. Sec. 2, cols. 1–3 (Dec. 10, 1985); Gordon T. Ownby, *Law School News*, L.A. Daily J., 12 cols 1, 2 (Jan. 13, 1986); John C. Metaxas, *Law Schools: No Pressure on Senior Professors to Publish, New Study Confirms*, Natl. L.J. 3, cols. 2, 3 (Dec. 30, 1985–Jan. 6, 1986); *Research by Harvard Law School Faculty Is Rated Tops*, Harvard L. Sch Bull. 35, col. 1 (Spring 1986); *Law School Faculty Receives National Acclaim for Scholarship*, K.U.L. Sch. News 1, col. 3 (Winter, 1986); *Publish or Perish Doesn't Seem to Apply*, Seattle's Weekly 7, col. 1 (Jan. 15–21, 1986).

The study generated considerable attention among legal educators, especially because it ranked law schools according to the total number of publications each of the school's senior faculty had produced in the window of time the study covered. The top ten law faculties were, in order, Chicago, Stanford, Harvard, Kansas, California (Boalt Hall), Tulane, Michigan, Pennsylvania, and Louisiana State. The empirical study's methodology was both defended and criticized. *See e.g.* David H. Kaye & Ira Mark Ellman, *The Pitfalls of Empirical Research: Studying Faculty Publication Studies*, 36 J. Legal Educ. 24 (1986).

3154. Swygert, *supra* n. 80.

3155. Swygert was an active member of Stetson's law faculty for twenty-six of his thirty-six years as a law professor.

terwards, he was presented with a Stetson College of Law "Distinguished Service Award."[3156]

(xv) Howard L. Oleck was born in 1911 in New York City. He fought in World War II, and afterwards practiced law in the Big Apple. When Oleck joined Stetson's College law faculty in 1979, he was a published novelist and poet, a member of the American Civil Liberties Union, an advocate for pacifism, a strong proponent of separation of church and state, a libertarian, and a harsh critic of what he called American "provincialism." At Stetson, he routinely challenged people's beliefs, sometimes to their annoyance. Colleagues and students saw him as a complex, but fascinating, individual.[3157]

Oleck earned his LL.B. degree from New York Law School in 1939, then practiced until he entered the U.S. Army's Officer's Candidate School at the outset of World War II.[3158] Initially sent to North Africa as a tank commander serving under General Patton, Oleck became an official military historian after the Army learned he had a skill for writing.[3159] He interviewed U.S. and Ally commanders following military engagements, then wrote up the details.[3160]

After entering legal education, Oleck first taught part-time at New York Law School, and then served as dean and a faculty member at Cleveland-Marshall College of Law, then at Wake Forest.[3161] In 1979, Dillon and the Stetson faculty invited Oleck to come to the College of Law. He remained at Stetson until his retirement. Throughout his career, Oleck was a prodigious scholar. His custom was to write four hours each morning. He authored numerous books, in-

3156. Dean Darby Dickerson bestowed the Distinguished Service Award on Professor Emeritus Swygert at the June 2005 annual meeting of The Florida Bar held in Orlando, Florida.

3157. The analysis set out in the text above of Professor Howard Oleck are the views of Professor Michael Swygert, co-author of this volume. Professor Swygert became a close friend of Professor Oleck. After his death, he was the executor of his estate. Swygert and Oleck spent many hours together, along with Professor James J. Brown, discussing intellectual and political issues. During these discussions, Oleck talked about his transformation from what he called a midwest traditionalist to a civil and political libertarian.

3158. *AALS 1977 Directory*, *supra* n. 3055, at 611.

3159. Information supplied to Professor Michael Swygert by Professor Howard Oleck (circa 1980) [hereinafter *Information*].

3160. *Id.*

3161. *AALS 1977 Directory*, *supra* n. 3035. Oleck loved teaching, and the following year accepted a faculty position at Cleveland-Marshall College of Law of Cleveland State University. Oleck stayed there twenty-six years, during which he served in various capacities: associate dean, acting dean, dean, and finally "Distinguished Professor of Law." He left in 1974 to join the faculty at Wake Forest University.

cluding a comprehensive treatise on non-profit business entities *Non-Profit Corporations, Organizations, and Associations.* At Stetson, he published its fourth edition.[3162] Oleck also authored a 3,000-plus page, six-volume annotated treatise titled *Modern Corporations Law.*[3163]

At Stetson, Oleck taught non-profit business entities and torts; established a Center for Non-Profit Organization Law; and loved to debate controversial ideas regarding legal education, especially with his colleague Swygert.[3164] The *Prelude* reported that "the Oleck-Swygert debates [led] to the initiation of a faculty discussion series."[3165] After Oleck retired from Stetson, many faculty members keenly felt his absence.

Short-Time and Visiting Faculty—During Dillon's deanship, the law school faculty and dean hired fourteen visiting professors, recognizing the advantages of introducing fresh perspectives and diverse experiences to the school. Visitors were also needed as temporary replacements of faculty member on sabbaticals or visiting at other schools.

In 1972, Dillon procured a $50,000 grant from the Arthur Vining Davis Foundation to assist hiring "an outstanding visiting professor on leave from another school."[3166] One visitor was Professor Robert Kovach of the University of Akron School of Law, who came in the fall of 1971.[3167] Unfortunately, during his second year at Stetson, he died at the age of fifty-four.[3168]

Following Kovach, three commercial law professors visited Stetson. The first was Professor Donald King of St. Louis University School of Law,[3169] who was already a recognized scholar when he visited during the 1973–74 academic year.[3170] A graduate of Harvard Law School, with an LL.M. from New York University, King and Stetson law professors Calvin Kuenzel and Bradford Stone co-authored a commercial law book.[3171] Stone had first come to Stetson as a

---

3162. Howard L. Oleck, *Non-Profit Corporations, Organizations, and Associations* (Prentice-Hall 1956).

3163. Howard L. Oleck, *Modern Corporations Law* (Bobbs-Merrill 1959)

3164. *See Information, supra* n. 3159.

3165. *See* Dan McCall, *Oleck-Swygert Debate Sparks Faculty Seminar*, Prelude 1, 2 (Feb. 1980).

3166. *Glance Backward, supra* n. 2600.

3167. *Death, Practice Claim Two Members of the Faculty*, 16 Stetson Law. 6 (Aug. 1973)

3168. *Id.*

3169. *College of Law Ready for New Academic Year, Three Faculty Members, One Visiting Professor Added to Staff*, 16 Stetson Law. 1, 1 (Aug. 1973).

3170. *Id.*

3171. *See* Donald B. King, Calvin A. Kuenzel & Bradford Stone, *Commercial Transactions under the Uniform Commercial Code and Other Laws* (Matthew Bender 1997).

visitor in 1974–75.[3172] A professor at Detroit College of Law, he was a graduate of the University of Michigan Law School, and had studied at the London School of Economics.[3173] In the mid-1980s, Stone returned to Stetson, this time as a regular member of the faculty.[3174]

In 1976–77, D. Fenton Adams became the third professor, who together comprised the commercial-law trilogy, to visit at Stetson. Adams was a member of the University of Mississippi School of Law faculty, and had earned his law degree at Dickinson Law School, where later he served as acting dean.[3175] Also, he once was assistant dean at the law school at Arkansas.[3176]

Another well-known scholar to visit Stetson during Dillon's deanship was Rubin G. Cohn, a retired professor of the University of Illinois College of Law. Cohen was an expert in administrative and constitutional law, and the principal drafter of the Illinois State Constitution.[3177] Other visitors at Stetson included John Hicks of the University of Tulsa, LL.B., Baylor, and LL.M, University of Illinois (1975–1976);[3178] Bong Ho Lee of Emory University Law School, former professor and dean of Seiji College in Tokyo, LL.M., Harvard, and Ph.D., University of London (1977–1978);[3179] Alfred W. Meyer of Valparaiso University School of Law, B.A., J.D., Valparaiso, LL.M., Harvard Law School (1978–1979);[3180] and Barry Hart Dubner, holder of four graduate law degrees, including an S.J.D. from New York University, and author of several books (1979–1980).[3181] Five others stayed and became regular members of the faculty: Jon W. Bruce,[3182] E. McGruder Faris,[3183] Michael I. Swygert,[3184] Charles C. McCarter,[3185] and James J. Brown.[3186] Finally, twenty other men and women became Stetson full-time faculty mem-

3172. Schaeffer, *New Faces, supra* n. 2969, at 7–8.
3173. *Id.*
3174. *See infra* nn. 3737–3754.
3175. *College of Law Starts Seventy-Seventh Year*, 19 Stetson Law. 1, 2 (Aug. 1976).
3176. *Id.* at 2.
3177. *AALS 1977 Directory, supra* n. 3035, at 201.
3178. *Expanded Faculty, supra* n. 3004.
3179. *School Starts, supra* n. 3057, at 1.
3180. *College of Law Begins 79th Year*, 21 Stetson Law. 1 (Aug. 1978).
3181. *AALS 1977 Directory, supra* n. 3035, at 258.
3182. *See supra* nn. 3129–3133 and accompanying text.
3183. *See infra* n. 3187.
3184. *See supra* nn. 3134–3156 and accompanying text.
3185. *See infra* n. 3187.
3186. *See infra* nn. 3618–30 and accompanying text.

bers during Dillon's administration, but each was on the faculty for three years or less.[3187]

One very key staff person during Dillon's era was Dorothy Bishop. Dillon has described Bishop as "the wind beneath the wings of the dean's office during my time there."[3188] As noted previously, Dean Harold Sebring hired Bishop in 1956 to perform various administrative duties.[3189] During the first nine

3187. The twenty were: Marion Fallwell (LL.B., LL.M., George Washington University (1969–1970); Joseph Long, first advisor to law review (1969–1970); Ridgely A. Scott, LL.M. University of Miami and former attorney-advisor to Chief Counsel of the Internal Revenue Service (1973–1975); James O. Davis, admiralty specialist in Tampa (1974–1978); Elihu H. Berman, A.B., J.D., Harvard University (1975–1976); Attorney Kenneth Deacon, Jr., (1976–1978); Robert A. Mellott B.S., U.S. Military Academy, J.D., University of North Carolina, and former assistant dean of the law school at North Carolina (1975–1976); Randolph A. Monsur, named in 1978 "outstanding professor" of the College of Law by SBA, a tax specialist with LL.M. in taxation from New York University (1976–1979); Millard W. Clark, Jr., another tax specialist with an LL.M. in tax from NYU (1976–1980); N. Terry Deutsch, Stetson law review advisor, honors graduate of University Maryland School of Law, two years in Somali in Peace Corps, and a teaching fellow at University of Illinois College of Law (1976–1978); and C. McFerrin Smith, III, executive director of the Florida Law Revision Council for five years, and former adjunct law professor at Florida State (1976–1977).

Others included Edward B. Craig IV, B.S., Tennessee, J.D., University of Florida (1977–1980); J. Baird Lefter, B.B.A., Emory, M.B.A., West Florida, and LL.M., New York University, and associate with Carlton, Fields, Ward, Emmanuel, Smith and Cutler in Tampa (1978–1979); Keith M. Casto, B.A., J.D., Stetson University, an attorney for the Environmental Protection Agency (1978–1979); E. McGruder Faris, B.S., J.D., Washington and Lee University, LL.M., Duke University, former member of Wake Forest University College of Law faculty, and author of West Hornbook on Law and Accounting (1979–1983); Mary Greenwood, former legal counsel to Winthrop College, an LL.M. degree with an emphasis in labor law from George Washington University (1978–1980); Elvin C. Lashbrooke, Jr., A.B., M.A., J.D., LL.M., all from University of Texas, an M.B.A. from Michigan State, former mathematician and serviceman who worked in U.S. intelligence, author, including a co-authored book with Stetson professor Michael Swygert (1979–1981); Jonathan L. Alpert, judge of Florida Industrial Claims, B.A., John Hopkins, J.D., University of Maryland, and LL.M., Harvard Law School, and author of several books on Florida workers compensation, who is fondly remembered by his students for his "monologues and witticisms." (1979–1982); Keith F. Roberts, A.B., Stetson, M.A., J.D., Rutgers (Newark), member of Carlton, Fields law firm, taught land use planning and environmental law (1980–1981); James E. Byrne, B.A., Notre Dame; J.D., Stetson (class of,'77), LL.M., University of Pennsylvania (Spring of 1981); James F. Falco, A.B., Holy Cross, J.D., Villanova, LL.M., Temple University School of Law (1981–1982); and Beverly J. Greenley, B.A., Principia, J.D., University of Missouri, Columbia; LL.M., Washington University (1981–1983).

3188. *July 25 Dillon Conversation*, *supra* n. 2587.

3189. *See supra* n. 1953 and accompanying text.

Dorothy Bishop, Assistant to Six Deans

years of the College's existence on the St. Petersburg campus (1954–1963) the faculty did not have a secretary. In 1963, Dorothy Bishop, who had worked under the direction of Kay Eddy in the dean's office for the preceding seven years (she came in 1956), was assigned to be the assistant dean's secretary (Dillon had been assistant dean for four years at that time) and also secretary for the entire faculty. When Dillon was named to succeed Sebring in 1968, his first act was to offer the position of dean's secretary to Dorothy Bishop. She accepted.[3190]

As it turned out, Bishop worked with six deans of the College of Law: Harold Sebring, Richard Dillon, Bruce Jacob, Lizabeth Moody, Gary Vause, and Darby Dickerson. She retired in 2004, after serving the Stetson law school community for forty-eight years.[3191]

Dillon, likely echoing the sentiments of each dean Bishop worked with, described her importance to Stetson University College of Law:

> Dorothy Bishop made herself knowledgeable about every aspect of the College's operation, and I could always count on her to do the right thing. She was comfortable and efficient in dealing with the College's many constituencies, including presidents of the University, board members, and substantial donors. She served as a dependable resource for staff, faculty,

3190. *Aug. 20 Dillon-Manzanero Discussion*, *supra* n. 2720.
3191. *Id.*

> and students. When she was out of the office during the work day, and that was seldom, I felt like the electrical power to the building had been shut down and we were waiting for an auxiliary generator to kick in.[3192]

11.9 An Assessment of the Dillon Administration

At the suggestion of Dean Dillon, in 1979 a group of law school supporters and friends of the law school arranged for a twenty-fifth anniversary celebration of Stetson College of Law being a part of the Tampa Bay area community.[3193] Dillon called the group the "Suncoast Friends of Stetson." William F. Davenport of St. Petersburg chaired the Stetson Suncoast Friends, which included Horace A. Andrews, William J. Clapp, Kenneth C. Deacon, Earl B. Edington, Raymond O. Gross, John B. Lake, Paul May, and William Amory Underhill.[3194] On October 19, 1979, the Suncoast Friends, University administrators and trustees, members of the Board of Overseers, directors of the Charles A. Dana Law Center Foundation, and dean, faculty, and students of the College of Law came together to celebrate the school's twenty-fifth anniversary of its relocation to Gulfport. The Associate Attorney General of the United States, John H. Shenefield, spoke.[3195] Others also gave brief remarks, including Dillon.

With tongue in cheek, the dean told the assembled guests:

> In the last year of the College's operation in Volusia County, 1953–1954, President Edmunds was able to hold total expenses for the law school down to about $50,000. He had an efficient, economically run operation, in a low-rent barracks building at an abandoned air base North of DeLand, and what did he do? He moved it to St. Petersburg to a run-down, boom-time hotel.... Ladies and gentlemen, during the twenty-five years since the College has been one hundred and fifty miles beyond [Edmunds'] firm hand and watchful eye, annual operating costs and expenses have increased forty times to more than $2,000,000.[3196]

3192. Personal Ltr. from Richard T. Dillon, Dean Emeritus, Stetson U. College of L., to Michael I. Swygert, Prof. Emeritus, Stetson U. College of L. 28 (July 25, 2005) (quoted with permission of Richard T. Dillon).

3193. *See Stetson on the Suncoast, 1954–1979, A Community Salute* 1, 4 (Oct. 19, 1979) (a folded, four-page brochure distributed to attendees to the 25th celebration of the Stetson U. College of Law being located in Gulfport, Fla.) (on file at Stetson U. College of L., Gulfport, Fla.).

3194. *Id.* at 4.

3195. *Id.* at 3.

3196. *25th Anniversary Celebration, October 19, 1979* (untitled three page typed docu-

Interestingly, of those assembled at the school's 25th anniversary in Gulfport, only Richard Dillon had been present on the campus for the entire period, as a student, professor, assistant dean, and dean of the College of Law.

In the summer of 1980, Stetson University President Pope A. Duncan announced that Dean Dillon desired to relinquish his decanal responsibilities and return to full-time teaching on the law faculty.[3197] Duncan praised Dillon, noting that "he has brought the College of Law to the very pinnacle of its history."[3198]

There is no doubt about Dillon's significance to the law school. It has been recognized in several ways. In 1979, President Pope Duncan appointed Dillon the Charles A. Dana Professor of Law,[3199] an academic chair funded by the generosity of the Dana Foundation.[3200] In making the announcement, Duncan reviewed the dean's accomplishments, and exclaimed: "Dean Dillon is eminently qualified to be the first occupant of the first professorial chair in the history of the College of Law."[3201] Alumni of the College of Law also honored Dillon by naming him the 1978 recipient of the Ben Willard Award, an honor given each year by the Stetson Lawyers Association to "a Stetson lawyer who has put forth extra effort, which has resulted in direct benefit to the citizens of Florida and has added distinction to the legal profession.[3202] Ben Willard was a graduate of Stetson College of Law and a long-time jurist in Dade County.[3203]

In September 2004, Richard T. Dillon, Dean Emeritus and Charles A. Dana Professor Emeritus of Law of the law school, was inducted into the Stetson College of Law Hall of Fame, one of the original seventeen inductees to receive the College's highest honor.[3204]

An article in the *Stetson Lawyer* describes how the College of Law underwent dramatic change during Dillon's deanship. The title left little to read:

---

ment setting out the remarks Richard Dillon, Dean, Stetson University College of Law, read to the guests at the school's twenty-fifth celebration of its move to St. Petersburg-Gulfport, Florida, in 1954.) (Oct. 19, 1979) (on file at Stetson U. College of L., Gulfport, Fla.).

3197. Memo. from Pope A. Duncan, Pres., Stetson U., to Bd. of Trustees, Stetson U., and Bd. of Overseers, Stetson U. College of L. (July 24, 1980) (copy of file at Stetson College of L., Gulfport, Fla.).

3198. *Id.*

3199. *President Names Dillon First Dana Professor*, 23 Stetson Law. 9, 9 (Feb. 1979) [hereinafter *President Names Dillon*].

3200. *See supra* n. 2647 and accompanying text.

3201. *President Names Dillon*, *supra* n. 3199, at 9.

3202. *Dean Dillon Honored by Alumni*, 21 Stetson Law. 3, 3 (Aug. 1978).

3203. *Id.*

3204. Frank Klim, *Stetson University Hall of Fame*, 44 Stetson Law. 26 (Fall 2004).

"Dean Dillon's Administration Characterized by Physical Improvements and Academic Growth—Faculty Doubled, Book Collection Tripled, Fiscal Structure Strengthened."[3205] No doubt, Dillon's success in procuring substantial gifts combined with emphasis on fiscal responsibility were crucial for the school's moving forward. Wallace Storey, who had been an officer of both the College of Law Board of Overseers and of the Charles A. Dana Law Center Foundation, in 1990 wrote a letter to Professor Gary Vause in which Storey commented that Dillon had "a great genius in building a healthy reserve to attract healthy matching gifts to carry the school over emergencies."[3206]

The Sebring and Dillon building campaigns for the most part were completed by the mid-1970s, thereby allowing Dillon and the faculty to focus on improving the school's academic standards, raising admission requirements, hiring faculty who would be strong teachers, and increasing faculty scholarship.[3207] Dillon's raising the quality of both students and faculty was his most long-lasting and significant contribution to the College. He worked with three Stetson University presidents: Paul F. Geren, John Edwin Johns, and Pope A. Duncan. Dillon held each in high regard.[3208] Dillon relinquished the deanship of the College of Law in the summer of 1981, but remained on the faculty as a full-time member.[3209] Then, after serving his alma mater for thirty-three continuous years, Richard T. Dillon retired from Stetson University College of Law on August 15, 1990.[3210]

3205. *Dillon's Administration*, *supra* n. 2787, at 5.

3206. Ltr. from Wallace L. Storey, Atty. at L., former officer, Stetson U. College of L., Bd. of Overseers, to W. Gary Vause, Prof. of L., Stetson U. College of L. (July 24, 1990) (on file at Stetson U. College of L., Gulfport, Fla.).

3207. Vause, *Dillon Years*, *supra* n. 2581, at 28.

3208. Ltr. from Richard T. Dillon, Dean Emeritus, Stetson U. College of L., to Michael I. Swygert, Prof. Emeritus Stetson U. College of L. 1, 15 (June 2005) (on file at Stetson U. College of L., Gulfport, Fla.).

3209. *In re: Faculty, Richard T. Dillon*, 29 Stetson Law. 7, 7 (Spring 1990).

3210. *Id.*

CHAPTER TWELVE

Concern for Students; Campus Renovation; Greater Alumni Support; Increased Diversity—Dean Jacob

12.1 A Different Dean

After a six-month national search for a new dean, one that produced several strong candidates, Stetson University President Pope Duncan appointed Bruce R. Jacob, then dean of the Walter F. George School of Law at Mercer University, to be dean of Stetson College of Law.[3211] Jacob was the favorite of the search committee chaired by Professor Calvin Kuenzel, and consisting of Amory Underhill ('36), chairperson of the Board of Overseers; Cecil Bailey ('27), president of the Charles A. Dana Law Center Foundation; Earl Edington, past-president of the University Board of Trustees; Douglas Lee, University Vice President for development; and four College of Law professors: McGruder Faris, Ruth Thurman, Robert Bickel, and William Eleazer.[3212] With outstanding credentials—his resume had "111 separate listings"[3213]—Jacob returned to his law school alma mater in the summer of 1981. A 1959 Stetson graduate, Jacob was the eleventh dean in the then eighty-first year of the law school's existence.[3214]

a. Bushrod

Jacob was dean of the Stetson College of Law from 1981 through 1994. His title as dean notwithstanding, many Stetson alumni throughout that pe-

---

3211. *Bruce Jacob, '59, Will Succeed Dillon as Dean*, 25 Stetson Law. 1, 1 (May 1981).

3212. *Id.*

3213. *Id.*

3214. The earlier Stetson College of Law deans were, in order, Farrah, Rasco, Tribble, Raymond, Lambert, Howes, Haslup, Hilkey, Sebring, and Dillon.

Dean Bruce R. Jacob

riod called him "Bushrod."[3215] Therein lies a revealing story about Jacob's character.

The anecdote begins in 1957, shortly after Bruce enrolled as a law student at Stetson. He was sitting in a constitutional law class taught by Professor Roy Howes. Jacob recalls, "I loved to hear Dr. Howes talk about the history and background of the Constitution."[3216] In one class, Howes spoke about Montesquieu's *Spirit of the Laws* and urged the students to read the seminal book.[3217] Another day, the class discussed the case of *Corfield v. Coryell*, decided by a federal judge named Bushrod Washington. Howes told the students that the judge was George Washington's nephew, noting that "Bushrod spit tobacco" while presiding over court. Howes urged his class to "read about Bushrod Washington."[3218] Jacob relates what happened next:

> When [Howes] said to read about the judge, I was intrigued and wrote in my class notes: "Read about Bushrod Washington." My friend sitting next to me saw what I had written and he couldn't stop laughing. He and

3215. Jacob explains: "In law school we all had nicknames. One day, when I was Dean, my secretary, Dorothy Bishop, received a phone call from a former classmate of mine, Circuit Judge John Miller in Ft. Lauderdale. He said 'Tell 'Bushrod' that 'Bwana' is on the phone.'"

3216. Jacob, *Recollections*, *supra* n. 1678, at 1.

3217. *Id.*

3218. *Jacob Interview*, *supra* n. 2280, at 30.

> the other students [who had been in law school longer] would never read Montesquieu or about Bushrod Washington because they knew these readings were not required, [that] there would be nothing on the exam about these subjects.... After class he told the other students what I had written in my notes. And from that day to this my nickname has been "Bushrod."[3219]

Though a few still call Jacob "Bushrod," most faculty, staff, and students refer to him as "Bruce," "dean," or "professor." Today, when Jacob teaches *Corfield v. Coryell* in his constitutional law class, he tells his students about how he got the name "Bushrod," adding that they can call him that if they wish.

Born in 1935 in Chicago, Illinois, Jacob spent his early childhood in Indiana, then moved back to Illinois for a few years.[3220] When sixteen, he and his family moved from Hinsdale, Illinois, to Sarasota, Florida.[3221] In high school, he participated in high school football, track, basketball, and was state champion in the half mile. His athletic skills earned him a partial track scholarship at Florida State University. A serious student, Jacob achieved the highest academic average of varsity athletes at FSU during his attendance, being a member of the FSU varsity basketball and track teams. Also, he received a partial scholarship to play in the first violin section of the University's symphony orchestra.

Jacob received his B.A. degree from FSU in 1957, and then earned his J.D. degree in 1959 from Stetson College of Law. President of the Student Bar Association, Jacob graduated second in his class. Over time, Jacob was admitted to practice in Florida, Illinois, Massachusetts, and Ohio,[3222] and Jacob accepted a job as Special Assistant and Assistant Attorney General, State of Florida.[3223] In that position,[3224] he argued on behalf of Florida—the respondent—in the landmark United States Supreme Court case of *Gideon v. Wainwright.*[3225] Jacob soon left his position as assistant attorney general and joined the Florida law firm of Holland, Bevis & Smith (later Holland & Knight), where he remained until 1964, when he left the firm to earn a graduate (LL.M.) degree in law from Northwestern University School of Law.

3219. Jacob, *Recollections*, *supra* n. 1678, at 1.

3220. *AALS 2004–2005 Directory*, *supra* n. 3045, at 600.

3221. Bruce Vielmetti, *Dean Pulled Stetson Up a Notch*, St. Pete. Times B-1 (June 20, 1994).

3222. *Id.*

3223. Jacob, *Gideon*, *supra* n. 2474.

3224. 372 U.S. 335 (1963).

3225. Jacob, *Gideon*, *supra* n. 2474, at 181.

He next joined the Emory University School of Law faculty in 1965, teaching both criminal law and criminal procedure.[3226] At Emory, he started a program to provide legal assistance to inmates incarcerated in the United States Penitentiary in Atlanta. In one case, he was appointed by the Supreme Court to represent a federal inmate in *Kaufman v. United States*.[3227] Jacob decided to attend Harvard Law School to obtain an S.J.D. degree. There, he served as a research associate at the Center for Criminal Justice at Harvard University Law School (1969–70), and then as a staff attorney at the Cambridge Legal Assistance Office (1970–71), where he supervised Harvard Law students in the defense of criminal cases of indigent defendants.[3228]

By 1971, Jacob had become an experienced criminal defense and poverty lawyer. He accepted the position of associate professor on the tenure track at Ohio State University College of Law.[3229] In 1973, he was named Professor of Law and Director of Clinical Programs at Ohio State, positions he held until 1978, when he became dean of the Mercer University School of Law.[3230] Mercer had neither a placement office, nor funds to hire a placement director, so Jacob's wife, Ann, served as the school's volunteer director. In 1981, Jacob relinquished his Mercer deanship when he became dean and vice-president of Stetson University College of Law.[3231]

b. Hopes and Expectations

In October 1981, Carlos Enriquez, editor of the Stetson law school student newspaper, *Prelude*, interviewed the law school's new dean, Bruce Jacob.[3232] According to published excerpts, Jacob described his role and policies as "different from [those of] former Dean Dillon's," pointing out that "I don't know enough about the way things were done when [Dillon] was dean, but I know we have different personalities, so obviously there will be some differ-

3226. *Id.*

3227. Jacob won the case and Harold Kaufman was released about eleven years before he normally would have been discharged from federal custody. Kaufman then infiltrated organized crime in New Jersey for the F.B.I. and was responsible for sending a number of members of organized crime to prison. His experience turned into a movie entitled "A Deadly Business." Alan Arkin played Kaufman's part. Kaufman was placed in the Federal Witness Protection Program.

3228. *Id.*

3229. *Id.*

3230. *AALS 2004–2005 Directory*, *supra* n. 3045, at 600.

3231. *Id.*

3232. *Carlos Enriquez Interview with Dean Jacob*, 11 Prelude 1 (Oct. 1, 1981).

ences."[3233] Jacob explained that he had enjoyed his time as a Stetson law student due to positive relations he had had with Dean Sebring, Justice Brand, Dick Dillon and others, and his friendships with fellow students. Jacob said that he wanted "to make Stetson a very happy and pleasant place for students, but this doesn't mean," he added, "that it's not going to be tough academically."[3234] Jacob commented that he hoped to foster a new attitude of friendship at the school:

> Since this is a relatively small school [around 500 students at the time], one of its potentials is to develop close relationships among students, faculty and staff. This is one advantage we have to offer, and I want to encourage it. Everybody ought to know everybody here; law school should be a friendly experience where lifetime friendships are formed.[3235]

Jacob's desire that the law school become a more user-friendly community reflected, and still reflects, his positive, yet realistic view of human nature. "There's something beautiful in every human being," he told the *Prelude* reporter, adding, "I have liked just about every [person] I have ever known, including clients who were criminals."[3236] Above all, Jacob emphasized that he especially respected "people who are concerned about other people."[3237]

When it came to the new dean's expectations, Jacob, like Dillon before him, clearly understood that running a law school is a joint-governance operation involving both the dean and the faculty. "There are many goals to be accomplished," he said, "but I am skeptical about how much difference the dean alone can make," explaining his view that the dean is analogous to the president or governor, and the faculty to Congress or the Legislature.[3238] Working together, Jacob believed, the school would move forward.

c. Goals—Change Attitudes and Make School Friendlier

Though he gave credit to his predecessor, Dean Dillon, and to the faculty for successfully raising academic standards during the 1970s, Jacob nonethe-

---

3233. *Id.* at 2.

3234. *Id.*

3235. *Id.*

3236. *Id.* at 1. Jacob helped obtain the release of two Atlanta inmates who had been exceptionally able jailhouse lawyers, and put them to work helping him supervise Emory Law students "working on legal matters of inmates in the Emory Legal Assistance for Inmates" program that he had established. Their salaries were paid under a National Legal Aid and Defender Foundation grant.

3237. *Id.*

3238. *Id.* at 2.

less believed that the school's tough grading pattern throughout that decade, high academic attrition rates, and the rigidity of the administration and staff enforcement of "strict rules," caused many law students to harbor feelings of hostility toward the school both during and after their tenure there.[3239] The hostile attitudes, moreover, persisted at the school when Jacob became dean. He based his belief "on my observations, on discussions I had with students, faculty members, and alumni at the time, and on the written evaluations of faculty teaching by students."[3240] Looking back two decades later, Jacob comments that his "greatest problem" was "to improve the attitudes of our students toward their faculty, their administration and school."[3241] He explains why changing the school's atmosphere and the attitudes of students, faculty, and staff were necessary:

> My philosophy has always been that law school should be a pleasant place. It does not have to be an unpleasant environment for students to learn. During my early days here, I found that students were extremely unhappy with staff, among other things, and I was not at all happy with the attitude of some of our staff toward our students.[3242]

Not long after becoming dean, Jacob suggested to the faculty and staff that the students were the school's "customers," and that "they are paying a great deal of money to [Stetson] and that our salaries depend upon the students."[3243] He told the staff that they should assume they were working "at a luxury hotel and the students were our guests."[3244] In short, Dean Bruce Jacob wanted to transform the school's atmosphere.

Jacob had no intention, however, that by making the school friendlier he would precipitate a relaxation of academic standards. During his deanship, Stetson graduates scored 100 percent on one bar examination, and usually

---

3239. Bruce R. Jacob, *Report on the Bruce Jacob Deanship At Stetson University College of Law, 1981–1994*, at 1, 2 (2000) (on file at Stetson U. College of L., Gulfport, Fla.) [hereinafter Jacob, *Report on Deanship*]. Jacob wrote: "Probably the most important task as dean was to build goodwill and good feelings about the law school among all of its constituencies—students, faculty, staff, university administrators, alumni, and the community." *Id.*

3240. *Id.* at 2.

3241. *Id.*

3242. *Id.*

3243. *Id.* at 3.

3244. *Id.* According to Jacob, during his thirteen years as dean he fired or cause to resign fourteen faculty and staff members because of their negative attitudes toward students. He insisted that new staff members be hired through a national search, and that students be included in interviewing candidates, telling him who they preferred.

ranked first or second among Florida law schools. When the thirteen years of Jacob's deanship are combined, Stetson's cumulative passing percentage during that period was first in the state.[3245]

12.2 Upgrading Student Morale

a. Open-Door Policy

In furtherance of his desire to change attitudes and make the school a friendlier place for the administration, staff, faculty, and students to interact, Jacob opened his office door to any student who had a complaint.[3246] In his own words:

> I took steps to improve the attitudes of our students toward their faculty, administration, and school. One step was to establish an open-door policy. Anyone at the College could come directly to me with any kind of complaint. And when I received a complaint that had merit, I acted on it.[3247]

Professor Bob Batey comments: "He listened to everyone on the faculty, even the most blathering of our colleagues."[3248] Not only did Jacob require the staff to emulate his open-door style of management, he also encouraged his faculty to be more accessible to students. He emphasized to the faculty that ABA standards required the posting of office hours. By the end of his deanship, most faculty members welcomed students into their offices, a practice consistent with Jacob's view that the students "are our customers." A later Stetson law school dean looking back commented, "Dean Jacob was a very student-oriented dean.[3249]

3245. Jacob, *Report on Deanship, supra* n. 3239, at 11.

3246. *See* Robert D. Batey, *Bruce Jacob: An Appreciation*, 21 Stetson L. Rev. 299 (1992); Vause *Centennial History, supra* n. 595, at 187–88.

3247. Jacob, *Report on Deanship, supra* n. 3239, at 2.

3248. Robert D. Batey, *A Good Dean and the Best of Colleagues*, 39 Stetson Law. 5, 5 (Summer 1994) [hereinafter Batey, *A Good Dean*].

3249. Vause, *Centennial History, supra* n. 595, at 187. Only one time did Jacob's open-door policy displease a few members of the faculty. In addition to the student eating area in the Stetson Inn, there was (and remains) a separate dining area reserved for faculty and their guests. To satisfy the requests by some faculty for privacy, he asked the school's business manager to put up a wall and door between the faculty area and the students. However, the wall was not placed where Jacob had requested it, and ended up enclosing more space than was needed by faculty. Jacob ordered it torn down and did not replace it immediately. Instead, he pondered whether the wall was a good idea in the first place. He considered the physical separation of faculty from students, especially by a closed barrier between his two principal constituent groups, contrary to his goal of maximizing student-faculty interaction, and de-emphasizing the hierarchical structure typical of law

Bruce Jacob and his wife Ann opened yet another door to Stetson law students, the one to their St. Petersburg home. Near the beginning of each school year, Bruce and Ann held a reception to welcome new students.[3250] Jacob also inaugurated an annual school-sponsored party for the graduating class, often at his and Ann's home.[3251]

b. Student Evaluations of Faculty

As discussed earlier, though students asked for the privilege to evaluate faculty teaching during previous administrations, the majority of the faculty (and the dean) believed that student evaluations of faculty would be counter-productive.[3252] In contrast, Dean Jacob felt student evaluations of faculty were essential. Many of the younger and more recently hired members of the faculty thought so, too.[3253] Consequently, upon the urging of Jacob, in 1982 the College of Law faculty adopted an anonymous student evaluations of faculty policy, one that continues through today.[3254] The primary purpose of the student

---

schools. When the new school year began in mid-August, a not insignificant number of faculty members were disturbed that the Stetson "wall had come tumbling down." Whichever side of the door one stood, it really was an open and shut issue. Eventually, Jacob was won over by the need for some faculty privacy and he had the wall and door rebuilt, but this time where he originally had asked that it be placed. Professor Michael Swygert recalls the door-removal event (though does not remember the year) and, in full disclosure, confesses he was among those who at the time felt the physical barrier should have remained. A new door of separation was installed, in part based on the argument that students were talking so loudly around the corner from the faculty eating area that members of the faculty had difficulty communicating among themselves.

3250. *Jacob Interview, supra* n. 2280, at 45.

3251. *Id.*

3252. *See supra* nn. 2892–2903 and accompanying text.

3253. The faculty in these two groups included Jonathan Alpert, Bob Batey, Bob Bickel, James J. Brown, Jon Bruce, Bill Eleazer, McGruder Faris, Beverly Greenley, Elvin Lashbrooke, Howard Oleck, and Michael Swygert. Not every one necessarily supported student evaluations, but of the eleven, at least eight or nine did so, according to Professor Swygert's recollection.

3254. Vause *Centennial History, supra* n. 595, at 187. The process has changed little since its adoption twenty-three years ago. Near the end of each semester, students in each class are handed a form to fill out and provide comments on their instructor, who is absent while students complete their evaluations. Students may not put names or other identifying information on their evaluations. One student is assigned to gather and count the completed forms, put them in an envelope, seal it, and take the envelope to the College of Law Registrar's Office, where they are placed in a safe. Only after all grades have been turned into the Registrar's office are the evaluations of a particular class made available for the teacher of that class to review. Prior to all grades being turned in, the only persons granted access to

evaluations of professors is to provide criticisms and constructive input to the instructor, in the hope he or she will improve his or her teaching effectiveness.[3255] Another purpose of student evaluations of faculty is to provide information to the dean when annually adjusting faculty salaries.[3256] Jacob says, "I read every evaluation every year" of each faculty member.[3257]

It appears that Jacob's open-door policy and beginning student evaluations of faculty helped raise student morale during his deanship. But there were other causes as well. To make the school more student-oriented, Jacob added a new subdean to serve as assistant dean for student affairs, Professor Robert Bickel, who had earlier severed as an assistant dean under Dillon.[3258]

A factor contributing to low student morale when Jacob became dean was Stetson's grading system. Students complained that in seeking jobs they were at a disadvantage to other schools because Stetson was on a 3.0 grading system, while the other Florida law schools were on a 4.0 system. Thus, students argued, if a Stetson student with a 2.4 grade point average was competing with a University of Florida student with a 3.0, the Florida applicant might get the job even though the Stetson 2.4 was the equivalent of a 3.4 on the University of Florida standard. Initially, Jacob was skeptical whether this was true, but after talking with numerous lawyers, he realized that they were confused over Stetson's grading system. Consequently, he and the faculty changed Stetson's grading to a 4.0 system.[3259]

The law school's responsiveness to student concerns helped in the recruitment of new students, as the number of applicants climbed to almost 3,000 annually during Jacob's deanship. Near the end of his tenure, roughly one in five of those who applied was accepted, as the school was able to become more selective.[3260]

---

any teacher's student evaluations are the dean and associate dean for academic affairs. Later, when a specific member of the faculty is under review for retention, promotion, or tenure, the members of the Promotion and Tenure Committee of the College have limited access to that professor's cumulative teaching evaluations.

3255. *Id.*

3256. Jacob, *Report on Deanship*, *supra* n. 3239, at 2.

3257. *Id.* Jacob reports that the students' attitude towards faculty improved dramatically during the next thirteen years while he was dean. At first, students as a group were hostile toward faculty, poking fun at many of them and using a very angry tone in their comments. However, by the end of his deanship, students as a whole seemed to genuinely like and appreciate the faculty.

3258. *Id.* at 5; *see also* Vause, *Centennial History*, *supra* n. 595, at 189.

3259. *Id.*

3260. Personal ltr. from Bruce R. Jacob, Dean Emeritus, Stetson U. College of L., to Michael I. Swygert, Professor Emeritus, Stetson U. College of L. (July 27, 2005) (on file with

Bruce Jacob's emphasis upon improving the law school for its customers—the students—continued with his expanding the placement office staff[3261] and appointing students to certain faculty committees, thereby involving them directly for the first time in the administration of the College of Law.[3262] According to Jacob, all the measures he implemented helped transform Stetson's atmosphere into "a happy and pleasant place for students."[3263]

12.3 A More Diversified Student Body

a. Legal Education Turns Back on African-Americans

In 1869, George Lucas Ruffin was the first African-American to graduate from an American law school (Harvard).[3264] In 1974, Thomas E. Stringer, Sr., was the first African-American to graduate from Stetson College of Law.[3265] During the 105 years separating these two events, African-Americans were conspicuously absent from the legal profession. According to the renowned American legal educator Ernest Gellhorn,[3266] the reason for so few African-American attorneys was persistent and widespread racial discrimination and, to a lesser degree, economic hardship.[3267] The statistics are revealing: Gellhorn found that as late as 1968—three years before Tom Stringer enrolled at Stetson College of Law—fewer than 3,000 of the approximately 300,000 attorneys in the Unites States were African-Americans.[3268] That number constituted one percent of the legal profession, even though African-Americans made up twelve percent of the population.[3269] This meant that while one in 628 Americans was a lawyer, only one in 7,100 African-Americans was so.[3270] These dis-

Michael I. Swygert, Professor Emeritus, Stetson U. College of L.) [hereinafter *July 27 Jacob Letter*].

3261. Jacob, *Report on Deanship*, *supra* n. 3239, at 5.

3262. Vause, *Centennial History*, *supra* n. 595, at 187.

3263. *See Carlos Enriquez Interview with Dean Jacob*, *supra* n. 3232, at 2.

3264. Gellhorn, *supra* n. 480.

3265. *See supra* nn. 2914–2931 and accompanying text.

3266. Ernest Gellhorn had a distinguished career in legal education, serving on the faculties of both Duke University and University of Virginia law schools, and later professor and dean of Arizona State University College of Law. He also served as an officer of the Association of American Law Schools. *AALS 1977 Directory*, *supra* n. 3035, at 323.

3267. *See Gellhorn*, *supra* n. 480, at 1069–1088.

3268. *Id.* at 73.

3269. *Id.* at 1073.

3270. *Id.*

parities were further magnified in the South. Mississippi, for example, reportedly had nearly one million African-Americans in 1968, but only nine of whom were lawyers.[3271] The numbers were only slightly better when it came to law students. Of all graduates of America's law schools in 1968, only 200 of roughly 10,000 were African-Americans.[3272]

Professor Gellhorn published the above statistics in the *Duke Law Journal* in an article titled "The Law Schools and the Negro."[3273] Based on the disturbing findings of his study, Gellhorn challenged the nation's law schools to actively recruit a much larger group of African-American law students, an objective that required making available sufficient scholarship funds, thereby enabling more African-Americans to afford law school.[3274]

b. Florida: The Twenty-Eight-Year Struggle of Virgil Hawkins

The University of Florida's (UF) original charter provided that the University shall admit no persons except "white male students." UF was not alone in denying consideration of African-Americans and women to apply to law school.[3275] Prior to the 1980s, women and African-Americans in significant numbers did not enroll in the nations's law schools.[3276] But from 1980 onward, doors opened wider.

What caused American law schools to change their racial and gender profiles? Many factors, of course, came together. First was a group of courageous individuals willing to fight to bring down discriminatory barriers. In Florida, one such person was an African-American named Virgil Hawkins. A second group was those law school administrators and faculty who pushed to diversify their schools on the basis of race, gender, and ethnicity. One such administrator was Stetson College of Law Dean Bruce R. Jacob.

In 1949, Virgil Hawkins applied for admission to the University of Florida College of Law.[3277] By doing so, he became the first African-American in Florida's history who sought to attend law school. Hawkins was a man of color, and came from a poor and uneducated family.[3278] A graduate of Bethune-

3271. *Id.* at 1074.

3272. *Id.* at 1078.

3273. *See* Gellhorn, *supra* n. 480.

3274. *Id.* at 1076–1088.

3275. Stevens, *Law Education, supra* n. 196, at 18.

3276. *Id.*

3277. Lawrence A. Dubin, *Virgil Hawkins: A One-Man Civil Rights Movement*, 51 Fla. L. Rev. 913, 916 (Dec. 1999) [hereinafter Dubin, *Virgil Hawkins*].

3278. *Id.* at 914–917.

Cookman College, Hawkins was hired to be its director of public relations.[3279] While working at Bethune-Cookman, he mailed his application to the UF law school. It was rejected.[3280]

Professor Lawrence Dubin of the University of Detroit Mercy School of Law writes that Hawkins went to the courts seeking redress for being denied admission to law school not once, but *twelve* times, including five petitions to the Supreme Court of Florida, and three writs of certiorari to the United States Supreme Court, followed by more petitions and appeals to the United States Fifth Circuit Court of Appeals, and to the U.S. District Court. After Hawkins lost his third appeal to the Florida Supreme Court,[3281] his attorneys filed a second writ of certiorari with the U.S. Supreme Court,[3282] which granted the petition and remanded the case to the Florida Supreme Court in light of the Court's decision—handed down only seven days earlier—in *Brown v. Board of Education*,[3283] which held that governmental institutions, including public schools, cannot segregate students on the basis of race.[3284] Following remand, Florida's Supreme Court denied (for the fourth time) Hawkins' request for an order that he be admitted to the University of Florida College of Law, but did appoint a fact-finder to determine when, or even if, Hawkins should be admitted so as to prevent "grave and serious problems affecting the welfare of all students."[3285]

The Florida Court's decision was not unanimous, as two judges dissented.[3286] One was Harold L. Sebring (who later that year became dean of Stetson College of Law).[3287] In a dissenting opinion, Sebring noted that judicial duties must take precedence over personal views.[3288] Sebring's dissent was contrary to his position in the earlier Hawkins' appeals, where he had upheld Hawkins' exclusion on the basis of race, noting that there was little harm since Hawkins could apply to Florida A. & M. University's law school in Tallahassee, a school that accepted "Negroes."[3289] To his credit, Sebring understood that under the U.S. Supreme

3279. *Id.* at 916.

3280. *See generally* Samuel Selkow, *Hawkins: The United States Supreme Court and Justice*, 31 J. Negro Educ. 97 (1962).

3281. *State ex rel. Hawkins v. Board of Control*, 60 So. 2d 162 (Fla. 1952).

3282. Dubin, *Virgil Hawkins, supra* n. 3277, at 928.

3283. 347 U.S. 483 (1954).

3284. Dubin, *Virgil Hawkins, supra* n. 3277, at 929.

3285. *State ex rel. Hawkins*, 83 So. 2d 20, 24 (Fla. 1955); *see also* Dubin, *Virgil Hawkins, supra* n. 3277, at 930–32.

3286. Dubin, *Virgil Hawkins, supra* n. 3277, at 932.

3287. *See supra* nn. 1902–1907 and accompanying text.

3288. *Hawkins*, 83 So. 2d at 31, 33.

3289. *See* Brown, *Affirmative Inaction, supra* n. 2913, at 213–215.

Court's *Brown* decision, Florida's Supreme Court had had no choice but to hold that "if Hawkins was qualified to be admitted to the University of Florida law school if White, then he had to be admitted though he was Black."[3290]

By 1955, the National Association for the Advancement of Colored People (NAACP) had become involved in the Hawkins' case. NAACP's top lawyer, Thurgood Marshall (who had argued the petitioner's position in the *Brown* case) filed Hawkins' third writ of certiorari to the U.S. Supreme Court,[3291] requesting it strike down the University of Florida racial barrier. In a per curiam opinion, the Court held that Hawkins was "entitled to prompt admission under the rules and regulations applicable to other qualified candidates," again remanding the case to Florida.[3292] Florida's highest court, nonetheless, continued to defy the U.S. Supreme Court,[3293] deciding that the UF law school's segregation policy was legally valid and could continue to be implemented.[3294]

In response, Hawkins' attorneys again went to the U.S. Supreme Court, but this time (October 1957) the Court declared relief must come from U.S. district court.[3295] But it did not happen. In 1958, Hawkins dropped his suit against UF, and soon thereafter, UF admitted George Starke to its law school.[3296] Starke thereby became the first African-American to be admitted at UF.[3297]

A few years later, in 1962, Virgil Hawkins enrolled in Boston's New England School of Law from which he subsequently graduated. But because the school was not then ABA approved, he was ineligible to take Florida's bar examination.[3298] Seventy-one years old and twenty-eight years after applying to the UF law school, Hawkins finally gained admission to The Florida Bar in 1977.[3299] He practiced until he was seventy-eight years old, during which he "represented a multitude of clients, most of whom paid him little or no fees for his services."[3300]

3290. *Id.*

3291. *Id.*

3292. *Florida ex rel. Hawkins v. Bd. of Control,* 350 U.S. 413, 414 (1956).

3293. *State ex rel. Hawkins v. Bd. of Control,* 93 So. 2d 354 (Fla. 1957).

3294. Dubin, *Virgil Hawkins, supra* n. 3277, at 935, 937–939. Professor Dubin describes Florida Supreme Court 1957 decision as articulating "some of the most racist ideas ever written in a judicial opinion." *Id.*

3295. *Florida ex rel. Hawkins v. Board of Control,* 355 U.S. 839 (1957).

3296. Dubin, *Virgil Hawkins, supra* n. 3277, at 941, 942.

3297. *Id.*

3298. *Id.* at 943–945.

3299. *Id.* at 947.

3300. *Id.* at 953. During his last two years in practice, several grievances were filed against Virgil Hawkins. On April 18, 1985, he surrendered his Florida license to practice law. Three years later, in 1988, Virgil Hawkins died—he was eighty two. *Id.*

c. Stetson: Increasing Percentage of Minority Students

As discussed previously,[3301] Stetson College of Law, in lockstep with virtually all southern law schools, made no effort to integrate African-Americans into its student body through the 1950s and most of the 1960s, well beyond the U.S. Supreme Court case of *Brown v. Board of Education.*[3302] True, the *Brown* decision did not apply to private law schools such as Stetson, yet its conclusion that "separate is inherently unequal" articulated a moral principle that many felt *ought to* apply to *all* educational institutions. Nonetheless, most southern law schools continued to refuse to admit African-Americans, thereby seeming to ignore the core moral principle of racial equality.[3303] Only after the AALS established a new qualification for membership—one that required schools to not deny admission on the basis of race—did the doors begin to open, albeit slowly, to African-Americans.[3304] As discussed previously, at Stetson College of Law, the first African-American to graduate from the school was Thomas E. Stringer, Jr., in 1974.[3305]

Bruce Jacob estimates that when he became Stetson's dean in 1981, there were between fifteen and twenty minority students out of roughly 500 students, or 3 to 4 percent of the total.[3306] Many of these were Hispanic, several second generation Americans from parents and grandparents of Cuban ancestry who had migrated to Tampa in the late 1890s and in the early decades of the twentieth century.[3307]

By the fall of 1988, a total of thirty-five minority students comprised 6.8 percent of the student body, a number including fourteen African-Americans.[3308] At the College's December 23, 1989, graduation, Louis Whitehead (from St. Petersburg) commented that he was one of four African-Americans in his graduating class, four being at that point the highest number in the school's history. The others were M. Elizabeth Benson (Philadelphia), Gregory McKeithen (Electra, Alabama), and Yate Cutliff (St. Petersburg).[3309] A second-year African-American law student, Ingrid Lecounte-Frances from Miami told the *St. Petersburg Times*: "Stetson really has been great to us, constantly giving

3301. *See supra* nn. 2493–2495 and accompanying text.
3302. 347 U.S. 483 (1954).
3303. *See supra* nn. 2494–2496 and accompanying text.
3304. *See supra* nn. 2496–2498 and accompanying text.
3305. *See supra* nn. 2415–2416 and accompanying text.
3306. Jacob, *Report on Deanship, supra* n. 3239, at 19.
3307. *See supra* n. 250 and accompanying text.
3308. Jacob, *Report on Deanship, supra* n. 3239, at 19.
3309. *Id.*

their support and encouragement."[3310] The *Times* story noted that "Whitehead, who works actively with the black students at Stetson, gives much of the credit for an aggressive minority recruiting program to Bruce Jacob, the current dean of the school."[3311] The aggressive recruitment of minorities under Jacob continued. In the fall of 1993, 112 minority students out of 647 students were enrolled, more than 17% of the total.[3312] Of these, forty-three were Hispanics, thirty-four were African or Island Americans, eighteen Asian, and three Native Americans.[3313]

Jacob's efforts to recruit minority students included joining with the deans of the state's other law schools in preparing a proposal they presented to the Florida Post-Secondary Education Planning Commission, asking for state funds to help minority students attend law schools.[3314] Jacob explains:

> The reason for this is that it was very difficult to attract black students unless we could give them a lot of scholarship money. They came largely from families that did not have much in the way of financial resources. Hopefully, this is gradually changing, but when but when I was dean, to bring in more black students, we had to have scholarship money, and this was not easy to come by. The proposal was accepted and is now known as the Minority Participation and Legal Education Program, or the MPLE Program. Many of our [Stetson] minority students received financial aid through this program.[3315]

Not only did Jacob help get money from the outside for minority scholarships, he also raised the school's internal scholarship budget during his deanship. Again, he explains how he did so:

> I always insisted during the budget process that our scholarship budget increase at twice the percentage rate as the rest of the budget. In other words, if the next year's budget was increasing by 6 percent, I insisted that the scholarship budget increase by 12 percent. By the time I left the deanship, our scholarship budget was approaching one-and-a-half million dollars.[3316]

3310. *Id.*
3311. *Id.*
3312. *Id.*
3313. *Id.*
3314. *Id.* at 19–20.
3315. *Id.* at 20. The State's MPLE program no longer exists.
3316. *Id.*

Looking back on his thirteen years as dean, Jacob says that, "we made tremendous efforts to recruit more minorities and provide scholarships for them."[3317] His efforts succeeded, as revealed by the proportional increases in the number of minority students during his deanship.[3318] Jacob adds:

> The profession of lawyer is a public profession, and we owe it to society to produce competent, ethical lawyers. But, also, it seems to me that we owe an obligation to provide minority clients who want them with lawyers of their own race or sex. That, to me, is one of the important reasons why we needed to increase our numbers of minority students. Also, it was the right thing to do."[3319]

Fifteen years after Jacob's left the deanship, Stetson College of Law continued to increase its percentage of minority students in proportion to the total student body. According to a study by Vernellia R. Randall, professor of law at Dayton (who teaches a course titled Race and Racism in American Law),[3320] Stetson College of Law's minority students comprised approximately 18 percent of the student body during the 2003–2004 academic year.[3321] By the fall of 2005, the numbers had risen to 24 percent.[3322]

Hispanics, Asians, and women, in contrast to African-Americans, have had an easier time in gaining admission to the Stetson College of Law. As discussed earlier, women were accepted during the school's first decade and have been ever since.[3323] Moreover, no evidence has been found showing that the school denied admission or, for that matter, discouraged women, Asian, African-American, and Hispanics to apply.

Nonetheless, reflecting national trends, Stetson had relatively few minority law students during the first sixty-five years of its existence. Beginning in the late 1960s, however, and accelerating throughout the 1970s, women applied and were admitted to the College in greater numbers.[3324] The upward trend in the proportion of women to the entire student body continued throughout

---

3317. *Jacob Interview*, *supra* n. 2280, at 82.

3318. *A Quiet Resolve, after 13 Years as Dean, Bruce Jacob Steps Aside*, 34 Stetson Law. 2, 3 (Summer 1994) [hereinafter *A Quiet Resolve*].

3319. *July 27 Jacob Letter*, *supra* n. 3260.

3320. *AALS 2004–2005 Directory*, *supra* n. 3045, at 869.

3321. Vernellia Randall, *The 2004 Whitest Law School Report*, http://academic.udayton/race/o3justice/LegalEd/Whitest/HWLS0403.htm (accessed Apr. 12, 2004).

3322. The 2005 statistics were provided by the Stetson University College of Law Office of Admissions.

3323. *See supra* nn. 496–508 and accompanying text.

3324. *See supra* nn. 2617, 2779, and accompanying text.

Jacob's administration. He notes that the percentage of women during his deanship rose from about 30 percent in 1981, to above 50 percent in 1993–94, his last year as dean.[3325] He takes no credit for the rise, however, explaining:

> I had absolutely nothing to do with that. That was a trend throughout the country. Every law school was getting more and more women, and so that was a national trend. But that was a wonderful trend, because if we hadn't had all those good women students, I think we would have been in difficulty financially.[3326]

d. Faculty Diversity

The sharply increased diversification in reference to race and gender of the student body during Jacob's administration was reflected in the composition of the faculty as well. When Jacob took over the deanship from Dillon in 1981, no African-Americans, Hispanics, or Asians were on the faculty, though there was one, but only one, woman—Ruth Thurman.[3327] When Jacob retired from the deanship in 1994, "there were two African-Americans professors, Dorothea Beane and Daryl Wilson; and one Hispanic professor, Manuel Ramos."[3328] Professor Ramos, however, voluntarily left the school at the end of the 1994–95 academic year, one year following a controversy regarding his renewal, a subject discussed later in this chapter.[3329] The second Hispanic to join the Stetson law faculty occurred in 1998, when Luz E. Nagle, a native of Colombia, was hired. She was the first Hispanic professor to gain tenure and become a full-time professor at the College of Law, and remains a member of the Stetson law faculty.[3330]

When it comes to women, three women were hired as Stetson faculty members during the Dillon administration (Leeman, Schaeffer, and Thurman),[3331] while nine were hired during Jacob's deanship (Beverly Greenley, Suzanne Armstrong, Dianne Clark, Rebecca Morgan, Dorothea Beane, Marleen O'-Connor, Joryn Jenkins, Roberta Flowers, and Terry Pollman.)[3332] In contrast, the number of African-American professors who had been hired as full-time faculty members by 2004 was six: Beane, Wilson, Robert Davis, Mary Scriven,

---

3325. Jacob, *Report on Deanship*, *supra* n. 3239, at 18.

3326. *Jacob Interview*, *supra* n. 2280, at 82.

3327. Jacob, *Report on Deanship*, *supra* n. 3239, at 13.

3328. *Id.*

3329. *See infra* nn. 3568–3601 and accompanying text.

3330. *Nagle Becomes Stetson's First Hispanic Full Law Professor,* 45 Stetson Law. 13, 13 (Summer 2005); *Stetson Law Professor's Hard Ascent*, St. Pete. Times B-1 (Dec. 20, 2004).

3331. *See supra* nn. 2951, 2957, 3004, and accompanying text.

3332. Bishop, *List*, *supra* n. 2351, at 3–12.

Madison Mosley, and Cynthia Hawkins-Leon, with at least one additional African-American expected to join the faculty in fall 2006.[3333] In the 1990s, Ester Kim became the first Asian-American to join the law school's faculty, though the visiting professor remained only two years.[3334]

By spring 2005, the number of women was approaching fifty percent of the full-time teaching faculty. That year, the fifty-three-member Stetson full-time teaching faculty consisted of twenty-four women and twenty-nine men. Sixteen of the twenty-four women held professorial positions, while eight were instructors. In addition, there were eighteen women in adjunct positions.[3335] At the same time, twenty-four of the men were professorial rank, while two were instructors.[3336] Through the 1960s, however, no Jewish faculty candidates were hired. In the 1960s, Jacob was considered for a teaching position but was not hired because, he believes, "the faculty mistakenly thought I was Jewish and that the University trustees would not approve my appointment."[3337] During Jacob's deanship, several Jewish faculty were hired.

Today, Bruce Jacob is pleased with the faculty's diversity when compared with the faculty's composition in 1981 when he became dean. Then, it was composed entirely of white males with one exception, one white female. Though Dillon was the first to hire women on the faculty, Jacob's administration was the first to hire African-Americans and Hispanics.[3338] By the fall of 2005, the combined number of women and traditional minority students was slightly higher than the number of white male students (though not of the tenured faculty), making the latter the new "minority."

12.4 Major Renovations and Campus Additions

a. The Walls Came (Nearly) Tumbling down

In fall 1981, Jacob, shortly after becoming dean, was visited by a City of Gulfport, Florida, fire inspector.[3339] Following an examination of campus buildings,

3333. *Id.*

3334. *Id.*

3335. *Id.*

3336. *July 27 Jacob Letter*, *supra* n. 3260, at 3.

3337. Notes on Manuscript Draft from Bruce R. Jacob, Dean Emeritus, Stetson U. College of L., to Michael I. Swygert, Prof. Emeritus, Stetson U. College of L. (Sept. 25, 2005) [hereinafter Jacob, *Sept. 25 Draft*].

3338. *See supra* nn. 3568–3601 and accompanying text.

3339. Jacob, *Report on Deanship*, *supra* n. 3239, at 23.

the inspector "found almost 100 fire code violations."[3340] Surprised, Jacob walked through the campus with the inspector, who pointed out the infractions. "I was convinced after seeing these," Jacob notes, "that he was accurate in his findings; we remedied these violations within a year at a cost of about $20,000."[3341]

Other than the fire code problems, Jacob at first believed the campus buildings were in good shape. Dillon felt so too, Jacob says.[3342] After all, Dillon had installed new air conditioning units in the Stetson Inn, had the Mann Lounge and Sebring Courtroom renovated, and had to budget significant expenditures for maintenance of campus properties.[3343] So, after correcting the fire code problems, Jacob believed that the campus "facilities" problems were past. Not so. In the mid-1980s, an architect informed Jacob that the school's main building was in dire straits. As reported in the *St. Petersburg Times,* "Chunks of plaster are falling on students. Floors are rotting, and handrails are rusting."[3344] Problems of serious decay included the central bell tower of the old Rolyat Hotel,[3345] student dormitory rooms, Great Hall, Mann Lounge, the kitchen and dining room area, and various offices. With outward manifestations of structural problems, Jacob hired architect Charles Canerday to investigate.[3346] Carnerday's findings appeared in an article in the *Stetson Reporter*:

> Numerous examples of the unexpected decay were found by [the] supervising architect. All sorts of structural nightmares were discovered. The ground floor was so rotted and termite-ridden that it had to be replaced with concrete. The second floor joists were in better shape, but the workers had to add more joists and levelers to prop up the sagging beams.[3347]

What became clear to Jacob was that the dormitory area, in particular, was unsafe.[3348] He explains:

3340. *Id.*

3341. *Id.; see also Jacob Interview, supra* n. 2280, at 56, 57.

3342. *Id.*

3343. *See supra* nn. 2600–2615 and accompanying text.

3344. Susan Eastman, *Hallowed Halls Are Crumbling—Poor Construction Costly to Stetson*, St. Pete. Times, City Sec. 1 (Sep. 11, 1988) [hereinafter Eastman, *Hallowed Halls*].

3345. *See infra* nn. 2951, 2957, 3004, and accompanying text.

3346. Eastman, *Hallowed Halls*, *supra* n. 3344, at 1. Charles Canerday was head of Charles Canerday & Associates Architects, AIA. *Id.*

3347. Rick Boucher, *Renovation Plan Meets Today's Needs*, 28 Stetson Law. 12, 12 (1988) [hereinafter Boucher, *Renovation*].

3348. Jacob, *Report on Deanship*, *supra* n. 3239, at 25.

> Termites had eaten through many of the beams and supporting columns, and dry rot was found throughout the buildings. When we learned this, we had to immediately evacuate the students and find housing for them away from campus ... After the building was evacuated, it was completely renovated.[3349]

Prior to actual renovation, Jacob faced a tough choice. Either the entire dormitory wing of the Stetson Inn had to be torn down and a new structure erected, or the existing building would have to be gutted, leaving only the original walls and ceiling, requiring that all the living quarters would have to be rebuilt from within with new walls, doors, windows, plumbing, wiring, and central air conditioning. It turned out that the complete tear down plus rebuilding would cost about the same as a new building from ground up.[3350] Jacob and a majority of the faculty were determined to preserve the distinctive Mediterranean Revival architecture style in accordance with the plan of the original Rolyat Hotel, and to be architecturally consistent with other units of the Stetson Inn.[3351] The preservation and renovation choice trumped the demolishment and new construction alternative.[3352] As Canerday explained:

> While it is essential to modernize the rooms, it is also important to maintain the Mediterranean Revival architectural style. To this end, all doors and windows will remain in the same locations to keep the facade unchanged. The result of this project will restore the original style, while updating and modernizing the mechanical and electrical needs.[3353]

Canerday told the *St. Petersburg Times* that even though the 1925 Rolyat Hotel structures "look good, they didn't build them very good in those days."[3354] The architect predicted it would take at least four years to renovate

3349. *Id.* at 26.

3350. *Jacob Interview*, *supra* n. 2280, at 57.

3351. Boucher, *Renovation*, *supra* n. 3347, at 12.

3352. Notes from Bruce R. Jacob, Dean Emeritus, Stetson U. College of L., to Micheal I. Swygert, Prof. Emeritus, Stetson U. College of L. (Aug. 29, 2005) [hereinafter, Jacob, *Aug. 29 Notes*].

3353. Boucher, *Renovation*, *supra* n. 3347, at 12.

3354. Eastman, *Hallowed Halls*, *supra* n. 3344, at 1. Charles Canerday, the architect who oversaw the Stetson Inn's Renovation, commented that during the hotel building boom of the 1920s, when "builders were rushing productivity, they threw in whatever was laying around and called it building material." *See* Boucher, *Renovation*, *supra* n. 3347, at 12.

the building's old hotel rooms, Great Hall, the granary, and the bell tower.[3355] He was right. The massive project cost several million dollars and was financed primarily through funds from the Rosa Estate (discussed earlier).[3356]

b. Renovations

In addition to rebuilding the Stetson Inn's dormitory rooms from the inside out, Jacob oversaw several other campus improvements. These included: renovations of Stetson's Inn's six guest apartments; the Great Hall (redoing air conditioning and adding new lighting); the Mann Lounge (for the second time);[3357] enlargement of the business office; construction of new offices for faculty and staff members and for the law review; renovation of the Classroom H courtroom; adding more seminar rooms and small meeting rooms; installing an elevator in the bell tower for access to the second and third floors; repainting campus buildings back to the original colors used when the hotel was built; and renovation of the Crummer building classrooms into facilities having tiered seating and curved tables, thereby enabling students to better interact with the instructor and with other students.[3358]

One renovation Jacob had no choice in making was the entrance to Great Hall. In the mid-1980s, Gulfport fire department officials advised the dean that the layout of the hall was in violation of the city's fire code. The massive, intricately carved wooden doors (original to the 1925 Rolyat Hotel) opened inwardly into Great Hall and thereby violated the city's fire code requiring that doors to enclosed rooms must open to the outside.[3359] The problem was that the doors, structurally, could not be rehung to open outward. Jacob asked architect Dale Sprankle to come up with a solution.[3360] Sprankle suggested that a set of glass doors be installed that would open outward, while keeping the stately wooden doors in a permanent open position on the inside.[3361] The glass doors were added, thereby preserving the wooden doors while being in compliance with the fire code standards.[3362]

3355. *Id.*

3356. *The Margin of Excellence, Estate Gift Provides Needed Expansion*, 27 Stetson Law. 8, 8 (Fall 1987) [hereinafter *Margin of Excellence*].

3357. The first renovation occurred in Dillon's administration.

3358. Jacob, *Report on Deanship*, *supra* n. 3239, at 26.

3359. Bruce R. Jacob, *Annual Report to Dr. Pope Duncan* 1, 3 (July 17, 1986) (on file at Stetson U. College of L., Gulfport, Fla.) [hereinafter Jacob, *1986 Report*].

3360. *Id.*

3361. *Id.*

3362. *Id.* at 4.

c. *James and Ruth Nemec Office Complex*

Jacob's making the campus more efficient and responsive to the needs of the College of Law continued. In 1986, the dean solved what faculty called the teaching disaster of "Classroom A," the largest and most difficult room to teach on campus (acoustics were horrible), located on the first floor of Crummer Hall. The architect suggested severing it into two sections.[3363] The western segment became a significantly smaller lecture hall (in 2004 converted into a tiered modern classroom).[3364] At the same time, the eastern segment was converted into offices to accommodate the Development and Alumni Relations Department along with several offices for faculty and staff.[3365]

In 1989, Stetson University President H. Douglas Lee officially named the new classroom and lecture hall the *James and Ruth Nemec Auditorium*, and the adjacent office complex the *James and Ruth Nemec Office Complex.* The *Stetson Lawyer* reported, "The naming of the College's largest classroom pays tribute to two Stetson alumni" for their establishing a $500,000 trust for the law school, to use at the school's discretion.[3366] James Nemec had won a football scholarship to Stetson University in 1930. He earned a degree in business administration, followed by an LL.B. degree—later changed to a J.D.—from the law school in 1936.[3367] Nemec practiced law in Palm Beach County and served as an officer of the County Bar Association while actively participating in both The Florida Bar Association and the Florida Trial Lawyers Association.[3368] He met his future wife, Ruth Bartlett, when they both were students. She graduated from Stetson in 1938, and later did graduate work at Columbia University.[3369] The Nemecs were among many Stetson alumni whom Jacob visited as part of his fund-raising activities, a topic discussed below.[3370]

d. *Carey & Florin Courtroom; New Faculty Offices*

At the suggestion of Overseer member Dick Jacobs, Dean Bruce Jacob hired architect Dale Sprankle to design a master plan to guide the future develop-

3363. *Margin of Excellence*, *supra* n. 3356, at 8.

3364. *Id.*

3365. *Id.*

3366. *Id.*

3367. *Id.*

3368. *Id.*

3369. *Id.*

3370. *See supra* nn. 3396–3446 and accompanying text; *see also* Jacob, *Report on Deanship*, *supra* n. 3239, at 11.

ment of the school's Gulfport campus.[3371] After Sprankle completed the plan in 1984, Jacob submitted it to the University President, Board of Trustees, and Board of Overseers for approval. All did so in 1986.[3372]

In the planning process, Jacob and Sprankle considered what new structures the school would need in coming years, and where on campus they should be located.[3373] At first, the school's most pressing need was a facility to house additional students, either on campus or nearby. After the Rosa money became available in the mid-1980s, with the help of Business Manager Joe Estenes, the College purchased and renovated an off-campus apartment complex.[3374] But additional new facilities became necessary as the school's programs and faculty continued to expand. To help fill the need, the College embarked on a program of purchasing houses and apartments near the law school to provide housing, primarily for married students. Today, the College owns over fifty homes and apartments in the vicinity of the law school, in addition to one off-campus apartment complex.

By the mid-1980s, the school needed two additional courtrooms. Professor Eleazer, together with other faculty, judges, and lawyers, had put together a trial advocacy project that had become the highest-rated law-school advocacy program in the country.[3375] Besides the Sebring Courtroom, the make-do courtroom in Classroom "H," and a very small courtroom on the second floor of the Rolyat tower, additional spacious and state-of-the-art courtrooms were needed to meet the student demand for trial advocacy training.

But the school had another priority as well. By the late 1980s, the faculty had grown, and additional offices had to be provided.[3376] To accommodate a new courtroom and faculty offices, Jacob and the faculty facilities committee agreed that a new building should be constructed. With backing from Trustees, Overseers, and faculty, a plan was conceived to connect the new structure with the Crummer classroom facility.[3377] The building would be built in the Renaissance Revival architectural style. The work proceeded, and

3371. Jacob, *Report on Deanship*, *supra* n. 3239, at 24.

3372. Jacob, *1986 Report*, *supra* n. 3359, at 4.

3373. *Id.*

3374. *Margin of Excellence*, *supra* n. 3356, at 8.

3375. *See infra* ch. 13.

3376. Beginning in the late 1970s and accelerating in the 1980s, the College of Law faculty grew primarily due to expansion of the curriculum in both skills and substantive law areas, the latter reflecting the growth and development of newer specialities in law practice such as environmental, real estate finance, poverty, pension, sports and entertainment, and elder law areas, among others.

3377. Jacob, *Aug. 29 Notes*, *supra* n. 3352.

the structure was completed in the summer of 1993. In addition to a spacious and technologically savvy new courtroom, the facility included eleven spacious faculty offices.[3378]

The funding for the courtroom came from five partners of the then-existing Clearwater, Florida, law firm of Carey & Florin, who gifted the College of Law with a quarter of a million dollars in honor of the school's trial advocacy program.[3379] While Tom Carey, a noted trial attorney, earned his law degree at Suffolk University, the four other donors were Stetson law school graduates: William Florin ('80), Thomas Roebig ('86), James Huddlestun ('87), and Michael Walker ('87).[3380] The Carey & Florin Courtroom was dedicated on November 5, 1993, in recognition of Professor Robert Bickel.[3381] Assistant Dean Thomas E. Allison (Stetson law, '77) spoke to the eighty guests on the "importance of alumni giving back," and thanked Messieurs Carey, Florin, Roebig, Huddlestun, and Walker for their donation. It was the largest gift to the trial program in the law school's then ninety-three-year history.[3382]

12.5 Alumni Morale and Fund Raising

a. Raising Alumni Morale

After Jacob retired from the deanship at the end of the 1993–94 academic year, the *Stetson Lawyer* featured a lengthy tribute commenting on the goals Jacob had accomplished.[3383] Brian S. Thomas and Paula J. Reed wrote that one of Jacob's "greatest strengths was his relationship to the alumni, [a group] he has brought closer to their law school," noting that the dean spent "thousands of hours" traveling around the state and meeting with alumni, and that his efforts made a significant difference.[3384]

In a report summarizing his deanship, Jacob listed as number two (behind building student morale), his success in increasing the level of "good feelings"

3378. Bruce R. Jacob, *Dean's Pages*, 33 Stetson Law. 2, 3 (Summer 1993) [hereinafter Jacob, *Dean's Pages*].

3379. *Carey & Florin Courtroom Dedicated*, 34 Stetson Law. 4, 4 (Winter 1993) [hereinafter *Carey & Florin*].

3380. *Id.*

3381. *Id.*

3382. *Id.*

3383. *See A Tribute to Bruce R. Jacob, Dean, 1981–1994*, 34 Stetson Law. cover pg. (Summer 1994).

3384. *A Quiet Resolve*, *supra* n. 3318, at 2, 4.

among alumni toward the school.[3385] Many graduates from the 1960s and 1970s retained negative feelings about their experience at the law school.[3386] The reasons, of course, varied. Some found they did not like law study, while others found the work too demanding. Such reactions are typical of some students at any law school. At Stetson, however, many students of that era were displeased over how they perceived they were treated by their instructors. A number of students felt that a few professors had demeaned them in class.[3387]

Interviews of several Stetson law alumni and a few members of today's law faculty who taught in the 1970s recall that there were students back then who, years later, as alumni continued to harbor ill feelings about their law school experience.[3388] Soon after taking office, Jacob says he realized the depth of the morale problem.[3389] In a report, he wrote:

> Many of the graduates of the 1970s had formed what they called the "I Won't Give a Dime Club." They disliked the school so much that they had vowed that they would never give any money to Stetson. This attitude had to be changed.[3390]

Furthermore, Jacob learned that other alumni—those who had graduated in the 1960s during the Sebring administration—were upset for altogether different reasons.[3391] Jacob explains:

> [Beginning in the 1960s], the school had allowed some LL.B. degree holders to exchange their LL.B. diplomas for J.D. degrees [in accordance with what nearly all American law schools did], but a fairly large group of alumni were not allowed to do so.
>
> For many years, a person could come to law school after three years of college. If the student came from Stetson after three years, [at graduation from law school] that person received a B.A. or B.S. degree on the basis of spending one year here at the law school. However, students coming

3385. Jacob, *Report on Deanship*, *supra* n. 3239, at 6.

3386. *See supra* nn. 3239–3245 and accompanying text.

3387. What certain students considered to be a confrontational—some would say "put down"—psychological climate and pedagogy found in a few classes at Stetson during a couple of decades was in no way particular to Stetson. The popular book and resulting movie, *Paper Chase*, reflects the pedagogy of classroom put down and resulting fear it engenders, in this instance occurring at Harvard Law School.

3388. *See infra* nn. 3389–3395 and accompanying text.

3389. Jacob, *Report on Deanship*, *supra* n. 3239, at 7.

3390. *Id.* at 7.

3391. *Id.* at 6.

President Pope Duncan

> from other colleges and universities after only three years did not receive a bachelor's degree after completing a year of law study [at Stetson].[3392]

The school took the position that Stetson LL.B. graduates who had not earned a Stetson undergraduate degree were ineligible to exchange their LL.B. degrees for the J.D. degrees.[3393] According to Jacob, many alumni among this group "had become alienated from the law school, and some of them had vowed never to give any money."[3394] Jacob asked Stetson President Pope Duncan and the law faculty to change the policy, thereby permitting all Stetson LL.B. graduates to convert their degrees to J.D.s. The University went along, and many formerly alienated alumni became staunch supporters of the school, according to Jacob.[3395]

b. Networking Alumni

Another goal Jacob set out during his deanship was "to develop a strong network of alumni."[3396] At the time he became dean, the school had a national alumni association and national officers, but the alumni met infrequently and were not well organized geographically. Jacob was determined to correct these problems and in time did so. He gives much of the credit to several alumni who worked with him. He mentions especially his law school classmate John

3392. *Id.*
3393. *Id.*
3394. *Id.*
3395. *Id.* at 7.
3396. *Jacob Interview*, *supra* n. 2280, at 48.

Guyton ('58), as well as Paul May ('79), Deborah Werner ('83), and Martin Rice ('74).

Near the outset of Jacob's administration, alumnus John Guyton talked with him about fund raising.[3397] Jacob told Guyton that before he became dean, few alumni gave to the law school. Guyton asked what the numbers were, and Bruce replied that less than 100 had made gifts the year prior to his becoming dean.[3398] Guyton, a businessman, suggested that the College of Law needed an office of development, where a person trained in fundraising would work with Jacob full-time raising monies.[3399] But before a professional fundraiser could hope to be successful, the school needed to inspire alumni to regain interest in the school. That's where Paul May, of Ft. Lauderdale, and Deborah Werner, of Tampa, played a big role. Jacob enlisted the two to assist him in putting together local and regional alumni organizations throughout Florida and beyond. They divided the alumni of the College into sixteen districts, fifteen in Florida and the sixteenth for graduates residing outside the state. Jacob explains:

> We divided the state of Florida and out-of-state alumni into [several] groups—each one [covering] a geographic area—and we began the process of electing officers in each group ... We started a fund raising office here on campus to help out, but it took a tremendous amount of work. I probably spent more time in fund raising work than in anything else.[3400]

Jacob initiated an annual telephone campaign, lasting as long as six days per year, in which alumni volunteers, faculty and College officials contacted alumni and asked each to contribute a financial gift to the school.[3401] Jacob's work with alumni throughout Florida took great effort, but it succeeded. By the end of his deanship, he had appointed alumni officers in each district of the state. With assistance from alumni from each district, the school, Jacob says, held up to "twenty-five alumni events each year," including breakfasts, lunches, dinners, and receptions.[3402] Alumni including Bill Whitaker, Ray

3397. Telephone Conversation between Michael I. Swygert, Prof. Emeritus, Stetson U. College of L., and John T. Guyton, Emeritus Member, Stetson U. College of L. Bd. of Overseers (July 29, 2005) [hereinafter *Guyton Conversation*].

3398. *Id.*; *see also* Jacob, *Report on Deanship*, *supra* n. 3239, at 8. "The year before I became dean, the school raised $74,000 ... The number of donors [was] less than 100." *Id.*

3399. *Guyton Conversation*, *supra* n. 3397.

3400. *Id.* at 48, 52.

3401. *July 27 Jacob Letter*, *supra* n. 3260.

3402. Jacob, *Report on Deanship*, *supra* n. 3239, at 7.

Steinhardt, and Clyde Wilson, Jr., often paid for these events during the 1980s. The numerous alumni social gatherings continue today, and remain important for increasing alumni support and awareness of school information. Jacob explains:

> By getting alumni at the district level involved, we [began] to develop a cadre of leaders of our alumni association. Our national officers came from the ranks of those who have done a good job at the district level. We [also] established an annual weekend in late March or early April each year to bring our alumni back to the campus for an alumni weekend, including class reunions.[3403]

In 1992, the spring alumni weekend drew 148 persons for a "grand reception and dinner." Then, in 1994, 255 attended the reception and dinner, and 115 at a luncheon in the school's courtyard the next day.[3404] But by far the largest gathering of alumni on campus during Jacob's deanship occurred in the spring of 1993, when 350 alumni and guests came back to Stetson. The highlight was a roast of Professor Calvin Kuenzel.[3405]

c. *Professor Kuenzel's Trial*

Tying together the annual spring alumni gathering with a roast of Stetson's most-talked-about professor—Cal Kuenzel—was an astute move. Stetson College of Law alumni from far and wide came back to get revenge and laugh at the expense of their former professor. On March 19, 1993, "Cool Cal, the Students' Pal" was indicted, tried, and convicted before a crowd of cheering and jeering former students, families, and friends.[3406] The trial occasion took place in the Grand Ballroom of the recently renovated Vinoy Hotel in downtown St. Petersburg. It was a prosecution to remember.

After a "pre-trial reception, followed by a four-course gourmet dinner," Kuenzel was read the indictment:

> 1. Intentional infliction of emotional distress;
> 2. Student molestation (being hit by erasers) and other violations of human rights;
> 3. Criminal conversion of the Uniform Commercial Code; and,
> 4. Classroom terrorism and other crimes against nature.[3407]

3403. *Id.* at 8.
3404. *Id.*
3405. *Id.*
3406. Paula J. Reed, *Cal's Day in Court*, 33 Stetson Law. 8, 8 (Summer 1993).
3407. *Id.* at 8, 9.

Assistant Director of College Relations Paula J. Reed later wrote up a summary of the trial in the *Stetson Lawyer* and the description that follows is largely her account.[3408] Former Cal student Brian Bolves ('82), dressed in robe and wig as the bailiff, "boldly called order to the court, and announced that presiding judge, William 'Lightnin' Blews ('66)," was entering the courtroom. The evidence against the renowned Stetson professor included "hundreds of letters" from Cal's former students, and the testimony of six witnesses.[3409]

Richard C. McFarlain ('64), in noting that Cal used the Socratic teaching method, pointed out that "Socrates, you recall, took hemlock, poured to him by his devoted students."[3410] Daniel N. Burton ('64), told the court that Cal's problems began when his family came to America "in a dinghy behind the Mayflower."[3411] Then, Second District Court of Appeal Judge David F. Patterson ('64) testified that Kuenzel's "sadistic method of teaching was nothing more than a deep-seeded, unholy, perversion; a combination of Napoleon and Darth Vader," adding that he was humiliated in class when Cal told him that the appellant in the admiralty case under discussion was "10,000 feet of pieces of wood."[3412]

Judge Susan F. Schaeffer ('71), both a student and later colleague of Kuenzel, began by noting that a roast of Cal would not be complete without at least one woman giving evidence. She reportedly recounted, in some ironic detail, the "defendant's love for women."[3413] Schaeffer also noted that Kuenzel insisted that students know inside and out "Section 2-207 [of the Uniform Commercial Code]," a topic he tortured students in contract classes, but Schaeffer snipped, "As a lawyer and judge for twenty-two years, I have never been confronted, ever, with anything pertaining to 2-207."[3414] Then, one of the organizer's of the "trial," Paul M. May ('80), told the story of his last class with Kuenzel. He asked all the students to walk into a non-plussed Cal's class with their heads covered by paper shopping bags. This, May argued, proved that he had gone insane as a result of the infliction received "from the dreaded Cal."[3415]

But Paul May provided even more dramatic evidence to prove his point. Earlier in the evening of the trial, he distributed about 360 paper supermar-

3408. *Id.* at 8–10.
3409. *Id.* at 9.
3410. *Id.*
3411. *Id.*
3412. *Id.*
3413. *Id.*
3414. *Id.* at 10.
3415. *Id.*

ket shopping bags to those in the audience. Later, during the trial, May told about Cal's class with the hooded students. May then turned to the hundreds of spectators and asked them to put their paper bags over their heads.[3416] Kuenzel roared. Judge James C. Dauksch of the Fifth District Court of Appeal was the final witness who thanked the court for the opportunity to give something back to Calvin Kuenzel.[3417]

Despite the indictment, trial, and conviction of Professor Kuenzel by his former students, all the alumni present that evening appeared to have a genuine admiration, appreciation, and affection for their former professor, giving him a standing ovation at the close of the evening.[3418] Though many of the alumni likely held differing opinions about Kuenzel while in law school, it was obvious that his former students—now successful lawyers and judges—years later shared an understanding of what they had learned from their former professor."[3419]

d. Fund Raising Efforts Succeed

During the prior Dillon administration, the dean and members of the Overseers centered fundraising efforts on procuring large gifts and, as detailed in the previous chapter, their efforts were largely successful.[3420] Though it was through Dillon's efforts that the school ultimately received the largest gift in its history—the Rosa estate money[3421]—relatively few of the College's alumni

---

3416. *Id.*

3417. *Id.* Stories told tongue-in-cheek about how Professor Calvin Kuenzel's classroom teaching affected students have flourished for decades. A few examples heard by Professor Swygert include an alumnus recalling trying to explain to his wife that his "D" grade in contracts was one of the higher grades Cal gave. Another speaks about her panic attacks when entering a courtroom, dreading the judge's first question, knowing that if she responded in Cal's manner—"Judge, the answer is in your question"—she would be held in contempt. Yet another alum tells that when he hears someone ask, "What do you think?" that question still causes his mind to go completely blank, thirty-five years after Cal first asked him that question. Finally, a frustrated former student of Cal claims that a few years after she graduated, she prohibited her children from watching *Paper Chase*—a movie portraying a cranky, demanding, and totally frightening law professor named Kingsfield—because of the pain it would cause her to relive the experience of Cal's class.

3418. *Id.*

3419. Professor Swygert believes that Professor Kuenzel's roast in 1993 was one of the more entertaining and satisfying evenings he attended at Stetson, entertaining due to roasters and their witty remarks; satisfying because the evening's events revealed that Stetson alumni truly shared a deeply felt appreciation and affection for their professor and for the benefits of their Stetson law school education.

3420. *See supra* nn. 2618–2708 and accompanying text.

3421. *See supra* nn. 2659–2694 and accompanying text.

had participated in supporting the school financially during his administration.[3422]

After becoming dean, Jacob set for himself a goal: to increase the amount of funds given by alumni in the annual fund drive "ten times before stepping down from the deanship."[3423] He met the goal. In a report on his deanship, Jacob wrote:

> The year before I became dean, the school raised about $74,000. In the year in which I left, we raised over $740,000. The number of donors increased from less than 100 in 1980–81, to 1,776 during my last year as dean, 1993–94. Dean Circle Members, those who give at least $1,000 per year, in my final year totaled 116, more than [the] total donors in the year before I arrived.[3424]

In 1995, during Jacob's deanship, the Stetson Lawyers Association, in concert with the Stetson University's National Alumni Association, established "The Stetson Society" to recognize those individuals who advise the University or the College of Law that they have included Stetson as a beneficiary in their wills or estate plans.[3425] William Gillespie ('56) and his wife Sally Gillespie, were the initial co-chairs of The Stetson Society.[3426]

According to the *Stetson Lawyer,* the percentage of alumni who gave to the school the year prior to Jacob's deanship when compared with the percentages near the end reveals a vast increase.[3427] The reported numbers were: 4 % of the alumni contributed to the College of Law in 1981, compared with 27 % who did so in 1993.[3428] At that time, the 27 % rate was the highest rate of alumni giving at any Florida law school.[3429] In addition, during Jacob's thirteen-year deanship, the amount of the school's endowment grew "from $1.6 million in 1981 to $6.2 million in 1993."[3430]

Stetson law alumni contributing more money in greater amounts received a boost in 1988, when the *St. Petersburg Times* presented the law school a challenge gift of $125,000, payable in $25,000 increments, "conditioned upon Stet-

3422. Jacob, *Report on Deanship, supra* n. 3239, at 8.

3423. *Id.*

3424. *Id.* at 8–9.

3425. *The Stetson Society*, 33 Stetson Law. 12, 12 (Summer1993).

3426. *Id.*

3427. *A Quiet Resolve, supra* n. 3318.

3428. *Id.* at 4.

3429. Stetson Director of Development Brian Thomas was the source of this information, according to Bruce Jacob. *See* Jacob, *Aug. 29 Notes, supra* n. 3352.

3430. *Id.*

son College of Law alumni in the Tampa Bay area contributing $25,000 or more per year to the alumni fund."[3431] The *Times* Chairman of the Board Eugene Patterson announced the gift, one Stetson University President Doug Lee described as one of "the significant events in the history of Stetson College of Law."[3432]

Several major gifts came in during Jacob's administration. The largest was the several million dollar, Rosa-estate gift, following the death of the donor's spouse.[3433] Jacob points out that, though the Rosa funds came in during his administration, he could not take credit, as "the commitment [to make that gift] was made [to Dillon] before I became dean."[3434] Still, Jacob sought large gifts and grants and was successful in obtaining several. A major $500,000 gift was made by Tampa lawyer Hugh F. Culverhouse, then-owner of the National Football League's Tampa Bay Buccaneers.[3435] The money was used to endow "The Hugh F. Culverhouse Chair."[3436] Jacob was pleased, thanking the Culverhouse family for its generosity and support of Stetson College of Law.[3437] Still another significant gift, $250,000, came from the law firm of Carey & Florin, discussed earlier.[3438] Finally, the generous gift from Ruth and James Nemec, also noted earlier, was made to support new construction on the campus.[3439]

In 1993, Joseph J. Reiter ('68), gave a $100,000 gift to the school to name a renovated classroom.[3440] Other alumni contributing equal amounts during Jacob's deanship included Cecil Bailey, Roy Speer (businessman and founder of the Home Shopping Network), Mada Fraser Babcock McLendon, Ruth Ives, Emily Larkin, Murray Sams, and the Florida Power Corporation.[3441]

Jacob attributes the school's success in substantially increasing alumni giving during his deanship to many factors, and mentions not only his own ef-

3431. *College of Law Announces Challenge Gift from the St. Petersburg Times*, 27 Stetson Law. 1, 1 (Mar. 1988).

3432. *Id.*

3433. *See supra* n. 2685 and accompanying text; Jacob, *Report on Deanship*, *supra* n. 3239 and accompanying text.

3434. Jacob, *Report on Deanship*, *supra* n. 3239, at 10.

3435. *Culverhouse Endows Law Chair*, St. Pete. Times 3 (Apr. 18, 1987). Like the Rosa gift, the Culverhouse pledge was made prior to Jacob becoming dean. *See* Jacob, *Report on Deanship*, *supra* n. 3239, at 10.

3436. *Id.*

3437. *Id.*

3438. *See supra* nn. 3379–3380 and accompanying text.

3439. *See supra* n. 3336 and accompanying text.

3440. *Recent Major Gifts*, 34 Stetson Law. 25, 25 (Winter 1993).

3441. Jacob, *Report on Deanship*, *supra* n. 3239, at 9–10.

Benefactors James and Ruth Nemec

forts, but also those of Stetson University President Doug Lee.[3442] Jacob and Lee set aside one day each month for calling on prospects, both when Lee was University vice president for development, and later when he became presi-

President H. Doug Lee

3442. *Id.* at 11.

dent.[3443] In addition to these monthly excursions, Jacob himself, or with Brian Thomas, the school's director of development—sometimes with Overseers, including John Guyton—called on hundreds of individuals, corporations, and foundations in his efforts to raise funds to benefit the College of Law.[3444] Again, these efforts paid off. Among the contributors were the Saunders Foundation of Tampa[3445] and the Nichols Foundation of New York City. The Nichols money was used to establish a Nichols Foundation Speakers Series at the school.[3446]

12.6 New Academic Programs and Clinics: Elder Law; Judicial Interns

Stetson College of Law added several new programs during Dean Jacob's administration, including an elder law clinic, a joint J.D.-M.B.A. program, a federal judicial internships program, and a pro bono requirement for graduation. In addition, a committee headed by Professor Jerome Latimer made substantial revisions to the Student Code of Professional Responsibility.[3447]

a. Elder Law Clinic and Stetson College of Law Center for Law and Aging

In 1984, on behalf of the law school, Stetson law professor Ronald Halpern applied for a grant under Title III of the Older Americans Act to fund the start of an Elder Law Clinic at the College.[3448] Prior to joining the Stetson faculty in 1983, Halpern was Executive Director of Gulf Coast Legal Services, Inc., and before that, Director of the Legal Aid Society of Dayton, Ohio.[3449] In the summer of 1985, the school learned that its application was approved by the na-

---

3443. *Id.*

3444. *Id.*

3445. Brian Thomas, *Stetson Law Receives $25,000 Grant from Saunders Foundation* (Stetson U. College of L. Aug. 25, 1993) (news release).

3446. Brian Thomas, *Nichols Foundation Endows Lecture Series at Stetson College of Law* 1, 2 (Stetson U. College of L. Feb. 4, 1994) (news release).

3447. *See* Memo. from Jerome Latimer, Prof. of L., Stetson U. College of L., and Chair, Honor Code Comm., to Dean and Faculty, Stetson U. College of L. (Feb. 24, 1987) (on file at Stetson U. College of L., Gulfport, Fla.).

3448. Telephone Interview by Michael I. Swygert, Professor Emeritus, Stetson U. College of L., with Rebecca Cohen Morgan, Boston Asset Mgt. Distinguished Prof. of L., Stetson U. College of L. (Aug. 1, 2005) [hereinafter Aug. 1 Morgan Interview].

3449. *Faculty Forum, Faculty Notes*, 26 Stetson Law. 11, 12 (special ed. 1984).

Rebecca Morgan

tional board of the Legal Services Corporation, and that the College would receive an $80,000 grant to fund an elder law clinic for two years.[3450] In addition, the law school received a $10,000 grant from the Florida Bar Foundation to support the new clinic.[3451]

After interviewing several candidates, the dean and faculty chose Stetson law alumnus Rebecca Cohen Morgan ('80) to direct the new Elder Law Clinic.[3452] Arriving at Stetson in the fall of 1985, Morgan put in place Stetson's in-house elder law clinic in just three months.[3453] The new center opened in January 1986.[3454]

Morgan was well-qualified for her new position. She became interested in elder law issues when a Stetson law student in the late 1970s.[3455] Following her graduation, Morgan joined Gulf Coast Legal Services to furnish legal services

---

3450. Jacob, *1986 Report*, *supra* n. 3359, at 6.

3451. *Id.* Typical legal problems of the elderly involve, among others, Medicare, Medicaid, guardianships, incapacity, planning for incapacity, alternatives to guardianships, right to die, nursing homes, housing income, long-term care planning, and legal issues related to death and dying. *See* Rebecca Cohen Morgan, *Curriculum Vitae*, 1 (Aug. 2, 2004).

3452. *Id.*

3453. *Aug. 1 Morgan Interview*, *supra* n. 3448.

3454. *Id.*

3455. *New Assistant Dean of Student Services, Rebecca Morgan*, 1 The Law. 21, 21 (Fall 1989).

to elderly clients soon after the agency had received funding pursuant to provisions of the Older Americans Act, Title III.[3456] For five years, she served as Title III Project Director of the program for elderly persons who were eligible for legal aid.[3457] Working with supervising attorney Marion McGrath, Morgan had honed her legal skills and increased her knowledge of elder law by the time she joined the Stetson law faculty in 1985.[3458]

Following the expiration of the two-year Legal Services grant to Stetson, the clinic procured funds for a third year of operations from the U.S. Department of Education.[3459] In time, the College became the clinic's principal supporter. Since the early years of the program, the Elder Law Clinic has offered Stetson students opportunities to represent low-income elderly people in the Tampa Bay region, providing legal services under guidance of supervisory attorneys.[3460] Working with Gulf Coast Legal Services for a few years as an in-house clinic on the school's campus, the Elder Law Clinic subsequently was moved to the Gulf Coast Legal Services offices, where it remains today as one of several external clinics of the College.[3461]

In 1995, the focus on elder law became national when the Stetson University College of Law Center for the Study of Law and Aging was established. Later, Morgan was named director of what became known as the Center for Excellence in Elder Law, a post she continues to hold.[3462] Additional information regarding Professor Morgan's state and national involvement in elder law is reported subsequently.[3463]

b. Federal Judicial Internship Program

At the time of its creation in 1988, the Federal Judicial Intership Program was described as a "relatively uncommon program nationally." Since then, the program has afforded hundreds of Stetson law students the opportunity to

---

3456. Michael I. Swygert, Prof. Emeritus, Stetson U. College of L., Interview with Rebecca Morgan, Boston Asset Mgt. Prof. of L., Stetson U. College of L. 1, 8 (May 17, 2004) [hereinafter *May 17 Morgan Interview*].

3457. *Aug. 1 Morgan Interview*, *supra* n. 3448.

3458. *May 17 Morgan Interview*, *supra* n. 3456, at 9, 10.

3459. E-mail from Rebecca C. Morgan, Dir., Ctr. for Excellence in Elder L., to Silvia Manzanero, Paralegal, Stetson U. College of L. (Aug. 29, 2005).

3460. Michael P. Allen, *Passion for Caring Drives Stetson's Elder Law Pioneer*, 44 Stetson Law. 16, 17 (Fall 2004).

3461. *Aug. 1 Morgan Interview*, *supra* n. 3448.

3462. *Recent Publications, Presentations, Awards, and Activities of Stetson Law Faculty, Rebecca C. Morgan '80*, 44 Stetson Law. 8, 10 (Fall 2004).

3463. *See infra* nn. 4481–4485 and accompanying text.

Judge Elizabeth Kovachevich

clerk on a part-time basis for federal judges.[3464] Judge Elizabeth Kovachevich ('61), of the United States District Court for the Middle District of Florida, has been the court's administrator of Stetson's internship program, while Professors Michael Finch and Michael Allen have served as the law school's administrators.[3465] Finch notes that Judge Kovachevich "has given her unrelenting efforts" to the program's success.[3466] She says that she is pleased to see that so many Stetson law students have the "unparalleled opportunity in professional education.[3467]

The program has provided up to seventy-five students a year the opportunity to intern with federal judges for academic credit. One reason so many students are able to participate in the program is because the Middle District of Florida is "one of the ten busiest federal court districts in the nation."[3468] Those selected into the program are kept well-occupied. An article in the *Stetson Lawyer* describes interns' responsibilities:

> The student's commitment to the program is considerable. Each student is expected to spend at least one full day each week "in chambers," and is

3464. *A Courtroom Campus: Stetson's Federal Judicial Internship Program*, 34 Stetson Law. 22, 22 (Winter 1993).

3465. *Id.*

3466. *Id.*

3467. *Id.*

3468. *Id.* at 23.

> expected to devote an additional eight to ten hours to research and writing projects outside chambers. Periodic meetings are held of all student participants, where guest speakers and the students discuss issues arising in the federal court system.[3469]

Within the first few years of its beginning, several Middle District judges and magistrates have participated in Stetson's Federal Internship Program in addition to Judge Kovachevich, including: Steven Merryday, Ralph Nimmons, Mary Scrivens, Elizabeth Jenkins, Charles Wilson, and Thomas Wilson, along with several others.[3470] The quality of the students who are assigned to the program is the responsibility of Professor Finch, who attempts to insure that only academically sound and highly motivated students are selected to be judicial interns. He attributes the success of the judicial assistance program to judges who are willing to welcome interns into their chambers.[3471] Finch observes that: "Federal judges are sometimes thought to be remote, platonic authorities of limited accessibility. The judges in [Stetson's] program are just the opposite. They take their educational roles seriously, and they take our students seriously."[3472]

Understandably, given the educational, placement, and career benefits of the Federal Judicial Internship Program, applications to be selected as an intern to a federal judge exceed the available openings.

c. *Expansion of Clinics*

By 1987, Stetson's second- and third-year students could choose to participate in one of seven clinics for which they would receive academic credit.[3473] The Elder Law Clinic that began in January 1986 (described above)[3474] gave students opportunities to represent elderly clients "who met the federal guidelines for eligibility" for legal assistance.[3475] In the fall of 1986, Stetson established another public service agency, called the Federal Civil Rights Clinic, resulting from discussions between Professor Michael Finch and (then) Chief Judge Terrel Hodges of the U.S. District Court for the Middle District of

---

3469. *Id.* at 22.

3470. *Id.*

3471. *Id.*

3472. *Id.* at 23.

3473. *Stetson Offers Participation in Clinics*, 27 Stetson Law. 11, 11 (Fall 1987) [hereinafter *Stetson Clinics*].

3474. *See infra* nn. 3448–3463 and accompanying text.

3475. *Stetson Clinics*, *supra* n. 3473, at 11.

Florida.[3476] Tampa attorney Karen Buesing co-directed the new Clinic. The Civil Rights Clinic permitted students to represent indigent victims (including those in jail) of alleged employment discrimination under federal laws, and of other civil rights protections guaranteed under the Constitution and federal laws and regulations.[3477]

Meanwhile, the Stetson Labor Law Clinic became associated with Stetson's Center for Labor-Management Dispute Resolution. Furthermore, in 1983, Stetson University President Pope Duncan and Dean Jacob approved the College's creating a Center for Labor-Management Dispute Resolution.[3478] Associate Dean Gary Vause proposed the idea, and in 1984 he resigned as associate dean to become the Center's director.[3479] A re-structural Labor Law Clinic was an outgrowth of the Center for Labor-Management Dispute Resolution, and was under the directorship of Vause. The Clinic afforded students the opportunity to work at either the Tampa regional office of the National Labor Relations Board, or at the headquarters of the Florida Public Employee Relations Commission in Tallahassee.[3480]

Concurrently, students in Stetson's older Civil Clinic rendered legal assistance to clients of various legal services organizations throughout the greater Tampa Bay region, including the Bay Area Legal Services of Tampa.[3481] The students worked in legal services offices in Clearwater, St. Petersburg, Bradenton, Sarasota, and Tampa.[3482] In 1987, Stetson students began to represent clients "in-house," that is, on the school's Gulfport campus, in a pro bono program with the St. Petersburg Bar Association.[3483]

A new Criminal Appeals Clinic was related to the first clinic established at the school—the Public Defender Clinic.[3484] The Criminal Appeals Clinic allowed eligible students to work with attorneys in the Sixth Judicial Circuit Public Defender Office in representing indigent criminal defendants in post conviction proceedings.[3485] Dean Jacob instructed the Clinic's students. Meanwhile,

3476. *Id.*

3477. *Id.*

3478. *Stetson's New Labor-Management Center*, Stetson Law. 13 (spec. ed. Summer 1984).

3479. *Id.*

3480. *Stetson Clinics, supra* n. 3473.

3481. *Id.*

3482. *Id.*

3483. *Id.*

3484. *See supra* nn. 2443–2460 and accompanying text.

3485. *Id.*

Justice John Paul Stevens with Stetson Students
Rosemarie Williams and Irene Rodriguez

Stetson's original two clinics continued to operate—the Public Defender Clinic and the Prosecution Clinic. Professor Latimer served as co-director of the Public Defender Clinic along with Chief Assistant Public Defender Dudley Clapp.[3486] The Prosecution Clinic continued to be operated under the direction of State Attorney James T. Russell and Assistant State Attorney Fred Schaub.[3487]

12.7 Student Activities

a. New Groups and Organizations Flourish

Student groups and organizations proliferated throughout Jacob's deanship. New clubs included: Entertainment, Arts & Sports Law Society (EALS); the Stetson chapter of Florida Young Democrats; the Federalist Society; the Stetson Poets Workshop; Stetson chapter of the Florida Association of Women Lawyers (FAWLS); the "Ball-Busters," a short-lived women's basketball team; the ABA Law Student Division; Volunteer Income Tax Student Assistance Service; and *Stetson Intramural Law Journal.*

EALS began in the fall of 1988, and within a year "boasted nearly 100 members."[3488] Among others, Stetson law graduate Richard McKay, then the head

3486. *Id.*

3487. *Id.*

3488. *New Student Groups*, The Law. 6 (Fall 1989) (a law school publication much like the *Stetson Lawyer,* but this publication had only one issue, followed by resumption of issues of the *Stetson Lawyer*) [hereinafter *New Student Groups*].

attorney for the Tampa Bay Buccaneers and Stetson adjunct professor of law, and Ronald Sikes, attorney for Universal Studies in Orlando, addressed the EALS members.[3489]

In 1989, Stetson students started a chapter of the Florida Young Democrats (YDs). In its first year, the YDs sponsored both blood and food drives for the community and helped with logistics for Stetson's Law Day for prospective students.[3490] Arguably at the other end of the political spectrum, in the early 1990s, Stetson students and faculty members organized a chapter of the Federalist Society, a national organization of conservative lawyers, judges, law professors, and students. The national chapter was headed by former U.S. Attorney General Edwin Meese.[3491]

Perhaps the most interesting new campus organization during Jacob's deanship was the "Stetson Poets Workshop," consisting of a small number of students and three professors: Joryn Jenkins (the group's leader), Bradford Stone (a life-long fancier of poetry), and a visiting professor from Brigham Young University, Douglas Parker.[3492] An article in the *St. Petersburg Times* sums up its improbability:

> It's 2 o'clock on a sunny Wednesday afternoon, and most law students are sitting rigidly in contracts, frozen with the fear that they'll be called on next ... But in a small second-floor conference room at Stetson University College of Law, four students and three faculty members are engaged in a most unlegal [sec] activity ...
>
> The group is a sort of underground poets' society in the most unlikely of places, artists afloat in a world where emotions are second to logic, and language is used to indict and attack, not to inspire.[3493]

The participating student poets and literary critics—Michael Boswell, Jeffrey Picker, Brad Lang, and Pamela Woolley—surely found it an atypical law school experience.[3494]

3489. *Id.*

3490. *Id.*

3491. Though the exact date of the founding has not been found, Professor Swygert was present at the organizational meeting. Professor Swygert was also a member of the Society for two or three years until he remembered he had been raised to be a liberal Democrat.

3492. Jeanne Malmgren, *Rhymes and Misdemeanors*, St. Pete. Times Floridian sec. 1 (Apr. 19, 1994).

3493. *Id.*

3494. *Id.*

In the early 1980s, Stetson's women law students changed their organization's name from "Women and the Law" to "FAWLS," (The Florida Association of Women Law Students). The group became one of the more active student organizations, sponsoring seminars, bringing in speakers for "brown-bag" lunches, and holding a series of "dinners with professors."[3495] In 1981, FAWLS's state organization began an annual writing competition, open to all women law students in Florida. Stetson's students participated.

Soon after the Stetson FAWLS chapter came into being, it began to hold an annual reception to honor members of the Tampa Bay judiciary. The area's judges were invited, as were Stetson's faculty and students. It was designed to be an elegant, semi-formal evening with gourmet food and quality beverages. This level of sophistication, of course, deserved a proper venue. To that end, FAWLS held several of the fêtes at the St. Petersburg Museum of Fine Arts, as well as at the Salvador Dali Museum.

Stetson's women students not only held what many believed was the best social occasion of the year, they also beat the men (at least once) in basketball. An article in the *Prelude* reported that for the first time, women "have gotten up a team and are playing competitive ball."[3496] Meanwhile, Stetson men played Stetson faculty in basketball. Reportedly, the faculty team was composed of "Prof. Thomas 'con-man' Marks"; "the D-fensive threat of Kal [sic] 'I wanna renegotiate my contract' Kuenzel"; "Charles 'all-night-long' McCarter"; "Bev 'don't call me Horace' Greeley"; and "Prof. Bobby 'in your face, ain't no trace from outer space, get off my case, to your place, ace, 360 scissor slam bam thank you ma'am, disgrace dunk' Bickel."[3497]

During Jacob's era, Stetson students began VITA, an acronym standing for "Volunteer Income Tax Assistance," a program developed by the American Bar Association, Law Student Division.[3498] The program consisted of law students who volunteered to help area people who were "unable to fill in their federal income tax returns."[3499] Starting in 1982 at the St. Petersburg Don Vista Community Center, Stetson students met with community taxpayers seeking assistance in completing their tax forms.[3500]

Finally, Stetson students when Jacob was dean solicited and edited articles for a new publication for the area's legal community—the *Stetson Intramural*

3495. *Women-in-Law*, 14 Prelude 6, 6 (Mar. 1983).

3496. Mohammed Melvin, *Jock Itch*, 11 Prelude 5, 5 (Oct.1, 1981).

3497. *Id.*

3498. *ABA Law Student Division Update*, 11 Prelude 1, 1 (Nov. 13, 1980).

3499. *Id.*

3500. *VITA*, 14 Prelude 3, 3 (Jan. 1983).

Law Journal (not to be confused with either the Stetson *Intramural Law Review* or the *Stetson Law Review*, discussed earlier).[3501] The first issue of the biannual *Intramural Law Journal* was published in October 1989.[3502] It consisted of comments and articles written by students and faculty members.[3503] The quality was quite good. Such was not the "Ann Slanders" advice column published occasionally in the student newspaper, the *Prelude*. "Ann Slanders" wrote responses to letters from mythical readers.[3504] One example: "Dean Ann, Every time I get called on in class I am unprepared. It seems I only get called on when I am unprepared. What can I do?" Ann Slanders' response:

> This happens to all of us. You need to learn the art of offensive hand raising. Do not let them get you on the defensive by asking you the question first. [Just] raise your hand once at the beginning of each semester in each class, ask the longest, most detailed question you can think of, and [I] guarantee that the prof. will stay as far away from you as he can all semester.[3505]

b. Student Competitions: Client Counseling; Negotiations; Moot Court

The 1980s at Stetson College of Law included student trial advocacy teams winning state, regional, and national championships.[3506] By the middle of the decade, Stetson was receiving national recognition for its advocacy program, being ranked number one in the nation by the magazine *U.S. News & World Report* on several occasions.[3507]

But Stetson's success in skills competitions went beyond its trial teams. In another area, Stetson teams also brought home trophies—client counseling. Beginning in the mid-1980s and continuing through the present, Stetson law students have participated in client counseling competitions around the country and the world. In 1989, a Stetson team won the national championship of the American Bar Association National Client Counseling Competition.[3508] The team then went to the International Client Counseling Com-

3501. *See supra* nn. 2806–2871 and accompanying text.

3502. *New Student Groups*, *supra* n. 3488, at 6.

3503. *Id.*

3504. Ann Slanders, *Isn't That Special!!!!* 23 Prelude 4, 4 (1987).

3505. *Id.*

3506. *See infra* ch.13.

3507. *See infra* nn. 3376–3378 and accompanying text.

3508. *Client Counseling Competition,* 1989–1991 Off. Bull. Stetson U. College of L. 35 (1989) [hereinafter *Client Counseling*].

petition in Baltimore, Maryland, where they tied for first place with Great Britain.[3509]

The Stetson team was the designated representative of the United States.[3510] Members of this national and international championship team were students Laura Featherhoff, Debbie Westmoreland, Liz Mulligan, and David Sharp (student coach).[3511] Stetson professor Rebecca Morgan coached the team with assistance from law alumnus Nick Karamessinis.[3512] To reach the national championship, Stetson defeated five other law schools.[3513] Over the years, Stetson's client counseling teams have consistently performed well, for example, coming in first place four times at the regionals of the ABA National Tournament.[3514]

In yet another skills area—negotiations—Stetson teams have done quite well. In both 1985 and 1986, the school's negotiation team went undefeated in ABA southeast regional.[3515] The team members were Matt Towery, Fred Rudzik, Linster Brinkley, and Ron Cook.[3516] In 1985, Stetson professors John Cooper and Richard Gershon instituted a new national competition held on campus—the Stetson University College of Law National Tax Moot Court Competition. "[3517] The Stetson-sponsored competition has taken place every year since.[3518] In its initial year, thirteen law school teams came from various regions of the country to Gulfport. Stetson's two teams finished first and second.[3519] In the early years of the Tax Moot Court Competition, Stetson students who took first or second place included Donald Smucker, Magda McSwain, Julia Walker, Ed Williams, Eric Abrahamson, and Russell Hintze.[3520] This competition transitioned to the Florida Bar and continues through today.

The number of other student moot court teams participating during the 1980s and 1990s gets longer each year. The better known include the National

3509. *Client Counseling Team Wins International Competition*, 28 Stetson Law. 2, 2 (Spring 1989) [hereinafter *Team Wins*].

3510. *Id.*

3511. *Id.*

3512. *Id.*

3513. *Client Counseling*, *supra* n. 3508, at 2.

3514. *It's Team Spirit; That Does It at Stetson*, 27 Stetson Law. 5, 7 (Fall 1987) [hereinafter *Team Spirit*].

3515. *Id.* at 6, 7.

3516. *Id.*

3517. Jacob, *1986 Report*, *supra* n. 3359, at 6.

3518. Stephanie Vaughan, *Stetson Moot Court Board Recent Awards* 5 (unpublished ms. 2005) (copy on file at Stetson U. College of L., Gulfport, Fla.).

3519. *Team Spirit*, *supra* n. 3514, at 6, 7.

3520. *Id.* at 7.

Moot Court Competition, sponsored by the Association of the Bar of the City of New York, and the Phillip Jessup International Moot Court Competition.[3521] Others include the Robert Orseck Memorial Moot Court Competition, the Robert F. Wagner Labor Law Moot Court Competition (New York City), the Florida Worker's Compensation Institute Moot Court Competition, and the Giles Sutherland Rich Intellectual Property Moot Court Competition.[3522] The moot court program in recent years has been directed by Professor Stephanie Vaughan.

c. A Death on Campus

Students were not the only ones moving about during this period. For six years, no one on campus could miss him, sneaking around all over the campus, night and day, lurking into student rooms and faculty offices uninvited. Arrogant as he could be, he exhibited few manners, getting up in a class and just leaving, or, worst of all, messing up the school's commencement program. On one memorable occasion, "he" became entangled in President Doug Lee's feet as the president was addressing the law graduates. Lee exclaimed: "What's this cat doing here?" Jacob took the microphone and said, "It's Porkchop, our cat," to thunderous cheering from the graduates.[3523] The beloved feline died on September 7, 1991. Porkchop was not just any old cat, he was "the premier" cat among those felines that made Stetson College of Law their home. Moreover, Porkchop was the weightiest.[3524] An article in the *Stetson Lawyer* lamented that "all of us will miss the presence of his bulk sprawled in the horseshoe driveway.[3525] A student writing Porkchop's obituary in the *Prelude* opined that "graduation won't be the same without our cat crossing the podium."[3526]

12.8 Strategic Planning and Application for Coif

a. Strategic Planning

In late 1987, Dean Jacob and the faculty embarked on an intensive strategic planning process, one lasting several years.[3527] The impetus came from Stet-

3521. *Id.*
3522. *Id.*
3523. Jacob, *Aug. 29 Notes*, *supra* n. 3352.
3524. *In Memory of Porkchop the Cat*, 31 Stetson Law. 15, 15 (Fall 1991).
3525. *Id.*
3526. *Id.*
3527. Jacob, *Report on Deanship*, *supra* n. 3239, at 29.

son University President H. Doug Lee who, prior to his Stetson presidency, had been the University's vice president for planning and development.[3528] Lee, who became the eighth president of the University on November 6, 1987,[3529] requested each school within the institution to prepare a strategic, five-year plan that would set out goals to make each school stronger.[3530]

At the law school, the first task was to reconsider the law school's mission. That task turned out to be challenging. While some faculty members thought the school should espouse that it strove to inculcate moral values, in addition to training students to be competent and ethical lawyers, others believed that moral principles as distinct from professional ethics were too subjective and that, in any event, teaching morality was not the mission of a law school. One professor who felt the matter of moral values should be part of the school's expressed mission wrote an article published in *Boston College Law Review* promoting the concept[3531] (later criticized in a responsive article in the *Journal of Legal Education*).[3532]

A significant part of the strategic planning process, one that took a protracted time to finish, was undergoing a self-study that identified the College's strengths and weaknesses. This was followed by the faculty and dean formulating specific goals for the school, and then devising steps that the school should take over two, three and five-year periods to realize those goals.[3533] Through weekend retreats and special meetings, the faculty spent hundreds of hours discussing what the school's aspirations should be, then what specific steps the school would have to do to attain those goals.

Jacob believes that the faculty, by becoming involved in this strategic long-range planning process, "I think, really helped the law school move forward."[3534] In a later report, Jacob wrote: "We did not accomplish all of the steps or achieve all of the goals, but the process gave direction to our efforts to constantly improve the law school."[3535]

3528. *Jacob Interview*, *supra* n. 2280, at 66.

3529. *Resolution by the Dean and Faculty, Stetson University College of Law, in Honor of H. Douglas Lee* (Dec. 19, 1987).

3530. *Id.*

3531. *See* Michael I. Swygert, *Striving to Make Great Lawyers—Citizenship and Moral Responsibility: A Jurisprudence for Law Teaching*, 30 B.C. L. Rev. 803 (May 1989).

3532. Lee Modjeska, *On Teaching Morality to Law Students*, 41 J. Leg. Ed. 71 (1991). Professor Modjeska's critique of Swygert's thesis was responded to by Stetson's Professor Peter Lake. *See* Peter F. Lake, *Make Lawyers, Not Lethal Sheep*, 42 J. Leg. Ed. 271 (1992).

3533. *Jacob Interview*, *supra* n. 2280, at 66, 67.

3534. *Id.* at 67.

3535. Jacob, *Report on Deanship*, *supra* n. 3239, at 29.

b. Seeking Order of the Coif

One of the goals of the strategic plan that was not achieved was the school's gaining admission to the Order of the Coif, an honorary organization having chapters at roughly forty to forty-five percent of ABA-approved law schools in the year 2000.[3536] Jacob describes the school's unsuccessful effort as "my major disappointment as dean."[3537] He explains some of the steps he took before the school formally applied:

> To become eligible [for Coif], I took steps to increase the median faculty salary to that of the top forty percent among law schools, since about forty percent were members of Coif. Because faculty scholarship was the main interest of Coif, I instituted a program of providing summer research grants for faculty to increase their scholarly output. This program was very successful.[3538]

The dean began to hold annual faculty retreats to, among other things, move toward meeting the requirements for a Coif chapter.[3539] In 1989, the faculty met for two days at the University of South Florida's retreat at Chinsegut Hill near Brooksville, where they deliberated on the "attainment of those distinctions which would qualify the College of Law for membership in Order of the Coif."[3540] Jacob observed that a faculty retreat "is an opportunity for focused and extended collegial discussion of the College's major goals and plans."[3541]

After contacting Coif officials, Coif assigned a consultant to work with Stetson's administrators and faculty in helping the school prepare an application for a Coif chapter.[3542] Subsequently, following two years of the consultant's advice, the school, according to Jacob, had "complied with all Coif requirements,"[3543] and the Coif-appointed consultant then told Jacob that Stetson was "ready to apply."[3544] But then a new problem unexpectedly arose. Jacob explains:

> At the last minute [the consultant] asked whether we had a grade-normalization policy in place. We said no and also pointed out that there

3536. *Id.* at 32.

3537. *Id.*

3538. *July 29 Jacob Letter*, *supra* n. 3260.

3539. *Faculty Gathers for Annual Retreat*, 29 Stetson Law. 9, 9 (Spring 1990).

3540. *Id.*

3541. *Id.*

3542. Jacob, *Report on Deanship*, *supra* n. 3239, at 32.

3543. *Id.*

3544. *July 29 Jacob Letter*, *supra* n. 3260.

> was nothing in the written Coif requirements for such a policy. Our consultant said ... "You have to have a grade normalization policy anyway." We decided to wait a year, to allow time to adopt a grade normalization policy for our school.[3545]

Thus, in the fall of 1993, Stetson College of Law filed its application to Coif for a chapter, believing that it had satisfied all the requirements, both written and unwritten, as described by the Coif consultant. Not long thereafter, Jacob received a phone call from a representative of Coif who told him that the governing board of the organization had "changed considerably" from the year earlier.[3546] This turned out to be bad news for Stetson. Jacob tells why:

> The new board had decided to only accept one law school each year, and that they had already decided which school they [were letting in] that year. They recommended that we withdraw our application and file instead the following year.[3547]

In the spring of 1994, Jacob completed his thirteen years as dean of the College of Law. He took a sabbatical leave, and thus was not at the school that fall. He expected that the faculty would file another application with Coif.[3548] To Jacob's amazement, however, that did not happen. "The faculty voted not to apply," Jacob notes, and to this day still "expresses bewilderment" at why they did not do so, especially when the school, in his judgment, "was so close to getting a Coif chapter."[3549]

Part of the explanation for inaction may be because several members of the faculty continued to be disturbed over Coif's advising the school to withdraw its 1993 application. Those faculty members underscored that the Coif consultant had led the dean and the faculty to believe that the College of Law had met all of Coif's requirements and that it would be granted a chapter. Thus, the faculty's reactions to Coif's advising the school to withdraw its application were disappointment and frustration. A few members were angry.[3550]

3545. *Id.*

3546. Jacob, *Report on Deanship*, *supra* n. 3239, at 32.

3547. *Id.*

3548. *Id.*

3549. *Id.*

3550. Though Professor Michael Swygert remembers those Stetson faculty members who argued that Stetson should not again apply for a Coif chapter, he believes there is no reason that they be specifically identified in this history. He can reveal, however, that at least one of those who felt that way was a member of Coif himself.

In 2005, reflecting back on the school's failed effort, Jacob believes that even so, certain benefits to the school resulted.[3551] "The years spent trying to attain our goal were valuable," he says, adding, that they "helped provide direction and purpose, and thereby made us a better law school."[3552] Among the positives, faculty research and writing increased.[3553]

12. 9 Faculty Concerns

a. Cash Surplus and Tuition

In December 1992, three members of the Stetson faculty, concerned that the school was taking in more students than the budget called for—thereby producing excess revenues—sent a memorandum to the law faculty and to Dean Jacob. In their memorandum, professors Michael Finch, Michael Swygert, and Gary Vause criticized the dean for what they perceived to be the law school's producing yearly cash surpluses by basing the school's annual budgets on fewer students than were expected to enroll.[3554] They also criticized the dean's fundraising efforts.[3555] When it came to Jacob's fundraising efforts, the memorandum's authors were off the mark. As recounted earlier,[3556] Jacob expended great time and effort in successfully cultivating alumni and in raising funds. Jacob believes the faculty may not have understood the success of his efforts.[3557]

Jacob reacted to the critical memorandum with disbelief.[3558] To begin with, he could not understand why the authors had not first discussed with him the issues before distributing the memo to the faculty. Consequently, he believed that he was blind-sided. Jacob believed that the memo's authors did not know the facts, that they were ignorant as to why the school had been receiving more revenue than it needed to cover expenses to build financial reserves.

Jacob's critics believed the school was getting larger to produce more revenue. Jacob explained that when he was dean at Mercer (which had 400 stu-

---

3551. *See* Michael I. Swygert, *Bruce R. Jacob: A Dean for All Seasons*, 21 Stetson L. Rev. 307, 309 (1992) (Jacob exemplifies Winston Churchill's belief that "it is far more valuable to be an actor than a critic." *Id.*).

3552. Jacob, *Report on Deanship*, *supra* n. 3239, at 33.

3553. *Id.*

3554. *See* Memo. from Michael Finch, Michael Swygert, and W. Gary Vause to Dean Bruce Jacob and the Faculty of the College of Law (Dec. 1992).

3555. *Id.*

3556. Jacob, *1986 Report*, *supra* n. 3359, at 3240.

3557. Jacob, *Report on Deanship*, *supra* n. 3239, at 33.

3558. *Id.* at 34.

dents at the time), he realized that the school was too small to operated efficiently in the students' best interests; for example, that the small number of students caused prospective employers not to come to the Mercer for interviews.[3559] He concluded that a law school needed to have a larger number of students, a figure between 500 to 600 students, which he felt was the optimum size for a law school, noting that "many of the nation's great schools" including Yale, Stanford, Chicago, Cornell, Northwestern, Vanderbilt, and Duke had student bodies within that range.[3560] After becoming dean at Stetson, Jacob allowed its student body to rise to an average of 550 enrollees, where it hovered for several years.

Then, around 1989, both the number and quality of applications to the school rose sharply.[3561] This presented Stetson an opportunity. Jacob explains:

> Professor Cal Kuenzel, as chair of the admissions committee, came to me and said ... "let's take more while we are receiving such good applications. Put some of that extra income aside for the future when we aren't getting such good applicants. Then we can take fewer students and still make our budget."[3562]

Kuenzel's suggestion seemed a good idea to Jacob. He allowed the school's enrollment to rise from around 550, to an average of 600-plus per year. The tuition revenues generated as a consequence of a larger student body resulted in larger year-end cash reserves. Jacob writes: "Some of the additional money was being used for construction purposes on the campus and some was being saved."[3563] Moreover, Jacob points out: "Many of the facilities used by present students were paid for in part with tuition monies received from students in years past,"[3564] adding that allocating a portion of present income for future use did not violate ABA standards for accreditation or AALS membership requirements. Jacob believes that "Kuenzel probably could have ended the controversy if he had explained the reason for taking more students. However, he did not come forward."[3565]

No Stetson law school dean has ever decided alone what the school's next year budget will be. Though the dean oversees the budget's preparation, the

---

3559. *July 27 Jacob Letter*, *supra* n. 3260.
3560. *Id.*
3561. *Id.*
3562. *Id.*
3563. *Id.*
3564. *Id.*
3565. Jacob, *Sept. 25 Draft*, *supra* n. 3337, at 775.

University President, the Board of Overseers, and the Board of Trustees must approve the final budget.[3566] As regards the dean's and the faculty's realms of responsibility, Jacob notes that "the dean has to have ultimate authority over the budget, because he or she is the person held responsible if the law school incurs financial difficulties."[3567]

b. A Divided Faculty: Renewal of Manuel Ramos

Manuel Ramos joined the faculty of the Stetson College of Law in January 1992.[3568] A native of Cuba, Ramos spent his youth in Florida and Virginia.[3569] He graduated from Yale University *magna cum laude* with honors in sociology.[3570] At Yale, he won the Wrexham Prize for the best senior thesis.[3571] Following graduation, he wrote articles for magazines and newspapers, including *The Washington Post.*[3572]

Ramos next went to the University of Virginia, where he earned his law degree.[3573] After law school, he took a job as staff attorney for the U.S. Commission on Civil Rights in Washington, D.C., working on a study on "how various cities and their agencies responded to battered women."[3574] Leaving government, Ramos then joined the San Diego law firm of Lewis, D'Amato, Brisbois & Bisgard, said to be the "fastest growing law firm" of less than 100 members.[3575] The firm represented lawyers sued for malpractice.

According to *St. Petersburg Times* Reporter Bruce Vielmetti, Ramos decided to leave law practice "because he sought a slower pace," returning to Florida, where he accepted Stetson's offer to teach.[3576] He was the first Hispanic professor to be employed at the Stetson law school, and the first His-

3566. Memo. from Bruce R. Jacob, Dean Emeritus, Stetson U. College of L., to William F. Blews, William Reece Smith, Jr., and Judge Thomas Stringer (Mar. 20, 1998) (on file at Stetson U. College of L., Gulfport, Fla.

3567. *Id.*

3568. *Faculty Forum, Manuel Ramos*, 32 Stetson Law. 12, 13 (Summer 1992) [hereinafter *Faculty Forum, Ramos*].

3569. Bruce Vielmetti, *Stetson Struggles to Diversify*, St. Pete. Times B-4 (June 20, 1994) [hereinafter Vielmetti, *Stetson Struggles*].

3570. *Faculty Forum, Ramos, supra* n. 3568, at 13.

3571. *Id.*

3572. *Id.*

3573. Vielmetti, *Stetson Struggles, supra* n. 3569, at 4.

3574. *Faculty Forum, Ramos, supra* n. 3568, at 13.

3575. Nancy Rivera, *Southland Business: Fastest-Growing Law Firms*, L.A. Times V-4 (Oct. 6, 1985.)

3576. Vielmetti, *Stetson Struggles, supra* n. 3569, at 4.

panic to attain tenure.[3577] Ramos taught property law and an advanced course in attorney malpractice. Everything seemed fine until he came up for renewal.

As is the case at most law schools, new professors at Stetson for the first few years have no guaranteed job security. They are referred to as "non-tenured faculty." Ramos was in that group, though he held a "tenure-track" appointment, meaning that after serving a certain number of years, and after demonstrating that his work met the school's requirements for tenure, he would be granted that status. At many law schools, faculty members disagree whether a non-tenured colleague should be renewed, often due to questions about the quality of the applicant's teaching and/or scholarship.

Manuel Ramos came up for renewal at Stetson College of Law ten months after he began teaching his first year at Stetson.[3578] At the beginning of the 1992 fall semester, he and the rest of the faculty took part in a two-day, faculty off-campus retreat. The retreat's agenda focused on the school's self-study—a report required periodically by the ABA, as part of its approval (accreditation) process, that requires the school to prioritize and articulate its goals.

One issue discussed was the racial and ethnic diversification of the faculty. At that time, one other faculty besides Ramos was a minority—Professor Dorothea Beane, an African-American hired in 1990.[3579] Ramos also noted that the law faculty, with one exception, had voted in favor of "affirmative action."[3580]

During the discussions about faculty diversification, Professor Ramos declared that he would not vote to hire any Anglo/white males until the gender, ethnic, and racial makeup of the faculty mirrored the representation of these groups in Florida.[3581] Jacob remembers that Ramos' statement "angered some members of the faculty."[3582] One professor in particular was upset, declaring that he could not believe his colleague could be a racist.[3583]

Later that semester, at a November meeting of tenured faculty, the issue of the renewal of Professor Ramos for another year came up—an issue that the

3577. *Id.*

3578. Jacob, *Report on Deanship*, *supra* n. 3239, at 34.

3579. Bishop, *List*, *supra* n. 2351, at 6.

3580. Manuel R. Ramos, *Legal and Law School Malpractice: Confessions of a Lawyer's Lawyer and Law Professor*, 57 Ohio St. L.J. 863, 901 (1996) [hereinafter Ramos, *Malpractice*].

3581. *Id.*

3582. Jacob *Report on Deanship*, *supra* n. 3239, at 34.

3583. Ramos, *Malpractice*, *supra* n. 3580, at 900. Co-author Michael Swygert was present at the retreat and affirms what Manuel Ramos writes about the racist charge in his article in the *Ohio State Law Journal.*

faculty was required to make a recommendation to the dean under the school's policies. In a split decision, the faculty voted not to renew the Ramos contract.[3584]

Ramos had taught at Stetson for one complete semester at that point, and it was uncommon for a law school not to renew someone after so short a period.[3585] After conferring with the chair and members of the promotions and tenured committee, Jacob was able to reverse the vote on procedural grounds.[3586] But that was not the end of the story. Jacob believes that his action in obtaining the reversal caused some members of the faculty to become angry.[3587]

In early 1993, the tenure committee once again voted on the renewal of Professor Ramos. At this point, he had completed two semesters of teaching and was in his third. According to those present, the vote was close, but the majority was against renewal.[3588] Ramos himself acknowledged his unorthodox teaching approach contributed to the faculty's decision.[3589] Dean Jacob was not present for the vote, but sent a recommendation in favor of renewal to the President. Jacob later wrote that the only reason of substance for Ramos' non-renewal was "his view on affirmative action—his remarks at the [earlier] faculty retreat."[3590] In his report, Jacob claimed that many faculty members viewed Ramos as an extremist, given his stated policy of not hiring white males irrespective of qualifications until racial, gender, and ethnic balances had been achieved.[3591]

Jacob submitted to University President Doug Lee the recommendation of the tenure committee that Ramos not be renewed. Pursuant to the bylaws, however, he had the right to send his independent recommendation.[3592] He did so, recommending that Ramos be retained for another year. President Lee went along. Jacob then advised Ramos that his contract was being extended for another year, the majority vote of the tenured faculty against renewal notwithstanding[3593] Jacob describes the faculty's reaction:

> This infuriated many members of the faculty. Some of them thought that I did not have the power as dean to give a contrary recommendation to

3584. Jacob, *Report on Deanship, supra* n. 3239, at 35.
3585. Ramos, *Malpractice, supra* at 902.
3586. Jacob, *Report on Deanship, supra* n. 3239, at 35.
3587. Ramos, *Malpractice, supra* at n. 108.
3588. *July 27 Jacob Letter, supra* n. 3260.
3589. Ramos, *Malpractice, supra* at 907.
3590. Jacob, *Report on Deanship, supra* n. 3239, at 35.
3591. *Id.*
3592. *Id.* at 26.
3593. *Id.*

> the president, and some thought that I should have told the [promotions and tenure] committee of my decision and given the committee notice, so that they could contact the president ... and argue that Ramos should [not be renewed].[3594]

Under University and law school bylaws, there was no question that Jacob had the power to present to the president a recommendation contrary to the recommendation of the tenure faculty. The issue that most displeased many faculty members was that Jacob neither notified them, nor gave them opportunity to send comments to the University president. Jacob responds:

> The bylaws did not require me to notify faculty and also there wasn't time for this. If there had been, I would have given them the opportunity to send their views to the president. As it was, I talked to several and summarized for President Lee the comments that had been made by Ramos' detractors at the meeting. The bylaws required that if Ramos was to be terminated, I had to place a termination letter in his hands by a certain date. I had advised the faculty chair of the committee of this and asked him to set the meeting at an early enough date to allow me to obtain approval of the president and get the letter to Ramos by the deadline.[3595]

Without question, the faculty's criticism of his action angered Dean Jacob.[3596] He felt he was right, given that he was of the opinion the majority of the tenured faculty voted against Ramos because of his unwavering position on not hiring white males.[3597]

A year later, an ABA/AALS periodic inspection of Stetson College of Law took place. The ABA inspectors discussed the Ramos issue with the dean and members of the faculty. At the exit interview with the dean and with Professor Bickel (who had assisted Jacob in preparing for the inspection), the inspectors said that based on interviews they conducted with everyone involved, they agreed with Jacob's opinion that the primary reason the faculty committee had voted against Ramos' renewal was his position on affirmative action,

---

3594. *Id.*

3595. *July 27 Jacob Letter*, *supra* n. 3260. The chairperson did not comply with my request, and when the committee voted, they left me with only three working days to summarize the action of the committee for the president; to decide whether I should join in the committee's recommendation or send my own contrary recommendation; to allow the president time to phone me or other faculty members for further clarification; for the president to decide himself whether to terminate Ramos; and for him to notify me of his decision and to enable me to get a letter typed and in Ramos' hands by the deadline.

3596. Jacob, *Sept. 25 Draft*, *supra* n. 3337, at 783

3597. *See Jacob Interview*, *supra* n. 2280, at 90–100.

based on the statement he had made at the faculty retreat. Therefore, the action by the tenured faculty "was inappropriate."[3598] Moreover, the inspectors told Jacob he had done the right thing in making his contrary recommendation."[3599] The ABA/AALS, in its report on the school, said that Stetson's procedure for evaluating and voting on retention of new faculty members should be changed. The Ramos matter made it clear that Stetson's procedure was adversarial, when it should have been a nurturing process. A few years later, the faculty did adopt new policies and procedures.[3600] And, perhaps more importantly, let the history be clear: during the 1994–95 academic year, Stetson's tenured faculty voted *in favor* of Ramos, and he was granted tenure at Stetson College of Law. Subsequently, Ramos left Stetson to accept a position at Tulane University Law School.[3601]

c. A Divided Faculty

Even prior to the controversy engendered by the Ramos matter, the faculty of the College of Law was dividing into two groups. One generally consisted of those who had been at the school the longest, and for the most part, tended to be satisfied with things as they were. In contrast, the other group, comprised largely of younger and newer members, wanted changes. The issues included: the tenure process and requirements; reform of the curriculum; the size (number of students) of the law school; and the size and diversity of the faculty.[3602] One other concern was how the faculty and dean participate in the "joint-governance" of the law school, a requirement of the ABA.[3603] Issues such as those listed above come up at most law schools. At times, divisions of opinion became entrenched. This happened at Stetson College of Law from around 1990 through the following decade.

Many factors contribute to divisions and discord on a faculty, one being its sheer size and another relating to how fast it grows. From 1990 onward, Stet-

---

3598. Jacob, *Report on Deanship*, *supra* n. 3239, at 39.

3599. *Id.*

3600. *July 27 Jacob Letter*, *supra* n. 3260.

3601. Jacob, *Report on Deanship*, *supra* n. 3239, at 38.

3602. *July 27 Jacob Letter*, *supra* n. 3260.

3603. Standards of the American Bar Association require that a law school faculty participate in the governance of the law school on issues affecting the academic standards and quality of the institution, including making the initial recommendations on hiring, retention, promotion, and tenure of faculty; setting the requirements for admission, grading, retention, and graduation of students; overseeing all academic programs, especially the curriculum; and determining what courses students must take, as well as those that are considered electives.

son's faculty grew in number at a relatively rapid rate. This can and did cause friction at Stetson between so-called "old-guard" faculty and newer, often younger, members of the faculty.

All of these events, fears, and mistrust came together at Stetson law school during the last few years of the Dillon administration and accelerated during the deanships of Bruce Jacob and Lizabeth Moody, as newer and younger faculty rapidly increased in number, but with the "old guard" still in power. In any event, by 2005, faculty members hired since 1990 outnumbered those who were hired before.[3604]

12.10 Hiring a Diverse Faculty: New Staff

a. An Overview

During the thirteen years of Jacob's administration, the faculty hired forty-two new full-time and visiting faculty members.[3605] The number included several women: Joryn Jenkins, Suzanne Armstrong, Dorothea Beane, Judith Royster, Roberta Flowers, Marleen O'Connor, Rebecca Morgan, Diane Clark, Terrill Pollman, and Lizabeth Moody (successor dean to Bruce Jacob); two African-Americans, Dorothea Beane and Darryl Wilson; and one Hispanic, Manuel Ramos.[3606]

Among the forty-two appointments, seven were distinguished professors who held Stetson's Culverhouse Chair visiting professorships: Morgan Shipman (Ohio State), Alfred Conard (Michigan), Allan Farnsworth (Columbia), Harry Krause (Illinois), Douglas Parker (Brigham Young), and John Cribbet (dean at San Diego, and former dean and chancellor at Illinois).[3607] Dean Jacob appointed four persons to be Distinguished Professorial Lecturers: Professor J. Tim Reilly, Judge John M. Scheb, and attorneys Cary R. Singletary and Wm. Reece Smith, Jr.[3608] Visitors from law schools (other than Culverhouse chair holders) included professors Nathaniel Gozansky (Emory University), Robert Ashford (Syracuse University), Gary Minda (Brooklyn Law School), and Patricia Fry (University of Missouri).[3609]

Thirteen of thirty full-time professors hired during Jacob's deanship remained on the faculty in the fall of 2005: professors Dorothea Beane, James J. Brown, Thomas Allison, John Cooper, Darryl Wilson, Marleen O'Connor-

3604. *See* Bishop, *List*, *supra* n. 2351, at 1–10.
3605. *Id.*
3606. *Id.*
3607. *Id.*
3608. *Id.*
3609. *Id.*

Feldman, Peter Lake, Rebecca Morgan, Roberta Flowers, Steven Everhart, Michael Finch, Royal Gardner, and Lizabeth Moody. Seventeen appointees no longer on the faculty included one who died, Suzanne Armstrong; one who retired, Bradford Stone; eleven who moved to other universities (including three who were offered faculty chairs): Patrick Longan (Mercer University), Mark Brown (Capital University), and Charles Elson (University of Delaware); one who became dean at the Texas Wesleyan law school, then at the University of Charleston, S.C., Richard Gershon; one who became a federal magistrate, Mary Scriven; and three who returned to law practice.

Several professors hired during the Jacob era are described in other chapters of this volume: Professors Mark Brown,[3610] Manuel Ramos,[3611] Steven Everhart,[3612] Roberta Flowers,[3613] Rebecca Morgan,[3614] Bradford Stone,[3615] Ronald P. Halpern,[3616] and Lizabeth Moody.[3617]

b. New Faculty Members Contribute to the College

(i) James J. Brown, a holder of the Attorneys' Title Insurance Fund Endowed Professorship, came to Stetson law school as a visiting professor in the fall of 1981. Within a few months, Jacob and the faculty offered Brown a tenured position. At the time, he was tenured at Nova Southeastern Law Center, having joined Nova's faculty in 1976 after six years on the faculty at the University of Missouri-Kansas City.[3618]

Brown, born in Cleveland, Ohio, in 1937, is a polio survivor of the 1946 epidemic.[3619] He earned a B.S. degree in 1960 from University of Pennsylvania's Wharton School of Finance, where he was a member of the varsity debate team.[3620] In 1964, Brown received the J.D. degree with Honors from Cleveland State University College of Law, where he served as the editor-in-chief of the law review and was a member of the school's moot court team. In law

3610. *See infra* nn. 3687–3695 and accompanying text.

3611. *See supra* nn. 3578–3565 and accompanying text.

3612. *See infra* nn. 4061–4066 and accompanying text.

3613. *See infra* nn. 4045–4058 and accompanying text.

3614. *See supra* nn. 3452–3468 and accompanying text.

3615. *See infra* nn. 3737–3754 and accompanying text.

3616. *See supra* nn. 3448–3451 and accompanying text.

3617. *See infra* nn. 4076–4099 and accompanying text.

3618. *AALS 2004–2005 Directory*, *supra* n. 3045, at 312.

3619. Written Comments from James J. Brown, Prof. of L., Stetson U. College of L., to Michael I. Swygert, Prof. Emeritus, Stetson U. College of L. (Nov. 2005).

3620. James Jay Brown, *Curriculum Vitae* 1 (June 19, 2005) (on file at Stetson U. College of L., Gulfport, Fla.) [hereinafter Brown, *Curriculum Vitae*].

James J. Brown

school, he received the Judge S.H. Silbert, the Baldwin, and the Phi Alpha Delta awards.[3621] After graduation, Brown practiced in Cleveland for four years,[3622] then was accepted into a graduate program at Washington University School of Law in St. Louis, where he studied land use planning and local government law. He earned the LL.M. degree in May 1970.[3623]

Since joining Stetson, with its barrier-free campus, Brown devoted his time to developing his expertise in property and land-use planning, which have been his teaching areas. In addition, for nearly a decade, the *Stetson Law Review,* under Brown's guidance, has published an annual symposium on local government law sponsored by The Florida Bar's City, County, and Local Government Law Section.[3624] The annual symposium attracts top legal experts in government law from all over the nation, and the school has been recognized and praised for the quality of its publication.

His Florida Bar membership opened opportunities for service and scholarship. Twice, Brown chaired or co-chaired The Florida Bar's Government Regulation of Land Committee. He also has served twenty-eight years on the Executive Committee of the Bar's Real Property, Probate and Trust Law Section. Brown has maintained strong ties with Florida practitioners as a mem-

3621. *Id.*

3622. *AALS 2004–2005 Directory*, *supra* n. 3045, at 312.

3623. Brown, *Curriculum Vitae, supra* n. 3620, at 1.

3624. *Id.*

ber of the Executive Committee of the Bar's City, County, and Government Law Section.[3625] An active member of the Bar's Environmental and Land Use Law Section, Brown served on its Executive Council and was publication co-chair and editor from 1984 through 1997. For his activities, Brown has received the Stephens Register Memorial Award and the Service Award from the Environmental and Land Use Section of the Bar; a Service Award from the Bar's City, Council, and Government Law Section; and the Annual Service Award from the Bar's Real Property, Probate, and Trust Law Section.[3626]

While at Stetson, Brown has authored numerous publications, and has edited or co-edited several books. Moreover, he has served as the compiler of supplements to the E.C. Yokley treatise on *Zoning Law and Practice* (eight volumes), and has authored more than twenty articles and book reviews.[3627] In 1994, Brown received the Homer and Dolly Hand Award for Excellence in Faculty Research.[3628] He has served as president of the American Society of Writers on Legal Subjects (SCRIBES) and has served on its board of directors. In addition, Brown has been associated with the Urban Land Institute in Washington, D.C.[3629]

Collegial, hard working, willing to take on time-consuming commitments, James J. Brown has been a sturdy supporter of the law school. His contributions were recognized in 2005 when Dean Darby Dickerson named him the inaugural Attorneys' Title Insurance Fund Professor of Law.[3630]

(ii) Professor Michael S. Finch joined the Stetson law faculty in 1982.[3631] Finch earned his B.A. degree with honors in 1975 from Oberlin College in Ohio, where he majored in philosophy. In college, Finch was editor of the Oberlin undergraduate *Journal of Philosophy*.[3632] After college, he enrolled in Boston University School of Law, where he was note and case editor of the school's law review, earning his J.D. degree in 1978.[3633] Years later, Finch stud-

3625. *Id.*

3626. *Id.* at 2.

3627. *Id.* at 3, 4.

3628. *Id.* at 2.

3629. *Id.*

3630. *See Gifts Establish Two New Endowed Professorships—Attorney's Title Insurance Fund Professorship-Major*, 45 Stetson Law. 37, 37 (Spring 2005); *Stetson University College of Law Receives Major Gift from Attorney's Title Insurance Fund, Inc.*,www.law.stetson.edu/communications/news.asp?id=149 (Feb. 15, 2005) (news release).

3631. *AALS 2004–2005 Directory*, *supra* n. 3045, at 459.

3632. *Faculty Forum, Professor Michael Finch*, 26 Stetson Law. 11, 11 (Summer 1984) [hereinafter, *Faculty Forum Finch*]; *see also The Faculty of the College of Law, Stetson University College of Law 1993–1994*, at 6 (1993).

3633. *Id.*

Michael S. Finch

ied at Harvard Law School.[3634] There, he served as co-director of Harvard's Education Arbitration Project.[3635] He studied empirical research methods with professors Lloyd Onlin and Paul Weilor. Finch received his S.J.D. in 1990.

Initially admitted to practice in Connecticut, Finch later became admitted to the bars of Vermont, Florida, and Montana.[3636] After graduating from Boston College, he associated with the Stamford, Connecticut, law firm of Cummings and Lockwood, and subsequently moved to the St. Johnsbury firm of Downs, Rachlin and Martin.[3637] In New England, Finch practiced in the areas of labor, commercial transactions, and appellate work. He authored three articles published in law journals while in practice.[3638]

At Stetson, Finch teaches civil procedure, conflicts of law, federal jurisdiction, and various seminars, including one on empirical and statistical legal research called Law and Behavioral Science.[3639] A demanding teacher, he challenges students to understand the deeper dimensions of law, often using a multi-disciplinary teaching approach combining economic, sociologic, jurisprudential, and

3634. *Faculty Profiles*, 1985–1986 Off. Bull. (Stetson U. College of L.) 18, 21 [hereinafter *1985 Faculty Profiles*].

3635. *Id.*

3636. *AALS 2004–2005 Directory*, *supra* n. 3045, at 459.

3637. *Id.*

3638. *1985 Faculty Profiles*, *supra* n. 3634, at 21.

3639. *Faculty Forum Finch*, *supra* n. 3632, at 11.

statistical analyses. As discussed earlier, Finch is one of the founders and serves as supervisor of Stetson's Federal Court Internship Program.[3640]

Based on the frequency and places his work is cited, Finch is a first-rate scholar. His scholarship encompasses public-sector labor law, conflicts of laws, federal jurisdiction, law and scientific evidence, civil procedure, and death penalty cases.[3641] While working toward his Harvard S.J.D. degree, Finch and Harvard College instructor Trevor Nagle directed the Educational Arbitration Project in Cambridge, funded by grants from Harvard University and the Charles E. Culpepper Foundation, plus a personal research grant Finch received from Stetson law school.[3642] He has published extensively,[3643] and his works have been cited by several courts, including by the United States Supreme Court.[3644] He is a contributing author in a national anthology on conflicts of laws, a leading resource for law professors and attorneys around the country.[3645] A repeat recipient of the Homer and Dolly Hand Award for faculty scholarship, he and his colleague Michael Allen recently co-authored a book on federal civil procedure, titled *An Illustrated Guide to Civil Procedure*, published by Aspen Publishers, Inc.[3646] In recent years, Finch has focused on law and scientific evidence. He serves on the Board of Advisors of Daubert Tracker, a leading research source on expert witnesses, and has been invited to be co-editor of a new journal—*Psychological Evidence and Law.*

Having an extraordinary lexicon, he writes with precision and clarity. Because his writing skills and expertise on complex litigation are well known, Finch frequently is asked by law firms to draft appellate briefs in challenging cases. In addition, faculty colleagues frequently ask Finch to review drafts of the articles they are working on. Certain faculty members—for example, Steven Everhart—point to him as the person who provided them the most help when they began to write.[3647]

3640. *See supra* nn. 3322–3333 and accompanying text.

3641. *Faculty Forum Finch*, *supra* n. 3632, at 11.

3642. *Id.*

3643. *See e.g.* Michael Finch, *Choice of Law Problems in Federal Courts: A Retrospective on the Restatement (Second)*, 24 Stetson L. Rev. 653 (1995).

3644. *See Lockhart v. McCree*, 476 U.S. 162 (1986) (citing Mark Ferraro, *The Empirical Challenge to Death—Qualified Juries: On Further Examination*, 65 Neb. L. Rev. 21 (1986) and relied on in both the majority and the dissenting opinions).

3645. *See A Conflict of Laws, Anthology* (Gene Shreve ed., Anderson Pub;g. Co. 1997).

3646. Michael P. Allen & Michael S. Finch, *An Illustrated Guide to Civil Procedure* (forthcoming Aspen Publishers 2006).

3647. Interview by Michael I. Swygert, Stetson U. College of L., with Stephen M. Everhart, Prof. of L., Stetson U. College of L. 21 (May 17, 2004) [hereinafter *Everhart Interview*].

(iii) Professor Suzanne R. Armstrong joined the Stetson faculty in 1983. One person was especially pleased Armstrong did so—Bruce Jacob. Armstrong, as a law student, had been an administrative assistant to Jacob, then dean of Walter F. George School of Law of Mercer University.[3648] Jacob was aware that Armstrong not only was a hard worker, but also that she possessed a keen mind. She graduated from Mercer with a J.D. degree *cum laude*, and had been managing editor of the school's law review.[3649]

Born in 1945 in Laramie, Wyoming, Armstrong earned her B.A. degree in 1967 from the University of Wyoming, followed by an M.A. in 1971 from the University of South Carolina.[3650] She taught English for several years before entering law school at Mercer. After graduation, she clerked for Judge Peter T. Fay of the United States Court of Appeals for the Fifth Circuit in Miami.[3651] After clerking, she joined the Tampa firm of Carlton, Fields, Ward, Emmanuel, Smith & Cutler, where she engaged in general and appellate practice.[3652]

At Stetson, Armstrong taught civil procedure, research and writing, and contracts, and authored several articles on procedure,[3653] as well as a work related to her pro bono representation of an indigent defendant before the Eleventh Circuit U.S. Court of Appeals.[3654]

Two years after coming to Stetson, Armstrong learned she had cancer. In a letter to Stetson students in the *Prelude*,[3655] she acknowledged that she had to cancel classes while undergoing chemotherapy treatments, telling them, "I could have never survived it without you," and thanking them for the "great role you have played."[3656] Professor Armstrong declared her determination to survive. She wrote:

> Last spring, I faced 149 freshmen, all primed and ready for an exam, knowing if my doctors were to be believed, I wouldn't see the class graduate [two years later]. While they were taking the exam, I battled the fear and anger that accompanies news of impending death ... Had I finally

3648. Rebecca Morgan, *Dedication*, 20 Stetson L. Rev. 1, 2 (Fall, 1990) [hereinafter Morgan, Dedication].

3649. *Faculty Notes, Suzanne R. Armstrong*, 26 Stetson Lawyer 11, 12 (Summer 1984); *see also Faculty Profiles, Suzanne R. Armstrong*, 1985 Off. Bull. (Stetson U. College of L.) 18.

3650. *Faculty Notes, Suzanne R. Armstrong*, *supra* n. 3649, at 12.

3651. *Id.*

3652. *Id.*

3653. *Id.*

3654. *See* Suzanne R. Armstrong, *Self-Incrimination and the Insanity Plea; out of Mouths of Babes*, 66 Denver U. L. Rev. 81 (1988).

3655. Suzanne R. Armstrong, *An Open Letter*, 20 Prelude 8, 8 (Apr. 15, 1986).

3656. *Id.*

been given a burden too heavy to bear? And then the solution hit me; I had to see them graduate. I could fight that long.[3657]

Suzanne Armstrong fought that long, and several graduations beyond. But death finally came on July 9, 1990, five years after she had been told she had only a short time to live. Up until the last weeks of her life, Armstrong continued contributing to the law school by teaching, researching, and writing. At the time of death, she was working with Professor Finch on a treatise on Florida practice and procedure.[3658]

During her time at Stetson, Armstrong researched how to best computerize the faculty secretarial offices, making specific recommendations of what needed to be purchased.[3659] Connie Evans, Director of Faculty Support Services, recalls Armstrong "spending a lot of time getting us organized," adding, "I would give anything if she could just come back and see [how] we've taken some of her ideas and have progressed over the years."[3660]

In Armstrong's memory, the College established a Suzanne R. Armstrong Memorial Fellowship and renamed the research and writing teaching fellows, "Armstrong Teaching Fellows."[3661] In an issue of the *Stetson Lawyer* dedicated to Armstrong, her friend and colleague Professor Rebecca Morgan wrote: "Suzanne was a living definition of courage."[3662]

(iv) Professor I. Richard Gershon came to the Stetson law school in the fall of 1984. An Atlanta native, Gershon earned his B.A. degree from the University of Georgia in 1978; in 1981, a J.D. degree from the University of Tennessee; and an LL.M. in taxation from the University of Florida in 1983.[3663] He worked briefly as a special assistant attorney general for Georgia, then joined the law faculty at Ohio Northern University.[3664] After one year, Gershon left Ohio Northern to accept Stetson's offer to join the faculty.[3665]

At Stetson, Gershon and a colleague, John Cooper, founded the Stetson Tax Moot Court Competition, discussed earlier.[3666] During the six years Gershon

---

3657. *Id.*

3658. Morgan, *Dedication*, *supra* n. 3648, at 2.

3659. *Id.*

3660. *Evans Interview*, *supra* n. 3126, at 17, 18.

3661. Morgan, *Dedication*, *supra* n. 3648, at 2, 3.

3662. *Id.*

3663. *In re Faculty, New Associate Dean, I. Richard Gershon*, 28 Stetson Law. 14, 15 (Fall 1988) [hereinafter *New Associate Dean Gershon*].

3664. *1985 Faculty Profiles*, *supra* n. 3634, at 21.

3665. *Id.*

3666. *See supra* nn. 3517–3520 and accompanying text.

served on the faculty, he coached Stetson's tax moot courts, several of which won first or second places in national competitions.[3667] At Stetson, Gershon's writings focused on taxation, authoring the book *A Student's Guide to the Internal Revenue Code,* and co-authoring with colleagues Thomas Allison and Rebecca Morgan *Life Planning in Florida.*[3668]

In the fall of 1988, Bruce Jacob appointed Gershon associate dean for academic affairs.[3669] Jacob later praised all his subdeans, commenting that "Becky Morgan, Bob Batey, and Richard Gershon were very loyal and very able associate deans during my last years in the deanship.[3670] Gershon left Stetson in 1990 to become dean of a new law school in Fort Worth, Texas. Presently, he is dean at a new law school in Charleston, South Carolina.

(v) Professor John Frederick Cooper comes from a military family. He spent a portion of his youth in Japan where his father, an Army officer, served on the staff of General Douglas MacArthur.[3671] Back in the states, Cooper graduated from Culver Military Academy in Indiana, then went to the College of William & Mary, where he earned his B.A in 1972.[3672] Following military service (which included being trained as a U.S. Army paratrooper), Cooper decided to go to law school. He enrolled at the University of Oklahoma Law Center, where he earned a J.D. degree in 1979.[3673] There, he was an editor on the *Oklahoma Law Review* and was elected to the Order of the Coif.[3674] He also served as research assistant to Professor Fred Miller, a recognized authority in commercial law.[3675]

Before coming to Stetson, Cooper practiced in Oklahoma City and served as an Assistant Attorney General for the State of Oklahoma.[3676] In practice, Cooper authored a book for practitioners on organizing and dissolving Oklahoma corporations, a precursor of his later scholarship.[3677] He developed an

3667. *New Associate Dean Gershon, supra* n. 3663, at 15.

3668. *Id.*

3669. *Id.* at 14.

3670. Jacob, *Report on Deanship, supra* n. 3239, at 40.

3671. Conversation between John F. Cooper, Prof. of L., Stetson U. College of L. and Michael I. Swygert, Prof. Emeritus, Stetson U. College of L. (circa 1990).

3672. John Frederick Cooper, *Resume* 1 (Mar. 4, 2005) (on file at Stetson U. College of L., Gulfport, Fla.) [hereinafter Cooper, *Resume*].

3673. *Id.*

3674. *The Faculty of the College of Law, 1993–1994* 24 at 8 (Stetson U. College of L. 1993) (on file at Stetson U. College of L., Gulfport, Fla.) [hereinafter *Faculty 1993*].

3675. Cooper, *Resume, supra* n. 3672, at 1.

3676. *AALS 2004–2005 Directory, supra* n. 3045, at 374.

3677. Cooper, *Resume, supra* n. 3672, at 2.

John F. Cooper

expertise in corporate and tax law while, at the same time, nourishing a growing interest in the problems of Native Americans.

In 1985, Stetson invited Cooper to join the faculty as a visiting assistant professor of law.[3678] He did so, and his status was quickly changed to a regular tenure-track member of the faculty. In the fall of 2005, Professor Cooper began his twenty-first year as a tenured member of Stetson's faculty.

Cooper's teaching is concentrated in the tax realm.[3679] His courses include federal taxation, state & local taxation, and international taxation. In addition, he teaches estate planning, state tax, and state constitutional law.[3680] In 1993, Stetson University College of Law recognized Cooper's teaching skills by presenting him the University's Excellence in Teaching Award. He also has been a recipient of the University's Homer and Dolly Hand Award for Excellence in Faculty Research. In 2001, Dean Gary Vause bestowed on Professor Cooper the Dean's Award for Extraordinary Service to the College of Law.

Twice, Cooper co-chaired dean search committees, and has also chaired faculty curriculum reform, tenure and promotion, financial aid, and appointments committees.[3681] For six years, he advised the *Stetson Law Review* and several times he coached moot court teams.[3682] In the summer of 2003,

3678. *AALS 2004–2005 Directory*, *supra* n. 3045, at 374.

3679. Cooper, *Resume*, *supra* n. 3672, at 2–3.

3680. *AALS 2004–2005 Directory*, *supra* n. 3045, at 374.

3681. Cooper, *Resume*, *supra* n. 3672, at 4.

3682. *Id.*

Cooper served as resident director of the College of Law summer abroad program in Granada, Spain.[3683] Dean Darby Dickerson appointed Cooper interim director of the College's Graduate and International Programs[3684] and later promoted him to be Associate Dean of International and Cooperative Programs.[3685]

Regarding research and scholarship, Cooper has compiled an impressive record. His state constitutional law publications, co-authored with Professor Marks, were noted earlier.[3686] Among the articles and book chapters Cooper has authored, one article in particular deserves special mention, a work that necessitated that he rummage through hundreds of old files in the basement of Princeton University's library. The resulting article documents how Russian immigrant Mennonites were persecuted in the United States because of their religious-based objections to military service in World War I. Cooper's work fills a significant gap in American history.

(vi) Professor Mark R. Brown, currently holder of the Baker Hostetler Chair and Professor of Law at Capital University Law School in Columbus, Ohio, joined the Stetson law faculty in 1986.[3687] He is a 1981 graduate of Dayton University, and a 1984 honors graduate of the University of Louisville, Louis D. Brandeis School of Law.[3688] In law school, Brown was president of the Brandeis Society, and was an editor of the school's *Journal of Family Law*.[3689] He then clerked for Judge Harry W. Wellford of the United States Court of Appeals for the Sixth Circuit.[3690] Later, he earned an LL.M. degree from the University of Illinois while teaching legal research and writing to the law school's students.[3691]

At Stetson, Brown taught civil rights and constitutional law. He was active in the Florida chapter of the American Civil Liberties Union, representing ACLU clients in several pro bono cases. His scholarship has been published in important law reviews, and he has co-authored a book on litigating constitutional issues under Section 1983 of the United States Code.[3692] An expert on civil rights,

3683. *Id.*

3684. *Three Faculty Promoted to Decanal Positions*, 44 Stetson Law. 4, 4 (Spring 2004).

3685. *Id.*

3686. *See supra* n. 2995 and accompanying text.

3687. *AALS 2004–2005 Directory*, *supra* n. 3045, at 313.

3688. *Id.*

3689. *Id.*

3690. *Faculty 1993*, *supra* n. 3674, at 8.

3691. *The Faculty of the College of Law*, 1991–1992, Off. Bull., (Stetson U. College of L.) 12, 13 [hereinafter *1991 Bulletin*].

3692. *Id.*

Thomas E. Allison

he chaired both the AALS Section on Civil Rights and the ABA Subcommittee on Section 1983 Litigation.[3693] At Stetson, Brown was selected by the United States Supreme Court to be a Judicial Fellow for the Court's 1993–94 term.[3694] There, he worked for the late Chief Justice of the United States, William H. Rehnquist.[3695]

(vii) Professor Thomas E. Allison is a successful lawyer who became a successful law teacher, then a successful law school administrator. Allison taught on the Stetson faculty for a few years on a part-time basis, then in 1985 became a permanent member.[3696] A holder of four university degrees, Allison earned his B.S. from Tulane University in 1973, an M.B.A. from Florida State University in 1974, followed by a J.D. from Stetson in 1977, and finally an LL.M. from the University of Florida in 1978.[3697]

For several years, Allison practiced with the firm of Allison & Heistand, where he was a partner for eight years before joining the Stetson faculty.[3698]

3693. *AALS 2004–2005 Directory*, *supra* n. 3045, at 313.

3694. *U.S. Supreme Court Chooses Professor Mark Brown as Judicial Fellow*, 33 Stetson Law. 12, 12 (Summer 1993).

3695. *Id.* From the hundreds of applicants for the Supreme Court Judicial Fellow position, only one is chosen, and that year, it was Stetson's Professor Mark Brown. Brown left Stetson in 2000 to accept the position at the Capital.

3696. *AALS 2004–2005 Directory*, *supra* n. 3045, at 225.

3697. *Id.*

3698. *Id.*

Allison is Florida Bar Board certified in taxation and is a certified financial planner.[3699] He has chaired committees of The Florida Bar dealing with trusts and estates and estate planning. At Stetson, Allison teaches agency and partnership, property, estate and gift taxation, estate planning, and trusts and estates. Together with professors Rebecca Morgan and Richard Gershon, Allison co-authored *Life Planning in Florida*.[3700] In addition to teaching, he has served the College in various administrative capacities, first as assistant dean to Jacob, later as associate dean during Dean Moody's administration, and more recently as vice dean during most of Vause's deanship.[3701] In 2003, Allison returned to full-time teaching. Personable, laid back, always courteous, and having a sharp wit, Professor Tom Allison is a tonic the school periodically has needed in moments when the seas become rough.

(viii) Professor Marleen A. O'Connor in 1984 graduated first in a class of 999 students from DePaul University in Chicago, Illinois, earning a B.S. *summa cum laude*, with a dual major in accounting and economics.[3702] After passing the C.P.A. examination, O'Connor entered Duke Law School, where she served as an articles editor on the *Duke Law Journal*.[3703] She graduated from Duke's law school with honors in 1987, then became associated with the Atlanta law firm of King & Spalding.[3704] In 1988, O'Connor joined the Stetson College of Law faculty.[3705] At Stetson, she teaches business associations, agency and unincorporated entities, securities regulation, and law and economics.

During her years thus far on Stetson's law faculty, O'Connor has produced quality scholarship. Her work has appeared in a score of publications, including *Cornell Law Journal, University of Pennsylvania Law Review, Fordham Law Review, Washington & Lee Law Review, George Washington Law Review, North Carolina Law Review, University of Cincinnati Law Review*, and most recently, the *University of Southern California Law Review*.[3706] Many of her articles deal

---

3699. *1991 Bulletin, supra* n. 3691, at 12.

3700. *See* Thomas I. Allison, I. Richard Gershon & Rebecca C. Morgan, *Life Planning in Florida* (D&S Publishers 1988).

3701. *AALS 2004–2005 Directory, supra* n. 3045, at 225.

3702. *The Faculty of the College of Law, 1993–1994 Bulletin* 19 (Stetson U. College of L. 1993) [hereinafter *1993 Bulletin*].

3703. *Id.*

3704. Marlene A. O'Connor, Curriculum Vitae 1 (May 4, 2005) (on file at Stetson U. College of L., Gulfport, Fla.) [hereinafter O'Connor, *Curriculum Vitae*].

3705. *1993 Bulletin, supra* n. 3702, at 17.

3706. O'Connor, *Curriculum Vitae, supra* n. 3704, at 2, 3.

Marleen A. O'Connor

with a subject she pioneered—the undervaluation of "human capital" as a business asset.[3707]

O'Connor's cutting-edge scholarship has garnered her recognition throughout the country, and she has been invited to speak at scores of institutions, including Harvard, Cornell, U.C.L.A., Massachusetts Institute of Technology, Pennsylvania, George Washington, Washington & Lee, Florida, Cincinnati, Buffalo, Catholic, British Columbia, and Georgetown.[3708] O'Connor has participated in national programs of the AALS, the Law and Society Conference (eleven years in a row), the Economic Policy Institute, the Brookings Institution, the National Annual Labor Conference, the Society for the Advancement of Socio-Economics, and the Critical Legal Studies Conference, among others.[3709]

3707. *See e.g.* Marlene A. O'Connor, *American Corporate Governance and Resilient Families: Investing in Children's Human Capital in Turbulent Times*, 77 So. Cal. L. Rev. 1255 (2004); *The Human Capital Era: Reconceptualizing Corporate Law to Facilitate Labor-Management Corporations*, 78 Cornell L. Rev. 899 (1993).

3708. O'Connor, *Curriculum Vitae*, *supra* n. 3704, at 3, 4.

3709. *Id.* Professor O'Connor's scholarly activities include serving as a member of: Alfred P. Sloan Project on Dispute Resolution and Corporate Governance, U.C.L.A. Law School (2004–present); Brookings Institution Task Force on Intangibles (1977–2000); Property Consulting Group, Robin Malloy, Director, Syracuse Law School (2004–present); and, Labor's Capital Project on Pension Funds and Responsible Investing (sponsored by the United Steel Workers of America and the Ford and Rockefeller Foundations (1998). Id.

Stetson University College of Law has recognized O'Connor's scholarship by twice awarding her the Homer and Dolly Hand Award for Excellence in Faculty Research (1991 and 2003).[3710] In 1990, the *Stetson Law Review* gave her an Award for Scholarship and Teaching. Other recognitions include her receiving an Alfred P. Sloan Foundation grant for research in 2002, and being awarded the "Best Paper Prize" at the International Conference of Socio-Economics.[3711] In 2000, Professor O'Connor was named associate director of The George Washington University Law School International Institute for Corporate Governance and Accountability.

(ix) Professor Dorothea Beane, born in Plainfield, New Jersey, received her B.A. degree from Drew University in 1974, where she majored in history with minors in sociology and political science.[3712] From Drew, she entered Rutgers University Center for Law & Justice at Newark, where she earned her J.D. degree in 1977.[3713]

Dorothea Beane joined the Stetson law faculty in 1990, having eleven years of civil litigation experience. Ten of those years, she represented the United States government. She began her federal career in Washington, D.C., in 1977 as trial attorney with the Torts Branch of the Civil Division of the U. S. Department of Justice.[3714] There, she represented federal agencies in U.S. District and Appellate Courts, and supervised government attorneys involved in tort litigation in various U.S. Attorney offices.[3715] Beane left the Department of Justice in 1982 and practiced with the Washington, D.C., law firm of Robinson and Geraldo.[3716] In 1983, she returned to government service after being appointed an Assistant United States Attorney for the Middle District of Florida, working with the Jacksonville and Ocala divisions.[3717] For two years she served as a general civil litigation lawyer, and in 1985 was promoted to senior litigating attorney, working primarily in commercial and medical malpractice litigation.[3718]

In 1986, Beane received the U.S. Attorney General's Award for Sustained Superior Performance of Duty.[3719] Though she "loved" her work at the De-

3710. *Id.*

3711. *Id.*

3712. Dorothea Beane, Curriculum Vitae 1 (2005) (on file at Stetson U. College of L., Gulfport, Fla.) [hereinafter Beane, *Curriculum Vitae*].

3713. *Id.*

3714. *Id.*

3715. *Id.*

3716. *Id.*, at 2; *see also AALS 2004–2005 Directory*, *supra* n. 3045, at 262.

3717. *Id.*

3718. Beane, *Curriculum Vitae*, *supra* n. 3712, at 2.

Dorothea Beane

partment of Justice, in 1990 she left to accept an offer from Stetson College of Law to become a professor of law.[3720]

At Stetson, Beane teaches federal civil procedure, pretrial practice, federal litigation internships (a program she initiated and oversees with attorneys in federal agencies in Florida), alternative dispute resolution (including negotiations), international human rights law, and law of international tribunals.[3721] In addition to her expertise in civil litigation and federal practice, after coming to Stetson, Beane has intensified her focus in the areas of international human rights, both in teaching and scholarship. Frequently, she travels to The Hague to observe the workings of the International Criminal Tribunal for the Former Yugoslavia, the International Court of Justice, and the Permanent Court of International Arbitration. There, she has made friends with several jurists, including Appellate Judges Navi Pillay and Gabrielle Kirk McDonald.[3722]

3719. *1993 Bulletin*, *supra* n. 3702, at 12.

3720. Beane, *Curriculum Vitae*, *supra* n. 3712, at 1, 2. During the years Dorothea Beane worked in the U.S. Department of Justice, eleven different government agencies awarded her numerous "letters of commendation." The agencies issuing the commendations included the Federal Bureau of Investigation (FBI), U.S. Dept. of Justice, U.S. Dept. of Energy, U.S. Labor Depart., U.S. Dept. of Agriculture, U.S. Dept. of the Navy, U.S. Treasury Dept., U.S. Postal Service, U.S. Marshals Service, U.S. Bureau of Alcohol, Tobacco and Firearms, and Office of the Judge Advocate General. *See id.* at 7.

3721. *Id.* at 4.

3722. *Recent Events, Professor Dorothea Beane Visits International Criminal Court*

Judge Pillay and Professor Beane put together a program that enabled Stetson law students to visit The Hague in 2005 to observe the proceedings of the international courts and to meet with several judges.[3723] The students and Beane also visited the Human Rights Court in Freiburg, Germany.[3724]

Due to her interest in international human rights and international tribunals, Beane has been invited to speak at universities and institutes around the world, including Oxford University in England (where she also did graduate course work at New College in international human rights), George Washington University, and the University of Innsbruck, Austria. She attends various international conferences, such as a 1998 United Nations Diplomatic Conference in Rome, Italy.[3725] In addition to overseeing the College's Summer Abroad Program at the Institute of Social Studies in The Hague,[3726] Beane has taught human rights and humanitarian law in Stetson's summer program in Tallinn, Estonia (the same year she was appointed faculty advisor for Stetson's American-Caribbean Law Initiative).[3727]

Professor Beane's scholarship includes: *AIDS Crisis and the Health Care Community*,[3728] *The International Tribunal for the Former Yugoslavia: A Progress Report*,[3729] *The Yugoslav Tribunal and Deferral of National Prosecutions of War Criminals*,[3730] *After the Dusko Tadic War Crimes Trial: A Commentary on the Applicability of the Grave Breaches Provisions of the 1949 Geneva Convention*,[3731] *Human Rights in Transition: Freedom from Fear*,[3732] *Catching the Chameleon: When Is the Treating Physician an Expert?*,[3733] *Pleasing and Disclosure of Damages in Federal Courts: No Cat and Mouse Game*,[3734] and *Are Governments Employees Proper Qui Tam Plaintiffs?*[3735]

Stetson U. College of Law 1, www.law.stetson.edu/recentevents/BeaneICC.asp (July 14, 2004)

3723. *Id.*

3724. Notes from Lisa Smith, Research Asst., to Michael I. Swygert, Prof. Emeritus, Stetson U. College of L. (Oct. 9, 2005) (on file at Stetson U. College of L., Gulfport, Fla.).

3725. Beane, *Curriculum Vitae*, *supra* n. 3712, at 3, 4.

3726. *Id.*

3727. *Id.*

3728. 45 Mercer L. Rev. 633 (1994).

3729. The Irish Times (Dublin) (Oct./Nov. 1966) (co-authored with Liz Heffernam).

3730. 13 ASIL Insight 1 (Oct. 1966).

3731. 27 Stetson L. Rev. 589 (1998).

3732. 6 Wash. & Lee, Race, Ethic & Ancestry L.J. 1 (2000).

3733. 51 Fed. Law. 4 (May 2004) (co-authored with Theodore Karatinos).

3734. 3 Fed. Discovery News 4 (Mar. 1997).

3735. 14 J. Leg. Med. (1993).

Bradford Stone

Throughout her work at Stetson, Beane has participated in numerous professional organizations, many relating to the American, National, and Federal bar associations. She serves as vice-president of the United Nations Affairs, International Law Section of the National Bar Association. As noted earlier, Professor Beane was the first African-American hired by Stetson College of Law in its 105-year history, and that occurred in 1990.[3736] Her presence at Stetson has helped the College to grow in important ways, particularly in overcoming what some may perceive as stereotypical thinking regarding race.

(x) Professor Bradford Stone, born in 1929, earned his A.B. from the University of Michigan in 1951, where he majored in political science and wrestled on the university's team. Stone then enrolled in Michigan's law school, receiving his J.D. degree in 1954, after which he was admitted to the Michigan Bar.[3737] From 1954 through 1956, Stone served in the U.S. Army at Fort Still, Oklahoma. He then took a year to study at the London School of Economics.[3738] From 1958 through 1963, Stone worked as a corporate attorney in the legal division of Burroughs Corporation at its Detroit headquarters.[3739]

3736. *See supra* nn. 3032–3033 and accompanying text.

3737. Bradford Stone, *Resume* 1 (May 1992 and addendum 2005) (on file at Stetson U. College of L., Gulfport, Fla.) [hereinafter Stone, *Resume*].

3738. *Id.*

3739. *AALS 2004–2005 Directory*, *supra* n. 3045, at 999.

In 1963, Brad Stone began his twenty-four years on the Detroit College of Law faculty. There, he taught commercial transactions, creditors' rights, secured transactions, and a commercial transactions seminar.[3740] In addition, Stone was appointed director of the Legal Drafting Program and, for a time, served as the faculty advisor to the school's national moot court teams.[3741] During his years on the DCL faculty, he visited at the University of Michigan Law School, Stetson University College of Law,[3742] and the J. Reuben Clark Law School of Brigham Young University.[3743]

Throughout his career in legal education Stone has authored numerous books. He wrote the first edition of the *Uniform Commercial Code in a Nutshell* that was published by West Publishing Co. in 1975.[3744] The book has proven to be very popular with law students across the country and, since its original publication, has gone through five subsequent editions, the most recent sixth edition published in 2005.[3745]

In addition to his *Commercial Law Nutshell,* Stone began to write a series of books for West on legal forms. The first series consisted of nineteen volumes of *Modern Legal Forms* published in 1973, which Stone annually updated.[3746] He also was responsible for volumes twelve to fifteen of *West's Legal Forms* (2d. ed.), that he also subsequently updated. Then, in 1986, he revised volumes twenty-six through twenty-nine of *West's Legal Forms—Specialized Forms.*[3747] In a project for the Michigan Institute of Continuing Legal Education, in 1964 Stone co-authored a Michigan *Desk Reference to the Uniform Commercial Code.*[3748] While a member of the Detroit College of Law faculty, he authored three law review articles.[3749]

3740. Stone, *Resume*, *supra* n. 3737, at 2.

3741. *Id.*

3742. *See supra* nn. 3172–3174 and accompanying text.

3743. *AALS 2004–2005 Directory*, *supra* n. 3045, at 999. In addition, Professor Stone was a visiting lecturer at University of Michigan Graduate School of Business Administration, teaching a course in business law from 1959 through 1973. *See* Stone, *Resume*, *supra* n. 3737, at 2.

3744. *Id.*

3745. *Id.* at addendum.

3746. Stone, *Resume*, *supra* n. 3707, at 4.

3747. *Id.* In addition to the West Legal Forms series, Bradford Stone was responsible for authoring and annotating *Michigan's Compiled Laws Annotated—Uniform Commercial Code Forms with Practice Comments* (West 1971) (with annual supplements through 1986), as well as putting out a second edition in 1992. *Id.*

3748. *Id.*

3749. *Id.* They were published in the Wayne State, Detroit College, and the Brigham Young Law Reviews. *Id.*

In the spring of 1987, Bradford Stone came to Stetson's law school to visit for the second time.[3750] The faculty was seeking someone to teach commercial law. With the encouragement of Professor Kuenzel, Stone said he was interested in the position. Thereupon, Dean Jacob and the faculty offered Stone a permanent position. After coming to Stetson, Stone taught sales, secured transactions, commercial paper, creditors' rights, international sales of goods, and international transactions.[3751] Three summers he taught international sales transaction in Spain as part of Stetson's international summer programs.[3752]

Stone first learned about Stetson from his friend Cal Kuenzel, whom he met at a New York University Commercial Law Workshop in 1964. As discussed earlier, the two—along with four others who became acquainted at that conference (professors King, Lauer, Littlefield and Joe McKnight)—authored a joint case book on commercial law, currently in its fifth edition. In 1987, Stone became a full-time member of the Stetson faculty.[3753] With the retirement of Dean Emeritus Richard Dillon, first holder of the Charles A. Dana Professorship, he was appointed the second Charles A. Dana Professor of Law of Stetson University. Bradford Stone retired from the College of Law in fall 2005 after eighteen years of productive service.[3754]

(xi) Professor Peter Francis Lake in 2005 was named the third recipient of the Charles A. Dana Chair of Stetson College of Law.[3755] He joined the school's faculty in the fall of 1990, after practicing four years in the international law firm of Cahill Gordon & Reindel at its New York City headquarters.[3756] Lake earned his A.B. degree *magna cum laude* in 1981 from Harvard University, where he majored in philosophy and was a member of Phi Beta Kappa.[3757] At Harvard College, he served as teaching assistant to Harvard Law School Professor Charles Fried, and was the recipient of a John Harvard Scholarship (honorary), the Detur Prize, and a grant from the Mark DeWolfe Howe Fund for study and research in legal history.[3758]

3750. Bishop, *List*, *supra* n. 2351, at 4.

3751. Professor Stone also assisted in coaching Stetson Moot Court teams when commercial law issues were involved.

3752. *See infra* nn. 4236–4257 and accompanying text.

3753. *Id.*

3754. *Professors Stone; Swygert Retire*, 45 Stetson Law. 13, 13 (Spring 2005).

3755. *Peter Lake Appointed to Charles A. Dana Chair*, 45 Stetson Law. 8, 8 (Spring 2005).

3756. *1991 Bulletin*, *supra* n. 3691, at 16.

3757. *Id.*

3758. Peter Francis Lake, *Curriculum Vitae* 1 (2004) (on file at Stetson U. College of L., Gulfport, Fla.) [hereinafter Lake, *Curriculum Vitae*].

Peter Lake

Lake entered Harvard Law School in 1981 and graduated in 1984 with a J.D. degree, *cum laude*.[3759] During law school, he served on the board of editors of the *Harvard International Law Journal*, and received the Laylin Prize for the best paper written by a student in the field of public international law.[3760] In addition, Lake was selected to be research assistant for Harvard Law School professors Lloyd Weinreb and Henry Steiner, and for Harvard School of Public Health professor Wendy Mariner.[3761]

After law school, Lake clerked one year for Bruce M. Selya, Judge of the United States District Court for the District of Rhode Island (who later was elevated to the United States Court of Appeals for the First Circuit). The following year, he clerked for Neil Lynch, Associate Justice of the Massachusetts Supreme Judicial Court.[3762] After clerking, he joined Cahill Gordon & Reindel, where he specialized in insurance and bankruptcy practice, as well as in First Amendment law with Floyd Abrams, a leading expert in the field whose clients included the *New York Times*.[3763]

Though he had offers from other schools, Peter Lake chose to join the Stetson law faculty in the fall of 1989. At Stetson, Lake teaches courses in torts, in-

3759. *Introducing the Newest Members of the Stetson Faculty, Professor Peter Lake*, 30 Stetson Law. 8, 8 (Fall 1990) [hereinafter *Newest Faculty-Lake*].

3760. *Id.* at 1, 3.

3761. *Id.* at 3.

3762. *Newest Faculty-Lake, supra* n. 3759, at 8.

3763. *Id.*

surance, jurisprudence, client counseling, and law and higher education, and has served as coordinator of the school's honors program.[3764] He has earned several teaching awards, including: Stetson University College of Law Outstanding Teacher (1995); Student Bar Association Professor of the Year (1996); SBA Excellence Award (2000); Stetson Business Law Society Golden Apple Achievement Award (2000); and SBA Best Professor for First-Year Students (2003) and (2004).[3765] Lake has twice received the Homer and Dolly Hand Award for Excellence in Faculty Research.[3766]

Lake, along with his colleague Robert Bickel, has co-authored a book on the legal rights and responsibilities of the "modern university."[3767] Lake has also authored or co-authored a score of articles and book reviews, many related to issues in law and education, but several dealing with either torts or legal philosophy.[3768] Having been cited in several judicial opinions,[3769] Lake is frequently asked to speak at national conferences, conclaves, and workshops.[3770]

Lake serves as a member of the Board of Editors of the *Journal of College and University Law* (published at Notre Dame Law School). He and Professor Bickel work together in the field of law and higher education. Their expertise is known throughout the country.[3771] As a result, they serve as consultants to several colleges and universities regarding legal issues associated with higher education. At Stetson, they co-direct Stetson's Center for Excellence in Higher Education Law and Policy.[3772]

(xii) Professor Charles M. Elson, a graduate of Harvard University and University of Virginia School of Law (Order of the Coif), joined the Stetson faculty in 1990.[3773] While in law school, Elson clerked part-time for J. Harvie

---

3764. Lake, *Curriculum Vitae, supra* n. 3758, at 2.

3765. *Id.*

3766. *Id.*

3767. *See* Robert D. Bickel & Peter F. Lake, *The Rights and Responsibilities of the Modern University: Who Assumes the Risks of College Life?* (Carolina Academic Press 1999).

3768. Professor Lake's writings have appeared in journals and law reviews, including: *Journal of Legal Education*; *New York Law Journal*; *Idaho Law Review*; *Missouri Law Review*; *Nebraska Law Review*; *DePaul Law Review*; *Columbia Transnational Law Journal*; *Albany Law Review*; *Brooklyn Law Review*; *Campus Law Enforcement Journal*; *American Bar Association Journal*; and *Journal of College and University Law*. *See* Lake, Curriculum Vitae, *supra* n. 3758, at 4, 5.

3769. *Id.*

3770. *Id.* at 6, 7.

3771. *See infra* nn. 3927–3936 and accompanying text.

3772. *Faculty Forum, Peter Lake Appointed*, 45 Stetson Law. 8, 8 (Summer 2005).

3773. *Members of the Stetson Faculty, Professor Charles Elson*, 30 Stetson Law. 8, 8 (Fall 1990).

Wilkinson III, Judge of the United States Court of Appeals for the Fourth Circuit.[3774] After graduating, he clerked for the Honorable Elbert P. Tuttle, Senior Judge of the United States Court of Appeals for the Eleventh Circuit.[3775] Elson next joined the New York City law firm of Sullivan & Cromwell, where he practiced in the areas of corporate finance, mergers, and acquisitions.[3776]

At Stetson, Elson taught securities regulation, corporations, agency and seminars. His scholarship has focused on corporate law and executive compensation. At Stetson, one of Elson's works was published in the *Cornell Law Review*.[3777] His interest in corporate law led him to put together a national conference on corporate law. One of the speakers was Professor Stewart J. Schwab, who later became the dean of Cornell Law School. In 1993, Elson was selected as a Fellow of the Heritage's Foundation Salvatori Center for Academic Leadership, an organization "which emphasizes preservation of the principles of American liberty."[3778] At Stetson, Elson founded the school's chapter of the Federalist Society, a national group of politically conservative judges, lawyers, and law students. Charles Elson remained at the Stetson College of Law for several years, then accepted a chaired professorship at the University of Delaware.

(xiii) Professor Patrick E. Longan, a Texas native, was hired by Stetson in 1991. He received his undergraduate education from Washington University in St. Louis, majoring in economics and political science.[3779] After graduating in 1979, Longan went to England to earn a master of arts degree in economic policy and planning from the University of Sussex.[3780] He returned to the States and entered the University of Chicago Law School. Longan received his J.D. degree in 1983 from Chicago, then clerked for Bernard M. Decker, Senior Judge, United States District Court for the Northern District of Illinois.[3781] Following his clerkship, he practiced law in Dallas, Texas, including six years with Andrews & Kurth.[3782] His eventual goal was to teach.

3774. *Id.*

3775. *Id.*

3776. *Faculty 1993*, *supra* n. 3674, at 8.

3777. Charles M. Nelson, *Enron and the Necessity of the Objective Proximate Monitor*, 88 Cornell L. Rev. (2001).

3778. *Professor Charles Elson Selected as Salvatori Fellow*, 33 Stetson Law. 13, 13 (Summer 1993).

3779. *Professor Patrick E. Longan, New Faces*, 31 Stetson Law. 12, 12 (Fall 1991) [hereinafter *New Faces-Longan*].

3780. *Id.*

3781. *AALS 2004–2005 Director*, *supra* n. 3045, at 704.

3782. *Id.*

In 1991, Longan accepted Stetson's offer and began a new career in legal education.[3783] At Stetson, he taught civil procedure and professional responsibility. Though his work at Stetson was first rate, Longan was not entirely pleased with the direction the school was taking. He and several of his colleagues felt that Stetson was making a mistake by increasing each year the size of its student body.[3784]

When Longan announced that he was leaving Stetson to accept a chaired professorship at Mercer University Law School, his colleagues were happy for him, but saddened that Stetson law school was losing a valuable faculty member. In the fall of 2000, Patrick E. Longan became the William Augustus Bootle Chair in Professionalism and Ethics at Mercer Law School.[3785]

(xiv) Professor Darryl C. Wilson, born in Chicago in 1961, went to college at Southern Methodist University in Dallas, Texas, with a four-year academic scholarship.[3786] At SMU, Wilson was a teaching assistant and a member of the varsity football team.[3787] In 1982, he graduated with honors, earning both a bachelor of business administration (B.B.A.), and a bachelor of fine arts (B.F.A.).[3788] Subsequently, Wilson went to University of Florida College of Law,[3789] where he earned his J.D. in 1984. In law school, he was a Virgil Hawkins[3790] Teaching Fellow, a faculty research assistant, and an instructor for the Council for Legal Education Opportunity (CLEO), and was invited to join the UF law review.[3791] Initially after law school, he worked for the Center for Governmental Responsibility in Gainesville.[3792] He later earned an LL.M. degree in intellectual property from John Marshall Law School in Chicago.[3793]

Wilson began his practice in Chicago as a Reginald Herber Smith Community Law Fellow, where he worked at the Cook County, Illinois, Legal Assis-

---

3783. *New Faces-Longan*, *supra* n. 3779, at 12.

3784. Patrick Longan and Michael Swygert were members of a faculty committee that urged the law school administration not to allow the school's enrollment to go above 550 students.

3785. *AALS 2004–2005 Directory*, *supra* n. 3045, at 704.

3786. Darryl C. Wilson, *Curriculum Vitae* 2 (May 31, 2005) [hereinafter Wilson, *Curriculum Vitae*].

3787. *Id.*

3788. *AALS 2004–2005 Directory*, *supra* n. 3045, at 1085.

3789. *Id.*

3790. Wilson, *Curriculum Vitae*, *supra* n. 3786, at 2.

3791. *Id.*

3792. *Id.*

3793. *AALS 2004–2005 Directory*, *supra* n. 3045, at 1085.

Darryl C. Wilson

tance Foundation, a congressionally funded national public interest law program.[3794] As staff attorney, Wilson litigated property disputes on behalf of poor people, and also represented clients in bankruptcy and employment areas. In addition, he served as the pro bono coordinator for the Legal Assistance Foundation.[3795]

After two years, Wilson left the Foundation to become in-house counsel for a Chicago-based corporation, where his practice focused on trademark and copyright issues.[3796] He also spent a year as regional counsel for UAW-Ford Legal in Lansing, Illinois. Then, in 1989, Wilson opened his own law offices in Chicago, Darryl C. Wilson & Associates, where for three years he practiced both real and intellectual property law. Concurrently, he taught bar review courses for Minority Legal Education Resources, Inc.[3797] Leaving Chicago in 1992, Wilson went to Detroit to accept a position as a visiting professor at Detroit College of Law (later affiliated with Michigan State University).[3798] Stetson learned about Wilson by way of Bradford Stone.[3799] Upon Stone's recommendation, Wilson visited Stetson. The school made him an offer, and he joined the faculty in the fall of 1994.[3800]

3794. *Id.*

3795. Wilson, *Curriculum Vitae, supra* n. 3786, at 1.

3796. *Id.*

3797. *Id.*

3798. *AALS 2004–2005 Directory*, *supra* n. 3045, at 1085.

3799. Conversation between Michael I. Swygert, Prof. Emeritus, Stetson U. College of L. and Darryl C. Wilson (circa spring 2005).

3800. *Stetson Welcomes New Faculty*, 34 Stetson Law. 20, 20 (Summer 1994).

At Stetson, Wilson teaches property, trademarks, unfair competition, patents, copyrights, sports law, entertainment law, and international intellectual property. In 1997–98, Wilson was named Stetson's "Teacher of the Year." He also was honored with the Homer and Dolly Hand Excellence in Faculty Research Award in 1999.[3801]

Wilson's publications include a casebook on sports law co-authored with M. McKinnon and R. McCormick (published in 1996 by Lupus Publications, with a second edition in 1998). He has been the revisor of the real estate law sections in *Florida Lawyer's Guide*, and has published articles on the challenges facing minority law schools,[3802] Title IX Problems and the role of the NCAA,[3803] computer crime,[3804] elder law issues involving real property,[3805] and the relationship between sports and intellectual property.[3806] In the summer of 2005, Wilson completed an article titled "*Waltzing to R.A.P.*," which he describes as "a short article on how I teach the rule against perpetuities."[3807] It will appear in the *Creighton Law Review*.

Throughout Wilson's eleven years at Stetson, he's been the school's advisor to both Stetson's Black Law Students Association (BLSA), and to the school's Entertainment and Sports Law Society, while also serving as a coach for various moot court and ADR teams.[3808] He has chaired faculty committees on curriculum, distinguished speakers and guests, facilities, scholarship, graduate and international programs, admissions, and appointments.[3809] In addition, he serves on the AALS Committee on Recruitment and Retention of Minority Law Teachers, the executive committee and current chair of the AALS Sports Law Section, and the Sixth Judicial Circuit of Florida Judicial Nomination Commission. From 2000 through 2004, he chaired the National Bar Associa-

---

3801. Wilson, *Curriculum Vitae*, *supra* n. 3786, at 1.

3802. *See* Darryl C. Wilson, *"Black" Law Schools Face Challenges of a New Day*, 18 Black Issues in Higher Educ. 104 (Apr. 12, 2001).

3803. *See* Darryl C. Wilson, *Title IX's Collegiate Application Raises Serious Questions Regarding the Role of the NCAA*, 31 John Marshall L. Rev. 1201 (1988).

3804. Darryl C. Wilson, *Viewing Computer Crime: Where Does the Systems Error Really Exist?* 11 Computer L.J. 265 (1991).

3805. Darryl C. Wilson, *Elder Law Issues in the Basic Real Property Course*, 30 Stetson L. Rev. 353 (2001).

3806. Darryl C. Wilson, *The Legal Ramifications of Saving Face: An Integrated Analysis of Intellectual Property and Sports*, 4 Villanova Sports & Ent. L.J. 227 (1997) (later excerpted in *Sports and the Law: A Modern Anthology* (Carolina Academic Press, 1999)).

3807. Wilson, *Curriculum Vitae*, *supra* n. 3786, at 3.

3808. *Id.* at 4.

3809. *Id.*

Royal C. Gardner

tion Law Professors Division.[3810] Moreover, he is a Website developer of BlacklawProfessors.net, a certified arbitrator and mediator, and serves on various panels, including the National Arbitration Forum (NAF), and the World Intellectual Property Organization (WIPO).[3811]

As for his expertise in intellectual property, Wilson travels widely to speak on that subject, as well as on sports and entertainment law and matters concerning minorities in legal education.[3812]

(xv) Professor Royal C. Gardner graduated *magna cum laude* from both Georgetown University (A.B., 1985), and Boston College Law School (J.D., 1988).[3813] In law school, Gardner was executive member of the *Boston College Law Review* and was elected into Order of the Coif. He also served as a law tutor in the school's academic support program.[3814]

After graduating, Gardner clerked for Francis J. Boyle, Judge of the United States District Court for the District of Rhode Island.[3815] Afterwards, Gardner became assistant to the General Counsel, Department of the Army, in the

3810. *Id.* at 5.

3811. *Id.*

3812. *Id.* at 6, 7.

3813. *New Faculty, Royal C. Gardner*, 34 Stetson Law. 20, 20 (Summer 1994) [hereinafter *New Faculty, Gardner*].

3814. Royal C. Gardner, Curriculum Vitae 3 (2004) (on file at Stetson U. College of L., Gulfport, Fla.) [hereinafter Gardner, *Curriculum Vitae*].

3815. *AALS 2004–2005 Directory*, *supra* n. 3045, at 492.

Washington, D.C., Office of the General Counsel. There, he served as the Department's principal wetland attorney, advising the assistant Secretary of the Army (Civil Works) on matters related to the administration of the provisions of the Clean Water Act.[3816] Gardner later became Assistant for Safety, Security, and Dismantlement Activities in the Office of the Assistant Secretary of Defense (Nuclear Security and Counterproliferation), at the Pentagon.[3817] There, he helped negotiate and draft international agreements with Russia, Ukraine, Kazakhstan, and Belarus regarding the dismantlement of the former Soviet Union's nuclear weapons.[3818]

Gardner joined the Stetson faculty in the fall of 1994. Over the past eleven years he has taught torts, environmental law, international environmental law, and introduction to the United States legal system (in international programs sponsored by the school).[3819] Not long after arriving at Stetson, professors Gardner and Dickerson created Stetson's International Environmental Law Moot Court Competition, which in October 2005 held its tenth annual competition.[3820] Gardner also oversees the school's environmental law internship program, which places students in part-time jobs with federal, state, and local environmental agencies.[3821]

In 1999, Gary Vause succeeded Lizabeth Moody as dean of the College of Law and named Gardner Stetson's Director of Graduate and International Programs. As director, he administered the school's LL.M. program in international law and business and put together the program for the Scandinavian/Baltic Institute on Emerging Markets and Transitional Democracies in Tallinn, Estonia. He also oversaw Stetson's International Dispute Resolution Program in Granada, Spain.[3822] In the summer of 1999, Concordia International University in Tallinn invited Professor Gardner to teach international environmental law in Estonia.[3823]

In the area of scholarship, Gardner has researched and authored a score of articles. His work has been published in journals, including *Stanford Environ-*

3816. *New Faculty, Gardner, supra* n. 3813, at 20.

3817. *Id.*

3818. Gardner, Curriculum Vitae, *supra* n. 3814, at 1.

3819. *Id.*

3820. *Gardner Selected to Lear New Biodiversity Institute, U.S. Ramsar Committee*, 45 Stetson Law. 14, 14 (Summer 2005) [hereinafter Gardner, *Biodiversity*]; *see also 10th Annual International Environmental Moot Court Competition* (six-page printed brochure 2005) (on file at Stetson U. College of L., Gulfport, Fla.).

3821. *Id.*

3822. *Id.*

3823. *Id.*

mental Law Journal,[3824] *Harvard Environmental Law Review*,[3825] *UCLA Journal of Environmental Law*,[3826] *Iowa Law Review*,[3827] and *University of Cincinnati Law Review*.[3828] He is a the recipient of the Homer and Dolly Hand Award for Excellence in Faculty Research.[3829]

In 2002, Dean Vause appointed Gardner associate dean for academic programs.[3830] Two years later, Dean Darby Dickerson promoted Gardner to vice dean.[3831] In the fall of 2005, Gardner left that post upon his selection to head a new Stetson University "Institute for Biodiversity Law and Policy,"[3832] an institute to serve "as an interdisciplinary focal point for education, research and service activities related to global, regional, and local biodiversity issues."[3833] That same spring, Gardner was selected as chair of the United States National Ramsar Committee, a body that oversees U.S. cooperation with other countries under terms of the Ramsar Convention on Wetlands, an international treaty signed in Iran in 1971.[3834] Gardner had been the official United States Delegate to the Eighth Conference of the Contracting Parties to the Ramsar Convention in Valencia, Spain, November 2002.[3835] Another new hire that year was Professor Steven Everhart. His contributions to Stetson were previously outlined in Chapter Eleven.

(xvi) Professor William Reece Smith, Jr., graduated first in his class with high honors from the UF College of Law in 1949, where he was editor-in-chief of the *Florida Law Review*, president of the student bar association, an elected

---

3824. Royal C. Gardner, *Invoking Private Property Rights for Environmental Purposes: The Takings Implications of Government-Authorized Aerial Pesticide Spraying*, 18 Stanford Envtl. L.J. 65 (1999).

3825. Royal C. Gardner, *Exporting American Values: Tenth Amendment Principles and International Environmental Assistance*, 22 Harv. Envtl. L. Rev. 1 (1998).

3826. Royal C. Gardner, *Public Participation and Wetlands Regulation*, 10 UCLA J. Envtl. L. & Policy 1 (1991).

3827. Royal C. Gardner, *Banking on Entrepreneurs: Wetlands, Mitigation Banking, and Takings*, 81 Iowa L. Rev. 525 (1996) (reprinted in 34 Pub. Land & Resources L. Dig. 11 (1997)).

3828. Royal C. Gardner, *Taking the Principle of Just Compensation Abroad: Private Property Rights, National Sovereignty, and the Cost of Environmental Protection*, 65 U. Cin. L. Rev. 539 (1997).

3829. *AALS 2004–2005 Directory*, *supra* n. 3045, at 492.

3830. *Id.*

3831. *Three Faculty Promoted to Faculty Positions*, 44 Stetson Law. 4, 4 (Spring 2004).

3832. Gardner, *Biodiversity*, *supra* n. 3820, at 14.

3833. *Id.* Professor Gardner's work in the Pentagon on biodiversity matters prepared him for his position as Director of the Stetson Institute for Biodiversity Law and Policy.

3834. *Id.*

3835. Gardner, *Curriculum Vitae*, *supra* n. 3814, at 8.

Stetson benefactor and distinguished professorial lecturer William Reece Smith, Jr.

member of the University Executive Council, and selected for membership in the Florida Blue Key.[3836] From Florida, Smith went to Oxford University as a Rhodes Scholar, where he studied private international law and where he also played varsity lacrosse and basketball.[3837] Returning from Oxford, Smith accepted an offer to join the University of Florida law faculty, where he remained one year (1952–53) teaching contracts, conflict of laws, and legal writing.[3838]

Smith then associated with the Tampa, Florida, law firm that became Carlton Fields. In short order, he was asked by three senior partners — Giddings E. Mabry, Judge O.K. Reaves, and Doyle E. Carlton (former Governor of Florida) — "to go over to the new [Stetson law school] campus in Gulfport and help with the teaching because some faculty had declined to move from DeLand."[3839] Being a new associate and knowing that Mabry, Reaves, and Carlton were all members of the Stetson University Board of Trustees, "I did what my new bosses asked me to do," Smith says.[3840]

3836. Biographical Summary, William Reece Smith, Jr. 1 (six-page typed document supplied from law firm of Carlton Fields, Tampa Office, Aug. 2005) (copy on file at Stetson C. of L. Archives, Gulfport, Fla.) [hereinafter *Smith, Biographical Summary*].

3837. *Id.* at 2.

3838. *Id.*

3839. Letter from Wm. Reece Smith, Jr., Chair Emeritus and Senior Member, Carlton Fields, Attys. at Law and Distinguished Professorial Lecturer, Stetson U. College of L., to Michael I. Swygert, Prof. Emeritus, Stetson U. College of L. (Aug. 2, 2005).

3840. *Id.*

During the law school's first year at Gulfport, Smith taught conflicts of laws, federal pleadings and practice, and common law practice.[3841] He remained an adjunct member of Stetson's law faculty through the spring of 1957, when he turned all his energies to his firm. Smith did not return to the Stetson faculty until 1991, when Dean Jacob offered him the position of Distinguished Professorial Lecturer, a position he accepted and continues to hold.[3842] During the thirty-four years prior to Smith's return to the Stetson faculty, he was associated with Carlton, Fields, Emmanuel, Smith & Cutler, P.A., first as a member, then shareholder, and later president, chair, and finally and currently, as chair emeritus.[3843] Jacob introduced Smith at the College's 1990 spring graduation, where Smith gave the commencement address. Jacob described the speaker as "one of the truly great attorneys in the United States," noting that Smith had served as president of The Florida Bar, the American Bar Association, and the International Bar Association in London, England.[3844] Had there been time, Jacob could have described scores of additional achievements and honors that Stetson's commencement speaker had compiled.[3845] Among them, Smith was the recipient of the ABA Gold Award, the Association's most prestigious honor; The Florida Bar Foundation's Medal of Honor; the holder of eleven honorary doctorate degrees (including one from Stetson University); and an initial inductee in the Stetson College of Law Hall of Fame. In addition, the law school established the "Wm. Reece Smith, Jr., Award for Outstanding Public Service."[3846] In announcing the award, Jacob commented:

3841. *Id.* Reece Smith comments that his teaching common law pleading in 1954 at Stetson College of Law may have been the last time it was "taught in Florida or elsewhere in the country." *Id.*

3842. *Smith, Biographical Summary*, *supra* n. 3836, at 3.

3843. Carlton Fields, Attorneys at Law, Attorneys, *Wm. Reece Smith, Of Counsel*, www.carltonfields.com/rsmith/ (accessed July 19, 2005).

3844. Bruce R. Jacob, *Introduction of Wm. Reece Smith, Commencement, May 12, 1990*, 30 Stetson Law. 29, 29 (Fall 1990) [hereinafter Jacob, *Reece Smith*].

3845. For twenty-five years, Smith has served on the Council (ruling body) of the American Law Institute; has been president of both the American Bar and Florida Bar Foundations and of both the American and Florida Bar Endowments; president of the National Conference of Bar Presidents; trustee or fellow of Bethune-Cookman College, Stetson University, and University of Tampa; member of the advisory boards of Florida, Miami, Florida State, and Stetson law schools, University of South Carolina, and chair, Council of Advisors, University of South Florida; fellow of International Academy of Lawyers, American College of Trial Lawyers, and International Society of Barristers; interim president, University of South Florida; and the list goes on. *Smith, Biographical Summary*, *supra* n. 3836, at 2–6.

3846. Jacob, *Reece Smith*, *supra* n. 3844, at 29.

> Reece Smith has devoted much of his professional life to improving the delivery of legal services. He has been a staunch advocate for legal services for the poor and is probably responsible more than any other single individual for maintaining these services for those who cannot afford them. While president of the American Bar Association, he established the Private Bar Involvement Program which regenerated interest in *pro bono* work on a nationwide basis.[3847]

Jacob then honored Smith by naming him the first recipient of the award bearing his name.[3848]

In January 2004, Stetson law school dedicated a new courtroom at its recently opened Tampa Law Center. It is officially named the William Reece Smith, Jr., Courtroom.[3849]

In the spring of 2005, Smith's name became the basis of a prestigious title at Stetson. The Joy McCann Foundation established an endowed professorship in the name of Reece Smith.[3850] The Foundation's $500,000 gift endowed a chair that is to be awarded to a full-time College of Law professor "with a demonstrated commitment to both professionalism and the mentoring of students."[3851] Joy McCann Dougherty, chair of the McCann Foundation, emphasized that the Foundation was pleased "to support Stetson by honoring Reece."[3852] Professor Roberta Flowers was named the first holder of the William Reece Smith Distinguished Professorship. In the fall of 2005, Wm. Reece Smith, Jr., eighty years young, continued to teach professional responsibility and legal ethics to the next generation of Stetson lawyers.

Other faculty hired during the Jacob administration, several of who stayed only a short time, include Elizabeth Diane Clark, a graduate of University of Pennsylvania School of Law. She joined the Stetson faculty in 1984 from Carlton Fields, where she practiced commercial law.[3853] Clark also served as the administrative assistant to Reece Smith during his presidency of the American Bar Association.

3847. *Id.*

3848. *Id.*

3849. Davina Y. Gould, *Tampa Courtroom Named to Honor Wm. Reece Smith, Jr.*, 44 Stetson Law. 29, 29 (Spring 2004).

3850. *Majored Gifts Establish Two New Endowed Professorships, William Reece Smith, Jr., Distinguished Professorship*, 45 Stetson Law. 37, 37 (Spring 2005).

3851. *Id.*

3852. *Id.*

3853. *Faculty Profiles*, *supra* n. 3649, at 14.

Other relatively short-term members of the faculty who contributed to the school's academic advance were: Charles M. Waygood, a 1960 Stetson law school graduate who first taught at Stetson as an assistant professor in the 1961–62 academic year,[3854] then rejoined the faculty in 1987 after retiring from a New York City law firm. At Stetson, Waygood primarily taught alternative dispute resolution and trial advocacy. He also helped coach the school's trial teams. For the 1992–93 academic year, he served as assistant dean to Bruce Jacob.[3855] Beverly Greenley joined the faculty in 1981 and remained two years.[3856] David Zlotnick, a Harvard Law School graduate and former clerk of the Honorable John Steadman, Jr., Judge of the U.S. Court of Appeals for the District of Columbia, came to Stetson in 1993 and left in 1995. Zlotinick still is in academia. Jerome Kramer was a visiting trial advocacy professor from 1983 through 1987. Joryn Jenkins was on the faculty, teaching bankruptcy for two years, 1992 through 1994. Ronald Halpern was hired in 1983 and resigned in 1987 from the faculty after four years. Terrill Pollman spent three years on the Stetson law faculty before going to the University of Illinois, then on to the law school at the University of Nevada, Las Vegas, where she holds a chair.

Another person attaining faculty status was Sally Ginsberg Waters. She was hired as a reference librarian in 1982 and continues at Stetson today; she earned both juris doctorate and master of library science degrees from the University of South Carolina.[3857] In 1983, Waters began teaching legal research and writing, along with legal bibliography.[3858] Subsequently, she was given adjunct faculty status.[3859] Waters continues to teach and serve as a Reference and Instructional Services Librarian.[3860]

During Jacob's deanship, many staff changes took place. Four persons in particular deserve mention for the contributions they gave to the school: Albert A. Lane, Jean Hinkle, Joseph E. Estenes, Jr., and Connie Evans. After retiring from the Army, Al Lane was hired by Dean Dillon to be the comptroller and business manager of the College in 1972.[3861] He earned an M.B.A. from Harvard University while in service and had served as comptroller of the

---

3854. *See supra* nn. 2396–2400 and accompanying text.

3855. *Law School Announces New Deans*, 33 Stetson Law. 3, 3 (Fall 1992).

3856. The information in this paragraph regarding the years of service of the professors listed comes from the list of Dorothy Bishop; *see* Bishop, *List*, *supra* n. 2351, at 4–8.

3857. *Faculty Notes, Sally Ginsberg Waters*, 26 Stetson Law. 12, 12 (Summer 1984).

3858. *Id.*

3859. *AALS 2004–2005 Directory*, *supra* n. 3045, at 150.

3860. *Id.*

3861. *Changes at Stetson, Albert A. Lane*, 26 Stetson Law. 9, 9 (Summer 1984).

Connie Evans, Director of Faculty Support Services

United States Military Academy at West Point.[3862] He was admired by both deans he worked with—Richard Dillon and Bruce Jacob—who both have high praise for his work at the school. Lane retired from Stetson in the summer of 1983.[3863]

Jean Hinkle succeeded Al Lane as comptroller and business manager. Hinkle had been bursar of the College for several years. She retired at the end of the 1983–84 academic year after twenty years of professional service to the school.[3864] Hinkle's successor was Joseph E. Estenes, Jr., hired by Dean Jacob in 1984 to be the school's comptroller and business manager. Estenes earned B.S. and M.B.A. degrees from Seton Hall University.[3865] Before coming to Stetson, he had been business manager of Monmouth College and vice president for business affairs at Westminister Choir College.[3866] Dean Emeritus Bruce Jacob comments on the significance of Estenes:

> I believe Joe Estenes has saved us hundreds of thousands of dollars and perhaps millions through his skill as chief financial officer. In construction projects alone, through his ability to get quality work done at the lowest possible cost, he has saved [the College of Law] huge amounts of

3862. *Id.*
3863. *Id.*
3864. *Id.*
3865. *Id.*
3866. *Id.*

money. Furthermore, he has brought order and organization to our business and physical plant operations.[3867]

Connie Evans was hired in 1982 as a part-time clerk in the office of faculty secretaries (as it was then known).[3868] Carol Teagarden, office supervisor, asked Evans to do copying work. She did, and more, helping the faculty organize files, and assisting in coordinating secretarial services. In 1987, Dean Jacob asked Evans to become the supervisor.[3869] She reluctantly did so, and soon began to develop a center for faculty support services, one that many faculty members say may be the best in the country. Edward D. Ohlbaum, Professor of Law and Director of Trial Advocacy at Temple University School of Law, after spending a semester as Stetson's visiting Culverhouse Professor, presented Evans with a plaque with the inscription: "Still Waters Run Deep. To the Number One Secretarial Pool in Academia for Their Gracious Spirit, Efficient Labors, and Energetic Spirit. Presented by a grateful fan, Edward D. Ohlbaum, Culverhouse Visiting Professor of Law."[3870] Evans recalls that when Ohlbaum left to return to Temple, he said that he "very badly wanted to pack all of us up to take us [with him], because he had never worked with such an efficient group of support staff, and he wanted to take us [to Temple]."[3871]

The sentiment of visitors coming to Stetson has been mirrored by Stetson professors visiting other schools. Professor Swygert, during his years at Stetson, visited five other law schools, and each time he returned he told Evans that Stetson's faculty support services were superior to those he had observed at the other schools. Other Stetson faculty have had similar experiences. Evans notes that it is not uncommon for a Stetson faculty member visiting at other schools to still ask for Stetson faculty support, because the services at the another school were wanting.[3872] When Lizabeth Moody became dean, she promoted Evans to Director of Faculty Support Services, the position she holds today.[3873] At some point, Stetson Business Manager Brian Boardman suggested that the word "secretaries," be replaced with the more professional description of "faculty support staff."[3874] Today, Stetson's faculty support staff includes administrative specialists, notaries, computer wizards, and paralegals.

3867. Jacob, *Report on Deanship*, *supra* n. 3239, at 40.
3868. *Evans Interview*, *supra* n. 3126, at 5, 6.
3869. *Id.*
3870. *Id.* at 54.
3871. *Id.* at 53.
3872. *Id.* at 19.
3873. *Id.* at 20.
3874. *Id.* at 36.

In December 2002, Evans received a standing ovation in the packed Great Hall of the College of Law when Dean W. Gary Vause presented her with the 2002 Dean's Award for "grateful recognition and sincere appreciation for extraordinary service to the College of Law."[3875] In presenting the award, Vause told the crowd:

> Connie is loved by all who work with her. She and her staff always get the job done on time with a smile, and they are always willing to take on whatever the faculty presents to them. She is a wonderful colleague and a wonderful representative of the College."[3876]

Evans responded that "receiving the Dean's Award will always be my most memorable experience working here, but I couldn't be where I am today without the support and hard work of my staff."[3877] In May 2006, Ms. Evans retired from the College.

12.11 Continuing Legal Education: 1975–Present

a. Jacob Establishes CLE Office; Appoints Director

In 1981, when Jacob became Dean, the College's continuing legal education offerings were "about three per year."[3878] They consisted of Judge Alexander Paskay's annual bankruptcy seminar,[3879] Professor Robert Bickel's annual Law and Higher Education Conference,[3880] and Professor Gary Vause's annual Labor and Employment Law Conference.[3881] Throughout Jacob's first decade as dean, the CLE offerings rarely went beyond six per year. What programs were offered tended to be developed by Stetson faculty members. For example, Stetson sponsored CLE programs on Real and Personal Property Financing, first in Tampa, and the following year in Miami, Orlando, and Tampa. The programs were put together by Professor Swygert.[3882] But there was no central

3875. *Faculty Support Services Director Connie Evans Receives 2002 Dean's Award*, 43 Stetson Law. 14, 14 (Spring 2003).

3876. *Id.*

3877. *Id.*

3878. Jacob, *Report on Deanship*, *supra* n. 3239, at 22.

3879. *See infra* nn. 3895–3908 and accompanying text.

3880. *See infra* nn. 3910–3934 and accompanying text.

3881. Professor Vause came to Stetson with an expertise in labor law, having specialized in that area of practice for several years. Dean Dillon encouraged Vause to put together labor law conferences, which Vause did for nearly two decades.

3882. Professor Swygert brought in national as well as local speakers. They included Professor Jon W. Bruce of Vanderbilt University School of Law, a specialist on real estate fi-

Jan Majewski, CLE Director

coordination of CLE events during that period, and Judge Paskay complained that the content of Swygert's programs at times overlapped his bankruptcy seminars (and they did). If CLE programs were to expand, they had to be coordinated by one person. Jacob understood the benefits of having a director.

As the campus renovations neared completion in late 1990, the dean announced that the school had the space to house an office of continuing legal education. He felt strongly that Stetson College of Law should expand its CLE courses.[3883] Moreover, the faculty, as part of the strategic planning process, decided that developing a larger, high-quality CLE program should be one of the school's main goals, since CLE offerings could enhance the school's reputation by providing a valuable service to the bench and bar.[3884] To oversee and expand the CLE program, Jacob appointed Jan F. Majewski, a lawyer who prior to coming to Stetson worked for the National Institute of Municipal Law Offices in Washington, D.C. Ten years after Majewski took charge of Stetson's CLE programs, the school's programs increased several fold from what they had been when he arrived.[3885]

During the first academic year that Majewski directed Stetson's CLE Program—1991 to 1992—he scheduled eleven conferences on subjects consist-

nancing, and the Honorable Robert E. Ginsberg, Chief Judge of the United States Bankruptcy Court for the Northern District of Illinois, an expert on how UCC Article Nine security interests are treated in bankruptcy.

3883. Bruce R. Jacob, *Message from the Dean*, 31 Stetson Law. 2, 2 (Fall 1991).

3884. *July 27 Jacob Letter*, *supra* n. 3260.

3885. Jacob, *Report on Deanship*, *supra* n. 3239, at 22.

ing of: law and religion; condominium law; school law; international trade law; health law; elder law; and legal issues in police administration; in addition to annual conferences on law and higher education, labor and employment law, and bankruptcy.[3886] That year, 2,029 registrants attended these programs, which provided 128 hours of CLE credits in Florida.[3887] The following year began with Stetson's second annual elder law program, a two-day program that included a pre-seminar workshop on elder abandonment (sometimes referred to as "granny dumping").[3888] During Majewski's second year as CLE Director, Stetson sponsored seventeen CLE programs, including in two new areas, mortgage foreclosures and mediation techniques.[3889] Again, over 2,000 attended the programs. By 1994, Stetson's CLE programs took place in Tampa and Orlando as well as in Clearwater, St. Petersburg, and Gulfport.[3890] Majewski's successful efforts in developing and managing the Stetson CLE program became widely known. In 2002, he was elected president of the Association for Continuing Legal Education, a body composed of about 500 members representing 270 CLE providers across the United States and Canada.[3891] Dean Vause applauded Majewski's election, noting that Stetson's CLE programs had expanded to thirty a year, and that nearly 3,000 attendees took part.[3892]

Through the fall of 2005, Stetson's CLE offerings have continued to address topical subjects while providing valuable CLE credits to lawyers. In 2004, after the opening of the Stetson's new Tampa Law Center, the school hosted a variety of programs that ranged from one-hour luncheon offerings to conferences lasting several days.[3893] In recent years, CLE topics have expanded to include Social Security disability law, appellate advocacy, mediation training, construction law, and special needs trusts, in addition to the school's traditional offerings in elder law, health law, employment law, and

3886. Jan F. Majewski, *Stetson Prepares for a New and Exciting Year of CLE Programming*, 31 Stetson Law. 14, 14 (Fall 1991).

3887. Jan F. Majewski, *CLE Department Expands*, 32 Stetson Law. 19, 19 (Summer 1992).

3888. Jan F. Majewski, *CLE Report*, 33 Stetson Law. 21, 21 (Fall 1992).

3889. Jan F. Majewski, *Benefits of Stetson CLE Go Beyond Credit Hours*, 33 Stetson Law. 11, 11 (Summer 1993).

3890. *Id.*

3891. Davina Gould, *Stetson U. College of Law* (Stetson U. College of L. Sept. 13, 2002) (news release) (on file at Stetson U. College of L., Gulfport, Fla.).

3892. *Id.*

3893. *Stetson's CLE Office to Offer Programs on New Topics in New Locations*, 43 Stetson Law. 13, 13 (Fall 2003).

Judge Alexander L. Paskay

the two longest running CLE programs—bankruptcy, and law and higher education.[3894]

b. Judge Paskay's Annual Bankruptcy Seminars

On November 12–13, 1976, Alexander L. Paskay, United States Bankruptcy Judge for the Middle District of Florida and adjunct Professor of Law at Stetson College of Law, chaired a seminar titled Bankruptcy Law and Practice.[3895] Held at the Host Airport Hotel in Tampa, it was sponsored by Stetson College of Law and represented a seminal event in the history of continuing legal education at the school. Paskay's conference was the first of what, by 2005, had become a thirty-year string of national and international conferences on bankruptcy law.

The idea behind the conference first came from Dean Richard Dillon, who in the spring of 1976 asked Professor Ruth Thurman (then head of CLE programs) to talk with Judge Paskay about the possibility of the judge and Stetson putting on a bankruptcy seminar as part of the school's CLE offerings.[3896] Judge Paskay—who already had established a national reputation in the bankruptcy bar and judiciary—was excited about the venture, and invited the best

---

3894. *Id.*

3895. *Bankruptcy Seminar Scheduled for Nov. 12–13*, 19 Stetson Law. 2, 2 (Aug. 1976) [hereinafter *Bankruptcy Seminar*].

3896. *See supra* nn. 3021–3024 and accompanying text.

possible faculty he could find to come to Tampa. The faculty included Professor Vern Countryman of Harvard Law School; Professor and Associate Dean Lawrence P. King of New York University Law School; and Professor Frank Kennedy of University of Michigan Law School—all leading experts on bankruptcy law in the country.[3897] In addition, Judge Paskay invited both George Brody, U.S. Bankruptcy Judge for the Eastern District of Michigan, and well-known bankruptcy attorney, Daniel R. Cowens, of Cowens and Murphy, San Francisco (a former U.S. Bankruptcy judge himself for the Northern District of California).[3898]

Stetson's second annual Bankruptcy Law and Practice was held in Tampa in November 1977. In addition to professors Vern Countryman and Frank Kennedy, other prominent visitors included George Treister, a prominent Los Angeles lawyer and part-time instructor in bankruptcy at Stanford; U.S. Bankruptcy Judge William L. Norton of Georgia; U.S. Bankruptcy Judge Joseph Lee of Kentucky; and Chicago bankruptcy lawyer Norman H. Nachman.[3899] The Florida Bar approved the seminar for designation re-certification credit of twelve hours.[3900]

Stetson's third annual Stetson Seminar on Bankruptcy Law and Practice took place the following year, again at the Host Hotel in Tampa.[3901] Once again, Judge Paskay assembled a faculty comprised of many of the nation's leading bankruptcy law experts, including: Professor David Epstein of the University of Texas Law School (later dean of Emory Law School); Professor Lawrence King of New York University Law School; former Houston, Texas, U.S. Bankruptcy Judge Arthur Moller; U.S. Bankruptcy Judge Conrad Cyr of Maine; and U.S. Bankruptcy Judge William Norton of Georgia.[3902] With high quality programming and well known faculty, Judge Paskay continues to attract bankruptcy lawyers from across the country to the Stetson-sponsored national seminars. Today, the programs have gone global.

In 1994, Paskay and Stetson began to offer international bankruptcy law seminars. The first was held in Budapest, Hungary, and drew 120 attendees, including eighty European lawyers.[3903] In addition to Judge Paskay, American participants included Leonard Gilbert, President of Carlton, Fields,

3897. *Bankruptcy Seminar*, *supra* n. 3895, at 2, 3.
3898. *Id.*
3899. *Bankruptcy Seminar November 17–18*, 20 Stetson Law. 2, 2 (Aug. 1977).
3900. *Id.*
3901. *Third Annual Seminar*, 21 Stetson Law. 2, 2 (Aug. 1978).
3902. *Id.*
3903. *Id.*

Ward, Emmanuel & Cutler, Tampa; Claude Rice, Senior Member, McDowell, Rice & Smith, Kansas City; U.S. Bankruptcy Judge Paul Glen, attorney Lynn Van Hyning Ramey, Stetson law, '88, of Rumberger, Kirk & Caldwell, P.A., Tampa, and United States Bankruptcy Trustee, Sara Kisler, Stetson law, '82, of Tampa.[3904] Using wireless headphones to listen to simultaneous live translators, the attendees participated in all discussions, be they in English or Hungarian.

In 2001, Stetson's Second International Bankruptcy Symposium also took place in Budapest, while the third was held in Vienna, Austria, in the summer of 2002.[3905] The Vienna program covered two areas of bankruptcy law and elder law, the latter chaired by Professor Rebecca Morgan.[3906] Next, Montreal, Quebec, Canada, was chosen for Stetson's Fourth International Bankruptcy Symposium to take place in the summer of 2004.[3907] The three-day program included the host country's top bankruptcy official, Marc Mayrand, Canada's Superintendent of Bankruptcy.[3908]

As of the fall of 2005, Judge Alexander Paskay continues teaching bankruptcy law and practice at Stetson College of Law, as he has done for thirty-plus years. Moreover, he continues to put together and moderate domestic and international symposia, seminars, and conferences on bankruptcy law and practice with the zest of a man half his age. Judge Alexander Paskay's contributions to Stetson law school and to its graduates have been substantial. In December 2005, the school named its annual bankruptcy conference for Judge Paskay.

c. *Professor Bickel's Law and Higher Education Conferences*

(1) An Innovative Commingling of Lawyers and Clients

As discussed previously, before joining the Stetson faculty, Professor Robert Bickel served as general counsel for Florida State University and had authored a book on law and higher education.[3909] In the fall of 1978, he approached

---

3904. *Id.* at 6, 7.

3905. Frank Klim, *Stetson University College of Law to Host International Elder Law and Bankruptcy Programs in Italy*, www.law.stetson.edu/new/italy.htm (Apr. 9, 2002) (news release).

3906. *Id.*

3907. Stetson U. College of L., Off. of Commun., *Stetson Law to Present International Bankruptcy Symposium, June 15–18 in Canada*, www.law.stetson.edu/Communications/news.asp?id=81 (Mar. 19, 2004) (news release).

3908. *Id.*

3909. *See supra* n. 3086.

Dean Dillon and suggested that Stetson host an invitational national seminar where participants would discuss legal issues pertaining to higher education.[3910] Bickel explains:

> I informed Dean Dillon that I felt that the matter of higher education law, the way in which law relates to the very administration of higher education itself, and the law and policy questions that are unique to American higher education, was undeveloped. There was no reason why a discourse on that subject could not be developed here as well as it could any place else.[3911]

For years, Bickel attended meetings of the National Association of College and University Attorneys (NACUA) as Florida State's general counsel, and he knew that these meetings involved lawyers of colleges and universities talking among themselves with no input or dialogue with their institutions' administrators.[3912] Bickel realized that something was missing. Again, he explains:

> It occurred to me that, having practiced seven years and having built an internal university relationship between legal counsel and policy administrators, the development of higher education law should involve a discourse that would bring policy makers and higher education lawyers together.[3913]

The innovation of the suggested discourse, Bickel points out, was that it had to be interdisciplinary—that lawyers and clients would be in the same room, talking about important issues.[3914] He believed that the dialogue would deepen mutual understanding of issues. Moreover, university attorneys would no longer serve only as responders, but would also assist in developing policies for higher education in relation to legal issues.[3915]

(2) The First Law and Higher Education Conference: 1980

Dean Dillon fully supported Bickel's innovative idea. In January 1980, Stetson launched its first Law and Higher Education Conference.[3916] Bickel invited various higher education associations, and college presidents, along with col-

3910. Bickel Interview, *supra* n. 2746, at 34.
3911. *Id.*
3912. *Id.* at 35.
3913. *Id.* at 36.
3914. *Id.*
3915. *Id.*
3916. *Id.* at 37.

lege attorneys who were leaders in NACUA, to a conference at the Don Cesar Hotel in St. Petersburg Beach.[3917] Bickel describes the results:

> A grand total of ninety-three people came, sixty-three of whom were speakers. They attended each others' programs. To be honest, it was more of a round table than what you would think of as a conference ... We were happy with the results. The dialogue seemed meaningful and it seemed different. It was not traditional for lawyers and policy folks to relate to each other in this way until we did it. We decided to do it again, and the Conference evolved over time.[3918]

Bickel enlisted the American Council on Education to be a co-sponsor of the conference, a move that enhanced the acceptance rate of those invited to participate. After all, over a quarter of a century ago, relatively few college administrators knew Bickel, and even fewer knew much about Stetson College of Law. The event's title, however, was topical, inviting and informative: "Law and Higher Education: Issues and Challenges in the 1980s; A Conference Jointly Sponsored by the American Council on Education and the Stetson University College of Law."[3919]

In what became a characteristic feature of Bickel's conferences, he invited speakers consisting of a mix of college and university administrators; university general or assistant general counsels; representatives of higher education foundations and associations; and federal government officials dealing with education issues.[3920]

Issues covered included the impact of federal legislation on higher education; mandatory retirement and age discrimination; recent court decisions in-

3917. *Id.*

3918. *Id.* at 37, 38.

3919. *Law and Higher Education, Issues and Challenges in the 1980s* 1 (Jan. 1980) (brochure) (copy on file at Stetson U. College of L., Gulfport, Fla.).

3920. *Id.* at 2–6. Participants at the inaugural event included: Armando M. Rodriguez, Commissioner, U.S. Equal Employment Opportunity Commission; Jean Frohlicher, Counsel of the U.S. Senate Committee on Labor and Human Resources; Thomas R. Wolanin, Staff Director, Subcommittee on Postsecondary Education, U.S. House Committee on Education and Labor; David M. Rabban, Associate General Counsel, American Association of University Professors; Norman A. Wiggins, President, Campbell University; Casey Mahon, General Counsel, University of Iowa; Stephen B. Burbank, General Counsel, University of Pennsylvania; Jeffrey Orleans, Special Assistant to the President, University of North Carolina; R. Claire Guthrie, General Counsel, American Council on Education; Patricia Hollander, General Counsel, American Association of University Administrators; and Susan Fratkin, Director of Programs, National Association of State Universities and Land-Grant Colleges.

terpreting college and university catalogs involving contract law principles; equal employment opportunity and affirmative action programs; institutional response to handicapped employees as well as students; administrator liability; and legal issues related to tenure.[3921]

(3) 1981 Conference on Federal Tax Policy and Higher Education

The success of the 1980 conference caused Bickel to push ahead for a sequel the following year, one that again was held at the Don Cesar Resort Hotel. The principal topic of the conference was federal tax policy and its impact on higher education.[3922] Two U.S. Congressmen spoke on how tax laws affected colleges and universities: the Honorable Thomas N. Kindness, Member, Judiciary Committee, U.S. House of Representatives, and the Honorable James M. Shannon, Member, Ways and Means Committee, U.S. House of Representatives.[3923] At the second conference, several well-known national universities were represented, including Yale (by Linda Koch Lorimer, Assistant General Counsel); Brown (by Beverly Ledbetter, University Counsel); Texas (by Stephen Monti, Assistant to the President); University of California, Berkeley (by Michael R. Smith, Vice-Chancellor for Legal Affairs); and Johns Hopkins (by Estelle A. Fishbein, General Counsel, and President, National Association of College and University Attorneys).[3924] Bickel brought in another co-sponsor in addition to the American Council on Education—the American Association of University Administrators.[3925] The 1981 conference drew 125 attendees, and the following year attendance rose to 180.[3926] Its notoriety and appeal have risen ever since.

(4) Growth in Numbers and Importance

While the tenth annual conference was in the planning stage, a lengthy article in the *Stetson Lawyer* documented the importance of university law and

---

3921. *Id.*

3922. *Forums Focus on Legal Problems of Bankruptcy, Higher Education, and Religious Organizations; Law and Higher Education*, 25 Stetson Law. 3, 3 (May 1981).

3923. *Id.*

3924. A Conference Jointly Sponsored by Stetson University College of Law, the American Council on Education, and The American Association of University Administrators *Law and Higher Education Issues for 1981*, 1 (Jan. 11–14, 1981) (brochure) (on file at Stetson U. College of L., Gulfport, Fla.).

3925. *Id.* at 1.

3926. *Bickel Interview*, *supra* n. 2746, at 38.

how Stetson's annual conferences on law and higher education brought the country's experts together.[3927] The article noted that each year the conference was having a greater impact as it drew more attorneys and officials involved with higher education. One year, U.S. Supreme Court Justice Clarence Thomas, then head of the EEOC, was on the program.

In 2001, Stetson's National Conference on Law and Higher Education drew its largest enrollment, between 600 and 700 registrants representing over 400 American colleges and universities.[3928] That year marked the twenty-first Annual National Conference on Law and Higher Education. The event included both pre- and post-conference sessions, and covered five full-working days with twenty-five different seminars.[3929]

(5) 25th Conference Anniversary: 50th Anniversary of *Brown v. Board of Education*

In 2004, the Twenty-Fifth Annual National Conference on Law and Higher Education was held at the Sheraton Sand Key Resort in Clearwater Beach, Florida. The highlight was an all-day "Special 50th Anniversary Symposium on *Brown v. Board of Education,* and the Principle of Equality in Higher Education."[3930] Speakers included: Professor John Hope Franklin of Duke University; James T. Patterson, Ford Foundation Professor of History at Brown University; John Seigenthaler, founder of the First Amendment Center at Vanderbilt University and former President of the American Society of Newspaper Editors; Theodore M. Shaw, Associate Director and Counsel for the NAACP Legal Defense and Education Fund, Inc., and Adjunct Professor of Law, Columbia Law School; Eugene Patterson, former Editor, *Atlanta Constitution*; Robert Belton, Professor of Law, Vanderbilt University Law School; Raymond O. Arsenault, Professor of History, University of South Florida; and Jack Bass, Professor of History, College of Charleston, and author of *Unlikely Heroes.*[3931]

Beginning with the twenty-sixth annual conference in 2005, Stetson's newly established Center for Excellence in Higher Education Law and Policy became

---

3927. *See Legal Forum, Leadership in Continuing Legal Education: Stetson's National Conference on Law & Higher Education*, 1 Stetson Law. 16, 16–18 (Fall 1989).

3928. *Id.*

3929. *Id.*

3930. *25th Annual National Conference on Law and Higher Education* 2 (Feb. 2004) (program) (on file at Stetson U. College of L., Gulfport, Fla.).

3931. *Id.* at 2.

the official sponsor.[3932] The 2005 conference also marked the beginning of Stetson's Center jointly cooperating with Oxford University's Center for Higher Education Policy Studies.[3933]

Stetson College of Law has reaped enormous benefits by its long association and sponsorship of Professor Bickel's annual law and higher education conferences. Bickel, himself, is happy how it turned out, commenting, "I think, however my career evolves, I'll consider the National Conference on Law and Higher Education to be my most meaningful contribution to this law school, its student body, and the school's image in the country."[3934] His efforts and success have not gone unnoticed.[3935] The American Law Institute and American Bar Association Committee on Continuing Legal Education have awarded Professor Robert Dale Bickel the Harrison Tweed Award for his outstanding contributions to continuing legal education.[3936]

12.12 Dean Jacob's Administration: An Assessment

From the time Bruce Jacob entered Stetson College of Law in the fall of 1957 as a first-year law student through the present (the spring of 2006), the school has held for him "a very special meaning."[3937] The relationship has been reciprocal. His colleague, Robert Batey, has described Jacob as a "good dean and the best of colleagues."[3938]

Looking back with historical perspective, it is truly impressive how much Jacob accomplished during his thirteen years as dean: a turnaround in student and alumni morale;[3939] strengthening career services for students; networking and strengthening alumni organizations;[3940] increasing the percentage of alumni fundraising donations from 3 percent to as high as 27 percent;[3941] mod-

3932. *26th Annual National Conference on Law and Higher Education* 3 (program) (on file at Stetson College of L., Gulfport, Fla.).

3933. *26th Annual National Conference on Law and Higher Education*, (Mar. 1995) (recent events).

3934. *Bickel Interview*, *supra* n. 2746, at 33, 34.

3935. *See supra* nn. 3091–3092 and accompanying text.

3936. Soud, *National Award*, *supra* n. 3075.

3937. Dorothy Bishop, *A Personal Tribute to Our Dean: Bruce R. Jacob*, 31 Stetson Law. 18, 20 (Fall 1991).

3938. Batey, *A Good Dean*, *supra* n. 3248, at 6.

3939. *See supra* nn. 3235–3251; 3383–3395 and accompanying text.

3940. *See supra* nn. 3396–3304 and accompanying text.

3941. *See supra* nn. 3422–4346 and accompanying text.

ernizing the curriculum and instituting student evaluations of teachers;[3942] beginning a merit system for compensating faculty;[3943] diversifying both the student body and the faculty;[3944] expanding the school's clinical programs;[3945] beginning federal judicial internships;[3946] procuring funding to start the elder law clinic;[3947] enlargement of the student body;[3948] diversifying, enlarging, and strengthening the faculty;[3949] maintaining high bar passage rates (the cumulative results for Jacob's thirteen years as dean indicate that Stetson had the highest passage rate of any Florida law school during that period);[3950] providing the funding necessary for Stetson's trial advocacy program, helping it to become the highest ranking program in the nation;[3951] creating an office and director for continuing legal education (and strongly supporting the successful bankruptcy and law and higher education annual conferences);[3952] major renovation of campus buildings;[3953] the purchase of Rosa building for married student housing;[3954] bringing to campus some of the nation's best-known and highest respected law professors as Culverhouse Chair visitors;[3955] providing funds for the expansion of law library from 153,277 to 323,453 volumes;[3956] and commencement of long-range strategic planning involving faculty and administrative staff of the school.[3957]

3942. *See supra* nn. 3252–3263 and accompanying text.

3943. *See* Jacob, *Report on Deanship*, *supra* n. 3239, at 15.

3944. *See supra* nn. 3306–3338 and accompanying text.

3945. *See supra* nn. 3473–3487 and accompanying text.

3946. *See supra* nn.3464–3472 and accompanying text.

3947. *See supra* nn. 3448–3463 and accompanying text.

3948. *See supra* nn. 3561–3564 and accompanying text.

3949. *See supra* nn. 3605–3860 and accompanying text.

3950. Jacob, *Report on Deanship*, *supra* n. 3239, at 22, 23. "Our cumulative passing total, in terms of percentage takers over the entire thirteen-year period, was the highest of the law schools in the state, including the University of Florida." *Id.*; *Stetson Leads State in Bar*, 34 Stetson Law. 23, 23 (Summer 1994). "Stetson maintains the highest cumulative passing rate of all Florida law schools over last decade with an 89.43 percent." *Stetson Leads State in Bar*, *supra* n. 3950, at 23; *see also* Bruce R. Jacob, *Annual Report to President Pope Duncan* 10, 11 (July 17, 1886) (covering years 1984, 1985, and 1986); *Bar Exam Results*, 27 Stetson Law. 19, 19 (Fall 1987); *Florida Bar Exam Results*, 28 Stetson Law. 5, 5 (Fall 1988); *Every Recent Stetson Grad Passes Bar Exam*, St. Pete. Times B-8 (Apr. 20, 1989).

3951. *See supra* nn. 3506–3507 and *infra* nn. 4036–37.

3952. *See supra* nn. 3878–3894 and accompanying text.

3953. *See supra* nn. 3339–3382 and accompanying text.

3954. *See supra* n. 3556 and accompanying text.

3955. *See supra* n. 3607 and accompanying text.

3956. Jacob, *Report on Deanship*, *supra* n. 3239, at 23.

3957. *See supra* nn. 3527–3535 and accompanying text.

True, Jacob had a few disappointments: the Ramos situation,[3958] some critical faculty,[3959] and failure to attain a chapter of Order of the Coif.[3960] Yet even in those instances Jacob shined—by standing firm on principle regarding the way he felt the faculty had mistreated Professor Ramos;[3961] by being proven right when it came to fundraising and the school the budgeting for future needs;[3962] and for establishing the goal of seeking Coif and, in pursuit of that objective, causing faculty scholarship to improve and grade patterns to normalize, both being requirements for Coif certification.[3963] As dean of Stetson University College of Law, Bruce Jacob moved the school up the ladder, modernized its programs, renovated its campus, maintained its academic standards, and prepared the school for a new chapter in its 105-year on-going history.

3958. *See supra* nn. 3578–3601 and accompanying text.

3959. *See supra* nn. 3536–3550 and accompanying text.

3960. *See supra* nn. 3596–3600 and accompanying text; *see also* Jacob, *Report on Deanship*, *supra* n. 3239, at 33.

3961. *Id.* at 36.

3962. *See supra* nn. 3563–64 and accompanying text.

3963. *See supra* nn. 3551–53 and accompanying text.

CHAPTER THIRTEEN

The Nation's Top-Rated Advocacy Program

Stetson University College of Law for over two decades has won national recognition[3964] for its advocacy program and for the consistent success of its trial teams in winning major competitions.[3965] *U.S. News & World Report* has ranked Stetson's advocacy program the best in the nation eight years out of the last twelve, and second best in three of the other four years.[3966] Though numerous judges, attorneys, and faculty have contributed to the program's success, the person most responsible is Stetson University Distinguished Professor Emeritus of Law William R. Eleazer. While Eleazer's background, education, and United States Marine Corps service were discussed earlier,[3967] this

3964. *See e.g.* Christopher G. Frey, *ATLA Team Wins Two First Places*, 22 Prelude 1, 8 (Apr. 1, 1987); *It's Team Spirit That Does It at Stetson*, 27 Stetson Law. 5, 5 (Fall 1987); *Stetson's Trial Advocacy Team Continues National Winning Streak* 2 (Spring/Summer 2000); *Stetson Trial Team Brings Home the National Championship (Again)!* 30 Stetson Law. 3, 3 (fall 1990); *Stetson Trial Team Continues to Win*, 29 Stetson Law. 1 (Spring 1990); *Stetson University College of Law Ranked # 1 in Trial and Appellate Advocacy*, 36 Stetson Law. cover pg. (Spring 1996); *Trial Team Continues to Shine*, 39 Stetson Law. 2, 2 (Winter 1999); *Trial Teams Continue Winning Tradition*, 39 Stetson Law. 2, 2 (Spring 1966); *Trial Teams Set Unprecedented Record, Five National Competitions in One Year*, 34 Stetson Law., 14, 15 (Summer 1994).

3965. *See e.g. Best Graduate Schools*, 128 U.S. News & World Rpt. 56 (Apr. 10, 2000); *Best Graduate Schools*, 126 U.S. News & World Rpt. 95 (Mar. 19, 1999); *Best Graduate Schools*, 124 U.S. News & World Rpt. 77 (Mar. 2, 1998); *America's Best Graduate Schools*, 122 U.S. News & World Rpt. 67 (Mar. 10, 1997); *America's Best Graduate Schools*, 120 U.S. News & World Rpt. 82 (Mar. 18, 1996); *America's Best Graduate Schools*, 118 U.S. News & World Rpt. 84 (Mar. 20, 1995).

3966. *U.S. News & World Report* ranked Stetson first or tied for first in the nation in 1995, 1996, 1997, 1998, 2002, 2003, 2005, and 2006, and second in 2000, 2001, and 2004.

3967. *See supra* nn. 3105–3128 and accompanying text.

chapter focuses on his building Stetson's trial advocacy program over the twenty-year period he directed it.[3968] Some of what follows is taken from an article authored by Professor Eleazer and published in the *Stetson Law Review* in 2000.[3969]

Stetson's College of Law excellence in trial advocacy over the past quarter of a century is not something new for its graduates. Long before *U.S. News & World Report* named Stetson's trial advocacy program number one in the nation,[3970] the College had been producing capable and successful trial lawyers throughout its 105-year history.[3971] Eleazer notes that Stetson law school has long been known for educating "practitioners,"[3972] more so than academics, business leaders, or politicians (though Stetson has produced its share of each).[3973] Stetson graduates, he says, are often designated "great practitioners," which means graduates having "lawyering and trial skills to practice in a general way the profession of law."[3974]

When did Stetson College of Law garner a reputation for being a school for practitioners? It began when the College opened its doors in 1900. Through the first decade of the twentieth century, Stetson was the only law school in Florida.[3975] When the school opened, Dean Albert Farrah and the faculty believed it was necessary for students to learn practical lawyering skills, especially

---

3968. Professor William Eleazer joined the faculty in 1979 and retired in 1999. Since his retirement, he has continued his close association with the College, on occasion teaching and judging simulated trials put on by students.

3969. *See* Eleazer, *Trial Advocacy, supra* n. 2780. Distinguished Professor Emeritus William Eleazer has granted Stetson University and the authors of this volume permission to borrow from this article without sentence by sentence attribution. The reader should understand, however, that the description of how the program developed to a large measure are the words previously written by Professor Eleazer and published in the *Stetson Law Review*.

3970. *See supra* n. 3976.

3971. The list of Stetson's widely recognized outstanding trial lawyers over its history is long. Several, *e.g.*, Maury Sams, and his son, Maury Sams, Jr., were mentioned earlier in this volume. Many Stetson alumni who became prominent trial attorneys contributed substantial time and effort in helping bring Stetson's trial advocacy program to prominence.

3972. Eleazer, *Trial Advocacy, supra* n. 2780, at 243.

3973. Examples in the academic field include Richard T. Dillon, dean of Stetson University

College of Law, 1968–1981; Bruce R. Jacob, thirty-five years in legal education and dean of Stetson, 1981–1994; and Dr. Karl M. Cuttler, Jr., president of St. Petersburg College since 1978. Examples in business include Roy M. Speer, Jr., a 1959 graduate and founder and retired Chief Executive Officer of Home Shopping Network, Inc. Examples in politics include David Sholtz, Governor of Florida, 1933–1937.

3974. Eleazer, *Trial Advocacy, supra* n. 2780, at 244.

3975. Vause, *Foundations for Excellence, supra* n. 308.

those involved in trials.[3976] Today's pedagogy of training law students in trial advocacy—using simulated jury trials—was the method used in fashion ninety years ago at Stetson. Mock trials were being held at the school from around 1915 onward. The following statement appeared in Stetson's 1917 yearbook, apparently written by a law student:

> I regret to say that in the moot court proceedings we were represented in rather ignominious fashion. Two of our members were convicted of murder, one of larceny and one for gross negligence. But let's cheer up; next year, we will sit in judgment over the rats. We also did jury duty; and here again we made proof that we are full-blooded Americans: The jury agreed in five minutes that the accused was guilty, but they wrangled for half an hour as to who should be foreman! And, I suppose, they never would have agreed on that point if it hadn't been for the supper bell![3977]

Thus, the seeds for Stetson's subsequent trial team were sown early in the College's 100-year-plus history.

13.1 Trial Advocacy in Gulfport

In the summer of 1954, Stetson College of Law moved from the DeLand campus of Stetson University to the law school's new Gulfport campus.[3978] By then, Stetson law graduates had already made names for themselves. At the dedication of the Charles A. Dana Library in March 1958, Governor Leroy Collins addressed the gathered dignitaries and took note that three Stetson law graduates were at that moment sitting justices on the Florida Supreme Court.[3979] Governor Collins suggested this fact proved that the Stetson law school had produced able practitioners, skilled in the law, who were ready to advance upward and become leaders in both the bar and the judiciary.[3980]

3976. The initial curriculum of the College of Law included a required course called "Practice Court." *See supra* nn. 368–371 and accompanying text.

3977. 10 *Oshihiyi* 41 (1917) (Stetson's yearbook). The junior class in 1917 consisted of thirty students, the largest ever at that time. One of its members was William Arthur Kelly, who practiced law in Akron, Ohio, 1919–1962, and argued two cases in the United States Supreme Court.

3978. *See supra* nn. 1875–1876 and accompanying text.

3979. *Bulletin of Stetson University College of Law* 10 (Aug. 1958). Although unidentified in Governor Collins's address, those justices were E. Harris Drew, chief justice at the time; Elwyn Thomas; and T. Frank Hobson.

3980. *Id.*

After the College of Law moved to Gulfport, the school announced a "unique program" of legal education, one that continued well into the 1960s. An annual bulletin of the College described the program as follows:

> *STETSON'S UNIQUE PROGRAM*
>
> The College operates under a somewhat different concept of legal training from that found in most law schools. The distinctive feature of Stetson's program is its adaptation of the British system of legal education to the conventional American system. For centuries, legal training in England has been built around close personal contact between law students and successful *practicing* lawyers, through their association in the famous Inns of Court—Gray's Inn, Lincoln's Inn, the Middle and Inner Temples. In these Inns, outstanding members of the English Bench and Bar share their wisdom and experience firsthand with embryo lawyers who someday will be expected to succeed them as leaders in their profession. Distinguished jurists also honor the students by their presence from time to time. On some occasions, actual court sessions of the Florida courts are held in the Courtroom of the College.[3981]

This description of Stetson's "unique program" was included in the school's annual announcements through 1969. How effective the claimed "inns-of-court" learning by osmosis approach may have been is unclear, but certain events occurred during the 1950s and '60s that directly relate to trial advocacy.

First, under the tutelage of Public Defender Robert Jagger, a 1958 Stetson law graduate, and Stetson Professor Paul Barnard, the school established Florida's Public Defender Clinic.[3982] Only a few years later and with the strong support of both Sixth Circuit Chief Prosecutor James Russell (also a Stetson law graduate) and Dean Richard Dillon, the College added a Prosecution Clinic.[3983] Professor Eleazer describes these developments as "true clinical pioneering by the College."

In the early 1960s, the law school instituted a formal course in trial practice similar to what Stetson had offered during its first two decades. The class included simulated jury trials held in the school's model courtroom.[3984] Eleazer

---

3981. *Bulletin of Stetson University College of Law: Announcements for 1961–1962,* at 5–6 (1961–1962) (emphasis in original). The "former Chief Justice of the Florida Supreme Court" referred to in the article was Harold L. Sebring, who became Stetson's dean in 1955. Jacob, *Remembering Sebring, supra* n. 1905, at 137.

3982. *See supra* nn. 2439–2459 and accompanying text.

3983. *See supra* nn. 2802–2803 and accompanying text.

3984. "TRIAL PRACTICE. 2 hours. A consideration of venue; service of process; pretrial procedures; charges; verdicts; new trial; judgment; executions; and practical application thereof at trial court level." *Stetson University College of Law: Catalogue 1960–1961: Fac-*

suggests that these three programs trained many of Florida's "finest trial advocates and jurists."[3985]

13.2 The NITA Program

In 1971, the National Institute for Trial Advocacy (NITA) came into being.[3986] Three organizations funded its creation: the ABA Section of Judicial Administration, the American College of Trial Lawyers, and the Association of Trial Lawyers of America.[3987] NITA's establishment was encouraged by the ABA and by its various task forces that urged that law schools needed to put greater emphasis on teaching legal ethics and lawyer skills, including, of course, trial advocacy. One ABA task force, headed by Cornell Law School Dean Roger Cramton, at one point issued a set of recommendations known as the "Cramton proposals," including the training of lawyers unfamiliar with trial procedures.[3988]

In 1972, NITA began to teach lawyers trial advocacy skills in programs using a "learning-by-doing" approach. Thereafter, NITA sponsored trial skills training courses throughout the country and continues to do so today. The program involves student-lawyers learning in small groups taught by experienced trial attorneys.[3989] Students are assigned to act as counsel and to perform short exercises involving the various components of a jury trial, beginning with the voir dire examination.[3990] The exercises are videotaped and each student's in-

---

ulty & Courses 21 (1960–61). By 1977 the Trial Practice course description included separate courses, civil trial practice and criminal trial practice, each for two hours credit, described as follows:

TRIAL PRACTICE (CIVIL). Preparation and trial of civil cases; including preparation of and arguments on pleadings, assembling facts and witness statements, pre-trial conferences, and actual trials before juries of fellow students.

TRIAL PRACTICE (CRIMINAL). Preparation and trial of criminal cases including pretrial motions and arguments thereon; jury selection and actual trials of criminal cases before student juries. *Stetson University College of Law: Bulletin 1977–1978*, at 29 (1977–1978).

3985. Eleazer, *Trial Advocacy*, *supra* n. 2780, at 246.

3986. *See* www.nita.org, accessed Sept. 7, 2005; *see also ABA Report on Lawyer Competency* (Summer 1979) ("the Cramton Report"); *see also* Stevens, *Law Education*, *supra* n. 196, at 239–241.

3987. *Id.*

3988. *Id.*

3989. *Bar Panel Bids Law Schools Stress Practical Training*, N.Y. Times A-10, col. 1 (Aug. 16, 1979); *see also* Eleazer, *Trial Advocacy*, *supra* n. 2780, at 247.

3990. Eleazer, *Trial Advocacy*, *supra* n. 2780, at 247.

dividual performance is then critiqued with the aid of the video playback.[3991] Building on these preliminary exercises, each student is then assigned to participate as counsel in a simulated jury trial from beginning to end and, at its conclusion, is again critiqued by NITA's teaching staff.[3992]

After the program became known to legal educators, they were able to see how the NITA-style of trial advocacy training could be adopted in law schools. Nonetheless, most schools did not do so (though Stetson was the exception), probably because of the high costs associated with implementing a NITA-style program due to the small teacher-student ration required. The NITA model calls for small classes with intensive, time-consuming instruction from the faculty. Consequently, a school has to hire additional faculty members with no offsetting gain in tuition revenue.

Even so, with increasing pressures put on law schools from accrediting agencies[3993] to add skills training programs, the legal education landscape began to change.[3994] In 1980, the ABA Section on Legal Education proposed that all accredited law schools be required to offer lawyering skills courses.[3995]

13.3 Stetson Adopts NITA Teaching Pedagogy

In the fall of 1979, Stetson hired two full-time professors to bolster its lawyering skills program, William R. Eleazer and Jonathan L. Alpert. Eleazer had extensive experience as a prosecutor. Alpert was an experienced civil trial attorney in Tampa.[3996] The two divided up the program, Eleazer to teach criminal trial advocacy, and Alpert to instruct in civil trial advocacy.[3997] Wanting to hone their teaching skills before the fall semester began, Eleazer and Alpert attended in the summer of 1979 a NITA-style trial-advocacy course.[3998] Impressed with the NITA method of teaching advocacy skills, they recommended such a program be implemented at Stetson.

3991. *Id.*

3992. *Id.*

3993. The American Bar Association and the Association of American Law Schools were the accrediting agencies.

3994. Stevens, *Law Education*, *supra* n. 196, at 240.

3995. *Id.*; *see also Bar Unit Urges Law Schools to Shift Emphasis*, *supra* n. 372.

3996. Interview by Michael I. Swygert, Prof. Emeritus, Stetson U. College of L., with William R. Eleazer, Distinguished Prof. Emeritus, Stetson U. College of L. 1, 14 (Apr. 17, 2004) [hereinafter *Eleazer Interview*].

3997. *Id.*

3998. *Id.*

That fall, with the approval and support of Dean Dillon, professors Eleazer and Alpert adopted the NITA methodology in teaching trial advocacy. They taugh a sufficient number of sections so that every Stetson student who wanted to take trial advocacy could do so.[3999]

Over time, the NITA-style program proved to be both popular and effective at the law school. Students were assigned to sections with a maximum of sixteen in each (later the maximum section size was reduced to twelve).[4000] An experienced full-time law professor or adjunct professor (usually an experienced trial lawyer or judge) was put in charge of each section. As student demand for the course rose, the hiring of additional part-time (adjunct professors) became necessary. While trial advocacy was not at that time, and is not today, a required course, during the 1980s and 1990s approximately eighty-five to ninety percent of eligible students opted to enroll in the course.[4001]

Today, Stetson's trial advocacy program and the philosophy underlying it have not significantly changed since 1979, when Eleazer and Alpert came to the College and first implemented the NITA-style methodology.[4002] Stetson's policy remains that every student who chooses to learn skills associated with trying a case before a jury be afforded that opportunity. The hands-on "learning-by-doing" teaching style continues to be used by Stetson's trial advocacy instructors, a method premised on repetitive student participation of trial exercises in a simulated courtroom environment.[4003]

Eleazer explains that students are eligible to take Stetson's basic trial advocacy course so long as they have taken, or take concurrently, a required course in evidence. He adds that the College continues to be committed to making sure that Stetson students have access to advocacy training, and that the school provides well-equipped modern courtroom facilities, thereby creating simulated real-world courtroom environments in which all exercises, trials, and instruction take place.[4004] The facilities grew from one courtroom in the 1950s to six courtrooms by 2005. One was built in 1990 on the second floor of the old Rolyat Hotel tower as part of a remodeling project. Each has video equipment for recording student performances and for facilitating critiques. Four of the courtrooms have jury rooms with video equipment that can be used to

---

3999. Eleazer, *Trial Advocacy*, *supra* n. 2780, at 247.

4000. *Id.*

4001. Although Trial Advocacy is not a required course, it is one of the courses available for students to satisfy the school's "skills requirement" for graduation.

4002. *Id.* at 248.

4003. *Id.*

4004. *Id.*

Dedication of Eleazer Courtroom (*left to right*): Keynote speaker and Former U.S. Attorney General Dick Thornburgh; AARP CEO William D. Novelli; Professor William Eleazer; Architect Charles Canarday; Jan Eleazer; Professor Rebecca Morgan; Dean Darby Dickerson; Professor Roberta Flowers; Linda Parker, wife of late Judge Jerry Parker; and Stetson Law graduate Shirin Vesely

record jury deliberations and to provide feedback to students.[4005] They consist of Classroom H; Room 203 courtroom in the tower; Dean Harold L. Sebring Courtroom, built in 1976;[4006] the Carey and Florin Courtroom,[4007] dedicated in 1993;[4008] the Wm. Reece Smith, Jr., Courtroom in Tampa, dedicated in 2004; and the newest, the William R. Eleazer Courtroom on the Gulfport campus, dedicated September 16, 2005.[4009]

A structured approach in teaching trial skills is maintained in all trial advocacy classes, ensuring that all students are instructed in jury selection, opening statements, direct and cross-examination of witnesses, making and meet-

4005. Professor Eleazer states that after consulting with other trial advocacy professors and trial team coaches, he learned that no other law school in the nation has four courtrooms on campus for use in teaching trial advocacy, certainly not four so well-equipped with video cameras.

4006. *See supra* nn. 2705–2708 and accompanying text.

4007. *Carey & Florin*, *supra* n. 3379, at 4.

4008. Members of the law firm who contributed a total of $250,000 to the building of Carey and Florin courtroom were Thomas Carey, W. H. Florin, Thomas D. Roebig, Jr., Michael L. Walker, and Dr. James Huddlestun. All but Thomas Carey are Stetson graduates, and Mr. Carey has been a long-time supporter of Stetson University College of Law. *See supra* nn. 3378–3382 and accompanying text.

4009. *See infra* n. 4075 and accompanying text.

ing objections, motions in limine, handling exhibits, examining expert witnesses, impeachment methods and techniques, preparing the "trial notebook," and closing arguments.[4010] In addition, instructors stress courtroom courtesies, ethics, and professional responsibility at each stage of instruction. They present students both civil and criminal trial problems. During the course, each student participates, first, in a short (two-hour) trial, and then in a four-hour simulated jury trial presided over by a judge from the local courts.[4011] As Eleazer describes it, the objective of the program is to prepare each student to be sufficiently versed in trial skills to perform competently in situations lawyers commonly face when they participate in trials.[4012]

In addition to this basic course in trial advocacy, Stetson offers instruction in advanced trial advocacy and also in specialized litigation, thereby giving students who expect to become trial attorneys after graduation opportunities for additional instruction.[4013] These advanced courses, like the basic course, remain popular with students.[4014]

13.4 Stetson's Trial Advocacy Competitions: 1980–1999

Stetson law school has always enjoyed a strong trial advocacy program, one that has produced outstanding trial lawyers. Consequently, earning national recognition for excellence in trial advocacy should not be surprising. Nonetheless, when in 1995 *U.S. News & World Report* named Stetson's program the number one program in the nation in the magazine's initial ranking of the top ten law trial advocacy programs, this news was an unexpected surprise to the Stetson community. Moreover, since 1995, *U.S. News & World Report* has continued to rank Stetson's trial advocacy program in the top five in the nation each year. In seven of those years, Stetson has been ranked number one, or tied for number one. In three years it was ranked second, and in one year, fourth.[4015]

4010. Eleazer, *Trial Advocacy*, *supra* n. 2780, at 248.

4011. *Id.* at 249.

4012. *Id.*

4013. *Id.*

4014. *Id.* at 249.

4015. Stetson was ranked number one in the nation in 1995, 1996, 1997, 1998, 2002, 2003, and 2005. The College was ranked second in 2000, 2001, and 2004, and its lowest ranking, fourth, occurred in 1999.

The question often is asked: "Just how did Stetson's trial advocacy program obtain such continuing high national honor?" In addition to the school's producing outstanding trial attorneys for decades, another factor has been Stetson's unprecedented success in national-level trial competitions over the past twenty-three years.

Despite the College of Law's relatively small enrollment, Stetson students over the past two decades have taken first place in twenty-one national-level trial competitions—more than any other law school in the nation.[4016] In addition to these twenty-one national championships, Stetson has won twenty-seven regional competitions, and thirty-one state competitions. During one three-year period in the 1990s, Stetson won more national-level trial competition championships than all other law schools in the nation *combined*. The names of all of the students who were members of these teams and their coaches through 1999 have earlier been published in the *Stetson Law Review*,[4017] and are not reproduced here. But given the impact on Stetson's reputation, it is appropriate to trace the history of Stetson's trial competition program below.

Trial competitions on a national level began in the 1970s. Initially, there were only two, but by the year 2000, the number had grown to seven major national trial competitions.[4018] These competitions require law students to

---

4016. The twenty-one Championships are as follows:

- The National Trial Competition: 1989, 1990, 1994, and 2001.
- ATLA's National Student Trial Advocacy Competition: 1993, 1994, and 1996.
- The National Invitational Trial Competition "Tournament of Champions": 1989, 1991, 1993, 1994, and 2004.
- The Cathy E. Bennett National Criminal Trial Competition: 1992, 1993, and 1995.
- The National Criminal Justice Trial Advocacy Competition: 1993, 1994, 1998, 1999, 2000, and 2002.

4017. *See* Eleazer, *Trial Advocacy*, *supra* n. 2780.

4018. The seven major competitions are as follows: The National Trial Competition, sponsored by the American College of Trial Lawyers and the Texas Young Lawyers Association; the National Student Trial Advocacy Competition, sponsored by the Association of Trial Lawyers of America (ATLA); the National Invitational Trial Competition,"Tournament of Champions," sponsored by the National Institute for Trial Advocacy; the Cathy E. Bennett National Criminal Justice Trial Competition, sponsored by The National Association of Criminal Defense Lawyers; the National Criminal Justice Trial Advocacy Competition, sponsored by the Criminal Justice Section of the American Bar Association; the National White Collar Crime Trial Competition, sponsored and hosted each year by Georgetown University, Washington, D.C.; and the William W. Daniel National Mock Trial Competition, sponsored by the Younger Lawyers Division of the State Bar of Georgia.

The National Invitational Trial Competition, "Tournament of Champions," now sponsored by the National Institute for Trial Advocacy, was originally sponsored by the Ohio

demonstrate their advocacy skills during a simulated jury trial of three to four hours, during which they are evaluated by experienced trial lawyers and judges. This is a significant test of the students' ability, and when applied over a period of years, is arguably the truest evaluation of how well advocacy training is being provided at a particular law school.

The two oldest, largest, and most prestigious student trial competitions are the National Trial Competition, sponsored by the American College of Trial Lawyers and the Texas Young Lawyers Association, and the National Student Trial Advocacy Competition, sponsored by the Association of Trial Lawyers of America (ATLA). These competitions, which are open to all accredited law schools, begin with regional trial competitions, from which the regional winners and co-winners proceed to the ATLA National Finals.

13.5 Stetson Trial Team Results through 1999

Eleazer gives much of the credit for the success of the Stetson Trial Teams to the early, continued, and unswerving support it has received from the faculty and administration. He says that he first heard of trial competitions and the potential they offered for teaching trial advocacy at a conference sponsored

---

Trial Lawyers Association. The often-told story of why it was established is interesting. Professor Eleazer explains:

> It seems that the National Trial Competition, which is held annually in Texas, was usually won by one of the schools from the South, and the perception by some was that southern schools had an advantage in Texas that would disappear if the competition were to be held in the North. Thus, the challenge was issued to the law schools across the nation with the best trial competition records to meet in Akron, Ohio, for three days of trial competition. The Ohio Chapter of the American College of Trial Lawyers sponsored the competition, which became known as the "Tournament of Champions." Invitations were extended to sixteen representative law schools, with at least one from each federal judicial circuit to ensure a good cross section of the country. The question to be answered was whether trial teams from the law schools of the South—the usual winners in Texas—could stand the test of "true trial advocacy skills" when judged by trial lawyers from the North, more specifically Ohio trial lawyers. The answer came when the semifinalists were announced after the first four rounds of the competition: Stetson, Wake Forest, Georgia State, and Texas Tech. Stetson went on to defeat Georgia State in the final round to win the first "Tournament of Champions" and put to rest the perceived unfair advantage of southern schools in the National Trial Competition because of its Texas location. Texas or Ohio—location simply makes no difference to Stetson trial teams.

by the Southeastern Association of Law Schools in the summer of 1980.[4019] Eleazer wanted to get involved, but knew it would involve extensive travel and expense, and thus needed Dean Dillon's approval. Eleazer describes Dillon's response:

> I came back to Stetson that fall and I approached Dean Richard Dillon, who like all the deans that followed him, was at all times very supportive of the idea. He provided us the funding necessary and said "go with it."[4020]

Thus, with full approval and support of the administration, Stetson's participation in trial competitions began, entering its first competition in the spring of 1981.[4021] It was a regional competition sponsored by the National Trial Competition in Fort Lauderdale, Florida, featuring law schools from the southeastern states. Although Stetson did not win this first opportunity, the team did reach the semifinals, and left with a determination to help build a winning program at Stetson. The following year, a Stetson team fared better in the same competition, advancing as co-winner of the regional competition to the national finals in Texas. The regional success continued in 1983, when a Stetson team was again a co-winner and advanced to the semifinal round of the national finals in Houston, Texas.

Then, in 1984, Stetson improved further, winning the regional of ATLA's National Student Trial Advocacy Competition and advancing to become a finalist in the ATLA Nationals in Washington, D.C. This was the first of many years of success by Stetson teams in the ATLA competitions. During the next fifteen years, Stetson teams won three ATLA National Championships and produced eight teams that were winners or co-winners in the regionals of the competition.

Stetson's regional and national success in the early 1980s was complemented by Stetson winning the first Florida State Bar Trial Competition in 1983—a competition open to all accredited Florida law schools. It was renamed the "Chester Bedell Memorial Trial Competition" in 1984. This victory began the start of Stetson's domination in The Florida Bar annual trial competitions. By 2000, Stetson had won first place in The Florida Bar competitions fourteen times of its then eighteen years in existence.

In 1985, the Academy of Florida Trial Lawyers established another important law school competition, the Florida Student Intrastate Mock Trial Com-

---

4019. *Eleazer Interview*, *supra* n. 3996, at 20.

4020. *Id.*

4021. The members of the first Stetson team (1981) were Kay Blanco, Baron Given, Robert Paver, Charlie Roberts, and Tom Whitaker. The greenhorn coach was Professor Eleazer. After graduation, the team members frequently returned in the fall semester to assist in the selection of the new team and, in the case of Robert Paver, to coach.

Coach Eleazer with 1991 Florida Bar Chester Bedell Memorial Trial Competition Champions Adam Littman, Marsha Massey, Grady Irvin, Jr., Amy Koltnow and George Guerra

petition, open to all Florida law schools. Stetson's trial team won first place in its first competition, and through 2000, won first place in eleven of the fifteen years the intrastate competition was held to that point.

Although the early years proved successful for Stetson's trial teams, 1989 marked a milestone in the school's trial competition program. That year, a Stetson team, coached by Fred Schaub, a member of Stetson's 1984 trial team, won its first national title—the National Trial Competition held in Houston, Texas. The following year, 1990, Schaub coached another Stetson team that again won the National Trial Competition, the first time that any law school had won the championship two years in a row. Schaub added to these accomplishments in 1994, when he took two Stetson teams, co-winners of the regional competition, to the National Finals, where they finished first *and* second, the first such one-two finish by any law school. Schaub proceeded to become the most successful trial competition coach in the nation, coaching Stetson teams to six national level championships, as well as three second-place finishes, two quarter-finalist finishes in national level competitions, ten regional championships or co-championships, and six state championships.[4022]

During Eleazer's period as head of the program, 1979–1999, many other Stetson trial team coaches joined Schaub in bringing state, regional, and national trial competition championship trophies back to the campus, and their

4022. Schaub coached Stetson's winning teams in the Chester Bedell Memorial Trial Competition in 1987, 1988, 1989, 1990, 1993, and 1995.

Coaches Eleazer and Fred Schaub with 1989 National Trial Team Champions Carol McMurray and Charles Samarkos

accomplishments served to establish and maintain Stetson's dominance in trial competitions. The phenomenal records established by these coaches merit special attention. They included Marie DeMarco, Kathy Tourville Hessinger, Shirin Mohammadbhoy Vesely, John Grant, Jaime Eagan, Professor W. McKinley Smiley, Professor Charles Waygood, Professor Jerry Kramer, Robert Tetreault, Jay Hebert, Mike Rachel, Bob Lang, Robert Paver, Brent Rose, Stacey Schroeder, Don Pumphrey, and Kristin Demers.[4023]

Stetson's trial competitions under Eleazer began in February 1981. Jacob became dean that fall, and like Dillon, Jacob fully supported Stetson's push into advocacy prominence. Jacob recalls:

> I realized that we could build a reputation in this area without spending an inordinate sum of money, and I knew that Eleazer would not spend money unnecessarily. Therefore, I gave him funds from the budget for trial competition.[4024]

4023. Ltr. from William R. Eleazer, Distinguished Prof. Emeritus, Stetson U. College of L., to Michael I. Swygert, Prof. Emeritus, Stetson U. College of L. 2 (Sept. 2, 2005) (on file at Stetson U. College of L., Gulfport, Fla.).

4024. Ltr. from Bruce R. Jacob, Dean Emeritus and Prof. of Law, Stetson U. College of L., to Michael I. Swygert, Prof. Emeritus, Stetson U. College of L. (Aug. 15, 2005) (on file at Stetson U. College of L., Gulfport, Fla.); *see also* Michael I. Swygert, *Bruce R. Jacob: A Dean for All Seasons*, 21 Stetson L. Rev. 307, 309 (Spring 1992). "He [Jacob] has given full

Like Eleazer, Jacob gives much of the coaching success of Stetson's trial teams during his deanship to others in addition to Eleazer, especially Fred Schaub. Jacob recollects that Schaub "practically lived at the school" when he was coaching trial teams. Jacob describes Schaub as being "one of the best trial advocacy coaches in the country."[4025]

13.6 Record of Stetson Mock Trial Victories, 2000–2005

At the end of the 1998–99 academic year, Professor "Bill" Eleazer chose to retire from Stetson University College of Law following twenty years of dedicated service. Hired in 1979 during Dean Dillon's administration, he led the advocacy program through the combined eighteen years of the Jacob and Moody deanships. No doubt, people associated with Stetson probably feared (while professors coaching other mock trial teams around the country likely hoped) that Eleazer's leaving Stetson would affect the winning pattern of Stetson's trial teams. But Stetson's victories have kept coming, and so have the top rankings in *U.S. News & World Report.*[4026]

Over the past six years, Stetson has won five national competitions: the 1999 ABA National Criminal Justice Trial Competition (Chicago); the 2000 ABA National Criminal Justice Trial Competition (Chicago); the 2002 National Trial Competition Championship Round (Dallas); the 2002 ABA National Criminal Justice Trial-Advice Competition (Chicago); and the 2004 National Tournament of Champions (NITA) (Los Angeles).[4027] The team and coaches felt that the 2004 NITA victory was particularly significant, first, because the competition is a "Tournament of Champions" where the top-rated sixteen trial advocacy teams are invited, and second, because Stetson had won the NITA national championship exactly ten years earlier in 1994.[4028]

Stetson Trial Advocacy Fellows Karen A. Williams and Pamela Cole Bell coached several championship teams during the years after Eleazer retired.

---

support to Professor William Eleazer's outstanding trial advocacy program." Swygert & Jacob, *supra* n. 4024, at 309.

4025. *Id.*

4026. *See supra* nn. 3965–3976 and accompanying text.

4027. Memo. from Pamela Cole Bell, Tr. Adv. Fellow, Stetson U. College of L., to Michael I. Swygert, Prof. Emeritus, Stetson U. College of L. 1–6 (May 2, 2005) (on file at Stetson U. College of L., Gulfport, Fla.).

4028. *Id.*

During this period, Stetson trial teams continued to perform well in regional and state competitions, winning first place ten times in five years. The state and regional victories include: the 2000 Chester Bedell Memorial Mock Trial Competition (Miami); both the 2000 and the 2001 ABA National Trial Competition Southeast Regionals (Clearwater); the 2001 and the 2003 Academy of Florida Trial Lawyers Honorable E. Earle Zehmer Memorial Mock Trial Competition (state champions); the 2004 and the 2005 National Trial Competition Southeast Regionals; the 2004 Association of Trial Lawyers of America National Student Trial Advocacy Competition, Southeast Regional; and the 2004 Chester Bedell Memorial Mock Trial Competition (state champion).[4029]

An article in the *Stetson Lawyer* reports on the team's success during the 2003–04 academic year: "The trial team had a strong run this academic year. Stetson swept Florida and our region," said Stetson professor and trial team advisor Pamela Cole Bell, '82, "We've won everything."[4030]

Beginning in 2005, Professor Lee Coppock took over the primary responsibilities for the College's trial program, including coaching the trial team, as the school's Trial Advocacy Fellow. Other Stetson law professors who have coached Stetson trial teams in recent years include William Eleazer, Steve Everhart, Roberta Flowers, Karen Williams, Pamela Cole Bell, and Kelly M. Feeley. Areas judges and lawyers who served as coaches include Robert Lang, Judge David Demers, Susan Demers, Kristin Demers-Crowel, Judge Jerry Parker, Stacey Schroeder, Jaime Eagan, Creighton Shafer, Donald Anderson, Thea Dalkalltsis, Dina Kenny, Natalie Silver, Lee Coppock, Don Pumphrey, Kenneth Foote, and Maria DiBlasio.[4031]

13.7 Stetson College of Law Center for Excellence in Advocacy

When Professor Eleazer retired in the spring of 1999 from the College of Law, a vacancy resulted that everyone knew would be hard to fill. One month after Eleazer retired, on July 1, 1999, Gary Vause succeeded Elizabeth Moody as dean of Stetson College of Law.[4032] Vause needed a person to lead the trial

4029. *Id.* at 2–6.

4030. *Advocacy Teams Continue Outstanding Performances in Competitions, Trial Team,* 44 Stetson Law. 7, 7 (Spring 2004).

4031. Records from Center for Excellence in Advocacy, Stetson U. College of Law (2005) (available at the Off. for Ctr. for Excellence in Adv., Stetson U. College of L., Gulfport, Fla.).

4032. *See infra* nn. 4297–4300 and accompanying text.

advocacy program in the manner Eleazer had done. Vause turned to Stetson Professor Roberta Kemp Flowers. Flowers joined the Stetson law faculty in 1993.[4033] Previously, she served four years in Miami as an assistant United States District Attorney for the Southern District of Florida, where she prosecuted public officials, drug traffickers, and other criminal defendants charged with major offenses.[4034] Prior to her work in Florida, Flowers served as a supervising trial attorney for Colorado's 18th Judicial District in Littleton, where she helped train newly appointed prosecuting attorneys.[4035]

Dean Vause was convinced Flowers had the right combination of experience, knowledge, and teaching savvy to lead a nationally recognized trial advocacy program. After selecting her, Vause established a "Center for Excellence in Advocacy at Stetson University College of Law."[4036]

The Center sponsors conferences and seminars and brings on campus nationally known speakers, sometimes in conjunction with an endowed speakers series. One example is Lawrence Fox, an "internationally recognized trial lawyer at the Philadelphia firm of Drinker, Biddle & Realth," who on January 29, 2004, gave the Wm. Reece Smith, Jr., Distinguished Lecture in Litigation Ethics at a Stetson Inns of Court Banquet.[4037] In addition to sponsoring speakers, the Center has promoted Stetson as a national focal point for advocacy in other ways.

With the assistance of Professor Flowers, the *Stetson Law Review* in 2004 published a "Center for Excellence in Advocacy Symposium" in conjunction with Center for Excellence in Elder Law.[4038] The authors included Judge O.H. Eaton, Jr., Circuit Judge for Florida's 18th Judicial Circuit,[4039] who wrote on capital punishment in Florida.[4040] Professor Michael P. Allen of the Stetson law faculty contributed an article on the controversy surrounding the life and

4033. Roberta Kemp Flowers, Resume 1 (n.d.) (on file at Stetson U. College of Law, Gulfport, Fla.) [hereinafter Flowers, *Resume*].

4034. *Id.* at 1.

4035. *Id.*; *see also* www.law.stetson.edu/faculty/flowers.asp (containing additional information about Professor Flowers's education, background, and activities at Stetson can be found).

4036. Roberta Kemp Flowers, *Introduction, Center for Excellence in Advocacy Symposium*, 34 Stetson L. Rev. 1 (2004).

4037. *Id.* at 2, 3 n. 11.

4038. *See Center for Excellence in Advocacy Symposium*, 34 Stetson L. Rev. (2004) [hereinafter *Center Symposium*].

4039. *Id.* at 2 n. 4.

4040. *See* O.H. Eaton, Jr., *Capital Punishment: An Examination of Current Issues and Trends and How These Developments May Impact the Death Penalty in Florida*, 34 Stetson L. Rev. 9 (2004).

death of Terri Schiavo, titled *Life, Death, and Advocacy: Rules of Procedure in the Contested End-of-Life Case.*[4041] The third lead article dealt with the Florida Evidence Code and the problems of distinguishing between issues of substance and procedure, and was authored by Michael P. Dickey, an attorney from Panama City, Florida.[4042] The final work was the published lecture of Lawrence J. Fox, mentioned above,[4043] titled, *Can Client Confidentiality Survive Enron, Arthur Anderson, and the ABA?*[4044]

As Director of the Center for Excellence in Advocacy, Flowers, along with Professor Charles Rose—appointed Associate Director of the Center in January 2006—oversee the skills and advocacy curriculum while supervising five clinics (Public Defender, Prosecution, Poverty, Local Government, and Elder Law);[4045] design and coordinate continuing legal education programs on advocacy; oversee Stetson's Moot Court Board, Mock Trial Team, and Client Skills Board; and supervise the American Mock Trial Association (AMTA) National Championship Competition (an intercollegiate event involving as many as 400 students).[4046] For the past several years, Pamela Cole Bell, Stetson's Trial Advocacy Fellow, has been the principal coach of Stetson's trial teams.[4047] As noted above, Professor Lee Coppock, beginning in the fall of 2005, took over that responsibility.

Meanwhile, the advocacy programs at Stetson continue to grow. In the summer of 2005, Flowers was in Granada, Spain, taking part in a "Comparative Advocacy Study-Abroad Program" that she designed.[4048] During the same summer, another Stetson trial advocacy professor, Stephen Everhart, was teaching law in China as a U.S. Fulbright professor.[4049] Everhart, who joined Stetson's law faculty in 1991, taught Chinese judges, lawyers, and law professors criminal law and civil law, evidence, and trial advocacy.[4050] In an interview, Professor Everhart commented:

4041. *See* Michael P. Allen, *Life, Death, Advocacy: Rules of Procedure in the Contested End-of-Life Case*, 34 Stetson L. Rev. 55 (2004).

4042. *See* Michael P. Dickey, *The Florida Evidence Code and the Separation of Powers Doctrine: How to Distinguish Substance and Procedure*, 24 Stetson L. Rev. 109 (2004).

4043. *See supra* n. 4036 and accompanying text.

4044. *See* 34 Stetson L. Rev. 147 (2004).

4045. Flowers, *Resume*, *supra* n. 4033, at 1.

4046. *Id.*

4047. *Id.*

4048. *Id.*

4049. Frank Klim, *Stetson Law Professor Receives Fulbright Scholarship to Teach in China* 1, www.law.stetson.edu/communications/news.asp?id=94(Apr. 29, 2004) (on file at Stetson U. College of Law, Gulfport, Fla.).

4050. *Id.*

> [Stetson's] moving into an area where we're going to have an international presence in advocacy training. Globalization is here, and Stetson can lead the way, training students, lawyers, law professors, and business executives all over the world in advocacy techniques ... We're moving in that direction and I think "Bobbi" [Professor Flowers] is exercising some tremendous leadership in it.[4051]

As a member of the Stetson faculty, Everhart has been among those who have coached Stetson trial teams to victory. In 1994, along with John Grant, he coached two Stetson mock trial teams that won national championships—first, the ABA Criminal Justice Trial Advocacy Competition in Chicago, and second, the National Invitational Tournament of Champions.[4052] For several years, he was a partner in the firm of Blews and Everhart. His partner was William F. Blews, Stetson class of '66 (later to be president of The Florida Bar).[4053] Everhart credits Blews as "his principal trainer as a lawyer."[4054]

13.8 A Look Ahead

After *U.S. News & World Report* announced their 2006 rankings (actually published in the spring of 2005), showing that Stetson College of Law was tied for first place in law school advocacy programs in the nation,[4055] and that the College had tied for third-place in its legal writing program,[4056] Stetson Dean Darby Dickerson issued this statement:

> Our faculty work very hard to teach students the skills, such as advocacy and legal writing, they need to be successful attorneys. Our students also work very hard to master these skills. These rankings reflect the thousands of hours of effort our faculty and students devote to achieving true excellence.[4057]

Then in the spring of 2006, *U.S. News & World Report* announced that Stetson's advocacy program was again the number one in the United States, while

4051. *Everhart Interview*, *supra* n. 3647, at 21.

4052. *Id.* at 10.

4053. Stephen M. Everhart, *Curriculum Vitae* 1 (2004) (on file at Stetson U. College of L., Gulfport, Fla.).

4054. *Everhart Interview*, *supra* n. 3647, at 6.

4055. *Stetson Ties as America's Top School*, *supra* n. 2979, at 3.

4056. *Id.*

4057. *Id.*

the school's legal writing program was ranked fourth best out of nearly 190 law schools. Professor Roberta Flowers, Stetson's Advocacy Center's Director, commented that the College of Law "is proud of its legacy of teaching students not only to think like lawyers, but also to act like lawyers."

Former Florida Bar President and Chair of the College of Law Overseers, alumnus William Blews has written that, "Stetson is a unique institution with a tradition of producing some of the finest trial lawyers in the nation."[4058]

Stetson's advocacy program—in addition to receiving annual recognition from *U.S. News & World Report*—has been honored by being named recipient of the prestigious Emil Gumpert Award, an award presented by the American College of Trial Lawyers to a law school selected for its outstanding trial advocacy program. The award is named for the late Emil Gumpert, chancellor-founder of the College of Trial Lawyers. Representatives of the American College of Trial Lawyers presented Stetson the award along with a $50,000 grant at Stetson's spring 1997 graduation.[4059]

Not only the program, but the program's designer—Professor and "Head Coach" Bill Eleazer—has also received national recognition. In 1996, the Roscoe Pound Foundation presented Eleazer with the Richard S. Jacobson Award for Excellence in Teaching Trial Advocacy, the most prestigious honor in the nation for a teacher of trial advocacy.[4060] Named for the first editor of *Trial* magazine, the Jacobson award "honors those who have demonstrated excellence in teaching trial advocacy, both in classroom and clinic settings."[4061] When Eleazer received the Jacobson Award, Stetson College of Law Dean Moody remarked:

> We are proud that Professor Eleazer has received this award which epitomizes the significant contribution he has made to Stetson and the legal pro-

---

4058. Vroman Graves Assocs., *Leaders in Trial Practice, The Employer's Guide* 3 (1995) (on file at Stetson U. College of L., Gulfport, Fla.).

4059. The award process is lengthy. Stetson applied in 1994. In 1996, representatives of the American College of Trial Lawyers (an "On-site Committee," which included Stetson alumnus Robert T. Scott) visited the law school campus to inspect the facilities, speak with faculty and students involved in the trial advocacy programs, and learn firsthand the true strength of the trial advocacy program. After the visit, the "On-site Committee" submitted a report to the full Gumpert Award Committee. In 1996, Stetson submitted a supplemental report to the Gumpert Award Committee. At its 1997 Spring Meeting, the Board of Regents of the American College of Trial Lawyers, acting on recommendation of the Gumpert Award Committee, voted to confer the 1997 Gumpert Award upon Stetson.

4060. *Professor Eleazer Receives National Teaching Award*, 1996 Stetson Law. 1, 1.

4061. *Id.*

> fession. Under his leadership, Stetson has developed what many believe to be the premier trial practice and advocacy program in the country.[4062]

There is no doubt that what Eleazer and those jurists, lawyers, and other professors who have participated in Stetson's advocacy program have accomplished, enhancing Stetson's law school's national reputation, while at the same time providing scores of its students solid training in trial practice. Of course, Stetson's advocacy program extends beyond trial advocacy to include appellate advocacy (national moot court) and in specialized advocacy programs, including the areas of: employment, tax, environmental, labor, and intellectual property, as well as in negotiations and counseling. (The school's extended advocacy programs and competitions they generate have already been noted in earlier chapters and will be highlighted in following chapters). In conclusion, Stetson's success in advocacy began with the work of the architect of the trial advocacy program—Distinguished Professor Emeritus of Law William R. Eleazer. The new College of Law courtroom dedicated in 2005 that bears his name is a fitting honor.[4063]

4062. *Id.*

4063. On September 16, 2005, the William R. Eleazer Courtroom of Stetson College of Law was dedicated. The courtroom is located in the completely renovated old library building, the Charles A. Dana Library. The Eleazer Courtroom is foremost in the nation for the accessability of facilities for individuals with disabilities and the elderly.

CHAPTER FOURTEEN

Deans Moody, Vause, and Dickerson

14.1 Lizabeth A. Moody, First Woman Law Dean in Stetson History

a. Winner of the "ABA Glass Cutter Award"

In the 1960s, Yale Law School graduate Lizabeth A. Moody joined the politically powerful Cleveland law firm of Metzenbaum, Gaines, Finley and Stern,[4064] where she rose to be one of the first women to become a partner in a major Cleveland law firm. During the noon hour one day, when no other lawyer was in the office, the firm's receptionist contacted Moody and said, "someone is on the phone wishing to talk with a lawyer."[4065] Moody took the call; she recalls the conversation:

> "This is Liz Moody. Can I help you?" The caller responded, "Oh, I'm sorry, I wanted to talk with a lawyer." I said, "Well, I'm a lawyer." He replied, "Well, I wanted to talk to a partner." I said, "Well, I'm a partner, "and he exclaimed, "Well, I'm not gonna talk to a woman."[4066]

Long before this incident, Moody had come to expect discrimination on account of her gender. After graduating in 1956 from Barnard College of Columbia University, she applied for admission to two law schools.[4067] Her advisor at Barnard urged that she apply to Yale. Thinking Yale might be a long shot because of its cost, Moody (a resident of Ohio) decided to apply to Ohio State

4064. *AALS 2004–2005 Directory*, *supra* n. 3045, at 776.

4065. Interview by Michael I. Swygert, Prof. Emeritus, Stetson U. College of L., with Lizabeth A. Moody, Dean Emeritus & Distinguished Prof. of L., Stetson U. College of L., 18, 20, 21 (May 17, 2005) (on file at Stetson U. College of L., Gulfport, Fla.) [hereinafter *Moody Interview*].

4066. *Id.*

4067. *Id.* at 4, 5.

Dean Lizabeth A. Moody

as a backup, believing that her record at Columbia and LSAT scores would cause her to be readily admitted to the state's university. Not so. While Yale accepted her, Ohio State told her not to send in her application. Moody explains: "Apparently, Ohio State College of Law did not admit women at that time."

Many schools did not. Harvard Law School did not accept women until 1950.[4068] Thus, it is not surprising that when Moody received her law degree in the late 1950s, women lawyers in the United States comprised only less than three percent of all attorneys, and many of them did not practice law.[4069]

After graduating in 1959 from Yale, Moody practiced law in Bridgeport, Connecticut, before moving with her husband, Alan Buchmann (also a Yale Law School graduate), to Cleveland, Ohio. There, Buchmann joined the city's largest law firm—Squires, Sanders and Dempsey.[4070] Moody was not so fortunate. She discovered that finding a Cleveland firm willing to hire a woman lawyer was, as she describes it, "a very hard job."[4071] Her luck changed, however, when she interviewed with a patent firm where the senior partner, J. Helen Slogh, daughter of the firm's founder, hired Moody.[4072] After practicing patent and trademark law a few years, she worked with Howard Metzenbaum

4068. Stevens, *Law Education*, *supra* n. 196, at 203, 204 n. 63.
4069. *Id.* at 234.
4070. *Moody Interview*, *supra* n. 4065, at 6, 7.
4071. *Id.* at 17.
4072. *Id.*

Stetson Law Library and Information Center

(later the United States Senator from Ohio) where she specialized in corporate transactional law.[4073]

Because of her own gender-discrimination experiences, Moody became involved in women's rights advocacy. She, along with other women lawyers, formed the Women's Equity Action League (WEAL).[4074] The group represented a plaintiff in a significant case advancing women's rights, *Cleveland Board of Education v. LaFleur.*[4075] The suit was consolidated with another action, and the two went to the United States Supreme Court via certiorari. Ruth Bader Ginsberg (later appointed an Associate Justice on the Court) was plaintiff's counsel in the companion case. Thereafter, Moody and Ginsberg were friends.[4076] Thus, in 2000, Dean Moody first thought of Justice Ginsberg as the person to dedicate Stetson's new Law Library and Information Center.[4077] Justice Ginsberg accepted Stetson's invitation.

Throughout Moody's career, she has worked to make the legal profession more accessible to women, serving as advisory council to the Women's Division of Ohio Bureau of Employment Services; president and trustee of the Women's Law Fund; president of Women's Equity Action League; a faculty member at the AALS Workshop for Women in Legal Education; a leader in

4073. *Id.*

4074. *Id.* at 21.

4075. 414 U.S. 632 (1974).

4076. *Moody Interview*, *supra* n. 4065, at 22.

4077. *See infra* nn. 4135–4136 and accompanying text.

the AALS Conference on Women in Law Teaching; and a commissioner on the Cleveland Bar Association Commission on Women and the Law.[4078] For her efforts to increase women's access to law practice, Moody has received several honors, including: Cleveland State University's "*International Women's Day Award* (1990); the *Josephine Irvin Award of Womenspace* "for contributions on behalf of women"; the YWCA "*Career Woman of Achievement in Education Award*"; and the American Bar Association Section on Business Law "*Glass Cutter Award*," for helping women lawyers "gain access to business and the legal profession."[4079] There is no doubt that women law students have viewed Moody's career as one to emulate.

Lizabeth Moody grew up in the mountains of eastern Tennessee. As a young child, Moody's circumstances did not bode well for a professional career.[4080] Her family was poor and had no formal education. Her father, who could neither read nor write, encouraged his Appalachian daughter to go to college and become a lawyer, advice she followed. Moody was intelligent, determined, and understood that education was the path to upward mobility. She excelled academically in high school and, based on her high school academic record, she was awarded a national, four-year scholarship from Junior Achievement, Inc., enabling her to attend any institution of higher learning in New York City.[4081] She chose Barnard College of Columbia University. There, she served as associate editor and, subsequently, editor of *Achievement Magazine*.[4082]

Years later, while working in the Metzenbaum law firm, Moody was a part-time lecturer at Cleveland-Marshall College of Law at Cleveland State University.[4083] In the fall of 1970, she joined the full-time faculty of Cleveland-Marshall and remained there until 1994, when she was appointed the twelfth dean of Stetson University College of Law. During her years on the Cleveland-Marshall faculty, Moody twice served as interim dean, and was the faculty representative to the University Board of Trustees.[4084] She also served as a visiting faculty member at the University of Toledo law school, the George Washington University National Law Center, and the University of Hawaii law school.[4085] Following her Stetson deanship, Moody returned to the University

4078. Lizabeth A. Moody, *Curriculum Vitae* 2–7 (May 2003) (on file at Stetson U. College of L., Gulfport, Fla.) [hereinafter Moody, *Curriculum Vitae*].

4079. *Id.* at 7, 8; *see also*, *Moody Interview*, *supra* n. 4065, at 43, 44.

4080. Moody, *Curriculum Vitae*, *supra* n. 4078.

4081. *Id.* at 2, 3.

4082. *Id.* at 3.

4083. *AALS 2004–2005 Directory*, *supra* n. 3045, at 772.

4084. *Id.*

4085. *Id.* at 24.

of Hawaii for one year as the Wallace Fugiyama Distinguished Visiting Professor of Law and, subsequently, as a visiting professor at Southern Methodist University School of Law.[4086]

Throughout her years in legal education, she has focused her teaching and scholarship on corporate law, nonprofit organizations, corporate planning, securities regulation (including international), and the legal profession.[4087]

What distinguishes Moody from previous Stetson law school deans has been her extensive involvement in the hierarchy of legal education. She has served as president and chief executive officer of Law School Admission Services; executive director of Law School Admission Council; delegate to ABA House of Delegates; council member of ABA Sections on Business Law and Legal Education and Admissions to the Bar. In addition, she has chaired the ABA Section's Law School Accreditation Committee, pre-law Committee, and Sub-Committee on Foreign Programs, and has served as a member and chair of numerous ABA and AALS site-evaluation teams.[4088] Moody is an elected member of the American Law Institute and has worked with both the National Conference of Bar Examiners and the National Conference of Commissioners on Uniform State Law.[4089] For her service, Moody received various recognitions, notably the "Ohio Bar Medal," and was named a "Life Fellow of the American Bar Foundation.[4090]

By 1994, when President Doug Lee invited Moody to be dean of Stetson College of Law, she was well entrenched in America's legal education establishment. In announcing Moody's appointment, Lee said: "She is one of the most talented administrators in legal higher education today," adding, "I would rank her among the most outstanding women in legal education."[4091]

b. Faculty Split Widens

Upon arriving at Stetson in the summer of 1994, Moody found a sharply divided faculty still steaming over the Ramos retention matter.[4092] Unfortunately, during Moody's first year as dean, the divisions deepened. The growing split became especially evident when the issue of retention of non-tenured

4086. Moody, *Curriculum Vitae*, *supra* n. 4078, at 1.

4087. *Id.* at 4.

4088. *Id.* at 3.

4089. *Id.* at 3, 4.

4090. *Id.* at 7.

4091. Paula Reed, *Stetson Announces New Dean* 1 (Stetson U. College of L. Apr. 19, 1994) (news release) (on file at Stetson U. College of L., Gulfport, Fla.).

4092. *See supra* nn. 3592–3595 and accompanying text.

faculty arose. And although the law school policy was that faculty's vote on any person's retention, promotion, or tenure was not to be disclosed, sometimes the votes were leaked to the *St. Petersburg Times*. In one instance, the paper reported that the faculty had voted thirteen to twelve against renewing the contracts of two professors.[4093] The vote represented only the tip of a cracking iceberg.

The divide was never as simple as old guard versus new guard, nor a division between tenured and untenured faculty. Rather, at the heart were two divergent social philosophies, though on the surface, the debate usually was over whether a particular non-tenured colleague had "earned" the privilege of being renewed. Underlying this issue was the matter of "meritocracy." What were a particular candidate's "merits"? At Stetson—as throughout legal education—a chasm developed between those who defined "meritocracy" under past criteria, and those who considered meritocracy within wider parameters encompassing life experiences and diversity in both upbringing and philosophy, as well as notions and ideas that were contrary at times to the faculty's majoritarian ethos.

In the fall of 1994, Stetson's law faculty consisted of thirty-three full-time members, twenty-three being tenured and ten not.[4094] Bruce Jacob was on sabbatical, as were professors James Brown, Tom Allison, John Cooper, and Brad Stone; Professor Richard Gershon was on leave.[4095] All six held tenured positions and several returned to participate when renewal, promotion, and tenure issues arose. One such occasion involved the retention of three non-tenured faculty members. The faculty voted to renew only one of the three. As to the other two, their fate was determined by one vote, according to numbers leaked to the *St. Petersburg Times*.[4096] After the vote, emotions among the faculty ran high, as the *Times* reported that a controversy had "erupted" at the school:

> [...] when the school's tenured faculty fired two professors by a 13 to 12 secret ballot. Since then, more than 200, or about a third, of the school's students have signed petitions protesting the action, and at least two professors have written letters of protest to University President H. Douglas Lee. On Wednesday, Lee visited the [school] to allow people to vent their feelings about the firings. However, he declined to overrule the decision.[4097]

4093. Ann Lindberg, *Stetson Law School Is Feeling the Pressure*, St. Pete. Times B-1 (Apr. 25, 1995) [hereinafter Lindberg, *Stetson Pressure*].

4094. Bishop, *List*, *supra* n. 2351, at 4–7.

4095. *Id.*

4096. Lindberg, *Stetson Pressure*, *supra* n. 4093, at 1, 7.

4097. *Id.*

Faculty polemics intensified following the vote. Two professors, Mark Brown and Manny Ramos, complained to the press about the faculty's non-renewal of two members. Brown, who was tenured, told the *Times*: "A majority of the tenured faculty do not believe in diversity," adding, "those faculty members think that the hiring of minorities or recruiting them is the same as taking a slot away from a deserving white person."[4098] Dean Moody retorted that the non-renewals "were a matter of merit, not race or politics." A few faculty members sided with Brown, while many agreed with Moody. Ramos told a reporter: "The only power the senior faculty has is to get rid of professors who are ideologically and culturally different."[4099]

Unfortunately, the emotive battles over who should be hired, renewed, or granted tenure, as well as over the governance relationship between the tenured faculty and the dean persisted throughout Moody's deanship. The continuing infighting among the faculty was upsetting not only to President Lee, but also to both the University Trustees and the College of Law Overseers. Stetson's situation was not unique. To put the divisiveness into historical perspective, similar highly emotional divisions have taken place at other law schools. Indeed, Harvard Law School's faculty infighting became the subject of a best-selling book, *Poisoned Ivy: How Egos, Ideology, and Power Politics Almost Ruined Harvard Law School*.[4100] Reflecting experiences at many law schools, near the end of Moody's tenure as dean, relations between her and several members of the senior faculty were strained so much so that at one point, she asked the entire faculty to attend an off-campus retreat, where professional conciliators attempted unsuccessfully to reconcile differences. For one thing, the divisions went beyond personality clashes.

Beginning in the early 1970s, law faculties debated more contentiously over issues of meritocracy, diversity, affirmative action, and faculty governance. Harvard Law School professor Duncan Kennedy was an early entrant in the debate, when in 1970 the *Yale Review of Law and Social Action* published what became a widely read article, "How the Law School Fails, A Polemic," in which Kennedy decried what he viewed as the hierarchical structure and elitist principles of American law schools.[4101] Meanwhile, back at Stetson, a more pragmatic concern took center stage—a new library.

4098. *Id.* at 7.

4099. Anne Lindberg, *Two Law Professors Lose Jobs at Stetson*, St. Pete. Times, N. Pinellas Sec. 3 (Apr. 23, 1995).

4100. *See* Eleonor Kerlow, *Poisoned Ivy: How Egos, Ideology, and Power Politics Almost Ruined Harvard Law School* (St. Martin's Press, 1994).

4101. 1 Yale Rev. of L. & Soc. Action 71 (1970).

c. *Moody Preserves ABA Accreditation; New Law Library Is Built*

When Moody stepped into the dean's chair, she was well aware that the College of Law had been put on notice years earlier that its library was on shaky grounds regarding ABA requirements, and that the problems were of such magnitude that a new structure might have to be built.[4102] The problem came to light in 1986 when the faculty adopted a long-range plan that included the need for additional library space.[4103] According to Librarian Emeritus Lamar Woodard, "the ABA picked it up and said, in effect, you say you need to do this, now when are you going to do it?"[4104] Woodard, Jacob, and Stetson architect Charles Canerday (whom Jacob had hired) visited law libraries in Chicago, Washington, D.C., Indiana, Virginia, and Arizona. "We spent a lot of time thinking about what we wanted to do," Woodard notes,[4105] adding, "He [Canerday] really came to understand what a law library was all about." Woodard concluded that Canerday "was able to design a building that got virtually everything we wanted."[4106] Moody pointed out, however, that the plans were significantly modified after she became dean.

In the early 1990s, a few people at the law school felt that a new building would be a waste of money, arguing that "libraries are going out of business, they will be totally eliminated in the future." In 2005, Woodard commented: "That, of course, didn't happen and it hasn't happened."[4107] Moody concurred: "Despite the fact that we now have all kinds of computers, law libraries are essential to a law school."[4108] She recognized that a library is not just a place for books, but is a place where students go to study—often in small groups where they discuss and think about law-related subjects surrounded by books. "The atmosphere of a library," Moody observed, "is useful to producing good lawyers."[4109]

By the time Moody became dean, Jacob, Woodard, and Canerday were well along in planning for a new library structure. But the University's central administration and a few members of the law faculty remained reluctant, preferring to expand and remodel the existing Dana Law Library.[4110] Moody told

---

4102. Memo. Lizabeth Moody, Dean Emeritus & Distinguished U. Prof., Stetson U. College of L., to W. Gary Vause, Dean, Stetson U. College of L. 1 (n.d) (circa 2001) [hereinafter *Moody-Vause Memo*].

4103. *Woodard Interview*, *supra* n. 3093, at 38.

4104. *Id.*

4105. *Id.* at 39.

4106. *Id.*

4107. *Id.* at 40.

4108. *Moody Interview*, *supra* n. 4065, at 37.

4109. *Id.*

4110. *Id.*

President Lee that the old building could not support "the kind of technology necessary for a modern law school,"[4111] a point with which Woodard agreed.[4112] "I argued," Moody noted, "that there was no way to have a first-rate law school without a totally new library."[4113] Earlier, Jacob also had urged that a new structure was necessary and had worked closely with Canerday and Woodard in its planning. But the final decision to go ahead was reached only during Moody's administration, when the University Board of Trustees and College Board of Overseers voted for construction of a new law library.

Working with architect Canerday, librarian Woodard, and business manager Joe Estenes, Moody oversaw the redoing of the building's exterior and interior design, a process that saw Jacob's original building plan downsized due to financial limitations. Even so, the new library turned out to cost more than nine million dollars.

At one point, Canerday told Moody that to build the new library in the Mediterranean Revival style consistent with the existing campus buildings would be too costly, noting that the tile roof alone would cost over a million dollars. Moody held firm, telling the architect, "Why not just do it?"[4114] As to the interior configuration, Moody insisted that the new structure have at least twenty study rooms for students, in addition to conference and seminar rooms.[4115] She explained: "I have something in mind where students can work on team projects, where they can work together in study groups, small rooms that will take four to six students.[4116]

The new library was finished in the summer of 1998, and it was everything Moody, Jacob, and the faculty had hoped it would be. The three-floor, 58,000-square-foot, state-of-the-art newly named Stetson Law Library and Information Center dazzled University and College administrators, trustees, overseers, students, alumni, and visitors.[4117] Accommodating not only the school's 350,000 and growing hard-bound book collection, but also thousands of government documents, and other traditional resource materials, the new center contained nineteen student group study rooms, 130 individual study carrels,

4111. *Moody-Vause Memo*, *supra* n. 4102, at 1.

4112. *Woodard Interview*, *supra* n. 3093, at 40, 41.

4113. *Moody-Vause Memo*, *supra* n. 4102, at 1.

4114. *Moody Interview*, *supra* n. 4058, at 40.

4115. *Id.*

4116. *Id.*

4117. Jeffrey T. Spoeri, *Stetson's New Library and Information Center Opens to Rave Reviews, Justice Ginsberg's Address at Dedication Praises the College's Technological and Scholarly Accomplishments*, 39 Stetson Law. 4, 5 (Fall 1998/Summer 1999) [hereinafter Spoeri, *New Library*].

four seminar rooms, eight conference rooms, and two computer classrooms with eighteen workstations in each.[4118] Moreover, the "stacks" were moveable (called "compact shelving") which, Woodard noted, allowed for future expansion of the College's collection "for thirty to thirty-five years."[4119] Every seat in the library was wired for connections with laptop computers, while each seminar and conference room was equipped with audiovisual equipment and wired for network access.[4120] Thus, Stetson's new Law Library and Information Center was both a functional and visual success. And, perhaps, of most significance, it was user friendly.

In comparison with its predecessor—where the majority of seats often went unoccupied—the new library burst with activity. One professor observed that whenever he entered, it seemed full of students who were working together in small rooms or individually at computerized desks.[4121] In addition, they were using the services of the research librarians; taking computer training classes; participating in seminars; attending various meeting and conferences; preparing for class; drafting legal documents; writing research papers; and, of course, using the vast resource materials available. Moody exclaims, that "yes, the new library draws the students there."[4122]

On December 5, 1998, on a stifling hot afternoon, more than 1,000 people attended the dedication of the Stetson Law Library and Information Center.[4123] Though the onlookers were extremely uncomfortable due to the heat and humidity, they came to hear U.S. Supreme Court Associate Justice Ruth Bader Ginsburg give the dedicatory address. Justice Ginsburg praised Stetson University College of Law for investing in the new, high-technology facility, and for making it a center for scholarship.[4124]

Funds for the new library came from several sources. The gifts included a $125,000 contribution from Barnett Charities, Inc., and Barnett Bank for a

4118. *Id.* at 6–7.

4119. *Woodard Interview, supra* n. 3093, at 40, 41.

4120. Spoeri, *New Library*, supra n. 4117, at 7.

4121. *Moody Interview, supra* n. 4065, at 37.

4122. *Id.* at 58.

4123. Spoeri, *New Library, supra* n. 4117, at 4.

4124. *Id.* at 5, 40. The platform party included Stetson University President Douglas Lee; College of Law Dean Lizabeth Moody; Board of Overseers President William Blews; U.S. District Court Chief Judge Elizabeth Kovachevich; Florida Supreme Court Chief Justice Major Harding; Associate Florida Supreme Court Justice Ben Overton; Stetson Professor, Law Librarian, and Director of Information Services Lamar Woodard; Gulfport, Florida, City Manager Robert Lee; St. Petersburg Bar Association President Pamela Campbell; Stetson Student Bar Association President Rhett Bullard; and Architect Charles Canerday.

Justice Ruth Bader Ginsburg at Library Dedication

business and banking collection in the new library.[4125] Sam Davis, II, president and CEO of Barnett Bank of Pinellas County, presented the gift to Dean Moody.[4126] Andrew Barnes, president and editor of the *St. Petersburg Times,* announced that the newspaper was giving $100,000 for the library.[4127] "Stetson law school is increasingly distinguished," Barnes noted, adding "we are proud to be able to continue backing its success."[4128] Another $100,000 donation came from alumnus Robert P. Rosin, class of '59, in memory of his parents, Marcus A. and Elsie P. Rosin.[4129] Law school alumnus John Guyton, '59, was chair of the development committee.[4130]

After Gary Vause succeeded Lizabeth Moody as dean in the fall of 1999, he asked her to describe what she felt was her most significant contribution to the law school during her deanship. Without hesitation, Moody replied. "The library."[4131]

d. An Interfaith Chapel and Meditation Room

The new library was the largest physical change on the campus during Moody's administration. The smallest was the conversion of a room in the

4125. *Recent Major Gifts*, 35 Stetson Law. 1, 1 (Fall 1995) [hereinafter *Recent Gifts*].

4126. *Id.*

4127. Brian Thomas, St. Petersburg Times *Commits $100,000 to Stetson College of Law* 1 (Stetson U. College of L. Mar. 31, 1995) (news release).

4128. *Id.*

4129. *Recent Gifts*, *supra* n. 4125, at 1.

4130. *Id.*

4131. *Moody-Vause Memo*, *supra* n. 4102, at 1.

Stetson Inn into an "Interfaith Chapel and Meditation Room." Ironically, it was the more controversial. The idea of a chapel arose during Jacob's deanship, when the Stetson chapter of the Christian Legal Society (SCLS) and its president, Frederick Graves, suggested the College offer space for prayer on the Gulfport campus to be accessible to students, faculty, and staff.[4132] Jacob was not persuaded, and nothing happened for several years. In the fall of 1995, after Moody became dean, the SCLS again broached the subject. Believing that the religious tradition and heritage of the University should be honored, Moody suggested that Room 308 (10 feet by 15 feet) in the Central Tower be converted for use as a chapel.[4133]

Though the dean favored the conversion,[4134] several faculty members opposed the idea, in particular Mark Brown.[4135] He urged his colleagues to squash the chapel plan, arguing that student tuition should not be used to support religion, that the name "chapel" relates only to the Christian religion, and that an educational institution not affiliated with a specific religious body should not align itself with religion in any manner.[4136] Brown told a *St. Petersburg Times* reporter, "The mission of a law school is legal education, not theology."[4137] Brown also carried his message to the student body.[4138] Those who spoke up were split on the chapel proposal; some suggested that an area on campus be set aside for reflection, prayer, and meditation, but not to call it a chapel.[4139]

Whereas Brown was the most vocal opponent to the chapel idea, Professor Swygert argued in behalf of the proponents.[4140] "In our drive to be tolerant of

---

4132. Ltr. from Michael I. Swygert, Prof. Emeritus, Stetson U. College of L., to H. Douglas Lee, Pres. Stetson U. 1 (Feb. 29, 1996) (on file at Stetson U. College of L., Gulfport, Fla.) [hereinafter *Lee Letter*].

4133. Nicole Piscopo, *Chapel Unable to Clear Its Name*, St. Pete. Times B-8 (Apr. 13, 1996) [hereinafter Piscopo, *Chapel*].

4134. *Moody-Vause Memo*, *supra* n. 4102, at 2.

4135. Piscopo, *Chapel*, *supra* n. 4133, at 8.

4136. *Id.*

4137. *Id.*

4138. *Id.*

4139. *Id.*

4140. At one point during the campus dialogue, Professors Brown and Swygert were invited by Rev. Pat Roberts of the Christian Broadcasting Network (CBN) to appear on "national television" and be interviewed about the Stetson "chapel controversy." Both agreed to do so, and a CBN reporter and crew from CBN's headquarters in Virginia Beach, Virginia, came to Stetson on May 1, 1996, to conduct the interviews. Segments appeared on an evening edition of the Pat Robert's CBN news. *See* Ltr. from Michael I. Swygert, Prof. Emeritus, Stetson U. College of L., to David Snyder, Congressional Correspondent, Christian Broad. Network (Apr. 20, 1996) (on file at Stetson U. College of L., Gulfport, Fla.).

all things," Swygert told the *St. Petersburg Times,* "somehow we're no longer tolerant of religion," adding, "soon we may learn that the University of Chicago faculty have renamed Rockefeller Chapel, the 'People's Multi-Purpose Edifice.'"[4141] Stetson's Student Bar Association endorsed the idea that an area simply be designated a "reflection room."[4142] The majority of the faculty voted that though a room could be used for prayer, reflection, or meditation, it should have no name.[4143]

Dean Moody forwarded both the faculty's no-name recommendation and the SBA's reflection room ideas to President Lee, who took them to the Executive Committee of the Board of Trustees.[4144] Taking an interesting spin on linguistic compromise, the Board's Executive Committee officially named room 308 in the Central Tower of the Stetson Inn, the "Interfaith Chapel and Meditation Room."[4145]

e. Faculty and Staff

During Moody's five-year administration, five full-time new faculty members joined the faculty, while eight visitors and several research and writing instructors were hired. In the summer of 1995, Darby Dickerson came to Stetson to teach legal research and writing.[4146] Within a year of her arrival, Moody appointed Dickerson director of Stetson's legal research and writing program. She later would become associate dean, vice dean, interim dean, then vice president and dean of Stetson University College of Law.[4147]

When Moody became Stetson's new dean in the summer of 1995, she brought with her from Cleveland Lynn A. Howell to be assistant dean, appointing her an administrative sub-dean only.[4148] In Cleveland, Howell had served as counsel to the Cleveland Bar Association, working in the areas of bar admissions, alternative dispute resolution, and the Commission on Women in

4141. *Id.*

4142. Ltr. from Members of Leg. Council, Student B. Assoc., Stetson U. College of L., to Michael I. Swygert, Prof. Emeritus, Stetson U. College of L. (Mar. 6, 1966) (emphasis in the original).

4143. Lee Letter, *supra* n. 4132, at 1.

4144. Paula J. Reed, *University Trustees Name Room at College of Law* 1 (Stetson U. College of L. Aug. 19, 1996) (news release).

4145. *Id.*

4146. *New Faculty Member Joins Stetson*, 35 Stetson Law. 21, 21 (Fall 1995).

4147. *See infra* nn. 4401–4479 and accompanying text.

4148. *Stetson Welcomes New Assistant Dean, Lynn A. Howell*, 35 Stetson Law. 20, 20 (Fall 1995).

Judge Mary S. Scriven

Law.[4149] She earned her J.D. degree from Cleveland-Marshall.[4150] She left Stetson in 2003.

During Moody's first full year as dean, she and the faculty hired three new professors and three instructors. They were Mary S. Scriven, Peter L. Fitzgerald, Julian R. Kossow, Stephanie A. Vaughan, Marsha B. Freeman, and Timothy Blevins.[4151] All began in the fall of 1996. Freeman and Blevins remained for only a short time, as did Scriven, while Fitzgerald, Kossow, and Vaughan stayed on.[4152]

(i) Mary Scriven joined the Stetson law faculty as a visiting professor of law on leave from Carlton, Fields, Wards, Emmanuel, Smith & Cutler.[4153] She earned an A.B. degree *cum laude* from Duke University, and a J.D. with honors from Florida State, and had clerked for the Honorable William Stafford, Judge, U.S. District Court for the Northern District of Florida.[4154] Scriven was at Stetson only briefly, however, as she accepted an offer to become a Magistrate Judge in the U.S. District Court for the Middle District of Florida, a position she holds today.[4155]

4149. *Id.* at 21.

4150. *Id.*

4151. Bishop, *List*, *supra* n. 2351, at 10–12.

4152. *Id.*

4153. *College of Law Welcomes New Faculty and Visitors, Mary S. Scriven*, 36 Stetson Law. 29, 29 (Fall 1996).

4154. *Id.*

4155. *Id.*

Peter L. Fitzgerald

(ii) Peter Lanston Fitzgerald spent fifteen years in the corporate legal department of International Business Machines (IBM) before joining the Stetson law faculty.[4156] At IBM, he was Counsel to IBM's Export Regulations Office, Washington, D.C.; a competition law specialist at IBM's European Headquarters, Paris, France; and a member of the litigation staff at IBM's Corporate Headquarters in Armonk, New York.[4157] Prior to his corporate work, Fitzgerald spent eight years in the U.S. Naval Reserve Intelligence Program, where he was assigned as a geopolitical analyst at the Navy's European Headquarters in London, and as Assistant Naval Attache for the Defense Attache's Office at the U.S. Embassy in Brussels.[4158]

Fitzgerald earned a B.A. degree in 1973 from the College of William & Mary; a J.D. degree in 1976 from the University of California, Hastings College of Law; and an LL.M. degree in European Legal Studies in 1981 from the University of Exeter in England.[4159] He also engaged in post-graduate research at the London School of Economics in 1977.[4160] At Stetson, he has taught international law, international business transactions, international trade regulation, electronic commerce law, and contracts.[4161] Fitzgerald's knowledge and teaching expertise in international law have become widely known, teaching at the Innsbruck Institute on World Trade Problems (summer 2003), and at

4156. *College of Law Welcomes New Visitors, Peter Lanston Fitzgerald,* 36 Stetson Lawyer 29 (Fall 1966) [hereinafter *College Welcomes*].

4157. Peter L. Fitzgerald, *Curriculum Vitae*, 2 (2005) (on file at Stetson U. College of L., Gulfport, Fla.) [hereinafter Fitzgerald, *Curriculum Vitae*].

4158. *Id.*

4159. *College Welcomes*, *supra* n. 4156, at 29.

4160. Fitzgerald, *Curriculum Vitae*, *supra* n. 4157, at 2.

4161. *Id.*

the Scandinavian/Baltic Institute on Emerging Markets in Tallin, Estonia (summer 2004).[4162] In addition, he was hired by George Washington University Law School in Washington, D.C., as an adjunct professor to teach international law.[4163]

In the spring of 2003, Fitzgerald was awarded a Fulbright grant to lecture at the University of Edinburgh.[4164] There, he developed a course in international trade and information technology law at the University's Arts & Humanities Research Board, Centre for Studies in Intellectual Property and Technology Law.[4165] Following his time in Scotland, Fitzgerald had high praise for the Fulbright program, noting: "It's clear that the exchange of views and the lasting ties the Fulbright program promotes are vitally important in today's increasingly complex and fractious world."[4166]

His international connections include: arbitrator on NAFTA Bi-National Dispute Resolution Panels, and a member of the NAFTA's International Roster; a member of Swedish Foreign Ministry Ad Hoc Working Group on Legal Safeguards and Targeted Sanctions; a member on the International Advisory Board, Sanctions Watch; and a director of the American Society of Comparative Law.[4167] He writes and speaks widely on international trade and technology issues. As one example, Fitzgerald addressed the U.S. economics sanction program at Jesus College, Cambridge University, at an International Symposium on Economic Crime[4168] and has testified before a congressionally created Judicial Review Commission on Foreign Assets Control.[4169]

At Stetson, Fitzgerald received the Homer and Dolly Hand Award for Excellence in Faculty Scholarship.[4170] He has co-authored a casebook on international business transactions and has written numerous articles, the publishers of which include the *Hastings Law Journal, Cornell International Law Journal, Vanderbilt Journal on Transnational Law, Temple International & Comparative Law Journal, New England Law Review, International Lawyer,*

4162. *Id.*

4163. *Id.*

4164. Frank Klim, *Stetson University College of Law Professor Receives Fulbright Scholar Award* 1 (Stetson U. College of L. Apr. 3, 2003) (news release) [hereinafter Klim, *Fitzgerald Fulbright*].

4165. *Id.*

4166. *Id.*

4167. Fitzgerald, *Curriculum Vitae, supra* n. 4157, at 3, 5.

4168. *Faculty Features,* 41 Stetson Law. 39, 40 (Spring/Summer 2001).

4169. Klim, *Fitzgerald Fulbright, supra* n. 4164, at 1.

4170. Fitzgerald, *Curriculum Vitae, supra* n. 4157, at 3.

and the *Foreign Service Journal*.[4171] Fitzgerald (along with Gary Vause, Lizabeth Moody, Luz Nagle, Dorothea Beane, Roy Gardner, Judge Alexander Paskay, and John Cooper) helped thrust Stetson College of Law into the global community.[4172]

(iii) Julian R. Kossow was hired in 1996 as an associate visiting professor to teach property and trusts and estates. A graduate of the University of Pennsylvania (B.A., 1955), and Georgetown University Law Center (J.D., 1967), Kossow clerked for Chief Judge David Bazelon of the U.S. Court of Appeals for the District of Columbia.[4173] He joined the faculty of Georgetown law school in 1969, where he remained through 1975, excepting one year when he taught at Haile Sellassie University in Addis Ababa, Ethiopia.[4174]

Kossow practiced in a Milwaukee law firm before becoming president of Kossow Development Company in Sarasota, Florida, a corporation he headed for eighteen years.[4175] Then, in 1994, he joined St. Thomas School of Law in Miami as visiting professor, then transferred to Stetson in 1996.[4176] During his years at Stetson, Kossow several times was named by the students the school's outstanding teacher. In 2004, Kossow left Stetson and became the Bode Visiting Professor of Law at Marquette University Law School in Milwaukee.[4177]

(iv) Stephanie E. Vaughan received her undergraduate degree at the University of Alabama, and in 1991 graduated from Stetson College of Law with honors.[4178] In law school, Vaughan was comments editor of the *Stetson Law Review*.[4179] She joined the Stetson faculty in 1996 as an adjunct, but soon became a full-time research and writing instructor.[4180] In 2000, Dean Gary Vause promoted Vaughan to be the associate director of Stetson's research and writing program, as well as the advisor to the school's moot court program.[4181] In the spring of 2005, Vaughan and Professor Jack Graves coached a Stetson moot court team to the world championship at an international competition in Vienna, Austria, in which 150 law schools competed from forty-seven coun-

4171. *Id.* at 2, 3.

4172. *See infra* nn. 4224–4245 and accompanying notes.

4173. *College of Law Welcomes New Faculty, Julian Kossow*, 36 Stetson Law., 29, 30 (Fall 1966) [hereinafter *Kossow Welcome*].

4174. *AALS 2004–2005 Directory*, *supra* n. 3045, at 655.

4175. *Kossow Welcome*, *supra* n. 4173, at 30.

4176. *AALS 2004–2005 Directory*, *supra* n. 3045, at 655.

4177. *Id.*

4178. *Faculty Forum*, 36 Stetson Law. 26, 31 (Fall 1996).

4179. *Id.* at 31.

4180. *Id.*

4181. Bishop, *List*, *supra* n. 2351, at 12.

Stephanie E. Vaughan

tries.[4182] (Stetson's world championship is discussed in more detail below.)[4183] In August 2005, Dean Dickerson appointed Vaughan director of the Tampa Law Center and acting director of the Legal Research and Writing program.

(v) Luz Estella Nagle is the only person in the 105-year history of Stetson University College of Law who has been the target of assassins, not once, but twice, before joining the faculty. Nagle was a judge in Medellin, Colombia, (her hometown) when the two attempts on her life occurred when her town was terrorized by drug lords.[4184] The terrorists especially went after judges who handled drug trafficking cases, as Nagle did.[4185] A story in the *Stetson Lawyer* describes her near assassinations:

> In October 1985, a gunman entered her office. Instinctively, she dropped to the floor and fired her pistol [which the police had previously issued her for protection], wounding her assailant. Only one month later, a motorcycle gunman pulled alongside her car and fired an automatic weapon. Fortunately, the young judge swerved her car, causing the [would-be] assassin to miss his mark.[4186]

4182. *World Champions*, 45 Stetson Law. 24 (Spring 2005) [hereinafter *World Champions*]

4183. *See infra* nn. 4448–4461 and accompanying text.

4184. "*La Chicita Bonita, Pero Bravita*", 35 Stetson Law. 16, 17 (Fall 2003) [hereinafter *La Chicita*].

4185. *Id.*

4186. *Id.* at 16.

Luz Estella Nagle

In Colombia, Nagle became known as "La chiquita bonita, pero bravita," or "the pretty, but brave little woman." Though she had for three years survived as a judge, after her brushes with death, Nagle decided to leave Colombia and, in 1986, came to the United States. She lived in California and did manual labor and worked as a private investigator while earning a graduate degree at U.C.L.A.[4187]

Though Nagle had earned a law degree (LL.D.) from the Universidad Pontificia Boliviariana in South America, to practice law in the United States she had to start law school over. In 1995, she earned a J.D. degree from William & Mary College of Law.[4188] Afterwards, she clerked on the Supreme Court of Virginia for two years, then worked for Microsoft Corporation as a commercial anti-piracy specialist in Ft. Lauderdale, Florida, prior to joining the Stetson faculty in 1998.[4189]

At Stetson, Nagle assisted in the school's establishing foreign programs, including one in Granada, Spain, where she taught one summer.[4190] She also has taught students at Andes Law School in Bogota, Colombia.[4191] In recognition of Nagle's international contributions, Dean Vause presented Nagle in 2000

4187. *Id.*

4188. *AALS 2004–2005 Directory*, *supra* n. 3045, at 795.

4189. *Id.* at 2.

4190. *Faculty News, Luz Estella Nagle*, 43 Stetson Law. 11, 12 (Spring 2003).

4191. *Id.*

the Dean's Award for Service to the College of Law.[4192] A prolific writer, the following year, she received the Homer and Dolly Hand Award for Excellence in Faculty Research.[4193] In December 2004, Nagle became the first Hispanic professor in the history of Stetson University College of Law to attain tenure.[4194] There, she has taught comparative business law, international criminal law, international law, and Latin American business law. Moreover, she has been active in various world organizations and as an advisor to governmental bodies, including: a member of Women in International Trade; co-chair of the International Bar Association; consultant to the Center for Terrorism; editor of the Journal of Iberoamerican Security; consultant to the FBI counter-terrorism team on Columbia; and a representative of the U.S. Department of Defense at both the Columbia War College and the Colombia Judge Advocate General School.[4195] Examples of Nagle's scholarship include: "Placing Blame Where Blame Is Due: The Culpability of Illegal Armed Groups and Narcotraffickers" in the *William & Mary Environmental Law & Policy Review*; and "Columbia Asylum Seekers" in the *Georgetown Immigration Law Journal*.[4196] In addition to writing, Nagle speaks at conferences and is a participant in panels and symposia, one being the Harvard-MIT Club of Bogota.[4197]

(vi) Richard B. Graves III, another new hire during Moody's deanship, earned four degrees: a B.A. from Washington & Lee, 1987; a J.D. from Stetson, 1991; an LL.M., Tulane, 2000; and an LL.M., Stetson, 2002.[4198] In addition to instructing legal research and writing, he has taught contracts and advanced legal research. During the 2004–05 and 2005–06 academic years, Graves was a visiting assistant professor at the University of Arkansas School of Law, Little Rock.[4199] Before joining the Stetson faculty, he served as judicial clerk on the U.S. District Court in New Orleans, and practiced law with a Houston, Texas, law firm.[4200] At Stetson, Graves authored articles published in national law reviews, and has received the Charles B. Seton Award in 2004 for his arti-

4192. *La Chicita*, *supra* n. 4184, at 16.

4193. *Id.*

4194. *See Nagle Becomes Stetson's First Hispanic Full Law Professor*, 45 Stetson Law. 13, 13 (Summer 2005); *Stetson Law Professor's Hard Ascent*, St. Pete. Times B-1 (Dec. 20, 2004).

4195. *Faculty Recent Publications, Presentations, Awards, and Activities, Luz E. Nagle*, 44 Stetson Law. 8, 11 (Fall 2004).

4196. *Id.*

4197. *Faculty Forum, Luz E. Nagle*, 44 Stetson Law. 12, 12 (Spring 2004).

4198. *AALS 2004–2005 Directory*, *supra* n. 3045, at 526.

4199. *Id.*

4200. *Id.*

cle "Globalization, Treaty Powers, and the Limits of the Intellectual Property Clause," published in the *Journal of the Copyright Society of the United States.*[4201]

(vii) Lawrence D. Rosenthal joined the faculty in 1998 as an instructor and associate director of Stetson's legal research and writing program.[4202] He earned a J.D. from Vanderbilt and an LL.M. from Georgetown. After five years at Stetson, Rosenthal left to become assistant professor of legal writing at Northern Kentucky University College of Law.[4203]

In addition to Vaughan, Graves, and Rosenthal, other legal research and writing instructors hired during the Moody administration included: Timothy Blevins, J.D., Thurgood Marshall School of Law, Houston;[4204] and Marsha Freeman, J.D., Touro College of Law, where she was visiting professor of legal research and writing.[4205]

Visiting faculty at Stetson during Moody's deanship included: Ester Kim; Jeffrey Grebe; Patricia B. Fry (Edward W. Hinton Professor of Law, University of Missouri, Columbia);[4206] Kimberly Colgate; Sandra L. Degraw (Professor of Law, South Texas College of Law);[4207] Carolyn Kinelski;[4208] and Edward D. Ohlbaum, who held the Culverhouse Chair visitorship in the spring semester of 1999.[4209] Ohlbaum, a trial-advocacy specialist, came to Stetson the year after William Eleazer had retired as head of the school's advocacy program.[4210] Ohlbaum was director of one of the country's top advocacy programs (in addition to Stetson), the one at Temple University School of Law in Philadelphia.[4211]

As regards the professional librarian staff, when Moody became dean, Lamar Woodard was the librarian. Other professional staff included: Pamela D. Burdett, Assistant Librarian for Public Services (B.A., Governors State University; M.A.L.I.S., University of South Florida); Dorothy Clark, Assistant Librarian for Public Services, (B.A., Boston University, M.L.S., Simmons College); Earlene Kuester, Series/Documents Librarian; (B.A., University of

4201. *Recent Publications, Richard B. Graves, III*, 44 Stetson Law. 8, 10 (Fall 2004).

4202. *AALS 2004–2005 Directory*, *supra* n. 3045, at 484.

4203. *Id.*

4204. *Stetson Strengthens Legal Research and Writing Program*, 36 Stetson Law. 30, 30 (Fall 1996).

4205. *Id.*

4206. *AALS 2004–2005 Directory*, *supra* n. 3045, at 484.

4207. *Id.* at 403.

4208. Bishop, *List*, *supra* n. 2351, at 10–13.

4209. *Id.*

4210. *See* Jacob, *Report on Deanship*, *supra* n. 3239, at 53.

4211. *Id.*

Wisconsin, M.A.L.I.S., University of South Florida); Madison Mosely, Reference Librarian, later to become head librarian, (B.A., Florida State University, M.L.S., University of North Carolina, Ph.D., Florida State University, J.D., Stetson University); Sally Waters, Reference Librarian (discussed earlier) (B.A., M.L.S., J.D., University of South Carolina);[4212] and Roman Yoder, Assistant Librarian for Technical Services (B.A., University of South Florida, M.L.S., Florida State University).[4213]

Yoder was well liked and highly respected by both the library staff and the faculty at Stetson law school. Often he took charge of the library when Woodard was away.[4214] Tragically, Yoder died of kidney disease. Reference Librarian Pamela Burdett recalled that Yoder "loved bluegrass music and he enjoyed philosophy and religion."[4215] His death deeply impacted faculty, staff, and students across the campus.

f. Professor Calvin Kuenzel Dies

On June 21, 1998, Stetson College of Law's most remembered teacher died at the age of seventy: Calvin A. Kuenzel, the L. LeRoy Highbaugh, Sr., Professor of Law.[4216] His Stetson career had spanned forty years.[4217] Moody expressed the sentiments of many: "Cal really was Stetson for all intents and purposes. He personified the Stetson law school experience for literally thousands of students, and his courses remain the most vivid memories for many of our graduates."[4218]

At a memorial service on August 21, several speakers praised Kuenzel, including University President Lee, who commented: "Without question, Cal Kuenzel was one of the landmark figures in Stetson University's history," adding, "he was easily the most feared and most loved man I ever heard described."[4219] The *Stetson Lawyer* quoted Professor Swygert: "I think that Calvin was an incomparable teacher of life," adding that "some people would say he taught contracts, but I think Cal taught deeper and more profound

4212. *See supra* nn. 3857–60 and accompanying text.

4213. *Library Staff*, 1995–1996 Bulletin 84 (Stetson U. College of L. 1995).

4214. Interview by Michael I. Swygert, Prof. Emeritus, Stetson U. College of L., with Pamela D. Burdett, Reference Libr., Stetson U. College of L. 17 (May 20, 2005).

4215. *Id.* at 18, 19.

4216. *Professor Calvin A. Kuenzel, 1928–1998*, 39 Stetson Law. 8, 8 (Fall 1988/Winter 1999).

4217. *Id.*

4218. *Id.*

4219. *Id.* at 9.

lessons."[4220] On a less serious note, Stetson alumnus William Blews added humor to the otherwise somber occasion, when he commented:

> [W]hen I first heard of Cal's death, I had this vision of Cal up at the Pearly Gates talking to St. Peter, reviewing his life, and St. Peter asking Cal why he should be admitted, to which, of course, Cal replied, "I don't know, what do you think?"[4221]

A plaque from an anonymous donor read:

> "What are you?" A question asked by Professor Kuenzel of first-year law students taking his contracts case. One student arrived at the answer long after the question was asked and after much thought: "I am my word." Professor Kuenzel taught us more than the laws—he taught us how to live it.[4222]

Other speakers at the Memorial Service included Rhett Bullard, judges Susan Schaeffer and David Patterson, and professors Bradford Stone and Thomas Marks, Jr.[4223]

g. *Stetson Expands Globally*

During Dean Jacob's administration, Professor Gary Vause began to teach a course in international business transactions.[4224] He realized that Stetson had an opportunity, Vause explained:

> I had taught International Business Transactions since 1985, and I could see that there was growing interest. I began to push hard for summer programs with foreign universities, for official visitation programs, and for an LL.M. program in international law. They all came to fruition.[4225]

In 1989, Gary Vause and his colleague John Cooper traveled to China to teach a two-month program in American law at the Beijing School of Eco-

---

4220. *Id.*

4221. *Id.*

4222. *Id.*

4223. *Id.*

4224. John F. Cooper, "*Gary, We Hardly Knew Ye*", 33 Stetson L. Rev. 7, 9 (2003) (part of a tribute titled *A Tribute to Dean W. Gary Vause* following his death due to cancer in the spring of 2003) [hereinafter Cooper, *Vause Tribute*].

4225. Frank Klim, *A Life of Service,* 33 Stetson L. Rev. 35, 35 (2003) (part of a tribute to Dean W. Gary Vause following his death from cancer in the spring of 2003) [hereinafter Klim, *Life of Service*].

nomics.[4226] Vause, who had taught in China several times earlier, once as a Fulbright scholar, was fluent in Mandarin Chinese.[4227] He had also taught in Brazil, where he lectured on international law in Portuguese, another language he had mastered after marrying his wife Celia (who is a native of Brazil).[4228] Vause wrote in Spanish and had a working knowledge of Russian.[4229] In 1992, he visited the Korean University Law School in Seoul, South Korea, with Stetson students Mike Choi and P.J. Bradley, to discuss the feasibility of cooperative projects between the Korean school and Stetson.[4230]

Perhaps because of his exposure to cultural diversity, Vause actively campaigned for Stetson's greater involvement in international law and for the school affording opportunities for its students to study in other countries. After Moody became dean, she appointed Vause associate dean of Stetson University College of Law,[4231] and in 1997, named him associate dean for graduate and international programs.[4232] Moody at that time was Chair of the ABA Committee on Approval of Foreign Programs.[4233]

In his new position, Vause contacted officials at Concordia International University in Tallinn, Estonia, about the possibility of joint sponsorship of a summer program in that country.[4234] Following Vause's visit to Estonia, the dean of the Concordia University law school journeyed to Gulfport to meet with deans Moody and Vause, where they agreed to establish "Scandinavia-Baltic Summer Institute on the Law of Emerging Markets and Transitional Democracies."[4235] With ABA approval, Stetson College of Law opened its first international program for law study in Tallin, Estonia, in the summer of 1998.[4236] Moody explains:

> Estonia was chosen in part because Central and Eastern Europe are a crucible for change, where significant social, political, and economic events

---

4226. Cooper, *Vause Tribute*, *supra* n. 4224, at 9.

4227. *Id.*

4228. *Id.* at 8.

4229. Leslie Reicin Stein, *Tribute to Gary Vause, A Personal Remembrance*, in *W. Gary Vause: A Life of Service*, 42 Fla. B. Checklist 1, 14 (Sept. 2003).

4230. *Faculty Forum, W. Gary Vause*, 39 Stetson Law. 18, 19 (Winter 1993).

4231. *Gary Vause Named Associate Dean*, 35 Stetson Law. 20, 20 (Fall 1995).

4232. Klim, *Life of Service*, *supra* n. 4225, at 38.

4233. Elizabeth A. Moody, Dean Emeritus, Stetson U. College of L., *Written Comments on Earlier Draft of This Book's Manuscript* 930 (Oct. 2005) (on file with Michael I. Swygert, co-author).

4234. *Id.* at 11.

4235. Dean Lizabeth A. Moody, *Dean's Message, Stetson Expands to Global Arena*, 38 Stetson Law. 2, 3 (Spring 1977).

4236. *Id.* at 3.

> combine and resonate across the globe. [These] countries are again the focus of great interest as the Cold War era fades into history. Estonia ... [is] a trading bridge between East and West.[4237]

Later, Oklahoma City University School of Law joined with Stetson and Concordia International University to jointly sponsor the Scandinavian/Baltic Institute on Emerging Markets in Transitional Democracies in Estonia.[4238]

Stetson commenced a second international law summer program[4239] during Moody's administration in Granada, Spain; one which continues today.[4240] The Granada program also is co-sponsored by Oklahoma City University School of Law in cooperation with the University of Granada.[4241] Subsequent to Dean Dickerson's appointment of Professor Cooper in 2003 as Associate Dean of International and Graduate Programs, Stetson law school added additional summer abroad programs, including one in Buenos Aires, Argentina; Freiburg, Germany; and the Hague, Netherlands.[4242] Professor Dorothea Beane was involved in starting up the Freiburg—Hague programs.

During Moody's deanship, the College of Law began a graduate masters of laws (LL.M.) program in international law and business,[4243] a program open to graduates of accredited law schools. Described as "an intensive one-year course of study, it leads to an advanced legal degree in International Law & Business."[4244] The law school has also instituted a two-year program for foreign lawyers leading to an American juris doctor degree.[4245]

4237. *Id.*

4238. *See* Stetson U. College of L., Off. of Intl. Programs, *Announcement: The Scandinavian/Baltic Institute on Emerging Markets in Transitional Democracies Summer Program in Estonia* (2004) (brochure).

4239. Mark D. Killian, *Stetson's Dean Moody Steps Down*, Fla. B. News 17 (Nov. 1, 1998) [hereinafter Killian, *Dean Moody*].

4240. *See* Stetson U. College of L., Off. of Intl. Programs, *Announcement: International Dispute Resolution Summer Program in Granada* 1 (2005) (brochure).

4241. *Id.* at 3.

4242. *See* Stetson U. College of L., Off. of Intl. Programs, *Announcement: the Summer Institute on International Law, Buenos Aires* 1 (2005) (brochure); Stetson U. College of L., Off. of Intl. Programs, *Summer Institute on International Law, Freiburg, Hague* 1 (2005) (brochure).

4243. Brian Thomas, *Stetson Law Considers Adding Part-Time Program* 2 (Stetson U. College of L. Apr. 9, 1998) (news release) [hereinafter Thomas, *Stetson Part-Time Program*].

4244. Stetson U. College of L., *Catalog: The Masters of Law, International Law & Business* 2 (2005) (fourteen-page catalogue).

4245. Stetson U. College of L., Off. of Intl. Programs, *Announcement: Two-Year Juris Doctor for Foreign Lawyers* 1 (2005) (brochure).

h. Moody Plans for Part-Time Program; Becomes Distinguished University Professor

Dean Moody recognized that Stetson College of Law had an opportunity to fill a major gap in legal education in Florida, one that would be especially beneficial to the greater Tampa Bay area—an evening, part-time program leading to the juris doctor degree.[4246] Such a program would allow students to continue to work full-time while pursuing a law degree part-time over a four- to five-year period. In April 1998, Moody announced that Stetson was considering adding a part-time program, commenting that "the Tampa Bay metropolitan area is the only regional population center that has no part-time or evening professional law program."[4247]

The part-time program earlier had been approved by both the law faculty and University administration.[4248] The faculty, however, had been divided over doing so, some arguing that having an evening program "lowered" the status of a law school in the eyes of many legal educators.[4249] Still others felt the new program would burden the faculty, as it would entail additional sections of required courses leaving little room for teaching electives. A few faculty members were concerned that the evening program might best be located off the Gulfport campus, requiring considerable commuting time.

Moody had appointed a joint committee of administrators and faculty to study the feasibility of the program.[4250] The committee consisted of professors Marks, Latimer, Kossow, Reilly, Thurman, and Swygert (chair), along with administrators Vause (associate dean), Majewski (CLE director), Joe Estenes (business manager), and Moody.[4251] After months of investigating and compiling demographic information about Hillsborough, Pinellas, Polk, Bradenton, and Sarasota counties, as well as the Interstate 4 corridor from Tampa to Orlando, the committee decided that it would be feasible for Stetson to offer a part-time program, especially if it were located in Tampa.[4252] The committee presented its proposal to the faculty. After lengthy discussions, the faculty

---

4246. Thomas, *Stetson Part-Time Program*, *supra* n. 4243, at 2.

4247. *Id.*

4248. Lizabeth A. Moody, *The College of Law Vigorously Approaches Its Second Century*, 39 Stetson Law. 2, 3 (Fall 1998/Summer 1999) [hereinafter Moody, *Second Century*].

4249. Co-author Michael Swygert chaired the special subcommittee to study the feasibility of a Stetson part-time program. The information in this paragraph is based on his recollections as chair of the committee.

4250. Moody, *Second Century*, *supra* n. 4248, at 3.

4251. Jacob, *Recollections, supra* n. 1678.

4252. *Id.*

narrowly voted to support the school's pursuing a part-time program, but one that had to be located in either Tampa or at the school's Gulfport campus.[4253]

Not long after beginning her fifth year as dean, Moody publicly announced that she wanted to return to full-time teaching after the 1998–1999 academic year, and to devote more time to her duties as Chair of the ABA Committee on Accreditation.[4254] Stetson President Lee noted that Dean Moody had achieved all her goals that they jointly established when she became dean, and pointed to completion of the new 58,000-square-foot Law Library and Information Center.[4255] Lee announced that the University had established a "Distinguished University Professorship," and that he had named Moody its first recipient.[4256] William Blews, chair of the College of Law Board of Overseers, commented that Dean Moody "had provided very effective leadership for the College of Law and had worked hard to enhance the law school's national reputation."[4257]

14.2 Dean W. Gary Vause: Stetson Enters the New Millennium

a. The Cuban Missile Crisis and Mandarin Chinese

The Cold War was broiling. The Cuban Missile Crisis between the United States and the Soviet Union was escalating to a point of unthinkable consequences. Russia was shipping missiles with nuclear warheads to Cuba to be implanted and aimed at America only ninety miles away. To say international tensions were high is to minimize the realities, especially after President John F. Kennedy ordered a U.S. Naval blockade of Cuba for the interdiction of Russia's nuclear weapons crossing the Atlantic on Soviet warships. For a few days in October 1962, a horrific prospect was in everybody's minds—nuclear war.[4258] Fortunately for the world, the Cuban Missile crisis ended when the Soviet Union turned its warships away from Cuba, thereby avoiding a military confrontation with the United States.[4259]

4253. *Id.*

4254. Killian, *Dean Moody*, *supra* n. 4239, at 17.

4255. *Id.*

4256. *Id.*

4257. *Id.*

4258. Sheldon M. Stern, *The Week The World Stood Still: Inside the Secret Cuban Missile Crisis* 2–7 (Stanford U. Press 2005).

4259. *See* Max Frankel, *High Noon in the Cold War: Kennedy, Khrushchev, and the Cuban Missile Crisis* (Presidio Press 2004).

Dean W. Gary Vause

Though nuclear war had been avoided, other problems remained. The Soviet Union had years earlier developed a hydrogen bomb, exploding a small version in 1953, followed by what was called the "RDS37," a monster, in 1955.[4260] In 1962, at the time of the Cuban Missile Crisis, American intelligence knew that Communist China was developing nuclear weapons, including a possible hydrogen bomb, or "H-Bomb." Deeply concerned, the U.S. directed intelligence services to gather as much information as they could about China's activities regarding development of hydrogen-enhanced nuclear warheads.[4261]

Shortly after the Cuban missile crisis, a twenty-year old young man—born and bred in the rural outskirts of Tallahassee, Florida—interrupted his studies at Florida State University and enlisted in the United States Air Force.[4262] As per Air Force custom, the young enlistee took a battery of tests, which revealed not only that he was exceptionally bright, but that he also possessed a special ability in foreign languages. As a result, the Air Force sent twenty-year-old William Gary Vause to Yale University for intensive, total immersion lan-

---

4260. *See* Richard Rhodes, *Dark Sun: The Making of the Hydrogen Bomb* (Simon & Schuster 1966).

4261. *See* Robert J. Donovan, *The Devastating Time: Truman, the Hydrogen Bomb, China and Korea* (Princeton 1979).

4262. Klim, *Life of Service*, *supra* n. 4225, at 36.

guage training.[4263] There, he became fluent in Mandarin Chinese within a year.[4264] By doing so, he was able to join the U.S. gathering intelligence concerning Communist China's nuclear program. Given Vause's proficiency in Mandarin, the Air Force sent him to "listen in" on the People's Republic of China communications,[4265] aboard U.S. aircraft flying out of the Kadena Air Base in Okinawa, Japan.[4266]

b. Newspapers, College, and Law School

Growing up on a farm near Tallahassee, Vause surely never imagined that one day he would be flying along the coast of the world's largest country, halfway around the world, speaking a language probably rarely if ever spoken in northern Florida in those days, and monitoring war preparations of what was then America's second most powerful enemy. His ancestors moved to the Florida panhandle in the early 1800s. None had a college education.[4267]

Vause was born in northern Florida in 1942. His father worked as a laborer in logging camps, where, on occasion, Vause would work along side his dad. Stetson University College of Law Director of Communications Frank Klim interviewed Vause about his boyhood.[4268] Klim writes that Vause's father would ask him, "Son, do you like doing this kind of work?" Vause responded, "No, I don't," to which his father replied: "If you don't get an education, you'll be doing this the rest of your life."[4269]

And get an education the son did. But first, Vause needed to find the economic means to do so, as his family did not have financial resources to pay for his college education. To earn money, for four years he arose each morning at 4 a.m. to deliver the *Florida Times Union,* then go to public school, followed each afternoon by delivering the *Florida Tallahassee Democrat* to hundreds of subscribers.[4270] During this time period, he drove over 200,000 miles in a Volk-

---

4263. Cooper, *Vause Tribute, supra* n. 4224, at 8.

4264. *See* Cary R. Singletary, *W. Gary Vause: Educator, Scholar, and Southern Gentlemen, in Memoriam, A Tribute to Dean W. Gary Vause,* 33 Stetson L. Rev. 58 (2003) [hereinafter Singletary, *Vause Tribute*].

4265. Dean Gary Vause told Professor Michael Swygert at a dinner in the Vause home in January 2000 about his intelligence work in the Air Force, specifically explaining how he rode in U.S. aircraft monitoring Chinese communications (in Mandarin) for the purpose of learning about China's ongoing program in developing a hydrogen bomb.

4266. Cooper, *Vause Tribute, supra* n. 4224, at 8.

4267. *See* Klim, *Life of Service, supra* n. 4225, at 35, 36.

4268. *Id.* at 23–39.

4269. *Id.* at 35.

4270. *Id.* at 36.

swagen. Vause recalled: "I would remove the passenger seat to get all those papers into the VW."[4271] In this manner, he made himself financially able to be "the first member of his family to attend college."[4272]

Vause's newspaper-delivery years began when he was in high school and continued during his first two years at Florida State University. Then, as explained above, he left Florida State to enroll in the Air Force.[4273] After Vause was honorably discharged from the Air Force, he enrolled at the University of Connecticut (UCONN), where he earned a B.A. degree. Thereafter, he entered UCONN's law school, and in 1970 he received a J.D. degree.[4274] While a law student, Vause was special projects editor of the *Connecticut Law Review*. Years later, he earned two additional law degrees—an LL.M. and an S.J.D.—both from the University of Virginia.[4275]

After graduating from UCONN law school, Vause founded the law firm of Vause, Sullivan, Lettick & Schoen in Hartford, Connecticut, where he concentrated his practice in public sector labor relations, municipal, and school law. Almost immediately, UCONN law school contacted Vause and asked if he would teach labor law on a part-time basis.[4276] He was pleased to do so, while at the same time serving as General Counsel for the Connecticut Association of Boards of Education.[4277]

c. *After a Serendipitous Visit, Vause Comes to Stetson*

In 1974, Vause traveled to Tallahassee, where he took and passed the Florida bar exam. Afterwards, he drove to Tampa to visit his sister.[4278] One afternoon, they toured the Stetson College of Law campus in Gulfport. It turned out to be a pivotal event in Vause's career. He had heard about Stetson and wanted not only to see the campus, but also to meet Dean Richard Dillon. Vause told Stetson University College of Law Director of Communications Frank Klim about the fateful meeting:

4271. *Id.*

4272. *Id.*

4273. *See supra* n. 4262 and accompanying text.

4274. *A Life of Service, W. Gary Vause, University Vice President and Dean, 1942–2002,* 43 Stetson Law. 1, 25, 26 (Spring 2003) [hereinafter *Dean Vause 1942–2002*].

4275. *AALS 2002–2003 Law School Directory* 987 (2002).

4276. *W. Gary Vause: A Life of Service, the Checkoff,* 42 Fla. B. News 1 (Sept. 2003).

4277. *A Joint Resolution by The Board of Trustees Stetson University and The Board of Overseers Stetson University College of Law In Honor of W. Gary Vause, a Tribute to Gary Vause,* 33 Stetson L. Rev. 3 (Fall 2003).

4278. *Id.*

> [I] stopped by with no appointment, and there sits Dorothy Bishop [Dillon's secretary]. I asked her if the dean was available. She said, "Do you have an appointment?" I said, "Well, actually, I don't." She went in and talked to the dean and came back and told me the dean would see me ... Dillon asked me about a problem he had with a new federal [labor] law. In about 15 minutes, I gave him the answer he needed. So that's how we started our relationship, pure serendipity.[4279]

A few months later, Dillon invited Vause to join the Stetson law faculty to be his assistant dean. Vause accepted, and the Connecticut firm of Vause, Sullivan, Lettick & Schoen lost its founding partner.[4280] Vause recalled that as assistant dean, he "handled anything the dean needed me to handle, and taught one or two courses per semester,"[4281] adding that he and Dillon "made the decision to hire faculty members who could bring more scholarship and publication" to the school, thereby recognizing "the need to change the profile of Stetson."[4282]

Vause served not only as an administrator during Dillon's deanship, he also held administrative positions under both deans Jacob and Moody.[4283] His strategic importance in Stetson's global outreach and international programs for foreign study is difficult to overstate. Many of his contributions have been noted earlier.[4284]

When it was learned that Lizabeth Moody would be stepping down as dean at the end of the 1998–1999 academic year, Stetson University President Doug Lee appointed a dean search committee consisting of alumni, members of both the College Board of Overseers and University Trustees, faculty, and students.[4285] Professor John Cooper co-chaired the search committee along with Board of Overseers President and Stetson law alumnus Marsha Griffin Rydberg ('76). Cooper had been a member of the search committee that had recommended Lizabeth Moody to be dean five years earlier,[4286] while Rydberg had an established record as an outstanding lawyer and civic activist in the greater Tampa community.[4287]

4279. *Id.* at 13.
4280. *Id.*
4281. *Id.*
4282. *Id.*
4283. Klim, *A Life of Service*, *supra* n. 4225, at 39.
4284. *See supra* nn. 4224–4236 and accompanying text.
4285. Vause, *Centennial History*, *supra* n. 595, at 191.
4286. *See supra* n. 4091 and accompanying text.
4287. Jeff Maine, *Marsha Griffin Rydberg, '76*, 33 Stetson Lawyer 24 (Fall 1992).

The national search resulted in a number of deans from other law schools applying for the Stetson post. After the finalists had been interviewed by the law faculty and the president, and the faculty had communicated its views to Lee, the president announced that the new "University Vice President and Dean of the College of Law, effective June 1, 1999, was Professor William Gary Vause of the Stetson College of Law Faculty."[4288]

d. SBA, Law Review

After becoming dean, Vause, like Jacob, advanced the theme of "students first."[4289] He favored an active student government and supported the thirty odd student organizations on campus.[4290] Vause was pleased that Stetson's Calvin A. Kuenzel Student Bar Association was named the "Outstanding Student Bar Association in America" for the 1999–2000 academic year by the ABA Law Student Division.[4291]

Another student organization, the *Stetson Law Review,* in the spring of 2002 hosted the National Conference of Law Reviews (NCLR), a group comprised of about 150 law journals and reviews. The session was put together by editors of the *Stetson Law Review* along with Associate Dean Darby Dickerson. After the program was over, participants from the other schools told Stetson students and administrators that they were pleased with both the efficiency and quality of the conference, so much so, that they selected Stetson to be the NCLR's national headquarters for five years, beginning 2003.[4292]

e. BLSA: Stetson's Black Law Students Association

During the administrations of both deans Vause and Dickerson, Stetson's Black Law Students Association (BLSA) became one of the more active student organizations on campus. Stetson alumni, Amelia G. Govan and Malcolm J. L.

4288. Vause, *Centennial History, supra* n. 595, at 191.

4289. *Id.* at 192.

4290. *Id.*

4291. Karen Altieri. *Stetson Student Bar Association Named Top in Nation,* (Stetson U. College of L. July 11, 2000) (news release). The announcement reads in part: "The award recognizes the best overall student bar association in the country. This accolade was presented to Stetson during the ABA's annual meeting in New York City. 'I am so proud of our students. This award is the most coveted award of the ABA Law Student Division,' said Assistant Dean Lynn Howell. Accepting the award on behalf of Stetson recent graduates were Melissa McCullough, immediate past president, and Wendy Pepper, immediate past vice president of the Stetson SBA." *Id.*

4292. Frank Klim, *Stetson University College of Law Selected as National Headquarters for Law Review Organization* (Stetson U. College of L. Apr. 23, 2002) (news release).

Judge Amelia Govan

Harper, founded Stetson's BLSA in 1979–80.[4293] Today, Judge Govan is a federal administrative law judge with the Labor Standards Bureau for the District of Columbia.[4294] Judge Harper is the chief administrative judge of the Administrative Hearing Division of the District of Columbia's Labor Standards Bureau.

Since its founding, BLSA has grown to become a dynamic and influential student organization. In the fall of 1999, BLSA began an annual Judge Thomas Stringer Youth Day, named in honor of the first African-American who graduated from Stetson College of Law. The annual event is intended to draw minority pre-law high school and college students to Stetson's campus to participate in discussions about the opportunities for going to law school and for minority lawyers in America.[4295] In November 2003, the honoree at BLSA's fourth annual Judge Thomas Stringer Youth Day was Judge Thomas E. Stringer himself.[4296] In 2005, Stetson law professor Dorothea Beane gave the keynote address at the annual Judge Thomas Stringer Youth Pre-Law Conference, an event jointly sponsored by BLSA and the Hispanic Bar Association.[4297] The first BLSA pre-law conference took place in February 2003 in connection with the

4293. E-mail from Darby Dickerson, V.P. and Dean, Stetson U. College of L., to Michael I. Swygert, Prof. Emeritus, Stetson U. College of L. (Mar. 17, 2005).

4294. *Id.*

4295. Frank Klim, *Stetson Black Law Students Association Celebrate Third Annual Judge Stringer Youth Day* (Stetson U. College of L. Nov. 19, 2002) (news release).

4296. *Benchmarks*, 30 Fla. B. News 23 (Dec. 1, 2003).

4297. *Judge Thomas Stringer Youth Pre-Law Conference*, (Stetson U. College of L. Feb. 4, 2005) (recent events).

national Minority Law Student Recruitment Month.[4298] Stetson's Hispanic Bar Association assisted in the conference.

One of the more popular BLSA events for years has been an annual art exhibit, where "ethnic and cultural works of local artists," many of whom are African-Americans, are on display. BLSA invites the entire Stetson and Tampa Bay community to visit and see the works, many of which can be purchased.[4299] In time, the annual event was expanded to honor area judges. In 2003, BLSA presented an award to the Honorable Frank Howard White (who had just retired from Florida's Sixth Judicial Circuit). Judge White was a graduate of both Howard University and of the Florida A&M School of Law.[4300]

Stetson's BLSA chapter has also expanded its activities to include students from other schools. In October 2002, it hosted students from nine Florida law schools in a program on "The Keys to Academic Success." Schools represented were members of the Southern Regional BLSA Association.[4301] Ya'Sheaka Campbell, President of BLSA at Stetson, commented that the academic retreat "helped illustrate Stetson's commitment to diversify, not only on this campus, but throughout the legal community."[4302] Law students from Florida State, Florida A&M, Nova Southeastern, Barry, Florida International, Florida Coastal, and St. Thomas came to Stetson. In another cooperative effort, BLSA and the St. Petersburg Bar Association placed in Stetson's Law Center in Tampa a traveling exhibit titled "A Legacy of Courage, Vision, and Hope," honoring the contributions of African-Americans to the legal profession in Pinellas County.[4303]

BLSA also has held annual brunches for alumni. In 2004, BLSA's first president, St. Petersburg attorney Laguerra Champagne, spoke at the BLSA alumni brunch.[4304] In 2005, BLSA used the annual alumni brunch to name the Stetson chapter the "Honorable Thomas E. Stringer, Sr., Chapter of the Stetson

---

4298. Davina Gould, *Stetson University College of Law to Host Minority Pre-Law Conference* (Stetson U. College of L. Jan. 29, 2003) (news release).

4299. Davina Gould, *Stetson Black Students to Honor Judge Howard White* (Stetson U. College of L. Apr. 1, 2003) (news release).

4300. *Id.*

4301. Frank Klim, *Stetson's Black Law Student Association Hosts Statewide Academic Retreat* (Stetson U. College of L. Oct. 24, 2002) (news release).

4302. *Id.*

4303. *Stetson Law Events Celebrate Black History Month,* 44 Stetson Law. 4, 4 (Spring 2004).

4304. Frank Klim, *Stetson College of Law Events to Celebrate Black History Month* 1 (Stetson U. College of L. Feb. 10, 2004) (news release).

Alumnus Grady Irvin, Jr.

Black Law Students Association."[4305] Stetson law graduate Grady Irvin, Jr. ('92) (who had represented several prominent persons in cases attracting national attention), gave the keynote address.[4306] Finally, in November 2005, BLSA members presented a "Nite of Soul" in the Great Hall, showcasing their talents. BLSA President Patice Holland and member Michael Davis headlined the event.[4307]

f. HBA: Stetson's Hispanic Bar Association

Beginning in 1997, the Stetson Hispanic Bar Association (HBA) has held an annual festive party and picnic in the courtyard for students, faculty, staff and their families. Latino music flows through the campus as salsa dance lessons are given to the rhythmically challenged. HBA members prepare Latin food and give cooking demonstrations. The event is one that attracts children of all ages and is a highlight of the social year at the school.[4308]

As noted above, the HBA has worked closely with the admissions staff of the College and in concert with the BLSA organization to recruit minority stu-

4305. *Stetson BLSA's Dedicates the Name of Its Chapter to Honor Judge Stringer* (Stetson U. College of L. Feb. 26, 2005) (recent events).

4306. Grady Irvin, Jr., *'92 Addresses BLSA Brunch; Chapter Named for Stringer, '74*, 45 Stetson Law. 45, 45 (Spring 2005).

4307. Bridgette Sanders, *Students Showcase Talents at Nite of Soul*, The Brief 8 (Nov. 15, 2005).

4308. Darby Dickerson, *Every Student Has a Story*, 43 Stetson Law. 1, 1 (Fall 2003).

dents to Stetson law school.[4309] Shortly after becoming dean, Vause appointed Pamela Coleman admissions director. A native of Trinidad, Coleman worked closely with both HBA and BLSA.[4310] A set back occurred, however, in 2001–2002, when Florida discontinued what was known as the Minority Participation in Legal Education Program, under which the state allocated scholarship funds to both public and private Florida law schools to support minority student recruitment.[4311] Realizing that the twin goals of raising the academic credentials of admitted students and increasing minority student enrollment required a major infusion of money for need-based and merit scholarships, Vause turned to the school's College Relations Office.[4312]

g. Asian American Law Association

In addition to BLSA and HBA, Stetson law students formed an Asian-American Law Association on campus in 2005. Organizing the AALA students was Grace Santos.[4313] Other organizations included Jewish, Christian, Republican, Democrat, Federalist, and International student groups.

h. A $12 Million "Cornerstone Campaign"

The College had a relatively small endowment when Vause became dean. During the preceding decade, the College Relations Office had focused primarily on alumni relations and the annual fund. Jacob's goals had been to increase both the percentage of alumni who contribute to the annual fund, and the total amount raised each year. As discussed, Jacob achieved those goals.[4314]

Dean Vause felt that the time had come to direct more effort toward eliciting major gifts. To further this priority, he hired new leadership in College Relations, bringing in Dotti E. Bressi, Ed.D.,[4315] as Associate Vice President. It turned out to be a strategic move. Bressi, who had extensive fundraising experience at the University of Tennessee College of Law, understood the process of putting together a campaign designed to raise large sums of money over and above the amounts collected through the annual fund drive.

In September 2002, the College announced a new fundraising campaign with a goal of raising $12 million by May 31, 2005. The proceeds were to be

---

4309. *See infra* nn. 4309–4310 and accompanying text.

4310. Vause, *Centennial History*, *supra* n. 595, at 192.

4311. *Id.* at 193.

4312. *Id.*

4313. Grace Santos, *Get Involved*, The Brief (Nov. 15, 2005).

4314. *See supra* nn. 3423–3424 and accompanying text.

4315. Vause, *Centennial History*, *supra* n. 595, at 193.

used for student scholarships, faculty chairs, and other academic enhancements.[4316] Called "The Cornerstone Campaign, Laying the Foundation for Tomorrow," the ambitious project represented the "biggest development effort in the College of Law's history."[4317] Co-chairs of the campaign were S. Sammy Cacciatore, Jr., a 1966 graduate of the law school, and William Reece Smith, Jr., Chair Emeritus of Carlton Fields, P.A., and distinguished professorial lecturer at Stetson. Matt Towery, a 1987 graduate of Stetson law school (who had earned his undergraduate degree at Cambridge University, England), chaired the law school's National Alumni Committee during the Cornerstone Campaign. Towery had been a campaign manager for U.S. Congressman Newt Gingrich and a former member of the Georgia House of Representatives.[4318] To begin the campaign, the Atlanta native pledged $100,000 to his law school.[4319]

In the summer of 2005, the results of the $12 million Cornerstone Campaign goal were announced.[4320] They were spectacular. The grand total came to $30,479,314, or over two-and-one-half times the original goal of $12,000,000.[4321] The total included approximately $17,850,000 in cashes, pledges, bequests, and trusts, as well as $10,000,000 in federal money.[4322] The latter amount included a $7,780,000 grant for Stetson's Clearinghouse for Science, Technology and the Law, a $1,000,000 grant for the Elder Consumer Protection Program, and $1,225,000 for the Tampa Law Center.[4323] The campaign's success was celebrated at Stetson's second annual induction of Hall of Fame Members in October 2005.[4324] Included among hundreds of major contributions and pledges were a $1 million testamentary trust for student scholarships from an alumnus who wished to remain anonymous;[4325] $1 million

4316. Frank Klim, *Stetson University College of Law Launches a $12 Million Campaign to Fund Scholarships, Professorships and Academic Enhancements*, (Stetson U. College of L. Sept. 19, 2002) (news release).

4317. Dotti E. Bressi, *Individual Giving Critical to College of Law Success*, 44 Stetson Law. 30, 30 (Fall 2004).

4318. *Campaign Chair Commits $100,000*, 43 Stetson Law. 34, 34 (Fall 2002). When he was thirty, Towery ran as the Republican nominee for Lt. Governor of Georgia.

4319. *Id.*

4320. *The Cornerstone Campaign; Laying the Foundation for Tomorrow, Announcement and Invitation to the Celebration* (Oct. 8, 2005) (on file at Stetson U. College of L., Gulfport, Fla.)

4321. Dotti E. Bressi, Stetson U. College of L., *Cornerstone Campaign Final Campaign Totals* (on file at Stetson U. College of L., Gulfport, Fla.).

4322. *Id.*

4323. *Id.*

4324. *Id.*

4325. *Alumnus Pledges $1 Million Testamentary Trust to Benefit Student Scholarships at Stetson Law*, 43 Stetson Law. 22, 22 (Fall 2002).

from Boston Asset Management, Inc., and the Center for Special Needs Trust Administration, Inc.;[4326] $700,000 from the Office of the Florida Attorney General to support a statewide program to educate elderly residents to avoid consumer fraud—money that resulted from a settlement reached between the attorney general's office and a Delaware-based firm facing allegations of deceptive practices;[4327] $500,000 from the Joy McCann Foundation to endow the William Reece Smith, Jr., Distinguished Professorship;[4328] and $250,000 from the Attorneys' Title Insurance Fund, Inc. to establish a faculty professorship.[4329]

In addition, a dozen major corporations and organizations made significant contributions, including: the *St. Petersburg Times*; The Florida Bar; C.M. Morgan Trust; the Florida Bar Foundation; the Dennis L. Fontaine Foundation; the American Association of Retired People (AARP); Florin Roebig, P.A.; Pinellas County Community Foundation; the American College of Trial Lawyers; the Nichols Foundation, Inc.; the Tampa Bay Bankruptcy Bar Association; the Saunders Foundation; the Legal Services Corporation; the Fort Myers Broadcasting Company; and Carlton Fields, P.A.[4330] Individual donors who have made major contributions in recent years include: Dale E. Anstine ('70); William F. Blews ('66); S. Sammy Cacciatore, Jr. ('66); Joy McCann Daugherty; Anthony J. Grezik ('53); E.V. McClurg ('69); Michael Mather ('65); William T. Moore ('52); James Nemec ('36) (deceased); William R. Nunno ('77); Joseph J. Reiter ('68); Murray Sams, Jr. ('49); Christian D. Searcy, Sr. ('73); Wm. Reece Smith, Jr.; Roy M. Speer, Jr. ('59); John W. Staunton ('97); Hon. Raphael Steinhardt ('63); Matthew A. Towery ('87); Gary R. Trombley ('73); J. Ben Watkins ('49); James L. Wilkes ('83); and John R. Woods ('51).[4331]

4326. Davina Gould, *Stetson University College of Law Receives $1 Million Pledge to Establish Faculty Chair in Elder and Disability Law*, (Stetson U. College of L. Feb. 4, 2003) (news release). Announcing the joint pledge was Leo Govoni, president of Boston Asset Management, and John Staunton, vice president of the Center for Special Needs Trust Administration, and a 1997 graduate of Stetson law school. *Id.*

4327. *Stetson Aims to Protect Seniors Against Fraud*, 29 Fla. B. News 18 (Dec. 15, 2002).

4328. *Major Gifts Establish Two New Endowed Professorships*, 45 Stetson Law. 37, 37 (Spring 2005).

4329. *Id.*

4330. The names listed above were supplied to the authors by the Stetson U. Office of College Relations in the summer of 2005.

4331. *Id.*

i. *Expansion of Physical Facilities; New Student Recreation Center*

During Vause's four-year deanship, he oversaw expansion and improvement of campus facilities. After taking office in 1999, he altered the priorities set out in the campus master plan by, first, paving over what was called "Sandspur Stadium," an unpaved parking area along 15th Avenue that alternated between dry and dusty and rainy and muddy, to the pleasure of hundreds of students.[4332]

Next, Vause moved up the date for the construction of a new student life and recreation center. The old Firestone recreation facility[4333] was too small and slated for removal.[4334] In the spring of 2001, construction on a new structure began. Called the Student Life and Recreation Center, a 13,500-square-foot two-story structure was built in the Mediterranean Revival style consistent with other campus buildings, and was dedicated in October 2002.[4335] Having an outdoor pool and lounge areas, the Center's first floor consisted of a fully equipped gymnasium for students and staff, a mail facility, and lounges and meeting rooms. The second floor housed the office of the assistant dean for student affairs, the offices of career services, and the headquarters of the student bar association. Together, the two construction projects cost over $4 million, and reportedly "were paid for without the necessity of deferred financing."[4336]

Vause made other campus improvements, including: additional paved parking areas adjacent to the Stetson Law Library; renovation of Classroom A; and remodeled offices for the associate dean for international programs, calendar and events, registrar, admissions, financial aid, college relations, and communications.[4337] But the most significant new facility Vause was responsible for was located twenty-four miles from the school's Gulfport campus in adjacent downtown Tampa.

j. *In Search of a Campus: "An Unparalleled Synergy"*

As noted earlier, in 1997, Dean Moody formed a faculty/administrative committee to examine the feasibility of offering a part-time evening program in Tampa.[4338] The resulting study revealed that there was a growing demand

4332. Vause, *Centennial History, supra* n. 595, at 194.

4333. *See supra* nn. 2651–2655 and accompanying notes.

4334. *Id.*

4335. Vause, *Centennial History, supra* n. 595, at 194.

4336. *Id.*

4337. *Id.*

4338. *See supra* nn. 4259–4265 and accompanying text.

for part-time legal education in the greater Tampa Bay metropolitan area.[4339] Given that Tampa was the largest major market in the United States that did not have an evening part-time program, several administrative officials and faculty members believed that if Stetson did not step up and fill the void, another law school would. A part-time program facilities sub-committee, comprised of professors Kossow, Marks, Swygert, and Associate Dean Vause, began to scout out possible sites and suitable buildings. The committee initially investigated the University of South Florida's campus on Fowler Avenue in north Tampa. Talks ensued between officials of the University of South Florida and Stetson over the possibility of Stetson renting a building on the USF campus.[4340] Though USF administrators seemed anxious to go ahead, Florida public officials were reluctant. Stetson officials also began to see difficulties with having an evening program at USF. First, the Tampa campus was located far from Gulfport, necessitating hour-long-plus drives each way. Another problem concerned possible bureaucratic entanglements with USF administration and members of the State Board of Regents.[4341] Even dwarfing these problems was Stetson's understanding that the ABA accreditation rules required that any building used by a law school must be *owned* by that school.[4342]

From that point on, the committee searched for a structure the school might purchase. Most buildings upon inspection, however, were found unacceptable. Then, in the heart of downtown Tampa, a building with historical significance was put on the market—the "old" United States Courthouse.[4343] A proud and stately structure with stairs leading to an impressive entrance set off by towering Greek columns, the courthouse's proportions were classic in design. The Tampa federal courts had relocated to a new building a few blocks away.

Like most federal buildings, the old Tampa courthouse was managed by the U.S. General Services Administration (GSA). Vause, Kossow, Swygert, and

4339. Vause, *Centennial History*, *supra* n. 595, at 195.

4340. *Id.*

4341. Associate Dean Vause and Dean Moody represented Stetson in what turned out to be only exploratory talks with USF officials. The discussants came to realize the large number of obstacles that would have to be overcome if USF and Stetson should enter into a campus-sharing arrangement.

4342. Vause, *Centennial History*, supra n. 595, at 196.

4343. The co-authors of this history—the late Dean Gary Vause and Professor Michael Swygert—were members of the committee which investigated the possible buildings and sites for the part-time, evening program the College of Law planned to implement. Much of the discussion that follows is based, first, on Dean Vause's early manuscript he prepared for this work, and, second, on Professor Swygert's recollections of the events. *See id.* at 195, 196.

Marks (among others from Stetson) were excited over the possibility of the College purchasing the historic courthouse, even though it was far too large to house only Stetson's evening program. That was not a significant detriment, however, as the school could lease the unneeded space to law firms or other law-related businesses, especially given the old courthouse's central location in the heart of Tampa's business and legal district.[4344]

Vause, Kossow, and Swygert traveled to Atlanta to discuss with GSA officials Stetson's purchase of the Tampa facility. There, GSA and Stetson representatives reviewed specific terms for the school's possible purchase. Subsequently, Stetson brought in an architect as well as a building engineer to determine the feasibility of transforming the courthouse into a structure accommodative with the law school's needs. But after the building engineer examined the old courthouse and found that asbestos-laced building materials were laden throughout the building, the attractiveness of the option lessened dramatically, even more so when it became clear that the GSA was not willing to remove the dangerous material. Stetson then calculated the cost of the school's doing so and decided it would be prohibitive.

With the old Tampa federal courthouse out of the picture, the search resumed.[4345] Vause and Kossow, with assistance of the Tampa Chamber of Commerce, continued to identify and then visit possible buildings. They began to also look at vacant land where Stetson could erect its own building.

In the fall of 2001, Vause (who two years earlier had become dean) learned that the City of Tampa was planning to sell 7.3 acres of land adjacent to the Hillsborough River, a few blocks north of downtown Tampa, and only a few hundred yards from the Ashley Street exit off Interstate 275.[4346] Though the property was in a somewhat depressed, mixed commercial and residential neighborhood, it was in the path of a downtown that could only grow northward. Thus, the area was ripe for restoration and new development. Tampa attorney Marsha Rydberg (Stetson alumnus, '76) pointed out that the parcel was in Tampa Heights, a historic Tampa community within the city's urban core.[4347]

Upon visiting the site, Vause quickly concluded that this was the best site for Stetson's satellite campus. Here, the dean's vision of the future of the law school could be realized. Marsha Rydberg has described his vision:

4344. *Id.*

4345. *Id.*

4346. *Id.*

4347. Marsha Griffin Rydberg, *A Lawyer's Lawyer, A Professor's Professor, A Dean's Dean, A Wonderful Person*, 33 Stetson L. Rev. 51, 53 (2003) [hereinafter Rydberg, *A Lawyer's Lawyer*].

Overseer President Marsha Rydberg

> He envisioned a fully accredited law school that spanned Tampa Bay. [His] vision was not one of a pedestrian office building that housed a few dreary classrooms, populated by weary professors and night-time law students ... Instead, Dean Vause conjured a gorgeous Mediterranean-style building, shared by a state appellate court and adjoining a park along the Hillsborough River.[4348]

Over the next several months, Dean Vause met with Tampa Mayor Richard Greco, the Tampa City Council, and other Tampa officials, as well as with officers of the Hillsborough County Bar Association and judges of Florida's Second District Court of Appeal in Lakeland about Stetson purchasing the property. As it turned out, each party had a stake in the outcome.[4349]

Greco and Vause discussed how the sale might be structured to enable both Stetson's purchasing of the property and Tampa's receiving the fair market value. According to Rydberg, Greco and Vause "had a special compatibility and shared a vision of having Stetson spur the development of historic Tampa Heights."[4350] Despite intense negotiations, the agreement did not come quickly, as several matters needed to be resolved. First, Stetson and Tampa, of course, had to agree on a price; second, one party would have to pay for removal of

4348. *Id.*

4349. Frank Klim, *Stetson University College of Law Closer to Agreement on Tampa Campus* (Stetson U. College of L. June 5, 2002) (news release).

4350. Rydberg, *A Lawyer's Lawyer*, *supra* n. 4347, at 53.

the old Tampa Police Station; third, Stetson needed to consummate the sale quickly; fourth, there was a question whether the city would retain and maintain the adjacent parkland along the river; and fifth, numerous zoning, easement, traffic, and other property considerations needed to be resolved. Rydberg, one of the lawyers working with Stetson in negotiating with Tampa, noted, "Dean Vause was at his best when he was negotiating a deal."[4351]

In the late fall of 2002, Stetson University and Tampa struck a deal. Mayor Greco exclaimed: "Stetson's Law Center and campus is a long-awaited dream that will soon become a reality and complete Tampa's goal as a center for academic excellence."[4352] Vause responded, "We are very excited about the purchase of this property in downtown Tampa. The Law Center and campus will be a major hub of legal activity for Tampa Bay."[4353] The terms of the sale included Stetson purchasing the 7.3-acre property for $1.2 million, plus paying the estimated $430,000 cost of tearing down the former Tampa Police Station. The College then would erect a three-story, 77,000-square-foot building that would include a courtroom along with class and seminar rooms, a library, offices, and conference center.

Concurrent with the negotiations between Vause, Greco, and the Tampa City Council, Stetson's dean met with judges of Florida's Second District Court of Appeal as a serendipitous opportunity had arisen. The court's Tampa Division was facing a "housing crisis," as it had to vacate the Hillsborough Courthouse because the structure was undergoing major renovations.[4354] Compounding the court's problem, the Florida Legislature failed to appropriate funds for the court to purchase land for a new courthouse. Upon learning these facts, Rydberg noted, "[H]e [Vause] seized the opportunity to offer the court a new home."[4355]

Following negotiations, on February 3, 2003, the Florida Second District Court of Appeal signed a historic lease with Stetson University College of Law, permitting the court to locate its Tampa branch in the new Stetson Law Center.[4356] At a news conference, the court's then Chief Judge Chris Altenbernd said: "Any university is proud to have a teaching hospital as part of its medical program, and I'm proud to announce that Tampa will be the first

---

4351. *Id.*

4352. Frank Klim, *Stetson University Purchases Downtown Property for Law Center and Campus* 1, 2 (Stetson U. College of L. Dec. 12, 2002) (news release).

4353. *Id.* at 1.

4354. Laura Kinsler, Tampa Trib., *Stetson Appeals to Second District Court,* lkinsler@tampatrib.com (accessed Feb. 4, 2005) [hereinafter Kinsler, *Stetson*].

4355. Rydberg, *A Lawyer's Lawyer, supra* n. 4347, at 53.

4356. Davina Gould, *Stetson University College of Law, Florida Second District Court of Appeal Sign Historic Agreement* (Stetson U. College of L. Feb. 4, 2003) (news release).

Drawing of Tampa Law Center

Groundbreaking for Tampa Law Center:
Dean W. Gary Vause, Stetson University President H. Douglas Lee and President of the Stetson Lawyers Association Carolyn DuPree Hill

place in Florida that is going to have a teaching court facility."[4357] Under the agreement, the court had exclusive use of the third floor of the Center to house the judges' chambers and a clerk's office, as well as offices for support staff. Dean Vause commented that the arrangement was "a perfect marriage for everyone involved," adding, "it serves the court and the law school because the court will be able to use our modern first-floor courtroom, and of course, it's a great advantage to our students to see the court in session."[4358] Rydberg may have said it best when she commented that the Tampa-Stetson-Second District Court of Appeal arrangement Vause had put together, "created an unparalleled synergy."[4359]

But there was yet another institution to be drawn into the fellowship—the Hillsborough County Bar Association. Its president, Gwynne Young, met with city and law school officials to consider moving the County bar association's headquarters to a new structure to be built on Stetson's Tampa campus.[4360] With the cooperation of Dean Vause and his successor, Dean Dickerson, Hills-

4357. *Id.*
4358. *Id.*
4359. Rydberg, *A Lawyer's Lawyer*, *supra* n. 4347, at 53.
4360. Kinsler, *Stetson*, *supra* n. 4354.

borough County Bar officials made plans to build its new headquarters adjacent to Stetson's Law Center.[4361]

The resulting assemblage of law students, working lawyers, and active jurists in one setting was a rarity in the history of American legal education. It blended the essential ingredients of the legal profession in one bowl: law students, legal educators, judges, lawyers, and bar officials, all intermingled on a single campus.

Vause was the person most responsible for pulling together the parts of this cooperative arrangement. What he accomplished may some day prove comparable in significance to the College's move to Gulfport in 1954.[4362] Both events were bold and daring. The law school's 1954 relocation from DeLand to Gulfport certainly made possible the school's subsequent progress. Likewise, the College's 2004 opening of the satellite Tampa Law Center and campus may turn out to be the school's most significant move in the 21st century. Whereas Stetson University President J. Ollie Edmunds brought about the law school's 1954 relocation, fifty years later, Stetson College of Law Dean W. Gary Vause engineered the 2004 purchase of a new campus in downtown Tampa.

Sadly, when the new Tampa Law Center officially opened in January 2004, Vause was not present; he had died eight months earlier, on May 9, 2003. After his death, Judge Thomas E. Stringer, Sr., wrote that Stetson's Tampa Law Center would not have been possible "without Gary's vision, leadership, and perseverance," concluding:

> This Center will forever stand for as a monument to his love for and commitment to Stetson, and his legacy will live on in each of the students who graduate and go on to epitomize the qualities of professional excellence for which Gary stood.[4363]

14.3 Approaching Death; Setting Up the Transition

a. Faculty Divisions Narrow

When Gary Vause became dean, he inherited the faculty divisions and unrest that had developed years earlier over the Ramos matter and then had intensified over subsequent appointment and non-renewal issues. By the fall of 1999, the two camps, each representing roughly half of the faculty, were well

4361. Graham Brink, *Stetson Opens Tampa Campus*, St. Pete. Times B-1 (Jan. 12, 2004).
4362. *See supra* Ch. 10.
4363. Thomas E. Stringer, Sr., *Gary Vause: A Great Leader*, 33 Stetson L. Rev. 81 (2003).

entrenched. Darby Dickerson recalls how when she came to the law school in 1995, various faculty members tried to enlist her on one side or another.[4364] It was not something she welcomed.[4365]

In the spring of 1999, when Vause became a candidate to succeed Moody as dean, the two faculty groups split on his candidacy. However, by the time the faculty voted on whether or not to send his name to President Lee as an "acceptable and qualified candidate," several members of the group who initially opposed Vause had changed their minds. Thus, by a comfortable margin, the faculty voted to recommend him to Lee.

As was also true of Dean Moody five years earlier, when Vause stepped into the dean's shoes in July 1999, he inherited a fractious and combative faculty. Even so, Dickerson notes, "Vause really got the trains moving again," adding that his "calmness and reaching out" to people who were "on the other side of the divide from him began to make a difference."[4366] Still, Dickerson points out, some of the divisions were so long standing that they could not be bridged, and Vause knew that.[4367] Nonetheless, his reaching out to both sides of the divide—thereby evidencing his independence from old alliances, and his calmness and professionalism in dealing with all his colleagues—caused the faculty to come closer together, thereby precipitating a transition from a combative and rancorous style of interaction to one of cooperation and relative harmony.

As it turned out, Vause had to engineer another transition, one he never had intended, but which fell upon him. Less than three years after becoming dean, W. Gary Vause was told he might have only a short time to live: he had colon cancer and it had reached an advanced stage.

b. Silent Preparations for a Successor

Though the precise date when Vause learned that he had colon cancer remains unclear, according to Celia Vause, his widow, he was aware of his illness for at least one year before his death in 2003.[4368] At one point, Vause went to Associate Dean Dickerson's office and asked if she would be vice dean, a position that Tom Allison then held, explaining that Tom wanted to go back to

---

4364. Interview by Michael I. Swygert, Prof. Emeritus, Stetson U. College of L., with Darby Dickerson, V.P. and Dean, Stetson U. College of L. 57, 58 (May 22, 2004) [hereinafter *Dickerson Interview*].

4365. *Id.* at 58.

4366. *Id.*

4367. *Id.*

4368. *Id.* at 61.

teaching full-time.[4369] After considering Vause's offer, Dickerson accepted and became Vice Dean of Stetson College of Law in July 2002, at that point not knowing of Vause's serious health problems.[4370]

Five months passed, during which Vause negotiated the purchase of land from the city of Tampa and procured an agreement with the Second District Court of Appeal to lease space in what would be Stetson's Tampa Law Center and Campus.[4371] Then, on a Sunday afternoon in mid-December of 2002, Vause called Dickerson into his office and said: "I have something to tell you."[4372] She describes what ensued:

> Very calmly, without changing his demeanor, he told me that he had terminal colon cancer. He explained to me the treatments that he had had and that, thus far, they had failed.... "Regardless of whether I live or I do not live, my doctors have told me that I cannot continue as dean," he said. "I intend to resign July 31 [2003] and [Stetson] needs to appoint an interim dean. I am recommending to [President Lee] that you be the interim dean."[4373]

The conversation "was a complete bombshell," Dickerson says.[4374] Vause wanted to remain dean as long as his health would allow, hopefully until July 31, 2003, when he would retire. As the year began, his immediate priority was to show Dickerson "as many things as possible" regarding the multifarious tasks and responsibilities of a dean, as she might be asked to serve as interim dean until a new dean could be chosen.[4375] Vause's goal was to make the decanal transition as smooth as possible when it became necessary.[4376]

c. *Death and Accolades*

Stetson students, staff, and faculty learned on April 23, 2003, that Dean Gary Vause would retire effective July 31 due to cancer.[4377] Knowing that Vause's health was slipping fast, President Lee, Interim Dean Dickerson, and Director of Communications Klim, among others, put together a special awards presentation to honor Gary's "twenty-eight years of extraordinary ser-

---

4369. *Id.*

4370. *Id.*

4371. *See supra* nn. 4354–4355 and accompanying text.

4372. *Dickerson Interview*, *supra* n. 4364, at 63.

4373. *Id.* at 64.

4374. *Id.* at 64, 65.

4375. *Id.* at 65.

4376. *Id.*

4377. Frank Klim, *Stetson University College of Law Dean Gary Vause Announces Retirement* 1 (Stetson U. College of L. Apr. 23, 2003) (news release).

vice to Stetson University College of Law." The award ceremony was supposed to highlight the school's commencement scheduled for Saturday May 10, 2004. The commencement took place, but the awards presentation did not, Gary Vause having had died the previous morning on Friday, May 9, 2004.[4378] Dickerson later wrote that Vause died "much too soon," noting that "he had so much left that he wanted to accomplish."[4379] His top priority was seeing the completion of the Tampa Law Center and Campus that he had spearheaded. "Though Gary did not live to see that day," wrote Dickerson, "he has left us with a powerful spirit."[4380]

The word of Vause's death shocked students, staff, faculty, alumni, and friends. A funeral mass was celebrated at the Most Holy Name of Jesus Catholic Church in Gulfport on May 12, 2003. In a eulogy, President Lee described Vause as a "Renaissance man,"[4381] while Professor James Brown described the late dean of Stetson's College of Law as a "builder, facilitator, and a courageous leader who was both dignified and humble."[4382]

In June 2003, family, friends, alumni, students, faculty, and staff of Stetson University College of Law came together in Great Hall to honor the memory of William Gary Vause. Speakers offered tributes to the person who had done so much for the school and who had meant so much to their lives. The most moving moment was a declaration of love from Gary's widow, Celia. Besides the oral tributes, several persons wrote homages to his memory in an *In Memoriam* special issue of the *Stetson Law Review.*[4383] Included were Judge Thomas Stringer, Sr., Chair of the law school's Board of Overseers;[4384] John Cooper, professor and interim director of graduate and international programs;[4385] Darby Dickerson, interim dean;[4386] Marsha Rydberg, member, Board of Overseer's (later, chair);[4387] Cary Singletary, attorney, arbitrator and one-

4378. Frank Klim, *Gary Vause, Stetson University College of Law Dean, Dies* 1, 2 (Stetson U. College of L. May 9, 2003) (news release).

4379. Darby Dickerson, *Lessons in Leadership*, 33 Stetson L. Rev. 29 (2003) [hereinafter Dickerson, *Lessons*].

4380. *Id.*

4381. Cooper, *Vause Tribute*, *supra* n. 4224.

4382. James J. Brown, *An Oral Tribute Annotated*, 33 Stetson L. Rev. 23, 28 (2003).

4383. *In Memoriam: A Tribute to Dean W. Gary Vause, 1942–2003*, 33 Stetson L. Rev. 1–90 (2003).

4384. *See* Thomas E. Stringer, Sr., *Gary Vause: A Great Leader*, 33 Stetson L. Rev. 81 (2003).

4385. Cooper, *Vause Tribute*, *supra* n. 4224, at 7–17.

4386. *See* Dickerson, *Lessons*, *supra* n. 4379.

4387. *See* Rydberg, *A Lawyer's Lawyer*, *supra* n. 4347.

time co-director with Vause of the Stetson Labor-Law Center;[4388] Thomas Sullivan, Vause's law former partner in Hartford, Connecticut;[4389] Frank Klim, Stetson Director of Communications;[4390] Elizabeth Kovachevich, Judge, U.S. District Court for the Middle District of Florida;[4391] Samuel Mandelbaum, an international law specialist who worked with Vause in the area of international trade and business development;[4392] Robert Batey, professor of law;[4393] Kalina Sarmov, Tampa attorney, Stetson alumnus, and co-author with Vause of two works on international business and labor law;[4394] Leslie Stein, general counsel, Verizon Data Services, Stetson alumnus, and instructor of "women in law" course;[4395] Frank Swacker, international lawyer and arbitrator;[4396] Ruth Thurman, professor of law;[4397] and Chad Strickland, Vause's nephew (the son of Gary's sister Suzanne), and Stetson law alumnus, class of '96.[4398]

Besides Dickerson, several persons at Stetson spent considerable time with Gary and Celia during Gary's final weeks, including professors John Cooper and Luz Nagle. Cooper observed:

> Facing a dread disease, he chose to soldier on ... And when he learned that he would lose his battle with cancer, he put his duties as dean first, planning for a smooth transition ... He faced death with a surpassing equanimity. He was even capable of making little jokes—evoking W.C. Fields when talking about using the cane he was obliged to walk with to ward off children and small dogs—thus showing a wry sense of humor that many of us never fully appreciated.[4399]

Cooper described Vause as "one of the most complex and multifaceted individuals he had ever met." In a tribute to his friend, Cooper proclaimed:

4388. Singletary, *Vause Tribute*, *supra* n. 4264.

4389. *See* Thomas Sullivan, *A Best Friend Recalled*, 33 Stetson L. Rev. 83 (2003).

4390. *See* Frank Klim, *Life of Service*, *supra* n. 4225.

4391. *See* Hon. Elizabeth A. Kovachevich, *Dean Gary Vause—Setting a Standard for Living*, 33 Stetson L. Rev. 41 (2003).

4392. *See* Samuel Robert Mandelbaum, *The Legacy of W. Gary Vause to International Legal Education and Practice in Florida*, 33 Stetson L. Rev. 43 (2003).

4393. *See* Robert D. Batey, *A Lesson in Courage*, 33 Stetson L. Rev. 21 (2003).

4394. *See* Kalina Sarmov, *One Life in Eternity*, 33 Stetson L. Rev. 55 (2003).

4395. *See* Leslie Reicin Stein, *A Personal Remembrance*, 33 Stetson L. Rev. 69 (2003).

4396. *See* Frank W. Swacker, *A Unique Individual*, 33 Stetson L. Rev. 87 (2003).

4397. *A Remembrance of Dean W. Gary Vause*, 33 Stetson L. Rev. 89 (2003).

4398. *See* D. Chad Strickland, *Gary Vause: A Perspective*, 33 Stetson L. Rev. 75 (2003).

4399. Cooper, *Vause Tribute*, *supra* n. 4224, at 17.

Dean Darby Dickerson

"Gary Vause died with honor, humility, good humor, and good will; he was courageous to the last. It is a final lesson we should never forget."[4400]

14.4 Dean Darby Dickerson Readies Stetson for a New Era

a. Coming to Stetson

Darby Dickerson explained that she first heard of Stetson when she "was a kid" when "the Hatters [of Stetson University] played the Carolina Gamecocks in basketball."[4401] A native South Carolinian, Dickerson spent her first sixteen years in Columbia, and then moved to a town outside Reading, Pennsylvania. An indication of her academic prowess was that by her final year in high school, she had earned college course credits at Albright College.[4402] In 1981, Dickerson enrolled at the College of William and Mary, where she completed her B.A. and M.A. degrees in three years.[4403]

4400. *Id.*

4401. *Dickerson Interview*, *supra* n. 4364, at 24.

4402. *Id.* at 2, 3.

4403. Darby Dickerson, *Summary Information and Curriculum Vitae* 4 (2005) (on file at Stetson U. College of L., Gulfport, Fla.) [hereinafter Dickerson, *Information*].

Dickerson knew she wanted to be a lawyer since she was twelve or thirteen. She originally wanted to work for the government, so she thought of going to law school in either Washington, D.C., or South Carolina.[4404] But the director of admissions at Vanderbilt University School of Law, Ann Brandt, changed Dickerson's mind. She met the admission's director at William and Mary's Career Services Department, where Dickerson worked as a "pre-law" staff member. Brandt convinced Dickerson to apply to Vanderbilt's law school. With Vanderbilt's offering financial assistance, she went, earning her J.D. degree in 1988.[4405] In law school, she was named Senior Managing Editor of the *Vanderbilt Law Review*, and was recipient of the "Law Review Candidate's Award" for the most outstanding contribution to the *Review* in 1988. That same year, she also won the Weldon B. White Prize for the best paper written on Tennessee law.[4406] Dickerson also served on the Vanderbilt Moot Court Board, where she was one of the finalists of the school's intermural competition.[4407]

Of Dickerson's many activities in law school, the most significant may have been her serving as research assistant to Professor Jon W. Bruce. Before joining the Vanderbilt faculty, Bruce had been a member of the Stetson law faculty from 1976 through 1981 (though he was a visitor at Vanderbilt during the 1980–81 academic year).[4408] At Vanderbilt, Dickerson worked with Bruce primarily on a treatise on easement law Bruce co-authored with his colleague, Professor James Ely.[4409] She was impressed by Bruce's work ethos, scholarship, and teaching proficiency (she took several of his courses)—so much so, that she aspired to become a law professor.[4410]

Vanderbilt asked Dickerson to serve as a student member on the committee. In reviewing the credentials of faculty candidates, she realized that after earning her law degree, it might be advantageous for her to seek a judicial clerkship.[4411] Dickerson applied to Harry W. Wellford, Judge of the United States Court of Appeals for the Sixth Circuit, who subsequently hired her.[4412] By coincidence, four years earlier a graduate of the University of Louisville

4404. *Dickerson Interview, supra* n. 4364, at 4.

4405. *Id.*

4406. Dickerson, *Information, supra* n. 4403, at 4.

4407. *Dickerson Interview, supra* n. 4364, at 6.

4408. *See supra* nn. 3129–3133 and accompanying text.

4409. *See supra* n. 3133.

4410. *Dickerson Interview, supra* n. 4364, at 8, 9.

4411. *Id.* at 10.

4412. *Id.* at 10, 11.

School of Law, Mark Brown, had also clerked for Judge Wellford.[4413] Brown soon thereafter joined the Stetson College of Law faculty.[4414]

Following her clerkship, Dickerson in 1989 joined the Dallas, Texas, law firm of Locke, Purnell, Rain, and Harrell as an associate in the commercial litigation department.[4415] During six years with the firm, besides practicing, she trained incoming litigation and bankruptcy associates, work, she says, "I enjoyed the most."[4416] The firm placed her in charge of continuing legal education for its litigation department. She liked her work at the firm, but her goal to join a law faculty had not ebbed. After contacting her mentor, Professor Bruce, she made a list of schools to which she might apply. Heading the list was Texas, followed by Stetson and several other law schools in the Southeast.

Why Stetson? Dickerson had become acquainted with the institution through fortuitous contact with several people from the law school. Foremost, of course, was Jon Bruce, who had taught and had gained tenure at Stetson. Another was Mark Brown, whom she met at periodic reunions of Judge Welford's former law clerks.[4417] But perhaps of most significance, several Stetson law students she witnessed in action.

While in practice, Dickerson served as Chair of the Texas Young Lawyer's Association National Trial Competition, an annual event held in Dallas.[4418] Overseeing the competition, Dickerson was impressed by Stetson's students winning both first and second place at the national competition. Along with members of the American College of Trial Lawyers, she sat as one of the judges. Stetson's two winning teams consisted of Angelo M. Patacca, Jr., and Karen A. Williams, versus Sharin Mohammedboy and David Paul.[4419] Stetson alumni Fred Schaub and Marie DeMarco coached both teams. Dickerson, who judged the final Stetson versus Stetson argument, recalled: "I was just so terribly impressed with the Stetson students."[4420]

One other Stetson person whom Dickerson knew was Professor Pat Longan.[4421] She first met Longan when they both served as adjunct professors at

4413. *Id.* at 23.

4414. *See supra* nn. 3687–3695 and accompanying text.

4415. Dickerson, *Information*, *supra* n. 4403, at 3.

4416. *Dickerson Interview*, *supra* n. 4364, at 18–21.

4417. *Id.* at 23.

4418. *Id.*

4419. *Id.* at 24, 25.

4420. *Id.* at 24.

4421. *See supra* nn. 3779–3785 and accompanying text.

SMU in the early 1990s.[4422] When Dickerson wrote Stetson of her interest in being considered for a faculty position, Longan was a member of the appointment committee and replied to her inquiry.[4423] In July 1995, Stetson hired Dickerson as assistant professor of law. Not only did she come with sterling recommendations, strong undergraduate and graduate degrees, and a clerkship on the Sixth Circuit, she also came with a record of achievements.

From 1992 until her arrival at Stetson, Dickerson was managing director of the *Scribes Journal of Legal Writing.*[4424] For her activities with the Texas Young Lawyers Association (that included being director, treasurer, and member of the executive committee), she received the President's Certificate of Merit Award in 1993, the President's Award in 1994, and the Association's Outstanding Award in 1995.[4425] That same year, she was named the outstanding lawyer in the city of Dallas, Texas. In an interview, Dickerson suggested that her being named the outstanding Dallas lawyer may have related to the fact that "I was somewhat famous among Dallas associates for the number of billable hours that I worked.[4426]

b. Rebuilding Legal Research & Writing Program; Work with ALWD

Upon her arrival at Stetson in July 1995, Dickerson taught legal research and writing, pre-trial practice, and a litigation ethics seminar. She remembers that on her first day on the job, Associate Dean Vause walked into her office and asked her to be in charge of the existing research and writing adjuncts and that she needed to hire four additional ones.[4427] Soon, by the start of classes in August, Dickerson was directing the work of nine R&W adjuncts, teaching, and running the Moot Court Board (that fielded as many as seventeen teams in various competitions).[4428] One year after directing the R&W adjuncts, Dean

---

4422. *Dickerson Interview*, *supra* n. 4364, at 27.

4423. *Id.*

4424. Dickerson, *Information*, *supra* n. 4403 at 7.

4425. *Id.* at 6.

4426. *Dickerson Interview*, *supra* n. 4364, at 26. No one at Stetson College of Law would doubt that Dickerson racked up the highest number of billable hours when she practiced law. If she was not traveling, raising money, or participating in state and national conferences, Dickerson typically arrived at school around 5:30 a.m., and worked into the evenings, and sometimes, well into the night. From the vantage point of her colleagues, from the moment Dickerson arrived on campus, she has never stopped working. She explains: "When I join an organization, I become very involved." *Id.*

4427. *Id.* at 32, 33.

4428. *Id.* at 34; *see also* Dickerson, *Information*, *supra* n. 4403, at 3.

Moody named Dickerson director of the school's R&W program. That same year, she and her colleague Roy Gardner began Stetson's annual International Environmental Law Competition.[4429] Beginning in 1997, Dickerson added law review advisor to her list of responsibilities. In 2000, Gary Vause appointed her associate dean of the College of Law, then in 2002 promoted her to vice dean.[4430]

Directors of research and writing programs at American law schools in 1995 formed an organization called the Association of Legal Writing Directors (ALWD).[4431] The following year, Dickerson attended its second annual meeting, where she became a member of AWLD's citation committee.[4432] Soon, she was named chair of the committee. In this connection, she asked her Stetson student assistant Fred Busack to analyze the sixteenth edition of the Bluebook (1996) of legal citations, a volume published for decades by law review students at Harvard, Yale, Pennsylvania, and Columbia. With Busack's help, Dickerson reviewed the sixteenth edition of the Bluebook, tracing its history and criticizing its periodic revisions, especially those changes adopted in the sixteenth edition. Her analysis was published in a 1996 issue of the *Stetson Law Review,* copies of which she took to the 1997 ALWD Board meeting.[4433] There, the ALWD governing body agreed with Dickerson's critique and revised edition.[4434] Soon thereafter, ALWD President Jan Levine, Associate Professor and Director of Legal Research and Writing at Temple University, along with Richard K. Neuman, Jr., Professor at Hofstra University School of Law, suggested to Dickerson that a common and simplified legal citation system needed to be established, not every few years rewritten by a different group of law students.[4435] Levine and Neuman said to Dickerson: "We want to write a citation manual under the ALWD name and we want you to be an author."[4436]

ALWD signed a contract with Aspen publishers in March 1999, with Dickerson to be an author. Aspen asked her to send a draft of the manual to New York within eight weeks. "So I killed myself," Dickerson said. "I showed up with the table of contents and hundreds of pages of rules of citation and met with

4429. Dickerson, *Information, supra* n. 4403, at 3.

4430. *See supra* n. 4370 and accompanying text.

4431. *Dickerson Interview, supra* n. 4364, at 37.

4432. *Id.*

4433. *See* Darby Dickerson, *An Un-Uniform System of Citation: Surviving with the New* Bluebook, 26 Stetson L. Rev. 53 (1996).

4434. *Dickerson Interview, supra* n. 4364, at 40, 41.

4435. *Id.*

4436. *Id.*

the editors."[4437] She continued to work through the summer of 1999. As a result, in 2000, Aspen published the first edition of the *ALWD Citation Manual: A Professional System of Citation*.[4438] Dickerson also authored a teacher's guide. By 2004, professors at approximately one hundred American law schools had adopted the ALWD Citation Manual, a number representing about 50 percent of the market.[4439] The significance of the new ALWD guide is reflected by the fact that following its publication, the seventeenth edition of the Bluebook came out one year earlier than normal, a revised edition that incorporated numerous changes Dickerson had first made in the ALWD Manual.[4440]

Stetson's law dean also significantly influenced the school's R&W program by reshaping its structure. Previously, each R&W instructor operated independently, there being little coordination and no common conceptual basis or shared goals. After taking over the R&W program, Dickerson established a uniform course of instruction for all R&W professors to follow. Understanding that the program's success depended on the quality of instruction, she made it a top priority to hire individuals with strong academic credentials and who were committed to teaching research and writing in a team effort. Though not all stayed, the cast of newly hired R&W instructors strengthened Stetson's program. They included: Stephanie Vaughan (subsequently Associate Director of R&W), Marsha Freeman, Darren Latham, Jennifer Anglim, Brooke Bowman (initially legal writing fellow, later special assistant to the dean), Ann Piccard (also coach of Stetson's National Civil Rights Moot Court Team), JoAnne Durako (also director for a time), Lawrence Rosenthal, Kelly Feeley (initially a legal writing fellow), Catherine Bohl, Richard Graves III, Jennifer Murphy, Catherine Cameron, Jeffrey Minneti, Bridget Remington, Candace Whitaker, and Carol C. McCrory.[4441]

All of Dickerson's efforts in revamping the R&W program paid off. In April of 2005, *U.S. News & World Report* ranked Stetson's legal writing program third best in the nation (tied with another program) out of 187 law schools.[4442] Not only was Stetson's R&W program recognized as one of the

---

4437. *Id.* at 44.

4438. *See* Association of Legal Writing Directors & Darby Dickerson, *ALWD Citation Manual: A Professional System of Citation* (Aspen L. & Bus. 2000). A second edition followed in 2003.

4439. *Burton Foundation Recognizes Dickerson, Wozniak with National Legal Writing Awards*, 45 Stetson Law. 6 (Spring 2005) [hereinafter *Burton Awards*].

4440. *Dickerson Interview*, *supra* n. 4364, at 50.

4441. Bishop, *List*, *supra* n. 2351, at 7–12.

4442. Darby Dickerson, *New Achievements Draw World's Attention to Stetson*, 45 Stetson Law. 2 (Spring 2005) [hereinafter Dickerson, *New Achievements*].

best, so too was its principal designer, Darby Dickerson. She received the 2005 Burton Award for Outstanding Contributions to Legal Writing Education.[4443] The award was given by the Burton Foundation.[4444]

c. Competitions

During Dickerson's administration through the end of calendar year 2005, both the Moot Court and Client Skills competitions expanded and had successful records. According to the *Stetson Lawyer*, in the 2003–04 academic year, Stetson's Moot Court Board under advisor Stephanie Vaughan won "several best brief awards and best oralist awards, and placed in the top three overall teams in virtually every competition entered since June."[4445] Meanwhile, Stetson's trial team advisor Pamela Cole Bell reported that the trial team "swept Florida and our region," exclaiming, "We've won everything."[4446] Concurrently, Client Skills Board Advisor Kelley Feeley, '95, announced that a Stetson negotiation skills team won the Robert Merhinge, Jr., National Environmental Negotiation Competition at the University of Richmond in Virginia, defeating both Georgetown and Richmond, while a Stetson client counseling team won third place in the Region Five competition at Mercer University.[4447]

d. World Championship

The 2004–05 competitions were highlighted by Stetson students winning the international William C. Vis International Commercial Arbitration Moot Court Competition in Vienna, Austria. Teams from 150 law schools representing forty-seven countries competed.[4448] To become world champions, the Stetson team won competitions against Columbia University law school, University of Vienna, National University of Singapore, Queen's University (Canada), and University of Notre Dame (Australia).[4449] By winning the world championship, Stetson was the first American law school to do so since Cornell had achieved the honor in 1996.[4450] Representing the victorious Stetson

---

4443. *Burton Awards*, *supra* n. 4439, at 6.

4444. *Id.* At the same time, Stetson law alumna Carrie Ann Wozniak, class of '04, was one of fifteen students in the country winning 2005 Burton Award for Legal Achievement.

4445. *Advocacy Board Awards, Advocacy Teams Continue Outstanding Performances in Competitions*, 44 Stetson Law. 7 (Spring 2004).

4446. *Id.*

4447. *Id.*

4448. *World Champions*, 45 Stetson Law. cover, 24, 25 (Spring 2005).

4449. *Id.* at 25.

4450. Interview by Michael I. Swygert, Prof. Emeritus, Stetson U. College of L., with Stephanie Vaughan, Assoc. Dir. of Leg. Research & Writing, Stetson U. College of L.; Jack

Vis World Champions (*left to right*):
Coach Jack Graves, Megan Schultz, Thomas Yaegers, Ryan Jones,
Katherine Hurst, Burks Smith, and Coach Stephanie Vaughan

College of Law were Katherine Hurst, Ryan James, Megan Schultz, Burks Smith, Tom Yeagers, and Kathryn Christian. Professors Stephanie Vaughan and Jack Graves coached the team.[4451]

Stetson first became involved in the Vis International Arbitration Competition upon hearing about it from Dean Emeritus Lizabeth Moody and her husband Alan Buchmann in the fall of 2002. Dean Vause talked to Dickerson about Stetson entering a team in the Vis competition. She in turn asked Vaughan to assemble a group of students to prepare for the 2003 world competition.[4452] Stetson's initial all-woman team consisted of Kristy Harrington, Victoria Cruz Garcia, Christine Jalbert, and Stephanie Zimmerman. At the 2003 international gathering, Kristy Harrington won one of the twenty-five honorable mention oralist awards out of 500 participants in the competition.[4453] The following year, Stetson students Ryan Burke, Burks Smith, Ven

Graves, Asst. Prof. of L., Stetson U. College of L.; and Stetson U. College of L. students Katherine Hurst, Ryan Jones, Megan Schultz, Burks Smith, Tom Yeagers, and Kathryn Christian, 4 (Apr. 2005) [hereinafter *Vaughan, et al. Interview*].

4451. *World Champions*, *supra* n. 4448, at 24.

4452. *Vaughan, et al. Interview*, *supra* n. 4450, at 6.

4453. *Id.* at 15.

Petty, and Sayten Ghandi represented the law school in Vienna. Smith was named one of the top twenty-five oralists of more than 600 participants at the 2004 competition.

Several persons assisted Vaughan and Graves in preparing the students for the 2005 competition. One was Dr. Eugen Salpius, an attorney from Salzburg, Austria, who was President of the Chartered Institute of Arbitrators, which Graves described as "the largest and most prestigious body of arbitrators in the world."[4454] Dr. Salpious flew to Tampa and worked ten days with the Stetson students. Graves and his colleague, Professor Bradford Stone, made sure Stetson's team was familiar with the governing laws: the United Nations Commission for International Trade Law (UNCITRAL); the International Sales of Goods (CISG), a 1980 Convention with more than 100 signatory states; and the UNCITRAL Model Law on International Arbitration.[4455] Graves taught a special class on CSIG.[4456] In addition to professional assistance, Stetson received financial support from the International Law Section of The Florida Bar to help defray the team's travel costs.[4457] Everything was in place.

Finally, in April 2005, the team, their coaches Graves and Vaughan, Dean Emeritus Moody, and Alan Buchmann traveled to Vienna. There, Stetson University College of Law's team won the world's championship. Afterwards, Graves commented: "I have never been more proud of a group of young men and women."[4458] Vaughan observed:

> This Team worked together in perfect harmony. They worked together as a cohesive unit for six months and traveled together for two weeks. Bringing home the world championship to the United States, and directly to Stetson, is indescribable. I have never been more excited for my students and Stetson.[4459]

Dean Dickerson also was pleased with the Stetson students' performance, pointing out that they argued the final round at "one of the largest advocacy competitions in the world before 1,700 observers, including prominent judges, attorneys, and professors from the international community."[4460] Dickerson

4454. *Id.* at 23.
4455. *Id.* at 2, 15.
4456. *Id.* at 15, 16.
4457. *Stetson Wins World Championship in Vienna*, The Brief 1 (Apr. 1, 2005).
4458. *World Champions*, *supra* n. 4448, at 25.
4459. *Id.*
4460. Dickerson, *New Achievements*, *supra* n. 4442, at 2.

noted that the closest U.S. law schools behind Stetson in the world competition were Columbia and Harvard.[4461]

Other Stetson advocacy teams have brought recognition to themselves and to the school in the first decade of the twenty-first century as well. For example, in one year—2004—Stetson's ABA Moot Court team defeated defending champion Yale Law School after beating Duke in the regional finals of the ABA National Appellate Advocacy Competition in Washington, D.C.[4462] Coached by Professor James Underwood, Stetson's team consisted of Brent Bigger, Erika Knowland Russell, and Dana Harris.[4463] That same weekend, Stetson's entry in the Philip C. Jessup International Law Moot Court Competition placed second in the Atlanta Regional, while winning the best brief award.[4464] Finally, three Stetson students advanced to the semi-final round in the Robert F. Wagner National Labor and Employment Law Moot Court Competition in New York City in March 2004, where they also were awarded the best brief award. Coached by Professor Jennifer Anglim, the team consisted of Mary Clapp, Chrysi Pejot, and Ashley Gay.[4465]

e. New Programs: Center for Excellence in Elder Law, et al.

Among the new initiatives implemented by Dickerson was a Jurist-in-Residence program, where a noted judge resides on the law school campus and serves for a semester as a distinguished professorial lecturer.[4466] Justice Andrew G.T. Moore II, retired justice of the Delaware Supreme Court, was the inaugural Jurist in Residence during the spring semester 2006. A New Orleans native and graduate of Tulane Law School, Justice Moore served on the Delaware Supreme Court for a dozen years before retiring from the bench.[4467] In addition to Justice Moore's appointment, Dickerson brought to Stetson several 'Distinguished International Fellows."

In another area, Dickerson strengthened the school's academic support service, using upper-level students called the "dean's fellows." The fellows helped

4461. *Id.*

4462. Frank Klim, *Stetson Law Moot Court Teams Excel in Competitions* 1 (Stetson U. College of L. Mar. 5, 2005) (news release).

4463. *Id.*

4464. *Id.*

4465. Frank Klim, *Stetson Law School Moot Court Team Wins Award at National Competition* 1 (Stetson U. College of L. Mar. 17, 2004) (news release).

4466. *Academic News, Justice Andrew Moore Serves as Inaugural Jurist in Residence*, 45 Stetson Lawyer 11 (Spring 2005).

4467. *Id.*

organize study groups, review practice examinations, organize course materials, and outline and answer questions.[4468]

Meanwhile, due primarily to the efforts of Professor Rebecca Morgan, Stetson University College of Law received substantial gifts and grants, enabling the school to establish a Center for Excellence in Elder Law. Dean Vause had appointed Morgan director of the Center. In April 2003, Morgan announced that the college had joined forces with the American Association of Retired People (AARP) to establish an academic journal on worldwide issues relating to aging and the law.[4469] Stetson's agreement with AARP required holding an annual conference that generated papers later published as articles in a new Stetson-centered publication—the *Journal of International Aging, Law and Policy*.[4470] Professors James W. Fox, Jr., and Richard B. Graves III, were appointed the journal's editors. The AARP undertaking joins other projects sponsored by the Elder Law Center, including: community consumer education programs; clinical elder law courses for students; and continuing legal education in elder law for practicing attorneys and business professionals.

During Vause's deanship, Professor Morgan also forged a unique public-private consortium to provide health law education programs. Stetson University College of Law, together with the University of South Florida School of Medicine, joined to form the Stetson-USF Health Law Consortium, designed to establish collaborative programs in continuing education, research, and policy development.[4471]

In addition to the recent elder and health law programs, Stetson College of Law in 2004 announced the formation of a National Clearinghouse for Science, Technology, and Law,[4472] noting that the purpose of the Clearinghouse was "to help the legal profession keep up with the cutting-edge crime-solving techniques and to train the next generation of scientific investigators."[4473] Due to the efforts of Florida Congressman C.W. Bill Young, the Clearinghouse re-

4468. *Id.* In the spring semester of 2004, fourteen upperclass students served as dean's fellows.

4469. Davina Y. Gould, *Stetson University College of Law and AARP Establish Journal, Conference on International Aging, Law, and Policy* (Stetson U. College of L. Apr. 29, 2003) (news release).

4470. *Id.*

4471. Darlene L. Kelly & Michael Hoad, *Stetson University College of Law and the University of South Florida Announce a New Health Law Consortium* (Stetson U. College of L. and U.S.F. Apr. 10, 2000) (joint-news press release).

4472. Frank Klim, *Stetson University College of Law Forms the Nation's First Clearinghouse on Science and Technology* 1 (Stetson U. College of L. Jan. 20, 1994) (news release).

4473. *Id.*

ceived significant federal funding.[4474] Professor Carol Henderson was and remains the national director of the Clearinghouse.

Henderson has served as co-editor of the *Encyclopedia of Forensic and Legal Medicine*, and has provided professional services to the Innocent Project of Florida.[4475] As part of her duties as head of the National Clearinghouse at Stetson, Henderson teaches a workshop in scientific evidence.[4476] She is a recognized authority in scientific evidence, criminal law, and ethics, and has presented lectures and workshops to thousands of forensic scientists and attorneys worldwide on the topics of scientific evidence, courtroom testimony, and professional responsibility. Moreover, Henderson has authored three books, including *Scientific Evidence in Civil and Criminal Cases*, and over forty articles on scientific evidence, law and ethics. She is an editor of the forthcoming *Encyclopedia of Forensic and Legal Medicine* (Academic Press, London) and a member of the Forensic Specialties Accreditation Board. In 1999, she received the American Academy of Forensic Sciences' Jurisprudence Section's Harold A. Feder Award, and was selected by the American College of Legal Medicine to deliver the Cyril Wecht Distinguished Lecture in Legal Medicine. In addition, she is a fellow in the American Academy of Forensic Sciences, and has served on its Board of Directors.[4477]

Henderson received her J.D. degree from the National Law Center, George Washington University, in 1980. She began her legal career as an Assistant United States Attorney in Washington, D.C. When she first came to Stetson in the fall of 2004, she was a visiting professor on leave from Nova Southeastern University, where she was a tenured professor of law and where she had taught for eighteen years. In the fall of 2005, the faculty and dean of Stetson College of Law invited Henderson to join the school's faculty as a tenured professor.[4478]

In summary, during the time Dickerson has been dean thus far, she and the faculty implemented several new programs. One practice, however, will be ending. With the faculty's approval, Dickerson announced that summer entry of new students will cease in 2006.[4479] From that point on, new first-year students will enter only at the start of the fall and spring semesters.

4474. *Id.*

4475. *Faculty Forum, Carol Henderson*, 45 Stetson Law. 8, 12 (Spring 2005).

4476. *Stetson C.S.I. Solves "Crime" During Workshop*, The Brief 4 (Feb. 2, 2004).

4477. Stetson U. College of L., *Faculty Home Page, Carol Henderson*, www.law.stetson.edu/faculty/henderson.asp (accessed Nov. 21, 2005).

4478. *Id.*

4479. *Academic News, College of Law Discontinues Entering Class*, 45 Stetson Law. 11, 11 (Spring 2005).

Kristen David Adams

f. New Faculty, 2000–2004

For the five-year period 2000 through 2004, Stetson College of Law hired twenty-nine new faculty members, a number including nine full-time research and writing instructors, two trial advocacy fellows, one elder law consumer protection fellow, and three visiting professors. In the fall of 2000, three persons joined the Stetson faculty: Kristen David Adams, B.A., Rice University, J.D., Emory University, LL.M., Yale Law School; James J. Fox, Jr., B.A., University of North Carolina, J.D., University of Michigan; and Kelly M. Feeley, B.S., Florida State University, J.D., Stetson University. Six joined the faculty in the fall of 2001: Michael Allen, B.A., University of Rochester, J.D., Columbia University; Robert N. Davis, B.A., University of Hartford, J.D., Georgetown University; Janice Kay McClendon, B.A., University of Texas, J.D., University of Utah, LL.M., New York University; Madison Mosley, Jr., B.A., University of Florida, M.L.S., University of North Carolina (Greensboro), Ph.D., Florida State University, J.D., Stetson University; Carolyn J. Nygren, B.A., Tufts College, Ph.D., University of Chicago, J.D., Harvard Law School; and Theresa J. Pulley Radwan, B.A., University of Dayton, J.D., College of William and Mary.[4480]

Kristen David Adams, a tenured member of the Stetson law faculty, graduated from Emory Law School with honors in 1995 and received an LL.M. degree from Yale Law School in 2000. At Emory, she was a managing editor of the

4480. List of Stetson Law Faculty and Degrees (July 2005) (on file at Stetson U. College of L., Gulfport, Fla).

Emory Law Journal. Adams received an A.B. degree *cum laude* from Rice University in 1992. She is a member of both Phi Beta Kappa and Order of the Coif.

Between her two law degrees, Adams practiced law for four years in Atlanta, first with Alston & Bird, L.L.C., and later with Altman, Kritzer & Levick, P.C. Her practice included work in commercial litigation, products liability, medical products litigation, medical and psychiatric malpractice defense, intellectual property, and real estate litigation. During her tenure at Alston & Bird, she participated in developing the firm's Products Liability Advisory Committee. While practicing, Adams also was active in pro bono projects, including representing truants before the Fulton County Juvenile Court, co-chairing the Atlanta Legal Aid Society's annual Associate Fundraising Campaign, and serving as an Atlanta Legal Aid Litigation Fellow.

In 2005, Adams was elected into the American Law Institute. She has co-authored *The Practice of Law School: Getting in and Making the Most of Your Legal Education with Christen Civiletto Carey, Esq.* The book is intended to help new law students find out what to expect, how to make their law school experience both fulfilling and relevant to becoming lawyers. Dean Dickerson appointed Adams the holder of the Leroy Highbaugh, Sr. Chair in faculty research for the 2004–2005 and 2005–2006 academic years. During the 2005–06 academic year, she was preparing a commercial transactions casebook, to be published by West Group, and engaging in other research as her primary full-time responsibility. Adams is also the author of five articles.

James W. Fox, Jr., another tenured Stetson faculty member, joined the Stetson faculty in the fall of 2000. He graduated from the University of North Carolina and then attended the University of Michigan Law School, where he graduated *Magna Cum Laude* in 1990 and served as Editor in Chief of the *Journal of Law Reform.* He then clerked for Phyllis Kravitch on the United States Court of Appeals for the Eleventh Circuit. Fox was an associate with the Washington, D.C., firm of Covington & Burling, where his practice focused on complex tort and insurance litigation. He also served as a Temporary Staff Attorney for the Neighborhood Legal Services Program in Washington. Before joining the faculty at Stetson, Professor Fox taught at Mercer University Law School. He teaches Contracts, Poverty and Public Benefits Law, Insurance, and American Legal History.

Professor Fox has written on the history and theory of democratic citizenship and poverty, and on contract theory in journals such as the *Temple Political and Civil Rights Law Review*, the *Case Western Reserve Law Review*, the *Kentucky Law Journal*, and the *University of Pittsburgh Law Review.* Fox's research has also focused on the experience of Jim Crow by southern blacks and whites, and the possible meanings this experience could have for modern interpretations of the Fourteenth Amendment. Fox also has explored the con-

James W. Fox, Jr.

nections between mid-nineteenth-century contract ideology and interpretations of the Fourteenth Amendment.

New faculty in the fall of 2002 included Jack Graves, B.A., J.D., University of Colorado; James M. Underwood, B.A., Oklahoma Baptist University, J.D., Ohio State University; Pamela Cole Bell, B.A., J.D., Stetson University; and Brooke J. Bowman, B.S., Indiana University, J.D., Stetson University. Five were hired to begin in the fall of 2003: Paul J. Boudreaux, B.A., J.D., University of Virginia, LL.M., Georgetown University; Nicholas B. Cox, B.A., University of South Florida, J.D., Washburn University; Clark W. Furlow, B.A., Boston University, J.D., Emory University; Carol Henderson (discussed earlier), B.A., J.D., University of Florida; and Jeffrey J. Minneti, B.A., University of South Florida, and M.B.A., J.D., Samford University.

In the fall of 2004, ten new faculty members, arrived on the Stetson campus: Mark D. Bauer, B.A., University of Chicago, J.D., Emory University; Joan Catherine Bohl, B.A., Boston University, J.D., Suffolk University; Catherine Cameron, B.A., M.A., J.D., University of Florida; Lee A. Coppock, B.A., University of South Florida, J.D., Stetson University; Jo Anne Durako, J.D., University of Florida, Ed.M., Harvard University; Cynthia G. Hawkins-Leon, B.A., Wellesley College, J.D., Harvard Law School; Carol Cole McCrory (visitor), B.A., Queens College, M.A., University of South Florida, J.D., Stetson University; Joseph F. Morrissey (visitor), A.B., Princeton University, J.D., Columbia University; Jennifer E. Murphy, B.A., University of South Florida, J.D., Stetson University; and Charles H. Rose, III, B.A., Indiana University, J.D., Notre

Dame, LL.M., Judge Advocate General's School, U.S. Army.[4481] In the fall of 2005 and the spring of 2006, seven persons joined the Stetson faculty: Lee Coppock, B.A., University of South Florida, J.D., Stetson University College of Law; George E. Edwards (visitor), B.A., North Carolina State University, J.D., Harvard University; Martin A. Frey (visitor), B.S.M.E., Northwestern University, J.D., Washington University, LL.M., George Washington University; Douglas R. Haddock (visitor), B.A., J.D., University of Utah; William A. Kaplin (visitor), A.B., University of Rochester, J.D., Cornell University; Timothy S. Kaye (visitor), LL.B., University of Sheffield, UK, Ph.D., University of Warwick, UK; Lance N. Long (visitor), B.A., J.D., Brigham Young University; Ellen S. Podgor (Culverhouse Chair 2005–2006) (full professor 2006–), B.S., Syracuse University, J.D., Indiana University at Indianapolis, M.B.A., University of Chicago, LL.M., Temple University; Bridget Remington (visitor), A.B., Stanford University, M.A., University of Mississippi, J.D., Stetson University; Ruthann Robson (visitor), B.A., Ramapo College of New Jersey, J.D., Stetson University, LL.M., University of California at Berkeley; Candace Zierdt (visitor), B.A., J.D., University of Kansas, LL.M., Temple University.

g. Dr. Madison Mosley; Judge Robert Davis

Madison Mosley graduated from Stetson College of Law in 1992, and joined the library staff the following year.[4482] In addition to his Stetson law degree, Mosley earned a Ph.D. degree from the University of Florida and a graduate degree in library sciences from the University of North Carolina. At Stetson, he served as Reference Librarian until 1996, when Librarian Lamar Woodard appointed Mosley Associate Librarian. Subsequently, after Professor Woodard retired in February 2002, Dean Vause promoted Mosley to be Stetson's Law Librarian and Director of Information Services with the rank of associate professor.[4483] Tragically, Madison Mosley died on March 29, 2005, at the age of fifty-five.[4484] Dean Dickerson observed that he was "very dedicated to Stetson and the library," adding that "Dr. Mosley was a talented and a highly trained professional."[4485]

Outside of Stetson, Mosley served both as vice president (1998–1999) and president (1999–2000) of the Florida Library Association, and was active in

---

4481. *Id.*; *see also Stetson Welcomes New Law Faculty*, 44 Stetson Law. 12, 13 (Fall 2004).

4482. *Remembering Dr. Mosley*, 45 Stetson Law. 16, 16 (Spring 2005).

4483. *Stetson Community Leader Dr. Madison Mosley Dies*, The Brief 2 (Apr. 1, 2005) [hereinafter *Dr. Mosley Dies*].

4484. *Remembering Mosley*, *supra* n. 4482, at 16.

4485. *Id.*

Librarian Dr. Madison Mosley

the American Association of Law Libraries, the Association of College and Research Libraries, and the American Library Association Black Caucus.[4486] A member of The Florida Bar, Mosley taught as an adjunct at the University of South Florida School of Library and Information Services.[4487] In addition to his professional responsibilities at the College of Law, he served as a member of the Avon Park, Florida, City Council, and as chair of the City of St. Petersburg Citizen's Review Board. Mosley also was Parliamentarian of the City's African-American Voter Education Committee.[4488] Both at Stetson and in the community, Dr. Mosley was highly respected and well-liked.

Another popular Stetson law professor was Robert N. Davis, who came to the law school as a visitor in the fall of 2001 from the University of Mississippi College of Law.[4489] In short order, Davis became a permanent member of the Stetson faculty, but, as it turned out, not for long. On March 25, 2003, President George Bush nominated Davis to be a federal judge on the United States Court of Appeals for Veterans Claims.[4490] The nomination was confirmed by

4486. *Staff Updates, Dr. Madison Mosley*, 41 Stetson Law. 48, 48 (Spring/Summer 2001); *see also Dr. Mosley Dies*, *supra* n. 4483, at 2.

4487. *Id.*

4488. *Id.*

4489. *AALS 2004–2005 Directory*, *supra* n. 3045, at 399.

4490. *Stetson Law Professor Confirmed as Federal Judge*, 45 Stetson Law. 3, 3 (Spring 2005).

the United States Senate on November 29, 2004, and Judge Davis took office in January 2005. On February 1, 2005, the oath of office was administered to Judge Davis on Stetson's campus by Stetson alumnus Judge Thomas Stringer, Sr.[4491] Prior to his appointment, Davis taught courses on national security, terrorism, and constitutional issues at Stetson. Davis was an experienced arbitrator and while at Stetson served on various alternative dispute resolution panels, including those of the American Arbitration Association and the U.S. Postal Service. Judge Davis also served on an arbitration panel with the U.S. Olympic Committee.[4492] Following the September 11, 2001, terrorist attacks on the World Trade Center, Davis, a retired Naval officer, was called back to duty to work with the U.S. Navy Reserves Joint Intelligence Directorate at Tampa's MacDill Air Force Base.[4493]

h. Hall of Fame

Dean Darby Dickerson in 2004 established a law school "Hall of Fame," honoring the "dedication and contributions of alumni, faculty and friends" of Stetson University College of Law.[4494] The dean chaired a ten-member committee that selected the inaugural inductees. The initial members, with a brief description of each, were: Edith M. Atkinson ('22), Stetson's first woman graduate to become a judge, and a pioneer in Florida's juvenile justice system;[4495] Charles A. and Eleanor N. Dana, who, along with the Dana Foundation (discussed earlier),[4496] were major financial supporters of the College of Law; Richard T. Dillon ('57), who joined the faculty after graduating and became the dean of the College of Law for a thirteen-year period, during which the school became stronger both academically and financially;[4497] J. Ollie Edmunds ('28), a Jacksonville lawyer who became president of Stetson University and remained associated with the University for sixty years, and who engineered the move of the law school from DeLand to Gulfport.[4498]

4491. *Id.*

4492. *Investiture of Federal Judge for Former Professor Robert Davis* (Stetson U. College of L. Feb. 1, 2005) (news release).

4493. *Id.*

4494. *In Depth: Business of Law, Seventeen Members Inducted into Stetson Charter Hall of Fame*, Tampa Bay Business Journal (Oct. 15, 2004) (available at www.bixjournals.com/tampabay/stories/2004/10/18).

4495. Frank Klim, *Stetson College of Law Hall of Fame*, 44 Stetson Law. 26, 27 (Fall 2004) [hereinafter Klim, *Hall of Fame*].

4496. *See supra* nn. 2618–2648 and accompanying text.

4497. *See supra* ch. 11.

4498. *See supra* ch. 8.

Justice Frederick B. Karl

Others included: Bruce Jacob ('61), who was dean of the school from 1981 through 1994, and who was responsible for increasing student and alumni morale and renovation, and expansion of the campus; Frederick B. Karl ('49), who spent almost his entire career in public service as Justice of the Florida Supreme Court (one of seven Stetson law grads to do so),[4499] state senator, member of the state house of representatives, state public counsel, county attorney and administrator, city attorney, gubernatorial candidate, and hospital CEO;[4500] Elizabeth A. Kovachevich ('61), who is a judge (former chief judge) on the United States District Court for the Middle District of Florida, member of the College Board of Overseers, and founder of the federal internship program for Stetson students;[4501] Calvin Arnold Kuenzel, who was the first holder of the LeRoy Highbaugh Sr., Professorship;[4502] James Nemec ('36), and Ruth Bartlett Nemec, major benefactors both of the University and the College of Law, who together established the James and Ruth B. Nemec scholarship fund at the law school;[4503] and Perry Nichols ('37), successful trial lawyer and president of both the American Trial Lawyers Association and the Inter-

4499. The others were Roy H. Chapman, Elwyn Thomas, Vassar B. Carlton, T. Frank Hobson, Hap P. Dekle, and E. Harris Drew.

4500. Klim, *Hall of Fame*, *supra* n. 4495, at 26.

4501. *See supra* nn. 3164–3172 and accompanying text.

4502. *See supra* n. 4216 and accompanying text.

4503. Klim, *Hall of Fame, supra* n. 4495, at 27.

national Trial Lawyers Association, and a charter member of the Stetson Law Center Foundation and College of Law Board of Overseers, each of which he chaired.[4504]

In addition, the original Hall of Famers included: Harold L. "Tom" Sebring, dean of the College of Law from 1955 to 1968, who was a former chief justice of the Florida Supreme Court, judge on the Nuremberg War Crimes Tribunal, and head football coach at the University of Florida;[4505] William Reece Smith, Jr., chair emeritus of the law firm Carlton Fields in Tampa, and who has served as president of the American and International Bar Associations, National Conference of Bar Presidents, American Bar Foundation, and American Bar Endowment, as well as interim president of the University of South Florida, and who today holds the title of distinguished professorial lecturer at Stetson law school;[4506] Lewis H. Tribble ('15), former dean of the College of Law, who was a member of the faculty for seventeen years, including ten as dean, and who was responsible for obtaining Stetson law school's accreditation and for keeping the school going during the depression;[4507] William Amory Underhill ('26), trustee of Stetson University who chaired the College Board of Overseers for eighteen years, and who received Stetson's highest honor in 1988, "the Doyle E. Carlton Award for outstanding service to the University and to higher education;"[4508] W. Gary Vause, late dean of Stetson College of Law who spearheaded the search and then negotiated the agreements for construction of the Tampa Law Center (whose contributions to the school were discussed earlier);[4509] and Judge Susan F. Schaeffer ('71), who became the eighteenth inductee of the Stetson College of Law Hall of Fame in February 2005,[4510] a Stetson law student, then a Stetson law professor, who subsequently became a highly acclaimed jurist.[4511]

i. Hall of Fame—2005 Inductees

Stetson University College of Law inducted ten additional alumni, faculty, and friends into its Hall of Fame in 2005. They included: William R. Eleazer, who served twenty-five years on the Stetson faculty and who built Stetson's

4504. *Id.*

4505. *See supra* ch. 10.

4506. Klim, *Hall of Fame, supra* n. 4495, at 27; *see also supra* nn. 3836–3852 and accompanying text.

4507. *See supra* ch. 5.

4508. Klim, *Hall of Fame, supra* n. 4495, at 27.

4509. *See supra* nn. 4224–4236, 4280–4400, and accompanying text.

4510. *Susan Schaeffer, '71, Inducted into Hall of Fame,* 45 Stetson Law. 4, 4 (Spring 2005).

4511. *Id.*

nationally recognized, number-one ranked trial advocacy program; E. Harris Drew ('23), who served two decades as a member of the Florida Supreme Court, including two terms as chief justice, was president of The Florida Bar and the Stetson Lawyers Association, and who was winner of Stetson's Ben C. Willard Award; Ruth Fleet Thurman ('63), who holds the distinctions of being the first female tenured professor at the College of Law and the only woman in her graduating class; William J. Clapp, who played a pivotal role in convincing Stetson University trustees and President Ollie Edmunds that St. Petersburg/Gulfport was the ideal place to relocate the College of Law, and who helped organize a community fundraising campaign to make the move financially possible; and Gardner W. Beckett, Jr. ('57), a celebrated civil rights attorney who during his career donated countless hours of legal representation through the American Civil Liberties Union and who was recognized with the Nelson Poynter Award, Florida's highest award in civil liberties, who won three cases before the United States Supreme Court, and who was president of the board of directors for the Stetson University Law Center Foundation.

Others were: Murray Sams, Jr. ('49), who has been a member of the American College of Trial Lawyers, a board member of the International Academy of Trial Lawyers, president of the International Society of Barristers, and the Florida Bar Board of Legal Specialization and Education, and who was a member of the College of Law Board of Overseers and the Charles A. Dana Foundation; Mary Stewart Howarth-Hewitt ('08), who was the first woman in Florida to go to law school and earn a law degree, admitted by the Florida Supreme Court to practice on June 20, 1908; James T. Russell ('54), who was elected to the Florida Legislature in 1958, and who served as a judge for several municipalities and a City Attorney, in 1965 became an assistant state attorney, then in 1969, state attorney for the 6th Judicial Circuit, a position he held until January 1992, and who in the 1970s helped create a new prosecution clinic at the College of Law; Robert E. Jagger ('58), who spent more than three decades as Public Defender of Pinellas-Pasco county, and who in 1963, together with Stetson professor Paul Barnard and 6th Judicial Circuit Senior Judge John Bird, organized the state's first clinic education program at the College of Law; and Walter Mann, who for more than 25 years was a moving force in the development of Stetson University College of Law, who generously gave time and resources, and who was an organizer of the College of Board of Overseers and its first president from February 1961 until February 1967, who was later elected treasurer of the board, serving from 1969 until his death in 1981, who was a long-term member of the University Board of Trustees, and who had been an investment banker in New York City.

Overseer President William F. Blews

Sammy Cacciatore

j. Alumni

Given the thousands of Stetson law alumni, this history can only mention a few. Several already have been acknowledged in preceding chapters. Here, a few additional law school alumni are briefly noted.

Stetson's graduating lawyers who have excelled in trial work include: Perry Nichols ('37); Sammy Cacciatore ('46); Murray F. Sams, Jr. ('49); Henry M. Searcy ('50); Michael Maher ('61); William F. Blews ('66); Joseph Reiter ('68); and Christian D. Searcy ('73). Stetson graduates have included scores of judges, among them seven members of the Florida Supreme Court—Roy H. Chapman, Elwyn Thomas, T. Frank Hobson, E. Harris Drew, Hal P. Dekle, Vassar B. Carlton, and Frederick B. Karl. Stetson federal judges include two members of the United States Court of Appeals for the Fifth Circuit, David W. Dyer and Louis Willard Strum, as well as several district United States District Court judges, among whom are George H. Whitehurst, Robert Munroe, Susan Bucklew, and Elizabeth Kovachevich.

Stetson United States Congressmen have included E. Clay Shaw, Jr., and Joseph E. Hendrick. Clay Shaw, ('66), has represented South Florida since 1981. By 2005, he was second in seniority among Republicans on the strategic House Ways and Means Committee. A 2005 newspaper story reported that he would likely be a future candidate to be chair of that "powerful" committee.[4512] For

4512. Bill Adair, *For Pragmatic Legislator, It's a Fight for a Key Job: Rep. Clay Shaw Seems*

Judge Susan Bucklew

years, Shaw served as the chair of the Social Security Subcommittee of the House, and has been one of the Congressional leaders in efforts to reform the Social Security system. In 1996, he authored the 1996 Welfare Reform Act.[4513]

U.S. Congressmen E. Clay Shaw

Fit to Be the Next Ways and Means Chairman, but He'll Have to Struggle for It, Like All Else, St. Pete. Times B-1, 1 (June 13, 2005).

4513. *Id.*

Carl M. Kuttler, Jr. (*Courtesy of St. Petersburg College*)

A former mayor of Fort Lauderdale, Congressman Shaw was an associate municipal judge and chief city prosecutor prior to running for Congress.[4514] James Short ('83), a blind native-American, became general counsel of the Seminole Indian Tribe (who came close to assassination by a fellow member of the Tribe's counsel).

Stetson law alumni who have achieved in areas other than the law include: Carl Martin Kuttler, Jr. ('65), president of St. Petersburg College; honorary alumnus Nelson Poynter ('62), former Chief Executive Officer of the St. Petersburg Times, Inc.; Roy M. Speer, Jr. ('59), founder of Home Shopping Network; Thomas James, Chairman of the nation-wide investment company Raymond James and Associates; Russell A. Rasco, former dean, University of Florida law school; Ted Cassidy ('55), actor in both television series and movies; George Winston ('71), professional pianist; Gary Larsen ('78), who worked as a comedian to pay his law school tuition; Robert Mathews ('49), who manufactured and sold mayonnaise to pay his law school tuition; Michael McDonnell ('69), folk-singing guitar and banjo player; Robert L. Ulrich ('63), mayor of St. Petersburg; Frances "Dolly" Hand ('49), community and cultural activist in southeast Florida; Steven M. Millsaps ('85), founder and owner of a software company; and Fred Ridley ('76), Tampa attorney and winner of the

4514. *Id.* at 2.

Nelson Poynter

U.S. Amateur Golf Championship when he was a law student who, in 2005, was president of the United States Golf Association.[4515]

14.5 Conclusion: A Look Ahead

As the writing of this history comes to a close near the end of 2005, Darby Dickerson is in her third year as dean of Stetson University College of Law. Over a century earlier, Stetson College of Law opened as the first law school in Florida, and for nearly a decade was the only law school in the state. Today, Florida has ten law schools. Legal education in the state, as elsewhere, is undergoing significant change. Today, certain law schools stress teaching technical rules of law, and neither expect nor reward faculty research and scholarship. At the other extreme are those schools which attempt to emulate Harvard, Yale, and Stanford, where faculty research and scholarship are given top priority, and professors may teach only six or seven hours in an entire academic year.

Dickerson sees virtues in each of these models, but understands that a particular law school has to evolve in part to respond to its own market forces.

4515. The information in the above paragraph come from various sources, most from newspaper stories that are on file in the Stetson Law Library in catalogues in which Stetson news stories have been posted.

Changing market conditions explain Stetson's part-time program in Tampa, and especially locating it on a "satellite" campus near the center of the largest business and law center in Florida.

As to Stetson's future, Dickerson perceives its mission as one of preparing men and women not only to be "outstanding lawyers," but also to become "leaders" in a rapidly changing global community.[4516] This means that Stetson cannot have "a trade school mentality."[4517] To produce both able lawyers and competent leaders requires, among other things, that professors raise in the classroom a broad range of public policy, jurisprudence, and social science issues and perspectives, including those involving economics, history, psychology, sociology, public policy, and global political considerations. In addition, Dickerson believes that faculty research and writing is a necessity. "To be a complete teacher," she says, "you need to be a good scholar," adding, "It forces you to delve deeply into one's subject."

By developing a focused philosophy of legal education and by having an understanding and appreciation of the legal profession's increasingly competitive and changing dimensions, Dean Darby Dickerson remains confident that Stetson University College of Law will meet the new challenges and, in the process, will reap increasing recognition for educating men and women who are both skilled lawyers and responsible leaders, professionals able to serve their clients' and the public's interests. That is the mission of the Stetson University College of Law.

4516. *Dickerson Interview*, *supra* n. 4364, at 92.
4517. *Id.*

Final Thoughts

"Maybe we should add a law program." So pondered Stetson University President John F. Forbes. The year was 1898. With encouragement from Florida jurists and lawyers, Forbes followed through and Stetson University College of Law opened in DeLand in 1900 with five white male students (all Floridians). Today, 106 years later, the law school has over 1,000 students attending classes on campuses in Gulfport and Tampa. As an acorn germinates and grows into a great oak, provided the soil is nourishing and environmental conditions are favorable, so too an idea takes hold and evolves into a great institution, if good people are committed and circumstances are conducive for development.

The history of Stetson University College of Law is a story of how John Forbes's idea came to fruition. It is the story of people associated with the institution who made both good and poor decisions along the journey, and of circumstances and events that created both opportunities and hardships. In Stetson's case, good people, fortuitous circumstances, and generous benefactors ultimately came out on top. The resulting synergy turned a once-struggling law school into the prestigious College of Law it is today, a school that has talented and diverse students, fine teachers, recognized scholars, innovative programs, an acknowledged supremacy in advocacy, strong administrators, and supportive alumni and friends.

Throughout its existence, Stetson University College of Law was affected by crucial economic and political events: the slow healing of the nation's sectional wounds following the Civil War and its aftermath; the human and economic sacrifices brought on by World War I, the Great Depression, World War II, and the Vietnam War; and assassinations, including two U.S. Presidents (McKinley and Kennedy), Senator Robert Kennedy, and the Reverend Martin Luther King, Jr.

The school has played its part in historically significant social changes. Both through its teachings and by example, Stetson College of Law became an active participant in breaking down entrenched racial, ethnic, and gender biases;

in contributing to a more compassionate society based on principles of human dignity, freedom, and equality; in raising the standards of the legal profession and the efficacy of legal education; and in increasing the awareness of the importance of international law. When the College began in1900, in Volusia County, Florida, the phrase "global community" was unknown. One hundred and six years later, however, the law school holds, or has held, classes and educational programs in Argentina, Austria, Canada, Colombia, Estonia, Germany, Hungary, Mexico, the Netherlands, and Spain, and in the spring of 2006 was planning a program in China.

Since Stetson's first class graduated in 1902, several thousand lawyers have earned degrees from the College, the majority in Gulfport, where the facilities remain something to behold. Many students and professors who have studied or taught at the Gulfport campus believe it is the most beautiful and welcoming law school campus in the country, and they may be right. The buildings constructed in the distinctive Mediterranean Revival architectural style, and the gorgeously landscaped grounds are a far cry from the school's cramped and shoddy facilities at the abandoned Air Naval Station near DeLand during the late 1940s and early 1950s.

When Stetson law school opened in 1900, there was no law school building, only a small space in Elizabeth Hall on the campus of John B. Stetson University. That fall, the school's five students were taught by three full-time instructors, one of whom was the dean. The library had fewer than 200 books. No secretaries, librarians, or administrative personnel were on the payroll; just as well, since the school's budget for its first year was likely less than $5,000, and student tuition was $66 a year. Travel to and from DeLand was difficult, since most roads were dirt and automobiles were scarce. In the fall of 1901, the law school moved into the new Flagler Hall, built to house both law and engineering programs, and was financed by the famous oil and railroad tycoon Henry Flagler.

On several occasions during the College's first half century, it nearly closed: first, after the State's second law school sprung up at the University of Florida in 1909. Then, but for the efforts of Stetson's President Lincoln Hulley and the school's second law dean, Richmond Rasco, Stetson College of Law would not have survived. Another near closure came after the American Bar Association (ABA) implemented stricter standards for law school approval in 1921. If Stetson was not ABA "approved," its law graduates faced the prospect of not being allowed to sit for state bar examinations. Fortunately, the College's third dean, Lewis Tribble, spearheaded the school's gaining both ABA approval and membership in the Association of American Law Schools (AALS). Two decades later, the College faced closure for economic reasons due to a massive decline in enrollment after America's entry into World War II. In fact, the school did close for two years, but re-opened with a large influx of veterans after the war.

The most serious threat to the College's future, however, occurred in the early 1950s when the ABA declared said it would no long approve the law school because of its rundown physical facilities, low admission and retention academic standards, and due to the absence of decanal and faculty autonomy from the University's central administration. The dire warning caused the University's Board of Trustees and President J. Ollie Edmunds to make a fateful decision: the College of Law would be moved to a metropolitan community of Florida with a large population that would afford the school greater visibility and, thereby, hopefully attract more students. A competition ensued among Jacksonville, Pensacola, Tampa, Orlando, and St. Petersburg. A group headed by a power company executive, William Clapp, represented St. Petersburg and won the prize, resulting in the University purchasing an abandoned hotel property in adjacent Gulfport. Thus, in the summer of 1954, after more than half a century in DeLand, Stetson University College of Law moved onto the grounds of the vacant 1920s former resort, and by doing so, gave the school not only a new campus, but more importantly, revitalized vitality.

Following relocation to Florida's west coast, Stetson College of Law virtually remade itself. At the beginning of the 2005–2006 academic year, the College had 1,013 enrolled students—consisting of: 538 women (53%); 475 men (47%); and 242 minorities (24% of the student body), composed of sixty African-Americans; 119 Hispanics; twenty-six Asians; and five Native Americans. Meanwhile, the full-time law faculty grew from three in 1900 to fifty-eight in 2005, including twenty-five women, thirty-three men, four African-Americans, and two Hispanics. The library had 410,000 volumes and a staff of eight professional librarians along with twelve supporting personnel. Excluding the faculty, the College of Law employed in excess of 120 persons. In the academic realm, by 2006, the law school had established four "Centers for Excellence:" Advocacy; Elder Law; Higher Education Law and Policy; and International Law and Business.

The most enduring story of Stetson University College of Law has been and continues to be its graduates. Back in 1903, a young man graduated at the second commencement of the budding law school in DeLand. His name was O.K. Reaves (when he was born, his father allegedly said, "He's O.K."). Reaves practiced law in Bradenton for twelve years, and for a time represented Manatee County in the Florida House of Representatives. In 1915, he was appointed circuit judge for the Sixth Judicial Circuit, then encompassing several counties on Florida's west coast.

In the early decades of the twentieth century, racially motivated lynchings were taking place in Florida, including Hillsborough County.[4518] Those who committed the cold-blooded murders were rarely held accountable, and public officials seldom denounced the atrocious crimes. One exception was Judge O.K. Reaves. In 1921, Judge Reaves wrote a letter to the *Bradenton Herald* newspaper in which he condemned the lawless perpetrators.[4519] He wanted the public to know that lynchings violated the Constitution of the United States of America, that all people were guaranteed due process under the law, and that "lynchings had no legal justification whatsoever, none." In the ensuing decades, Judge O.K. Reaves never forgot the value of his legal training at Stetson College of Law. For many years, he served on the University's Board of Trustees.

The 1900 Stetson University College of Law and the school with the same name today outwardly bear little resemblance. Yet the school's core mission remains the same. For over a century, men and women of Stetson College of Law have sought to instill in Stetson law students knowledge, skills, judgment, and ethical and behavioral norms characteristic of the most respected and successful lawyers. This has been and continues to be the school's continuing mission. As this history has aspired to demonstrate, the most valuable and enduring legacy of Stetson University College of Law is its graduates. Judge O.K. Reaves is but one among thousands.

4518. Ingalls, *supra* n. 66, at 51–73; *see generally* Richardson, supra n. 474. For a good discussion of the experiences of African-Americans in Florida from the time Stetson College of Law was founded that focuses on the early decades on the Twentieth Century, *see* Jones, *supra* n. 67.

4519. Wm. Reece Smith, Jr. *Historical Profiles of Carlton, Fields, Ward, Emmanuel, Smith & Cutler, P.A.* 18 (86 page unpublished manuscript) ((May 1992) (on file at Stetson U. College of L., Gulfport, Fla). Smith is former President of the American Bar Association and The Florida Bar and today is Chairman Emeritus of the Board of Carlton Fields and Distinguished Professorial Lecturer at Stetson University College of Law.

ADDENDUM ONE

Stetson University Presidents

John F. Forbes	1885–1903
Lincoln Hulley	1904–1934
William Sims Allen	1934–1947
J. Ollie Edmunds	1948–1967
Paul F. Geren	1967–1969
John E. Johns	1969–1976
Pope A. Duncan	1977–1987
H. Douglas Lee	1987–present

ADDENDUM TWO

Deans of Stetson University College of Law

Albert J. Farrah	1900–1909
Lincoln Hulley (president, acting)	1909–1914
Richmond A. Rasco	1914–1921
Lincoln Hulley (president, acting)	1921–1929
Lewis H. Tribble	1929–1938
Paul Raymond	1938–1941
Thomas F. Lambert (acting)	1941–1942
Roy F. Howes (school closed)	1942–1946
Lemuel A. Haslup	1946–1953
Charles J. Hilkey (acting)	1953–1955
Harold J. "Tom" Sebring	1955–1968
Richard T. Dillon	1968–1981
Bruce R. Jacob	1981–1994
Lizabeth A. Moody	1994–1999
W. Gary Vause	1999–2003
Darby Dickerson (acting)	May 2003–February 12, 2004
Darby Dickerson	2004–present

Bibliography

Books

A Conflict of Laws, Anthology (Gene Shreve ed., Anderson Publg. Co. 1997).

A Guide to the History of Florida (Paul S. George ed., Greenwood Press 1989).

Edward N. Akin, *Flagler: Rockefeller Partner and Florida Baron* (Kent State U. Press 1988).

American Bar Association on Lawyer Competency (ABA 1973).

American Higher Education: A Documentary History vol. 1 (Richard Hofstadter & Wilson Smith eds., U. Chi. Press 1961).

Raymond Arsenault, *St. Petersburg and the Florida Dream: 1888–1950* (Donning Co. 1988).

Richard Baepler, *Flame of Faith, Lamp of Learning: A History of Valparaiso University* (Concordia Publg. House 2002).

John Bartlett, *Familiar Quotations* (Emily Morison Beck ed., 15th ed., Little, Brown & Co. 1980).

Charles A. Beard & Mary R. Beard, *A Basic History of the United States* (Garden City Publg. 1944).

Camaliel Bradford, *Webster, Daniel*, in *Encyclopedia Britannica* vol. 23 (William Yust ed., U. Chi. 1946).

Caroline Mays Brevard, *A History of Florida: From the Treaty of 1763 to Our Times* (James Alexander Robertson ed., Fla. St. Historical Socy. 1924).

Lynne S. Brown, *Gulfport, Florida* (Arcadia Publg. 1999).

W. Paul Burman, *The First German War Crimes Trial: Desk Notebook of the Doctors' Trial, Held in Nuremberg, Germany, December 1945 to August 1947* (Documentary Publications 1985).

Robert S. Carr & John G. Beriault, *Prehistoric Man in South Florida*, in *Environments of South Florida: Present and Past* (P.J. Gleason ed., 2d ed., Miami Geological Socy. 1984).

Bruce Catton, *The Civil War* (Am. Heritage Press 1971).

Celebrating Florida's First 150 Women Lawyers (Wendy S. Loquasto ed., Fla. B. & Fla. Assn. of Women Laws., Lexis Publg. 2000).

Whittaker Chambers, *Witness Whittaker Chambers* (Random House, Inc. 1952).

David Leon Chandler, *Henry Flagler: The Astonishing Life and Times of the Visionary Robber Baron Who Founded Florida* (MacMillan Publishers Co. 1986).

Eugene Francis Clark, *Dartmouth College*, in *Encyclopedia Britannica*, vol. 7 (William Yust ed., U. Chi., 1946).

David R. Colburn, *Florida Politics in the Twentieth Century* in *New History of Florida* 344–372 (Michael Gannon ed., U. Press Fla. 1996).

James B. Conant, *Thomas Jefferson and the Development of American Public Education* (U. Cal. Press 1962).

Peter Del Swords & Frank K. Walwer, *The Costs and Resources of Legal Education: A Study of the Management of Educational Resources* (Colum. U. Press 1974).

Helen Parce DeLand, *Story of DeLand and Lake Helen, Florida* (Academic Press 1928).

John Dewey, *My Pedagogic Creed* (Kellogg 1897).

Robert J. Donovan, *The Devastating Time: Truman, the Hydrogen Bomb, China and Korea*, (Princeton 1979).

Max Frankel, *High Noon in the Cold War: Kennedy, Khrushchev, and the Cuban Missile Crisis* (Presidio Press 2004).

Lawrence M. Friedman, *A History of American Law* (2d ed., Simon & Schuster 1986).

Walter P. Fuller, *St. Petersburg and Its People* (Great Outdoors Publg. Co. 1972).

Michael V. Gannon, *Florida: A Short History* (U. Press Fla. 1993).

Harry C. Garwood, *Stetson University and Florida Baptists: A Documentary History of Relations between Stetson University and the Florida Baptist Convention* (Fla. Baptist Historical Socy. 1962).

George Washington Goethals & Clarence Ridley, Panama Canal, History, in *Encyclopedia Britannica* vol. 171 (William Yust ed., U. Chi., 1946).

Karl H. Grismer, *The Story of St. Petersburg, Florida* (P.K. Smith 1948).

Walter Hagen, *The Walter Hagen Story* (Simon & Schuster 1956).

Albert J. Harno, *Legal Education in the United States* (Bancroft-Whitney Co. 1953).

Barbara J. Harris, *Beyond Her Sphere: Women and the Professions in American History* (Greenwood Press 1978).

Hugh Hawkins, *Between Harvard and America: The Educational Leadership of Charles W. Eliot* (Oxford U. Press 1972).

Rackham Holt, *Mary McLeod Bethune* (Doubleday 1964).

John P. Howe, *Chicago, University of*, in *Encyclopedia Britannica* vol. 5 (William Yust ed., U. Chi. 1946).

Elbert Hubbard, *Little Journeys to the Homes of Great Business Men: John B. Stetson* (Roycrofters 1911).

Charles Evans Hughes, *The Supreme Court of the United States* (Colum. U. Press 1927).

James Willard Hurst, *The Growth of American Law: The Law Makers* (Little, Brown & Co. 1950).

Robert P. Ingalls, *Urban Vigilantes in the New South: Tampa, 1882–1936* (U. Tenn. Press 1988).

Marquis James, *The Life of Andrew Jackson: Part One—The Border Captain* (Bobbs-Merrill Co. 1938).

Paul Johnson, *A History of the American People* (Weidenfeld & Nicolson 1997).

Maxine D. Jones, *The African-American Experience in Twentieth Century America*, in *The New History of Florida* (Michael Gannon ed., U. Press Fla. 1996).

David M. Kennedy, *The American People in the Great Depression: Freedom from Fear*, in *Oxford History of the United States* (Oxford U. Press 2003).

Eleonor Kerlow, *Poisoned Ivy: How Egos, Ideology, and Power Politics Almost Ruined Harvard Law School* (St. Martin's Press 1994).

Christopher Columbus Langdell, *A Selection of Cases on the Law of Contracts* (Little, Brown & Co. 1871).

Frederick DeLand Leete, *The DeLand Family in America, a Biographical Genealogy* (DeLand, Fla. 1943).

Anthony Lewis, *Gideon's Trumpet* (Random House 1964).

Gilbert L. Lycan, *Stetson University: The First 100 Years* (Stetson U. Press 1983).

Lee Manchester, *The Lake Placid Club, 1890–2002* (Adirondack Publg. Co. 2003).

Sidney Walter Martin, *Florida's Flagler* (U. Ga. Press 1949).

Master Builders: A Guide to Famous American Architects (Diane Maddex ed., Preservation Press 1985).

David McCullough, *The Path between the Seas: The Creation of the Panama Canal, 1879–1914* (Simon & Schuster 1977).

George McKenna, *American Populism* (G.P. Putman's Sons 1974).

Marian C. McKenna, *Tapping Reeve and the Litchfield Law School* (Oceana Publications 1986).

Raymond A. Mohl & George E. Pozzetta, *From Migration to Multiculturalism: A History of Florida Immigration*, in *New History of Florida* (Michael Gannon ed., U. Press Fla. 1996).

Edmund Morris, *The Rise of Theodore Roosevelt* (Coward, McCann & Geoghegan 1979).

Edmund Morris, *Theodore Rex* (Random House 2001).

New Perspectives on Charles Wilson Peale (Lillian B. Miller & David C. Ward eds., U. Pittsburgh Press 1991).

Official Guide to ABA-Approved Law Schools (2005 ed., ABA & LSAC 2006).

Herman Oliphant, *Summary of the Studies of the Legal Education by the Faculty of Law of Columbia University* (Colum. U. 1938).

Herbert L. Packer & Thomas Ehrlich, *New Directions in Legal Education* (McGraw-Hill 1973).

Clifton Paisley, *The Red Hills of Florida* (U. Ala. 1989).

George W. Pettengill, Jr., *The Story of Florida Railroads 1834–1903* (Ry. & Locomotive Historical Socy. 1952).

Samuel Proctor, *Napoleon Bonaparte Broward: Florida's Fighting Democrat* (U. Fla. Press 1950).

Samuel Proctor, *Prelude to the New Florida, 1877–1919*, in *New History of Florida* (Michael Gannon ed., U. Press Fla. 1996).

Alfred Z. Reed, *Training for the Public Profession of Law* (Charles Scribner's Sons 1921).

Alfred Z. Reed, *Training for the Public Profession of Law: Historical Development and Principal Contemporary Problems of Legal Education in the United States with Some Account of Conditions in England and Canada* (ABA 1921).

Richard Rhodes, *Dark Sun: The Making of the Hydrogen Bomb* (Simon & Schuster 1966).

Joe M. Richardson, *The Negro in the Reconstruction of Florida* (Fla. St. U. Studies No. 46, 1965).

John Ritchie, *The First Hundred Years: A Short History of the School of Law of the University of Virginia for the Period 1826–1926* (U. Press Va. 1978).

William W. Rodgers, *Fortune and Misfortune: The Paradoxical Twenties*, in *New History of Florida*, Michael Gannon ed., U. Press Fla. (1996).

John L. Rosser, *A History of Florida Baptists* (Broadman Press 1949).

Daniel L. Schafer, *U.S. Territory and State*, in *New History of Florida* (Michael Gannon ed., U. Press Fla. 1996).

Michael G. Schene, *Hopes, Dreams and Promises: A History of Volusia County, Florida* (News-J. Corp. 1976).

Arthur M. Schlesinger, Jr., *The Age of Jackson* (Little, Brown & Co. 1945).

J. Irving Scott, *The Education of Black People in Florida* (Dorrance Publg. Co. 1974).

James B. Scott, *The American Law School* (publisher unavailable 1906).

Charles Coleman Sellers, *Charles Wilson Peale with Patron and Populace: A Supplement to Portraits and Miniatures by Charles Wilson Peale* (Am. Phil. Socy. 1969).

Charles Coleman Sellers, *Portraits and Miniatures of Charles Wilson Peale* (Am. Phil. Socy. 1952).

Thomas L. Shaffer & Robert S. Redmount, *Lawyers, Law Students and People* (Shepard's 1977).

William Bristol Shaw, John Batterson Stetson, in *Dictionary of American Biography* vol. 17 (Charles Scribner's Sons 1943).

Wm. Reece Smith, Jr. *Historical Profiles of Carlton, Fields, Ward, Emmanuel, Smith & Cutler, P.A.* (May 1992) (unpublished manuscript).

Sheldon M. Stern, *The Week the World Stood Still: Inside the Secret Cuban Missile Crisis* (Stanford U. Press 2005).

Robert Stevens, *Law School: Legal Education in America from the 1850s to the 1980s* (U.N.C. Press 1983).

Ambrose L. Suhrie, *Teacher of Teachers* (Richard R. Smith 1955).

Michael Irven Swygert, *And, We Must Make Them Noble, A Contextual History of the Valparaiso University School of Law: 1879–2004* (Carolina Academic Press 2004).

Telford Taylor, *The Anatomy of the Nuremberg Trials: A Personal Memoir* (Knopf 1992).

Charlton W. Tebeau, *A History of Florida* (U. Miami Press 1980).

The AALS Directory of Law Teachers 1977 (Am. L. Found. 1977).

The AALS Directory of Law Teachers 2004–2005 (West Publg. Co. 2004).

The Story of the Florida Bar—A History (Fla. B. n.d.).

Alain Touraine, *The Academic System in American Society* (McGraw-Hill 1974).

Trials of War Criminals before the Nuremberg Military Tribunals under Control Council Law 10, vol. 1 (Govt. Prtg. Off. 1950).

Vroman Graves Assocs., *Leaders in Trial Practice, The Employer's Guide* (1995).

Charles Warren, *History of the American Bar* (Little, Brown & Co. 1913).

Edward C. Williamson, *Florida Politics in the Gilded Age, 1877–1893* (U. Press of Fla. 1976).

Periodicals

NOTE: Any periodicals or clippings that have no date are on file at Stetson U. College of L. Archives, Gulfport, Fla.

Benchmarks, 30 Fla. B. News 23 (Dec. 1, 2003).

Bill Adair, *For Pragmatic Legislator, It's a Fight for a Key Job: Rep. Clay Shaw Seems Fit to Be the Next Ways and Means Chairman*, St. Pete. Times (June 13, 2005).

Along Florida's West Coast, Special to The New York Times, N.Y. Times 22 (Feb. 16, 1936).

America's Best Graduate Schools, 128 U.S. News & World Rpt. 56 (Apr. 10, 2000).

America's Best Graduate Schools, 126 U.S. News & World Rpt. 95 (Mar. 19, 1999).

America's Best Graduate Schools, 124 U.S. News & World Rpt. 77 (Mar. 2, 1998).

America's Best Graduate Schools, 122 U.S. News & World Rpt. 67 (Mar. 10, 1997).

America's Best Graduate Schools, 120 U.S. News & World Rpt. 82 (Mar. 18, 1996).

America's Best Graduate Schools, 118 U.S. News & World Rpt. 84 (Mar. 20, 1995).

Army Orders and Assignments, Special to The New York Times, N.Y. Times 30 (Aug. 20, 1935).

Jack Averitt, *In, Around Statehouse,* Indianapolis Times (June 14, 1970).

Jack Averitt, *Skipping Law Exams Ends in Court Hassle,* Indianapolis Times (June 11, 1970).

Bar Panel Bids Law Schools Stress Practical Training, N.Y. Times A-10 (Aug. 16, 1979).

Bath Houses to Be Erected; Cadets to Use New Treasure Island Center for Beach, Aquatic Activities (a news story in what was likely either in the *St. Petersburg Times* or the *Evening Independent* (May 2, 1937)).

Bill Beck, *He Gave to Florida: Spring Baseball; A Billion Dollar Industry* 39 (n.d.) (newspaper clipping, likely from Tampa Bay area newspaper, circa 1970s).

Dick Bothwell, *Stetson at Twenty,* St. Pete. Times (Sept. 29, 1974).

Myra Bradwell, *Admission of Women to the Bar,* 11 Chi. Leg. News 179 (1879).

Lowell Brandle, *Sebring Decides to Accept Post as Stetson Dean,* St. Pete. Times sec. 1, 15 (July 2, 1955).

David Briggs, *The Sacred & the Secular: A Scholarly Struggle,* St. Pete. Times E4 (Sept. 12, 1992).

Graham Brink, *Stetson Opens Tampa Campus,* St. Pete. Times B1 (Jan. 12, 2004).

Buildings Dedicated at Stetson Law School, St. Pete. Times A2 (Mar. 7, 1969).

Burger Urges Curbs on Trial Lawyers Not Fully Trained, N.Y. Times 1 (Nov. 27, 1973).

Tom Carney, *The Downfall of Handsome Jack,* 1 Old Pinellas Press 2 (1992).

Culverhouse Endows Law Chair, St. Pete. Times 3 (Apr. 18, 1987).

Dean Sebring, Noted Jurist, Law Dean Dies, St. Pete. Times B13 (July 27, 1968).

Dean Tribble, DeLand Sun (Sept. 9, 1931).

Dr. Paul Raymond Returns to Take Up Duties of Law Dean, DeLand Sun 1 (Aug. 9, 1938).

Duke Law Dean Joins Stetson, N.Y. Times 25 (Mar. 4, 1956).

Hamilton Dunn, *Florida, Stetson University's College of Law: It's Taylor Spelled Backwards* (undated newspaper clipping, likely from Tampa Bay area newspaper, circa 1954–1955).

Susan Eastman, *Hallowed Halls Are Crumbling—Poor Construction Costly to Stetson,* St. Pete. Times City sec. 1 (Sep. 11, 1988).

Editorial, *Intellectual Climate Moving South,* St. Pete. Times 8 (Mar. 5, 1956).

End of an Era, DeLand Sun News 1 (Feb. 20, 1954).

Every Recent Stetson Grad Passes Bar Exam, St. Pete. Times B8 (Apr. 20, 1989).

Florida Baptist Witness (Sept. 10, 1985).

Peter B. Gallagher, *Jim Bob Tinsley Chronicles Life and Music of Cowboys,* St. Pete. Times (n.d.).

Norman Gelman, *To Stetson Law School Dean, Every New Job Has Been More Enticing Than the Last*, 74 St. Pete. Times 4 (Sept. 29, 1957).

Bob Harig, *Hagen's Approach: Be a Real Swinger,* St. Pete. Times C1 (Aug. 14, 1989).

Scott Taylor Hartzell, *Gulfport Owes It All to Catalog Mogul Roebuck,* St. Pete. Times Neighborhood Sec. 2 (Feb. 18, 2004).

Scott Taylor Hartzell, *Jungle Sparkled as 1925 Hotel Boom's Crown Gem,* St. Pete. Times S. Pinellas Sec. 1 (Apr. 11, 2001).

Carol Jeffares Hedman, *Pasco County Politicians Make Mark in Legislature,* Tampa Trib. F6 (Pasco ed.) (July 13, 2004).

Ed Hirshberg, *Tampa Bay Transformations: Hotels to Universities,* Fla. Gulf Coast Living 20 (April/May 1981).

Honor Court, DeLand Sun News 8 (Nov. 11, 1949).

Dudley S. Johnson, *Henry Bradley Plant and Florida,* 45 Fla. Historical Q. 118 (Oct. 1966).

James A. Jones, Jr., *Former WAC Ties for Most Time in Military,* Bradenton Herald Local sec. 1 (Aug. 17, 2003).

Mark D. Killian, *Stetson's Dean Moody Steps Down*, Fla. B. News 17 (Nov. 1, 1998).

Jeff Klinkenberg, *Thanks Babe,* St. Pete. Times E1 (Mar. 21, 2004).

Jerome C. Latimer, *Stetson University: Clinical Programs—Pioneering, Innovative, and Effective*, Fla. B.J. 43 (July/Aug. 1991).

Anne Lindberg, *Stetson Law School Is Feeling the Pressure,* St. Pete. Times B1 (Apr. 25, 1995).

Anne Lindberg, *Two Law Professors Lose Jobs at Stetson*, St. Pete. Times N. Pinellas Sec. 3 (Apr. 23, 1995).

Jeanne Malmgren, *Rhymes and Misdemeanors*, St. Pete Times (n.p.) (Apr. 19, 1994)

Walter Mann, *Winter Haven Pioneer, Receives Honorary Degree*, Winter Haven News 2 (May 23, 1973).

Jean Miller, *Updated Elegance: Designer Takes Pride in Restoring a Part of Stetson's Past*, St. Pete. Times F1 (Oct. 5, 1975).

Muriel Mendels Bride; Former New Jersey Girl Is Wed in South to James D. Hedges, N.Y. Times 22 (Feb. 16, 1934).

Nobel Laureate Visits Stetson, 29 Fla. B. News 35 (May 15, 2002).

Bette Orsini, *Men, Men, More Men, and Stetson Gals Talk Taxes*, St. Pete. Times E7 (Oct.17, 1954).

People You Should Know, Dean Lemuel Allen Haslup (n.d.) (clipping from unidentified newspaper).

Peter Kramer, *An Informal Visit with Mr. Sebring of Stetson*, St. Pete. Times 10 (Nov. 28, 1965).

Nancy Piscopo, *Chapel Unable to Clear Its Name*, St. Pete. Times B8 (Apr. 13, 1996).

Presentation Day—A Yearly Occurrence of Great Advantage to a Florida College, Jacksonville Times Union (Feb. 23, 1902).

Response on Behalf of Newly Admitted Members, Fla. B.J. 528 (Nov. 1957).

Nancy Rivera, *Southland Business: Fastest-Growing Law Firms*, L.A. Times V4 (Oct. 6, 1985).

Rolyat Pronounced Architectural Gem; Pasadena's Highly Picturesque Spanish Hostelry Is Acclaimed as a Distinct Addition to the Fine Show Places of the Country, 2 Pasadena Progress 1 (Nov. 5, 1925).

Scott E. Schiltz, *Judicial Profile: Honorable Susan F. Schaeffer*, Newsltr. (Clearwater B. Assn.) 1 (Dec–Jan. 2002).

Schools, N.Y. Times, Classified sec. (Aug. 7, 1949).

William D. Slicker, *The Building Boom in St. Petersburg: A Photographic Essay*, 11 Tampa Bay History 22 (Fall/Winter 1989).

Leslie Reicin Stein, *Tribute to Gary Vause, A Personal Remembrance*, in *W. Gary Vause: A Life of Service*, 42 Fla. B. Checkoff 1 (Sept. 2003).

Stetson Aims to Protect Seniors against Fraud, 29 Fla. B. News 18 (Dec. 15, 2002).

Stetson Appoints Six Full-Time Professors, St. Pete. Indep. A7 (Sept. 10, 1975).

Stetson Law Dean, Judge Harold Sebring, St. Pete. Indep. C6 (July 26, 1968).

Stetson Law Professor's Hard Ascent, St. Pete. Times B1 (Dec. 20, 2004).

Suniland: The Magazine of Florida 112 (Nov. 3, 1925) (published monthly by the Peninsular Publg. Co., Tampa, Fla.).

The Adoption of Student Practice Rules, Fla. B.J. 35 (July/Aug. 1991).

The Last Dance, Adirondack Life Mag. 42 (Apr. 1987).

The Rolyat Hotel, St. Petersburg, Florida, N.Y. Times, Classified Sec. (Dec. 24, 1929).

Bruce Vielmetti, *Dean Pulled Stetson Up a Notch*, St. Pete. Times B1 (June 20, 1994).

Bruce Vielmetti, *Stetson Struggles to Diversify*, St. Pete. Times B4 (June 20, 1994).

Tom Zucco, *Outstanding in His Field; Part of Babe Ruth's Legacy Lives in St. Petersburg*, St. Pete. Times D4 (Mar. 2, 1998).

Academic Journals

Bar Unit Urges Law Schools to Shift Emphasis, 18 Chron. Higher Educ. 6 (June 1979).

Mark F. Boyd, *The First American Road in Florida: Pensacola-St. Augustine Highway, 1824*, 14 Fla. Historical Q. 73 (Oct. 1935).

Anthony Chase, *The Birth of the Modern Law School*, 23 Am. J. Leg. History 329 (1979).

James W. Covington, *The Tampa Bay Hotel*, 26 Tequesta 1 (1966).

Henry J. Doherty, *Jacksonville as a Nineteenth Century Railroad Center*, 58 Fla. Historical Q. (Apr. 1980).

Charles D. Farvis, *The Courts of Territorial Florida*, 19 Fla. Historical Q. 346 (Apr. 1941).

Robert P. Ingalls, *General Joseph H. Wall and Lynch Law in Tampa*, 63 Fla. Historical Q. 51 (July 1984).

Sidney Johnston, *The Historic Stetson University Campus in DeLand, 1884–1934*, 70 Fla. Historical Q. 281 (Jan. 1992).

JoEllen Lind, *Trailblazers: The Changing Role of Women in American Legal History*, 7 Amicus 12 (Winter 1994).

Janet Snyder Matthews, *He Carried His Life in His Hands: The Sarasota Assassination Society of 1884*, 58 Fla. Historical Q. 1 (July 1979).

Samuel Proctor, *The National Farmers' Alliance Convention of 1890 and Its "Ocala Demands,"* 28 Fla. Historical Q. 161 (Jan. 1950).

Henry Wade Rodgers, *Law School of the University of Michigan*, 1 Green Bag 189 (1889).

Henry Wade Rodgers, *Law Department of Michigan University*, 3 W. Jurist 129 (1899).

Samuel Selkow, *Hawkins: The United States Supreme Court and Justice*, 31 J. Negro Educ. 97 (1962).

Charles Coleman Sellers, *Charles Wilson Peale and John Beale Bordley*, 12 Pharos 20 (Summer–Fall 1969).

Robert Stevens, *Two Cheers for 1870: The American Law School*, 5 Persps. on Am. History 403 (1971).

Maurice M. Vance, *Northerners in the Late Nineteenth Century Florida: Carpetbaggers or Settlers?* 38 Fla. Historical Q. 1 (July 1959).

Mary Young, *Indian Removal and Land Allotment: The Civilized Tribes and Jacksonian Justice*, 64 Am. Historical Rev. 31 (Oct. 1958).

Law Reviews

A Joint Resolution by the Board of Trustees Stetson University and the Board of Overseers Stetson University College of Law in Honor of W. Gary Vause, a Tribute to Gary Vause, 33 Stetson L. Rev. 3 (2003).

A Labor of Love: A Final Interview with Dean Paul E Raymond, 30 Stetson L. Rev. 57 (2000).

Robert D. Batey, *A Lesson in Courage,* 33 Stetson L. Rev. 21 (2003).

Robert D. Batey, *Bruce Jacob: An Appreciation,* 21 Stetson L. Rev. 299 (1992).

Robert D. Batey & Scott William Fitzpatrick. *The Early Years of the* Stetson Law Review, 30 Stetson L. Rev. 213 (2000).

Cynthia Grant Bowman, *Women and the Legal Profession,* 7 Am. J. Gender Soc. Policy & L. 149 (1998).

James J. Brown, *An Oral Tribute Annotated,* 33 Stetson L. Rev. 23 (2003).

Mark R. Brown, *Affirmative Action: Stories from a Small Southern School,* 75 Temple L. Rev. 201 (2002).

Paul D. Carrington, *The Aims of Early American Law Teaching: The Patriotism of Francis Lieber,* 42 J. Leg. Ed. 339 (1992).

Paul D. Carrington, *Teaching Law in the Antebellum Northwest,* 23 U. Tol. L. Rev. 3 (1992).

Paul D. Carrington, *The Revolutionary Idea of University Legal Education,* 31 Wm. & Mary L. Rev. 527 (1990).

Paul D. Carrington, *Teaching Law and Virtue at Transylvania University: The George Wythe Tradition in the Antebellum Years,* 41 Mercer L. Rev. 673 (1990).

Center for Excellence in Advocacy Symposium, 34 Stetson L. Rev. (2004).

John F. Cooper, "*Gary, We Hardly Knew Ye,*" 33 Stetson L. Rev. 7 (2003).

Jane A. Dall, *Determining Duty in Collegiate Tort Litigation: Shifting Paradigms of the College-Student Relationship,* 29 J.C. & U.L. 485 (2003).

Darby Dickerson, *Lessons in Leadership,* 33 Stetson L. Rev. 29 (2003).

Nancy E. Dowd, Kenneth B. Nunn & James E. Pendergast. *Diversity Matters: Race, Gender, and Ethnicity in Legal Education,* 15 U. Fla. J.L. & Pub. Policy 11 (2003).

Virginia G. Drachman, *Women Lawyers and the Quest for Professional Identity in the Late Nineteenth-Century America,* 88 Mich. L. Rev. 2414 (1990).

Lawrence A. Dubin, *Virgil Hawkins: A One-Man Civil Rights Movement,* 51 Fla. L. Rev. 913 (1999).

William Eleazer, *Trial Advocacy at Stetson: The First Hundred Years,* 30 Stetson L. Rev. 243 (2000).

Harry First, *Competition in the Legal Education Industry (1),* 53 N.Y.U. L. Rev. 311 (1978).

Harry First, *Competition in the Legal Education Industry (2): An Antitrust Analysis,* 54 N.Y.U. L. Rev. 1049 (1979).

Roberta Kemp Flowers, *Introduction, Center for Excellence in Advocacy Symposium*, 34 Stetson L. Rev. 1 (2004).

Ernest Gellhorn, *The Law Schools and the Negro*, 1968 Duke L.J. 1069.

Ruth Bader Ginsburg, *Remarks in Celebration of Stetson's Law Library and Information Center*, 28 Stetson L. Rev. 2 (1998).

In Memoriam: A Tribute to Dean W. Gary Vause, 1942–2003, 33 Stetson L. Rev. (2003).

Bruce R. Jacob, *Memories and Reflections about* Gideon v. Wainwright, 33 Stetson L. Rev. 181 (2003).

Bruce R. Jacob, *Remembering a Great Dean: Harold L. "Tom" Sebring*, 30 Stetson L. Rev. 71 (2000).

Robert E. Jagger, *Stetson: The First Public Defender Clinic*, 30 Stetson L. Rev. 189 (2000).

Frank Klim, *A Life of Service*, 33 Stetson L. Rev. 35 (2003).

Elizabeth A. Kovachevich, *Dean Gary Vause—Setting a Standard for Living*, 33 Stetson L. Rev. 41 (2003).

Peter F. Lake, *Make Lawyers, Not Lethal Sheep*, 42 J. Leg. Educ. 271 (1992).

Jerome C. Latimer, *Confrontation after* Crawford: *The Decision's Impact on How Hearsey Is Analyzed Under the Confrontation Clause*, 36 Seton Hall L. Rev. 328 (2006).

Samuel Robert Mandelbaum, *The Legacy of W. Gary Vause to International Legal Education and Practice in Florida*, 33 Stetson L. Rev. 43 (2003).

Thomas C. Marks, *From "Professor Kuenzel" to "Cal"*, 28 Stetson L. Rev. 991 (2000).

Lee Modjeska, *On Teaching Morality to Law Students*, 41 J. Leg. Educ. 71 (1991).

Rebecca Morgan, *Dedication*, 20 Stetson L. Rev. 1 (1990).

Charles M. Nelson, *Enron and the Necessity of the Objective Proximate Monitor,* 88 Cornell L. Rev. (2001).

Manuel R. Ramos, *Legal and Law School Malpractice: Confessions of a Lawyer's Lawyer and Law Professor*, 57 Ohio St. L.J. 863 (1996).

Marsha Griffin Rydberg, *A Lawyer's Lawyer, A Professor's Professor, A Dean's Dean, A Wonderful Person*, 33 Stetson L. Rev. 51 (2003).

Kalina Sarmov, *One Life in Eternity*, 33 Stetson L. Rev. 55 (2003).

Warren A. Seavey, *The Association of American Law Schools in Retrospective*, 3 J. Leg. Educ. 153 (1952).

A.W.B. Simpson, *The Rise and Fall of the Legal Treatise: Legal Principles and the Forms of Legal Literature*, 48 U. Chi. L. Rev. 632 (1981).

Cary R. Singletary, *W. Gary Vause: Educator, Scholar, and Southern Gentlemen*, 33 Stetson L. Rev. 58 (2003).

J.B. Spence & Jeffery Roth, *Closing the Courthouse Door: Florida's Spurious Claims Statute*, 10 Stetson L. Rev. 398 (1981).

D. Chad Strickland, *Gary Vause: A Perspective*, 33 Stetson L. Rev. 75 (2003).

Thomas E. Stringer, Sr., *Gary Vause: A Great Leader*, 33 Stetson L. Rev. 81 (2003).

Russell N. Sullivan, *Professional Organizations and Legal Education*, 4 J. Leg. Educ. 401 (1952).

Thomas Sullivan, *A Best Friend Recalled*, 33 Stetson L. Rev. 83 (2003).

Thurman, Ruth Fleet, *A Remembrance of Dean W. Gary Vause*, 33 Stetson L. Rev. 89 (2003).

Frank W. Swacker, *A Unique Individual*, 33 Stetson L. Rev. 87 (2003).

Michael I. Swygert, *Striving to Make Great Lawyers—Citizenship and Moral Responsibility: A Jurisprudence for Law Teaching*, 30 B.C. L. Rev. 803 (May 1989).

Michael I. Swygert & Jon W. Bruce, *The Historical Origins, Founding, and Early Development of Student-Edited Law Reviews*, 36 Hastings L.J. 739 (1985).

Michael I. Swygert, *Bruce R. Jacob: A Dean for All Seasons*, 21 Stetson L. Rev. 307 (1992).

Michael I. Swygert, *Calvin Arnold Kuenzel, Master Teacher*, 28 Stetson L. Rev. 1001 (2000).

James E. Tribble, *The Life and Times of Dean Lewis H. Tribble*, 30 Stetson L. Rev. 19 (2000).

W. Gary Vause, *Foundations for Excellence—The History of Stetson University College of Law*, 16 Stetson L. Rev. 295 (1987).

W. Gary Vause, *Occupational Safety and Health Law for Agricultural Employment*, 8 Stetson L. Rev. 13 (1978).

Miscellaneous Publications

Building Begun on Hotel Rolyat, 1 Pasadena Progress 1 (Nov. 2, 1924) (semi-annual brochure published by Pasadena Estates, Inc., of St. Petersburg, Fla., for a short time in the 1920s).

Charles Evans Coe, *The Seminoles Right to Lands* (1897) (pamphlet indexed and located in the National Archives, Washington, D.C.).

Description of Construction of Hotel Rolyat Now Stetson University College of Law 1 (undated, typed document with no name of the author, located at Stetson U. College of L. Archives, Gulfport, Fla.).

Fla. Mil. Acad., *1933 Commencement Exercises* 1 (brochure) (on file at Stetson U. College of L., Gulfport, Fla.).

Fla. Mil. Acad., *An Accredited University Preparatory School, Reserve Officers Training Corp, College Entrance Board Examination Center, Designated as an Honor Military School by the U.S. War Department* (1939) (72 unnumbered pages in a hardback book).

Fla. Mil. Acad., *The Dugout of 1948* (1948) (approximately 149 unnumbered pages except for advertisements at end).

Pasadena-on-the-Gulf, Florida's $100,000,000 Development—"A Slice of Old Spain" 2 (several pages—though not paginated—printed and undated document, presumably a Pasadena-on-the-Gulf promotional brochure, probably issued by the development's owners in 1926 or 1927).

The Rolyat (1926) (promotional brochure).

Stetson Publications

NOTE: Stetson Collegiate, *The* Yearbook, *and* Stetson Reporter *and miscellaneous items pre-1954 are all available in the Stetson U. Archives, DeLand, Fla. The* Stetson Law News, Stetson Lawyer, *and* Prelude *and various miscellaneous items post-1954 are kept at the Stetson U. College of L. Archives in Gulfport Fla.*

Stetson Collegiate

An Aunt's Letter to Her Nephew, Stetson Collegiate 2 (Oct. 26, 1908).

Arthur L. Auvil, *College of Law*, Stetson Collegiate 3 (Feb. 14, 1906).

Arthur L. Auvil, *College of Law*, Stetson Collegiate 5 (May 9, 1906).

Class History-Law Department, Stetson Collegiate 8 (Apr. 1902).

College of Law: Little News Notes about Our Lawyers, Stetson Collegiate 3 (Jan. 16, 1906).

John. B. Stetson University, Stetson Collegiate 16 (Apr. 1902) (advertisement).

Kent Club, Stetson Collegiate 6 (Oct. 24, 1907).

Law Department, 3 Stetson Collegiate 4 (Oct. 1901).

Law School Flourishing This Year; Larger Than Ever, Stetson Collegiate 1 (Oct. 31, 1913).

Law School Seniors Plead Cases: Men of '07 Wield Sword of Justice, Stetson Collegiate 1 (Apr. 24, 1907).

Law Senior Class Report, Stetson Collegiate 5 (1909).

Lehman McKinney, *Class History-Law Department*, Stetson Collegiate 7 (Apr. 1903).

Senior Class Day, 4 Stetson Collegiate 4 (May 1902).
Stetson University, 10 Stetson Collegiate (Dec. 1899) (advertisement).
The College of Law: Lawyers Are Busy with Practice Court: Pelot Acquitted of Murder, Stetson Collegiate 1 (Apr. 18, 1906).
University Opening and New Teachers, 3 Stetson Collegiate 2 (Oct. 1900).

Stetson Yearbook—Oshzhzyi

A Short Lecture on Blackstone; College of Law, Oshzhzyi 50 (1911).
College of Law, Oshzhzyi 65 (1921).
College of Law, Oshzhzyi 62 (1920).
College of Law, Oshzhzyi 41 (1917).
College of Law, Oshzhzyi 57 (1915).
Junior Law Class of 1920–21; College of Law, Oshzhzyi 73 (1921).
LL.B's to Be; College of Law, Oshzhzyi 52 (1917).
Senior Law; College of Law, Oshzhzyi 67 (1919).

Stetson Reporter

12 Stetson Rptr. 1 (Jan. 30, 1948).
12 Stetson Rptr. 1 (Oct. 29, 1947).
Betty Lou Alexander, *Law School Has 29 Women Grads, Mrs. Howarth Was First to Receive Her Law Degree*, 3 Stetson Rptr. 2 (Dec. 8, 1937).
Allow Sixty Days for Law Decision, 66 Stetson Rptr. 3 (Feb. 27, 1953).
Amory Underhill Heads Young Dems., 1 Stetson Rptr. 3 (Mar. 25, 1936).
Attorney General Approves Legal Aid Clinic, 4 Stetson Rptr. 1 (Mar. 1, 1939).
Austrian Law Scholar Engaged as Lecturer at College of Law 4 Stetson Rptr. (Sept. 23, 1942).
Baker and Cobb Split Law Prize, "Divorce Traffic" Is Subject for D.H. Redfearn Law Essays, 3 Stetson Rptr. 1 (May 18, 1938).
Cary D. Landis, State's Attorney General Passes Away Tuesday; One Time on Stetson Law Faculty, Stetson Rptr. 1 (May 11, 1938)
Cherry Is Chosen Law Group Proxy, 5 Stetson Rptr. 1 (Sept. 27, 1939).
College of Law Adds C.J. Hilkey to '51 Staff, 65 Stetson Rptr. 4 (Oct. 26, 1951).
College of Law Invaded by Girls; Four Co-Eds Register for Legal Study Here, 8 Stetson Rptr. 3 (Oct. 7, 1943).
College of Law Regains Standing, 4 Stetson Rptr. 1 (Nov. 11, 1939) (quoting a story from the *Orlando Sentinel*).
College of Law Revamped: Law Library Has Many Changes, 4 Stetson Rptr. 8 (Sept. 21, 1938).
College of Law Summer Program Given; Military and Constitutional Law Will be Stressed, 7 Stetson Rptr. 1 (May 6, 1942).

Dean Tribble Leaves Stetson, 5 Stetson Rptr. 1 (Sept. 13, 1939).

Delta Theta Phi Installs Officers; Leeds New Dean, 13 Stetson Rptr. 2 (May 19, 1950).

Dr. Howes Challenges Grads to Carry out Stetson Ideals, 8 Stetson Rptr. 1 (Feb. 3, 1943).

Dr. J.J. Kindred Gives $1,000 for New Law Building, 1 Stetson Rptr. 1 (May 13, 1936).

Editorial, *Law School to Jacksonville May Not Be a Catastrophe,* 5 Stetson Rptr. 2 (Feb. 21, 1940).

Egbert Rosecrans Tells Legal Frat of Famous Trial; State Used Robbery as Step to Murder Charge, Stetson Rptr. (Feb. 19, 1936).

Enrollment Reaches All-Time High Here, 5 Stetson Rptr. 1 (Feb. 15, 1939).

Mac Ferguson, *Legal Language,* 6 Stetson Rptr. 4 (Oct. 30, 1940).

Jerry Fine, *The Barrister's Bar,* 65 Stetson Rptr. 2 (Dec. 7, 1951).

Francis Biddle to Speak on Third Law School Day, 6 Stetson Rptr. 1 (Mar. 12, 1941).

Garwood Appointed New Dean, Lambert Will Head Law School; Outstanding Men Replace Davis and Raymond. Former Dean Raymond Will be Assistant Attorney General, 7 Stetson Rptr. 1 (Sept. 18, 1941).

Fred Hope, *Law Briefs,* 13 Stetson Rptr. 4 (Apr. 21, 1950).

Fred Hope, *Law Briefs,* 63 Stetson Rptr. 4 (Feb. 3, 1950).

Fred Hope, *Legal Briefs,* 13 Stetson Rptr. 5 (Jan. 20, 1950).

Fred Hope, *Law Briefs,* 13 Stetson Rptr. 8 (Oct. 28, 1949).

Hotel Putnam Scene of Initiation Banquet Legal Fraternity, 1 Stetson Rptr. (Apr. 29, 1936).

Judge Frederick Speaks of Ethics to Law Students, 1 Stetson Rptr. 1 (Mar. 11, 1936).

Krewe Initiates Campus Leaders; Year-Old Organization Has Helped Stetson Go Forward, 1 Stetson Rptr. 1 (May 13, 1936).

Lambert Resigns Deanship for Board of Economic Warfare Job, 7 Stetson Rptr. 1 (Feb. 4, 1942).

Sylva Landress, *Bar Association Names R. Milan President at Meet; New Head Is Stetson Alumnus,* 6 Stetson Rptr. 1 (Apr. 2, 1941).

Last Year Law School Grads Succeed in Chosen Field, 5 Stetson Rptr. 6 (Sept. 13, 1939).

Law Association Formed Wednesday, 4 Stetson Rptr. 1 (Oct. 12, 1938).

Law Briefs, 13 Stetson Rptr. 4 (Apr. 14, 1950).

Law Classes Suspend for 43–44 Session, Board Calls Effects of War Disastrous to Enrollment, 8 Stetson Rptr. 1 (Feb. 24, 1943).

Law Frat Plans Student Practice: Senior P.A.D. Law Students Will Work with Attorneys, 3 Stetson Rptr. 6 (Mar. 2, 1938).

Law Professors Attend Groups, 4 Stetson Rptr. 3 (Dec. 14, 1938).

Law School Competitions Are Part of Re-Modeled School, 4 Stetson Rptr., 8 (Sept. 21, 1938).

Law School Day Is Saturday May 6; Dean Paul Raymond Announces Program of Events; Law Club Competition Finals Will be Held in Stover Little Theatre; Supreme Court Justices Will Preside, 4 Stetson Rptr. 1 (May 3, 1939).

Law School Enrollment Reaches All-Time High, 12 Stetson Rptr. 6 (Oct. 1, 1947).

Law School Grads Earn Distinction, Stetson Alumni Gain Honors on Bench, at Bar, Abroad, 3 Stetson Rptr. 6 (Nov. 10, 1937).

Law School Moves, 68 Stetson Rptr. 1 (Oct. 1, 1954).

Law School Sets Seven Moot Trials, 67 Stetson Rptr. 7 (Oct. 30, 1953).

Law School to Move to Air Base, 11 Stetson Rptr. 3 (May 26, 1947).

Law Summer School Offers Nine Courses, 5 Stetson Rptr. 4 (May 22, 1940).

Lawyers Organize, 1 Stetson Rptr. 1 (Oct. 25, 1935).

Lawyers to Have Six-Day Week Second Semester, 5 Stetson Rptr. 1 (Jan. 17, 1940).

Leading Article in Law Paper Written by Paul Raymond; Treatise on Moral Liability in Criminal Law Is Featured, 1 Stetson Rptr. 1 (Apr. 18, 1936).

Legal Aid Clinic to be Instituted Here, 3 Stetson Rptr. 4 (June 1, 1938).

Legal Aid Clinic, 4 Stetson Rptr. (Sept. 21, 1938).

Legal Bigs Here for Law School Day; State Supreme Court Justices Will Hear Law Club Finals, 6 Stetson Rptr. 1 (Apr. 30, 1941).

Legal Forum, 11 Stetson Rptr. 1 (Apr. 1, 1947).

Legal Fraternity Installs Officers, Robert H. Gamble Leads Installation Services Here, Stetson Rptr. (Apr. 27, 1938).

Legal Language, 12 Stetson Rptr. 8 (Oct. 22, 1947).

Legal Language, 5 Stetson Rptr. 4 (May 22, 1940).

Legal Language, 4 Stetson Rptr. 3 (May 24, 1939).

Legal Language, 4 Stetson Rptr. 4 (Mar. 29, 1939).

Legal Language, 5 Stetson Rptr. 2 (Sept. 13, 1939).

Legal Language, 4 Stetson Rptr. 7 (Mar. 1, 1939).

Legal Language, 4 Stetson Rptr. 5 (Nov. 19, 1938).

Legal Talk, 5 Stetson Rptr. 3 (Jan. 17, 1940).

Local Chapter of Phi Alpha Delta Has Many Famous Alumni Members; David K. Brewer Chapter Famed for Jurists and Governors, 3 Stetson Rptr. 8 (May 11, 1938).

Mandatory Registration Today at High School Gymnasium; Every Male Student between 21 and 36 Required to Sign Up, 6 Stetson Rptr. 1 (Oct. 16, 1940).

Many New Faculty Members Appointed, Three New Men on Law School Staff, 7 Stetson Rptr. 4 (Sept. 17, 1941).

John Mattingly, *Barrister's Bar,* 67 Stetson Rptr. (Nov. 6, 1953).

John Mattingly, *Barrister's Bar,* 67 Stetson Rptr. 1 (Oct. 23, 1953).

John Mattingly, *Barrister's Bar,* 67 Stetson Rptr. (Oct. 16, 1953).

Member of Law Faculty Honored, 3 Stetson Rptr. 2 (Dec. 8, 1937).

New Argument Plan Provides Practice for Law Students; Unique System Takes Place of Law Club Competition, 6 Stetson Rptr. 1 (Mar. 12, 1941).

New Million-Dollar Law School Site Is Patterned after English Legal Inns, 67 Stetson Rptr. 1 (Dec. 11, 1953).

Outstanding Man Added to Faculty of Law School; Appointment Follows Resignation of Professor Tribble, 5 Stetson Rptr. 6 (Sept. 13, 1939).

P.A.D. to Initiate Renowned Writer: Charles Francis Coe Will Join the David J. Brewer Chapter, 3 Stetson Rptr. (Mar. 9, 1938).

Pearson Continues on Law Faculty, 66 Stetson Rptr. (Aug. 29, 1952).

Phi Alpha Delta Legal Frat Tours Tallahassee; Hears Court Arguments, 13 Stetson Rptr. 2 (May 19, 1950).

Phi Alpha Delta Pledges Six, 2 Stetson Rptr. (Sept. 30, 1936).

Phi Makes Plans for Parade, 3 Stetson Rptr. 6 (Mar. 2, 1938).

Posniak to Speak before Legal Frat, 3 Stetson Rptr. (Dec. 8, 1937).

Proceedings of the Second Annual Law Day, 5 Stetson Rptr. 1 (Apr. 6, 1940).

Raymond Prepares Volume Dealing with Parole Problems of Nation, 4 Stetson Rptr. 4 (Oct. 13, 1937).

Joy Reese, *Thomas Lambert Is Talented New Law Professor, Rhodes Scholar Comes to DeLand from California,* 6 Stetson Rptr. 1 (Sept. 11, 1940).

Relocation: The Law School, 66 Stetson Rptr. 1 (May 1, 1953).

Sears Addresses Lawyers Tuesday, Will Speak on AAA Decision in PAD Room, Science Hall, 1 Stetson Rptr. (Jan. 29, 1936).

Seven Law Students Contribute to Bar Journal; Students Write Case Comments for Magazine, 5 Stetson Rptr. 6 (Nov. 15, 1939).

Sid Taylor Wins in Contracts Case, 2 Stetson Rptr. 3 (Apr. 28, 1937).

Solomon Will Head Legal Fraternity, 3 Stetson Rptr. (Apr. 6, 1938).

Son of Stetson—Hendricks—Takes Congress Place; "Little Joe" Assumes High Office in Nation's Capital, 2 Stetson Rptr. 1 (Jan. 6, 1938).

Stetson Law Graduate Is ESA General Counsel, 64 Stetson Rptr. 1 (Jan. 5, 1951).

Stetson Law Prof Co-Author of Book, 65 Stetson Rptr. 3 (Apr. 18, 1952).

Stetson Law Professor Charles Hilkey Holds Prominent Government Position, 66 Stetson Rptr. (Mar. 6, 1953).

Stetson Law School Announces Plans for Summer Enrollment, 11 Stetson Rptr. 6 (Feb. 14, 1947).

Stetson Law School Celebrating 50th Anniversary this Year; Justices Here, 63 Stetson Rptr. 2 (Apr. 28, 1950).

Thomas Law Club Fetes Chapmans; Advisors Dekle, Kirkland to Speak; Law Profs. Sextet Is the Highlight, 4 Stetson Rptr. 2 (May 3, 1939).

To Honor Alumnus, 14 Stetson Rptr. 30 (May 25, 1951).
Trustee Committee Holds Key to Future of Law School; Board Discusses Plans at Annual Meeting to Move College of Law, 5 Stetson Rptr. 1 (Feb. 21, 1940).
Trustees Agree to Move Law School, 66 Stetson Rptr. 1 (May 1, 1953).
Two Law Professors Chosen for National Committee; Association of American Law Schools Chooses Futch, Tribble; Recognize Stetson, 1 Stetson Rptr. 1 (Mar. 4, 1936).
Aubrey Vincent, *Trial and Error,* 7 Stetson Rptr. 7 (Jan. 21, 1942).
Aubrey Vincent, *Trial and Error,* 6 Stetson Rptr. 25 (Mar. 19, 1941).
Whitechair Addresses Graduates, 15 Stetson Rptr. 1 (Jan. 18, 1952)
Wilson Will Change Law Club Procedure, 4 Stetson Rptr. 3 (May 31, 1939).
Francis Winters, *Moot Court Capers,* 3 Stetson Rptr. 5 (May 11, 1938).
Woman Presides over Law Court, 67 Stetson Rptr. 7 (Mar. 19, 1954).

Stetson Law News

Calvin A. Kuenzel, 2 Stetson L. News 4 (Nov. 1958).
Distinguished Jurists among New Faculty Members, 2 Stetson L. News 2 (Nov. 1958).
Governor Speaks at Dedication of Law Library, 1 Stetson L. News 1 (Apr. 1958).
Lawyerettes Aid Children's Hospital, 2 Stetson L. News, No. 1, 6 (Nov. 1958).
Library Donations, 1 Stetson L. News 3 (Jan. 1958).
Paul Barnard, 2 Stetson L. News 4 (Nov. 1958).
Stanley Millege, 2 Stetson L. News 4 (Nov. 1958).
Stetson L. News 1 (Jan. 1958).
Stetson's Bar Passage Rate Was 83% on the August 1958 Examination—36 Stetson Grads Pass Bar, 2 Stetson L. News 3 (Nov. 1958).
Student Paper Available, 1 Stetson L. News 4 (Jan. 1958).
Top Legal Talent of Nation at Mid-Winter Trial Seminar, 1 Stetson L. News 2 (Apr. 1958).

Stetson Lawyer Report

Law Library Nearing Completion, 1 Stetson's Law. Rpt. 1 (Oct. 1957).

Stetson Lawyer

1 Stetson Law. 1 (Oct. 1957).
2 Stetson Law. 3 (Apr. 1959).
2 Stetson Law. 8 (Apr. 1959).
100%, 43 Try, 43 Pass, 13 Stetson Law. 4 (Dec. 1969).
100%, Feb. 1971 Exam—Enrollment Records Shattered through 1970–1971, 14 Stetson Law. 3 (May, 1971).

100% on March 1970 Exam—Successful Candidates, Spring Candidates Pass Spring Bar Examination, 13 Stetson Law. 3 (July 1970).

100% on March 1966 Exam, 100% on March 1967 Exam—Stetson Again Hits Jackpot: Grads Excel on Bar Exam, 100 Percent Passing, 10 Stetson Law. 7 (May 1967).

100% on March 1965 Exam—Score: Stetson 100% on March Bar Exam, 8 Stetson Law. 4 (June 1965).

100%—Twenty Six of Twenty Six Pass Bar, 9 Stetson Law. 4 (June 1966).

$100,000 Gift, 13 Stetson Law. 1 (Dec. 1969).

150,000th Library Book Accessioned in March; Volume Count Has Doubled in Law Seven Years, 24 Stetson Law. 1 (May 1980).

19 Stetson Law. 7 (Aug. 1976).

1966 Annual-Mid-Winter Trial Seminar, 9 Stetson Law. 1 (Feb. 1966).

1967 Annual Stetson Mid-Winter Trial Seminar, 10 Stetson Law. 2 (Feb. 1967).

97% on August 1966 Exam—Exam Results Reveal Stetson Grads Excel, 10 Stetson Law. 7 (Nov. 1966).

97% on March 1964 Exam—Bar Exams No Bar to College of Law Grads, 7 Stetson Law. 3 (July 1964).

98% on the August 1967 Exam—Stetson Grads Again Lead Bar Examinees, 11 Stetson Law. 7 (Nov. 1967).

A Courtroom Campus: Stetson's Federal Judicial Internship Program, 34 Stetson Law. 22 (Winter 1993).

A Glance Backward—Past Five Years Have Been Years of Steady Progress at College of Law, 16 Stetson Law. 3 (Aug. 1973).

A Life of Service, W. Gary Vause, University Vice President and Dean, 1942–2002, 43 Stetson Law. 1 (Spring 2003).

A Quiet Resolve, after 13 Years as Dean, Bruce Jacob Steps Aside, 34 Stetson Law. 2 (Summer 1994).

A Tribute to Bruce R. Jacob, Dean, 1981–94, 34 Stetson Law. 1 (Summer 1994).

Academic News, College of Law Discontinues Entering Class, 45 Stetson Law. 11 (Spring 2005).

Academic News, Justice Andrew Moore Serves as Inaugural Jurist in Residence, 45 Stetson Law. 11 (Spring 2005).

Advocacy Board Awards, Advocacy Teams Continue Outstanding Performances in Competitions, 44 Stetson Law. 7 (Spring 2004).

Advocacy Teams Continue Outstanding Performances in Competitions, Trial Team, 44 Stetson Law. 7 (Spring 2004).

Michael P. Allen, *Passion for Caring Drives Stetson's Elder Law Pioneer*, 44 Stetson Law. 16 (Fall 2004).

Alumnus Pledges $1 Million Testamentary Trust to Benefit Student Scholarships at Stetson Law, 43 Stetson Law. 22 (Fall 2002).

Anticipated Inroads on Enrollment by Draft Boards, 11 Stetson Law. 1 (May 1968).

Assistant Professors, 4 Stetson Law. 5 (Oct. 1960).

Bankruptcy Seminar November 17–18, 20 Stetson Law. 2 (Aug. 1977).

Bankruptcy Seminar Scheduled for Nov. 12–13, 19 Stetson Law. 2 (Aug. 1976).

Bar Exam Results, 27 Stetson Law. 19 (Fall 1987).

Robert D. Batey, *A Good Dean and the Best of Colleagues*, 39 Stetson Law. 5 (Summer 1994).

Beloved Professor, Distinguished Milledge, 69, Dies Suddenly, 9 Stetson Law. 5 (Nov. 1965).

Dorothy Bishop, *A Personal Tribute to Our Dean: Bruce R. Jacob*, 31 Stetson Law. 18 (Fall 1991).

Booker Will Join Notre Dame Faculty This Fall, 11 Stetson Law. 4 (May, 1968).

Rick Boucher, *Renovation Plan Meets Today's Needs*, 28 Stetson Law. 12 (1988).

Dotti E. Bressi, *Individual Giving Critical to College of Law Success*, 44 Stetson Law. 30 (Fall 2004).

Bruce Jacob, '59, Will Succeed Dillon as Dean, 25 Stetson Law. 1 (May 1981).

Burton Foundation Recognizes Dickerson, Wozniak with National Legal Writing Awards, 45 Stetson Law. 6 (Spring 2005).

Campaign Chair Commits $100,000, 43 Stetson Law. 34 (Fall 2002).

Carey & Florin Courtroom Dedicated, 34 Stetson Law. 4 (Winter 1993).

Changes at Stetson, Albert A. Lane, 26 Stetson Law. 9 (Summer 1984).

Client Counseling Competition, 20 Stetson Law. 7 (Aug. 1977).

Client Counseling Team Wins International Competition, 28 Stetson Law. 2 (Spring 1989).

College of Law Announces Challenge Gift from the St. Petersburg Times, 27 Stetson Law. 1 (Mar. 1988).

College of Law Begins 79th Year, 21 Stetson Law. 1 (Aug. 1978).

College of Law First on Mrs. Dana Personal List, 22 Stetson Law. 1 (Feb. 1979).

College of Law Launches New Development Program, Gifts Provide for Erection of Two New Buildings to Meet Growing Demand for Legal Education, 8 Stetson Law. 1 (Mar. 1965).

College of Law Looks to Future; 1968–1969 Academic Year Heralds Many Changes, 12 Stetson Law. 1 (Feb. 1969).

College of Law Ready for New Academic Year, Three Faculty Members, One Visiting Professor added to Staff, 16 Stetson Law. 1 (Aug. 1973).

College of Law Starts Seventy-Seventh Year, 19 Stetson Law. 1 (Aug. 1976).

College of Law Welcomes New Faculty and Visitors, Mary S. Scriven, 36 Stetson Law. 29 (Fall 1996).

College of Law Welcomes New Faculty, Julian Kossow, 36 Stetson Law. 29 (Fall 1996).

College of Law Welcomes New Visitors, Peter Lanston Fitzgerald, 36 Stetson Law. 29 (Fall 1996).

College Receives $200,000 from Dana Foundation; Latest Grant for Library Expansion Swells Total of Dana Gifts to More than $1,000,000, 14 Stetson Law. 1 (May 1971).

Crummer, Dana Halls to be Dedicated; Formal Ceremonies Will Be Part of Two-Day Program of Events Honoring Stetson Donors, 12 Stetson Law. 1 (Feb. 1969).

Dana Foundation Grant Benefits Law School, 22 Stetson Law. 1 (Feb. 1979).

Dana Library Symbolizes College of Law's Growth, 18 Stetson Law. 1 (Aug. 1975).

Darby Dickerson, *New Achievements Draw World's Attention to Stetson,* 45 Stetson Law. 2 (Spring 2005).

Dean Dillon Honored by Alumni, 21 Stetson Law. 3 (Aug. 1978).

Dean Dillon's Administration Characterized by Physical Improvements and Academic Growth, 25 Stetson Law. 4 (May 1981).

Death, Practice Claim Two Members of the Faculty, 16 Stetson Law. 6 (Aug. 1973).

Dedication of Harvey Firestone III Memorial Recreation Center, 17 Stetson Law. 1 (Aug. 1974).

Darby Dickerson, *Every Student Has a Story,* 43 Stetson Law. 1 (Fall 2003).

Dillon Succeeds Sebring as Dean, September 1, 11 Stetson Law. 1 (Mar. 1968).

Dormitory Area Is Now Fully Air-Conditioned, 13 Stetson Law. 2 (July 1970).

Kay Eddy, *New Faces, Retirements Characterize 1971–1972,* 15 Stetson Law. 2 (Aug. 1972).

Enrollment Records Shattered through 1970–1971, 14 Stetson Law. 3 (May 1971).

Enrollment Statistics, 4 Stetson Law. 7 (Oct. 1960).

Estate Gift Provides Needed Expansion, 27 Stetson Law. 8 (Fall 1987).

Exchange Program, 5 Stetson Law. 4 (Oct. 1961).

Faculty Doings, 5 Stetson Law. 7 (Oct. 1961).

Faculty Features, 41 Stetson Law. 39 (Spring/Summer 2001).

Faculty Forum, 36 Stetson Law. 26 (Fall 1996).

Faculty Forum, Carol Henderson, 45 Stetson Law. 8 (Spring 2005).

Faculty Forum, Faculty Notes, 26 Stetson Law. 11 (Spec. Ed.) (1984).

Faculty Forum, Luz E. Nagle, 44 Stetson Law. 12 (Spring 2004).

Faculty Forum, Manuel Ramos, 32 Stetson Law. 12 (Summer 1992).

Faculty Forum, Peter Lake Appointed, 45 Stetson Law. 8 (Summer 2005).

Faculty Forum, Professor Michael Finch, 26 Stetson Law. 11 (Summer 1984).

Faculty Forum, W. Gary Vause, 39 Stetson Law. 18 (Winter 1993).

Faculty Gathers for Annual Retreat, 29 Stetson Law. 9 (Spring 1990).

Faculty News, Luz Estella Nagle, 43 Stetson Law. 11 (Spring 2003).

Faculty Notes, Sally Ginsberg Waters, 26 Stetson Law. 12 (Summer 1984).

Faculty Notes, Suzanne R. Armstrong, 26 Stetson Law. 11 (Summer 1984).

Faculty Recent Publications, Presentations, Awards, and Activities, Luz E. Nagle, 44 Stetson Law. 8 (Fall 2004).

Faculty Sets Standard of Attire, Appearance, 13 Stetson Law. 5 (Dec. 1969).

Faculty Staff Enriched by Three New Members, 13 Stetson Law. 6 (Dec. 1969).

Faculty Support Services Director Connie Evans Receives 2002 Dean's Award, 43 Stetson Law. 14 (Spring 2003).

Faculty Vacations, 6 Stetson Law. 2 (Nov. 1962).

Faculty, Staff Enriched by Three New Members, 13 Stetson Law. 6 (Dec. 1969).

Few New Faces on 1974–1975 Law School Faculty, 17 Stetson Law. 7 (Aug. 1974).

Florida Bar Exam Results, 28 Stetson Law. 5 (Fall 1988).

Florida Bar Property Institute at Stetson, 9 Stetson Law. 7 (Nov. 1965).

Former Mercer Instructor Joins Faculty, 8 Stetson Law. 2 (Nov. 1961).

Forums Focus on Legal Problems of Bankruptcy, Higher Education, and Religious Organizations; Law and Higher Education, 25 Stetson Law. 3 (May 1981).

Foundation Changes Name to Honor Dana, 22 Stetson Law. 1 (Feb. 1979).

Freshman Statistics, 20 Stetson Law. 2 (Aug. 1977).

Gardner Selected to Lead New Biodiversity Institute, U.S. Ramsar Committee, 45 Stetson Law. 14 (Summer 2005).

Gary Vause Named Associate Dean, 35 Stetson Law. 20 (Fall 1995).

Gifts Establish Two New Endowed Professorships—Attorney's Title Insurance Fund Professorship-Major, 45 Stetson Law. 37 (Spring 2005).

Davina Gould, *Tampa Courtroom Names to Honor Wm. Reece Smith, Jr.*, 44 Stetson Law. 29 (Spring 2004).

Graduate Evans Named Librarian, Professor, 11 Stetson Law. 6 (Nov. 1967).

Harold "Tom" Sebring, 1898–1968: Scholar, Athlete, Lawyer, Jurist, Legal Educator and Former Dean, 12 Stetson Law. 1 (Feb., 1969).

Harvey Firestone, Jr., Is Commencement Speaker; Thirty-Six Graduates to Receive Degrees in Spring Exercises, 2 Stetson Law. 1 (Apr. 1959).

Harvey S. Firestone, Jr., Dead at Age 75; Was One of the College of Law's Major Benefactors, 16 Stetson Law. 1 (Aug. 1973).

Homecoming 1975 Style, Varied Programs Attract over 300 Alumni, Guests, 18 Stetson Law. 4 (Aug. 1975).

Illinois Justices Establish Book Memorial to Harvey Firestone III, 5 Stetson Law. 7 (Oct. 1961).

In Memory of Porkchop the Cat, 31 Stetson Law. 15 (Fall 1991).

In re Faculty, New Associate Dean, I. Richard Gershon, 28 Stetson Law. 14 (Fall 1988).

In re: Faculty, Richard T. Dillon, 29 Stetson Law. 7 (Spring 1990).

International Law Society Returns to the Stetson Campus, 31 Stetson Law. 11 (Spring 1991).

Introducing the Newest Members of the Stetson Faculty, Professor Peter Lake, 30 Stetson Law. 8 (Fall 1990).

Grady Irvin, Jr., *'92 Addresses BLSA Brunch; Chapter Named for Stringer, '74*, 45 Stetson Law. 45 (Spring 2005).

It's Team Spirit That Does It at Stetson, 27 Stetson Law. 5 (Fall 1987).

Bruce R. Jacob, *Dean's Pages*, 33 Stetson Law. 2 (Summer 1993).

Bruce R. Jacob, *Introduction of Wm. Reece Smith, Commencement, May 12, 1990*, 30 Stetson Law. 29 (Fall 1990).

James T. Brand, 7 Stetson Law. 1 (Mar. 1964).

Judge Dayton Called, New Faces, Retirements 1971–1972, 15 Stetson Law. 3 (Aug. 1972).

Judge Dekle, '40, Seeks to Succeed Justice Drew, '12, 13 Stetson Law. 3 (Dec. 1969).

Frank Klim, *Stetson College of Law Hall of Fame*, 44 Stetson Law. 26 (Fall 2004).

Mary Ann S. Kokoszyna, *June Issue of Law Review Readied for Publication*, 25 Stetson Law. 2 (May 1981).

Kuenzel New Assistant Dean Will Teach, 13 Stetson Law. 1 (Dec. 1969).

"*La Chicita Bonita, Pero Bravita*," 35 Stetson Law. 16 (Fall 2003).

Labor Forums, 5 Stetson Law. 5 (Oct. 1961).

Landscaping Is Planned as New Structures Rise, 11 Stetson Law. 1 (Nov. 1967).

Lasseter Bows Out as Fund's Chief Executive, 10 Stetson Law. 5 (May 1967).

Law Review Establishes J. Ben Watkins Award, 34 Stetson Law. 24 (Winter 1993).

Law School Announces New Deans, 33 Stetson Law. 3 (Fall 1992).

Learning; Versatility Characterize Largest Faculty: Aim to Develop Lawyers, Not Legal Technicians, Says Dean, 4 Stetson Law. 5 (Oct. 1960).

Legal Forum, Leadership in Continuing Legal Education: Stetson's National Conference on Law & Higher Education, 1 Stetson Law. 16 (Fall 1989).

Library Gift, 23 Stetson Law. 1 (Feb. 1979).

Maestros, 17 Stetson Law. 5 (Aug. 1974).

Jeff Maine, *Marsha Griffin Rydberg, '76*, 33 Stetson Law. 24 (Fall 1992).

Jan F. Majewski, *Benefits of Stetson CLE Go beyond Credit Hours*, 33 Stetson Law. 11 (Summer 1993).

Jan F. Majewski, *CLE Department Expands*, 32 Stetson Law. 19 (Summer 1992).

Jan F. Majewski, *CLE Report*, 33 Stetson Law. 21 (Fall 1992).

Jan F. Majewski, *Stetson Prepares for a New and Exciting Year of CLE Programming*, 31 Stetson Law. 14 (Fall 1991).

Major Gifts Establish Two New Endowed Professorships, William Reece Smith, Jr., Distinguished Professorship, 45 Stetson Law. 37 (Spring 2005).

Many "Firsts" on Dean-to-Be's Record, 11 Stetson Law. 2 (Mar. 1980).

Members of the Stetson Faculty, Professor Charles Elson, 30 Stetson Law. 8 (Fall 1990).
Lizabeth A. Moody, *Dean's Message; Stetson Expands to Global Arena*, 38 Stetson Law. 2 (Spring 1977).
Lizabeth A. Moody, *The College of Law Vigorously Approaches Its Second Century*, 39 Stetson Law. 2 (Fall 1998/Summer 1999).
Nagle Becomes Stetson's First Hispanic Full Law Professor, 45 Stetson Law. 13 (Summer 2005).
New Assistant Dean of Student Services, Rebecca Morgan, 1 Stetson Law. 21 (Fall 1989).
New Course Bolsters Basic Writing Skills, 12 Stetson Law. 2 (Feb. 1969).
New Courtroom Planned in Memory of Late Dean, 18 Stetson Law. 7 (Aug. 1975).
New Faces, Retirements Characterize 1971–1972, 15 Stetson Law. 2 (Aug. 1972).
New Facilities Gift of Harvey Firestone, Jr., 4 Stetson Law. 6 (Oct., 1960).
New Faculty Member a Teacher for 21 Years, 11 Stetson Law. 6 (Nov. 1967).
New Faculty Member Joins Stetson, 35 Stetson Law. 21 (Fall 1995).
New Faculty, Royal C. Gardner, 34 Stetson Law. 20 (Summer 1994).
New Student Groups, Stetson Law. 6 (Fall 1989).
New Students May Receive Summer Grants, Part of Stepped-up Recruiting Program to Offset Anticipated Inroads on Enrollment by Draft Boards, 11 Stetson Law. 1 (May 1968).
News from Alumni Files, 5 Stetson Law. 8 (Nov. 1962).
"Not Guilty" Is Verdict in Law School Trial, 65 Stetson Law. 3 (Nov. 16, 1951).
Notes from Alumni Files, 5 Stetson Law. 8 (Oct. 1961).
Past Year One of Growth, Achievement and Firsts, 13 Stetson Law. 1 (July 1970).
Peter Lake Appointed to Charles A. Dana Chair, 45 Stetson Law. 8 (Spring 2005).
Plans Being Prepared for Library Expansion, 12 Stetson Law. 2 (May, 1969).
President Names Dillon First Dana Professor, 23 Stetson Law. 9 (Feb. 1979).
Professor Calvin A. Kuenzel, 1928–1998, 39 Stetson Law. 8 (Fall 1988/Winter 1999).
Professor Charles Elson Selected as Salvatori Fellow, 33 Stetson Law. 13 (Summer 1993).
Professor Eleazer Receives National Teaching Award, 1966 Stetson Law. 1.
Professor Patrick E. Longan, New Faces, 31 Stetson Law. 12 (Fall 1991).
Professors Stone and Swygert Retire, 45 Stetson Law. 13 (Spring 2005).
Public Defender Clinic Conceived as a Learning through Service Program, 6 Stetson Law. 3 (May 1963).
Raleigh Greene New President of Law Center Foundation, 25 Stetson Law. 2 (May 1981).
Recent Articles by Stetson Professors, 11 Stetson Law. 3 (Nov. 1967).
Recent Major Gifts, 34 Stetson Law. 25 (Winter 1993).

Recent Major Gifts, 35 Stetson Law. 1 (Fall 1995).

Recent Publications, Presentations, Awards, and Activities of Stetson Law Faculty, Rebecca C. Morgan '80, 44 Stetson Law. 8 (Fall 2004).

Recent Publications, Richard B. Graves, III, 44 Stetson Law. 8 (Fall 2004).

Recent Writing Activity by Faculty, 17 Stetson Law. 1 (Aug. 1974).

Record Enrollment as College Enters 70th Year, 13 Stetson Law. 1 (Dec. 1969).

Paula J. Reed, *Cal's Day in Court*, 33 Stetson Law. 8 (Summer 1993).

Remembering Dr. Mosley, 45 Stetson Law. 16 (Spring 2005).

Retiring Librarian Describes Four-Year Term as One of "Substantial Progress", 8 Stetson Law. 3 (June 1965).

Runyon's Death Recalls Local Bid for Stetson, 2 Stetson Law. 1 (May 1968)

School Starts with Early Calendar and New Faculty, 20 Stetson Law. 1 (Aug. 1977).

Score: Stetson 100% on Bar Exam, 8 Stetson Law. 4 (June 1965).

Sebring Administration at College of Law an Era of Development and Progress, 11 Stetson Law. 2 (Nov. 1967).

Sebring Successor: "An Excellent Choice", 11 Stetson Law. 2 (Mar. 1968).

Second Annual Legal Institute and Law Day Activities Are Planned for Tomorrow at 2 p.m., 65 Stetson Law. 1 (Apr. 25, 1952).

Some Highlights of Dedication Festivities of Eleanor Dana Hall and H. Jackson Crummer Hall, 12 Stetson Law. 4 (May 1969)

Adrian G. Soud, *Professor Robert Bickel Wins National Award*, 38 Stetson Law. 34 (Fall 1997).

Space Seminar Highlights Law Day, 1961, 5 Stetson Law. 1 (Oct. 1961).

Jeffrey T. Spoeri, *Stetson's New Library and Information Center Opens to Rave Reviews, Justice Ginsberg's Address at Dedication Praises the College's Technological and Scholarly Accomplishments*, 39 Stetson Law. 4 (Fall 1998/Summer 1999).

St. Petersburg Woman Wills College of Law $250,000 for Purchase of Library Books, 5 Stetson Law. 1 (Apr. 1962).

Staff Updates, Dr. Madison Mosley, 41 Stetson Law. 48 (Spring/Summer 2001).

Standard Appearance and Attire, 13 Stetson Law. 5 (Dec. 1969).

Stetson Announces Expanded Faculty, 18 Stetson Law. 2 (Aug. 1975).

Stetson Announces Student Bar Association Officers, 40 Stetson Law. 1 (Fall 2000).

Stetson ATLA Trial Team Places First and Second in State Competition, 27 Stetson Law. 5 (Fall 1987).

Stetson Grad Named Business Manager, 8 Stetson Law. 2 (Nov. 1964).

Stetson Grads Again Lead Bar Examinees, 11 Stetson Law. 7 (Nov. 1967)

Stetson Hosts Florida Bar CLE Courses, 19 Stetson Law. 3 (Aug. 1976).

Stetson Law Events Celebrate Black History Month, 44 Stetson Law. 4 (Spring 2004).

Stetson Law Professor Confirmed as Federal Judge, 45 Stetson Law. 3 (Spring 2005).
Stetson Law Review *May Soon Be a Reality*, 13 Stetson Law. 5 (Dec. 1969).
Stetson Mid-Winter Trial Seminar, 8 Stetson Law. 2 (Mar. 1965).
Stetson Offers Participation in Clinics, 27 Stetson Law. 11 (Fall 1987).
Stetson Professor on ATLA Ethics Committee, 13 Stetson Law. 2 (Dec. 1969).
Stetson Strengthens Legal Research and Writing Program, 36 Stetson Law. 30 (Fall 1996).
Stetson Ties as America's Top School for Advocacy; Legal Research and Writing Ties as Nation's Third Best, 45 Stetson Law. 3 (Spring 2005).
Stetson Trial Team Brings Home the National Championship (Again)! 30 Stetson Law. 3 (Fall 1990).
Stetson Trial Team Continues to Win, 29 Stetson Law. 1 (Spring 1990).
Stetson University College of Law Ranked # 1 in Trial and Appellate Advocacy, 36 Stetson Law. 1 (Spring 1996).
Stetson Welcomes New Assistant Dean, Lynn A. Howell, 35 Stetson Law. 20 (Fall 1995).
Stetson Welcomes New Faculty, 34 Stetson Law. 20 (Summer 1994).
Stetson Welcomes New Law Faculty, 44 Stetson Law. 12 (Fall 2004).
Stetson's CLE Office to Offer Programs on New Topics in New Locations, 43 Stetson Law. 13 (Fall 2003).
Stetson's New Labor-Management Center, Stetson Law. 13 (Spec. ed., Summer 1984).
Stetson's Success Was 100% on the August 1969 Bar Examination—100%, 43 Try, 43 Pass Latest Bar Examination, 13 Stetson Law. 4 (Dec. 1969).
Student Lounge Becomes Walter Mann Lounge, 18 Stetson Law. 6 (Aug. 1975).
Survey of Past Quarter of a Century Shows Abundant Evidence of Qualitative Growth, 22 Stetson Law. 1 (Feb. 1979).
Susan Schaeffer, '71, Inducted into Hall of Fame, 45 Stetson Law. 4 (Spring 2005).
The Margin of Excellence, Estate Gift Provides Needed Expansion, 27 Stetson Law. 8 (Fall 1987).
The Stetson Society, 33 Stetson Law. 12 (Summer 1993).
Third Annual Seminar, 21 Stetson Law. 2 (Aug. 1978).
Three Faculty Promoted to Faculty Positions, 44 Stetson Law. 4 (Spring 2004).
Trial Team Continues to Shine, 39 Stetson Law. 2 (Winter 1999).
Trial Teams Continue Winning Tradition, 39 Stetson Law. 2 (Spring 1996).
Trial Teams Set Unprecedented Record, Five National Competitions in One Year, 34 Stetson Law. 14 (Summer 1994).
Trustee's Gift Tops New Book Donations, 7 Stetson Law. 3 (July 1964).
U.S. Supreme Court Chooses Professor Mark Brown as Judicial Fellow, 33 Stetson Law. 12 (Summer 1993).

Varied Programs Presented at Inns of Court Dinners; Speakers Include the Attorney General, a County Solicitor, a Conservationist, Practicing Lawyers, 14 Stetson Law. (May 1971).

Vause, W. Gary. *Milestones in Stetson Law School History—The Dillon Years*, 30 Stetson Law. 22 (Fall 1990).

Vause, W. Gary. *The Dillon Years*, 30 Stetson Law. 1 (Fall 1990).

West Point Professor Joins Teaching Staff, 10 Stetson Law. 3 (Nov. 1966).

Woman Chancellor of New Legal Fraternity, 11 Stetson Law. 6 (Mar. 1968).

Women Vie with Men for Grades, Scholarships, 10 Stetson Law. 1 (Nov. 1966).

World Champions, 45 Stetson Law. 24 (Spring 2005).

Stetson Prelude

ABA Law Student Division Update, 11 Prelude 1 (Nov. 13, 1980).

Laura Alcott, *Stetson Women's Association Welcomes New Wives*, 4 Prelude 3 (July 4, 1973).

Suzanne R. Armstrong, *An Open Letter*, 20 Prelude 8 (Apr. 15, 1986).

Carlos Enriquez Interview with Dean Jacob, 11 Prelude 1 (Oct. 1, 1981).

Client Counseling Competition Nears, Prelude (Nov. 8, 1978).

Tom Drage, *Inns of Court*, 1 Prelude 3 (Oct. 15, 1971).

Entertainment: Prelude *Guide to Extracurricular Fun*, Prelude 3 (Nov. 8, 1977).

Cheryl Flax-Davidson, *Women in Law Hosts Interesting Speakers*, Prelude 6 (Nov. 8, 1977).

Christopher G. Frey, *ATLA Team Wins Two First Places*, 22 Prelude 1 (Apr. 1, 1987).

Future of Teacher Evaluations Is in Doubt, Prelude 2 (Feb. 1980).

Marc Gilner, *Former Prof. Cushman, Newcomer Batey Join Faculty*, Prelude 3 (Sept. 30, 1977).

Jim Hardman, *Law Review Plans National Publication*, Prelude 1 (Feb. 2, 1978).

Honor Court, 3 Prelude 7 (Oct. 1972).

Peter Keating, *Phi Alpha Delta Law Fraternity*, 4 Prelude 9 (Apr. 30, 1973).

Bob Kunkel, *Editors' Notes*, 1 Prelude 1 (Oct. 1. 1971).

Mohammed Melvin, *Jock Itch*, 11 Prelude 5 (Oct. 1, 1981).

Mrs. Eddy Retires, Prelude 2 (Oct. 15, 1971).

Prelude 3 (Apr. 1980) (untitled, an entire page consisting of fifty bar graphs, five columns wide, and ten columns high, with five lines in each column).

Prelude 6 (Feb. 24, 1988) (unavailable title or author name).

William Prosser & Karl Llewellyn, *Embrace Me, Non-Negotiable You*, Prelude 2 (Sept. 30, 1977).

Public Defender Clinic, 1 Prelude 1 (Oct. 29, 1971).

Vicki Rubel, *Wives*, 3 Prelude 1 (Oct. 1972).

Ann Slanders, *Isn't That Special!!!!* 23 Prelude 4 (1987).
Students Meet with Accreditation Committee, Prelude 1 (Apr. 1980).
VITA, 14 Prelude 3 (Jan. 1983).
Women-in-Law, 14 Prelude 6 (Mar. 1983).

The Brief

Bridgette Sanders, *Students Showcase Talents at Nite of Soul*, The Brief 8 (Nov. 15, 2005).
Grace Santos, *Get Involved*, The Brief (Nov. 15, 2005).
Stetson C.S.I. Solves "Crime" During Workshop, The Brief 4 (Feb. 2, 2004).
Stetson Community Leader Dr. Madison Mosley Dies, The Brief 2 (Apr. 1, 2005).
Stetson Wins World Championship in Vienna, The Brief 1 (Apr. 1, 2005).

Miscellaneous College Publications, Speeches, and Releases

10th Annual International Environmental Moot Court Competition (2005) (six-page printed brochure).
25th Anniversary Celebration, (Oct. 19, 1979) (untitled three-page typed document setting out the remarks Dean Richard Dillon, read to the guests at the school's twenty-fifth celebration of its move to St. Petersburg/Gulfport, Fla., in 1954).
25th Annual National Conference on Law and Higher Education (program) (Feb. 2004).
26th Annual National Conference on Law and Higher Education (program) (Feb. 2005)
26th Annual National Conference on Law and Higher Education (recent events) (Mar. 2005).
A Conference Jointly Sponsored by Stetson University College of Law, the American Council on Education, and The American Association of University Administrators, *Law and Higher Education, Issues for 1981* (Jan. 11–14, 1981) (brochure).
About Your Law School (circa 1900).
Address at Reunion, Stetson and Florida Law Students, Albert John Farrah 1863–1944 (Ala. L. Sch. Found. 1985) (containing address, papers, and letters).
Karen Altieri, *Stetson Student Bar Association Named Top in Nation* (Stetson U. College of L. July 11, 2000) (news release).
Dorothea Beane, *Curriculum Vitae* (2005).

Biographical Summary, William Reece Smith, Jr. (Aug. 2005) (six-page typed document given to the Author by the law firm of Carlton Fields, Tampa Office).

Dorothy Bishop, *List of Law Faculty and Dates of Appointment from 1954 through 2004* (2004).

Dotti E. Bressi, *Cornerstone Campaign Final Campaign Totals* (2005).

James Jay Brown, *Curriculum Vitae* (June 19, 2005).

Classmates Unveil Portrait of Marine Hero, 5 Stetson-Ltr. 6 (DeLand, Fla. June 1957).

Codicil to Last Will and Testament of John T. Rosa (unexecuted and undated except for 1979).

Darby Dickerson, *Summary Information and Curriculum Vitae* (2005).

Fiftieth Anniversary of the Stetson University College of Law Move to Gulfport, Florida, Banquet Dinner (Sept. 2004) (videotapes).

Firestone Tapestry Given to Stetson University College of Law (an undated copy of a two-page professional evaluation and assessment of the gift).

Full-Time Faculty Policies, *Consensual Relations Policy* (Stetson U. College of L. 2005).

Gift from L. LeRoy Highbaugh, Jr., Dorothy L. Highbaugh, to John B. Stetson University (Apr. 3, 1973) (a one-page typed document signed by Mr. and Mrs. Highbaugh, and by Stetson University Business Manager, H. Graves Edmundson).

Davina Gould, *Stetson University College of Law to Host Minority Pre-Law Conference*, (Stetson U. College of L. Jan. 29, 2003) (news release).

Davina Gould, *Stetson Black Students to Honor Judge Howard White* (Stetson U. College of L. Apr. 1, 2003) (news release).

Davina Gould, *Stetson U. College of Law* (Stetson U. College of L. Sept. 13, 2002).

Davina Gould, *Stetson University College of Law and AARP Establish Journal, Conference on International Aging, Law, and Policy* (Stetson U. College of L. Apr. 29, 2003) (news release).

Davina Gould, *Stetson University College of Law Receives $1 Million Pledge to Establish Faculty Chair in Elder and Disability Law* (Stetson U. College of L. Feb. 4, 2003) (news release).

Davina Gould, *Stetson University College of Law, Florida Second District Court of Appeal Sign Historic Agreement* (Stetson U. College of L. Feb. 4, 2003) (news release).

Investiture of Federal Judge for Former Professor Robert Davis (Stetson U. College of L. Feb. 1, 2005) (recent events).

Bruce R. Jacob, *Orientation Remarks Regarding the History of Our Law School*, 3 (Gulfport, Fla. n.d.).

Bruce R. Jacob, *The John T. Rosa Bequest to the Stetson College of Law* (1985) (submitted to the executors of the John T. Rosa Estate).

John B. Stetson University Commencement 1942; Graduation Exercises Program (Stetson U. June 1, 1942).

John F. Forbes, *President's Statement—Presentation Day 1902* (Stetson U. 1902).

John Frederick Cooper, *Resume* (Mar. 4, 2005).

John Paul Stevens, *Remarks* (St. Petersburg, Fla. 1989).

Judge Thomas Stringer Youth Pre-Law Conference (Stetson U. College of L. Feb. 4, 2005) (recent events).

Darlene L. Kelly & Michael Hoad, *Stetson University College of Law and the University of South Florida Announce a New Health Law Consortium,* (Stetson U. College of L. & U.S.F. Apr. 10, 2000) (joint-news release).

Frank Klim, *Gary Vause, Stetson University College of Law Dean, Dies* (Stetson U. College of L. May 9, 2003) (news release).

Frank Klim, *Stetson Black Law Students Association Celebrate Third Annual Judge Stringer Youth Day* (Stetson U. College of L. Nov. 19, 2002) (news release).

Frank Klim, *Stetson College of Law Events to Celebrate Black History Month* (Stetson U. College of L. Feb. 10, 2004) (news release).

Frank Klim, *Stetson Law Moot Court Teams Excel in Competitions* (Stetson U. College of L. Mar. 5, 2005) (news release).

Frank Klim, *Stetson Law Professor Receives Fulbright Scholarship to Teach in China,* www.law.stetson.edu/communications/news.asp?id=94 (Apr. 29, 2004).

Frank Klim, *Stetson Law School Moot Court Team Wins Award at National Competition* (Stetson U. College of L. Mar. 17, 2004) (news release).

Frank Klim, *Stetson University College of Law Closer to Agreement on Tampa Campus* (Stetson U. College of L. June 5, 2002) (news release).

Frank Klim, *Stetson University College of Law Dean Gary Vause Announces Retirement* (Stetson U. College of L. 1 Apr. 23, 2003) (news release).

Frank Klim, *Stetson University College of Law Forms the Nation's First Clearinghouse on Science and Technology* (Stetson U. College of L. Jan. 20, 1994) (news release).

Frank Klim, *Stetson University College of Law Launches a $12 Million Campaign to Fund Scholarships, Professorships and Academic Enhancements* (Stetson U. College of L. Sept. 19, 2002) (news release).

Frank Klim, *Stetson University College of Law Professor Receives Fulbright Scholar Award* (Stetson U. College of L. Apr. 3, 2003) (news release).

Frank Klim, *Stetson University College of Law Selected as National Headquarters for Law Review Organization* (Stetson U. College of L. Apr. 23, 2002) (news release).

Frank Klim, *Stetson University Purchases Downtown Property for Law Center and Campus* (Stetson U. College of L. Dec. 12, 2002) (news release).

Frank Klim, *Stetson's Black Law Student Association Hosts Statewide Academic Retreat* (Stetson U. College of L. Oct. 24, 2002) (news release).

Law and Higher Education, Issues and Challenges in the 1980's (Jan. 1980) (brochure).

Lemuel A. Haslup, *Faculty File* (n.d.).

Library Staff, 1995–1996 Bulletin (Stetson U. College of L.).

Lincoln Hulley, *President, Stetson College of Law* (1909) (handwritten ad).

List of Stetson Law Faculty and Degrees (July 2005).

Lizabeth A. Moody, *Curriculum Vitae* (May 2003).

Marlene A. O'Connor, *Curriculum Vitae* (May 4, 2005).

One of America's Most Interesting Law Schools (1956) (a twenty-four-page advertising brochure containing mostly pictures of the Gulfport campus).

Peter Francis Lake, *Curriculum Vitae* (2004).

Pope A. Duncan, *Leaders of Stetson: Dr. Paul A. Raymond* (Dec. 28, 1990).

Paula J. Reed, *Stetson Announces New Dean* (Stetson U. College of L. Apr. 19, 1994) (news release).

Paula J. Reed, *University Trustees Name Room at College of Law* (Stetson U. College of L. Aug. 19, 1996) (news release).

Records from Center for Excellence in Advocacy (Stetson U. College of Law 2005).

Resolution by the Dean and Faculty, Stetson University College of Law, in Honor of H. Douglas Lee (Dec. 19, 1987).

Richard T. Dillon, *Commencement Address* (Stetson U. College of L. May 9, 1981).

Richard T. Dillon, *Address to Stetson Lawyers Association* (Washington, D.C. Spring 1973).

Royal C. Gardner, *Curriculum Vitae* (2004).

Susan Shulins, *Women of Stetson, Creating a Foundation for Change* (2003) (ten-printed pages brochure).

Standard of Appearance and Attire, Stetson University College of Law (Nov. 12, 1969) (a three-inch by seven-inch single page (light green)).

Stephen M. Everhart, *Curriculum Vitae* (2004).

Stetson BLSA Dedicates the Name of its Chapter to Honor Judge Stringer (Stetson U. College of L. Feb. 26, 2005) (recent events).

Stetson College of Law Begins Its 61st Year with Largest Faculty in Its History (1961) (six-page, legal size typed paper, author unknown).

Stetson U. College of Law Purchase Order to Mead Data Control, Inc. (May 8, 1980).

Stetson News Release (n.d.; 1950; Oct. 1951; Apr., 1952; Aug. 14, 1953; Dec. 5, 1953).

Stetson on the Suncoast, 1954–1979, A Community Salute (Oct. 19, 1979) (a folded, four-page brochure distributed to attendees to the 25th celebration of the Stetson U. College of L. being located in Gulfport, Fla.).
Bradford Stone, *Resume* (May 1992, addendum 2005).
The Cornerstone Campaign; Laying the Foundation for Tomorrow (Oct. 8, 2005) (announcement & invitation to the Celebration).
The Last Will and Testament of John T. Rosa (Feb. 20, 1976).
The Sebring Courtroom (Stetson U. n.d.) (brochure).
Brian Thomas, *Nichols Foundation Endows Lecture Series at Stetson College of Law* (Stetson U. College of L. Off. of Pub. Rel. Feb. 4, 1994) (news release).
Brian Thomas, St. Petersburg Times *Commits $100,000 to Stetson College of Law* (Stetson U. College of L. Mar. 31, 1995) (news release).
Brian Thomas, *Stetson Law Considers Adding Part-Time Program* (Stetson U. College of L. Apr. 9, 1998) (news release).
Brian Thomas, *Stetson Law Receives $25,000 Grant from Saunders Foundation* (Stetson U. College of L. Aug. 25, 1993) (news release).
U. of Med. & Dentistry of N.J. *News Release*, (2001).
W. Gary Vause. "*Prominent*" *Stetson Law Graduates* (n.d.) (handwritten notes).
Darryl C. Wilson, *Curriculum Vitae* (May 31, 2005).

Annual Announcements and Catalogues

Annual Announcement and Catalogue (John B. Stetson University, 1899, 1900, 1901, 1909, 1910, 1911, 1913, 1914, 1915, 1916, 1960).
Client Counseling Competition, 1989–1991 Off. Bull. (Stetson U. College of L. 1989).
College of Law, John B. Stetson U. Bull. (1948, 1949, 1958, 1961).
International Dispute Resolution Summer Program in Granada (Stetson U. College of L., Off. of Intl. Progrs. 2005) (brochure).
Summer Institute on International Law, Buenos Aires (brochure).
Summer Institute on International Law, Freiberg, Hague (Stetson U. College of L., Off. of Intl. Progrs. 2005) (brochure).
The Masters of Law, International Law & Business (Stetson U. College of L. 2005) (catalog).
Off. Bull. (Stetson U. College of L.) (1977, 1985, 1991, 1993).
The Scandinavian/Baltic Institute on Emerging Markets in Transitional Democracies Summer Program in Estonia (Stetson U. College of L., Off. of Intl. Progrs. 2004) (brochure).

Two-Year Juris Doctor for Foreign Lawyers (Stetson U. College of L. Off. of Admissions 2005) (brochure).

Formal Reports

NOTE: All reports and unpublished manuscripts and memoranda pre-dating 1954 on file at Stetson University Archives, DeLand, Florida. Post-1954 texts are on file at Stetson U. College of Law Archives, Gulfport, Florida.

ABA, *ABA Report on Lawyer Competency* (Summer 1979).

ABA, *Report of the Committee on Legal Education of the American Bar Association* (1891, 1930, 1979).

ABA, *Reports of the American Bar Association* (1878, 1879, 1893, 1894, 1931).

ABA, *The American Lawyer: Statistical Report* (Am. B. Found. 1968).

William Sims Allen, *Annual Report of the President of Stetson University to the Board of Trustees* (1927, 1936, 1938, 1940, 1942, 1943, 1946, 1947).

Assn. of Am. L. Schs., *Annual Meeting, Program and Reports of the Committees* (1963).

Assn. of Am. L. Schs., *Report on Stetson University College of Law* (1940).

Assn. of Am. L. Schs., *Resolution adopted at the Annual Meeting* (Dec. 28–30, 1951).

Administrative Office of the United States Courts.

Board of Overseers, Stetson U. College of L., *American Bar Association Relationships* (n.d.) (circa 1963).

Board of Overseers, Stetson U. College of L., *A Resolution in Honor of Thomas E. Stringer, Sr.* (Dec. 3, 2003).

David Dickson, *Committee Report to College of Law Faculty* (Sept. 20, 1965).

J. Ollie Edmunds, *Annual Report of the President of Stetson University to the Board of Trustees* (1949, 1952, 1951, 1953, 1954, 1955, 1960, 1961).

John F. Forbes, *Annual Report of the President of Stetson University to the Board of Trustees* (1899, 1900, 1901).

Forbes-Stetson Controversy Folder.

Lemuel A. Haslup, *Annual Report of the President of Stetson University to the Board of Trustees* (1949).

John G. Hervey, *ABA Inspection Report, John B. Stetson University College of Law, DeLand Florida* (May 7, 1951; Apr. 4, 1952).

Charles Hilkey, *Annual Report on Stetson University College of Law to the University to the President* (Oct. 1954).

Lincoln Hulley, *Annual Report of the President of Stetson University to the Board of Trustees* (1922, 1923, 1925, 1930).

Bruce R. Jacob, *Annual Report on Stetson University College of Law to the University President* (July 17, 1986).

Bruce R. Jacob, *Report on the Bruce Jacob Deanship at Stetson University College of Law, 1981–1994* (2000).

President of the Board, *Report to the Board of Overseers of Stetson University College of Law* (Oct. 22, 1960).

Private Reports from Stetson: $250,000 Given University for New Law Center (Sep. 1955).

Private Reports from Stetson: Justice Sebring Heads Stetson Law School (Oct. 1955).

Private Reports from Stetson: Law Center Campaign Reaches Its Objective (Nov. 1956).

Josef Redlich, *The Common Law and the Case Method in American University Law Schools, a Report to the Carnegie Foundation for the Advancement of Teaching* (Found. 1914).

Harold L. Sebring, *A Few Facts about the College of Law, Acquisition of Property* (Feb. 20, 1957) (twelve-page report distributed to the newly appointed members of the Board of Overseers, along with five appendices).

Harold L. Sebring, *A Five-Year Report of Progress; Stetson University College of Law, 1954–1959* (July 28, 1959) (on file at Stetson U. College of Law, Gulfport, Fla.).

Harold L. Sebring, *Annual Reports on Stetson University College of Law to Board of Overseers* (1955, 1957, 1958, 1959, 1967).

Harold L. Sebring, *New Members of Stetson College of Law Faculty Fall Semester 1960–1961* (1960).

Harold L. Sebring, *Stetson University College of Law from 1954 to 1968* (Feb. 1968).

Harold L. Sebring, *Stetson University College of Law: Past, Present, Future, 1954–1959* (n.d.) (circa 1959–1960).

Russell N. Sullivan, *ABA Inspection Report, Stetson University College of Law, Gulfport Florida* (1957).

Telford Taylor, *Final Report to the Secretary of the Army on the Nuremberg War Crimes Trial under Control Council Law No. 10* (William S. Hein & Co. 1997).

U.S. Census Bureau, *Florida: Population of Counties by Decennial Census: 1900 to 1990* (Govt. Prntg. Off. 1995).

U.S. Census Bureau, *Twelfth United States Census* (Govt. Prntg. Off. 1900).

U.S. Census Bureau, *United States Summary: Population and Housing Units 1790 to 1990* (Govt. Prntg. Off. 2004).

James Vescovi, *A Survey of Columbia Law School's Expanding Curriculum*, Colum. L. Sch. Rpt. 9 (Spring 2003).

J. Lamar Woodard, *Report on Charles A. Dana Law Library* (Mar. 31, 1981).

Faculty and Board Minutes

Stetson Law Center Foundation Directors Minutes (Oct. 9, 1959; June 2, 1967).

Stetson University Board of Overseers Minutes (Feb. 20, 1957; Nov. 13, 1953; May 24, 1957 (special)).

Stetson University Board of Trustees Minutes (Feb. 15, 1940; January 8, 1944; Oct. 3, 1952; Apr. 30, 1953; Nov. 13, 1953; Dec. 3, 1953 (special); Feb. 21, 1957).

Stetson University College of Law Faculty Minutes (Sept. 29, 1938; Jan. 5, 1939; May 25, 1939; Aug. 3, 1939; Sept. 21, 1939; Apr. 28, 1940 (special); Aug. 13, 1940; Nov. 7, 1940; Sept. 17. 1941; Oct. 29, 1941; Mar. 17, 1943 (special); Sept. 1945; Oct. 5, 1949; Jan. 25, 1950; Oct. 25, 1950; Sept. 9, 1965; Sept. 17, 1956; 1975–1980).

Unpublished Manuscripts and Scholarly Memoranda

Olga Bowen, *Henry A. DeLand* (1969).

Olga Bowen, *The Stetson College of Law* (1969).

Olga Bowen, *John Franklin Forbes* (1968).

Olga Bowen, *History of Stetson University* (Stetson U. 1967).

Olga Bowen, *William Sims Allen* (1967).

Olga Bowen, *Lincoln Hulley* (1964).

Olga Bowen, *John B. Stetson* (n.d.).

Florida — Tampa and Its Neighbors (unpublished, undated two-page printed document, circa mid-1930s).

W.S. Gordis, *John B. Stetson University: History and Reminiscence* (unpublished ms. 1946).

Bruce R. Jacob, *Memorandum to File on History of the Law School* (July 27, 1987).

Bruce R. Jacob, *My Recollections What It Was Like to Be a Stetson Law Student and Graduate; the Move of the Law School to Gulfport* (Sept. 1, 1999).

Wm. Reece Smith, *Historical Profiles of Carlton, Fields, Ward, Emmanuel, Smith & Cutler, P.A.* (May 1992).

W. Gary Vause, *Centennial History of the Stetson University College of Law* (unfinished ms. 2003).

Jerry Woods Weeks, *Florida Gold: Emergence of the Florida Citrus Industry, 1865–1895* (unpublished Ph.D dissertation, U.N.C. 1977).

Oral History Interviews

NOTE: Transcripts of the oral histories listed below are on file at Stetson University College of Law in Gulfport, Florida with the exception of the Lycan-Brown Interview.

Interview by Gilbert Lycan with Russell Brown, former Pres. of the Stetson U. Alumni Assn. (Dec. 1, 1977).

Interview by Prof. Michael I. Swygert, Prof. Emeritus, Stetson U. College of L., with Walter F. Pratt., Jr., Assoc. Dean & Prof. of L., Notre Dame L. Sch. (Feb. 2002).

Interview by Todd Richardson with Ray Jordan (Oct. 9, 1986).

Interview by W. Gary Vause, Dean Emeritus, Stetson U. College of L., with Richard T. Dillon, Dean Emeritus, Stetson U. College of L. (Oct. 24. 1986).

Interview by Bruce Jacob, Dean Emeritus, Stetson U. College of L., with Cecil Bailey, former Pres. of Stetson U. College of L. Bd. of Overseers (Jan. 13, 1986).

Interview by Bruce Jacob, Dean Emeritus, Stetson U. College of L. with Joe Ann Taylor Van Gelder, Stetson U. alumnus (Apr. 25, 2005).

Interview by Bruce Jacob, Dean Emeritus, Stetson U. College of L., with Ray Jordan, Libr., Stetson U. College of L. (Oct. 21, 1985).

Interview by Bruce R. Jacob, Dean Emeritus, Stetson U. College of Law, with Amory Underhill, former Pres. of Stetson U. College of L. Bd. of Overseers (June 10, 1986).

Interview by Bruce R. Jacob, Dean Emeritus, Stetson U. College of L., with J. Ben Watkins, former member of Stetson U. College of L. Bd. of Overseers (Oct. 21, 1999).

Interview by Carrie Lambeth, with John Wood, Stetson U. College of L. alumnus (July 18–19, 2001).

Interview by Dorothea Bressi, Assoc. V.P., Stetson U. College of L., with Judge Melvin Orfinger, Stetson U. College of L. alumnus (n.d.).

Interview by Maria Guerrero, Stetson U. College of L. student, with Elsie M. O'Laughlin, Stetson U. College of L. alumna (Nov. 2, 2001).

Interview by Michael I. Swygert, Prof. Emeritus, Stetson U. College of L., with the Hon. Alexander Paskay (Apr. 23, 2005).

Interview by Michael I. Swygert, Prof. Emeritus, Stetson U. College of L., with William R. Eleazer, Distinguished Prof. Emeritus, Stetson U. College of L. (Apr. 17, 2004).

Interview by Michael I. Swygert, Prof. Emeritus, Stetson U. College of L., with Stephen M. Everhart, Prof. of L., Stetson U. College of L. (May 17, 2004).

Interview by Michael I. Swygert, Prof. Emeritus, Stetson U. College of L., with Lizabeth A. Moody, Dean Emeritus & Distinguished Prof. of L., Stetson U. College of L. (May 17, 2005).

Interview by Michael I. Swygert, Prof. Emeritus, Stetson U. College of L., with Pamela D. Burdett, Ref. Libr., Stetson U. College of L. (May 20, 2005).

Interview by Michael I. Swygert, Prof. Emeritus, Stetson U. College of L., with Darby Dickerson, V.P. & Dean, Stetson U. College of L. (May 22, 2004).

Interview by Michael I. Swygert, Prof. Emeritus, Stetson U. College of L., with Rebecca Morgan, Boston Asset Mgt. Prof. of L., Stetson U. College of L. (May 17, 2004).

Interview by Michael I. Swygert, Prof. Emeritus, Stetson U. College of L., with Thomas C. Marks, Jr., Prof. of L., Stetson U. College of L. (Apr. 8, 2004).

Interview by Michael I. Swygert, Prof. Emeritus, Stetson U. College of L., with the Hon. Thomas E. Stringer, Judge, Fla. Second Dist. Ct. of App. (Apr. 7, 2004).

Interview by Michael I. Swygert, Prof. Emeritus, Stetson U. College of L., with Robert Batey, Prof. of L., Stetson U. College of L. (Apr. 8, 2004).

Interview by Michael I. Swygert, Prof. Emeritus, Stetson U. College of L., with Robert Bickel, Prof. of L., Stetson U. College of L. (Apr. 14, 2004).

Interview by Michael I. Swygert, Prof. Emeritus, Stetson U. College of L., with J. Lamar Woodard, Prof. Emeritus & Libr. Emeritus, Stetson U. College of L. (Apr. 21, 2004).

Interview by Michael I. Swygert, Prof. Emeritus, Stetson U. College of L., with Connie Evans, Dir. of Faculty Support Servs., Stetson U. College of L. (May 13, 2005).

Interview by Michael I. Swygert, Prof. Emeritus, Stetson U. College of L., with Ruth Fleet Thurman, Prof. of L., Stetson U. College of L. (May 18, 2004).

Interview by Michael I. Swygert, Prof. Emeritus, Stetson U. College of L., with Bruce R. Jacob, Dean Emeritus, Stetson U. College of L. (Apr. 14, 2004).

Interview by Michael I. Swygert, Prof. Emeritus, Stetson U. College of L., with Judge Susan Schaeffer, Cir. Judge of the Sixth Jud. Cir. (Jan. 20, 2005).

Interview by Michael Swygert, Prof. Emeritus, Stetson U. College of L., with Jerome C. Latimer, Prof. of L., Stetson U. College of L. (Apr. 2, 2004).

Interview by Michael Swygert, Prof. Emeritus, Stetson U. College of L., with Richard Dillon, Dean Emeritus, Stetson U. College of L. (Dec. 29, 2004).

Interview by Michael I. Swygert, Prof. Emeritus, Stetson U. College of L., with Coaches & Members of the 2005 Stetson VIS World Championship Team: Stephanie Vaughan & Jack Graves, Profs., Stetson U. College of L., and Katherine Hurst, Ryan Jones, Megan Schultz, Burks Smith, Tom Yeagers, & Kathryn Christian, students, Stetson U. College of L. (Apr. 2005).

Bruce R. Jacob, *Reflections and Memories of Justice Harold L. "Tom" Sebring and Justice E. Harris Drew* (Fla. Sup. Ct. Historical Socy. Nov. 2, 1990) (video recording).

Telephone Interviews

Telephone Conversation between Michael I. Swygert, Prof. Emeritus, Stetson U. College of L., with Rebecca Cohen Morgan, Boston Asset Mgt. Distinguished Prof. of L., Stetson U. College of L. (Aug. 1, 2005).

Telephone Conversation between Michael I. Swygert, Prof. Emeritus, Stetson U. College of L., with John T. Guyton, alumnus, Stetson U. College of L. & Emeritus Member, Stetson College of L. Bd. of Overseers (July 29, 2005).

Telephone Interviews by Michael I. Swygert, Prof. Emeritus, Stetson U. College of L., with Richard T. Dillon, Dean Emeritus, Stetson U. College of L. (Jan. 27, 2005; May 4, 2005).

Telephone Interview by Michael I. Swygert, Prof. Emeritus, Stetson U. College of Law, with Joseph W. Bradham, Jr., alumnus of the Fla. Military Academy (Oct. 4, 2004).

Telephone Interview by Michael I. Swygert, Prof. Emeritus, Stetson U. College of Law, with Lisa Smith, Esq., Stetson U. College of L. student, & Flagler College alumna (Aug. 27, 2004).

Telephone Interview by Bruce R. Jacob, Dean Emeritus Stetson U. College of Law, with Sidney Taylor, alumnus, Stetson U. College of L. (June 1, 2001).

Conversations

Conversation between Bruce Jacob, Dean Emeritus, Stetson U. College of L., and Arthur Morris, former member Bd. of Trustees, Stetson U. College of L. (Apr. 1995).

Conversations between Silvia Manzanero, Paralegal, Stetson U. College of L., and Richard T. Dillon, Dean Emeritus, Stetson U. College of L. (Aug. 3, 2005; Aug. 20, 2005).

Conversations between Michael I. Swygert, Prof. Emeritus, Stetson U. College of L., and Richard T. Dillon, Dean Emeritus, Stetson U. College of L. (Jan. 29, 2005; May 7, 2005; May 9, 2005; July 24, 2005; July 25, 2005).

Conversation between Michael I. Swygert, Prof. Emeritus, Stetson U. College of L., and Bruce Jacob, Dean Emeritus, Stetson U. College of L. (Feb. 2005; Apr. 2005; July 10, 2005).

Conversation between Michael I. Swygert, Prof. Emeritus, Stetson U. College of L., and Connie Evans, Dir. of Faculty Support Servs., Stetson U. College of L. (June 12, 2005).

Conversations between Michael I. Swygert, Prof. Emeritus, Stetson U. College of L., and Darby Dickerson, V.P. & Dean, Stetson U. College of L. (Apr. 2005).

Conversation between Michael I. Swygert, Prof. Emeritus, Stetson U. College of L., Kristen David Adams, Assoc. Prof. of L., LeRoy Highbaugh Sr. Chair, Stetson U. College of L., Thomas C. Marks, Jr., Prof. of L., Stetson U. College of L., and Richard T. Dillon, Dean Emeritus (January 2005).

Conversation between Michael I. Swygert, Prof. Emeritus, Stetson U. College of L., and John F. Cooper, Prof. of L., Stetson U. College of L. (circa 1990).

Letters

NOTE: All letters and memoranda pre-dating 1954 on file at Stetson University Archives, DeLand, Fla. Post-1954 texts are on file at Stetson U. College of Law Archives, Gulfport, Fla.

Ltr. from A. Hollis Edens, Pres., Duke U., to J. Ollie Edmunds, Pres., Stetson U. (Dec. 13, 1950).

Ltr. from Albert Farrah to John Forbes (June 22, 1900).

Ltr. from Arthur N. Morris, Member, Bd. of Trustees, Stetson U., to H. Graves Edmondson, Comptroller, Stetson U. (Oct. 31, 1960).

Ltr. from Bernard C. Gavit to Dean L.A. Haslup (Jan. 17, 1947).

Ltr. from Bruce R. Jacob, Dean Emeritus, Stetson U. College of L., to Dr. Pope Duncan, Pres., Stetson U. (July 17, 1986).

Ltr. from Charles J. Hilkey, Dean, Stetson U. College of L., to Harvey Firestone, Jr. (Jan. 6, 1955).

Ltr. from Charles Tom Henderson to Dean L.A. Haslup (Aug. 2, 1948).

Ltr. from Cliff B. Gosney, Jr., to W. Gary Vause (Apr. 2, 1999).

Ltr. from David Dickson, Prof. of L., Stetson U. College of L., to Perry Nichols, Pres., Bd. of Oversees, Stetson U. College of L. 2 (Nov. 3, 1965).

Ltr. from David F. Cavers et al., Prof. Harvard L. Sch., to the Deans and Faculty Members of Association Schools (Mar. 26, 1951).

Ltr. from David J. Kadyk to Dean W. Gary Vause (Apr. 6, 1999).

Ltr. from Dean H.A. Haslup to Dean Bernard C. Gavit (Feb. 7, 1947).

Ltr. from Dossie C. Hull to J. Ollie Edmunds (n.d).

Ltr. from Eric Johannesen, Preservation Officer at W. Res. Historical Socy., Cleveland, Ohio, to "Dean of the College of Law, Stetson University" (Oct. 7, 1989).

Ltr. from F.D.G. Ribble, Pres., Assoc. of Am. L. Schs., to J. Ollie Edmunds, Pres., Stetson U. (Jan. 14, 1952).

Ltr. from Gov. Doyle E. Carlton to Georgiana Sheldon, Dir. of Admiss., Stetson U. College of L. (Jan. 10, 1955).

Ltr. from H. Graves Edmondson, V.P. & Bus. Manager, Stetson U., to Bruce R. Jacob, Dean, Stetson U. College of L. (Jan. 26, 1982).

Ltr. from H.A. DeLand, Pres. & Manager, Monroe Co. Chem. Corp., to Mrs. S.E. Stetson (Mar. 28, 1906).

Ltr. from H.W. Arant to William Sims Allen (Mar. 1, 1937).

Ltr. from Harold L. Sebring, Dean, Stetson U. College of L., to the Honorable Doyle E. Carlton, former Gov., Fla. (June 16, 1959).

Ltr. from Harry R. Trusler to Lincoln Hulley (May 18, 1908).

Ltr. from I. Ollie Edmunds, Pres., Stetson U., to Presidents or Deans of Eleven Southern Universities (Nov. 29, 1950).

Ltr. from Innes Henry to J. Ollie Edmunds (Feb. 28, 1954).

Ltr. from J. Ollie Edmunds, Pres., Stetson U., to Walter Mann, member, Bd. of Trustees, Stetson U. (Oct. 18, 1960).

Ltr. from James A. McLaughlin to Judge J. Ollie Edmunds (Dec. 19, 1939).

Ltr. from James Perkins to Lincoln Hulley (July 1, 1909)).

Ltr. from Jo Ann Van Gelder, alumnus of Stetson U. College of L., to Frank Klim, Exec. Dir. of Commun. (July 10, 2004).

Ltr. from John F. Forbes to Florida Newspaper Editors (May 16, 1900).

Ltr. from John Forbes to E.W. Huffcutt (Oct. 23, 1899).

Ltr. from John Forbes to J.C. Davant (Sept. 27, 1899).

Ltr. from John Forbes, Pres., Stetson U., to Henry Flagler (Mar. 17, 1899).

Ltr. from John G. Hervey, ABA Consultant on Leg. Educ., to Harold L. Sebring, Dean, Stetson U. College of L. (Sept. 14, 1955).

Ltr. from John Warren, Jr., to John B. Stetson L. College (Feb. 4, 1981).

Ltr. from Jonathan A. Bush, Adjunct Prof., Columbia U., to Darby Dickerson, V.P. & Dean, Stetson U. College of L. and Madison Mosley, Libr., Stetson U. College of L. (Mar. 2, 2004).

Ltr. from Joseph A. Peel, Jr., Pres. PAD, to J. Ollie Edmunds, Pres. Stetson University (Feb. 2, 1949).

Ltr. from Joseph W. Bradham to Michael I. Swygert, Prof. Emeritus, Stetson U. College of L. (Oct. 7, 2004).

Ltr. from L.A. Haslup to John B. Stetson, Pres., Stetson U. (Oct. 17, 1949).

Ltr. from Lewis H. Tribble to Lincoln Hulley (Jan. 10, 1916).

Ltr. from Lincoln Hulley to A.A. Murphree, Pres., U. Fla. (May 16, 1913).

Ltr. from Lincoln Hulley to F.W. Sams. and D.F. Pattishall (n.d.).

Ltr. from Lincoln Hulley to George B. Selden (n.d.).

Ltr. from Lincoln Hulley to I.L. Farris (n.d.).
Ltr. from Lincoln Hulley to John B. Stetson, Pres., Stetson U. (Mar. 29, 1932).
Ltr. from Lincoln Hulley to Nine School Deans (U. Ala., U. Chi., Cornell, U. Mich., U. Tenn., U. Tex., U. Va., Wash. & Lee, and Yale) (Mar. 22, 1922).
Ltr. from Louis Massey to Lincoln Hulley, Pres., Stetson U. (Apr. 20, 1907).
Ltr. from Lynne Brown, Gulfport, Fla. Historian, to Michael I. Swygert, Prof. Emeritus, Stetson U. College of L. (Aug. 2005).
Ltr. from M.H. Mabry, Clerk of the Fla. Sup. Ct., to Lincoln Hulley (May 22, 1914).
Ltr. from Members of Legislative Council, Student B. Assoc., Stetson U. College of L., to Michael I. Swygert, Prof. Emeritus, Stetson U. College of L. (Mar. 6, 1966).
Ltr. from Michael I. Swygert, Prof. Emeritus, Stetson U. College of L., to H. Douglas Lee, Pres. Stetson U. (Feb. 29, 1996).
Ltr. from Michael I. Swygert, Prof. Emeritus, Stetson U. College of L., to David Snyder, Congressional Correspondent, Christian Broad. Network (Apr. 20, 1996).
Ltr. from Mrs. Robert S. (Geraldine G.) Salisbury to Bruce R. Jacob, Dean, Stetson U. College of L. (June 6, 1983).
Ltr. from Signed Student-Petitioners to Dean L.A. Haslup (July 20, 1948) (one page petition, three pages of signatures, 146 signatures).
Ltr. from Paul E. Raymond to W. Gary Vause, Dean, Stetson U. College of L. (July 24, 1999).
Ltr. from R.A. Rasco, Dean, Stetson U. College of L., to Lincoln Hulley, Pres., Stetson U. (Feb. 11, 1915).
Ltr. from R.F. Howes, Prof., Stetson U. College of L., to Dr. Bernard C. Gavit, Sec., Assn. of Am. L. Schs. (July 11, 1942).
Ltr. from Richard T. Dillon, Dean Emeritus, Stetson U. College of L., to Creighton Gilbert (Apr. 15, 1960).
Ltr. from Richard T. Dillon, Dean Emeritus, Stetson U. College of L., to John Warren, Jr. (Mar. 29, 1982).
Ltr. from Bruce R. Jacob, Dean Emeritus, Stetson U. College of L., to _________ (Nov. 1, 1989).
Ltr. from W.S. Allen, Pres., Stetson U., to Dean L. Haslup (Mar. 6, 1947).
Ltr. from W.F. Davenport, Jr., to, W. Gary Vause, Assoc. Dean, Stetson U. College of L. (Apr. 5, 1999).
Ltr. from W.S. Allen to the John B. Stetson U. Bd. of Trustees (Sept. 19, 1947).
Ltr. from W.S. Allen, Pres., to R.F. Howes, Dean, Stetson U. College of L. (Mar. 7, 1942).

Ltr. from Wallace L. Storey, Atty. at L., former officer, Stetson U. College of L. Bd. of Overseers, to W. Gary Vause, Prof. of L., Stetson U. College of L. (July 24, 1990).

Ltr. from Will Shafroth to Lincoln Hulley, Pres., Stetson U. (June 6, 1930).

Ltr. from William H. Maness, Stetson U. College of L. alumnus, to W. Gary Vause, Dean, Stetson U. College of L. (Apr. 5, 1999).

Ltr. from William R. Eleazer, Distinguished Prof. Emeritus, Stetson U. College of L., to Michael I. Swygert, Prof. Emeritus, Stetson U. College of L. (Sept. 2, 2005).

Ltr. from William Sims Allen to H.W. Arant, Sec., Am. Assoc. of L. Schs. (Feb. 22, 1937).

Ltr. from William Sims Allen to Judge O.K. Reaves, member, Stetson U. Bd. of Trustees (Feb. 4, 1939).

Ltr. from Wm. Hugh McEniry, Jr., and Lemuel A. Haslup to Dr. J. Ollie Edmunds and Dr. H.C. Garwood (Apr. 27, 1948).

Ltr. from Wm. Reece Smith, Jr., Chair Emeritus & Senior Member, Carlton Fields, Attys. at L., & Distinguished Professorial Lecturer, Stetson U. College of L., to Michael I. Swygert, Prof. Emeritus, Stetson U. College of L. (Aug. 2, 2005).

Ltrs. from Ambrose Suhrie to Lincoln Hulley (Aug. 1, 1909; July 11, 1909).

Ltrs. from Bruce R. Jacob, Dean Emeritus & Prof. of L., Stetson U. College of L., to Michael I. Swygert, Prof. Emeritus, Stetson College of L. (July 10, 2005; July 27, 2005; July 29, 2005; Aug. 15, 2005).

Ltrs. from Creighton Gilbert, Curator, John & Mable Ringling Museum of Art, to Richard T. Dillon, Dean, Stetson U. College of L. (Apr. 6, 1960; Apr. 23, 1960).

Ltrs. from Dean L.A. Haslup to J. Ollie Edmunds, Pres., Stetson U. (Aug. 4, 1948; July 30, 1948; Nov. 19, 1949).

Ltrs. from L.A. Haslup to the Law Alumni of the John B. Stetson U. (Oct. 25, 1947; Oct. 31, 1949).

Ltrs. from Lincoln Hulley to L.H. Tribble (Jan. 11, 1916; Sept. 19, 1932).

Ltrs. from Richard T. Dillon, Dean Emeritus, Stetson U. College of L., to Michael I. Swygert, Prof. Emeritus, Stetson U. College of L. (June 2005; July 25, 2005).

Ltrs. from Rufus C. Harris to Lewis Tribble, Dean, Stetson U. College of L. (Nov. 13–14, 1933).

Ltrs. from Walter Mann, member, Bd. of Trustees, Stetson U., to Dr. J. Ollie Edmunds, Pres., Stetson U. (Oct. 27, 1960; Nov. 4, 1960).

Attachments to Letters

Joseph W. Bradham, Jr., *Select History, Florida Military Academy Transition to Stetson University College of Law* (August 8, 2004) (two-page typed document attached to a handwritten letter from Mr. Bradham to Prof. Michael Swygert).

Joe Ann (Taylor) Van Gelder, *St. Patrick's Day* (1955) (a two-page attachment to letter from Jo Ann Van Gelder to Frank Klim).

Elizabeth B. Worth, *History of Frank Worth* (May 24, 1983) (one page, typed manuscript, originally included in letter from Mrs. Robert S. Salisbury to Bruce Jacob (June 6, 1983)).

Handwritten Notes and Comments

Note from Bruce Jacob Dean Emeritus, Stetson U. College of L., to Michael Swygert, Prof. Emeritus, Stetson U. College of L. (Feb. 22, 2005).

Note from Richard T. Dillon, Dean Emeritus, Stetson U. College of L., to Michael I. Swygert, Prof. Emeritus, Stetson U. College of L. (Jan. 2005).

Manuscript Comments from James J. Brown, Prof. of L., Stetson U. College of L., to Michael I. Swygert, Prof. Emeritus, Stetson U. College of L. (Nov. 2005).

Manuscript Comments from Bruce R. Jacob, Dean Emeritus, Stetson U. College of L., to Micheal I. Swygert, Prof. Emeritus, Stetson U. College of L. (Aug. 29, 2005).

Manuscript Comments from Bruce R. Jacob, Dean Emeritus, Stetson U. College of L., to Michael I. Swygert, Prof. Emeritus, Stetson U. College of L. (Sept. 25, 2005).

Manuscript Comments from Elizabeth A. Moody, Dean Emeritus, Stetson U. College of L., to Michael I. Swygert, Prof. Emeritus, Stetson U. College of L. (Oct. 2005).

Manuscript Comments from Lisa M. Smith, Esq., Research Asst., to Michael I. Swygert, Prof. Emeritus, Stetson U. College of L. (Oct. 9, 2005).

E-mails

E-mail from Paul D. Carrington, Henry Chadwick, Sr., Professor Emeritus, Duke U. School of L., to Michael I. Swygert, Professor Emeritus, Stetson U. College of L. (March 14, 2006).

E-mail from Brandi Palmer to Frank Klim, Davina Gould and Aaron Reincheld, Stetson U. College of L. Commun. Off. (Sept. 24, 2004) (forwarded to Dean Dickerson and Prof. Swygert).

E-mail from William R. Eleazer, Distinguished Prof. Emeritus, Stetson U. College of L., to Michael I. Swygert, Prof. Emeritus, Stetson U. College of L. (Mar. 21, 2005).

E-mail from Darby Dickerson, V.P. & Dean, Stetson U. College of L., to Michael I. Swygert, Prof. Emeritus, Stetson U. College of L. (Mar. 17, 2005).

E-mail from Rebecca C. Morgan, Dir., Ctr. for Excellence in Elder L., to Silvia Manzanero, Paralegal, Stetson U. College of L. (Aug. 29, 2005).

Telegrams

Telegram from Lewis H. Tribble, Dean, Stetson U. College of L., to Rufus C. Harris (Dec. 24, 1931).

Telegram from Lewis H. Tribble Dean, Stetson U. College of L., to Lincoln Hulley, Pres., Stetson U. (Dec. 24, 1931).

Memoranda

Memo. from Bruce R. Jacob, Dean Emeritus & Prof. of L., Stetson U. College of L., to W. Gary Vause, Dean, Stetson U. College of L., (n.d.).

Memo. from Bruce R. Jacob, Dean Emeritus, Stetson U. College of L., to William F. Blews, William Reece Smith, Jr., and Judge Thomas Stringer (Mar. 20, 1998).

Memo. from Jerome Latimer, Prof. of L., Stetson U. College of L. & Chair, Honor Code Comm., to Dean and Faculty, Stetson U. College of L. (Feb. 24, 1987).

Memo. from Lizabeth Moody, Dean Emeritus & Distinguished University Prof., Stetson U. College of L., to W. Gary Vause, Dean, Stetson U. College of L. (n.d.) (circa 2001).

Memo. from Michael Finch, Michael Swygert & W. Gary Vause to Dean Bruce Jacob and the Faculty of Stetson U. College of L. (1992).

Memo. from Pamela Cole Bell, Trial Advocacy Fellow, Stetson U. College of L., to Michael I. Swygert, Prof. of L., Stetson U. College of L. (May 2, 2005).

Memo. from Ann Hughes-Johnson to Gary Vause, Assoc. Dean, Stetson U. College of L. (Mar. 30, 1999).

Memo. from F.D.G. Ribble, Secretary-Treasury, Assoc. of Am. L. Schs., to the Member Schools of the Assoc. of Am. L. Schs. (Oct. 24, 1950).

Memo. from J. Ollie Edmunds, President, Stetson U., to Bd. of Trustees (Oct. 29, 1969).

Memo. from Pope A. Duncan, Pres., Stetson U., to Bd. of Trustees, Stetson U., and Bd. of Overseers, Stetson U. College of L. (July 24, 1980).

Memo. from Michael I. Swygert, Prof. Emeritus, Stetson U. College of L., to Faculty, Stetson U. College of L. (March 7, 1980).

Memo. from R.F. Howes, Dean, Stetson U. College of L., to J. Ollie Edmunds, Pres., Stetson U. (Mar. 1, 1943).

Memo. from the Comm. on Admissions, Stetson U. College of L., to J. Ollie Edmunds (Sept. 27, 1949).

Memo. from Walter Mann, Pres. Stetson U. College of L., Bd. of Overseers, to the Bd. of Overseers, Stetson U. College of L. & Bd. of Directors, Stetson L. Ctr. (May 4, 1959).

Memos. from Bruce R. Jacob, Dean Emeritus, Stetson U. College of L., to Michael Swygert, Prof. Emeritus, Stetson U. College of L. (Feb. 10, 2004; Apr. 26, 2004).

Memos. from J. Ollie Edmunds to L. A. Haslup, Dean, Stetson U. College of L. (July 23, 1948; Aug. 1948) (unsigned).

Judicial Cases

United States Supreme Court

Bradwell v. Ill., 83 U.S. 130 (1872).

Brown v. Bd. of Educ. of Topeka, 347 U.S. 483 (1954).

Brown v. Bd. of Educ., 349 U.S. 294 (1955).

Cleveland Bd. of Educ. v. LaFleur, 414 U.S. 632 (1974).

Crawford v. Washington, 541 U.S. 36 (2004).

Dartmouth College v. Woodward, 17 U.S. 518 (1819).

Fletcher v. Peck, 10 U.S. 87 (1810).

Florida ex rel. Hawkins v. Bd. of Control, 350 U.S. 413 (1956).

Florida ex rel. Hawkins v. Bd. of Control, 355 U.S. 839 (1957).

Gideon v. Wainright, 327 U.S. 335 (1963).

Lockhart v. McCree, 476 U.S. 162 (1986).

Stand. Oil Co. v. U.S., 221 U.S. 1 (1911).

Florida Supreme Court

Hulley v. Hunt, 57 So. 607 (Fla. 1912).

In re Criminal Procedure Rule No. 2, 167 So. 2d 574 (Fla. 1964).

John B. Stetson U. v. Hunt, 102 So. 637 (Fla. 1925).

State ex rel. Hawkins v. Bd. of Control, 60 So. Ed 162 (Fla. 1952).
State ex rel. Hawkins v. Bd. of Control, 93 So. 2d 354 (Fla. 1957).
State ex rel. Hawkins, 83 So. 2d 20 (Fla. 1955).

Statutes and Regulations

An Act to Incorporate an Institution of Learning at DeLand, Florida, under the Name of DeLand University, 1887 Fla. Laws ch. 3808, § 128.
Fla. Stat. § 239.01 (1969) (repealed 1979).
Fla. Stat. § 832.07(i)(a) (1964) (as revised).
1953 Fla. Laws ch. 28, § 704.
Pub. L. No. 78-346 (June 22, 1944) (the enabling legislation was officially known as the Servicemen Readjustment Act of 1944).

Miscellaneous Legal Documents

Aff. Richard T. Dillon (July 19, 1985).
Resolution of the Second Judicial Circuit for and in Leon County, Florida, on Behalf of the Tallahassee Bar Association in Honor of Louis Herndon Tribble (n.d.) (said to be filed in the "Records of the Circuit Court in and for Leon County, Florida, as a permanent testimonial to Lewis Herndon Tribble to the legal profession").

Online Resources

Ala. Lib. Assn., *Alabama Authors and Their* Works, www.lib.auburn.edu/madd/docs/ala_authors/f.html (accessed Oct. 29, 2004).
Biography of Henry A. DeLand, http://ourworld.compuserve.com/homepages/ndeland/Biography.htm (accessed May 26, 2004).
BabeRuth.com, *Biography*, www.baberuth.com/flash/about/biograph.html (accessed Dec. 30, 2004).
Bataan Death March, http://history.acusd.edu/gen/st/~ehimchak/death_march.html (accessed on Jan. 14, 2005).
Edna Buchanan, Miami Herald, *Fatal Politics*, http://history.jupiter.fl.us/kids/PI%20Menuu/miami_article.htm (accessed on May 10, 2005).
Biography of William Rainey Harper, www.lib.uchicago.edu/projects/centcat/centcats.pres.prescho01_01.html (accessed on June 13, 2004).

Rob DeLand, *The DeLand Family in America*, http://home2.owc.net/-rdeland/DeLandHome.html (last updated Oct. 24, 2003).

Carlton Fields, Attorneys at Law, *Wm. Reece Smith, Of Counsel*, www.carltonfields.com/rsmith/ (accessed July 19, 2005).

Florida Heritage Collection, *Economics and Society: Post-Civil War Florida 1865–1913: Reconstruction Era, 1865–1877*, http://palmm.fcla.edu/fh/outline/1865recon.html (last updated Jan. 7, 2002).

Florida Heritage Collection, *Florida Counties*, http://fdl.fcla.edu/fh/counties.html (updated Jan. 7, 2002).

Florida Supreme Court, *Justices of the Supreme Court, "The International Judge," Justice Harold L. Sebring*, www.flcourts.org/pubinfo/gallery/sebring.html (accessed Jun. 24, 2004).

Jack Fortes, *In Heyday, DeLand Was King for Citrus Cultivation*, www.informedvolusian.com/2003/Issue_3/Volusia%20History%20Fortes3A.htm (accessed Oct. 22, 2004).

IMDB, Earth's Biggest Movie Database, *The Strange One*, http://www.imdb.com/title/tt0051019/ (accessed May 10, 2005).

Bill Keeler, *DeLand Florida 1876–1896: A Tale of Two Families*, www.angelfire.com/ny5/fairporthistmuseum/deland.htm (accessed Oct. 22, 2004).

Laura Kinsler, Tampa Tribune, *Stetson Appeals to Second District Court*, lkinsler@tampatrib.com (accessed Feb. 4, 2005).

Henry B. Plant Museum, *The History*, www.plantmuseum.com/history/index.shtml; *select* "The History"; "Henry B. Plant Bio"; "1891 Hotel" (accessed Feb. 6, 2004).

Lois H. Hirsch, *"The Hat of the West" Is Born: John B. Stetson's Hats*, http://cheltenhamtownship.org/wallhouse/stetson.htm (accessed June 4, 2004).

History: The Bataan Memorial Death March, http://www.bataanmarch.com/history.htm (accessed on Jan. 14, 2005).

William R. Levesque, St. Pete Times, *Ailing Circuit Judge Susan Schaeffer to Retire, after a Distinguished 22 Years on the Bench, the Judge Will Leave at the End of the Year*, www.sptimes.com/11/03/news_pf/Tampabay/Ailing_Circuit_Judge_.shtml (accessed on Jan. 19, 2005).

NITA, www.nita.org (accessed Sept. 7, 2005).

Off. of Cultural & Historical Programs, *A Brief History of Florida*, http://dhr.dos.state.fl.us/facts/history/summary/ (2004).

Planet Fla., *The History of DeLand*, www.planetflorida.net/deland-hist/ (accessed Oct. 22, 2004).

Planet Smethport, *Home of Albert W. Johnson, Member of US Congress, 1963–1977*, www.smethport.org/franklinstreet/richmond.409/richmond.htm, (accessed May 14, 2004).

Pub. Broad. Serv., *Capture and Death March*, www.pbs.org/wgbh/amex/macarthur/sfeature/bataan_capture.html (accessed Jan. 14, 2004).

Pub. Broad. Serv., *The American Experience: MacArthur, The Siege of Bataan*, www.pbs.org/wgbh/amex/macarthur/sfeature/bataan_siege.html (accessed Jan. 14, 2004).

Vernellia Randall, *The 2004 Whitest Law School Report*, http://academic.udayton/race/o3justice/LegalEd/Whitest/HWLS0403.htm (accessed Apr. 12, 2004).

Recent Events: Professor Dorothea Beane Visits International Criminal Court Stetson U. College of Law 1, www.law.stetson.edu/recentevents/Beane-ICC.asp (July 14, 2004)

Edward P. Richards, III, LSU Law Center's Medical and Public Health Law, *The Nuremberg Code*, http://biotech.law.lsu.edu/Books/aspen/Aspen-The-8.html (accessed June 21, 2004).

William W. Rodgers, *A Documented History of the Incident Which Occurred at Rosewood, Florida, in January 1923*, http://dlis.dos.state.fl.us/fgils/rosewood.html (last updated Aug. 27, 2004) (report submitted to the Florida Board of Regents).

William J. Schellings, *The Role of Florida in the Spanish-American War 1898*, (unpublished Ph.D. dissertation, U. Fla. 1958) (located at Smathers Library, Special Collections).

Stetson U. College of L. Off. of Commun., *Stetson Law to Present International Bankruptcy Symposium, June 15–18 in Canada*, www.law.stetson.edu/Communications/news.asp?id=81 (Mar. 19, 2004).

Stetson U. College of L. Website, Faculty Home Page, *Carol Henderson*, www.law.stetson.edu/faculty/henderson.asp (accessed Nov. 21, 2005).

Stetson U. College of L., *Campus Tour, Stop One: Plaza Mayor*, www.law.stetson.edu/general/tour/a.asp (accessed January 2004).

Stetson U. College of L. Hall of Fame, www.law.stetson.edu/HallofFame/2005_inductees.Asp. (July 2005)

Stetson University College of Law Receives Major Gift from Attorney's Title Insurance Fund, Inc., www.law.stetson.edu/communications/news.asp?id=149 (Feb. 15, 2005).

Stetson University College of Law to Host International Elder Law and Bankruptcy Programs in Italy, www.law.stetson.edu/new/italy.htm (Apr. 9, 2002).

Tampa Bay Bus. J., *In Depth: Business of Law, Seventeen Members Inducted into Stetson Charter Hall of Fame*, www.bixjournals.com/tampabay/stories/2004/10/18 (Oct. 15, 2004).

Tampa Bay History Ctr., *Tampa's Contributions to the Spanish-American War*, www.tampabayhistorycenter.org/spanam.htm (accessed Oct. 27, 2004).

The Inflation Calculator, http://westegg.com/inflation (accessed Dec. 31, 2004).

Tropicals, *Hamlin Orange*, http://www.tropicalfruit.com/tfc/product.asp?ID=174 (accessed Oct. 22, 2004).

U. Fla. Archives, *University of Florida Timeline*, www.uflib.edu/spec/archome/Timeline.htm (last updated Apr. 27, 2000).

U. Neb., *The University of New Hampshire Army and Air Force ROTC Hall of Fame, Colonel Burnell V. Bryant, U.S. Army*, www.unh.edu/army/AlumniPage/bryant.html (accessed Jan., 2004)

U. Tampa, *History*, www.utampa.edu/aboutut/history-museum.html (accessed May 6, 2004).

Volusia Co. Heritage, *Henry DeLand*, http://volusiahistory.com/deland1.htm (accessed Oct. 22, 2004).

William Emery Baker, ftp://ftp.rootsweb.com/pub/usgenweb/fl/hernando/genealogy/baker.txt (accessed May 14, 2004).

Index